THE ARCHAEOLOGY OF ESSEX

Proceedings of the 1993 Writtle conference

edited by Owen Bedwin

Essex County Council
Planning Department
Chelmsford
1996

ISBN 185281 1226

© Essex County Council 1996
P O Milton B.Sc., A.R.I.C.S., M.R.T.P.I.
County Planner
County Hall
Chelmsford CM1 1LF

The information contained in this publication was, as far as is known, correct at the date of issue. Essex County Council cannot, however, accept responsibility for any error or omission.

All rights reserved. No part of this material may be reproduced or transmitted in any form or by any means, electronic or mechanical, photocopying, recording or otherwise, or stored in any retrieval system of any nature without the written permission of the copyright holder.

Cover illustration: Reconstruction of the Late Bronze Age settlement at Lofts Farm (by Roger Massey-Ryan)

CONTENTS

Contributors	v
Preface	vi
Foreword	vii
The Palaeolithic period in Essex *J J Wymer*	1
The Late Upper Palaeolithic and Mesolithic in Essex *R M Jacobi*	10
Essex c. 4000 - 1500 BC *Robin Holgate*	15
The archaeology of Essex c. 1500 - 500 BC *N Brown*	26
Re-thinking the later Bronze Age *Richard Bradley*	38
The Iron Age *P R Sealey*	46
Colchester; publications between 1978 and early 1994 *Philip Crummy*	69
The Roman towns of Essex *N P Wickenden*	76
The Roman countryside *C J Going*	95
Early Saxon Essex AD c. 400 - 700 *Susan Tyler*	108
Essex c. 700 - 1066 *Stephen Rippon*	117
Medieval Essex *Jennifer C Ward*	129
Standing timber-framed buildings *D F Stenning*	136
Essex Record Office sources for medieval archaeology *Janet Smith*	143
Post-medieval Essex *Paul Everson*	150
Industrial archaeology in Essex *John H Boyes*	160
Environmental archaeology in Essex *Peter Murphy*	168
Archaeological research and the Essex SMR *P J Gilman*	181

The chronicle of an archaeological unit (1968 - 1988) 192
N P Wickenden

Archaeology in Essex since 1945 199
Warwick Rodwell

Essex Archaeology: retrospect and prospect 207
D G Buckley

Index 219

Contributors

John Boyes
Industrial archaeologist

Richard Bradley
Department of Archaeology, University of Reading

Nigel Brown
Archaeology Section, Essex County Council Planning Department

David Buckley
Archaeology Section, Essex County Council Planning Department

Philip Crummy
Colchester Archaeological Trust

Paul Everson
Royal Commission on Historical Monuments of England, University of Keele

Paul Gilman
Archaeology Section, Essex County Council Planning Department

Chris Going
Consultant archaeologist (Roman specialist)

Robin Holgate
Luton Museum Service

Roger Jacobi
Department of Prehistoric and Romano-British Antiquities, British Museum

Peter Murphy
Centre of East Anglian Studies, University of East Anglia

Stephen Rippon
Department of Archaeology, University of Reading

Warwick Rodwell
Consultant archaeologist and architectural historian

Janet Smith
Essex Record Office

Paul Sealey
Colchester Museum

Dave Stenning
Historic Buildings and Conservation section, Essex County Council Planning Department

Susan Tyler
Consultant archaeologist (Saxon specialist)

Jennifer Ward
Goldsmiths College, University of London

Nick Wickenden
Chelmsford Borough Museums Service

John Wymer
Consultant archaeologist (Palaeolithic specialist)

(Ian Kinnes, Assistant Keeper, British Museum, also gave a paper at the Conference)

Preface

The publication in 1980 of the proceedings of the first conference on the archaeology of Essex (held at Clacton in 1978), was something of a landmark in the study of archaeology in the county. The proceedings, consisting of 19 contributions by 18 authors, covered the range from the Palaeolithic to AD 1500, and represented the first published account of the county's archaeology in a single volume.

By the late 1980s, however, it was becoming increasingly out of date, and it was clear that a revision was needed. For example, the chapter on the Bronze Age was based almost entirely on metalwork and pottery finds, whereas we now had a range of Late Bronze Age settlements, excavated on a large scale, plus considerable information about economy and environment.

Further impetus for revision came in the aftermath of PPG 16 (Provisional Planning Guidance Note 16), published by the Department of the Environment in late 1990. Among other things, this document stated that county archaeologists, and their staff, could recommend to district councils that archaeological evaluations be undertaken on sites which were the subject of planning applications. These were to be done *prior* to the determination of such applications, and the results were to be considered, along with all other relevant factors, in coming to a decision about them. PPG 16 also put the onus on developers to ensure that the archaeological implications of development were met, i.e. that rescue excavation resulting from the planning process should be properly funded.

For most planning authorities, 1991 was the year in which they came to terms with PPG 16. In Essex, the county council's archaeology section carried out a major internal re-organisation, resulting in the separation of the so-called curatorial functions (i.e. maintaining the Sites and Monuments Record and development control) from contractor's functions (i.e. fieldwork projects). By the end of 1991, the implementation of PPG 16 was reasonably well established in terms of working procedures within the county.

However, one obvious concern was beginning to emerge. In day-to-day dealings with planning officers, landowners, developers and their agents, development control archaeologists in Essex were frequently being asked to explain and justify the significance of particular archaeological deposits, since the scale of archaeological investigation requested would obviously have an impact on development costs. Nationally, too, there were misgivings about the upsurge of fieldwork, particularly evaluations, that followed from the implementation of PPG 16; to what aim was all this archaeological activity directed? In other words, although PPG 16 set out procedures, it did not provide priorities.

In early 1992, therefore, it was decided that the 1980 volume *Archaeology in Essex to AD 1500* should be revised, and that probably the best way to do this would be to organise a conference at which speakers would be invited to address themselves to two objectives. First, they should provide an up-to-date overview of the archaeology of the county on a chronological basis; secondly, they should identify research priorities to guide fieldwork over the next decade or so. The first objective would satisfy the need for a completely overhauled picture of the county's archaeology, incorporating the extra knowledge acquired since 1980; the second objective would meet the requirement for archaeological fieldwork to be clearly prioritised, so as to make best use of resources.

The county council's Environment committee was approached with the idea of holding such a conference, and gave its approval in April 1992. A programme of speakers was organised over the following few months, and the conference itself was held over a week-end in September 1993 at Writtle College. Nineteen speakers gave papers ranging from the Palaeolithic period to the Industrial Archaeology of the county, to an overall audience of c. 150 people.

This volume represents the written proceedings of that conference. There are 21 contributions from 20 authors; the two objectives noted above are clearly met, and, in addition, many of the contributors have provided very full bibliographies as an aid to further reading. The three final chapters, which were not presented at the conference itself, are accounts of particular aspects of the way in which archaeology has been organised and carried out in Essex, and are included because progress in a subject like archaeology can never be divorced from those who carry it out.

Owen Bedwin
Archaeology Section,
Essex County Council Planning Department

(Editor's note; all contributions, bar one, were substantially complete by December 1994, except where otherwise noted. Illustrations, where not provided by authors, were mainly by Iain Bell, with assistance from Stewart MacNeill, Nick Nethercoat and Roger Massey-Ryan.)

Foreword

In September 1993, I was happy to be able to make some introductory remarks at the opening session of the Archaeology of Essex Conference at Writtle. Now, I have the chance to provide a short foreword to the published proceedings of the Conference, which attracted a wide range of speakers from across the country.

What is very noticeable is the way in which the scope of the Conference has widened, since its predecessor was held in 1978 at Clacton. The inclusion of papers on Post-Medieval and Industrial Archaeology is a welcome departure. This has not, however, been at the expense of prehistoric concerns, where our understanding of the county's past has made great advances in the years since 1978.

The members of the Essex County Council Environment Committee and the Officers of the Council are all very much aware of the need to attend to the county's archaeological heritage. We shall, therefore, continue to monitor development proposals and to ensure that the appropriate archaeological responses are made in respect of the relevant sites.

Councillor John Gyford
Chairman of the Environment Committee

The Palaeolithic Period in Essex

J.J. WYMER

It is generally agreed that the great ice sheet which once covered most of Essex can be correlated with the Oxygen Isotope Stage 12 of the deep sea core chronology. In terms of the British Quaternary sequence this is known as the Anglian Stage. This ice sheet extended from the arctic to just north of the Thames Valley but no further south (Fig. 1).

The present estimate for the beginning of the Anglian Stage is 472,000 years. The till (Boulder Clay) of the ice sheet is not only a geological marker but it makes a starting point for this survey of the palaeolithic period as represented in Essex, for there is nothing yet found in Essex to demonstrate any human presence before it. However, there is now some evidence for the occupation of Britain prior to this glaciation, if not in Essex. The spectacular site at Boxgrove in Sussex (Roberts 1986) is associated with a high sea level of 45 metres above the present one and, on the basis of the mammalian faunal remains found with a hand-axe industry in primary context, is considered to be pre-Anglian. The discovery of the major part of a human tibia in December 1993 directly associated with the hand-axes emphasises the great importance of this site. Whether the individual concerned would be classified as *Homo erectus* or an archaic form of *Homo sapiens* cannot be ascertained on such a small fragment, but further excavation may reveal more of the skeleton. It is the oldest human bone to have been found in Britain.

Nearer to Essex, in north west Suffolk, is the site of High Lodge near Mildenhall (Ashton *et al.* 1992). There, a great raft of interglacial sediments has been transported bodily into the Anglian till, together with its contained archaeology including finely made flake tools but no hand-axes. This latter site is a very fortunate freak preservation for it is obvious that the pre-glacial landscape was destroyed by the passage of the ice sheets. Human groups may have been active in Essex at this time but any evidence they left behind them of their presence has been presumably destroyed. Even flint artifacts can be rendered unrecognisable by crushing and rolling by glacial agencies, but it is just possible that some may one day be found in the gravels covered by till in south east Essex, for these represent a precursor of the River Thames when it flowed well north of its present line north east towards Suffolk. These are known as the Kesgrave Sands and Gravels (Whiteman and Rose 1992). More recent courses of the Thames and Medway, but still pre-Anglian, are preserved on the Tendring Plateau (Bridgland 1994) but nothing palaeolithic has yet been found in them.

When the ice sheet did reach Essex, the Thames was flowing through the Vale of St. Albans towards Colchester. A lobe of ice blocked the river and it was diverted from

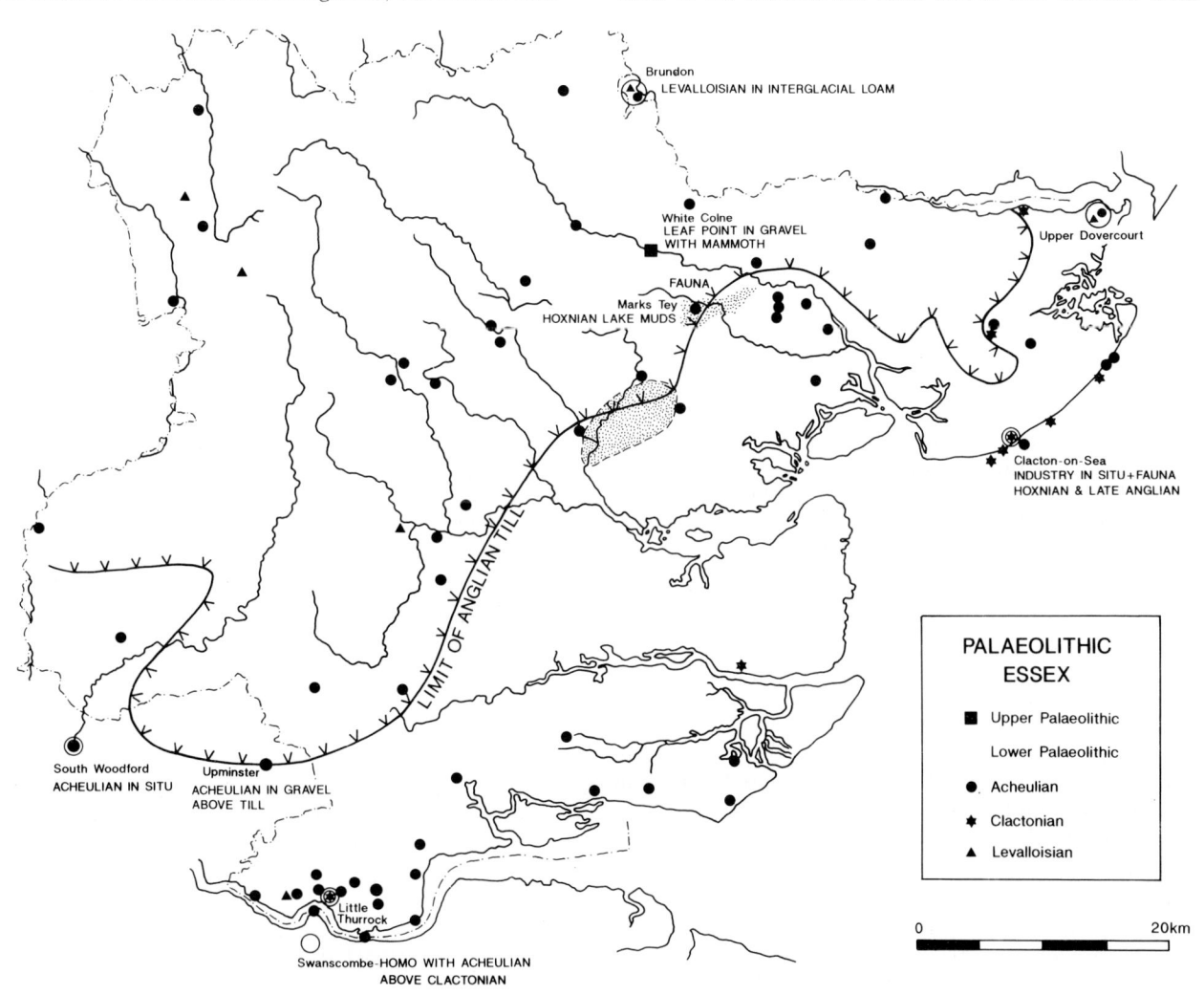

Fig. 1: Distribution of major Lower Palaeolithic sites in Essex related to the limit of the ice sheet of the Anglian Stage

Marlow in the Middle Thames Valley into its present valley system. This was a period of catastophic changes, for the ice sheet also dammed the drainage of the all the European rivers draining into the North Sea (Gibbard 1988) which breached the land bridge between the Pas de Calais and North Downs of Kent, causing the rivers to flow through what was to become the English Channel. When the ice eventually receded and late glacial episodes gradually softened into the milder climates of the beginning of the next interglacial stage (known as the Hoxnian Stage, see Table 1), the landscape of Essex bore considerable resemblance to that of the present day. The coastline was more distant but the rivers occupied their present valleys even if they flowed some 20-30 metres above their present heights O.D. in places. The Stour, Colne, Chelmer, Blackwater and Crouch would for the most part have been roughly where they are now. The one major exception was the Medway. It joined the Thames at Southend and the combined waters flowed north east towards Mersea and Clacton, beyond which it would have been estuarine. This would have been about 400,000 years ago and, as will be seen below, coincides with one of the most important palaeolithic sites in the county. Proglacial lakes remained, particularly in the Rivenhall, Marks Tey and Copford area, but these slowly silted up during this Hoxnian Stage. There is nothing to indicate that glaciers ever covered Essex again, although there were several very cold periods later in this Middle and Late Pleistocene period when ice advanced over the more northerly or Highland zones of Britain during some of them. Essex would have felt the brunt of periglacial climates on several occasions, when the landscape would have appeared like northern Canada with permafrost, ice-wedges, frost-heaving, pingoes and wide, braided river courses. Oscillations of sea level and climate affected the rivers, causing them to erode deeper channels and deposit sands and gravels along them. As each sea level dropped during the cold stages, due to the waters of the oceans being locked up as ice at the poles, so the rivers cut down and deposited their sediment. When the ice melted in the northern hemisphere so the sea level rose again, never it would seem as high as it was formerly, so the old flood plains were left high and dry as terraces. This is very significant, archaeologically, for it is in such terrace gravels that many of the palaeoliths are found. In the Middle and Upper parts of the Lower Thames Valley these terraces remain as step-like features, but Essex has never been very far from the North Sea and the rising sea level of interglacials has submerged the terraces in what are now the estuarine regions of the major Essex rivers. For example, the fine hand-axes which have been found at Rochford are in gravel at about present sea level whereas the same terrace gravel upstream in the Thurrock area is at about 20 m O.D. Actual subsidence of the whole of this part of south-east England also contributes to this complexity. The geological history of the Essex rivers throughout the 350,000 years or so of the palaeolithic period as represented in the county is epitomised in the terrace sequence of the Thames, shown diagrammatically on Fig. 2 below, as a result of the recent intensive studies by Gibbard (1985; 1994) and Bridgland (1994). The palaeoliths which are found within these terrace sediments can now be placed into a chronology with much greater confidence than was hitherto possible.

It can be seen from Fig. 3 that, apart from some of the difficulties in interpretation caused by oscillating sea levels, downwarping of the land and river diversions, erosion of a river to very low sea levels may cause it to deepen its valley so much that its gradient is steeper than later courses of the river. This can cause an inversion of the terrace sequence and this may have been the case with the Black Park Terrace. Bridgland (1994) extrapolates the gradient of this terrace from the Middle Thames and considers that it would have been at a lower level than the Boyn Hill Terrace from what is now central London eastwards. This is the interpretation used for Fig. 3 but it must be stressed that even with this it is difficult to reconcile the high level of the Dartford Heath Gravel (40 m O.D.) with the general surface level of the Boyn Hill-Orsett Heath Gravel downstream. Gibbard (1994) interprets the Dartford Heath Gravel as part of the Black Park Terrace. The resolution of this must await the confirmation of claims that a gravel-filled channel exists under the Dartford Heath Gravel at a level which would accord with the base level of the Lower Gravel at Swanscombe. Although just over the river from Essex, the famous Swanscombe Skull site must be noted here, for it gives a clear sequence of events for the interglacial stage following the recession of the Anglian ice sheet, referred to as the Hoxnian Stage (Table 1). Three different flint industries are stratigraphically separated within five major sedimentary divisions, with associated mammalian and molluscan fauna. This sequence can be used to help comprehend this part of the palaeolithic period in Essex where such well-preserved sequences are unknown. Whatever the relationship is with the Dartford Heath Gravel, it is clear that the Swanscombe sequence postdates the recession of the Anglian ice for the gravels there contain erratic rocks washed out of it. This was well after the actual diversion of the Thames as mentioned above, but probably at a time when the climate was still cold and solifluction was active on the bare valley sides. The very base of the Lower Gravel has been interpreted as a solifluction deposit by some, supported by claims of its "rough and tumble appearance", nests of frost-shattered flints and scratched flint flakes (see Bridgland 1994, 196-218 for the most detailed current summary of this internationally important site; also Conway and McNabb forthcoming). Others have refuted the presence of this solifluction deposit, but a likely explanation is that it does exist but only in localised patches, as later water-erosion in the Lower Gravel channel has removed much of it.

Significantly, flint flakes and a possible hand-axe at the base of this Lower Gravel would equate well with what is known from the Black Park Terrace Gravel in the Middle Thames Valley, where Acheulian hand-axes and flakes and cores as found in Clactonian Industries occur (Wymer 1968). The Black Park Gravel is considered to be the first Thames deposit after its diversion by the Anglian ice sheet, so could be contemporary with the basal (in part) Lower Gravel.

The Swanscombe sequence is summarised below, based on the tripartite division given by Conway and Waechter (1977):

Modern surface 32 m O.D.

PHASE III

Upper Gravel	Hill-wash and solifluction in cold climate	Derived hand-axes Rare faunal remains
Upper Loam	River deposit in cold climate	Acheulian Industry in primary context

PHASE II

Upper Middle Gravel	River gravel and sand	Acheulian Industry. Rich fauna. Human skull fragments
Lower Middle Gravel	River gravel and sand	Acheulian Industry. Rich fauna

THE PALAEOLITHIC PERIOD IN ESSEX

The Palaeolithic Sequence in Essex

British Quaternary Stage	Oxygen Isotope Stage (OIS)	Estimated years, BP	Lower Thames Terraces	Sites
FLANDRIAN	1		Floodplain	MESOLITHIC
		— 13,000 —		
DEVENSIAN	2		Maximum of glaciation	LATER UPPER PALAEOLITHIC EARLY UPPER PALAEOLITHIC White Colne leaf point
	3		Buried Channels	
	4			
	5a-d		EAST TILBURY MARSHES	▲ Tilbury
		— 110,000 —		
IPSWICHIAN	5e	— 120,000 —	Below f-p	None known
WOLSTONIAN	6		MUCKING	▲ Barling Magna ▲ Shoeburyness
		— 210,000 —		
	7			Aveley and Ilford brickearths
		— 260,000 —		■ Lion Pit Tramway, W. Thurrock
	8			
		— 302,000 —		
HOXNIAN	9		CORBETS TEY	▲ Belhus Park □▲ Purfleet ● Little Thurrock
		— 338,000 —		
	10	— 352,000 —	ORSETT HEATH	▲ Orsett Heath ● Clacton ▲● Swanscombe
	11			
		— 428,000 —		
ANGLIAN	12		Till	Major glaciation of Britain Thames diverted by ice into its present valley
		— 472,000 —		
CROMERIAN			Lower Kesgrave Sands and Gravels Terraces of the Tendring Plateau	Nothing known nearer than High Lodge, Suffolk

KEY

▲ Acheulian (hand-axes)

● Clactonian (cores and flakes)

■ Levalloisian (a technology rather than an industry, based on prepared cores)

□ Proto-Levalloisian

Table 1: The estimated years BP given are based on dates calculated for the various cold and warm stages identified by Oxygen isotope analysis of deep sea cores (Jones and Keen 1993, 4). It must be stressed that the correlation of marine and terrestrial events is by no means certain prior to OIS 5e. [N.B. Bridgland (1994,7) assumes OIS-7 between 186,000 and 245,000 years.]

PHASE I

Lower Loam	Channel fill of fine sediments	Clactonian Industry in primary context. Rich fauna
Lower Gravel	River gravel	Clactonian Industry. Rich fauna

CHALK OR THANET SAND BEDROCK

The mammalian faunal remains in Phases I and II are all interglacial species and include:

> Straight tusked elephant
> Rhinoceros
> Giant ox
> Giant, red, fallow and roe deer
> Horse
> Lion
> Wolf
> Marten
> Monkey
> Hare

These animals, coupled with the molluscs, give a vivid picture of the contemporary surroundings. There are also some bird bones and numerous small mammals. The latter are also useful for dating purposes as some of the species evolved relatively rapidly during the Pleistocene and their presence or absence is significant. Various changes are apparent upwards in the sequence, the most important one being the indication of the change towards cooler conditions during the time of the Upper Middle Gravel. Also, the presence of two distinctive molluscs (*Theodoxus serratiliniformis* and *Viviparus diluvianus*) after the deposition of the Lower Loam suggest that the Rhine and the Thames became confluent at this time, presumably through the rise of sea level during the closing part of the Hoxnian Interglacial.

As for the human skull fragments, they are regarded as those of a young female best described as an archaic form of *Homo sapiens*, probably ancestral to later Neanderthalers. With this impression of the opposite bank of the Thames to Essex during the period from about 440,000 to 350,000 years ago, the contemporary sites in Essex itself can now be considered.

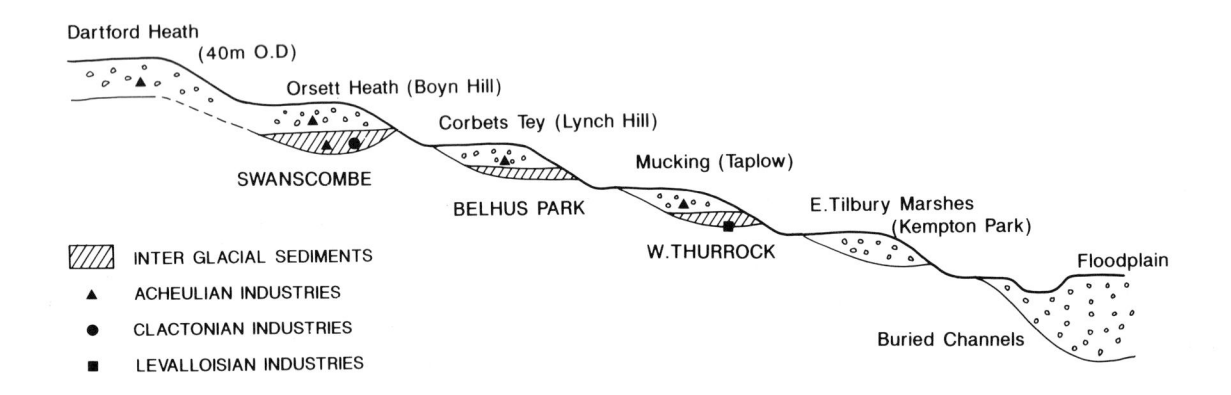

Fig. 2: Terraces of the Lower Thames Valley (after Bridgland 1994). Middle Thames Valley equivalents shown in brackets

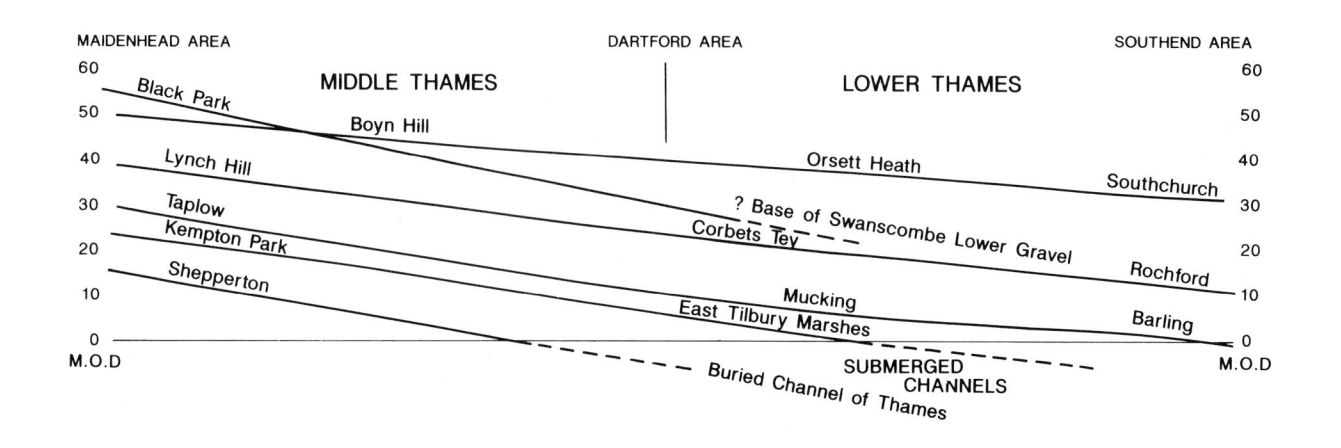

Fig. 3: Longitudinal profiles of the terraces of the Middle and Lower Thames

THE PALAEOLITHIC PERIOD IN ESSEX

When the Thames was flowing along the Lower Gravel channel at Swanscombe, it continued along the line of the present valley until just east of Southend where it joined the Medway and the combined waters flowed north east towards what is now the Blackwater. Little remains to substantiate this, but at Cudmore Grove, East Mersea, sections exposed in the cliff of organic estuarine silts are correlated by pollen analysis and palaeogeography with both the Swanscombe Lower Gravel and the Clacton sequence (Bridgland *et al.* 1988). The Clacton Channel deposits, once exposed along the cliffs at Clacton-on-Sea but now concealed by sea defences, have produced a wealth of archaeological material and information and are, of course, the type site of the Clactonian Industry.

Flint flakes and cores were known from Clacton, usually found on the beach when the cliff was naturally eroding, since the late 19th century. The site was already well known for its mammalian faunal remains, especially of straight-tusked elephant. It attracted the attention of S. Hazzledine Warren, who amassed a large collection of flints and also found the famous wooden spear, which is the oldest of the very few wooden arftifacts of the palaeolithic period found in Europe. The absence of hand-axes and the relative crudity of the flint working puzzled Warren and many other archaeologists, including the Abbe Breuil. The Abbe visited the site, examined the material and eventually wrote his paper on "Le Clactonien" (Breuil 1932) which was a landmark in palaeolithic studies. Excavations were carried out on a small scale in 1934 by Drs Oakley and Mary Leakey (Oakley and Leakey 1937) and demonstrated that although the upper estuarine beds were missing, the lower part of the Clacton Channel deposits continued from Clacton-on-Sea westwards to Lion Point, at Jaywick Sands. Major excavations were undertaken on the Golf Course during 1969 and 1970 by the University of Chicago (Singer *et al.* 1973). Boreholes were made on the site of the old Palace Hotel when it was demolished in 1979 and organic sediments of the Clacton Channel located at a depth of 15 m, thus beyond any threat from redevelopment of the site but also impractical to expose for research purposes. Further boreholes and a watching brief was conducted on the site of the former Butlins Holiday Camp in 1987 prior to its redevelopment. This was undertaken on behalf of the Essex County Council's Archaeology Section. Also in 1987 D.R. Bridgland conducted a series of small cuttings in the cliff on both sides of the pier and, after many years of controversey, demonstrated that the Clacton channel deposits were banked against the Holland Gravels (Bridgland *et al.* 1988)

There is a very extensive body of literature on this international site, which is now authoritatively summarised by Bridgland (1994). The actual Clactonian flint industry has been described by Warren (1951; 1958). It is an industry of cores and flakes. Some of the cores may have been used as choppers but micro-wear studies suggest the majority were for the production of flakes that could be used as they were or further trimmed into tools to serve some immediate purpose. Although there are a few distinctive aspects to the technology, there are no standardised tool forms or bifaces which could be termed hand-axes.

The Golf Course site produced a scatter of flintwork and broken mammalian bones in primary context (demonstrated by refitting pieces and the mint condition of many of the artifacts) on the south side of a small meander loop of the main river. Abraded artifacts in the gravelly beach may represent an earlier phase of the same industry, but the primary context site was clearly an interglacial one with a fauna that included horse, rhinoceros, fallow and red deer, Bos or Bison, giant beaver and numerous small mammals. Other sites in the Clacton Channel have produced remains of straight-tusked elephant, lion and pig.

Pollen analysis at the West Cliff in 1950 demonstrated the interglacial nature of the site, as did plant macro fossils found during the 1987 watching brief. Molluscs support it and it is reasonable to picture a wide river with minor abandoned channels flowing over a wide floodplain. The landscape was one of mixed deciduous woodland and open country with a climate much like that of the present day.

Nothing is known of the type of person who produced this industry. There has been much speculation in the past as to the possibility that it may have been someone at a different stage in human evolution to the Swanscombe remains, associated with hand-axes. However, as previously mentioned, hand-axes occur in Britain during the interglacial prior to the one represented at Clacton or the Lower Gravel at Swanscombe. Undoubtedly, simple Clactonian technique was often used in the more specialised hand-axe industries. J. McNabb (1993) has made an intensive study of the Clactonian Industry in Britain and concluded that the evidence is too slim to "warrant the continuing use of the name Clactonian, or the concept of a non-biface assemblage type." However, there is clear evidence from the Ural Mountains of Russia eastward, embodied in long stratigraphic successions of loess, that so-called pebble and flake industries occur at intervals over about 600,000 years with a total exclusion of hand-axes. Whether we have in Britain the appearance of two different traditions or the Clactonian Industry is merely another aspect of the Acheulian is one of the most intriguing aspects of the palaeolithic period and it is possible that the clue lies buried somewhere between Lion Point and the West Cliff at Clacton.

The estuarine beds overlying the West Cliff section at Clacton herald the onset of the high sea level towards the end of the Hoxnian Stage. It is possible that the few isolated finds of hand-axes in the Colchester area, and at Marks Tey, Feering, Kelvedon and Witham may owe their position to the existence of Hoxnian lakes. Hand-axes in the Boyn Hill Gravels at Orsett probably represent the artifacts from this period washed into the river as the climate deteriorated and a rejuvenated Thames flowed in braided courses with a cut and fill regime. This would have been at the beginning of the Wolstonian Stage (Table 1), possibly contemporary with the Upper Loam at Swanscombe, but this is a poorly understood part of the Quaternary sequence. All that can said at present is that the Wolstonian Stage as defined by the Geological Society of London's scheme for the British Quaternary (Mitchell *et al.* 1973) has to be modified by the twenty years of research since then. On the basis of the Oxygen Isotope chronology there must have been one or more major oscillations of climate with an interglacial usually described as occurring between the Hoxnian and the Ipswichian Stage. A major one probably correlates with OIS 7 as shown on the table. The whole matter is further complicated by the till at the Wolstonian type site now being considered to be of Anglian age. What does seem certain is the correlation of the Corbets Tey Gravel in the Lower Thames with the Lynch Hill Terrace of the Middle Thames. It is the latter which has produced some of the most prolific assemblages of palaeoliths in the Thames Valley, such as Furze Platt and Burnham, and there have been numerous discoveries of hand-axes in the Corbets Tey Gravel from South Ockendon to north-east London. The richest hand-axe site in Essex is the Pounds Farm or Gants Pit at Dovercourt. This is in terrace gravel of the River Stour at 27 m O.D. and is probably of this date. Roe (1968, 60) records 208 hand-axes from this site and a similar number of flakes.

Returning to the Thames Valley, the most prolific hand-axe sites in the Corbets Tey Gravel are mainly in the Greater London area, such as Chadwell Heath and numerous sites around Leytonstone and Wanstead. Although now just outside Essex, one must be mentioned for its

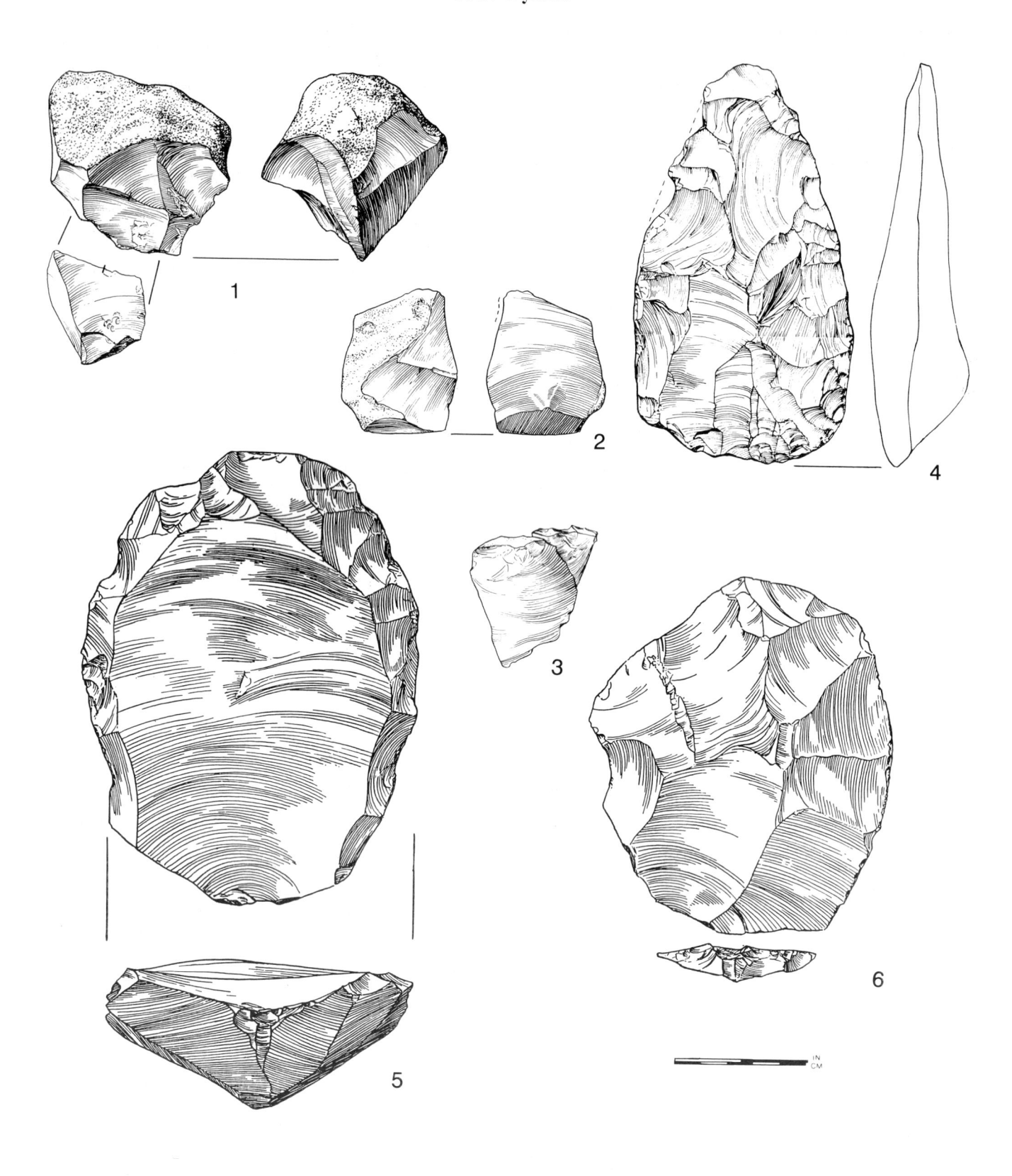

Fig. 4: Flint artifacts:
Clactonian Industry. From Clacton-on-Sea golf course excavations 1970:
1 Core with conjoinable flake
2 Flake with no retouch but microwear on edge represented by dotted line identified as caused by wood-whittling
3 Two refitted flakes
Acheulian Industry. From M11 excavation at South Woodford 1975:
4 Hand-axe in mint condition found in primary context
Levalloisian Industry. From Northfleet, Kent. Same industry as found in the Lion Pit Tramway Section 1984:
5 Large, struck 'tortoise' core
6 Flake struck from a core such as No.6. Note the faceting of the striking platform in order to produce the correct angle for the delivery of the final blow to detach the flake from the core

bearing it could have on other parts of the same terrace downstream. This is the site discovered in 1975 during the building of the M11 motorway. In a small area four hand-axes, the point of another and nine flakes were found in primary context lying on the gravel surface covered by 1-2 m of silty clay (Wymer 1985, 298). This is the only time that the "palaeolithic floor" postulated by Worthington Smith (1894) as exisiting over much of north-east London as far as the Roding has been seen since his own observations.

Palaeolithic hand-axe sites in the Thurrock area are numerous: mainly isolated finds but prolific at Chadwell St. Mary. However, there are also some very significant sites which must be mentioned: the Globe Pit at Little Thurrock, the Greenlands and Bluelands Pits at Purfleet, the Botany Pit also at Purfleet and Belhus Park at Aveley. All these sites add to an understanding of geological events during this long period and are associated with human activity.

The Globe Pit was dug for Chalk and Thanet Sand, in the process of which brickearth was removed from its northern end, and gravels both over the brickearth and an earlier deposit with the brickearth cut into and banked against it. In this latter deposit is a prolific Clactonian Industry whichappears to have been washed off a nearby river beach. Some of the flakes are virtually in mint condition (Wymer 1985, 307-310). The site is designated a Site of Special Scientific Interest by English Nature and some further excavations were conducted there in 1983 (Bridgland and Harding 1993) and considerably more artifacts were found, of the same flint industry but with the addition of two rolled flakes that may have come from the final stages of hand-axe manufacture.

The dating of this gravel at the Globe Pit with its Clactonian industry has been the subject of much dispute, as has been the brickearth which is banked against it. In the 19th century, this brickearth yielded a large number of faunal remains. It is clearly an interglacial fauna and has generally been equated with Swanscombe, thus of the Hoxnian Stage. Thus the stratigraphically earlier gravel would be an earlier stage of the same interglacial, equating very neatly the Clactonian Industry with its counterpart in the Lower Gravel at Swanscombe (see above). In order to explain the marked difference in altitude of the deposits at the two sites, a complex model of down-cutting and aggradation had to be employed (King and Oakley 1936). It is not necessary to labour the point here, but it is a classic example of archaeological typology taking precedence over geological considerations. Bridgland (1994, 235) places the gravel of the Globe Pit with its Clactonian Industry into the Corbets Tey Formation. This is regarded on the grounds of altitude and lithology as more recent than the higher Orsett Heath Gravel and equating with OIS 9 (Table 1). The interglacial brickearth is placed here, between the two cold phases which precede and follow it. This is contrary to the interpretations of others who would consider it no longer Hoxnian (OIS 11 sensu Swanscombe) but Ipswichian (OIS 5e) (Gibbard 1994, 62). In support of this dating are the other sites at Purfleet mentioned above in Corbets Tey Gravels (Bridgland 1994, 218-236). At Belhus Park, interglacial deposits are found between a lower and upper gravel. Some hand-axes have been found in the sandy gravel just above the interglacial sediments. A more complex site in the former Bluelands and Greenlands quarries (Palmer 1975) has yielded a sequence very similar to the Globe Pit, with flakes and cores which could be Clactonian in a thin basal gravel underlying interglacial sediments. There are no palaeoliths known from the latter, but the gravel above contains some hand-axes in its lower part and some Levalloisian flakes in its upper part. The nearby Botany Pit, on the north side of the outcrop of Chalk of the Purfleet anticline (now all quarried away) contained gravel which produced a prolific industry of flakes and cores, much of which is indistinguishable from the Clactonian industry but also demonstrating a Levallois-type faceting of the striking platforms (Wymer 1968, 312-314). However, no Levallois-type prepared cores (so-called tortoise cores) accompanied them, nor did any of the flakes appear to have been struck from such cores, so the industry is termed "Proto-Levalloisian."

This area of Thurrock is obviously a very critical one for this period and it is very unfortunate that so much has been dug away commercially in the past with so little record. Hopefully, what remains will receive adequate attention if it should be threatened.

If the Corbets Tey Gravel is traced downstream from Purfleet, it cannot be traced further east than Ockendon, where it meets the valley of the Mar Dyke, beyond which is higher ground of London Clay. This anomaly is explained by the former course of the Thames at the time having had to adjust to this topography, coupled with the barrier of the Purfleet anticline. The result that the Thames was diverted into a great meander loop, doubling back on itself and flowing east to west until it made a gap in the Chalk just west of Purfleet and resumed its normal direction. This also explains why the present Mar Dyke flows east to west here, as it follows the line of the old valley.

The latter part of the Corbets Tey Gravel aggradation is regarded as belonging to the oncoming cold conditions of OIS 8. Eventually, as the climate deteriorated further, a low sea level ensued and the Thames cut down accordingly, depositing the gravels of the Mucking Terrace. The important site at the Lion Pit Tramway Cutting at West Thurrock relates to this stage. A flint industry of well-developed Levalloisian cores and flakes occurs in the upper levels of a thin basal gravel. It may have moved slightly, but the mint condition of many of the artifacts and the presence of refitting material prove that it is contemporary with the deposition of the deposit or, perhaps more accurately, it was produced on the surface of it (Bridgland and Harding 1994). This was then covered by a thick, c. 12 m, of interbedded clays, silts and sands, considered to be intertidal or estuarine deposits, indicative of a rise of sea level in the next interglacial period.

However, a thin layer of brickearth within this sequence is a freshwater deposit and is correlated with the West Thurrock brickearth, well known from the late 19th century for its mammalian faunal remains. Bridgland's interpretation puts this brickearth into OIS 7, thus more recent than the fossiliferous brickearth mentioned above at Little Thurrock, which has been a matter of argument since it was first discovered. Archaeologically, it would seem that the Levallois artifacts can be correlated with confidence with the famous but un-dated Levallois site of Baker's Hole on the Kent side of the river (Wymer 1968, 354-356; Wenban-Smith 1993). This is supported by its altitude and that the basal gravel at the Lion Pit rests on Coombe Rock, which is also associated with the Baker's Hole industry.

Other sites in the Lower Thames Valley have been related to OIS 7, i.e. an interglacial between the Hoxnian and the Ipswichian, such as the brickearths at Aveley and Ilford with their rich mammalian remains (Sutcliffe 1985). However, this is not accepted by all Quaternary geologists (Gibbard 1994). There are no other comparable sites in Essex; the nearest is in the Stour Valley at Brundon, near Sudbury, Suffolk (Wymer 1985, 198-202). It might well be asked where are the sites in Essex of the Ipswichian Interglacial, as represented at the type site of Bobbitshole near Ipswich and Trafalgar Square in London. Perhaps, as far as the Lower Thames Valley is concerned, they have either been eroded away during the Last Glaciation or are submerged (Fig. 3). There is nothing in Essex to demonstrate any human presence during this stage, but this may be a national phenomenon, for, as yet, it is not possible to demonstrate with any certainty that the country was occupied at all. It also seems that the previous interglacial as represented at Lion Pit Tramway Cutting, Aveley and Ilford was only sparsely occupied. Nothing is known in Essex, although flakes and an atypical hand-axe are known from the brickearths of the Stour estuary at Stutton and Harkstead in Suffolk, thought to belong to this interglacial. A reason for this decreasing evidence for human occupation in the successive interglacials could perhaps be the existence of the English Channel, for there is no such sign of depopulations in Northern France during contemporary episodes. It was previously seen that the Straits of Dover were thought to have been breached during the Anglian Stage. At first, during interglacials, even during the times of maximum high sea level, crossing the waters with intervening islands and the opposite side reasonably close, might not have been difficult. However, each successive rise in sea level would have followed long periods of erosion of the Chalk, so that the crossing was wider until it eventually became too hazardous to attempt. A few hand-axes are known from the Mucking Gravel near Southend, especially at Barling Magna (Buckley 1977), and some other isolated finds may belong to this period prior to the Last Interglacial (i.e. Devensian Stage or OIS 5e). Against the suggestion that the Straits of Dover became an ever-increasing barrier to human movement, is the existence of palaeoliths in Britain during the Last Glaciation. However, the only evidence for Essex is the discovery of a few hand-axes of a form typical of the Mousterian of Acheulian Tradition found in the buried channel of the Thames at Tilbury (Wymer 1985, 302). Perhaps this could be explained by these artifacts representing a very late phase of the industry when the sea level was low enough to risk crossing. Certainly, the British equivalent of the Mousterian of Acheulian Tradition is very different from the French industry of the Early part of the Last Glaciation. Some independent evolution seems to have been likely. Yet, the Tilbury hand-axes indicate some people were about and, although no human skeletal remains have been found in Britain of this period, they would have been Neanderthalers.

The ice of the last ice sheet to cover Britain during the Devensian Stage came no nearer than the north coast of Norfolk. It reached its maximum about 18,000 years ago. The Upper Palaeolithic of north-west Europe is dated from about 40,000 years ago and there is one artifact found in Essex that probably dates to some time between the arrival in Britain of modern humans with Upper Palaeolithic industries and the maximum of the glaciation: a finely-made bifacial leaf point found at White Colne (Layard 1927). It was found in gravel underlying a Mesolithic site at a depth of "8 ft, in white sand overlying the blue loam which is below water level." The same gravel yielded a complete mammoth tusk, two teeth fragments, and molars of horse, aurochs and ibex.

The Later British Upper Palaeolithic is barely represented (see Jacobi in Chapter 2 of this volume). Again, it may be that the sites were mainly along the lower reaches of the Thames and other rivers and are now submerged.

Several isolated sites have not been mentioned in this survey as they can add little to our knowledge of the Palaeolithic apart from some idea of the general distribution of people at unknown times in this great span of time. There is also much that cannot be explained, such as the presence of sometimes unrolled hand-axes at Stone Point, Walton-on-the-Naze, but hopefully enough has been described to make it unnecessary to emphasise the importance of the area for unravelling some of the history of the earliest occupation of North West Europe during the last half a million years.

Bibliography and references
Details of the sites mentioned, and others, can be found in Wymer 1968 and 1985, which contain references to original sources. The CBA Gazetteer of British Lower and Middle Palaeolithic sites (Roe 1968) gives comprehensive lists of localities and museums where material is preserved. For an up-to-date summary of the British Palaeolithic period, consult "The Lower and Middle Palaeolithic Periods in Britain" (Roe 1981) and for a survey of Palaeolithic societies in Europe "The Palaeolithic Settlement of Europe" (Gamble 1986). For Quaternary geology: Evans 1975 and Sparks and West 1972 (introductory) and Jones and Keen 1993 (advanced). Contemporary fauna: Sutcliffe 1985 and Stuart 1982.

Ashton, N. M., Cook, J., Lewis, S. G. and Rose, J. (eds). 1992. *High Lodge. Excavations by G. de G. Sieveking, 1962-8 and J. Cook, 1988*, British Museum Press
Bridgland, D.R. 1994 *Quaternary of the Thames*, Chapman and Hall
Bridgland, D. R., Allen, P., Currant, A. P. et al. 1988. 'Report of the Geologists' Association Field Meeting in north-east Essex, May 22nd-24th 1987', *Proc. Geol. Ass.* 99, 315-33
Bridgland, D. R. and Harding, P. 1993. 'Middle Pleistocene Terrace deposits at Globe Pit, Little Thurrock, and their contained Clactonian industry', *Proc. Geol. Ass.* 104, 263-83
Bridgland, D. R. and Harding, P. 1994. 'Lion Pit Tramway Cutting (West Thurrock: TQ 598783)' in Bridgland, D. R., *Quaternary of the Thames*, 237-51
Breuil, H. 1932. 'Les Industries a Eclats du Palaeolithique Ancien. 1. Le Clactonien', *Prehistoire* 1, 125-90
Buckley, D. G. 1977. 'Barling Hall, Barling Magna TQ 937896', in Couchman, C. R. (ed.), 'Work of Essex County Council Archaeology Section 1977', *Essex Archaeol. Hist.* 11, 32-3
Conway, B. W. and McNabb, J. Forthcoming. Excavations at Barnfield Pit 1968-71
Conway, B. W. and Waechter, J. d'a 1977. 'Lower Thames and Medway valleys - Barnfield Pit, Swanscombe', in Shephard-Thorn, E. R. and Wymer, J. J. (eds), *South-East England and the Thames Valley, Guide Book for excursion A5 X INQUA Congress Birmingham*, Norwich: Geoabstracts, 38-44
Evans, J. G. 1975. *The environment of early man in the British Isles*, London: Paul Elek
Gamble, C. 1986. *The Palaeolithic settlement of Europe*, Cambridge: University Press
Gibbard, P. L. 1985. *The Pleistocene History of the Middle Thames Valley*, Cambridge: University Press
Gibbard, P. L. 1988. 'The history of the great northwest European rivers during the past three million years', *Phil. Trans. Roy. Soc. London*, B318, 559-602
Gibbard, P. L. 1994. *Pleistocene history of the Lower Thames Valley*, Cambridge: University Press
Jones, R. L. and Keen, D. H. 1993. *Pleistocene Environments in the British Isles*, Chapman and Hall
King, W. B. R. and Oakley, K. P. 1936. 'The Pleistocene succession in the lower part of the Thames valley', *Proc. Prehist. Soc.* 1, 52-76
Layard, N. F. 1927. 'A late Palaeolithic settlement in the Colne valley, Essex', *Antiq. J.* 7, 500-14
McNabb, J. 1993. *The Clactonian British Lower Palaeolithic technology in biface and non-biface manufacture*, Unpublished thesis, Inst. Archaeol. London
Mitchell, G. F., Penny, L. F., Shotton, F. W. et al. 1973. *A Correlation of Quaternary deposits in the British Isles*, Geological Soc. London Special Report, 4
Oakley, K. P. and Leakey, M. 1937. 'Report on the excavations at Jaywick Sands, Essex (1934)', *Proc. Prehist. Soc.* 3, 217-60
Palmer, S. 1975. 'A Palaeolithic site at North Road, Purfleet, Essex', *Trans. Essex Archaeol. Soc.* 7, 1-13
Roberts, M. B. 1986. 'Excavations of the Lower Palaeolithic site at Amey's Eartham pit, Boxgrove, West Sussex: a preliminary report', *Proc. Prehist. Soc.* 52, 215-45
Roe, D. A. 1968. *A Gazetteer of British Lower and Middle Palaeolithic sites*, CBA Res. Rep. 8
Roe, D. A. 1981. *The Lower and Middle Palaeolithic periods in Britain*, London: Routledge and Kegan Paul
Singer, R., Wymer, J. J. and Gladfelter, B. G. 1973. 'Excavation of the Clactonian industry at the golf course, Clacton-on-Sea, Essex', *Proc. Prehist. Soc.* 39, 6-74
Smith, W. G. 1894. *Man the Primeval Savage*, London: Stanford
Sparks, B. W. and West, R. G. 1972. *The Ice Age in Britain*, Methuen

Stuart, A. J. 1982. *Pleistocene vertebrates in the British Isles*, London; Longman

Sutcliffe, A. J. 1985. *On the track of Ice Age mammals*, British Museum (Natural History)

Warren, S. H. 1951. 'The Clacton Flint Industry: a new interpretation', *Proc. Geol. Ass.* 62, 107-35

Warren, S. H. 1958. 'The Clacton Flint Industry: a supplementary note', *Proc. Geol. Ass.* 69, 123-9

Wenban-Smith, F. 1993. 'Interim report on current Pleistocene Research in the Ebbsfleet valley, north west Kent', *Arch. Cant.* 110, 384-8

Whiteman, C. A. and Rose, J. 1992. 'Thames River sediments of the British Early and Middle Pleistocene', *Quat. Sci. Rev.* 11, 363-75

Wymer, J. J. 1968. *Lower Palaeolithic archaeology in Britain, as represented by the Thames Valley*, London: John Baker

Wymer, J.J. 1985 *The Palaeolithic sites of East Anglia*, Norwich: Geo Books

The Late Upper Palaeolithic and Mesolithic of Essex

R M Jacobi

The Late Glacial: 13-10,000 radiocarbon years BP

In the fifteen years since the publication of *Archaeology in Essex to AD 1500* we have learned an enormous amount more about the Late Glacial archaeology of Britain. This knowledge has particularly been augmented by the very careful application of accelerator mass spectrometry (AMS) radiocarbon dating to animal bones accidentally cut-marked by stone tools during dismemberment, artefacts such as barbed points made from bone or antler (see below), and human fossils. We also now possess many more radiocarbon dates for reliably identified faunal items (for a summary see Housley 1991).

As a result, we know that the earliest human re-occupation of Britain following the last ice maximum took place sometime between 13 and 12,500 radiocarbon years ago. It is also clear that elements of the Late Pleistocene fauna such as horse and reindeer were still present for a period of time after 10,000 years ago - the conventional end of the Pleistocene as measured in radiocarbon years.

Although short, as compared to the whole of the Pleistocene, the Late Glacial was marked by remarkable changes in annual temperatures and vegetation patterns. Their scale and rapidity almost certainly contributed to the disappearance from western Europe during the Late Glacial of species such as the mammoth - last recorded from Britain a few centuries before 12,000 BP (Lister 1991).

The principal features of these changes might be summarized as a rapid warming, perhaps beginning only ~ 13,000 BP, which resulted in a climate as warm as that of the present day by ~ 12,500 BP. This was followed, almost immediately, by a gradual cooling to a warmest summer month of ~ 10° C and a coldest winter month of ~ -17° C at ~ 10,500 BP. By ~ 9,800 BP the climate was again as warm as today (data from Atkinson *et al.* 1987). Between ~ 11,800 and 10,800 BP much of lowland Britain was covered by birch or birch and pine forest. Its replacement by open landscapes for the last part of the Late Glacial was due to low temperatures and destruction by massive forest fires, some triggered by volcanic eruptions.

Human re-occupation of Britain, as of much of northern Europe, corresponded closely with the warming of 13-12,500 years ago. For Britain archaeological radiocarbon dates are fewest for the period 11-10,000 years ago and it is not impossible that a break in human settlement corresponded to the maximum climatic downturn of 10,500 years ago.

Late Upper Palaeolithic find-spots in Essex are few, and their recognition depends upon artefact typology rather than context. That artefacts have been recovered from Late Glacial sediments at Broxbourne (E. Herts : Allison *et al.* 1952, 192-193) and at Sproughton (S.E. Suffolk : Wymer *et al.* 1975; Wymer 1976), localities not far beyond the county boundary, suggests that this need not always be the case.

In the absence of associated chronometric or environmental data it is only possible to divide these Essex finds into those likely to be older or younger than the climatic low of 10,500 years ago.

Older would be a shouldered and obliquely truncated blade found on the beach at Shoeburyness (Jacobi 1980a, fig. 4), a pair of broken Cheddar or Creswell points recently recognized at the British Museum amongst a multi-period collection made by S. Hazzledine Warren at the Lea Valley Co's pit at Hallsford (in the Roding Valley, east of Chipping Ongar), and some of the finds from beaches at Frinton and Walton-on-the-Naze. The finds from Walton include two partial Cheddar or Creswell points, several large convex-backed bi-points (Martingell and Jacobi 1979) and a large and atypical penknife point.

To the large tanged "points" illustrated in *Archaeology in Essex to AD 1500* (fig. 5) it is possible to add another picked up from The Wade, just south of Horsey Island (Warren 1912, pl. 14, 9 and 9b). While in 1980 continental analogues were emphasized, they can also be paralleled at Hengistbury Head (in Dorset : Barton 1992, fig. 4.25) where they form part of what has been termed a "straight-backed blade assemblage" (ibid., p.192). Its age remains to be precisely established, but somewhere between 12 and 11,000 radiocarbon years ago seems most probable. Whether the Essex examples also came from the same lithic context can only be discovered by excavation.

Younger than the climatic low of 10,500 years ago is the so-called "long blade" technology. As the name implies, one characteristic is the great size of some of the blades and of the cores when abandoned. Blades with their margins "bruised", possibly from chopping through antler (Barton 1986), can be numerous and the earliest true microliths to be found in Britain come from some of these find-spots. It is now apparent that these "long blade" find-spots date to the centuries immediately before and after 10,000 BP and are to be associated with a fauna of horse and reindeer (for more detailed descriptions and discussion see Barton 1991 and Cook and Jacobi, 1994).

The only Essex material which can confidently be considered part of such a "long blade" technology is from the shore of the River Stour to the N.N.E. of Wrabness Hall. Found by Warren in 1926 this small collection, now in the British Museum, includes an obliquely truncated bladelet (microlith), scrapers and burins as well as blades, flakes and cores. While there are re-fits, the material is clearly incomplete and presumably what was recovered is only part of a larger and once more informative assemblage.

Susceptible to no closer definition than Upper Palaeolithic, rather than Mesolithic, are isolated finds such as a blade from Tiptree Churchyard (Colchester and Essex Museum) and cores from Doreward's Hall, Bocking (Martingell and Clarke in Priddy (ed), 1987, p.141) and Southchurch Hall, Southend (Crowe, pers. comm.). Large blade cores have also been found on Hall Farm (McMaster 1978) and close to Brook Hall, Mount Bures (McMaster, pers. comm.).

At the beginning of this section reference was made to how much AMS radiocarbon dating had contributed to a better understanding of aspects of the Late Glacial. It has, for example, very successfully provided ages for "Creswellian" cave occupations (Jacobi 1991, table 13.1), and begun to demonstrate clear differences in the timing of human exploitation as between different upland areas. As yet there are too few radiocarbon dates and too few useful samples of Late Upper Palaeolithic material from lowland Britain to allow its integration into this developing picture. Such integration should now become an urgent research objective, and one to which the area of present-day Essex can be expected to contribute. Each of the finds noted above pinpoints an area where field-walking and watching-briefs might identify the sites whose excavation we so badly need.

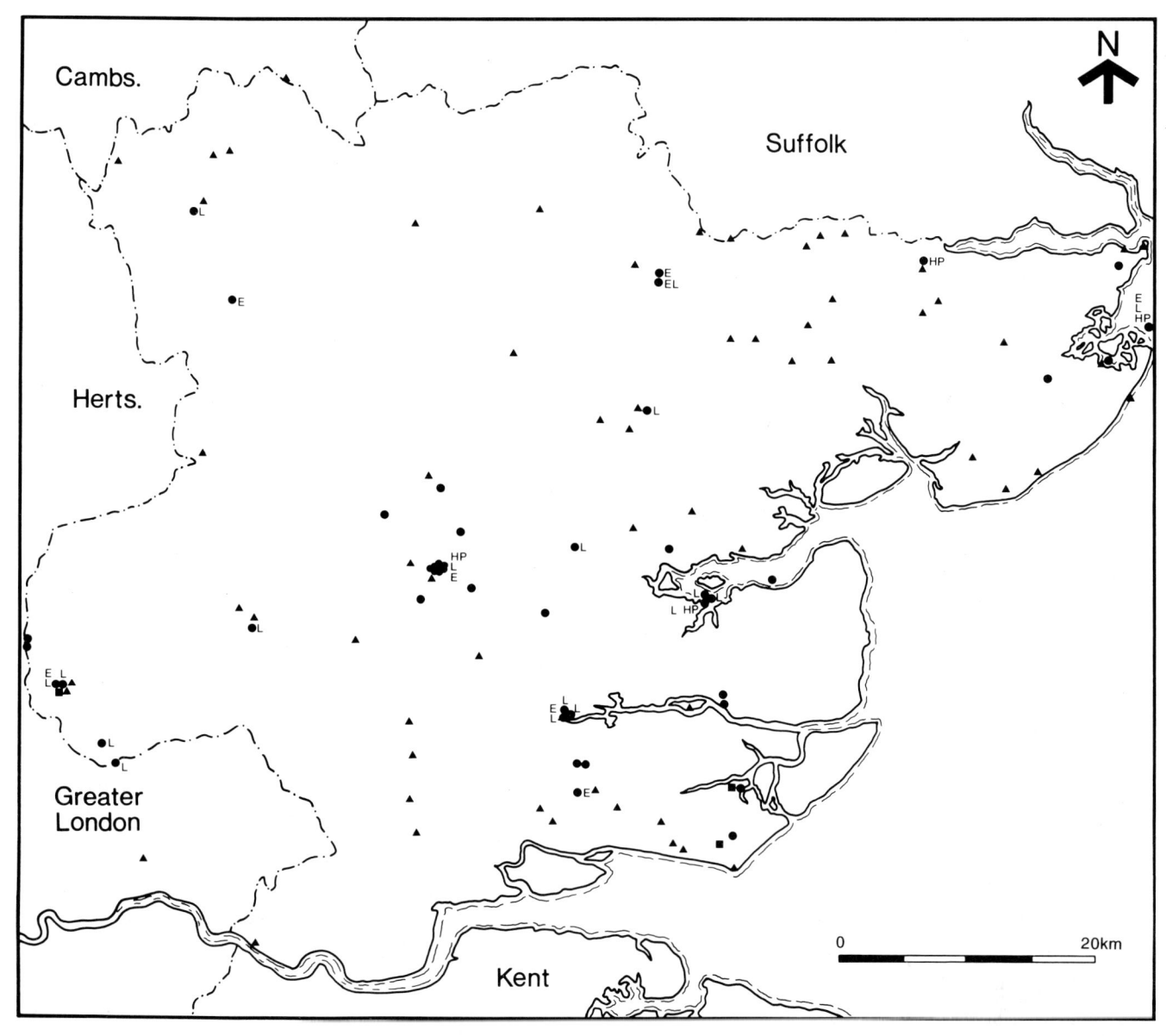

- ● — Mesolithic find spots identified by presence of microliths
- ■ — Mesolithic find spots identified by the presence of micro-burins
- ▲ — Mesolithic find spots identified by the presence of transversely sharpened core-adzes or sharpening-flakes

E - Early Mesolithic
L - Later Mesolithic
HP - Presence of "hollow-based point"

Fig. 1 Distribution of Mesolithic sites and finds.

The Mesolithic - introduction

Many of the older finds of Mesolithic material were described in *Archaeology in Essex to AD 1500* (Jacobi 1980b). Rather than simply repeating this information it seems more worthwhile to concentrate on some of the problems which we face in attempting to understand the archaeology of this period. It is these problems which must be taken into account when shaping any research strategy for the period as a whole, and the County in particular.

In 1980 it was generally accepted that technologies which we would describe as Mesolithic first appeared slightly before 10,000 years ago - the agreed radiocarbon boundary between the Pleistocene and Holocene. More recently, it has been argued that the earliest such technologies date to several hundred years after this boundary (Barton 1991). As noted above, a long blade technology and a fauna which included horse and reindeer could be found within these several hundred years.

The earliest dates for the British Neolithic are of ~ 5,400 radiocarbon years ago, and there is, to my mind, no credible evidence for a chronological overlap between Mesolithic and Neolithic technologies - at least in England and Wales.

The Mesolithic is equivalent to that part of the Holocene when most of lowland Britain was covered by a succession of forest types (Allen and Sturdy 1980, table I). Breaks occurred around lakes and along rivers, particularly where beavers had been active. As glacier ice melted and was returned to the oceans world sea-level continued to rise during most of the Mesolithic. One result would be the transformation of Essex from a land-locked plateau at the beginning of the period to an approximation of its present geography by its end.

Within this Early Holocene forest will have been populations of wild pig, red deer, roe deer, elk (moose) and wild cattle. By the end of the Mesolithic their hunting could, in the area of present-day Essex, have been combined with fresh- and salt-water fishing, the exploitation of migratory birds and sea-mammals, and the cropping of shell-fish beds. The relative proportions of hunting, fishing and gathering will have varied with local geography, and the economic potentials of many Essex locations will have changed dramatically during the Mesolithic as sea-levels rose replacing forests with coast, salt-marsh and tidal waters.

To my knowledge, no food residues have yet been recorded in association with Mesolithic artefacts at an Essex site. It is probably unnecessary to stress the need to explore any such association. This is a national, not just a local, priority.

Lithic finds
Most of what survives in Britain from the Mesolithic takes the form of lithic artefacts, of which the most diagnostic are microliths and transversely sharpened core-adzes. All too often these turn up within multi-period collections made during field-walking or recovered from mineral sediments exposed at inter-tidal level (Vincent and George 1980 and 1981), from surfaces beneath more recent structures or from the filling of later pits and ditches.

Conventionally, the period is divided into an Early and a Late Mesolithic (Jacobi 1973; Mellars 1974) with the boundary between the two at ~ 8,800- 8,500 radiocarbon years ago (for a display of radiocarbon dates see Myers 1988, fig. I). The division is principally based on changes in the size and shape of the microliths used as the tips and insets for an unknown range of equipment.

One aspect of the British Mesolithic which is gradually becoming more apparent, and which provides an interesting contrast to many areas of the European mainland, is how many Early Mesolithic find-spots there are in some parts of England and Wales. For Essex Early Mesolithic material can confidently be recognized from Hill Wood clay pit, High Beach, in Epping Forest (Jacobi 1980b, 14-17; Jacobi *et al.* 1979), White Colne (Jacobi 1980b, 17), Pledgdon, near Elsenham Cross (ibid.) and the Wyburn Height Estate, Thundersley (ibid., figs 8a and 8b). Of this, only the sample excavated in 1959-61 and 1977 from the western margin of Hill Wood clay pit is well documented (Marshall 1959; Jacobi *et al.* 1979). Early shapes of microlith are also present in many surface collections (as, for example, from Little Clacton: Martingell in Priddy (ed.), 1986) as well as amongst the finds from later period excavations (for example Chelmsford, site V: Healey pers. comm.).

The largest collections of Late Mesolithic microliths are from a three hundred metre length of the north bank of the River Crouch to the west of its junction with Fen Creek opposite Hullbridge, and from the two miles of beach south of Stone Point, Walton-on-the-Naze (Jacobi 1980b, 20-24). Not surprisingly, both collections are chronologically very mixed and also include what is, beyond ambiguity, a significant Early Mesolithic component. The description of the material from Walton as "flotsam" (ibid.) was inappropriate. Jetsam is, of course, the correct term.

Small numbers of late microlith shapes come from recently excavated sites where the standard of recovery has been high, as for example from Chigborough Farm, Kelvedon and Woodham Walter (Healey pers. comm.), or occur as rare components of the predominantly Early Mesolithic collections from White Colne and Hill Wood clay pit (Jacobi *et al.* 1979, fig. 2.12 and 2.13).

Without doubt chance recoveries will continue to provide the most frequent additions to our knowledge of Mesolithic Essex. For the South Benfleet area Crowe (1992) has drawn attention to an association between such finds and the Claygate/Bagshot ridge. It will be interesting to see whether further associations between the Mesolithic and particular sub-soil types become apparent as more areas are covered by systematic field-walking. Still more interesting would be any significant differences between Early and Late Mesolithic distributions. Such differences would not be unexpected given, as already noted, that the Mesolithic coincided with ongoing coastline recession and a well-documented sequence of forest types.

There is also good reason to believe that considerable changes in social and economic organization differentiate the Early from the Late Mesolithic. The former involved specialized subsistence economies organized solely from base-camps, the latter generalized subsistence economies with task-sites satellite to base-camps (Cane 1986). Our principal sources of information are the size and composition of stone tool assemblages and site-sizes - contrast, for example, data for Early Mesolithic sites in the Central Pennines (Stonehouse 1992) with those for Late Mesolithic sites (Radley *et al.* 1974). As yet, Essex has nothing to contribute to this data-base.

For it to do so, would require investigation of the best available approximations to single phase sites. In a lowland area, heavily cultivated from Neolithic times onwards, sites with the relevant level of integrity are clearly going to be hard to find. One obvious strategy would be to exploit those areas where lithics might have been rapidly trapped within, or beneath, fine-grained alluvial sediments.

Other cultures
So far discussion has been in terms of an Early and Late Mesolithic. As we have already seen, the period lasted for over four thousand radiocarbon years. Not surprisingly, there is evidence for temporal change within both Early and Late Mesolithic technologies. There is also increasing evidence for technologies with regional distributions. Best documented are find-spots clustered in the Weald of Surrey, Sussex and East Hampshire whose flint inventories include points with concave basal modification - so-called "Horsham" points (Clark 1934, fig. 9, 162-171).

Single examples of these points come from Mayland on the Blackwater (Vincent and George 1980, site 7) and Chelmsford (site AG : Healey pers. comm.) and four from Walton-on-the-Naze. A broken "Horsham" point in the Wellcome collection at the British Museum is provenanced to Lawford.

Other rare microlith shapes from Essex have the centres of their respective distributions in the Midlands and in Suffolk and Norfolk. Until we know more about the contexts of these Essex finds their significance is impossible to evaluate. If, however, there is any correlation with ethnicity they may hint at a fluidity of social boundaries in the area of present-day Essex.

Organic artefacts
The excavation of Star Carr was important for demonstrating that, where conditions for preservation were suitable, artefacts of bone, antler and wood could be expected from British sites of this period (Clark 1954). Sadly, this expectation has hardly been fulfilled.

The only artefact from Essex not made of stone, and whose likely Mesolithic age can be extrapolated from directly radiocarbon dated examples found elsewhere in Britain (see comments by Bonsall and C. Smith in Hedges *et al.* 1990, 105), was recovered from the Stour during bridge building at Wormingford (W.G. Smith 1898). It is part of a red deer antler beam, 59cm long, perforated at one end and with an elongated oblique truncation forming a blade at the other. This blade would have been orientated axe-wise to the handle which presumably once passed through the perforation. In current parlance it is an "unbalanced, or laterally perforated, antler beam mattock" (C. Smith 1989, 278). Although its upper end has been carefully trimmed, traces remain of a second, now partial, perforation. It would seem that the implement had snapped where first perforated and then been re-drilled lower down its shaft with any irregularities at the broken end being tidied up. The same pattern of events can be seen on an identical antler implement from the Thames at Kew (Museum of London : A.13647). Either these were treasured personal possessions, or their owners were loathe to simply throw away the time spent in preparing their blades.

W. G. Smith (1898, 312) thought that the Wormingford implement was a potter's tool - improbable given its suggested age - while Lovett (1898) argued that it might have been a bark-peeler. More recently, similar artefacts have been described as axes, picks or mattocks. However, none of these implied functions seems appropriate to the asymmetric polishing and rounding visible on their blades.

It doesn't need me to stress the necessity of following up any hint of a Mesolithic find-spot likely to produce bone, antler or wooden artefacts. Given the length of the period, it is impossible to believe that other sites as rich as Star Carr do not exist.

Absolute dating

That so much of the discussion has been couched simply in terms of an Early and Late Mesolithic disguises the fact that we know far less than we would like to admit about the detailed chronology of the period. No stratified sequence of cultural materials has ever been described for the British Mesolithic. The nearest approaches are reports of Early Mesolithic microlith types apparently deeper within a mineral profile than their Late Mesolithic equivalents (for example Froom 1976, fig. 63).

For this reason, creation of any sort of chronology has depended on the dating of individual find-spots and the extrapolation of these results to other localities, themselves undatable, but whose artefacts appear broadly similar. Radiocarbon dating has, of course, been the technique most used.

Bonsall (1976) rightly criticized the relevance and validity of some of these dates, and for much of Britain the situation has not markedly improved since. Most useful as potential dating samples are the charred shells from hazel nuts, where these have been collected as a food source, artefacts and by-products of bone and antler, animal bones and teeth with cut-marks and human bones or teeth. Generally, wood charcoals should be regarded as unsatisfactory dating material.

At the time of writing, the only radiocarbon date from Essex which is of un-ambiguous relevance to human activity during the period with which this chapter deals is for part of a "toothed" antler point found in 1974 on spoil beside a dis-used gravel-pit at Fisher's Green, Waltham Holy Cross. As is so often the case, this was an isolated find. Its age of 9,79±100 BP (OxA-1427 : Hedges *et al.* 1989, 216) provides us with a problem in that it overlaps dates for both the "long blade" technology (see above) and for the earliest Mesolithic, as well as the likely chronological boundary between an open-ground and a forest fauna.

While there is still a need to radiocarbon date more British Mesolithic assemblages, recent dendrochronological studies and the creation of the first calibration curves back to the end of the Pleistocene (Kromer and Becker 1993; Stuiver and Becker 1993) suggest that interpretation of some of these results may not be as straight-forward as hitherto perceived. Particularly troublesome are major "plateaux" in the calibration curves where radiocarbon dates remain constant over periods of several calendar centuries. The practical effect of these "plateaux" is that there will be portions of the Mesolithic during which events cannot be arranged in sequence using radiocarbon alone.

One spin-off of this situation may be to re-focus attention on pollen analysis, not just as a technique for environmental reconstruction, but as a valid means of relative dating - at least on a local basis. Recent work at Duvensee in North Germany (Bokelmann *et al.* 1981 and 1985) has shown how successfully radiocarbon dating and pollen analysis can be combined to order a number of spatially discrete find-spots, each of whose lithic inventories contains typological clues to the evolution of Early Mesolithic technologies over a much wider area of northern Europe.

Conclusions

So, what of the Essex Mesolithic? Perhaps this paper has treated aspects of it as something of an Aunt Sally, although the short-comings which I have attempted to highlight exist for most other areas of Britain as well. Clearly, if any progress is to be made towards a better understanding of the period and its dynamics, there is a need to integrate mapping of land-scapes with investigation of a range of single period sites whose plans have remained un-distorted by subsequent events. There is also a need to focus on localities where organic artefacts and food-residues are likely to be preserved. Ideally, any chronology should be supported by pollen analyses as well as by radiocarbon dating.

For many present-day counties this would, of course, be an impossible, or at best nearly impossible, set of objectives. Essex, however, is fortunate in that it includes part of the Lea Valley, an area known to contain organic sediments covering the whole of the Early Post Glacial and extending back into the Late Glacial (Allison *et al.* 1952). The existence of Mesolithic sites sealed beneath peat was demonstrated as long ago as the 1930s (Warren *et al.* 1934). Observations made in the 1970s revealed not only something of the great typological diversity amongst the Mesolithic material exposed by gravel-digging in the Broxbourne area, but also that this material could occur within, rather than always beneath, organic sediments (Reynier, in prep.). The limited radiocarbon and pollen studies undertaken at that time proved the susceptibility of these sites to both techniques.

Something of what we need to help comprehend the Mesolithic on a national scale must still survive in the Lea Valley. The time has come to go out and get it before it too ends up as quarry spoil.

Acknowledgements

I would like to thank Owen Bedwin for inviting me to write this paper. I also thank him, Elizabeth Healey and Hazel Martingell for much useful information about Essex finds.

Bibliography

Allen, R. H. and Sturdy, R. G. 1980. 'The environmental background', in D. Buckley (ed.), *Archaeology in Essex to AD 1500*, CBA Research Report, 34, 1-7

Allison, J., Godwin, H. and Warren, S. H. 1952. 'Late-Glacial deposits at Nazeing in the Lea Valley, North London', *Phil. Trans. Roy. Soc. London*, Series B, 236, 169-240

Atkinson, T. C., Briffa, K. R. and Coope, G. R. 1987. 'Seasonal temperatures in Britain during the past 22,000 years, reconstructed using beetle remains', *Nature*, 325, 587-592

Barton, R. N. E. 1986. 'Experiments with long blades from Sproughton, near Ipswich, Suffolk', in D.A.Roe (ed.), *Studies in the Upper Palaeolithic of Britain and Northwest Europe*, British Archaeological Reports, S296, 129-42

Barton, R. N. E. 1991. 'Technological innovation and continuity at the end of the Pleistocene in Britain', in N. Barton, A. J. Roberts and D. A. Roe (eds), *The Late Glacial in north-west Europe: human adaptation and environmental change at the end of the Pleistocene*, CBA Research Report, 77, 234-45

Barton, R. N. E. 1992. *Hengistbury Head, Dorset, volume 2: the Late Upper Palaeolithic and Early Mesolithic sites*, Oxford University Committee for Archaeology Monograph, 34

Bokelmann, K., Averdieck, F.-R. and Willkomm, H. 1981. 'Duvensee, Wohnplatz 8. Neue Aspekte zur Sammelwirtschaft im frühen Mesolithikum', *Offa*, 38, 21-40

Bokelmann, K., Averdieck, F.-R. and Willkomm, H. 1985. 'Duvensee, Wohnplatz 13', *Offa*, 42, 13-33

Bonsall, C. 1976. 'British Antiquity 1974-5: Palaeolithic/Mesolithic', *Archaeol. J.*, 132 for 1975, 302-309

Cane, T. R. 1986. *The socio-economic organisation of hunter-gatherers in the Mesolithic period of England and Wales* University of Manchester, unpublished Ph.D. thesis

Clark, J. G. D. 1934. 'The classification of a microlithic culture: the Tardenoisian of Horsham', *Archaeol. J.*, 90, 52-77

Clark, J. G. D. 1954. *Excavations at Star Carr*, Cambridge: University Press

Cook, J. and Jacobi, R. 1994. 'A reindeer antler or "Lyngby" axe from Northamptonshire and its context in the British Late Glacial', *Proc. Prehist. Soc.*, 60, 75-84

Crowe, K. L. 1992. 'Mesolithic flints from Badger Hall, South Benfleet, Essex', *Essex Archaeol. Hist.*, 23, 1-9

Froom, F. R. 1976. *Wawcott III: a stratified Mesolithic succession*, British Archaeological Reports British Series, 27

Hedges, R. E. M., Housley, R. A., Law, I. A. and Bronk, C. R. 1989. 'Radiocarbon dates from the Oxford AMS system: Archaeometry datelist 9', *Archaeometry*, 31(2), 207-234

Hedges, R. E. M., Housley, R. A., Law, I. A. and Bronk, C. R. 1990. 'Radiocarbon dates from the Oxford AMS system: Archaeometry datelist 10', *Archaeometry*, 32(1), 101-108

Housley, R. A. 1991. 'AMS dates from the Late Glacial and early Postglacial in North-west Europe : A review', in N. Barton, A.J. Roberts and D.A. Roe (eds), *The Late Glacial in north-west Europe: human adaptation and environmental change at the end of the Pleistocene*, CBA Research Report 77, 25-39

Jacobi, R. M. 1973. 'Aspects of the "Mesolithic Age" in Great Britain', in S.K. Kozlowski (ed.), *The Mesolithic in Europe*, 237-265, Warsaw : University Press

Jacobi, R. M. 1980a. 'Late-glacial settlement in Essex', in D. Buckley (ed.), *Archaeology in Essex to AD 1500*, CBA Research Report 34, 12-13

Jacobi, R. M. 1980b . 'The Mesolithic of Essex', in D. Buckley (ed.), *Archaeology in Essex to AD 1500*, CBA Research Report 34, 14-25

Jacobi, R. M. 1991. 'The Creswellian, Creswell and Cheddar', in N. Barton, A.J. Roberts and D.A. Roe (eds) *The Late Glacial in north-west Europe: human adaptation and environmental change at the end of the Pleistocene*, CBA Research Report 77, 128-40

Jacobi, R. M., Martingell, H. E. and Huggins, P. J. 1979. 'A Mesolithic industry from Hill Wood, High Beach, Epping Forest', *Essex Archaeol. Hist.*, 10 for 1978, 206-219

Kromer, B. and Becker, B. 1993. 'German oak and pine 14c calibration, 7200-9439 BC', *Radiocarbon* 35(1), 125-135

Lister, A. M. 1991 . 'Late Glacial mammoths in Britain', in N. Barton, A. J. Roberts and D. A. Roe (eds), *The Late Glacial in north-west Europe: human adaptation and environmental change at the end of the Pleistocene*, CBA Research Report 77, 51-9

Lovett, E. 1898. 'Observations on the implement made from a deer's antler in the museum of the Essex Field Club', *Essex Natur.*, 10, 351-3

Marshall, K. 1959. 'Excavations at a Mesolithic site near High Beach, Epping Forest', *Essex Natur.*, 30, 163.

Martingell, H. E. and Jacobi, R. M. 1979. 'A possible new Late-glacial find-spot in Essex', *Essex Archaeol. Hist.*, 10 for 1978, 233-4

McMaster, I. 1978. 'Flint core found at Hall Farm, Mount Bures, Essex', *Colchester Archaeol. Group Ann. Bull.*, 21, 11-2

Mellars, P. A. 1974. 'The Palaeolithic and Mesolithic', in C. Renfrew (ed.), *British Prehistory: a New Outline*, 41-99, London: Duckworth

Myers, A. M. 1988. 'Scotland inside and outside of the British mainland Mesolithic', *Scottish Archaeological Review*, 5(1-2), 23-29

Priddy, D. (ed.) 1986. 'Work of the Essex County Council Archaeology Section 1983-84', *Essex Archaeol. Hist.*, 16 for 1984-5, 82-122

Priddy, D. (ed.) 1987. 'Work of the Essex County Council Archaeology Section 1985', *Essex Archaeol. Hist.*, 17 for 1986, 141-155

Radley, J., Tallis, J. H. and Switsur, V. R. 1974. 'The excavation of three "narrow blade" Mesolithic sites in the Southern Pennines, England', *Proc. Prehist. Soc.*, 40, 1-19

Smith, C. 1989. 'British antler mattocks', in C. Bonsall (ed.), *The Mesolithic in Europe :Papers presented at the Third International Symposium, Edinburgh 1985*, 272-83, Edinburgh: John Donald

Smith, W. G. 1898. 'An implement made from a stag's antler, from Wormingford, Essex', *Essex Natur.*, 10, 310-312

Stonehouse, P. B. 1992. 'Two Early Mesolithic sites in the Central Pennines', *Yorkshire Archaeological Journal*, 64, 1-15

Stuiver, M. and Becker, B. 1993. 'High-precision decadal calibration of the radiocarbon time scale, AD 1950-6000 BC', *Radiocarbon*, 35(1), 35-65

Vincent, S. W. and George, W. H. 1980. *Some Mesolithic Sites along the Rivers Blackwater and Crouch, Essex*. Privately printed

Vincent, S. W. and George, W. H. 1981. *Some Prehistoric Sites along the Rivers Blackwater and Crouch, Essex*. Privately printed

Warren, S. H. 1912. 'The classification of the prehistoric remains of eastern Essex', *J. Roy. Anthrop. Inst.*, 42, 91-127

Warren, S. H., Clark, J. G. D., Godwin, H. and M. E. and Macfadyen, W. A. 1934. 'An Early Mesolithic site at Broxbourne sealed under Boreal peat', *J. Roy. Anthrop. Inst.*, 64, 101-28

Wymer, J. J. 1976. 'A long blade industry from Sproughton, Suffolk', *East Anglian Archaeology*, 3, 1-10

Wymer, J. J., Jacobi, R. M. and Rose, J. 1975. 'Late Devensian and Early Flandrian barbed points from Sproughton, Suffolk', *Proc. Prehist. Soc.*, 41, 235-41

Essex c. 4000-1500 BC

Robin Holgate

Introduction
Just over 20 years ago, A.C. Edwards (1978, 14) wrote: "(During the Middle Stone Age) great oak forests spread over the Essex claylands, making it difficult for all later invaders from the Continent to move inland from their settlements along the coast and the north side of the Thames. The only ways open to them were the corridors formed by the river valleys, and here they were able to make their homes on the waterside terraces of well-drained gravel. The people of the New Stone Age settled on the coast of the Tendring Hundred, in the Rochford Hundred, and in the Lea Valley." This view is simply a reiteration of the traditional view that pioneer farmers from the European continent colonised Britain at the start of the neolithic period, settling on the coast and along river valleys. Today, it is possible to present a more detailed view based on the results of archaeological and palaeoenvironmental studies undertaken in the last decade.

Up to the late 1970s, as John Hedges (1980, 26) stated in his presentation on neolithic Essex at the 1978 conference, there was limited scope for producing such an account due to the "fundamental lack of survey, excavation, and published information relating to the neolithic period". The same could be said of the earlier Bronze Age (cf. Couchman 1980, 40). Since the publication of the 1978 conference (Buckley 1980), in which Hedges (1980, 38) outlined the need for further aerial reconnaissance, surveys of existing sites, sample excavation of cropmark sites, surface collection surveys and the study of museum collections, much work has been done, primarily by the Essex County Council's Archaeology Section. The number of known neolithic and earlier Bronze Age cropmark sites has increased and a significant proportion of neolithic and later period cropmark sites have received some form of investigation in the field, as exemplified by the sample excavation of the long mortuary enclosure at Rivenhall End (Buckley et al. 1988). In addition, surface collection surveys have been undertaken as a routine part of evaluation work in areas of archaeological interest that have been subject to development, for example at Stansted airport (Brooks and Bedwin 1989), and as part of broader-based field projects, as exemplified by the Hullbridge Basin project (Wilkinson and Murphy 1986; 1987; 1988). Furthermore, studies of the neolithic and earlier Bronze Age material from Essex housed in museums throughout the country have been carried out, for example the study of flintwork as part of research on the neolithic settlement of the Thames basin (Holgate 1988a). A reasonable amount is also known about the palaeoenvironment of Essex, following on from the survey work undertaken in the Essex estuaries (Wilkinson and Murphy 1986; 1987; 1988; Murphy this volume).

There has therefore been an all-round increase in the information available for presenting a fresh account of neolithic and earlier Bronze Age Essex. This paper consists of four parts. First, a description of the environment and coastal changes during the neolithic period and earlier Bronze Age as a prelude to discussing the start of the neolithic period. Second, a review of the monuments, domestic sites and other classes of material that are presently known in Essex. Third, a discussion of settlement, economy and territorial organisation of Essex in the neolithic period and earlier Bronze Age, including a brief look at how developments in Essex relate to the Chilterns. Finally, some suggestions for future work.

Environmental background
The Mar Dyke pollen sequence is the only one compiled to date that spans the neolithic period and earlier Bronze Age (Murphy this volume). In the mid-4th millennium bc, deciduous woodland cover is present with lime dominant, followed by hazel and oak. In the early 3rd millennium bc, there is a decline in elm and an increase in *Plantago lanceolata* and cereal pollen, indicating that the elm decline is probably related to human activity. Palaeoenvironmental analysis of deposits in the Essex estuaries shows small clearings in the vicinity of earlier neolithic sites surrounded by large areas of woodland. It is not until the later Bronze Age that large-scale clearance of the woodland starts to take place (Murphy this volume). Little is known of the vegetation cover in other parts of Essex. Palynological analysis of post-glacial valley deposits, as are known to occur in the Lea, the Stort and other valleys, is clearly a priority for future work.

Changes in the altitude of sea level in all parts of south-east England have been generally consistent since the 6th millennium bc, although East Sussex and West Kent both experienced faster rates of sea-level changes in the 4th-2nd millennia bc than Essex and the Thames estuary (Long 1993, 198). This is probably due to differential movements of the earth's crust within south-east England, coupled with local variations in sediment supply and ground-water movements (Shennan et al. 1992, 164). From the work of Greensmith and Tucker (1973) on the Essex coast and Devoy (1980) on the outer Thames estuary, it is apparent that the sea level rose rapidly in the 6th-4th millennia bc (the Thames II transgression) to a high water mark of 2-5 m. below modern mean sea level by the start of the neolithic period. There were then minor fluctuations in the altitude of sea level until the early 2nd millennium bc (the Tilbury III regression) when there was a major transgression by the sea (the Thames III transgression: Devoy 1980; Wilkinson and Murphy 1986, 182). At the Stumble earlier neolithic site in the Blackwater estuary, borehole survey work indicated that the high water mark throughout the earlier neolithic and much of the later neolithic period was at the height of the present-day low water mark, with sea-level starting to rise at the end of the neolithic period (Wilkinson and Murphy 1988, 134). Thus from about 3500 to about 1800 bc, the present-day intertidal zone was dry land; estuaries, though, would not have been far away. Throughout the early 2nd millennium bc, the intertidal zone was initially blanketed by oak/alder fen before being submerged from around 1700 bc onwards.

The start of the neolithic period
By the end of the 5th millennium bc, the coastal zone and other river valleys were exploited by hunter-fisher-gatherers who lived by harvesting a variety of plant products supplemented by hunting, fishing and collecting shell-fish (Jacobi 1980). It is unlikely that they lived in one place throughout the year: coastal and riverine resources were probably exploited throughout the spring, summer and early autumn months with woodland areas being exploited as hunting grounds for deer, wild cattle and wild pig in the winter months. The start of the neolithic period, represented by the introduction of pottery, polished stone axes, cereals and domesticated animals, overlaps with the end of a period of sea level rise (the Thames II transgression) outlined above.

By 3100 bc, parts of Essex at least were occupied by communities who were cultivating cereals, keeping domesticated animals, making pottery and using ground stone axes and a new flint toolkit. There is some similarity in both the areas occupied and the flint sources exploited by the hunter and the farmer communities (cf. Holgate 1988a). Many questions remain unanswered. Precisely when was cereal cultivation, animal domestication and the concomitant changes in material culture introduced? Were they assimilated or developed by native hunter-fisher-gatherer communities, or introduced by colonising or invading farmers who then chose to develop their own unique styles of pottery, axes and flint implements?

My view is that farming was initially practised in Britain by the indigenous hunter-fisher-gatherer populations in the late 4th millennium bc, with a switch from reliance on mobile resources, for example deer and fish, to a dependence on immovable resources, namely cereals and domesticated animals, having occurred by the early 3rd millennium bc (Holgate 1988a; 1988b). This may have resulted from a decline in the availability of certain natural resources, perhaps influenced by changes in the coastal and estuarine configuration in response to rises in sea level, and a desire to try cultivating cereals and keeping domesticated animals to provide a more reliable food supply throughout the year. Indeed, this process is known to have occurred in Denmark and southern Sweden at about the same time (Rowley-Conwy 1983; Zvelebil and Rowley-Conwy 1984; Blankholm 1987) and, given Britain's comparable maritime position in north-west Europe, is worth further consideration as a model to explain the introduction of farming in Britain. Pottery manufacture and the production of a new range of flint implements would have been associated with the resultant changes in food production and preparation, along with other changes in work scheduling and life-style. However, there is insufficient reliably-dated archaeological material and associated environmental and economic information from 4th millennium bc contexts in southern Britain to test this model. It is certain, though, that communities using the new styles of pottery and flint implements were present in Essex, as in other parts of southern Britain, by the late 4th millennium bc and that these communities had started to leave permanent features in the landscape in the form of ceremonial monuments during the early 3rd millennium bc. These monuments included enclosures and, later, round barrows and ring ditches. Current knowledge of each of these categories of monument in Essex will be discussed in turn, followed by a discussion of domestic sites and other material remains.

Monuments

Causewayed enclosures

Causewayed enclosures date to the earlier neolithic period (3100-2600 bc), and their construction and main phases of use are often associated with plain bowl pottery. At the 1978 conference, sample excavations at the enclosure at Orsett, overlooking the lower Thames terrace (Fig. 1), were discussed by Hedges (1980, 31). Since then, a second causewayed enclosure has been discovered and sampled by excavation at Springfield Lyons (Buckley 1991). The Orsett enclosure consisted of three incomplete ditch circuits with an associated timber-palisade slot lying inside and concentric to the middle ditch (Hedges and Buckley 1978). Within the interior was a contemporary oval post-hole setting. Five radiocarbon dates were obtained using charcoal recovered from features on the site. With the exception of one date of 1,921 ± 62 bc (BM-1380), associated with the middle fill of the inner ditch, the dates were 2,583 ± 112 bc (BM-1214) from the primary silts of the middle ditch, 2,635 ± 82 bc (BM-1215) from the primary silts of the inner ditch, 2,776 ± 74 bc (BM-1378) from the palisade postpipe, 2,670 ± 43 bc (BM-1377) from a pit behind the palisade and 2,791 ± 113 bc (BM-1213) from a posthole situated centrally on the causeway entrance between the two palisade trench terminals. The fill of the inner ditch differed from that of the outer ditch: the lower, inner ditch fills contained intermittent deposits of charcoal-rich loams, pottery and flint resulting from successive placing or dumping of small amounts of material quickly covered with sand and gravel. Large quantities of Mildenhall-style plain bowl pottery and earlier neolithic flintwork were recovered from the ditch fills, with the inner ditch producing the greatest number of finds. A few sherds of Grooved Ware and beaker pottery were also recovered from upper ditch fills or features inside the enclosure.

At Springfield Lyons, excavation of a later Bronze Age enclosure also revealed a causewayed enclosure, this time consisting of a single arc of discontinous ditches on one of the highest points overlooking the Chelmer valley (Fig. 1). Features and superficial deposits associated with the causewayed enclosure produced over 2,000 Mildenhall-style plain bowl sherds. It is clear that some, if not most, of this material resulted from deliberate deposition in ditch segments or pits that were probably backfilled at the same time. Beaker sherds were also recovered from features and superficial deposits associated with the enclosure, whilst Grooved Ware sherds were recovered from superficial deposits and a number of small pits scattered across the excavated area (Brown, pers. comm.).

On the information available from these excavations, the use of these sites appears to date to the latter part of the earlier neolithic period. A variety of functions for causewayed enclosures have been proposed, ranging from exposure burial sites to high-status domestic sites. The material recovered from Orsett and Springfield Lyons suggests that both enclosures were places where pottery and other items were deliberately deposited in the ditch segments. This would be consistent with Smith's (1965, 19) interpretation of the Windmill Hill enclosure in Wiltshire and other enclosures with similar deposits as inter- or intra-group meeting sites. The range of activities practised at causewayed enclosures could have included the holding of initiation ceremonies, match-making and weddings, the exchange of stock and seed-corn and of more durable goods, and the performing of ceremonies to ensure the fertility of the flocks and herds and the growing of the corn, and finally to celebrate the harvest (Smith 1965, 19). Causewayed enclosures, placed either in the centre or at the periphery of occupied areas, probably played a vital role in the flow of commodities and produce, either within a community or between neighbouring communities. This topic will be considered further in the discussion below.

Long mortuary enclosures

The ploughed-out remains of thirteen elongated enclosures interpreted as either long barrows or mortuary enclosures have been identified by aerial photography (Fig. 2). Since the 1978 conference, the oblong enclosure at Rivenhall End has been sampled by excavation (Buckley et al. 1988) and excavations at Slough House Farm revealed a previously unidentified enclosure (Wallis and Waughman forthcoming). The Rivenhall End enclosure, which had either an internal bank or a low mound, produced a Mildenhall-style sherd from upper ditch fills; at the Slough House Farm enclosure, which consisted of a rectangular revetment slot flanked by large quarry pits, a beaker vessel had been deposited in a secondary context at one end of the revetment slot. A third millennium bc date is likely for these enclosures but further excavations are necessary to give more precise dating.

The Essex enclosures are located in the Blackwater, middle Chelmer and middle Stour valleys and in the Chelmer - Blackwater, Stour and Colne estuaries, with one enclosure situated some distance from a river between the

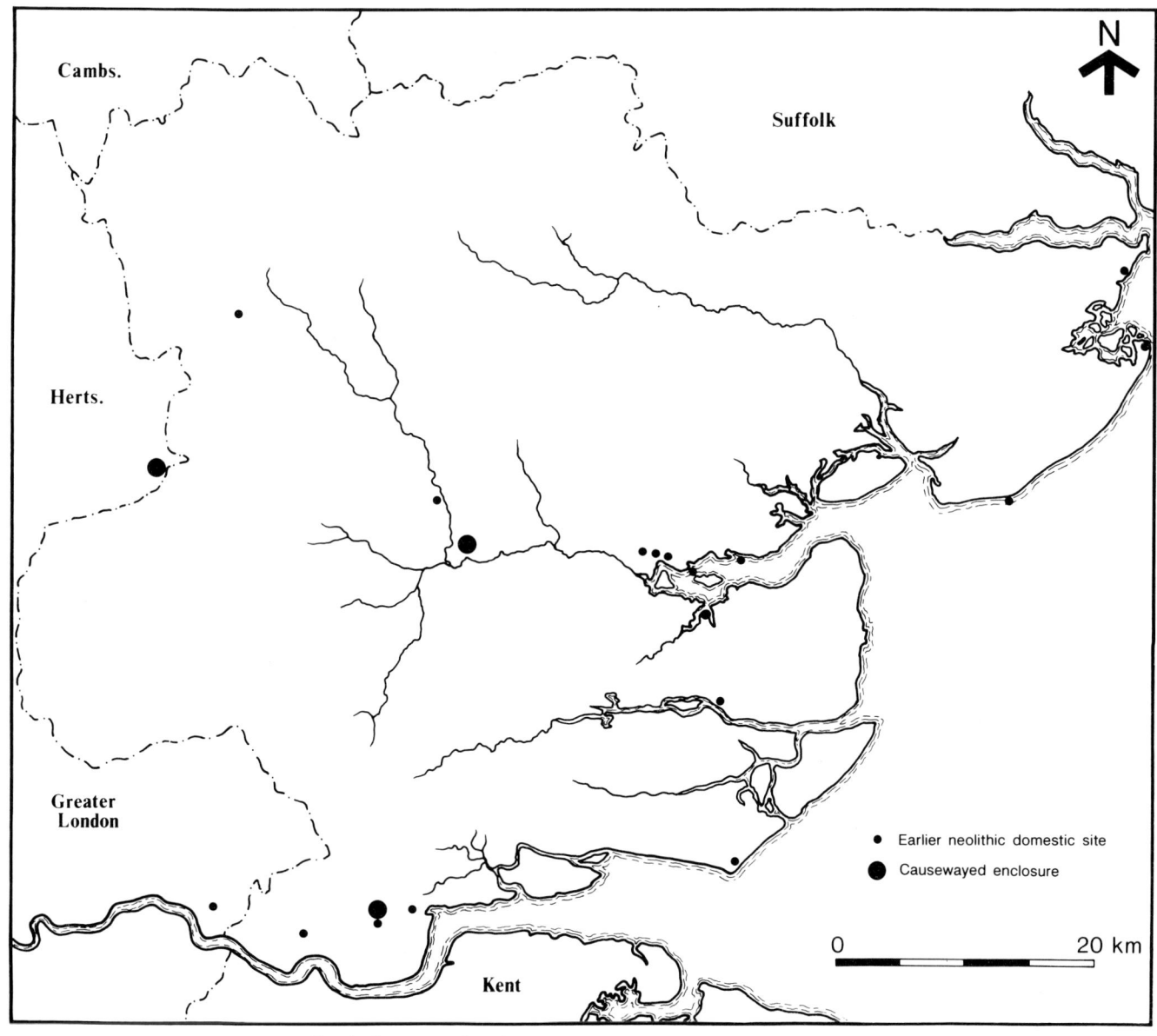

Fig. 1. Causewayed enclosures and earlier neolithic domestic sites.

Blackwater and Colne estuaries. In form, there are nine oblong, two small ovate and two large ovate enclosures. The limited investigation of the Essex sites has not added to the understanding of their function and it is still assumed, by analogy with sites excavated elsewhere in England, for example Barrow Hills, Oxfordshire (Bradley 1992), that they were used for mortuary or burial purposes in the mid-3rd millennium bc.

Cursus monuments
The Springfield cursus in the Chelmer valley is the only example of this type of monument known in Essex, although a second site is situated on the Suffolk border at Bures St Mary in the Stour valley (Fig. 2). Excavations at Springfield took place in the late 1970s and early 1980s (Hedges and Buckley 1981). The excavations revealed a sequence of deposits in the cursus ditch and associated features. There is a circular post-hole setting at the east end, with sherds of Peterborough Ware deriving from the post-hole fills which are similar to Peterborough Ware bowl fragments recovered from the ditch fills (Brown forthcoming). Large fragments of a Mortlake bowl were recovered from above the primary silts at the east end of the of the cursus, suggesting a mid-late 3rd millennium bc date for the monument. A third of the way along the southern cursus ditch from the east end is a segmented ring ditch which cuts into the cursus ditch. It produced Peterborough Ware sherds and a central feature, probably a grave, which contained three flint knives. In the top of the secondary silts in the northern cursus ditch near the circular post-hole setting, a deposit of burnt material with fragments of either one or two Grooved Ware vessels was recovered. Charcoal from the deposit yielded three radiocarbon dates: 2,170 ± 80 bc (HAR-6271), 2,040 ± 80 bc (HAR-6266) and 2,010 ± 80 bc (HAR-6268). The remains of an urn of biconical form were also recovered from a pit close to the post-hole setting and further urn fragments were recovered from secondary ditch silts. Fragments of both plain bowl and beaker pottery came from the cover loam at the west and east ends of the cursus respectively, but none were found in the ditch silts.

Traditionally, cursus monuments are considered to have been used for ceremonies of a processional nature in the late 3rd millennium bc (Atkinson *et al.* 1951). At the Springfield cursus, the deliberate deposition of pottery and other associated material took place throughout the late 3rd and early 2nd millennia bc. In this respect, the activities taking place at the Essex causewayed enclosures and at the Springfield cursus monument appear to overlap. It is thus possible, as suggested for the Essex causewayed enclosures, that the Springfield cursus was constructed for use as an inter- or intra-group meeting site.

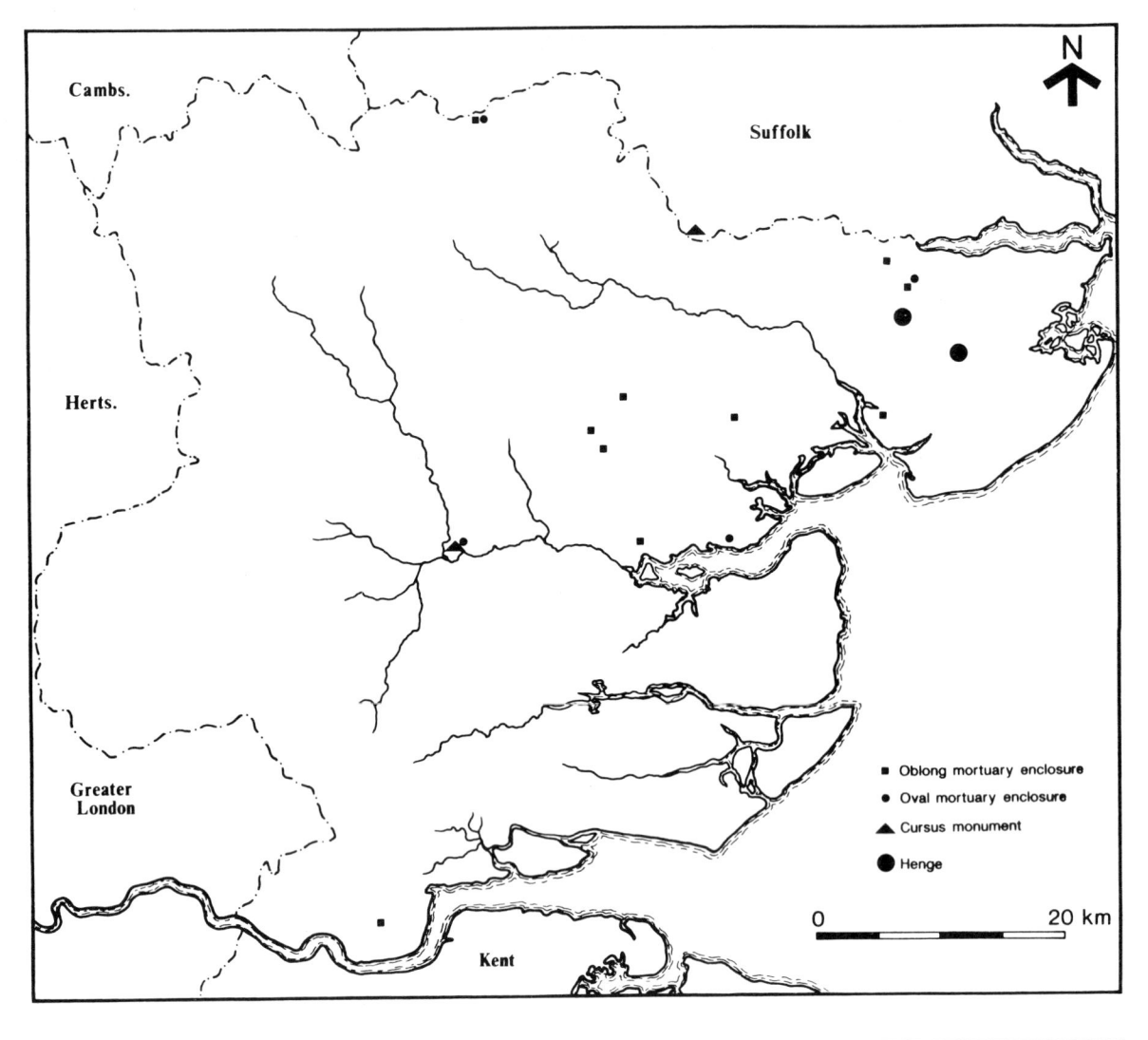

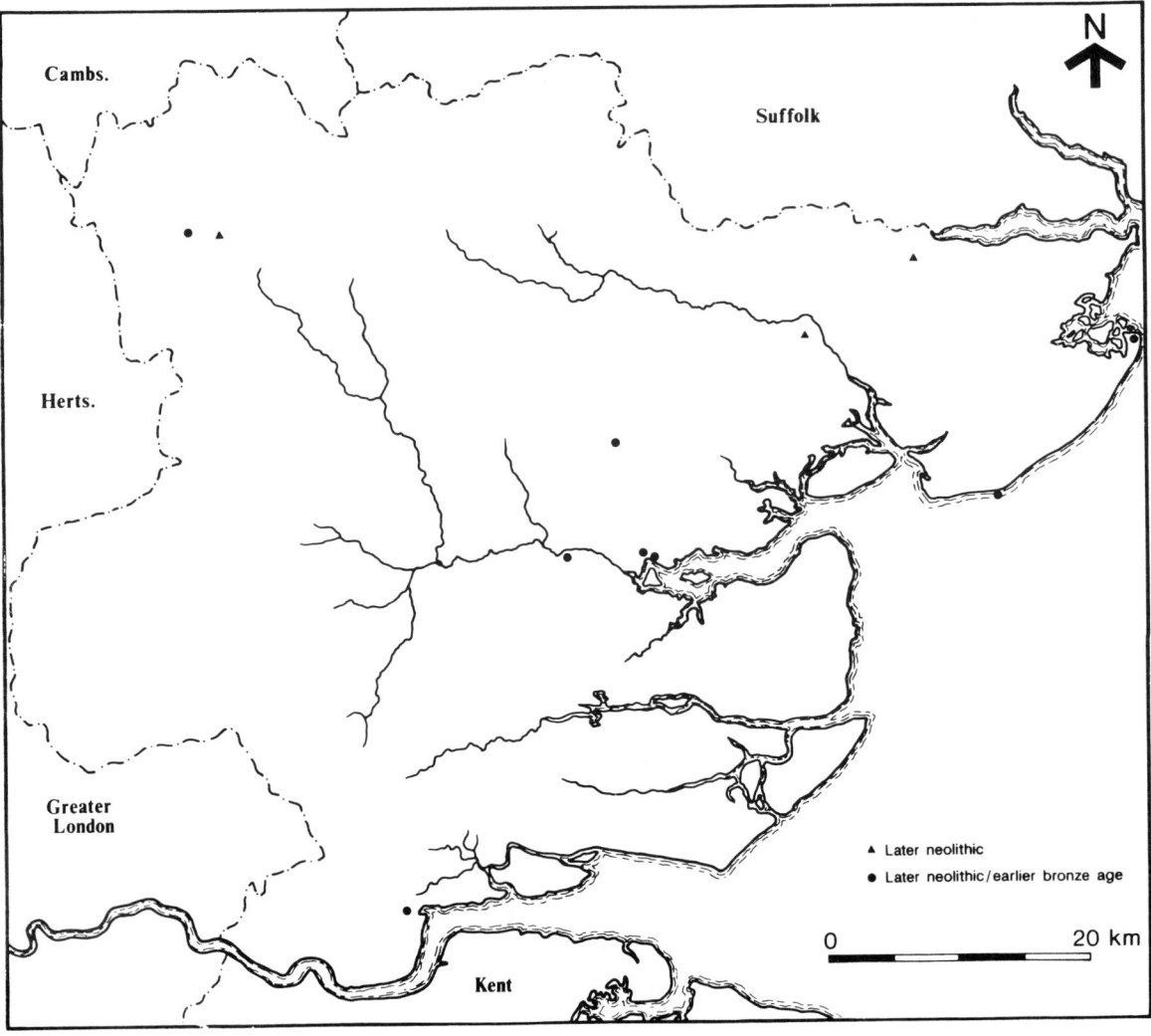

Fig. 2. Mortuary enclosures, cursus monuments, henges and later neolithic domestic sites.

Henges

A number of possible henge monuments, none of which had been excavated, was listed by Hedges (1980, 29-30) at the 1978 conference. Although these sites remain unexcavated, a comprehensive study of the aerial photographic evidence for henges in Britain has subsequently been undertaken by Harding and Lee (1987). Out of the 19 sites in Essex that were considered, only two are interpreted as possible henges (Fig. 2). These sites, both consisting of circular enclosures with two opposing entrances, are situated at Little Bentley and Little Bromley in the Stour valley (Harding and Lee 1987, 148-52). By analogy with similar sites from other parts of Britain, these sites date to the late 3rd and early 2nd millennia bc and were used for ceremonial purposes, in some cases linking in with the solar calendar.

Ring ditches and burials

Couchman (1980, 42) stated that in Essex "there are many ring-ditch cropmarks and several standing barrows; the few that have been excavated were either early or middle Bronze Age". Some of these ring ditches, though, could date to the neolithic period: such a site at Rainham, Greater London was excavated by Simpson and Smith in 1963. In the centre was a burial pit which yielded Mildenhall-style pottery whilst the ring ditch, in which large fragments of Mildenhall-style pottery were deposited, had been deliberately backfilled with material from the inner bank (Anon 1982, 7; Hedges 1980, 28). More recently, a segmented ring ditch of earlier neolithic date has been excavated at Brightlingsea (Lavender 1995). As with Rainham, considerable amounts of Mildenhall-style pottery were recovered from the ditch.

Some ring ditches of earlier Bronze Age date have produced burials, for example the cremation burial associated with a collared urn from a bowl barrow at Dedham (Longworth 1984, 198-9). Most ring ditches (Fig. 3) are situated in north-east Essex or on the river gravels of the Blackwater, Chelmer and inner Thames valleys, although there is a small cluster on the chalk dip slope in north-west Essex which is part of the Chiltern group of barrows and ring ditches (Priddy 1981, Fig. 34).

Numerous flat graves, some forming cemeteries, have been discovered on the river terraces. Beaker flat graves include an example at Orsett Cock, which contained two beakers and a bowl (Milton 1986), the grave with a beaker and eleven barbed and tanged arrowheads at Mucking (Jones 1973, 10) and the cemetery at Thorpe Hall, Southchurch in which one grave contained a flint dagger and a heap of cockle shells (Clarke 1970, 444 and 481). [The crouched inhumation associated with Grooved Ware from Southend Airport, noted by Hedges (1980), is now considered to be Iron Age in date on the basis of the pottery which accompanied it (K. Crowe, pers. comm.). The single small Grooved Ware sherd is thought to have been residual]. Cremation burials associated with collared urns include the cemetery at Alphamstone (Longworth 1984, 197-8), and the single burial at Rochford, where a possible example (represented by two sherds), in an inverted

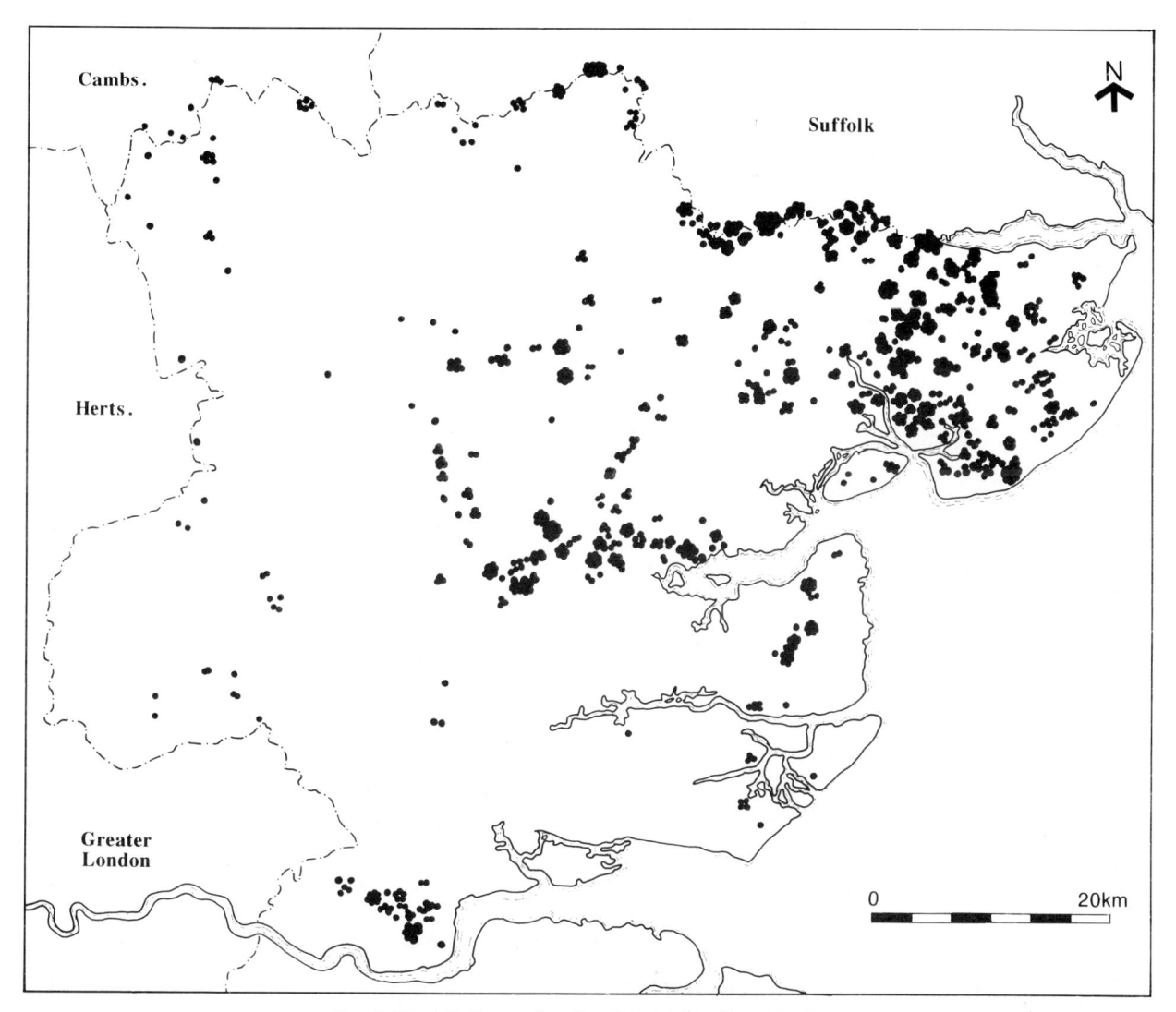

Fig. 3. Ring ditches and earlier Bronze Age domestic sites.

position, contained gold, amber and shale beads (Couchman 1980, 40). Couchman also highlighted the fact that collared urn finds all fall east of a line from Alphamstone to Orsett, whilst food vessels, which are believed to be contemporary, come from the west of the county. However, as only three food vessels are represented, further discoveries might disprove this apparent division.

Domestic sites

At the 1978 conference, Hedges (1980, 26) stated that "the present knowledge of Neolithic economy, settlement and intercommunal relationships here in Essex is, however, minimal". This is an area which has received further attention since then. The sub-soil features associated with domestic structures in the neolithic and earlier Bronze Age consist of either foundation trenches or post holes which, in an area which has been subjected to truncation by ploughing or other human or natural agencies, will only survive in exceptional circumstances (Holgate 1988a; 1988b, 104-5). Chigborough and the Stumble are rare examples where possible neolithic structural features have been discovered. In much of Essex, the base of pits and flintwork dispersed throughout the topsoil are likely to be all that remain of domestic sites.

Not all pits result from domestic activity: some, for example the isolated pit at Layer-de-la-Haye which contained a carinated bowl (Hedges 1982), are clearly non-domestic in nature and probably best interpreted as votive deposits (cf. Herne 1988, 26-7). However, pits containing pottery and flintwork from sites which have yielded flint assemblages containing a multiplicity of implements can be interpreted as the remains of domestic sites, as can discrete concentrations of flintwork from cultivated land which contain a substantial number and range of implements (Holgate 1988a, 51-61). Thus a study of the flints recovered from excavated neolithic contexts and from systematic surface collection surveys, along with collections in museums, is the way to identify domestic sites. It should be noted, though, that surface collection surveys have only covered a small fraction of Essex (Fig. 4). Given the small area covered, it is impossible to compile settlement distribution maps. Further survey work, combined with the opportune excavation of sites which could reveal the remains of neolithic and earlier Bronze Age domestic activity, should continue to be undertaken as a matter of priority.

Essex was amongst the first counties in England to yield neolithic and earlier Bronze Age domestic sites. In the late 1920s and early 1930s, when the first causewayed enclosures were being investigated (Curwen 1929; Leeds 1927) and controversy still raged over whether flint mines dated to the palaeolithic or the neolithic period (Clark and Piggott 1933), Warren was recording domestic features associated with neolithic and beaker pottery on the foreshore between the rivers Stour and Blackwater (Warren et al. 1936). At this time, archaeologists believed that neolithic people lived in pit dwellings and this view undoubtedly influenced Warren's accounts of the remains he discovered on the east coast of Essex. Warren discovered remains at Clacton, Dovercourt and Walton-on-the-Naze. He identified four classes of site: concentrations of artefacts 10 m in diameter that were considered to represent surface occupation or camp sites; round or oval pits 3-7 m in diameter that were interpreted as pit dwellings; pits 1 m in diameter that occurred below surface occupation and constituted cooking holes; patches of charcoal and fire-fractured flint that represented hearth sites. Whilst these remains undoubtedly result from domestic activity throughout the neolithic and earlier Bronze Age, recent work by Wilkinson and Murphy (1986; 1987; 1988) in the Essex estuaries, notably the excavations undertaken at the Stumble, indicates that structural remains were either overlooked or had not survived post-neolithic denudation.

Earlier neolithic domestic sites have been found predominately on the river terraces, although one is known on the edge of the chalk dip slope (Fig. 1). These sites are represented by flint scatters, for example Orsett Heath (Bingley 1978), and pits containing flints and pottery, as exemplified by Lofts Farm, Slough House Farm, Chigborough, Walton and Clacton (Brown 1988a; Wallis and Waughman forthcoming; Hedges 1980, 33). These sites might have differed in terms of organisation, economy and length of occupation. At Lofts Farm, the recovery of some indeterminate cereal and grass remains, along with fragments of hazelnut shell and a cherry stone, showed that some cereal cultivation and wild plant food gathering took place (Murphy 1988, 283). At the Stumble, the considerable quantities of cereal grains and spikelets of emmer wheat (*Triticum dicoccum*) and hazelnut shells (Wilkinson and Murphy 1987, 73), the wealth of pottery and the substantial flint assemblage, coupled with the presence of structural remains and middens, which showed that rubbish was being disposed of in specific places, all suggest a site occupied on a more permanent basis.

Concerning later neolithic sites, the river terraces and the chalk dip slope continued to be occupied (Fig. 2). Sites are represented by flint scatters, for example at Rivenhall End (Buckley et al. 1988), and pit clusters or deposits containing both flints and pottery, for example Wicken Bonhunt, Clacton, Lawford and Culver Street, Colchester (Wade 1980, 96; Hedges 1980, 33; Shennan et al. 1985; Crummy 1992). At Culver Street, large fragments of Grooved Ware were found in a small pit, along with a scatter of similar material and flints in the surrounding cover loam. The Grooved Ware had been placed in the pit so that one sherd rested on a stone that could be a rubbing stone for a quern; furthermore, the pit was located away from the main group of pottery (Brown 1992, 317). The contents of the pit appear to result from deliberate deposition, indicating that this practice, which occurs in later Bronze Age domestic sites as exemplified by Springfield Lyons, North Shoebury and Mucking (Brown and Lavender 1994), also took place on domestic sites during the later neolithic period.

Most of the later neolithic sites were also occupied during the beaker period, for example Wicken Bonhunt, Mucking, Walton and Clacton (Fig. 3: Wade 1980, 96; Hedges 1980, 33). At Clacton, two radiocarbon dates of 1,880 ± 80 bc and 1,800 ± 150 bc have been obtained using charcoal from a pit containing beaker pottery. Carbonised barley remains and hazelnut shells have also been recovered from beaker contexts at Clacton (Wilkinson and Murphy 1986, 186), along with fragmentary teeth of pig and probably cattle.

Other material

Stonework

As regards neolithic and earlier Bronze Age material culture, axes and pottery are the two main classes of artefact to discuss. The number of axes placed in causewayed enclosure ditches and in rivers suggests that apart from use for utilitarian purposes, for example woodworking, axes were also valued items that were used in making specialised deposits (Bradley 1990, 67-9). These deposits, consisting of the deliberate removal from the production, use and discard cycle that artefacts usually undergo, appear superficially to have been unreciprocated. However, anthropological theory concerning the reciprocity of gift exchange (Gregory 1982) suggests that the deliberate deposition of items in the ground could consti-

ESSEX C. 4000-1500 BC

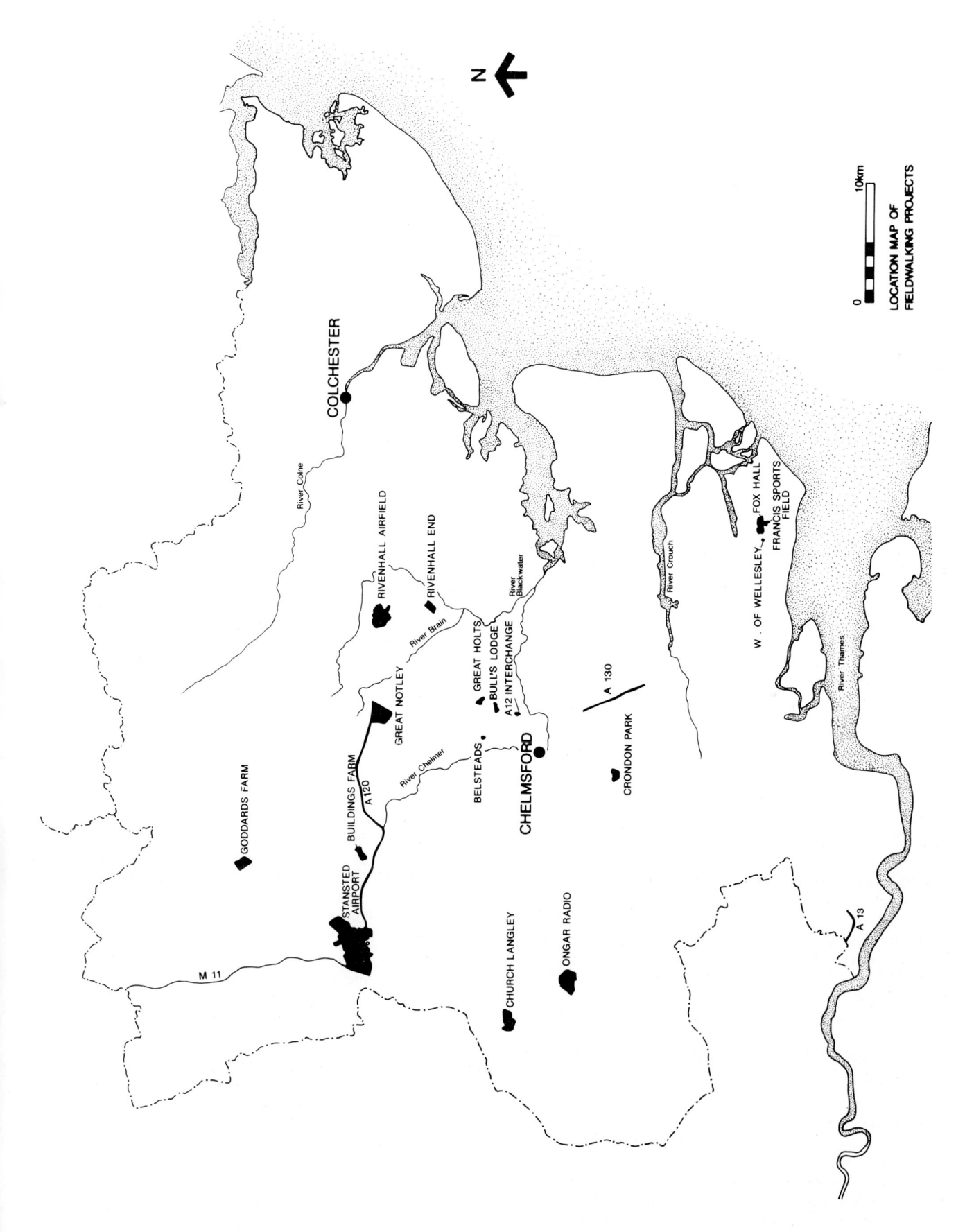

Fig. 4. Location of major surface collection survey projects undertaken in Essex.

tute votive offerings or the consumption of items of wealth to bestow status on the individuals concerned. Thus discoveries of complete neolithic axes could represent votive deposits as opposed to accidental losses whilst managing woodland or during domestic activity.

There are two main forms of flint axes that have been recovered from Essex: thick-butted and thin-butted axes. Thick-butted axes can be found in both earlier and later neolithic contexts whilst thin-butted axes, when found in association with other material, always occur in later neolithic contexts (Holgate 1988, 10). Both axe forms have been found throughout Essex (Fig. 5), perhaps indicating that the entire county was exploited, if heterogeneously, throughout the neolithic period. Some axes might have been fashioned using locally-available flint. The majority of flint axes, though, were produced using mined flint, some of which can be matched with the flint mined in Sussex (Craddock et al. 1983). Certainly, the flint axes and chisel recovered from the hoards found in southern Essex were manufactured using Sussex flint (Fig. 5: Craddock et al. 1983). These hoards consisted of a greenstone axe, three flaked and cutting edge-ground thin-butted flint axes, two flint axe preforms and a ground-edged sub-triangular knife from Chelmsford and two flaked and cutting edge-ground flint axes and a ground and polished flint chisel from Canewdon, whilst a third hoard of three flaked and cutting edge-ground thin-butted flint axes has been recovered from Stratford, Greater London close to the Essex county boundary. A significant proportion of the igneous stone axes (Fig. 5) originated from Cornwall (Cummins 1979), whilst five jadeite axes from Piedmont, north Italy have been found in the county. No specific pattern of deposition can be observed; axes can occur at monuments and, certainly from the later neolithic period onwards, in domestic contexts. Those axes recovered from watery contexts, along with the hoards, are likely to represent votive offerings.

Other flint artefacts which, like axes, might have formed specialised deposits are single piece sickles and daggers. Sickles, which could date to either the earlier or the later neolithic period (cf. Kinnes 1988, 3), have been recovered from south-east Essex and Walton. Daggers probably date to the early 2nd millennium bc and are known from the Grays area, Southchurch, Saffron Walden, Thundersley, Dunmow and Braintree. The Southchurch dagger was associated with a beaker burial (Clarke 1970, 444 and 481).

Shafthole implements, which probably date to the early and mid-2nd millennia bc (Smith 1979), have also been recovered from Essex. These include maceheads from northern and eastern Essex, a small group of battle axes from eastern Essex and a similar number of shafthole adzes from southern Essex (Hedges 1980, 37: fig. 14; Roe 1979; Martingell and Brice 1992; Merriman 1990). These items might have been singled out for selective deposition; battle axes, for example, can occur as grave goods and it is possible that those found in Essex accompanied earlier Bronze Age burials.

Bronzework
Copper flat axes are known from Shoebury (Couchman 1980, 40; Crowe 1992), Harlow (Brown 1988b), Tollesbury (Brown and Buckley 1985) and Gestingthorpe (Brown 1987), and the five axes from Great Baddow were also thought to have been flat (Evans 1881, 43). They overlap chronologically with shafthole axes and their use is likely to have been incorporated into the established pattern of votive deposition (cf. Needham 1988; Bradley 1990, 73).

Pottery
In a recent study, Herne (1988) has demonstrated that carinated bowls represent the earliest pottery horizon in Britain, dating between 3100 and 2850 bc. Carinated bowls have been found at four sites in Essex: Layer de la Haye, Clacton, Shoebury and Little Waltham (Herne 1988, 16). At Layer de la Haye, a complete carinated bowl had been placed in a shallow pit (Hedges 1982) and could thus be interpreted as a votive deposit.

Either overlapping chronologically with or succeeding carinated bowls is Mildenhall Ware: a decorated style of plain bowl pottery that occurs predominantly in East Anglia during the early and mid-3rd millennia bc. Brown (pers. comm.) has recently suggested a southern sub-division of Mildenhall ware amongst the earlier neolithic ceramic assemblages in Essex, which is present at Orsett, the Stumble and Springfield Lyons. Assemblages containing Mildenhall Ware have been retrieved from causewayed enclosures, long mortuary enclosures and domestic sites.

In the mid-3rd millennium bc, Peterborough Ware, Grooved Ware and beaker pottery was produced. These pottery styles probably overlap chronologically but more radiocarbon dates than those currently available are needed to resolve this issue (Cleal 1984, 157). Peterborough Ware from Essex includes the Mortlake bowl fragments deposited at the Springfield cursus (Brown forthcoming) and the two Ebbsfleet bowls recovered from a shallow pit at Waltham Abbey (Huggins 1970), all of which result from deliberate deposition. Pits and other features containing Grooved Ware have been discovered at a number of sites throughout Essex; to the list compiled by Hedges (1980, 33-4) can be added several recent discoveries, for example Brightlingsea, Chipping Hill, Witham, Great Baddow and Culver Street, Colchester (Brown pers. comm.; Flook and Bedwin 1993; Brown and Lavender 1994; Crummy 1992). The introduction of beaker pottery, accompanied by the earliest use of metalwork and the appearance of new forms of flint implements, for example daggers and barbed and tanged arrowheads, appear around 2,000 bc and perhaps represent a phenomenon similar to that characterised by carinated bowls. Both Grooved Ware and beaker pottery come from contexts associated with monuments, burials and domestic sites.

Discussion
At the 1978 conference, Hedges (1980, 38) stated that "Attempting to define land usage patterns or territorial organisation at the present time would be premature". Given the greater amount of archaeological information for the neolithic period and earlier Bronze Age that is now available, it is worth outlining a tentative sequence of settlement, economy and territorial organisation in Essex in the late 4th - early 2nd millennia bc.

The earliest neolithic material known in Essex, the carinated bowls, come almost exclusively from the river terraces in southern and eastern Essex. Early 3rd millennium bc domestic sites also occur predominantly on the river terraces but also exist on the chalk dip slope. Wheat was grown but wild plant foods continued to be gathered. Not all domestic sites were occupied throughout the year: there were sites at which horticulture, as opposed to agriculture, was practised whilst other parts of the landscape were exploited on a seasonal basis for the natural resources they contained and for grazing cattle. By the latter part of the earlier neolithic period, Mildenhall-style pottery was in use. It is possible to discern a southern sub-division of the Mildenhall style on sites across south and central Essex (Brown, pers. comm.). Those living in southern and eastern Essex might thus have formed a distinct social group with the causewayed enclosures at Orsett and Springfield Lyons situated on the periphery. The Boulder Clay plateau running west to north-east through the middle of Essex may have been largely unoccupied, as survey

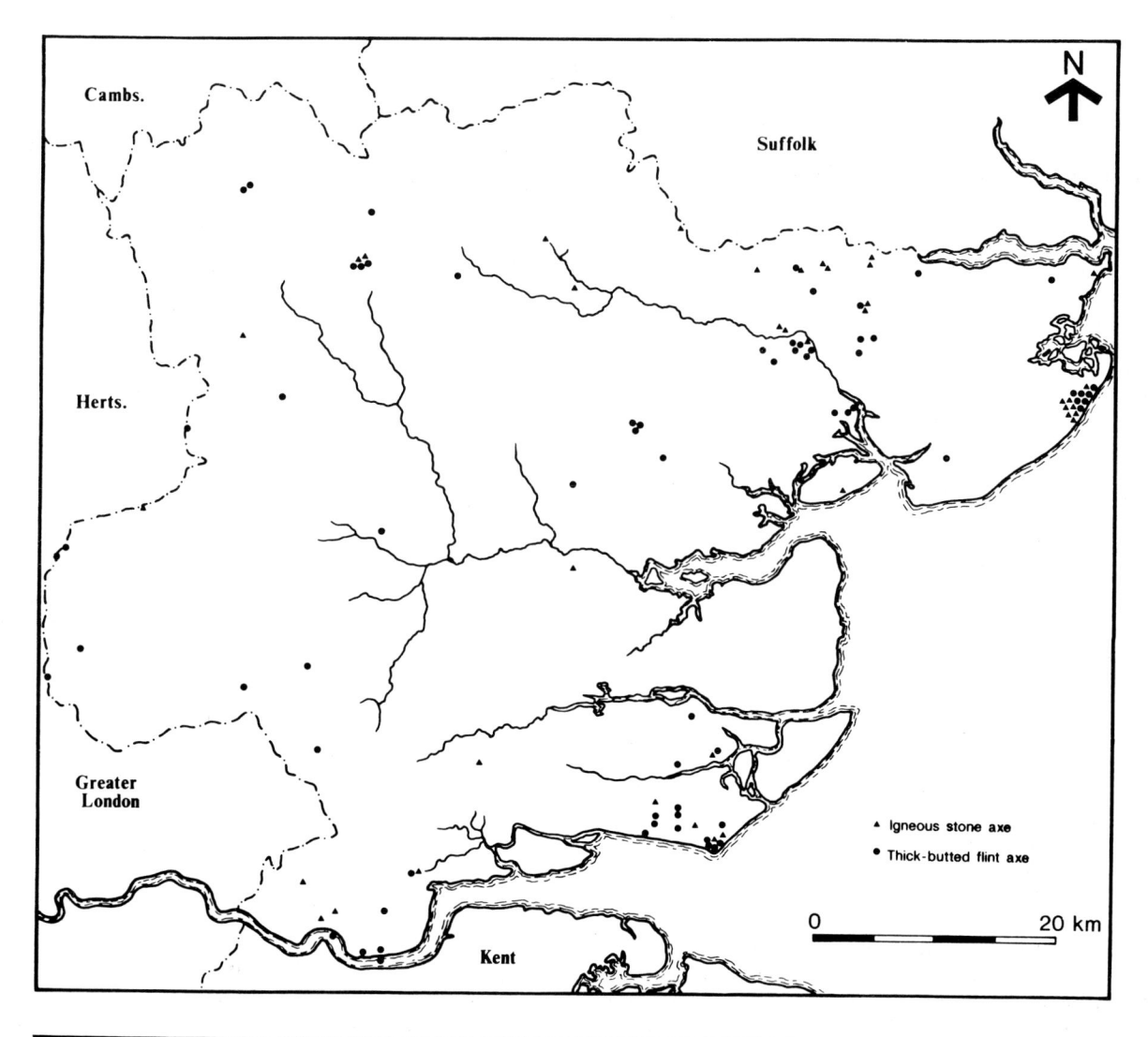

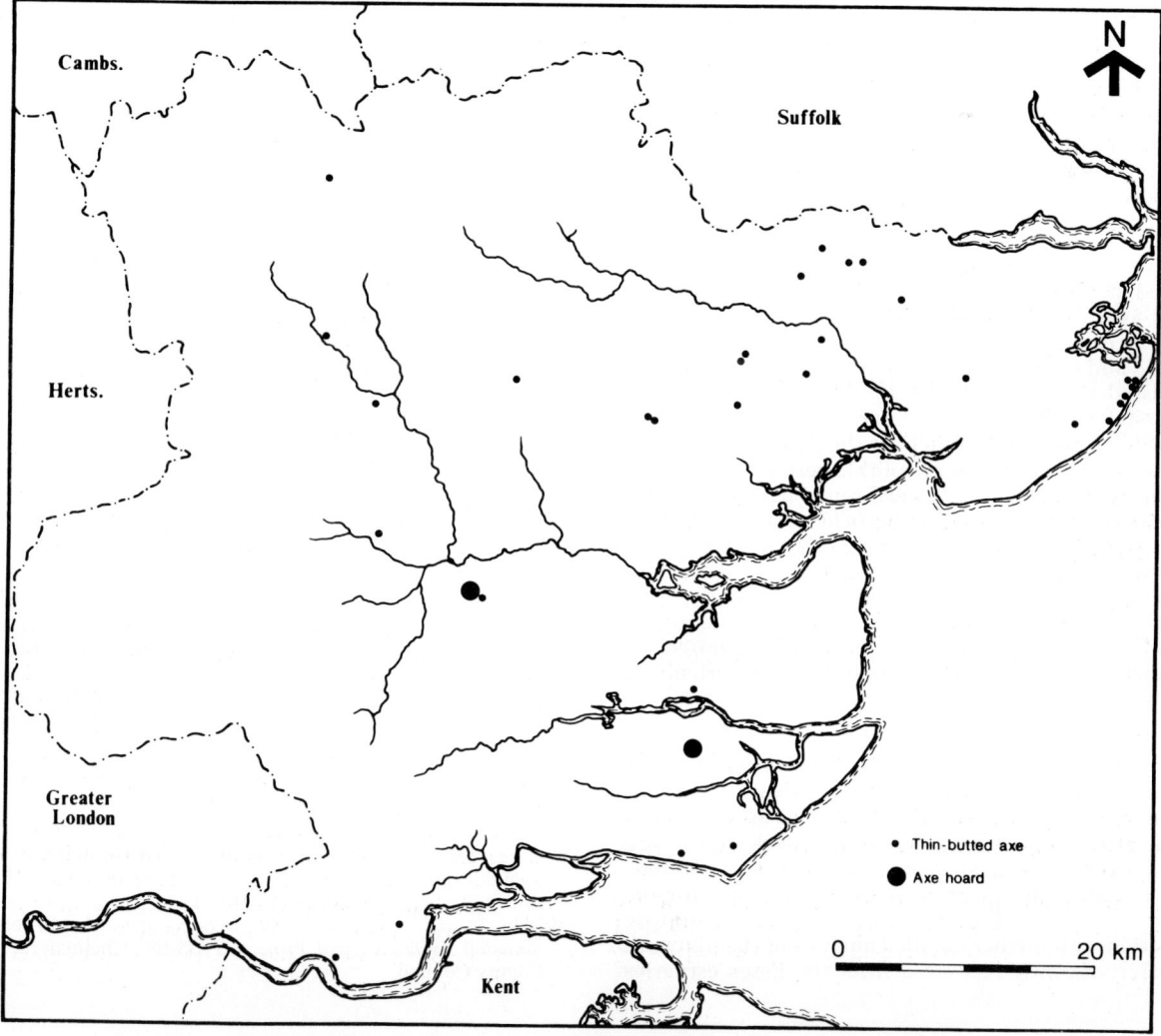

Fig. 5. Igneous stone axes, thick- and thin-butted flint axes and axe hoards.

work at Stansted (Brooks and Bedwin 1989) and in the vicinity of Great Chesterford (Williamson 1987) has not produced any traces of earlier neolithic domestic activity. North-west Essex, on the chalk dip slope, might have been occupied by people who were part of a social group centred on the Chiltern Hills, again with causewayed enclosures, namely Sawbridgeworth and Maiden Bower, situated on the periphery (Holgate 1988a, 116; 1995). These enclosures probably served as intercommunal meeting sites where ceremonies could be enacted and gifts exchanged. It is possible that the Springfield cursus, situated 1 km south of the Springfield Lyons causewayed enclosure, also served a similar function as an intercommunal meeting site. It is also worth noting that the siting within close proximity of one another at Springfield of a causewayed enclosure, a cursus monument, an oval barrow and ring ditches is the only example in south-eastern England of this grouping of 3rd and early 2nd millennia bc monuments comparable to the contemporary complex in the Abingdon area of the Upper Thames valley (Bradley 1992; Bradley and Holgate 1984).

During the later neolithic period and earlier Bronze Age, southern and eastern Essex and north-west Essex continued to be occupied with henges, round barrows and ring ditches being constructed, in some cases in areas that might have been freshly settled. There is minimal economic information available concerning farming practices and animal husbandry, and information on the nature of domestic sites is difficult to interpret (see above). However, by analogy with other parts of southern Britain as exemplified by the Upper Thames Valley, domestic sites were probably occupied on a permanent basis with agriculture being practised. In the Upper Thames Valley, there is an increase in domestic site numbers accompanied by the occupation of areas that had not previously been settled (Holgate 1988a, 117). In addition, traces of field boundary ditches have been discovered underlying earlier Bronze Age barrows at two sites in the Abingdon area, indicating that field systems were being laid out by the end of the later neolithic period (Holgate 1988a, 123-4). Later neolithic field systems are known elsewhere in England, for example at Fengate, Cambs. (Pryor 1978) and at West Heslerton, Yorks. (Powlesland 1986). This might have occurred in Essex; it certainly appears to have taken place in the Chilterns (Holgate 1995). Further surface collection survey work is necessary in order to test this suggestion. What is apparent is that the area between the Stour and Colne valleys was a focus for settlement, along with southern and north-west Essex. There is still no definitive evidence that the Boulder Clay plateau was occupied before the later Bronze Age, although some parts at least were being exploited for woodland resources during the earlier Bronze Age, as attested by the discovery of barbed and tanged arrowheads and associated flintwork at Stansted (Brooks and Bedwin 1989, 5); further field work could yield additional information to clarify the nature of this activity. Throughout the earlier Bronze Age, the areas settled in the later neolithic period continued to be occupied, with ring ditches and round barrows perhaps being sited in relation to existing field systems, although further fieldwork similar to that recently undertaken at Brightlingsea (Phil Clarke pers. comm.) is needed to investigate this further. Thus during the neolithic period and earlier Bronze Age, there is a switch in the investment of labour from the procurement of mobile resources to the management of specific tracts of land for agriculture and animal husbandry.

Future work

There are three main priorities for future work. First, further analysis and recording of material in museums and assessment of the results of recent fieldwork that is still at the post-excavation stage is necessary. For example, material recovered by Warren at Clacton and Walton-on-the-Naze (Warren et al. 1936) would repay a fresh study in conjunction with further detailed analysis of the flintwork and pottery recently recovered from the Essex estuaries (Wilkinson and Murphy 1986; 1987; 1988). This would help clarify the nature of currently-known pottery and flint assemblages.

Second, as stated at the 1978 conference, surface collection survey and aerial reconnaissance are a top priority (Hedges 1980, 34). The areas to focus on are south Essex, the Chelmer valley, the area between the Stour and Colne valleys, and north-west Essex. Local archaeological groups and societies have a vital role here. The survey work undertaken by the Manshead Archaeological Society of Dunstable in the area around Dunstable and Luton in the north Chilterns, which has led to the discovery of a number of mesolithic, later prehistoric and Romano-British domestic sites (Hudspith 1991; 1995) is a good example of both how this work can be organised and the results that can be achieved by amateur archaeologists.

Third, sample excavation of sites discovered by survey work is required. This includes evaluating all cropmark and other potential sites that become the subject of planning applications for development. Often, the investigation of later prehistoric and Romano-British sites yield neolithic or earlier Bronze Age material, for example Chipping Hill, Witham (Flook and Bedwin 1993) and Culver Street, Colchester (Crummy 1992). It is also necessary to undertake further palaeoenvironmental work in combination with the investigation of cropmark sites and artefact scatters. In addition to evaluation work, broad-based research projects similar to the Hullbridge basin and Brightlingsea projects should be undertaken in other parts of Essex, for example in the Lea, Stort, Chelmer, Stour and Colne valleys. It is hoped that projects of this nature would generate pottery and flint assemblages with associated environmental and economic information, in particular pollen and animal bone assemblages, and organic material that can be used to obtain radiocarbon dates. Securely-dated environmental, economic and artefactual material would shed light on a number of poorly-understood topics, for example the start of the neolithic period and the nature of domestic sites throughout the neolithic period and earlier Bronze Age.

The study of neolithic and earlier Bronze Age Essex has seen considerable advances since the 1978 conference, but much work still remains to be done by both amateur and professional archaeologists over the next 10-15 years.

Acknowledgements

I am indebted to Nigel Brown for supplying details of recent excavations undertaken by the Essex County Council's Archaeology Section, for discussing with me the results of his recent pottery studies and for commenting on a draft of this paper.

References

Anon. 1982. 'Archaeological Excavations at Rainham: a Passmore Edwards Museum Exhibition', *Essex J.* 17 (2), 6-9

Atkinson, R. J. C., Piggott, C. M. and Sanders, N. K. 1951. *Excavations at Dorchester, Oxon*, Oxford: Ashmolean Museum

Bingley, R. 1978. 'A Neolithic Site at Heath Place Farm, Orsett', *J. Thurrock Loc. Hist. Soc.* 21, 36-42

Blankholm, H. P. 1987. 'Late Mesolithic Hunter-Gatherers and the Transition to Farming in Southern Scandinavia', in Rowley-Conwy, P., Zvelebil, M. and Blankholm, H. P. (eds), *Mesolithic Northwest Europe: Recent Trends*, Sheffield: Dept. of Archaeology & Prehistory, 155-62

Bradley, R. 1990. *The Passage of Arms: an archaeological analysis of prehistoric hoards and votive deposits*, Cambridge: University Press

Bradley, R. 1992. 'The Excavation of an Oval Barrow beside the Abingdon Causewayed Enclosure, Oxfordshire', *Proc. Prehist. Soc.* 58, 127-42

Bradley, R. and Holgate, R. 1984. 'The Neolithic sequence in the Upper Thames Valley', in Bradley, R. and Gardiner, J. (eds), *Neolithic studies: a review of some current research*, Brit. Archaeol. Rep. Brit. Ser. 133, 107-34

Brooks, H. and Bedwin, O. 1989. *Archaeology at the Airport. The Stansted Archaeological Project, 1985-89*, Chelmsford: Essex County Council

Brown, N. 1987. 'Gestingthorpe', in Priddy, D. (ed.) 'Work of the Essex County Council Archaeology Section 1986', *Essex Archaeol. Hist.* 18, 88

Brown, N. 1988a. 'A Late Bronze Age Enclosure at Lofts Farm, Essex', *Proc. Prehist. Soc.* 54, 249-302

Brown, N. 1988b. 'Harlow, Holbrooks', in Priddy, D. (ed.) 'Work of the Essex County Council Archaeology Section 1987', *Essex Archaeol. Hist.* 19, 241-2

Brown, N. 1992. 'The prehistoric pottery', in Crummy, P., *Excavations at Culver Street, the Gilberd School, and other sites in Colchester 1971-85*, Colchester Archaeol. Rep. 6, 317-20.

Brown, N. 1995. 'Neolithic and Beaker Pottery', in *Excavations at North Shoebury: settlement and economy in south-east Essex 1500BC to AD1500*, E. Anglian Archaeol.

Brown, N. Forthcoming. Springfield Cursus Neolithic Pottery

Brown, N. and Buckley, D. 1985. 'Tollesbury', in Priddy, D. (ed.) 'Work of the Essex County Council Archaeology Section 1983-84', *Essex Archaeol. Hist.* 16, 91-4

Brown, N. and Lavender, N. J. 1994. 'Later Bronze Age sites at Great Baddow and settlement in the Chelmer Valley, Essex, 1500 to 500 BC', *Essex Archaeol. Hist.* 25, 3-14

Buckley, D. G. (ed.) 1980. *Archaeology in Essex to AD 1500*, Counc. Brit. Archaeol. Rep. 34

Buckley, D., Major, H. and Milton, B. 1988. 'Excavation of a Possible Neolithic Long Barrow or Mortuary Enclosure at Rivenhall, Essex, 1986', *Proc. Prehist. Soc.* 54, 77-91

Clark, J. G. D. and Piggott, S. 1933. 'The Age of the British Flint Mines', *Antiquity* 7, 166-83

Clarke, D. L. 1970. *Beaker Pottery of Great Britain and Ireland*, Cambridge: Univ. Press, 2 vols.

Cleal, R. 1984. 'The Later Neolithic in Eastern England', in Bradley, R. and Gardiner, J. (eds.) *Neolithic Studies: a review of some current research*, Brit. Archaeol. Rep. Brit Ser. 133, 135-58

Couchman, C. R. 1980. 'The Bronze Age in Essex', in Buckley, D.G. (ed.), *Archaeology in Essex to AD 1500*, Counc. Brit. Archaeol. Rep. 34, 40-6

Craddock, P. T., Cowell, M. R., Leese, M. R. and Hughes, M. J. 1983. 'The trace element composition of polished flint axes as an indicator of source', *Archaeometry* 25, 135-63

Crowe, K. L. 1992. 'An Early Bronze Age axe from North Shoebury', *Essex Archaeol. Hist.* 23, 115

Crummy, P. 1992. *Excavations at Culver Street, the Gilberd School, and other sites in Colchester 1971-85*, Colchester Archaeol. Rep. 6

Curwen, E. C. 1929. 'Excavations in the Trundle, Goodwood, 1928', *Sussex Archaeol. Collect.* 70, 33-85

Devoy, R. J. 1979. 'Post-glacial environmental change and man in the Thames estuary: a synopsis', in Thomson, F.H. (ed.), *Archaeology and Coastal Change*, Soc. Antiq. London Occ. Paper 1, 134-48

Edwards, A. C. 1978. *A History of Essex*, Chichester: Phillimore, 4th edition

Flook, R. and Bedwin. O. 1993. 'The excavations of 1988', in Rodwell, W. J., *The origins and early development of Witham*, Oxbow Monograph 26, 22-7

Greensmith J. T. and Tucker, E. V. 1973. 'Holocene transgressions and regressions on the Essex coast and outer Thames Estuary', *Geologie en Mijnbouw* 52, 193-202

Gregory, C. A. 1982. *Gifts and Commodities*, London: Academic Press

Harding, A. F. and Lee, G. F. 1987. *Henge Monuments and Related Sites of Great Britain: air photographic evidence and catalogue*, Brit. Archaeol. Rep. Brit. Ser. 175

Hedges, J. D. 1980. 'The Neolithic in Essex', in Buckley, D. G. (ed.), *Archaeology in Essex to AD 1500*, Counc. Brit. Archaeol. Rep. 34, 26-39

Hedges, J. D. 1982. 'Fields Farm, Layer de la Haye', in Priddy, D. (ed.), 'Work of the Essex County Council Archaeology Section, 1981', *Essex Archaeol. Hist.* 14, 111-32

Hedges, J. D. and Buckley, D. G. 1978. 'Excavations at a Neolithic Causewayed Enclosure, Orsett, Essex, 1975', *Proc. Prehist. Soc.* 44, 219-308

Hedges, J. D. and Buckley, D. G. 1981. *Springfield Cursus and the Cursus Problem*, Chelmsford: Essex County Council

Herne, A. 1988. 'A Time and a Place for the Grimston Bowl', in Barrett, J. C. and Kinnes, I. A. (eds.), *The Archaeology of Context in the Neolithic and Bronze Age: Recent Trends*, Sheffield: Dept. of Archaeology & Prehistory, 9-29

Holgate, R. 1988a. *Neolithic Settlement of the Thames Basin*, Brit. Archaeol. Rep. Brit. Ser. 194

Holgate, R. 1988b. 'A Review of Neolithic Domestic Activity in Southern Britain', in Barrett, J. C. and Kinnes, I. A. (eds.), *The Archaeology of Context in the Neolithic and Bronze Age: Recent Trends*, Sheffield: Dept. of Archaeology & Prehistory, 104-12

Holgate, R. 1995. 'Early Prehistoric Settlement of the Chilterns', in Holgate, R. (ed.), *Chiltern Archaeology: recent work*, Dunstable: Book Castle, 3-16

Hudspith, R. E. T. 1991. 'Fieldwalking at Houghton Regis and Caddington, South Bedfordshire 1988-90', *Bedfordshire Archaeol.* 19, 57-64

Hudspith, R. E. T. 1995. 'Fieldwalking in South Bedfordshire 1988-91', in Holgate, R. (ed.), *Chiltern Archaeology: recent work*, Dunstable: Book Castle, 131-9

Huggins, P. J. 1970. 'Waltham Abbey: monastic site and prehistoric evidence', *Trans. Essex Archaeol. Soc.* 2, 216-66

Jacobi, R. M. 1980. 'The Mesolithic of Essex', in Buckley, D. G. (ed.), *Archaeology in Essex to AD 1500*, Counc. Brit. Archaeol. Rep. 34, 14-25

Jones, M. U. 1973. 'An Ancient Landscape Palimpsest at Mucking', *Essex Archaeol. Hist.* 5, 6-12

Kinnes, I. A. 1988. 'The Cattleship Potemkin: Reflections on the First Neolithic in Britain', in Barrett, J. C. and Kinnes, I. A. (eds.), *The Archaeology of Context in the Neolithic and Bronze Age: Recent Trends*, Sheffield: Dept. of Archaeology & Prehistory, 12-18

Lavender, N. 1995. 'Brightlingsea, ring ditch at Moverons Pit', in Gilman, P. J. and Bennett, A., (eds), 'Archaeology in Essex 1994', *Essex Archaeol. Hist.* 26, 242

Leeds, E. T. 1927. 'A Neolithic site at Abingdon, Berks', *Antiq. J.* 7, 438-64

Long, A. J. 1992. 'Coastal responses to changes in sea-level in the East Kent Fens and southeast England, UK over the last 7500 years', *Proc. Geol. Assoc.* 103, 187-99

Longworth, I. H. 1984. *Collared Urns of the Bronze Age in Great Britain and Ireland*, Cambridge: Univ. Press

Martingell, H. and Brice, S. 1992. 'Shafthole implements from Paglesham and Rivenhall', *Essex Archaeol. Hist.* 23, 114-5

Merriman, N. 1990. 'A Shafthole Adze from Blackmore', *Essex Archaeol. Hist.* 21, 140-2

Milton, B. 1986. 'The Orsett 'Cock' Beaker Burial', in Priddy, D. (ed.), 'Work of the Essex County Council Archaeology Section, 1983-84', *Essex Archaeol. Hist.* 16, 87-91

Murphy, P. 1988. 'Plant macrofossils', in Brown, N., 'A Late Bronze Age Enclosure at Lofts Farm, Essex', *Proc. Prehist. Soc.* 54, 281-93

Needham, S. P. 1988. 'Selective deposition in the British Early Bronze Age', *World Archaeol.* 20, 229-48

Powlesland, D. 1986. 'Excavations at Heslerton, North Yorkshire 1978-82', *Archaeol. J.* 143, 53-173

Priddy, D. 1981. 'The Barrows of Essex', in Lawson, A. J., Martin, E. A. and Priddy, D., *The Barrows of East Anglia*, East Anglian Archaeology 12, 89-105

Pryor, F. M. M. 1978. *Excavation at Fengate, Peterborough, England: the second report*, Royal Ontario Museum Archaeological Monograph 5

Roe, F. E. S. 1979. 'Typology of stone implements with shaft holes', in Clough, T. H. McK. and Cummins, W. A. (eds.), *Stone Age Studies*, Counc. Brit. Archaeol. Res. Rep. 23, 23-48

Rowley-Conwy, P. 1983. 'Sedentary hunters: the Ertebolle example', in Bailey, G. (ed.), *Hunter-Gatherer Economy in Prehistory*, Cambridge: Univ. Press, 111-26

Shennan, S. J., Healy, F. and Smith, I. F. 1985. 'The Excavation of a Ring-Ditch at Tye Field, Lawford, Essex', *Archaeol. J.* 142, 150-215

Shennan, I., Orford, J. and Plater, A. 1992. 'Introduction', *Proc. Geol. Assoc.* 103, 163-5

Smith, I. F. 1979. 'The chronology of British stone implements', in Clough, T. H. McK. and Cummins, W. A. (eds.), *Stone Age Studies*, Counc. Brit. Archaeol. Res. Rep. 23, 13-22

Wade, K. 1980. 'A settlement site at Bonhunt Farm, Wicken Bonhunt, Essex', in Buckley, D. G. (ed.), *Archaeology in Essex to AD 1500*, Counc. Brit. Archaeol. Rep. 34, 96-102

Wallis, S. and Waughman, M. Forthcoming. *Archaeology and the landscape in the Lower Blackwater valley*, E. Anglian Archaeol.

Warren, S. H., Piggott, S., Clark, J. G. D., Burkitt, M. C. and Godwin, H. and M. E. 1936. 'Archaeology of the submerged land-surface of the Essex coast', *Proc. Prehist. Soc.* 2, 178-210

Warren, S. H. and Smith, I. F. 1953. 'Neolithic pottery from the submerged land-surface of the Essex coast', *Univ. London Inst. Archaeol. Ann. Rep.* 10, 26-33

Wilkinson, T. J. and Murphy, P. 1986. 'Archaeological Survey of an Intertidal Zone: the Submerged Landscape of the Essex Coast, England', *J. Field Archaeol.* 13 (2) 177-94

Wilkinson, T. J. and Murphy, P. 1987. *The Hullbridge Basin Survey, 1986*, Chelmsford: Essex County Council

Wilkinson, T. J. and Murphy, P. 1988. *The Hullbridge Basin Survey, 1987*, Chelmsford: Essex County Council

Williamson, T. 1987. 'The Development of Settlement in North West Essex: the results of a recent field survey', *Essex Archaeol. Hist.* 17, 120-32

Zvelebil, M. and Rowley-Conwy, P. 1984. 'Transitions to farming in northern Europe: a hunter-gatherer perspective', *Norwegian Archaeol. Review* 17, 104-28

The Archaeology of Essex, c. 1500-500 BC

N Brown

Introduction
This article briefly describes the archaeological evidence available from Essex, for a period of about 1000 years from mid 2nd millennium BC to the 1st half of the 1st millennium BC. Traditionally this would cover the Middle Bronze Age, Late Bronze Age and part of the Early Iron Age, and these broad divisions are retained below. Much of this period was discussed by Couchman in 1978 (Couchman 1980). At that time the evidence was almost entirely confined to finds of artefacts, mostly metalwork. Since then various programmes of fieldwork have added considerably to knowledge of settlement, and the present article largely concentrates on summarising this work.

Middle Bronze Age
There is a very large quantity of Deverel-Rimbury pottery from Essex (Brown 1995a), with over 400 surviving vessels (compare Ellison 1981 for central Southern England). The pots are mostly complete, or near complete examples from cremation burials, but include some rather more fragmentary material from settlement sites. Following publication of the Ardleigh cemetery (Erith and Longworth 1960), Deverel-Rimbury pottery from Essex has been more or less automatically regarded as part of the Ardleigh Group (eg. Couchman 1980, 42; Jones and Bond 1980, 471; Lawson 1984, 161). However, there are a number of differences, mainly in terms of decoration, between the ceramics of north and south Essex (Brown 1995a). The characteristic 'horseshoe handles' and profuse use of fingertip rustication, in a variety of motifs, of the Ardleigh Group, are almost absent on pottery from the south of the county (Fig. 2). Decoration on the southern material is largely confined to single horizontal rows of fingertip impressions, or applied cordons, on the body, and finger-impressed rims. Thus, two of the regional groups which characterise Deverel-Rimbury ceramics (Ellison 1975; 1980) appear to be present; the Ardleigh Group in north-east Essex and south-east Suffolk, and a southern group, in the Chelmer/Blackwater river system and along the Thames. This latter group can be considered as part of Ellison's (1980) Lower Thames Group, which was originally defined using pottery largely from Middlesex and the south side of the Thames (Ellison 1975). The difference between the two groups is strikingly represented in the fine wares; globular urns are present in the Ardleigh Group (Erith and Longworth 1960), but generally absent in the south. Indeed, Ellison (1975) noted the absence of fine ware as characteristic of her Lower Thames Group. However, there is a distinctive group of stamp-decorated vessels, often of bowl-like form, which may represent the fine-ware component of the Lower Thames Group. The most famous of these stamped pots is the bowl from Birchington, Kent (Powell-Cotton and Crawford 1924; Rowlands 1976); fragments of a number of similar vessels are present in the assemblage from North Shoebury (Brown 1984-5; 1995). A stamp-decorated pot has been recovered from Sipsons Lane, Middlesex (Cotton et al. 1986), and a vessel from Broadstairs, Kent (Champion 1982, fig.12.4) may belong with this material.

Interestingly, the areas covered by the two ceramic groups display differences in burial practice. Large cremation cemeteries with tight clusters of ring ditches are common in the area of the Ardleigh Group eg. Chitts Hill (Crummy 1977), Brightlingsea (Clarke 1991, and in prep.) and Ardleigh itself (Hinchliffe 1981; 1986 fig. 2). At Chitts Hill and Brightlingsea many of the cremation burials occurred as linear urnfields between the ring ditches. The urns recovered by Erith in the late 1950s, can now be seen to occupy a similar relationship to the cluster of ring ditches at Ardleigh (Brown forthcoming). By contrast, in south Essex dense clusters of ring ditches do not occur; instead ring ditches and their associated burials are more widely scattered, as at Orsett (Milton 1987), Slough House Farm (Wallis 1989; Wallis and Waughman forthcoming) and Mucking[1] (Jones and Bond 1980, fig. 1)

The distribution of metalwork remains largely as mapped by Couchman (1980), and is dominated by finds of single Palstaves. Hoards are few (Sealey 1981, Table 2) and concentrated in the south of the county (Couchman 1980, fig. 16). They vary from simple pairs of Palstaves such as those from Prittlewell (Pollitt 1953), and Grays (O'Connor 1980, 320), to complex examples like the fine late hoard of Rapiers and other objects from Orsett (Burgess 1974; O'Connor 1980). Another late deposit may be the Ballintober sword, apparently associated with a Palstave from Thorpe Hall Brickfield, Southchurch (Pollitt 1953; O'Connor 1980, 354). With the exception of the Navestock Hoard (O'Connor 1980, List 41, Map 19) ornaments are rare, a marked contrast with areas further north in East Anglia (Couchman 1980; Lawson 1984).

Deposition of metalwork in rivers is represented by a Tumulous sword and flanged axe from 'off Southend' (Rowlands 1976), a Rapier from the Blackwater (Rowlands 1976), and finds such as the late style Palstave, possibly of French origin, from Osea Island foreshore (Eddy 1982). Early flange-hilted swords, of Erbenhiem and Hemigkofen type, from the river Lea and Barking creek, appear to mark the eastern limit of a concentration of such swords in the Thames and its tributaries (O'Connor 1980, map 31).

Middle Bronze Age settlement sites in Essex remain elusive and are still largely confined to sites with occasional pits, such as those described by Couchman (1980, 42). The only clear candidate for a Middle Bronze Age building (Fig. 4) is a rectangular structure 8 x 2.8m from Howells Farm (Wallis and Waughman forthcoming), which had a complete cylindrical loomweight placed in one of its postholes. A large well, which produced Deverel-Rimbury pottery and cylindrical loomweights, has been recorded at Rook Hall on the gravels fringing the Blackwater estuary (Adkins et al. 1984-5). A similar example has recently been excavated nearby at Chigborough Farm (Waughman 1989, and Wallis and Waughman forthcoming). Such features appear to be characteristic of Middle and Late Bronze Age settlement around the Blackwater estuary; the environmental and other data from them are briefly discussed elsewhere (Murphy this volume). Settlements enclosed by substantial ditches are unknown. However, two large ditches have been recorded during excavation at Ardleigh (Hinchliffe 1981, 1986). One runs roughly north-east/south-west north of the cemetery, with a Radiocarbon date of 1310-840 cal bc (HAR-5126), the second runs east-west from south of the cemetery with a Radiocarbon date of 1495-1100 cal bc (HAR-5129). These features appear to partly define a flat plateau above the 30m contour line, although cropmark evidence indicates that they may be part of elongated rectilinear enclosures.

---

[1] Recent examination of finds from the ring ditches shown on the plan published by Jones and Bond (1980) has revealed that many are associated with later pottery often of Middle Iron Age date; only three of the ring ditches yielded Bronze Age material or radiocarbon dates.

THE ARCHAEOLOGY OF ESSEX, C.1500-500BC

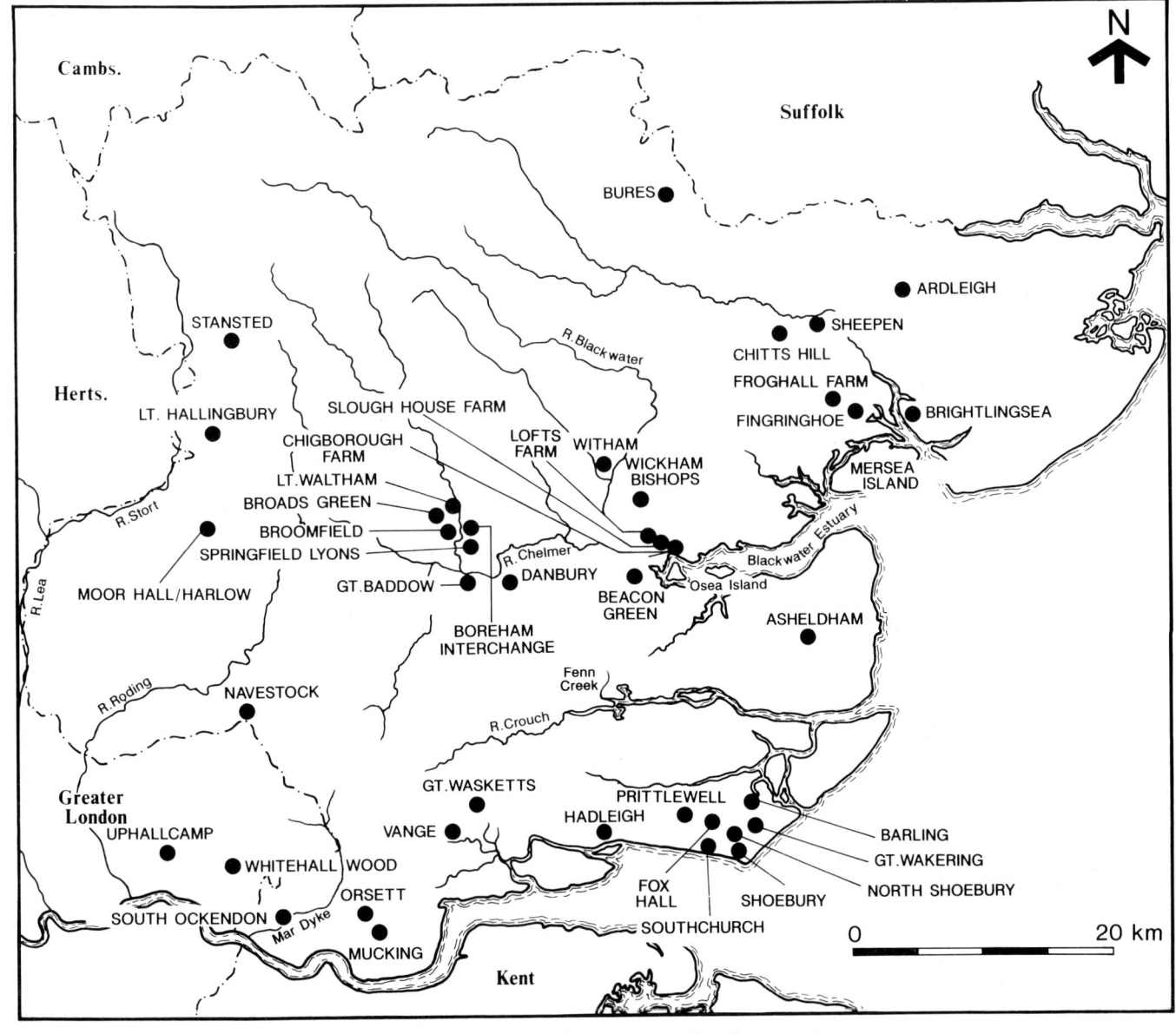

Fig. 1: Map showing places mentioned in the text.

A fragmentary system of shallow ditched rectangular fields recorded at Mucking appears to be of Middle Bronze Age date, and clearly pre-dates the Late Bronze Age circular enclosures (Jones and Bond 1980; Bond 1988).

The clearest settlement evidence comes from south-east Essex, and the most extensively excavated site is that at North Shoebury (Wymer and Brown 1995). This site was partly rescue recorded by D.G. Macleod of Southend Museum in 1971-2, during brickearth extraction, and partly excavated by Essex County Council in 1981. The Middle Bronze Age settlement had been damaged by later occupation, and consisted of a series of fragmentary rectilinear enclosures. These were bounded on the north and east sides by quite substantial V-profiled ditches up to 2m wide and 0.8m deep, but otherwise marked out by quite slight gullies. Set within these enclosures were clusters of small pits. In a number of cases the cohesive nature of the brickearth had preserved the original profile of the pits. This showed them to be miniature versions (about 1m diameter, 0.5m deep) of the classic beehive-shaped storage pits familiar from Iron Age sites on the chalk of southern England. In the area excavated in 1981, the pit groups lay in the western part of the enclosures; the eastern areas were largely blank. No traces of roundhouses were recovered, but it is possible that such structures had once existed in the apparently blank areas. The settlement may have been a linked group of compounds set within a wider field system, rather like the better preserved and intensively investigated sites on the chalk of southern England (e.g. Burstow and Holleyman 1957; Drewett 1982).

The rather sparse faunal (Levine 1995) and carbonised plant (Murphy 1995) remains from the settlement, perhaps unsurprisingly, indicate a mixed economy, with sheep, cattle and pigs kept, wheat and possibly oats grown. A single carbonised elder seed might attest to seasonal gathering of wild plant resources, whilst mussels were brought from the nearby coast. Fragments of Greensand and ferruginous sandstone querns attest to grain processing. Such stone is not available locally and must have come some distance, probably from south of the Thames (Buckley and Major 1995). The excavations produced large parts of at least seven cylindrical loomweights. Despite the different geographical setting, the economic evidence and range of resources exploited appear similar to that recovered from the downland sites (Drewett 1982).

Much of the ceramic debris recovered from North Shoebury appears to derive from placed deposits, rather than simple rubbish disposal. The faunal remains may also

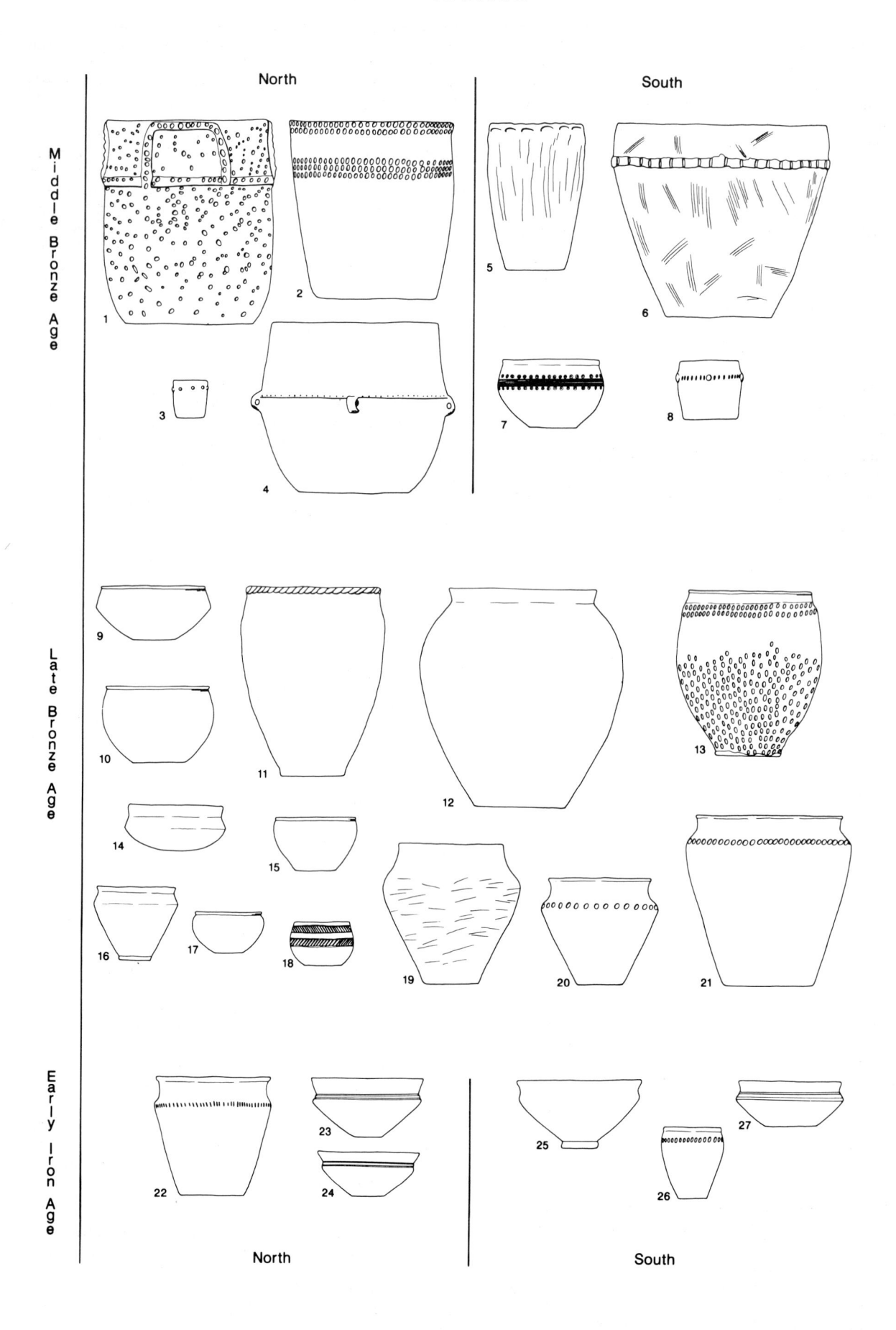

Fig. 2: Chronological development of pottery. All vessels shown are based on excavated examples from the county. The differences in ceramic styles between north and south Essex in the Middle Bronze Age are quite pronounced, particularly in terms of decoration. No such regional differences have so far been observed for the Late Bronze Age. In the Early Iron Age there may be regional variation with fine bowls mostly decorated in the north and mostly plain in the south.

have been treated in a similar manner (Brown and Wymer 1995). Deverel-Rimbury pottery and cylindrical loomweights from pits at Mucking also appear to derive from deliberately placed deposits, as may thirteen cylindrical loomweights found together in a clay pit at South Ockendon (Barford and Major 1992). Such structured deposition, and relative lack of faunal and plant remains, is again typical of settlement sites on the chalk (Barrett 1989).

An unurned cremation burial of a child was recovered 250m south-east of the main settlement area at North Shoebury; a second unurned cremation of an adult female was recovered in a test trench 400m to the south of the settlement. A radiocarbon date of 1855-1450 cal bc (HAR-4634) was obtained on charcoal from this burial, which lay close to two cropmark ring ditches. The relationship between these burials and the settlement appears to fit the pattern noted by Bradley (1981 fig. 7.5) for Deverel-Rimbury settlement and burial in southern England.

The settlement at North Shoebury was one of a series occupying the eastern end of the peninsula between the Thames and Roach estuaries (Brown and Wymer 1995). Contemporary occupation has been recorded to the north at Baldwins Farm, Barling (Couchman 1977), and at other sites in Barling and Great Wakering (K Crowe 1984-5 and pers. comm.). Whilst to the south, numerous finds of Deverel-Rimbury pottery in Southchurch and Shoebury, made in the course of brickearth extraction during the late 19th and early 20th centuries, demonstrate widespread occupation.[2]

Settlements such as North Shoebury were clearly not self-sufficient entities (Barrett and Needham 1988), but were embedded in a network of social exchanges. It may be that the ceramic groups noted above reflect areas within which the majority of social interaction took place. Although wider ranging contact clearly also occurred. Occasionally material evidence of such exchanges survives, in the form of the quernstones noted above, the broad similarity of ceramics on both sides of the North sea, with occasional, possibly imported, pots (O'Connor 1980, 282 and 286), and items of imported metalwork. The recovery of a paddle from the Crouch estuary radiocarbon dated to 1255-998 CAL BC (BM-2339) (Wilkinson and Murphy 1986; 1995) is a graphic reminder of the importance of waterborne transport, to which the numerous creeks and estuaries of the Essex coast are ideally suited. The paddle may have been used to power a boat like that recently recovered from Dover. Survey of the estuaries has also revealed a salt production site at Fenn Creek[3] (Wilkinson and Murphy 1986; 1995), charcoal from which produced a Radiocarbon date of 1412-1130 CAL BC (HAR-5734). Salt may well have been a valuable component in exchange relations and probably played a vital role in the changes in consumption and agricultural production noted below. A variety of wooden structures are now known within the intertidal zone of the Essex estuaries (below, Murphy this volume, and Wilkinson and Murphy 1995).

Late Bronze Age

The shift in the ceramic repertoire at about the beginning of the 1st millennium BC noted by Barrett (1980) in southern and eastern England is well attested in Essex (Fig. 2), and the general trend from plain ware to decorated assemblages is borne out by the stratified deposits from the Springfield Lyons enclosure ditch (Brown 1987 and in prep.). Many ceramic assemblages, both large and small, are now known from south and central Essex (Brown 1987; 1988 a and b; 1995b: Barrett 1978). There seems little evidence of differences in ceramic style between north and south Essex, such as those noted in the Middle Bronze Age (above). Instead, there is a broad similarity of ceramic style, with each site assemblage showing a wide range of minor variations of vessel form. However in north Essex, in the area of the preceding Ardleigh Group, relatively little post-Deverel-Rimbury pottery has been recovered, and the assemblages from Sheepen and Frog Hall Farm, Fingringhoe remain unpublished.

In common with Late Bronze Age pottery from the rest of southern Britain, the vessel forms appear to be derived from a combination of the preceding Deverel-Rimbury pottery (Brown 1988, 9), and Continental urnfield ceramics (Longley 1976, 65-74; Needham 1987, 116). Whilst the new ceramic styles might originate around the 10th century BC (Barrett 1980; Brown 1988, 6), dating evidence provided by metalwork associations and radiocarbon dates are consistently later (Field and Needham 1986; Needham 1993). Examples from Essex sites are radiocarbon dates from Mucking North and South Rings (Jones and Bond 1980; Bond 1988), and the Ewart Park bronze-casting moulds from Springfield Lyons (Needham 1987 and in prep.). Indeed the identification of a small pot as a 'deckseldoos' (O'Connor 1980, 286), found in direct association with Deverel-Rimbury vessels at Ardleigh Ring 3, would indicate Deverel-Rimbury pottery remained current into the 1st millennium BC. There may of course be differential development, with new ceramic styles being developed earlier in southern Essex, than in the area of the Ardleigh Group.

In marked contrast with the preceding period, there is a virtual absence of discernible burial practices during the Late Bronze Age (Needham 1995). However, there is some evidence to indicate that barrow construction continued into the Late Bronze Age at Ardleigh. Ardleigh Ring 5 (Erith 1975) had a central feature, associated with large parts of a shouldered jar, which can now be seen to be of classic Late Bronze Age type. Elsewhere, a penannular ditch about 150m south west of the Late Bronze Age enclosure at Lofts Farm (see below) was excavated under difficult circumstances by Maldon Archaeological Group (P Brown 1984-5 and pers. comm.). The central feature, an elongated rectangular pit appropriate to an inhumation grave, aligned north-east and south-west, contained a large jar of post-Deverel-Rimbury type. Unurned cremations within the Late Bronze Age site at Broads Green (Brown 1986b) may be contemporary with the other features. Cremations found within an unpublished palisaded rectilinear enclosure at Little Hallingbury recorded prior to construction of the M11 (Robertson 1975, 3.15) may also be of Late Bronze Age date. Some bodies may have been deposited in rivers in a similar manner to a variety of Late Bronze Age metalwork (Bradley 1990; Bradley and Gordon 1988) and a number of skulls from the Thames have been dated to the Middle and Late Bronze Age. Skulls have also been recovered from the Lea (Bradley and Gordon 1988). There is a remarkable discovery from Fenn Creek, of two skulls resting on a brushwood platform. The skulls were recovered in 1977 and passed to the British Museum, Natural History, via the Essex Police. The platform, which lay to the north of, and on the opposite bank from, the Fenn Creek saltern, was relocated in 1982 and a radiocarbon date of 927-823 CAL BC at one standard deviation (HAR-5222) obtained (Wilkinson and Murphy 1995).

Metalwork is dominated by material of the Ewart Park phase. In Essex, in common with much of East Anglia (Lawson 1984, 165) and the Lower Thames region (Needham 1987b, 120), Wilburton metalwork is strikingly absent. Similarly, Sompting and Breton axes together

---

[2] All this material is recorded in Brown (1995a).

[3] This saltern has been wrongly located at Walton-on-the-Naze by Darvill (1987, 129) and Parker-Pearson (1993, 121).

with other late, Llyn Fawr phase, metalwork is also largely absent (Sealey 1987). However, a recent hoard find from Barling may relate to a late stage of the Ewart Park phase (Crowe in prep.). Recent recovery of a complete Ewart Park sword from Mersea Island foreshore (Brown 1984-5) indicates deliberate deposition of metalwork in watery contexts, a practice well documented elsewhere.

Whilst the general distribution of metal finds remains largely as mapped by Couchman (1980, fig. 17), recent research and discovery have added detail to the distribution. In particular, metalwork from the Chelmer/Blackwater river system of central Essex appears broadly similar to the finds along the Thames Estuary to the south (Buckley et al. 1986; Brown et al. forthcoming). These finds help to bridge the apparent gaps in the distribution of particular metal types mapped by O'Connor (1980, eg. Ewart Park swords, Map 59, list 159; tanged leather-working knives Map 51, list 131) between concentrations along the Thames estuary and further north in East Anglia. It is therefore particularly interesting that Carps Tongue sword fragments are so far absent from hoard finds in the Chelmer/Blackwater area (Brown et al. forthcoming). The gap in the distribution of such sword fragments between the Thames estuary and north-east Essex, south-east Suffolk (O'Connor 1980, Map 58) may thus be genuine. The occurrence of Carps Tongue sword fragments in north-east Essex has been emphasised by the recently discovered Fingringhoe hoard (Sealey 1987; 1991).

Careful observation of the disposition of the objects in a recently discovered hoard from Great Wasketts, Basildon[4] shows they were packed tightly together, presumably having been deposited in a bag, with ingot fragments at the bottom and axes and other tools at the top. An account of the discovery of the unpublished Vange Hoard[5] (Col. Mus. Acc. No. 153, 196) also says that the objects were found in 'one compact group' again suggesting deposition in a bag. Both these hoards are from the heavy London clay area of south central Essex.

Two hoards from Wickham Bishops (Brown et al. forthcoming) found within 150m of each other display marked contrast in the type of objects present. Wickham Bishops I consisted mostly of small fragments of tools and Wickham Bishops II mostly of ingot fragments. This may suggest deliberate separation of types of metal artefact between the two hoards. Metal production is attested by large deposits of clay casting moulds from the ditch silts of the Springfield Lyons enclosure (Needham 1987b and in prep.). Fragments of similar moulds have been recovered from Mucking North Ring (Needham 1988).

There is now a wide variety of LBA settlement evidence from Essex. Most striking are a number of circular ditched enclosures, of a type now known to be distributed widely in eastern England (Champion 1980; Needham 1993). Five of these sites in Essex have been extensively excavated, or trial trenched, Mucking North Ring (Bond 1988), Mucking South Rings (Jones and Bond 1980), Springfield Lyons (Buckley and Hedges 1987 and in prep.), Gt Baddow (Brown and Lavender 1991; 1994) and Bures (Havis 1992). Many other sites have been provisionally identified from aerial photographs. These sites share much in common, notably circular form, substantial enclosure ditches and similar range of artefacts. However, these obvious similarities mask a considerable variation in detail; each site has a particular history and the extensively excavated enclosures show marked variation in internal arrangements (Needham 1993; Brown and Lavender 1994). This is perhaps most clearly demonstrated by the contrast between the layout of the Mucking North Ring and the plan of Springfield Lyons (Fig. 3). At Mucking North Ring, a large screen shields roundhouses in the west of the enclosure from anyone entering the main east entrance (Parker-Pearson 1993; Needham 1993). By contrast anyone entering through the imposing east entrance of Springfield Lyons would find themselves directly facing the substantial porch of a centrally placed roundhouse. Mucking North Ring and South Rings have considerable evidence for extra-mural occupation (Jones and Bond 1980; Bond 1988; Needham 1993). By contrast, extensive excavation outside the Springfield Lyons enclosure to the south and west, and trial trenching to the north and east has revealed almost no features of Late Bronze Age date. The Springfield site is overlain by an Early Saxon cemetery and Late Saxon settlement, both of which extended far beyond the limits of the Late Bronze Age enclosure. Examination of residual Late Bronze Age pottery from these Saxon features has revealed little from features outside the enclosure, and substantial quantities from features inside. The immediate vicinity of the Springfield enclosure therefore appears to have been kept clear (although a Late Bronze Age site has recently been excavated 800m to the north at the Boreham Interchange, see below). The occupants and activities taking place within the enclosed area appear to have been deliberately isolated in a manner anticipating the practice of the later 1st millennium BC (Bowden and McOmish 1987). Mucking South Rings, Springfield Lyons and Bures were all considered, on the basis of air photographs, to be henges before excavation. This may be more than a simple reflection of the difficulties of classifying, and dating enclosures solely from cropmark evidence. It is possible there was a conscious adoption of an archaic form for these Late Bronze Age sites (Clare 1987). It is now known that the Springfield Lyons site lay immediately west of a Neolithic Causewayed Enclosure (Buckley 1991; 1992) which may still have been visible in the Late Bronze Age. The Late Bronze Age enclosure, whose ditch has numerous causeways, could therefore be seen as a conflation of two types of Neolithic Monument, the circular form of the henge with a causewayed ditch, consciously imitating the adjacent Causewayed Enclosure.

The recent trial excavation of the Great Baddow enclosure (Brown and Lavender 1991; 1994), 2.8km south of Springfield Lyons site on the opposite bank of the Chelmer, besides confirming a Late Bronze Age date for the site, has revealed a number of differences between the two enclosures. The east entrance at Baddow lacks any sign of the impressive gate structure recorded at Springfield Lyons, and there was no sign of a post-built rampart or bank revetment. Indeed, the ditch silts contained evidence for the early collapse of an internal bank into the ditch. The apparent pairing of these two enclosures appears to be a widespread feature of such sites (Needham 1993), reflected in Essex by the two Mucking enclosures, the cropmark sites in Thurrock (Buckley and Hedges 1987, fig. 26) and further north in East Anglia by the sites at West Harling (Clark and Fell 1953).

Whilst there are clear ceremonial or symbolic aspects to these sites, it is evident that the occupants were deeply involved with agriculture and other aspects of production/consumption (salt at Mucking North Ring, metalwork at Springfield Lyons : Bond 1988; Needham 1987; 1993). Artefacts recovered from Springfield Lyons include a large pottery assemblage, loomweights, spindle whorls

---

[4] The hoard remains in the private possession of the finder. It was recovered about 700m west of an earlier find of a pair of socketed axes at Great Wasketts Farm (Brown 1986).

[5] The Vange hoard includes a winged adze, this is an addition to the three other winged adzes from Britain mapped by (O'Connor 1980, Map 47) and emphasises the concentration of these objects around the Thames Estuary.

North Ring Mucking

Springfield Lyons

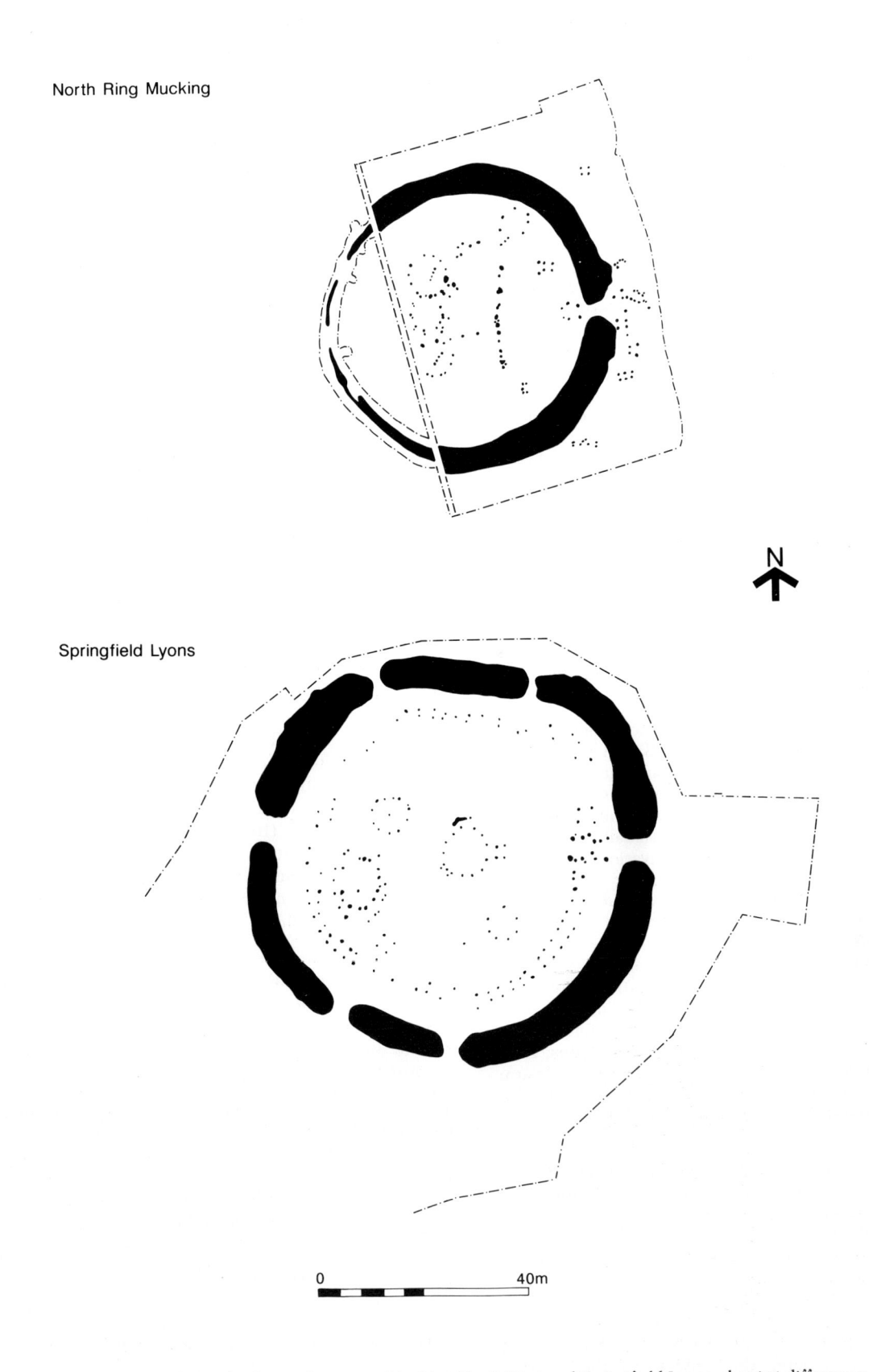

0   40m

Fig. 3: Comparative plans of the circular enclosures at Mucking North Ring and Springfield Lyons, showing differences in ditch form and internal arrangements.

and perforated clay slabs; carbonised plant remains indicate that crop processing took place within the enclosure (Murphy 1987).

Besides general rubbish disposal, there are a variety of what appear to be deliberately placed deposits at Springfield Lyons. These include substantial quantities of clay moulds for bronze casting, mostly of Ewart Park swords (Needham 1987a), deposited in the ditch butt ends north of the main east and west entrances. Large parts of pots, both coarse and fine wares, were recovered from pits in the vicinity of the central roundhouse.

Similar practices appear to have been carried out at a site at Boreham Interchange, 800m north of Springfield Lyons. This site was partly enclosed by a fairly narrow shal-

	Bread Wheat	Emmer	Spelt Barley	Hulled Barley	Naked Bean	Horse	Flax	Gold of Pleasure	Millet	Oats	Rye
Essex	*	*	*	*	*	*	*	-	-	*	-
N Europe	*	*	*	*	*	*	*	*	*	*	*

Table 1. Crops attested in Middle and Late Bronze Age sites in Essex and Northern Europe.

(Essex information derived from Murphy 1988, this volume and forthcoming. Information for Northern Europe from Harding 1989; Audouze and Büchenshütz 1991. Oats are sparsely represented in samples from Essex possibly as a weed.)

low ditch. There was no trace of domestic buildings within the enclosure, which was largely devoid of features, with the exception of clusters of pits, often containing apparently placed deposits of pottery and other artefacts. The western part of the curving 'enclosure' ditch had a number of partial recuts culminating in a V-shaped cut filled with a very dark artefact-rich deposit. A small rectangular post-built structure was subsequently placed just beside this part of the ditch. This structure is very similar in size and shape to one at Broads Green, and it is possible that these buildings may be shrines (Brown 1986). Pottery from the Boreham Interchange ditch was of Deverel-Rimbury character, whilst ceramics from the internal features were of Late Bronze Age type; sherds from the rectangular structure included fragments of an imported bowl.

Other forms of enclosed site[6] are also known, a rectangular double-ditched site at Lofts Farm (Brown 1988a) and a recently excavated D-shaped enclosure at Broomfield (Atkinson 1991; 1995). Both these enclosures were surrounded by comparatively slight ditches, and, unlike the circular enclosures were not sited in visually prominent locations. Although the Lofts Farm excavation had to concentrate within the enclosure, a number of features, including a large well, were recorded outside the enclosure, and it appears that occupation was not confined to the interior. Within the enclosure a central roundhouse was separated by a fence line from the largely empty northern part of the enclosure. The southern part was occupied by a variety of structures, with a long rectangular building in the south-east corner. Study of finds distributions for both Lofts Farm and Springfield Lyons, indicate spatial separation of activities within the enclosure (Brown 1988a; Murphy 1987; Parker-Pearson 1993, 120-21). Such spatial differentiation may also be apparent on open settlements (Brown 1989).

Structures within these settlements (Fig. 4) include two and four-post arrangements (eg. Lofts Farm, Brown 1988, fig. 8), occasional large rectangular buildings (Lofts Farm, Brown 1988a, figs. 8 and 10), and very small rectangular ?shrine structures recorded at Broads Green (Brown 1988b, fig. 3) and Boreham Interchange. However, the most common form of building is the roundhouse, almost invariably post-built (eg. Buckley and Hedges 1987, figs. 5 and 7, Bond 1988, figs. 8 and 9), an apparent exception being the building within Mucking South Rings (Jones and Bond 1980). This is a marked contrast with roundhouses of Middle Iron Age date which are generally marked by penannular gullies (eg. Little Waltham, Drury 1978; Uphall Camp, Greenwood 1988; Slough House Farm, Wallis and Waughman forthcoming). A similar contrast between Late Bronze Age and Iron Age buildings has been noted in the Upper Thames (Allen, Miles and Palmer 1984, 100).

A variety of unenclosed settlements are also known. At North Shoebury, a wide scatter of Late Bronze Age features, mostly ditches and groups of pits, was recorded to the south and east of the Middle Bronze Age settlement (Wymer and Brown 1995). Despite the proximity of the two settlements, the Middle Bronze Age site appears to have been deliberately avoided. The only Late Bronze Age features within the earlier settlement enclosures were three pits, two of which had what appear to be deliberately selected and placed deposits (Wymer and Brown 1995). The Late Bronze Age settlement was entirely recorded during rescue work in 1971-2. Few faunal and no plant remains were recovered; however dumps of mussel shell were noted and artefacts recovered included a typical range of Late Bronze Age pottery, together with spindle whorls, perforated clay slabs, occasional items of metalwork and bone tools (Fig. 5). Other sites include both extensive settlements (eg. Moor Hall, Harlow, Robertson 1975, 3.08) and smaller scatters of features (eg. Whitehall Wood, Upminster, Greenwood 1986). Their occurrence is by no means limited to gravel or brickearth-covered terraces. There are indications of settlement on low-lying London Clay areas (Brown 1988c), and widespread evidence of settlement on the fringes of the Boulder Clay plateau, wherever small streams or other features provided localised variation in the topography (Brown 1988b; 1989; Brown and Bartlett 1992).

Numerous wooden structures recorded in the estuaries indicate the importance of these coastal areas for a wide variety of activities (Murphy this volume). Radiocarbon dates indicate a pattern of activity originating in the Middle Bronze Age and continuing through the Late Bronze and Early Iron Age (Wilkinson and Murphy 1995).

There is considerable evidence for agricultural intensification at this time (Wilkinson 1988; Murphy 1988 and this volume). Carbonised plant remains indicate that the principal crops of the later first millennium BC had already been adopted by the Late Bronze Age, a process which clearly begins in the Middle Bronze Age. The range of cultivars is by no means confined to south-east Britain, but can be widely paralleled in southern Britain (e.g. Nowakowski 1991) and can be compared with evidence from northern Europe (Table 1).

---

[6] Hillforts may have some claim to be considered here. Two excavated sites, Asheldham Camp and Chipping Hill, Witham, have produced some Late Bronze Age evidence. At Asheldham Camp (Bedwin 1991), some pottery of Early Iron Age or possibly Late Bronze Age date was recovered, mainly from a buried soil beneath the bank. Pottery, more clearly of Late Bronze Age date, was recovered from buried soil and lower ditch silts at Chipping Hill (Rodwell 1993). The quantities of material are very small when compared with amounts recovered from excavation of definite Late Bronze Age enclosures. The Late Bronze Age pottery from these hillfort sites may best be regarded as residual.

Early Iron Age

In common with most of south-eastern Britain, the pottery of this period is clearly a development of earlier styles (Fig. 2). A variety of large assemblages are now known from Essex (eg. Lofts Farm well, Brown 1988a; Maldon, Beacon Green, Brown, 1992; North Shoebury, Brown 1995b; and Stansted SCS/CIS, Brown unpublished). Decoration used on fine angular bowls shows variation across the county. Such bowls from the north-east of the county and the Blackwater Estuary (eg. Barford forthcoming; Brown 1988a; 1992) are frequently decorated with horizontal grooved lines above the shoulder, typical of Cunliffe's Darmsden-Linton Group (Cunliffe 1968). The bowls themselves, by comparison with preceding ceramic forms, appear to be a highly standardised product, in terms of manufacture, form, decoration and colour (Brown 1988a, 272; 1992, 18). Whilst such bowls occasionally occur in material from sites along the Thames Estuary, large assemblages appear dominated by plain forms (Brown 1995b).

Burials of early Iron Age date are almost entirely absent, although a crouched burial in a storage pit was recovered from the Early Iron Age settlement at North Shoebury (Wymer and Brown 1995).

Despite a wealth of Late Bronze Age settlements, the Chelmer Valley has yielded little Early Iron Age material. The occupation sequence at Springfield Lyons comes to an end with a substantial deposit of ceramic debris, perhaps datable to the 7th century BC (Brown 1987 and unpublished). A possible post-built structure associated with a small quantity of Darmsden-Linton pottery has recently been recorded at Great Holts, Boreham. Elsewhere in the valley there is very little evidence of occupation, until the establishment of the earthworks on the Danbury Ridge, which have produced predominantly Middle and Late Iron Age pottery (Dunning 1934; Morris and Buckley 1978). By contrast, in the area around the Blackwater Estuary a number of sites are known. The well at Lofts Farm, in common with other similar features in the area (Brown 1988a), appears to have been deliberately backfilled with large dumps of pottery. Settlement is known at Slough House Farm (Wallis and Waughman forthcoming), and on a hilltop site at Beacon Green, Maldon. Here again substantial amounts of pottery were recovered, in this case from irregular pits. The settlement was later, at least partly, enclosed by a palisade. The relationship of this settlement with the earthwork at Maldon *burh* is uncertain (Bedwin 1992). There thus appears to be evidence for the deliberate filling of earlier features and a shift in settlement location during the Early Iron Age. The deposition of large quantities of pottery in pits of various kinds is a widespread phenomenon in the Early and Middle Iron Age (Hill 1989).

Some of the few Essex hillforts (Morris and Buckley 1978) may have been constructed at this time (Bedwin 1991). However, a major phase of occupation at a number of these sites appears to date from the Middle and Late Iron Age (Bedwin 1991; Greenwood 1988; Rodwell 1993).

Settlement shift during the Early Iron Age is by no means a universal occurrence. At Stansted, occupation on the fringes of the Boulder Clay plateau which began in the Late Bronze Age seems to have expanded in the Early Iron Age (Brooks and Havis in prep.). The expansion of earlier settlement is perhaps most clearly demonstrated at North Shoebury. Here, a series of rectilinear enclosures, partly defined by shallow ditches and gullies, lay either side of a trackway, developed from a ditched alignment of the Late Bronze Age (Wymer and Brown 1995). The settlement here included pits much larger than those of the Late Bronze Age. The site produced spindle whorls, loomweights and a bone weaving comb, and appears to have lasted into the 4th century BC. Elsewhere in south-east Essex similar evidence is known from Great Wakering (Crowe 1984-5 and pers. comm.) and settlement evidence has recently been excavated at Fox Hall (Ecclestone 1995). A shallow ditch, apparently of a settlement enclosure, has been recorded on a high bluff overlooking the Thames Estuary at Hadleigh (Brown 1987b).

Apart from a few ill-defined buildings noted by Drury (1980, 50), no houses of clearly Early Iron Age date are known; the exceptional structure at Ardleigh produced pottery best regarded as Middle rather than Early Iron Age (Erith and Holbert 1970). Similarly there is little information regarding the agrarian economy (Murphy this volume).

Priorities for Future Work

Publication of museum collections was identified as a high priority by Couchman (1980, 45), and this has begun to be addressed, along with publication of more recent finds (e.g. Buckley *et al.* 1986; Brown and Bartlett 1984-5; 1992; Sealey 1987, 1991; Brown 1991; Barford and Major 1992; Brown *et al.* forthcoming). However, much remains to be done; in particular a full catalogue of the Bronze Age artefacts held in Colchester Museum would be of great value. The Museum houses one of the finest and largest regional collections of Bronze Age material in Britain, and it is probable that its extent and importance is scarcely more appreciated now than it was thirty years ago (Erith 1963, 4).

Work is currently being undertaken to bring excavations at Ardleigh and Springfield Lyons to publication, and other recent projects are forthcoming. Certain other, older excavations would also repay study; amongst these two of the sites recorded during M11 construction in the early 1970s (Robertson 1975) would appear worthy of publication.

The recent publication of various parts of the Mucking excavations (Jones and Bond 1988; Bond 1988; Clark 1993) emphasises the importance of this extensively investigated landscape. There is little doubt that the evidence from Mucking could be used to provide insight into a number of the research objectives listed below. It is therefore crucial that the Middle Bronze Age, Late Bronze Age and Early Iron Age evidence be more fully published.

Further fieldwork might usefully focus on the following topics:-

Middle Bronze Age

Location and investigation of settlements should be a priority. Few such sites are known, and even fewer have been extensively excavated. The absence of settlement evidence is particularly striking within the area of the Ardleigh Group. The relationship of settlement to burial and of Middle to Late Bronze Age sites are likely to be fruitful areas of study.

Late Bronze Age

Settlement sites are much more extensively known, and this should provide the basis from which a more detailed understanding of the period can be developed. Fieldwork has concentrated on enclosed sites, and the location and extensive controlled excavation of open settlements is clearly required. The relationship of enclosed sites to the wider landscape is of particular interest. Sampling of further cropmark circular enclosures may allow the role played by the occupants of such sites to be better assessed. There is a clear imbalance between the recovery of plant, compared to faunal, remains. This can only be addressed by extensive excavation on calcareous subsoils. The brickearth of south-east Essex with its wealth of Middle and Late Bronze Age and Early Iron Age sites and

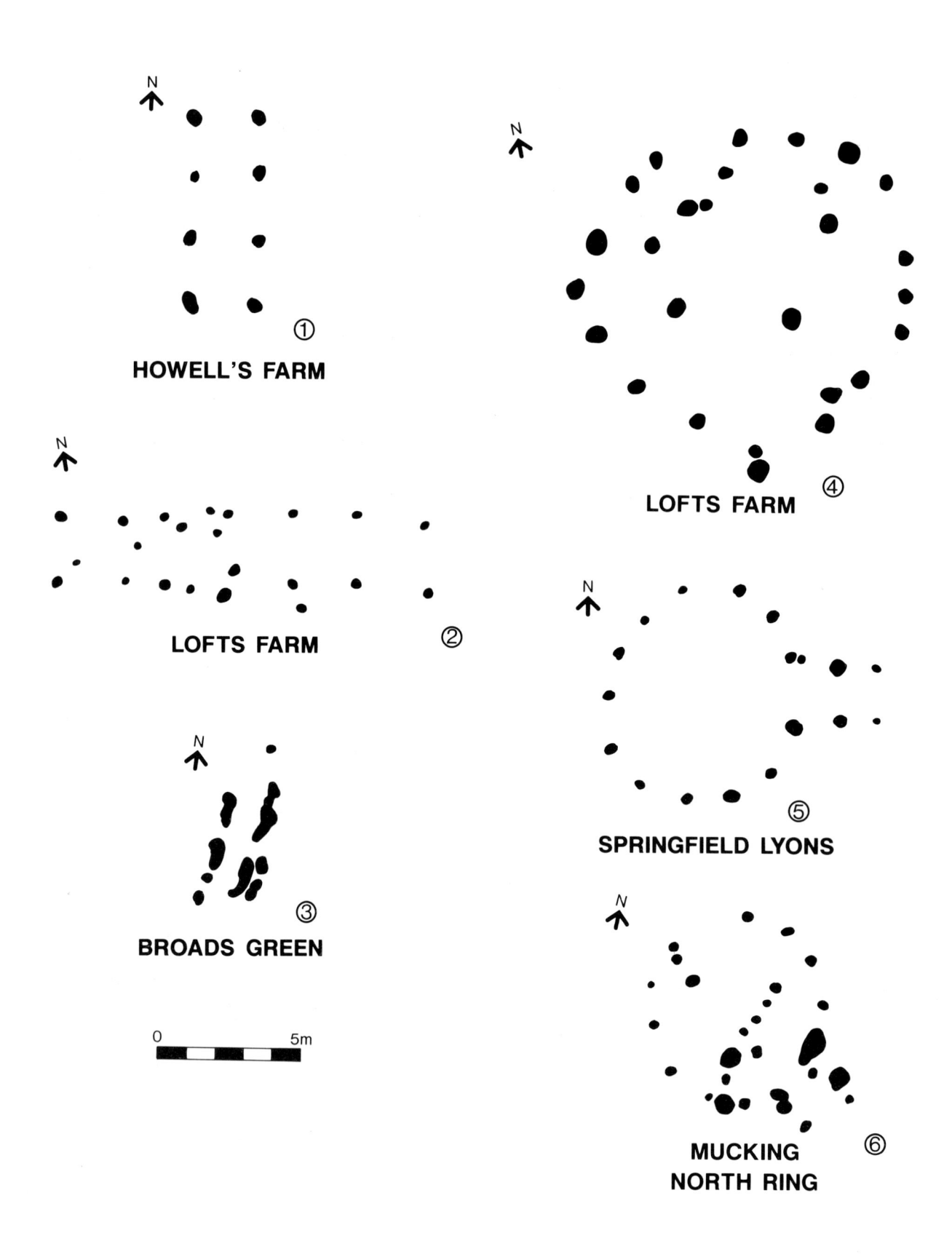

Fig. 4: Selected structures from excavated sites in Essex. There is some evidence to suggest that
Lofts Farm building (2) may have functioned as a longhouse, with a byre at the east end, and domestic activities
in the west (Brown 1988a). The Broads Green structure may be a shrine (Brown 1988b).
The posts of the houses from Springfield Lyons and Mucking North Ring, presumably represent roof supports.
The outer posts of the Loft Farm roundhouse may represent the wall-line,
with the irregular group of internal posts acting as roof supports.

THE ARCHAEOLOGY OF ESSEX, C.1500-500BC

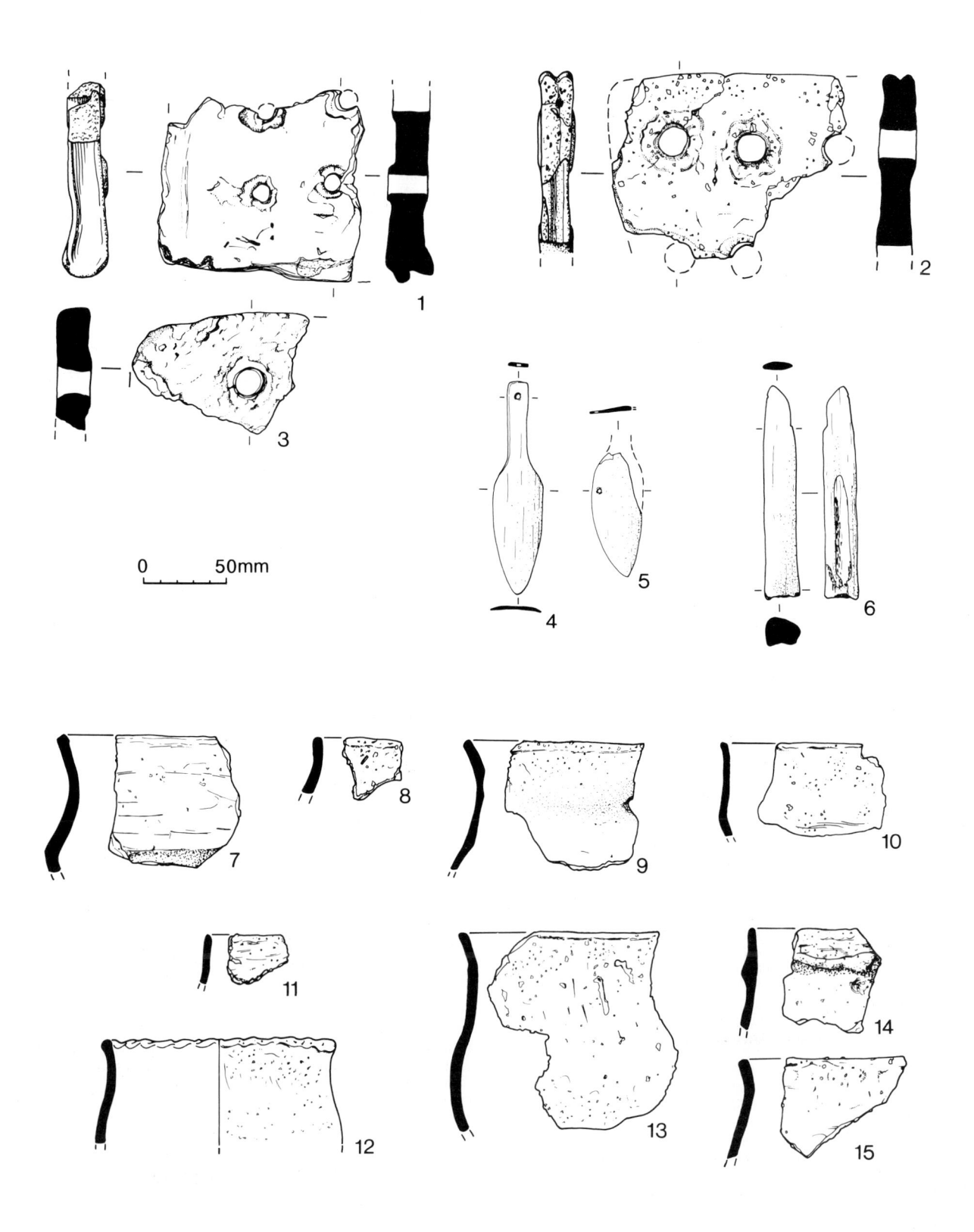

Fig. 5: Group of Late Bronze Age finds from a pit at North Shoebury. The perforated clay slabs are typical finds from settlements of this period, their function is uncertain. The bone objects are uncommon in Essex, where most excavated sites have been on acid gravels. The two finely made spatula-like objects (nos 4 and 5) may be paralleled by a group of 20 similar objects from All Cannings Cross (Cunnington 1923).

finds would be an obvious location. Suitable preservation may also be encountered on the fringes of the Boulder Clay plateau, and fieldwork here would be valuable since settlement is largely known through chance finds.

Early Iron Age
As with the Middle Bronze Age, location and investigation of settlement sites should be a priority. In particular the apparent absence of sites in the Chelmer Valley should be examined. There is clearly a contrast between the deliberate abandonment of some Late Bronze Age sites at this time and the development of others which may provide a useful focus for research.

Bibliography
Allen, T., Miles, D., and Palmer, S. 1984 'Iron Age buildings in the Upper Thames Region', in Cunliffe, B. and Miles, D. (eds) *Aspects of the Iron Age in Central Southern Britain*, 89-101

Atkinson, M. 1992. 'Broomfield', in Gilman (ed.) 'Archaeology in Essex 1991', *Essex Archaeol. Hist.* 23, 98-113

Atkinson, M. 1995. 'A Late Bronze Age enclosure at Broomfield, Chelmsford', *Essex Archaeol. Hist.* 26, 1-23

Audouze, F., and Büchenshütz, O. 1991. *Towns, Villages and Countryside of Celtic Europe*

Barford, P.M. Forthcoming. *Excavations at Little Oakley, Essex 1951-78: Roman Villa and Saxon Settlement*, E. Anglian Archaeol.

Barford, P.M., and Major H. 1992. 'Late Bronze Age Loomweights from Essex', *Essex Archaeol. Hist.* 23, 117-9

Barrett, J. 1978. 'The EPRIA prehistoric pottery', in Hedges, J. and Buckley, D., 'Excavations at a Neolithic causewayed enclosure, Orsett, Essex, 1975', *Proc. Prehist. Soc.* 44, 219-308

Barrett, J. 1980. 'The pottery of the late Bronze Age in lowland England', *Proc. Prehist. Soc.* 46, 297-330

Barrett, J. 1989. 'Food, Gender and Metal : Questions of Social Reproduction', in Sorensen, M. and Thomas, R. (eds) *The Bronze Age - Iron Age Transition in Europe*, Brit. Archaeol. Reps Int. Series 483, 304-320

Barrett, J., and Needham, S. 1988. 'Production, Circulation and Exchange : Problems in the interpretation of Bronze Age Bronzework', in Barrett, J. and Kinnes, I. (eds), *The Archaeology of Context in the Neolithic and Bronze Age: Recent Trends*, 127-40

Bedwin, O. 1991. 'Asheldham Camp - an early Iron Age hillfort : excavations 1985', *Essex Archaeol. Hist.* 22, 13-37

Bedwin, O. 1992. 'Early Iron Age settlement at Maldon and the Maldon *burh*; excavations at Beacon Green 1987', *Essex Archaeol. Hist.* 23, 10-24

Bond, D. 1988. *Excavation at the North Ring, Mucking, Essex*, E. Anglian Archaeol. 43

Bowden, M. and McOmish, D. 1987. 'The Required Barrier', *Scottish Archaeol. Review* 4, 76-84

Bradley, R. 1981 '"Various styles of urn": cemeteries and settlement in southern England c.1400-1000bc', in Chapman, R. and Kinnes, I. (eds), *The Archaeology of Death*, 93-104

Bradley, R. 1990. *The Passage of Arms: An Archaeological Analysis of Prehistoric Hoards and Votive Deposits*

Bradley, R., and Gordon, K. 1988. 'Human skulls from the River Thames, their dating and significance', *Antiquity* 62, 503-9

Brown, N. 1984-5. 'North Shoebury', in Priddy, D. (ed.), 'Work of the Essex County Council Archaeology Section 1983-4', *Essex Archaeol. Hist.* 16, 82-122

Brown, N. 1986. 'Basildon, Gt. Wasketts', in Priddy, D. (ed.), 'Work of the Essex County Council Archaeology Section 1985', *Essex Archaeol. Hist.* 17, 141-55

Brown, N. 1987a. 'Late Bronze Age Pottery', in Buckley, D. and Hedges, J., *The Bronze Age and Saxon Settlements at Springfield Lyons, Essex: An Interim Report*, Essex County Council Occ. Pap. 5

Brown, N. 1987b. 'Hadleigh, Chapel Lane', in Priddy, D. (ed.) 'Work of the Essex County Council Archaeology Section 1986', *Essex Archaeol. Hist.* 18, 88-103

Brown, N. 1988a. 'A Late Bronze Age enclosure at Lofts Farm, Essex', *Proc. Prehist. Soc.* 54, 249-302

Brown, N. 1988b. 'A Late Bronze Age settlement on the boulder clay plateau : excavations at Broads Green 1986', *Essex Archaeol. Hist.* 19, 7-14

Brown, N. 1988c. 'Wickford, Memorial Park', in Priddy, D. (ed.) 'Work of Essex County Council Archaeology Section 1987', *Essex Archaeol. Hist.* 19, 240-59

Brown, N. 1989. 'Great Waltham, Broads Green', in Bennett, A. and Gilman, P. (eds) 'Work of the Essex County Council Archaeology Section, 1988', *Essex Archaeol. Hist.* 20, 147-56

Brown, N. 1991. 'An Early Iron Age jar from North Shoebury', *Essex Archaeol. Hist.* 22, 164

Brown, N. 1992. 'Prehistoric Pottery', in Bedwin, O. 'Early Iron Age settlement at Maldon and the Maldon burh : excavations at Beacon Green 1987', *Essex Archaeol. Hist.* 23, 10-24

Brown, N. 1995a. 'Ardleigh reconsidered: Deverel-Rimbury pottery in Essex', in Kinnes, I. and Varndell, G. (eds), *"Unbaked Urns of Rudely Shape": Essays on British and Irish pottery for Ian Longworth*, Oxbow monograph 55

Brown, N. 1995b. 'Late Bronze Age and Early to Middle Iron Age Pottery', in Wymer, J. and Brown, N., Excavations at North Shoebury: settlement and economy in south-east Essex 1500BC-AD1500, E. Anglian Archaeol. 75, 77-87

Brown, N. Forthcoming. *The archaeology of Ardleigh, Essex: excavations 1955-80*, E. Anglian Archaeol.

Brown, N., and Bartlett, R. 1984-5. 'Harlow', in Priddy, D. (ed.) 'Work of the Essex County Council Archaeology Section 1983-4', *Essex Archaeol. Hist.* 16, 82-122

Brown, N., and Bartlett, R. 1992. 'A tanged chisel/leatherworking knife from Sheering, and prehistoric finds from the valley of the Pincey Brook', *Essex Archaeol. Hist.* 23, 115-6

Brown, N., and Lavender, N. 1991. 'Great Baddow, Manor Farm', in Gilman, P. (ed.) 'Excavations in Essex 1990', *Essex Archaeol. Hist.* 22, 148-61

Brown, N., and Lavender, N. 1994. 'Late Bronze Age Sites at Great Baddow and Settlement in the Chelmer Valley, Essex, 1500-500BC', *Essex Archaeol. Hist.* 25, 3-13

Brown, N., Crowe, K., and Northover, P. Forthcoming. 'Four Essex Hoards and a consideratoin of the metallurgy of copper ingots', *Antiq. J.*

Brown, P. 1984-5. 'Great Totham, Lofts Farm', in Priddy, D. (ed.) 'Excavations in Essex 1983-4', *Essex Archaeol. Hist.* 16, 123-39

Buckley, D. G. 1991. 'Springfield, Springfield Lyons', in Gilman, P. (ed.) 'Excavations in Essex 1990', *Essex Archaeol. Hist.* 22, 148-61

Buckley, D. G. 1992. 'Springfield Lyons', in Gilman, P. (ed.) 'Archaeology in Essex', *Essex Archaeol. Hist.* 23, 98-113

Buckley, D.G., and Hedges, J. D. 1987. *The Bronze Age and Saxon Settlements at Springfield Lyons, Essex: An interim report*, Essex County Council Occ. Pap. 5

Buckley, D. G., Brown, N., and Greenwood, P. 1986. 'Late Bronze Age hoard from the Chelmer Valley, Essex', *Antiq. J.* 66, 248-66

Buckley, D. G., and Major, H. 1995. 'Querns', in Wymer, J. and Brown, N. *Excavations at North Shoebury: settlement and economy in south-east Essex 1500BC-AD1500*, E. Anglian Archaeol. 75, 72

Burgess, C. 1974. 'The Bronze Age', in Renfrew, C. (ed.) *British Prehistory: a new outline*, 223-32

Burstow, G. P., and Holleyman, G. A. 1958. 'Late Bronze Age Settlement on Itford Hill, Sussex', *Proc. Prehist. Soc.* 23, 167-212

Champion, T. 1980. 'Settlement and environment in late Bronze Age Kent', in Barrett, J. and Bradley, R. (eds), *Settlement and Society in the British Later Bronze Age*, Brit. Archaeol. Rep. 83, 223-46

Champion, T. 1982. 'The Bronze Age in Kent', in Leach, P. (ed.), *Archaeology in Kent to AD1500*, CBA Res. Rep. 48, 31-39

Clare, T. 1987. 'Towards a reappraisal of henge monuments: origins, evolution and hierarchies', *Proc. Prehist. Soc.* 53, 457-78

Clark, A. 1993. *Excavations at Mucking Volume 1: The Site Atlas*, English Heritage Rep. 20

Clarke, C. 1991. 'Brightlingsea : A Bronze Age cemetery', *Current Archaeol.* 126, 272-3

Clark, J. G. D., and Fell, C. I. 1953. 'The Early Iron Age Site at Micklemoor Hill, West Harling, Norfolk and its Pottery', *Proc. Prehist. Soc.* 19, 1-40

Cotton, J., Mills, J., and Clegg, G. 1986. *Archaeology in West Middlesex*

Couchman, C., ed. 1977. 'Excavations in Essex 1976', *Essex Archaeol. Hist.* 9, 95-106

Couchman, C. 1980. 'The Bronze Age in Essex', in Buckley, D.G. (ed.) *Archaeology in Essex to AD1500* CBA Res. Rep. 34, 40-6

Crowe, K. 1984-5. 'Great Wakering Brickfields', in Priddy, D. (ed.), 'Excavations in Essex 1983-4', *Essex Archaeol. Hist.* 16, 123-39

Crummy, P. 1977. 'A Bronze Age cemetery at Chitts Hill, Colchester, Essex', *Essex Archaeol. Hist.* 9, 1-18

Cunliffe, B. 1968. 'Early Pre-Roman Iron Age communities in eastern England', *Antiq. J.* 48, 175-91

Cunnington, M.E. 1923. *The Early Iron Age inhabited sites at All Cannings Cross*

Darvill, T. 1987. *Prehistoric Britain* London: English Heritage

Drewett, P. L. 1982. 'Later Bronze Age downland economy and excavations at Black Patch, East Sussex', *Proc. Prehist. Soc.* 48, 321-409

Drury, P. J. 1978. *Excavations at Little Waltham 1970-71* CBA Res. Rep. 26

Drury, P. J. 1980. 'The early and middle phases of the Iron Age in Essex', in Buckley, D.G., (ed.) *Archaeology in Essex to AD1500* CBA Res. Rep. 34, 47-54

Dunning, G. C. 1934. 'Iron Age Pottery from Danbury, Essex', *Antiq. J.* 14, 186-90

Ecclestone, J. 1995. 'Early Iron Age settlement at Southend: excavations at Fox Hall Farm, 1993', *Essex Archaeol. Hist.* 26, 24-39

Eddy, M. 1982. 'Osea Island', in Priddy, D. (ed.) 'Work of the Essex County Council Archaeology Section 1981', *Essex Archaeol. Hist.* 14, 111-32

Ellison, A. 1975. *Pottery and settlements of the later Bronze Age in southern England*, unpublished Ph.D thesis University of Cambridge

Ellison, A. 1980. 'Settlements and regional exchange : a case study', in Barrett, J. and Bradley, R. (eds), *Settlement and Society in the British Late Bronze Age*, Brit. Archaeol. Rep. 83, 127-40

Ellison, A. 1981. 'Towards a socioeconomic model for the Middle Bronze Age in southern England', in Hodder, I., Isaac, G. and Hammond, N. (eds), *Pattern of the Past*, 413-438

Erith, F. H. 1963. 'The Rochford Gold Necklace and the Middle Bronze Age in Essex', *Col. Archaeol. Group Bul.* 6, 2-5

Erith, F. H. 1975. 'Ardleigh Ring Five', *Col. Archaeol. Group Bul.* 18, 2-4

Erith, F. H., and Holbert, P. R. 1970. 'The Iron Age "A" Farmhouse at Vinces Farm, Ardleigh', *Col. Archaeol. Group Bul.* 13, 1-24

Erith, F. H., and Longworth, I. H. 1960. 'Bronze Age urnfield on Vinces Farm, Ardleigh, Essex', *Proc. Prehist. Soc.* 26, 178-92

Field, D., and Needham, S. P. 1986. 'Evidence for Bronze Age settlement on Coombe Warren, Kingston Hill', *Surrey Archaeol. Collect.* 77, 121-51

Greenwood, P. 1986. 'A Late Bronze Age - Early Iron Age field system and settlement at Whitehall Wood, Upminster', *The London Archaeologist* 5, 171-5

Greenwood, P. 1988. 'Uphall Camp, Ilford', *Essex J.* 23, no. 1, 19-20

Harding, A. F. 1989. 'Interpreting the evidence for agricultural change in the Late Bronze Age in Northern Europe', in Nordström, H. and Knape, A. (eds) *Bronze Age Studies*, 173-81

Havis, R. 1992. 'Bures, Ferriers Farm', in Bennett, A. (ed.) 'Work of the Essex County Council Archaeology Section 1991', *Essex Archaeol. Hist.* 23, 91-7

Hill, J.D. 1989. 'Rethinking the Iron Age', *Scottish Archaeol. Review*, 6, 10-24

Hinchliffe, J. 1981. 'The Ardleigh Project : A summary', *Col. Archaeol. Group Bul.* 24, 2-5

Hinchliffe, J. 1986. 'Ardleigh', in *Preservation by Record: The Work of the Central Excavation Unit 1975-85*, 12-13

Jones, M. U. and Bond, D. 1980. 'Later Bronze Age settlement at Mucking, Essex', in Barrett, J. and Bradley, R. (eds), *Settlement and Society in the British Later Bronze Age*, 471-82

Lawson, A. 1984. 'The Bronze Age in East Anglia with particular reference to Norfolk', in Barringer, C. (ed.) *Aspects of East Anglian Pre-History*, 141-178

Levine, M. 1995. 'Animal Bone', in Wymer, J. and Brown, N., *Excavations at North Shoebury: settlement and economy in south-east Essex 1500BC-AD1500*, E. Anglian Archaeol. 75, 130-40

Longley, D. 1980. *Runnymede Bridge: excavations on the site of a Late Bronze Age settlement and waterfront*, Surrey Archaeol. Soc. Res. Rep. 6

Milton, B. 1987. 'Excavations at Barrington's Farm, Orsett Cock, Thurrock, Essex, 1983', *Essex Archaeol. Hist.* 18, 16-33

Morris, S., and Buckley, D. G. 1978. 'Excavations at Danbury Camp, Essex, 1974 and 1977', *Essex Archaeol. Hist.* 10, 1-28

Murphy, P. 1987. 'Environmental Evidence', in Buckley, D.G. and Hedges, J.D. (eds), *The Bronze Age and Saxon Settlements at Springfield Lyons, Essex*, Essex County Council Occ. Pap. 5, 12

Murphy, P. 1988. 'Plant Macrofossils', in Brown, N., 'A Late Bronze Age enclosure at Lofts Farm, Essex', *Proc. Prehist. Soc.* 54, 249-302

Murphy, P. 1995. 'Botanical Evidence', in Wymer, J. and Brown, N., *Excavations at North Shoebury: settlement and economy in south-east Essex 1500BC-AD1500*, E. Anglian Archaeol. 75, 146-50

Needham, S. P. 1987a. 'The Bronze Age' in Bird, J. and Bird, D.G., (eds), *The Archaeology of Surrey to 1540*, 97-138

Needham, S. P. 1987b. 'The metallurgical debris', in Buckley, D.G. and Hedges, J.D. (eds), *The Bronze Age and Saxon Settlements at Springfield, Essex: an interim report*, Essex County Council Occ. Pap. 5, 11

Needham, S. P. 1988. 'Industrial debris', in Bond, D. *Excavation at the North Ring, Mucking, Essex*, E. Anglian Archaeol. 43

Needham, S. P. 1993. 'The Structure of Settlement and Ritual in the Late Bronze Age of south-east Britain', in Mordant, C. and Richard, A. (eds), *L'habitat et l'occupation du sol à l'Age du Bronze en Europe. Actes du Colloque International de Lons-le-Saunier, 16-19 Mai 1990* Editors du Comité des Travaux historique et scientifique: Documents Préhistorique 4, 49-69

Needham, S. P. 1995. 'A bowl from Maidscross, Suffolk: burial with pottery in the post Deverel-Rimbury period', in Kinnes, I. and Varndell, G. (eds), *"Unbaked Urns of Rudely Shape": Essays on British and Irish pottery for Ian Longworth*, Oxbow Monograph 55, 159-72

Nowakowski, J. A. 1991. 'Trethellan Farm, Newquay : the excavation of a lowland Bronze Age settlement and Iron Age cemetery', *Cornish Archaeol.* 30, 5-242

O'Connor, B. 1980. *Cross Channel Relations in the Late Bronze Age*, Brit. Archaeol. Rep. Int. Series 91

Pollitt, W. 1953. *Southend Before the Norman Conquest*, Southend Museum Handbook No. 7

Powell-Cotton, P. H. G., and Crawford, O. G. S. 1924. 'The Birchington Hoard', *Ant. J.* 4, 220-6

Robertson, I. G. 1975. 'The Archaeology of the M11 Motorway in Essex, 1970-75', *Essex J.* 10, 68-91

Rodwell, W. 1993. *The Origins and Early Development of Witham, Essex*, Oxbow Monograph 26

Rowlands, M. J. 1976. *The production and distribution of metalwork in the Middle Bronze Age in Southern Britain* Brit. Archaeol. Rep. 3

Sealey, P. 1987. 'A Late Bronze Age Hoard from Fingringhoe', *Essex Archaeol. Hist.* 18, 7-15

Sealey, P. 1991. 'Some finds of the Bronze and Iron Ages in Essex', *Essex Archaeol. Hist.* 22, 1-12

Wallis, S. 1989. 'A Multi-Period site at Slough House Farm, Great Totham Parish', *Essex J.* 24, no.2, 29-43

Waughman, M. 1989. 'Chigborough Farm, Goldhanger: The first season's excavation of an early settlement', *Essex J.* 24, no.1, 15-8

Wallis, S., and Waughman, M. Forthcoming. *Archaeology and the Landscape in the Lower Blackwater Valley*, E. Anglian Archaeol.

Wilkinson, T. J. 1988. *Archaeology and Environment in South Essex: Rescue Archaeology along the Grays By-pass, 1979-80*, E. Anglian Archaeol. 42

Wilkinson, T. J., and Murphy, P. 1986. 'Archaeological Survey of an Intertidal Zone: the Submerged Landscape of the Essex Coast, England', *Journal of Field Archaeology* 13, no.2, 177-94

Wilkinson, T. J., and Murphy, P. 1995. *The Archaeology of the Essex Coast: Vol. 1 The Hullbridge Survey Project*, E. Anglian Archaeol. 71

Wymer, J., and Brown, N. 1995. *Excavations at North Shoebury: settlement and economy in south-east Essex 1500BC to AD1500*, E. Anglian Archaeol. 75

Rethinking the Later Bronze Age

Richard Bradley

Introduction

Archaeologists have always confronted the same dilemma. In order to make plans they have to synthesise what they know already. But every synthesis is premature and soon goes out of date. Some ideas seem to be doomed from the start, and new discoveries dispose of many more.

That may be why there has been so little interest in interpreting the archaeology of this period. It was in 1980 that John Barrett and I edited a series of conference papers under the ambitious title 'Settlement and Society in the British Later Bronze Age' (Barrett and Bradley 1980). Sixteen years later it would be difficult to do the same, and yet the need for such an overview is still more urgent now. There are more archaeologists working in the field, and with the advent of developer funding there are more opportunities for taking the initiative. Why, then, has the momentum been lost?

There are many reasons for that predicament. The syntheses offered in 1980 were premature, as we knew they would be, and they failed to predict the pattern of discovery over the next decade. Only Michael Rowlands' ambitious paper is still quoted with any regularity, and more as a contribution to social theory than as a programme for field research. The articles contributed by John Barrett, Ann Ellison and myself have not fared as well, and for a number of different reasons. Chronologies have changed, sometimes because key radiocarbon dates have been withdrawn or replaced. Field observations that had remained unchallenged for years lost their credibility overnight. There were also major changes in ways of thinking about the past. There was a weariness with the over-abstraction of processual archaeology with its bleak insistence on studying adaptation, and a greater concern with prehistory as the interpretation of human *practices* (Barrett 1993). Above all, the 1980s witnessed a growing convergence with the work of social anthropologists. This fired the imaginations and broadened the horizons of many of those studying the Bronze Age. No longer were they quite so prone to interpret the past in terms of their own experience, and with that change came the end of what John Barrett once described as the 'Good Housekeeping' model of prehistory.

Such changes have been exciting, but they can also be inhibiting, as familiar dogmas are overthrown. For example, studies of Bronze Age metalwork followed more or less the same course over many years: a process of cataloguing and comparison that laid down the terms for any discussion of sequence. But very little was said about why this material survived in the first place. Why had it not been reused? Was the deposition of so much metalwork one of the more important activities in Bronze Age society? That question had hardly been considered, so that now it looked as if we might need to start again (Bradley 1990). It is hardly surprising that we soon lost confidence in our ability to create a new order.

That failure of confidence perhaps went even deeper, for it also afflicted projects that had been published in preliminary form in the 1980 collection. In some cases, the final reports on that research are still awaited now, arousing the uneasy suspicion that the original observations might have been more complex - or less informative - than they once seemed to be. There have been significant changes of perspective. Thus Needham's excellent monograph on the rescue excavations at Runneymede Bridge (Needham 1991) raise a whole series of issues that were hardly latent in his interim report. Again Drewett's account of spatial patterning inside the houses at Blackpatch (Drewett 1982) seems less convincing now than it did when it was first published, simply because we have learned how to recognise structured deposition in Bronze Age settlements. What were refuse deposits in 1980 look more like intentional offerings today. In other cases, even the primary observations may have changed. The recent publication of work on the Marlborough Downs (Gingell 1992) employs a different chronological framework from the preliminary account.

If projects that were topical in 1980 still have to be published in detail, the same applies even more obviously to those conducted since then. Indeed, the rapid expansion of developer-funded excavations means that it is becoming difficult, even for a period specialist, to keep abreast of current fieldwork. To take a specific example, the Kennet valley has seen extensive activity by two archaeological units. Both have recently produced monographs on some of their excavations in this area (Butterworth and Lobb 1992; Moore and Jennings 1992), but the maps of Bronze Age settlement that they contain do not have the same information as one another. At the most basic level of all we are failing to communicate.

It might seem that these problems are unimportant - that they will be redressed as more projects appear in print - but that is to overlook the urgency of the present situation. English Heritage is already attempting to codify our state of knowledge in order to increase the number of Scheduled Monuments (Darvill *et al.* 1987). Whilst the Monuments Protection Programme provides a welcome opportunity to put a reasoned case for preservation, it presupposes a much greater understanding of the past than we are able to command at present. To be blunt, we are much more effective at collecting data than we are at analysing information.

The same problem applies to work funded by developers. In principle, this is another welcome initiative that could do much for Bronze Age studies. But once again research has fallen too far behind the pace of discovery, so that we are not as well informed as we should be on the significance of threatened monuments. Instead the main impact of evaluations (and I do not deny their usefulness) has been to encourage archaeologists to work in areas which had always seemed to be unoccupied. But to test a theory by accident is hardly a blueprint for the future.

This is precisely why the conference was so welcome. It allowed us to review what had been achieved and to consider it from a series of different perspectives. I have talked about the difficulty of coming to terms with Bronze Age archaeology, but I still believe in doing so. Now I must practise what I preach.

It is always too soon to synthesise, but it is always imperative to do so. The conference that resulted in the publication of 'Settlement and Society ...... ' certainly had some impact, as the published papers are cited in current accounts of prehistoric Britain. For that reason I shall take those articles as my starting point. I would like to trace some of the more recent developments in the archaeology of this period. There are a great many of them, and I shall have to be selective, but their very abundance and variety have a wider implication for the ways in which we do research. I shall advocate a rather different kind of landscape archaeology, and I shall reflect on some of the approaches that could be taken in the future. These need not be specific to the archaeology of Essex, but they might be more relevant here than in most parts of the country. As Nigel Brown's paper demonstrates so well, the work that has already been carried out in Essex has been of a very high standard.

A progress report

My title talks of 'rethinking' the Later Bronze Age. Even the definition of this term has changed. In 1980 it seemed as if we could break free of the constraints of metalwork typology, basing the period divisions on developments in the pattern of settlement. The Later Bronze Age combined the Middle and Late phases defined by typological studies and was really characterised by the reorganisation of food production across the country as a whole. In fact it would be true to say that it was only then that a fully agricultural society, with fixed land boundaries and archaeologically detectable settlements, became at all widely established in the British Isles. With those changes came the end of a number of older traditions, including the provision of burial mounds with grave goods and the special attention paid to much earlier monuments.

There is no doubt that this characterisation did identify some important points, but, like any model, in doing so it over-simplified the situation. This scheme now needs amending in at least two ways. It is clear that these changes were by no means synchronous. There are regions in which the first reorganisation of the landscape came, not in the Middle Bronze Age, but in the Late Bronze Age or even the Iron Age. Nor did all these developments establish themselves securely. Thus there are Middle Bronze Age enclosures in Cranborne Chase, but few Late Bronze Age sites (Barrett et al. 1991, chapters 5 and 6). By contrast, the river gravels around Reading show a dense distribution of Late Bronze Age settlements and fields, but there is little evidence of Early Iron Age activity (Butterworth and Lobb 1992; Moore and Jennings 1992). Moreover, some of these changes took place at a surprisingly local scale. Thus Middle Bronze Age occupation sites appear in dense clusters across quite limited areas and are virtually absent in others. For example, the Deverel-Rimbury sites investigated by Stone on the Hampshire/Wiltshire border have few counterparts on the eastern edge of Salisbury Plain, ten kilometres away, where the first period of intensive settlement was in the succeeding phase (Bradley et al. 1994).

If such cases extend the process of agricultural intensification across the earlier first millennium, we must also appreciate that its beginnings may lie further back than once seemed possible. There are settlements and field systems whose ceramic repertoire suggests an origin within the Early Bronze Age. Examples of this trend can perhaps be found at sites like Fengate which include pottery assigned to a pre-Deverel-Rimbury horizon (Pryor 1980). More striking still is the evidence from Dartmoor, where field systems, land boundaries and enclosed settlements again develop unexpectedly early (Fleming 1988). The pots from the Shaugh Moor settlement, for example, are mainly Biconical Urns (Tomalin in Balaam et al. 1982, 228-37). It has always seemed possible that the archaeologically visible enclosures of the uplands, which are so often found in association with Deverel-Rimbury ceramics, belong to a developed phase in the reorganisation of the landscape, a process which had already started on the most productive lowland soils. It will be especially important to date the beginnings of this development in eastern England, where there are already hints that it could have started at an early stage (Bradley 1993).

In order to explain these differences, I have been forced to go back to the more traditional terminology of an Early, Middle and Late Bronze Age. There is a further reason for doing so. In some areas of the landscape, recent research has shown that the process of agricultural change took quite distinct forms in these different periods. The clearest demonstration of this point is on the chalk, where it seemed as if early field systems and land boundaries might represent complementary aspects of a unitary system of land use, established in the middle of the Bronze Age. If anything, the fields seemed to have been established before the boundary ditches, which occasionally cut across them and put them out of use. Recent fieldwork on the edge of Salisbury Plain, the region in which these claims were first advanced, has upset this idea. Here the boundary ditches are not secondary to field systems at all. In fact they originated in the Late Bronze Age, during the first large-scale enclosure of the landscape (Bradley et al. 1994). In this case the field systems came later, in the Iron Age and Roman periods. Exactly the same sequence has been demonstrated on the Berkshire Downs (Ford 1982; Ford et al. 1988), but not, it seems, in south Dorset, or the Danebury study area where the traditional chronology may be correct (Lawson 1990; Papworth 1992; B. Cunliffe, pers. comm.).

If we were misled by over-estimating the scale of the new developments, we also tended to compare different features of the landscape as if they were portable artefacts. The work of the 1980s has shown that this was wrong. Andrew Fleming, for example, has argued that coaxial field systems were created during many different periods, from the Neolithic to the first millennium AD (Fleming 1987). In the same way, the longer land divisions that look so like the Dartmoor reaves may have had a more extended history. Those on the Wessex chalk are later than the boundaries on Dartmoor, and nearly all the excavated examples are Late Bronze Age or Iron Age in origin. Again there seems to have been more diversity than we were prepared to contemplate. Now it is the contrasts that really need explaining.

The same is true at a much more local level. In 1980 it was probably helpful to speak in general terms of an agricultural reorganisation, but sixteen years later we need to be more specific about what we mean. One result of increased settlement excavation has been to highlight the sheer diversity of Bronze Age land use. This was discussed by Nigel Brown in his report on the Lofts Farm enclosure (Brown 1988), and the same issues arise in the Kennet valley where one result of recent fieldwork has been to widen the range of Late Bronze Age activities still further (Bradley et al. 1980; Butterworth and Lobb 1992; Moore and Jennings 1992). Some sites may have been used mainly for cereal growing and others for farming livestock. Not all of them need have been occupied all year round, and there are further contrasts in the character of the storage structures, plant remains and evidence of craft production associated with the different sites. We can identify still broader patterns of similarity and contrast. Thus the pottery from the low-lying settlement complex at Reading Business Park (Moore and Jennings 1992) shows less variety than the finds from Aldermaston Wharf nearby, which seems to have been occupied all year round (Bradley et al. 1980). There is a greater density of pottery at Aldermaston Wharf despite the fact that it was settled for a shorter period, and it also includes a higher proportion of fineware, a characteristic which it shares with dryland sites further to the east. Other features may reflect the contrasting settings of these sites. It is often supposed that there is more evidence for textile production in the Late Bronze Age. Spindle whorls and loom weights are found extensively, but again there are striking contrasts within the Kennet and Middle Thames valleys. Both types of artefact occur together on the sites with well-drained soils, but all those settlements found in areas which were prone to flooding contain loom weights but no other artefacts associated with textile production. Perhaps spinning took place in settlements that could be occupied all year round, whilst weaving was a feature of those where activity was concentrated mainly in summer. The same contrast is suggested by finds of flintwork. Their density at the low-lying sites in Reading Business Park was roughly three times that at Aldermaston Wharf. All these suggestions are extremely tentative, but they serve to illustrate one point. They result from a series of rescue excavations that did not form part of any systematic programme of field work. Much more could surely be achieved by building such comparisons into the research design.

In some ways all these comments apply to classes of material which were already well known at the time of the 1980 collection. Fresh work has simply increased the range of variation. It has also led to changes of chronology. Over the same period there have been other, more dramatic, developments and these have resulted in the identification of new classes of monuments and the reassessment of others whose credentials had never been questioned.

Three classes of monument have assumed much greater prominence over the last few years. These are large open settlements, island sites and ringworks. Examples of all three were certainly known before 1980, but it has taken some time for their implications to become apparent. Open settlements, for example, had been documented since the pioneering excavations at All Cannings Cross (Cunnington 1923) and Plumpton Plain (Holleyman and Curwen 1935), but their real extent was unknown. They were certainly being found on the river gravels, where they could usually be identified by clusters of post holes and pits, and there was a feeling that sites that left so little obvious trace behind them might be under-represented among the results of rescue archaeology. This was probably true, and it explains why Late Bronze Age settlements are being found in greater numbers through systematic site evaluation. What was not apparent was that many comparable sites - probably even larger ones - had existed on the higher ground.

Again the problem was one of archaeological visibility. As long as rescue archaeology was guided by the evidence of earthworks and air photographs, Bronze Age settlement archaeology was bound to be dominated by enclosures. Such earthworks had been investigated since the end of the last century, but they had hardly received any attention for 50 years.

When the time came for a new campaign of field work on the chalk, it provided some unwelcome surprises. As expected, most of the enclosures had originated in the Middle Bronze Age and were associated with houses and fields (Barrett *et al.* 1991, chapter 4). But they had gone out of use by the Late Bronze Age, with the result that there now appeared to be a break in the sequence of activity that extended to the start of the Iron Age.

It might have been tempting to postulate a widespread period of desertion on the higher ground, and to suggest that this accounted for the increased density of Late Bronze Age findspots on the gravels, but, fortunately, in southern England we stopped short of making that mistake. Just as the full extent of the problem was becoming clear, English Heritage supported two rather unusual projects on the Wessex downland. The first was the excavation of the M3 extension at Winchester, where a large area free of cropmarks was investigated on an ambitious scale (Fasham *et al.* 1989). This work resulted in the discovery of an unexpectedly large number of post-built houses spanning the apparent hiatus between the Middle Bronze Age and the Iron Age. These buildings had not been enclosed by earthworks. A decade later, fieldwork took place in the Salisbury Plain Military Training Area (Bradley *et al.* 1994). One result of this work was to establish the history and relationships of the boundary ditches in this area, but it also afforded an opportunity to examine tracts of arable land which are ploughed only occasionally. These contained large quantities of Late Bronze Age pottery, with the result that we are now able to define a whole series of large unenclosed settlements on the higher ground, each of them at the centre of one of the land blocks defined by the linear ditches. Outside the Military Training Area, such settlements survive only as flint scatters, containing a range of artefacts that cannot really be dated.

The island sites are particularly difficult to discuss as much of the relevant work is recent and has still to be published. They may also overlap with a still more enigmatic class of wetland site represented by the extraordinary platform at Flag Fen. The distinctions between them can only be established by excavation.

Just two island sites have been investigated, although at different times other candidates have been suggested, particularly in the Thames valley. Both sites have certain characteristics in common. They occupied quite limited islands in the Thames and were fronted by a massive structure of upright posts. The first discoveries at Runneymede Bridge were summarised by Stuart Needham and David Longley in 1980, but since then the site has seen a sustained campaign of research excavation (Needham 1991 and 1992). This has helped to establish the extent and character of occupation there. The site contained a series of unusually rich midden deposits and also provided evidence of craft production. In addition, it contained the remains of several timber buildings, at least one of which adopted the rectangular groundplan more typical of sites on the Continent.

The second site was at Wallingford, higher up the Thames (Lambrick 1987). This was certainly an island in the Bronze Age, and again it was associated with a rich midden deposit. Unfortunately, in this case we do not know the nature of any associated structures. It does, however, command a stretch of the river which has produced a particular concentration of weapon finds, although most of these predate the material found on the island itself.

In 1980 it seemed likely that these sites were located in order to command the movement of prestige goods along the river. They might also have been involved in the production of such objects themselves. The islands were interpreted in similar terms to the ports of trade of the early medieval period which were being widely discussed at that time. If anything, opinion has shifted away from this model. With fresh discoveries at inland sites, there no longer seems to be such a remarkable concentration of craft production along the Thames itself, and more recent work has shown that equally rich midden deposits can be recognised at other sites. In fact, more are now known around the edges of the Wessex downland than in the Thames valley as a whole (for examples see Gingell and Lawson 1984, McOmish 1993 and Robinson and Swanton 1993). It may be better to regard these two islands as part of the widening variety of Late Bronze Age settlement sites in lowland Britain. Their most distinctive feature may prove to be their fine state of preservation. In this respect, they contrast with the other category of specialised site in this area, for the ringworks were generally discovered by air photography long after any surface deposits had been lost.

I need not say much about these ringworks, since their investigation seems to be an Essex speciality. Perhaps the most striking development of the last decade has been the pattern of discovery in eastern England. Although archaeologists have certainly been aware of the chances of finding these enclosures in other regions of the country, their only counterparts appear to be in Ireland (Bradley 1984, 124). So far, there are no convincing examples in the Midlands or the Upper Thames, and the one likely candidate on the Wessex chalkland is my own site at Rams Hill, which has now been re-dated to the Middle and Late

Bronze Age (Needham and Ambers 1994). Otherwise these are very much a North Sea phenomenon.

Having identified these sites, problems still remain. Were these self-sustaining settlements, or were they only the nucleus of larger open sites? The same question applies to those sites on islands. Were the circular structures inside the ringworks really houses at all, or were they public buildings? Can these earthworks have been central places when they may be found so close together? One of the achievements of excavation in Essex has been to provoke questions of this kind.

Already there are some intriguing patterns to consider. At Mucking North Ring (Bond 1988), it seems as if the highest proportion of fine pottery came from *outside* the enclosure. At both Thwing and Springfield Lyons other material may have been used to reinforce the boundaries of these sites: in one case the clay moulds placed in the principal entrances (Buckley and Hedges 1987), and in the other an enormous deposit of animal bones from the ditch (Mounteney 1981). At Mucking North Ring a cremation with two gold rings was also placed close to the entrance, whilst at Rams Hill each of the successive gates to the enclosure was associated with an animal burial (Bradley and Ellison 1975).

If the boundaries of these sites were so important, it becomes a major priority to determine which activities were allowed to take place inside them and which they were meant to exclude. Among those which are already evidenced in the literature, the most important is probably the preparation and consumption of food. These sites may also have played a central role in the production and distribution of metalwork, including a variety of weapons. To this we can add some recently published evidence of pottery manufacture and distribution (Wardle 1992). Ceramics were locally produced at most settlements in Late Bronze Age Yorkshire, but only those made at the enclosed sites seem to have had a wider circulation. The products of the ringwork at Thwing were the most extensively distributed of all.

The circular structures inside these sites raise other problems. Most of them are unusually large and those at Mucking South Rings and Thwing are of quite exceptional character (Jones and Bond in Barrett and Bradley 1980, 474; Manby, ibid, 343). Their sheer size makes it unlikely that they were used as domestic buildings, especially when so little room was left for activities to take place around them (cf. Clark and Fell 1953). They raise exactly the same questions as the enclosures in which they were built. Either they formed part of a larger complex, or their use would have been limited to special occasions.

I have already emphasised the importance of the perimeter earthwork on these sites. In most cases this was a bank and ditch, but there are now at least three sites - Rams Hill (Bradley and Ellison 1975), Thwing (Manby in Barrett and Bradley 1980) and Springfield Lyons (Buckley and Hedges 1987) - where the earthworks were reinforced by timber structures very like those found at hillforts. That comparison may be revealing because up to now it has been very difficult to establish the date at which British hillforts were first built.

Hillfort studies have seen many changes over the last twenty years. When the first radiocarbon dates were published, there was something of a fashion for discovering Bronze Age defended sites (Savory 1971), but a number of these claims have since been discounted. There were purely Iron Age defensive systems that overlay Bronze Age open settlements (cf Green 1981), and in those early days too little attention was paid to the quality and context of the samples submitted for dating (cf Guilbert 1980). There was also a plateau in the critical area of the radiocarbon calibration curve. As a result of all these misgivings, not much was said about Bronze Age hillforts in the papers published in 1980.

Sixteen years later, it seems as if the reaction has gone too far. There are hillforts like the Breiddin whose radiocarbon chronology seems entirely unambiguous (Musson 1991), and there are other sites such as Beeston Castle where Late Bronze Age artefacts are directly associated with the defences themselves (Ellis 1993, chapter 3). These sites are fewer in number than we might have expected some years ago, but they do have two important features in common. They can contain quite extensive settlements, including houses and raised storage structures, and their ramparts were reinforced by timbers in very much the same style as the ringworks on the east coast.

So far I have compared individual elements of the ringworks with features found at other classes of site in England and Wales. There are also the Irish parallels that I referred to earlier. Somewhat similar earthworks, associated with large circular buildings, are found at Rathgall (Raftery 1976) and Navan, the latter a site which enjoyed a particular eminence in the literature of the Early Medieval period (Lynn 1986; Mallory 1995). Very similar structures were built during the Irish Iron Age at sites like Dun Ailine and Tara (Lynn 1991; Cooney and Grogan 1991). It could be dangerous to extrapolate from such a distant comparison, but it does suggest one line of thought that is worth pursuing here. Although the Irish sites have been described as royal centres, they were essentially places of assembly, providing an arena for public transactions that attracted an audience from a wider area. That comparison runs counter to the intuitive interpretation of Bronze Age ringworks as residences of an elite, but there is no independent evidence to support this idea. As we have seen, their interpretation as self-contained settlements poses a number of problems.

One reason for taking this view is the discovery of two largely new kinds of site since 1980. Their very existence makes it more difficult to sustain any simple division between high and low status settlements. In each case they seem to provide indications of rather specialised gatherings. If the case is somewhat oblique, it still has interesting implications.

One of the most striking discoveries since 1980 has been the recognition of Late Bronze Age 'midden' sites; indeed, there may be a Middle Bronze Age example at Grimes Graves (Healy 1993). None has been published in full, but we have already come to recognise certain characteristics of these deposits. They consist of enormous accumulations of organic material, accompanied by a wealth of artefacts and food remains. Some of the contents of these middens seem to have been accumulated with a certain formality, and in this respect they recall the structured deposits found in the ditches of Late Bronze Age and Iron Age enclosures. In several cases the evidence for associated structures is surprisingly limited, leading to the paradoxical situation that some of the richest 'occupation sites' in the Late Bronze Age were also the most ephemeral.

We can compare that evidence with the excavated material from the wetland complex at Flag Fen - yet another new discovery that seems inconsistent with any simple division between high status and low status sites (Pryor *et al.* 1992). I wish to draw attention to just one feature: the material making up the timber platform at Flag Fen. From an early stage in the excavation it was difficult to understand why the site should contain so many structural timbers, and as the work proceeded, the case for postulating an *in situ* building became more difficult to sustain. The material of the platform certainly seems to have been taken from a rectangular building (or buildings) of considerable size. At the same time, these timbers showed little sign of use. The selection of different raw materials was also inconsistent with a stable or long-lasting structure. Now that we know that the Flag Fen complex is associated with numerous offerings - of weapons, ornaments, food and sacrificed animals - I wonder whether we are seeing evidence for the erection and dismantling of massive but temporary buildings associated with public ceremonial. If so, they may have been quite similar to the curious structure on the edge of the island settlement at Runneymede Bridge for which Needham favours an equally specialised role (Needham 1992, fig.7). Flag Fen is not a unique occurrence. There are reports of rather similar structures in the Trent Valley (Phillips 1941), Holderness (Smith 1911) and South Wales (Nayling 1993).

Building bridges
So far this paper has taken a traditional course and it might be expected to follow that to its logical conclusion. I have considered a number of developments in the archaeology of the Bronze Age, highlighting the contribution made by recent work at a number of sites. At this point two options might be open to us: to discuss possible strategies for future investigations of each type of monument separately: or to attempt to treat them together as components of a wider system.

There seems little sense in maintaining the divisions between all these different sites. Some of the distinctions look increasingly artificial as we recognise that a similar range of activities took place in and around them. We may do better to concentrate on tracing the history and distribution of a number of specific practices that are central to the evidence from this period. This approach would not only allow us to break down some of the categories that we ourselves have created, it could also allow work to expand beyond 'sites' altogether to investigate those various practices on a larger scale. As we shall see, that entails a rather different conception of landscape archaeology.

What are the common elements that link so many of these phenomena?

One of the most general was simply the creation of boundaries. These may have divided up the working landscape, but they did other things as well. They separated different people from one another, and they kept different kinds of activities apart. They are the outward manifestation of social distinctions that might have been every bit as subtle as those symbolised by Early Bronze Age barrows. Those divisions between places, between activities, and, above all, between different people were reinforced in a number of ways. They could be heightened by the construction of massive earthworks or their equivalents. It may be no coincidence that the same style of timber structure was built around the edges of the ringworks and also the early hillforts. It marked the perimeter of the island sites, and in one case in the Midlands, an important land boundary, Drays Ditches, was rebuilt in the same manner (Dyer 1981, pl. 18). In each case, the precise form of that division refers back to an exotic prototype, for this is how Continental hillfort ramparts were constructed.

Such barriers could also be reinforced by a variety of cultural deposits, and once again these cut right across our careful distinction between different classes of monument. Gold ornaments were deposited in the entrance of one of the ringworks in Essex (Bond 1988), but a very similar find is associated with the gateway of a large hillfort in Sussex (Bedwin 1983). Pits with specialised contents may have marked the edge of the island site at Runneymede Bridge (Needham 1992), but they also enclosed the hilltop at Danebury (Cunliffe 1984, 12), whilst a similar setting is found within the innermost enclosure at Haughey's Fort in Northern Ireland (Mallory 1995). Metalwork could be deposited in boundaries of all these kinds, from the Deverel-Rimbury earthwork at South Lodge Camp (Barrett et al. 1991, chapter 4) to the large Late Bronze Age enclosure at Petters Sports Field (O'Connell 1986). The same practice extends to the fortified hilltops at Drumcoltran (Coles 1893) and Norton Fitzwarren (Ellis 1989). Even where the metal objects themselves are absent, they can be represented by deposits of moulds, as we find in Essex at Springfield Lyons (Buckley and Hedges 1987) and again in Somerset at Norton Fitzwarren (Ellis 1989); mould fragments were also found with human skull fragments at the King's Stables, near Haughey's Fort (Lynn 1977; Mallory 1995). In the same way, human and animal remains can be associated with the perimeter of important enclosures, but they were placed with just as much formality in the filling of land boundaries on the Wessex chalk, where they were located some distance from any settlement site (Bradley et al. 1994). Given such an emphasis on boundary locations, the presence of weapons in rivers seems much less surprising.

Those tendencies are most clearly marked at the tantalising site of Flag Fen, for this combines many different elements. Again, a major barrier cut across the natural terrain, and along it were a series of structured deposits (Pryor et al. 1992). Not all the material was found together, and it seems as if there were conventions that determined which kinds of offering might be placed on either side of this division. There is even some oblique evidence that specialised buildings had been erected somewhere nearby and that they were soon dismantled. The remains of these structures were deposited in shallow water with just as much formality as the remains of whatever activities took place inside them. This is another area in which we may be perpetuating an unnecessary division in the archaeological record. Is it possible that Flag Fen was itself a midden site, rather like that at Potterne? In this case it was associated with a watery location rather than a dryland site. Among the features that these places share is the evidence for large-scale consumption, yet at neither site is there a compelling case for the prolonged use of any buildings. A paper published by Sonia Hawkes since the conference suggests yet another dimension to the question, for something rather similar may have happened at Longbridge Deverill Cow Down. Here there were three large circular structures, not unlike those found inside Late Bronze Age ringworks. They had been built in sequence and each of them had been burnt down with its contents inside it. None was replaced on the same spot. The excavator suggests an analogy with native American funeral practices (Hawkes 1994).

There are other more easily recognised activities that seem to have cross-cut the different classes of monument. For example, there is a notable concentration of metalwork deposits in the Chelmer Valley in Essex (Buckley et al. 1986), but there seems little reason to suppose that all of these were associated with the same kinds of site. We can compare that evidence with some recently reported finds from the West Berkshire Downs, where four collections of Bronze Age metalwork come from one small area. There are broken fragments, suitable for recycling, from the enclosure at Rams Hill (Bradley and Ellison 1975), and at a rather later stage in the sequence, there is evidence for bronze production on the nearby open site at Weathercock Hill; in this case the excavated material included part of a sword (Bowden, Ford and Gaffney 1993, 77-8). A newly discovered hoard belonging to the very end of the Bronze Age was found within a circular house inside a second open site on Tower Hill (D. Miles, pers. comm.), whilst at Waylands Smithy a small deposit, consisting of two bronze ornaments, had apparently been placed against the kerb of a megalithic tomb (Whittle 1991, 87-8).

By contrast, on the eastern edge of Salisbury Plain, there were no deposits of metalwork within the parts of the landscape defined by boundary earthworks. Just beyond that area, however, there was a substantial hoard containing a number of unfinished artefacts, and somewhere in the same valley a stone mould has also been discovered. In this case, the process of artefact production seems to have been excluded from the settled area (Bradley et al. 1994). If so, it may be no accident that it was in the same part of the landscape that flint nodules were collected and prepared for use in settlement sites elsewhere. Productive activities of more than one kind may have been confined to the edges of the landscape.

Yet another activity associated with that boundary area on Salisbury Plain was the creation of burnt mounds. These features have always been very difficult to interpret. Various explanations have been suggested, ranging from specialised cooking sites to saunas, and at present no agreement seems to be in sight (O'Drisceoil 1988). Isolated examples have been discovered with moulds or finds of metalwork, and both at Rathgall and at Thwing rather similar structures were found in the excavation of Bronze Age ringworks (Raftery 1976; T. Manby pers. comm.). For a long time the interpretation of burnt mounds was complicated by the mistaken idea that they were mostly a feature of the highland zone, where they might have been used in the course of hunting expeditions. That was quite misleading, and we now know that similar features can be found throughout southern and eastern England. Nor is it true that all these sites were found in isolation. As early as the 1930s, excavators working in Sussex were commenting on the concentrations of burnt flints found in Deverel-Rimbury settlements; indeed, Curwen seems to have been the first archaeologist to suggest a connection with saunas (Curwen 1934, 145-9). Fifteen years ago, an intact mound complete with its trough was excavated inside South Lodge Camp, where it was located beside two circular buildings (Bradley et al. 1991, fig. 5.13).

Burnt mounds are regularly encountered in field work in the Middle and Upper Thames valleys (S. Ford, G, Hey, D. Miles, pers. comm.) and some are associated with open settlements like those at Yarnton and Reading Business Park; another one has been excavated in south-west London (Bowsher 1991). Burnt flints may also be mixed with occupation debris. A recently published excavation at Kingston on Thames is a good illustration of this point (Serjeantson et al. 1992). We are still uncertain how these features were used, although the process clearly involved the heating of water in carefully constructed tanks. It remains a distinct possibility that meat was cooked on these sites. If so, we might compare that evidence for large-scale food preparation with the discovery of perforated clay slabs at settlements around the Thames estuary. In both cases, these finds may even provide oblique evidence of feasting.

Lastly we must break down the simple division between cemetery and settlement. This is familiar ground, but it is perhaps worth making two points. During the Middle Bronze Age, burials are poorly furnished. Not all of them may have been marked by mounds and, in contrast to earlier deposits, they are generally without grave goods (Bradley 1990, chapter 3). The one recurrent feature is their location near to occupation sites. It is at about the same time that the deposition of artefacts in rivers begins on a significant scale, and when formal burials disappear from the record during the Late Bronze Age the incidence of water deposits continues to rise (*ibid.*). It would be easy to suggest that these finds represent a form of surrogate burial, and there are even finds of Bronze Age skulls from wet deposits that might lend weight to that contention (Bradley and Gordon 1988; Cooney and Grogan 1991; Wilkinson and Murphy 1995, 132-5). But once again we must remember that the river finds overlap in many ways with other kinds of structured deposit. One example is sufficient to make my point. Human skulls may have been deposited with some of these objects, but this seems to have happened after they had lost their flesh. Other parts of the body are under-represented or absent. Taken at face value, that must suggest that human bones had circulated among the living in rather the same way as they did during the Neolithic. If so, the occasional pieces from occupation sites take on a new significance, and once again it becomes harder to study the archaeology of different kinds of site in isolation. The proper scale for our research must be the landscape as a whole.

'Landscape archaeology'
There are really two ways of thinking about landscape archaeology. One is in terms of fixed resources. This method privileges food production above any other kind of activity. It is an approach which emphasises adaptation, and as such it characterises the generalising principles of processual archaeology. It employs a battery of techniques borrowed from ecology and geography - techniques like Thiessen polygons and site catchment analysis - and in doing so it divides the archaeological record into foreground and background. Settlement sites are mapped onto resources, and there is only a thin line between reconstructing the past environment and imposing a model of precisely how it had to be used. In doing so it is easy to forget that people once lived inside those landscapes and that those people had minds of their own. They would have formed their own attachments to places and must have had their own experience of space: such conceptions are by no means universal (Thomas 1993). Prehistoric understandings of the world would have been just as complex as our own, but they would certainly not have been the same. A landscape that contained fields and houses would also include a whole network of places with their own significance: locations where certain things could happen and others where they were proscribed. Any landscape is also an arena in which social transactions unfold, so that changes in the way in which that space was organised must also have entailed changes in the way in which the world could be experienced (Pred 1986). And such experience might reach to the core of Bronze Age society. It is a product of modern social engineering to suppose that every development in the settlement pattern results from increased efficiency and levels of production.

From this perspective we can look back over everything I have said. In 1980 the Later Bronze Age was defined in terms of new methods of providing food. It was a time of fixed settlements and closer controls over agricultural land. But the work of the last sixteen years has steadily eroded any impression of familiarity. People may have ploughed rectangular plots of land, but they also placed human skulls in rivers. They may have utilised an improved range of agricultural tools, but they also made shields that could never be taken into battle. Their preoccupations and our own touch at only one point. It so happened that in the 1970s and early 1980s, the archaeology of agriculture was very high on the agenda. Having effected a match at that level we assumed that Bronze Age people had the same priorities as ourselves.

I have suggested that our perceptions of early landscapes were influenced by processual archaeology, and that many of its concerns were borrowed from other fields with an interest in generalisation. Now it is time to pay more attention to the specific content of the archaeology of individual areas, and that involves a much more flexible concept of the archaeological landscape, for it is not simply an extent of ground containing a number of monuments. It is an area in which many different activities took place, whose surviving residues amount to the sum total of the archaeological record. Whatever the short term pressures that influence the organisation of fieldwork, that is the whole from which we are selecting our samples. The record of Bronze Age activity is ultimately indivisible, and when we portion it out between specialist interests we very soon lose our bearings.

Summary

This paper has a very simple message. We should seek to reunite the different parts of the archaeological record, and we should use the results of that endeavour in research and education. There are things that we should do and practices we should avoid. I suggest the following rules of thumb:

1. We should not prejudge the nature or extent of Bronze Age settlement in any single area. That must be established by fieldwork, and it is imperative to date the changing patterns of land division on a local basis.

2. We should not study 'sites' in isolation. As I have suggested, there are benefits to be gained from informed and disciplined comparison. To secure the most informative results, suitable procedures have to be established before any fieldwork takes place.

3. We should not confine our fieldwork within the ostensible boundaries of those sites, for once again there are indications that as many activities took place outside them as happened within their area.

4. We should not study the more specialised sites in isolation from their wider setting. We now know that Middle Bronze Age cemeteries were closely linked to settlement sites. Was this also the case with burnt mounds or metal hoards?

5. We should abandon the conventional distinction between what we call 'sites' and 'chance finds'. If the deposits of elaborate artefacts were attended by special conventions, we should seek to study their placing in the wider landscape. In particular, I would advocate the routine use of metal detectors in the process of site evaluation.

6. We cannot manage a 'resource' unless it has some potential use. The Bronze Age archaeology of Essex is in good hands, and it is time to show how much it has to offer. New material will always come to light; interpretations will never stay the same. But interpretations are what we should provide, and they are what our public should expect.

References

Balaam, N., Smith, K. and Wainwright, G.J. 1982. 'The Shaugh Moor project: fourth report', *Proc. Prehist. Soc.* 48, 203-78

Barrett, J. 1993. *Fragments from Antiquity* Oxford: Blackwell

Barrett, J. and Bradley, R. (eds) 1980. *Settlement and Society in the British Later Bronze Age*, British Archaeol. Rep. 83

Barrett, J., Bradley, R. and Green, M. 1991. *Landscape, Monuments and Society: the Prehistory of Cranborne Chase* Cambridge: University Press

Bedwin, O. 1983. 'Miss P.A.M.Keef's excavations at Harting Beacon and nearby sites, 1948-52', *Sussex Archaeol. Collect.* 121, 199-202

Bond, D. 1988. *Excavations at North Ring, Mucking*, East Anglian Archaeol. 43

Bowden, M., Ford, S. and Gaffney, V. 1993. 'The excavation of a late Bronze Age artefact scatter on Weathercock Hill', *Berks. Archaeol. J.* 74, 69-83

Bowsher, J. 1991. ' A burnt mound at Phoenix Wharf, south-west London', in M. Hodder and L.Barfield (eds), *Burnt Mounds and Hot Stone Technology*, 11-19. Sandwell: Sandwell Metropolitan Borough Council

Bradley, R. 1984. *The social foundations of prehistoric Britain* Harlow: Longman

Bradley, R. 1990. *The passage of arms: an archaeological analysis of prehistoric hoards and votive deposits* Cambridge: University Press

Bradley, R. 1993. 'Where is East Anglia? Themes in regional prehistory', in *The Flatlands and Wetlands: Current themes in East Anglian Archaeology*, East Anglian Archaeol. 50, 5-13

Bradley, R. and Ellison, A. 1975. *Rams Hill - a Bronze Age defended enclosure and its landscape*, British Archaeol. Rep. 19

Bradley, R., Entwistle, R. and Raymond, F. 1994. *Prehistoric land divisions on Salisbury Plain. The work of the Wessex Linear Ditches project* London: English Heritage

Bradley, R. and Gordon, K. 1988. 'Human skulls from the River Thames, their dating and significance', *Antiquity* 62, 503-9

Bradley, R., Lobb, S., Richards, J. and Robinson, M. 1980. 'Two Late Bronze Age settlements on the Kennet gravels: excavations at Aldermaston Wharf and Knight's Farm, Burghfield, Berkshire', *Proc. Prehist. Soc.* 46, 217-95

Brown, N. 1988. 'A Late Bronze Age enclosure at Loft's Farm, Essex', *Proc. Prehist. Soc.* 54, 249-302

Buckley, D., Brown, N. and Greenwood, P. 1986. 'Late Bronze Age hoards from the Chelmer valley, Essex', *Antiq. J.* 66, 248-66

Buckley, D. and Hedges, J. 1987. *The Late Bronze Age and Saxon settlements at Springfield Lyons, Essex: an interim report* Chelmsford: Essex County Council

Butterworth, C. and Lobb, S. 1992. *Excavations in the Burghfield area*, Berkshire. Salisbury: Wessex Archaeology

Clark, J.G.D. and Fell, C. 1953. 'The Early Iron Age site at Micklemoor Hill, West Harling, Norfolk and its pottery', *Proc. Prehist. Soc.* 19, 1-40

Coles, F. 1893. 'The motes, forts and doons in the east and west divisions of the Stewartry of Kirkcudbright', *Proc. Soc. Antiq. Scotland* 27, 92-182

Cooney, G. and Grogan, E. 1991. 'An archaeological solution to the 'Irish' problem?', *Emainia* 9, 33-43

Cunliffe, B. 1984. *Danebury: an Iron Age hillfort in Hampshire, vol. 1*, CBA Res. Rep. 52

Cunnington, M. 1923. *The Early Iron Age inhabited site at All Cannings Cross* Devizes: George Simpson

Curwen, C. 1934. 'A Late Bronze Age farm and a Neolithic pit-dwelling on New Barn Down, Clapham, near Worthing', *Sussex Archaeol. Collect.* 75, 137-70

Darvill, T., Startin, B. and Saunders, A. 1987. 'A question of national importance: approaches to the evaluation of ancient monuments for the Monuments Protection Programme in England', *Antiquity* 61, 393-408

Drewett, P. 1982. 'Later Bronze Age downland economy and excavations at Blackpatch, East Sussex', *Proc. Prehist. Soc.* 48, 321-400

Dyer, J. 1981. *Hillforts of England and Wales* Princes Risborough: Shire

Ellis, P. 1989. 'Norton Fitzwarren hillfort: a report on the excavations by Nancy and Philip Langmaid between 1969 and 1971', *Somerset Archaeology and Natural History* 133, 1-74

Ellis, P. (ed.) 1993. *Beeston Castle, Cheshire* London: English Heritage

Fasham, P., Farwell, D. and Whinney, R. 1989. *The archaeological site at Easton Lane, Winchester* Winchester: Hampshire Field Club

Fleming, A. 1987. 'Coaxial field systems: some questions of time and space', *Antiquity*, 51, 188-202

Fleming, A. 1988. *The Dartmoor reaves* London: Batsford

Ford, S. 1982. 'Linear earthworks on the Berkshire Downs', *Berkshire Arch. J.* 71, 1-20

Ford, S., Bowden, M., Mees, G. and Gaffney, G. 1988. The date of the 'Celtic' field systems on the Berkshire Downs', *Britannia* 19, 401-4

Gingell, C. 1992. *The Marlborough Downs: a Later Bronze Age landscape and its origins* Devizes: Wiltshire Archaeological Society

Gingell, C. and Lawson, A. 1985. 'Excavations at Potterne, 1984', *Wiltshire Archaeol. Magazine* 79,101-8

Green, H.S. 1981. 'The dating of the Ivinghoe Beacon', *Records of Buckinghamshire* 23, 1-3

Guilbert, G. 1980. 'Dinorben C 14 dates', *Current Archaeology* 70, 336-8

Hawkes, S.C. 1994. 'Longbridge Deverill Cow Down, House 3: a major round house of the Early Iron Age', *Oxford Journal of Archaeology* 13, 49-69

Healy, F. 1993 'Review of I. Longworth *et al.* "Excavations at Grimes Graves, Norfolk, 1972-76, fascicule 3"', *Proc. Prehist. Soc.* 59, 417-8

Holleyman, G. and Curwen, C. 1935. 'Late Bronze Age lynchet settlements on Plumpton Plain, Sussex', *Proc. Prehist. Soc.* 1, 16-59

Lambrick, G. 1987. 'Wallingford by-pass: Late Bronze Age settlement', *South Midlands Archaeology* 17, 99-100

Lawson, A. 1990. 'The prehistoric hinterland of Maiden Castle, *Antiq. J.* 70, 271-87

Lynn, C. 1977. 'Trial excavations at the King's Stables, Tray townland, County Armagh', *Ulster J. Archaeology* 40, 42-62

Lynn, C. 1986. 'Navan Fort: a draft summary of D.M.Waterman's excavations', *Emainia* 1, 11-9

Lynn, C. 1991. 'Knockaulin (Dun Ailinne) and Navan: some architectural comparisons', *Emainia* 8, 51-6

McOmish, D. 1993. 'Salisbury Plain', *Current Archaeology* 135, 110-3

Mallory, J. 1995. 'Haughey's Fort and the Navan complex in the Late Bronze Age', in J. Waddell and E. Shee Twohig (eds), *Ireland in the Bronze Age*, 73-86. Dublin; Stationery Office

Moore, J. and Jennings, D. 1992. *Reading Business Park: a Bronze Age landscape* Oxford: Oxford Archaeological Unit

Mounteney, G. 1981. 'Faunal attrition and subsistence reconstruction at Thwing', in G.Barker (ed.), *Prehistoric Communities in northern England*, 73-86. Sheffield: Sheffield University Dept of Prehistory and Archaeology

Musson, C. 1991. *The Breiddin hillfort*, CBA Res. Rep. 76

Nayling, N. 1993. 'Tales from the riverbank: Bronze Age palaeochannels in the alluviated Nedern valley at Caldicot Castle lake, Gwent', in J.Coles, V.Fenwick and G.Hutchinson (eds), *A spirit of enquiry*, 72-6. Exeter: Wetland Archaeology Research Project

Needham, S. 1991. *Excavation and salvage at Runneymede Bridge, 1978: the Late Bronze Age waterfront site* London: British Museum Publications

Needham, S. and Ambers, J. 1994. 'Re-dating Rams Hill and reconsidering Bronze Age enclosure', *Proc. Prehist. Soc.* 60, 225-44

O'Connell, M. 1986. *Petters Sports Field, Egham: Excavation of a Late Bronze Age/Early Iron Age site* Guildford: Surrey Archaeological Society

O'Drisceoil, D. 1988. 'Burnt mounds: cooking or bathing?', *Antiquity* 67, 1-80

Papworth, M. 1992. 'Excavation and survey of Bronze Age sites in the Badbury area', *Proc. Dorset Nat. Hist. Archaeol. Soc.* 114, 47-76

Phillips, C.W. 1941. 'Some recent finds from the Trent near Nottingham', *Antiq. J.* 21, 133-43

Pred, A. 1986. *Place, practice and structure* Cambridge: Polity Press

Pryor, F. 1980. *Excavations at Fengate, Peterborough: the third report* Northampton: Northants Archaeological Society

Pryor, F. et al. 1992. 'Current research at Flag Fen, Peterborough', *Antiquity* 66, 439-531

Raftery, B. 1976. 'Rathgall and Irish hillfort problems', in D.Harding (ed.), *Hillforts: Later prehistoric earthworks in Britain and Ireland*, 339-59. London: Academic Press

Robinson, P. and Swanton, G. 1993. 'On Blagan Hill', *Current Archaeology* 134, 73-4

Savory, H. 1971. 'A Welsh Bronze Age hillfort', *Antiquity* 45, 251-61

Serjeantson, D., Field, D., Penn, J. and Shipley, M. 1992. 'Excavations at Eden Wharf II, Kingston, Surrey', *Surrey Archaeol. Collect.* 81, 71-90

Smith, R.A. 1911. 'Lake dwellings in Holderness, Yorkshire', *Archaeologia* 62, 593-610

Thomas, J. 1993. 'The politics of vision and the archaeologies of landscape', in B.Bender (ed.), *Landscape, politics and perspectives*, 19-48. Oxford: Berg

Wardle, P. 1992. *Earlier prehistoric pottery production and ceramic petrology in Britain* Oxford: Tempus Reparatum

Whittle, A. 1991. 'Wayland's Smithy, Oxfordshire: excavations at the Neolithic tomb in 1962-63', *Proc. Prehist. Soc.* 57.2, 61-101

Wilkinson, T. and Murphy, P. 1995 *Archaeology of the Essex Coast vol. I*, E. Anglian Archaeol. 71

The Iron Age of Essex

P. R. Sealey

This chapter reviews developments in our understanding of the Iron Age of Essex since the 1978 conference on the archaeology of the county. The period falls naturally into three phases:

(i) an early (initial) pre-Roman Iron Age (EPRIA), when flint-tempered Darmsden-Linton pottery was current, c.650-350 BC;

(ii) a middle pre-Roman Iron Age (MPRIA), characterised by sand-tempered pottery of the kind in use at Little Waltham and dated c.350-50 BC; and

(iii) a late pre-Roman Iron Age (LPRIA), distinguished by the grog-tempered and wheel-thrown pottery known as Belgic, lasting from c.50 BC until AD 43.

Each of these periods is described in turn, and a final section examines farming practice.

The early Pre-Roman Iron Age

A striking feature of Essex is the large number of late Bronze Age scrap metalwork hoards of the c.900-700 BC Ewart Park phase. It has been suggested that the failure to retrieve these hoards in prehistory can be explained by the introduction of iron in the succeeding Llyn Fawr (Hallstatt C) phase of the 7th century BC. As knowledge of the new metal spread, the demand for bronze slumped and much of the reserves stored in these hoards became redundant (Burgess 1979,275-6; Burgess and Coombs 1979,v-vi). But serious reservations have been expressed about this simple and dramatic model (Northover 1984,128; Needham 1986,60; 1990,133-7; Thomas 1989,275-6), largely because the Llyn Fawr industries show bronze working still in operation after the *floruit* of Ewart Park. But Llyn Fawr metalwork is not present in Essex (Sealey 1988,13) and it is possible to retain the Burgess thesis by postulating that regions without such metalwork were those where iron was adopted first, leaving districts such as Wessex - where Llyn Fawr industries are attested - as those that embraced iron at a later date.

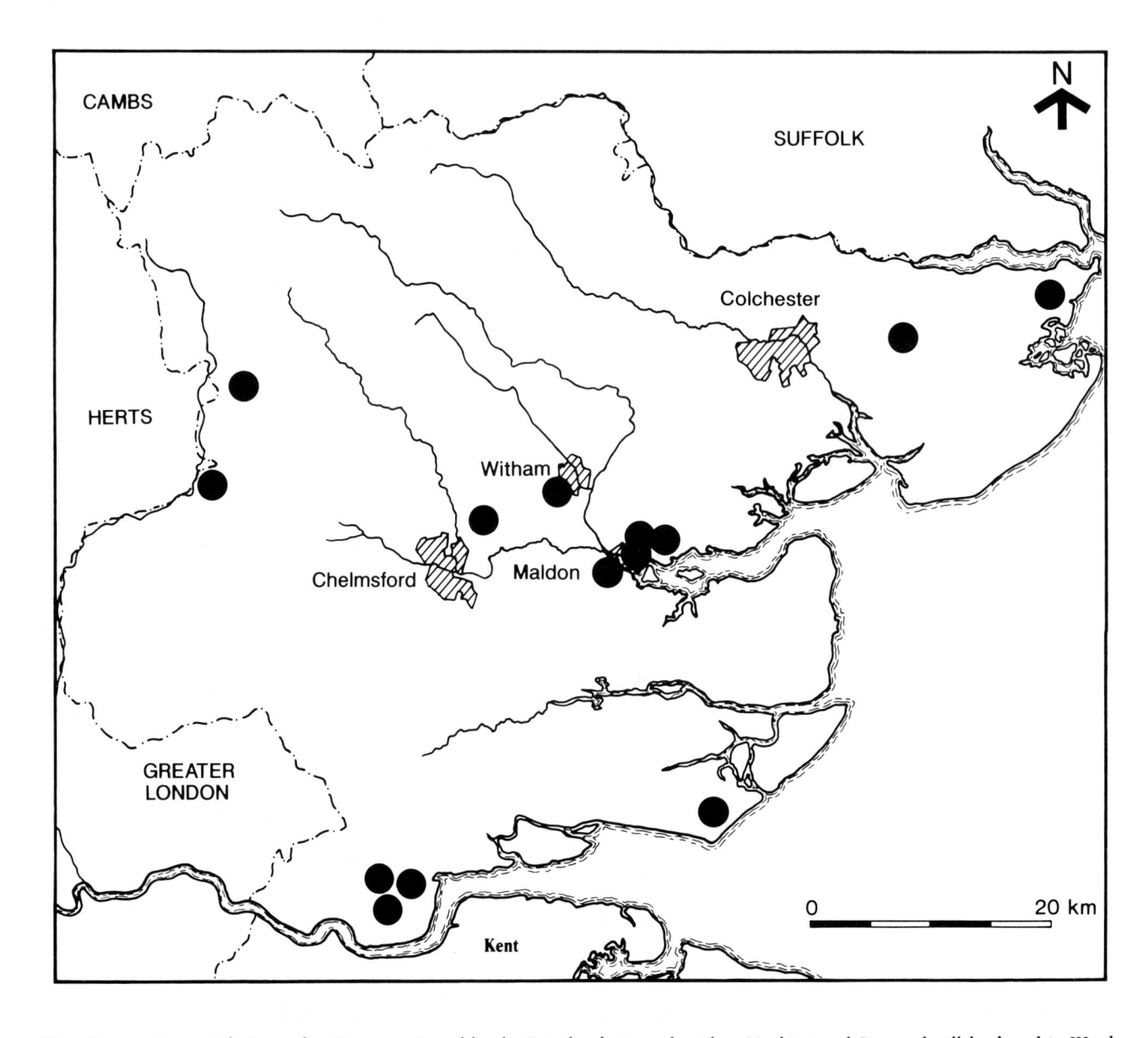

Fig.1 Sites in Essex with Darmsden-Linton carinated bowls. Details of sites other than Mucking and Stansted will be found in Ward Perkins 1937, Barrett 1978, Adkins *et al.* 1986, Brown 1988, Andrews and Priddy 1990, Bedwin 1992, and Wallis and Waughman forthcoming

Early Pre-Roman Iron Age Pottery

The 1978 conference was prepared for publication when Barrett (1978; 1980) demonstrated that what had been regarded as initial Iron Age pottery was in fact late Bronze Age. It has taken a decade to work out the implications for Essex, largely because published assemblages of the relevant pottery were not available for study then and it is only now that we can be confident the outlines of the ceramic sequence are secure.

The ceramic of the Essex EPRIA is the Darmsden-Linton pottery style-zone defined by Cunliffe (1968, 178-81, fig.1,184-90; 1974, fig.3:4,39, fig.A.11). Although this ware is found from Norfolk to Surrey, a recent distribution map shows a blank for Essex (Cunliffe 1991,fig.4.4) and Fig.1 is an attempt to correct the picture. It shows those sites in the county where the carinated tripartite bowls diagnostic of the style-zone have been reported.

The earliest group from Essex comes from a well at Lofts Farm, where it was stratified above late Bronze Age pottery (Brown 1988,figs 16-17,271-2,276,293). A date in the late 7th century BC seems reasonable. Later groups have the pedestal bases modelled on continental prototypes of 6th century BC and later date (Hodson 1962,142). A large assemblage from Maldon, Beacon Green, exemplifies this development (Brown 1992). An interesting minor element in both groups is the so-called haematite-coated ware (Middleton 1987), pointing to contact with Wessex. In the south of the country, shell-temper is sometimes found in EPRIA contexts. It was absent at Rectory Road in Orsett (Wilkinson 1988, 75), and only 3% by weight of the total pottery recovered at Hadleigh, but it dominates assemblages of this date at North Shoebury (Brown 1987b, 90; 1992, 18). Darmsden-Linton pottery developed from late Bronze Age antecedents by a process of organic typological evolution. Both styles of pottery have a coarse and fine ware element, and in both crushed burnt flint is the standard temper, although sand becomes increasingly common at the expense of flint in the EPRIA. Such is this similarity of fabric that assemblages dominated by coarse flint-tempered body sherds of late Bronze Age or EPRIA date can only be distinguished with difficulty.

Late Darmsden-Linton pottery that anticipates MPRIA ceramics is rare. N. R. Brown has drawn my attention to just such a group from the Stansted Airport Social Club Site which includes tripartite bowls with rounded profiles (Fig.2 nos 12-13). What might also be such transitional pottery has already been published from Orsett (Barrett 1978,280, fig.40 nos 40-7,282, fig.41,284, fig.42 nos 75-96). Pottery of this kind may have been current c.400-350 BC.

Early Pre-Roman Iron Age Settlement

Excavation of EPRIA settlements has been confined to Maldon, Ambresbury Banks and Asheldham Camp. Mindful of the scale of these sites, it is ironic that no house plan of the period has been recovered since 1978.

On top of the hill at Maldon, EPRIA pottery has been found in three different places. An open settlement there was subsequently defended by a timber palisade. Although the character of the occupation of the interior is unknown, it is clear that the settlement was extensive, running some 260 m from north to south. The palisade cut quarry scoops dug to extract clay for pottery and daub. Its construction must have involved the felling of large quantities of timber and it is evident that the site was significant. At the end of its history the palisade was systematically demolished but there is no evidence that this enclosed settlement was succeeded by a regular hill-fort (Bedwin 1992).

Excavations at Ambresbury Banks in Epping Forest (Alexander et al. 1979) have shown that the camp there was univallate with one entrance; it enclosed 5.5 ha. Pottery from beneath and within the rampart is dominated by flint-tempered sherds, with sand-tempered ware in a minority. This suggests construction in the EPRIA, before sand had replaced flint as the standard temper in the MPRIA. A sherd with finger-nail decoration on its flat rim was sealed beneath a collapse of rampart material at the entrance. The sherd is MPRIA and shows the camp defences had become dilapidated by then. The rampart was a simple dump construction, separated from the ditch by a berm; recuts of the ditch provided soil for a counter-scarp bank. The entrance roadway was metalled, with a camber. A drystone revetment wall of local conglomerate flanked the road as it passed through the rampart; there were wooden gateways at both ends. There was no sign of permanent occupation of the interior, and the modest quantities of pottery from the butt ends of the ditch at the entrance confirmed this. Presumably the camp was built as a temporary refuge for livestock and people when raids from neighbouring communities threatened; this is suggested by the entrance roadway, which shows that the brisk movement of traffic was envisaged when its metalling was laid.

Asheldham Camp (Bedwin 1991) is another defended site of the period, dated by pottery from the primary fill of the ditch and beneath the rampart. The camp itself was univallate and small, enclosing 3.5 hectares. Beneath the rampart was a buried soil; pollen analysis showed it had been cultivated but that the surrounding landscape was dominated by grassland with little in the way of arable. Extensive crop marks in the vicinity of Asheldham (Drury and Rodwell 1978,fig.2; Bedwin 1991,fig.1d) may be contemporary with the camp, amplifying this environmental evidence that the site was located in a relatively treeless agrarian setting. Although some EPRIA pottery was found in the interior of the camp, there was no real sign of permanent occupation. The cultivated character of the buried soil beneath the rampart suggests construction of the camp took place in an open landscape, rather than representing the defence of an existing settlement.

The Middle Pre-Roman Iron Age

The 1978 conference coincided with the publication of the Little Waltham report (Drury 1978a), a work that deserves recognition as a classic monograph: it defined for the first time the Essex MPRIA and we may start our survey of the period with subsequent research on the site itself.

Scientific analyses of twelve of the thirty iron artefacts from Little Waltham have now been published (Ehrenreich 1985,114,186-8,214). The excavator himself has proposed the rectangular structure at the heart of the Little Waltham village as a shrine (Drury 1980b,52 pace Wait 1985,161). Adjustment of the plan can give a square, rather than a rectangular structure (Grimes and Close-Brooks 1993,336,fig.22). Little Waltham and Stansted (see below) thus join a growing number of Iron Age sites in southern Britain where a nucleated settlement of round houses had just such a building at its centre (Drury 1980b,45-62; Grimes and Close-Brooks 1993,312-18,335-8).

No Iron Age coins were excavated at Little Waltham but N. P. Wickenden tells me that four have since been discovered some 750 m to the south. They are two gold staters (Gallo-Belgic E and British LB, both of the mid 1st century BC), a Class II potin and a bronze issue of ANDOCO: they serve as a reminder of the importance and potential of the site.

P. R. Sealey

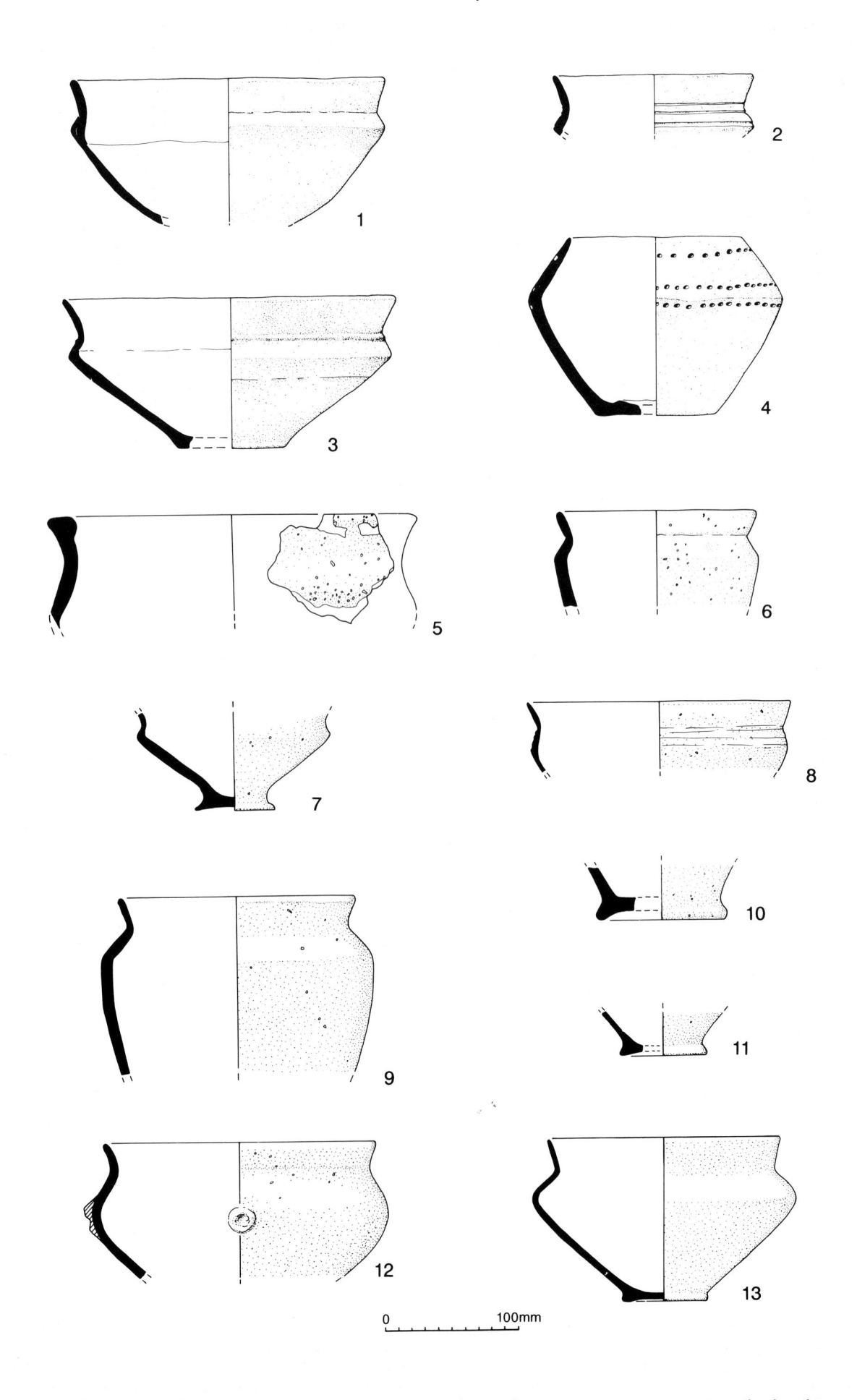

Fig.2 EPRIA Darmsden-Linton pottery. Nos 1-6, early Darmsden-Linton from Lofts Farm c.650-600 BC; nos 7-11, developed Darmsden-Linton from Maldon Beacon Green c.600-400 BC; nos 12-13, late Darmsden-Linton from Stansted Airport Social Club site c.400-350 BC (after Brown 1988 and Bedwin 1992)

THE IRON AGE OF ESSEX

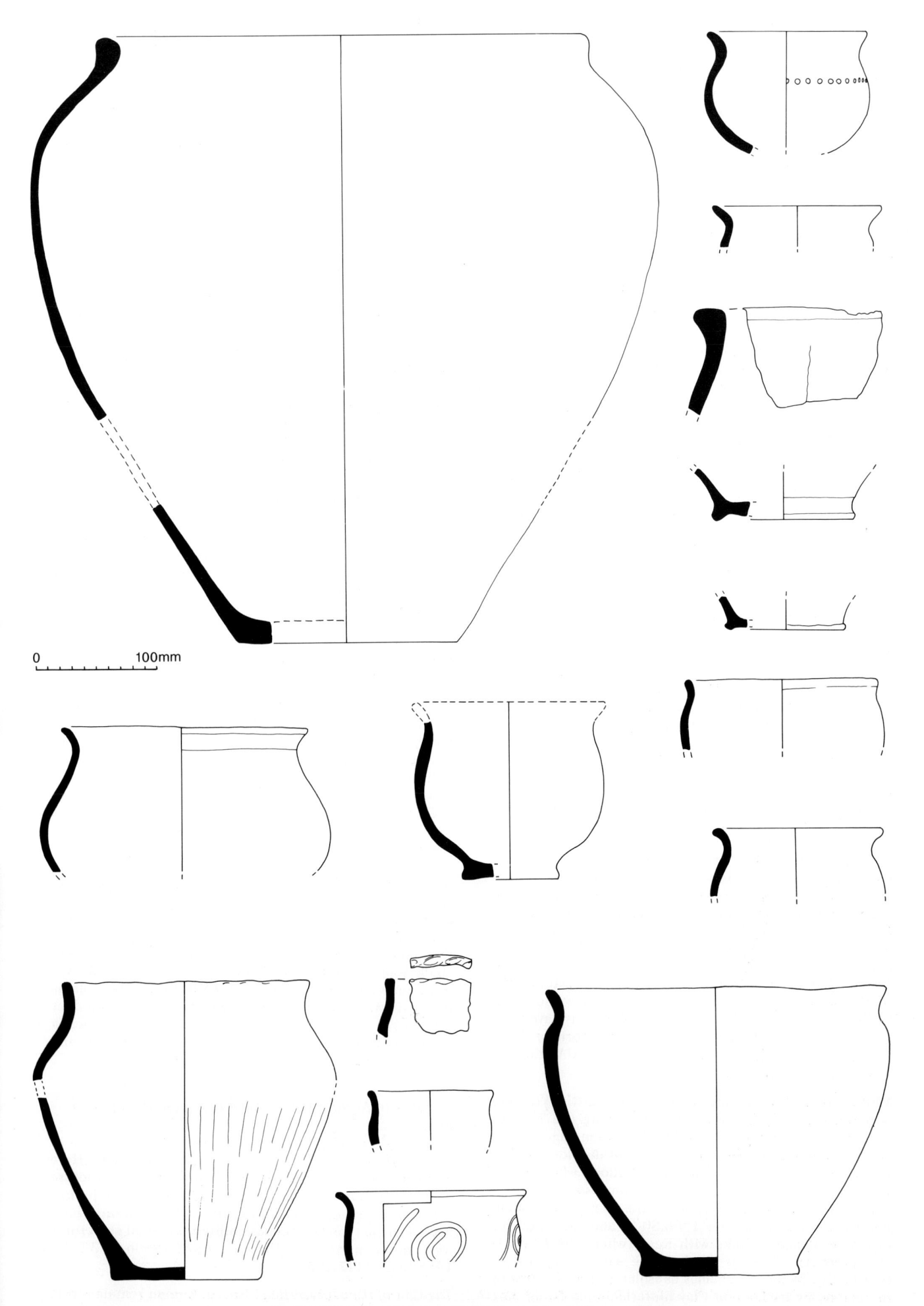

Fig.3 MPRIA pottery from Ardale School (after Wilkinson 1988)

Middle Pre-Roman Iron Age Pottery

Darmsden-Linton pottery was succeeded in Essex by sand-tempered wares of the kind represented at Little Waltham (Drury 1978a,51-85). The flint temper of the EPRIA recedes in importance: at Little Waltham, such vessels never make up more than 7 % of the total (*op. cit.*,table 10,58). Early MPRIA pottery assemblages may transpire therefore to be those with a higher incidence of flint temper. Such a group was found at Stock, where four pots of MPRIA form were all flint-tempered. The 4th-century BC date suggested for the find may not be unrealistic (Couchman 1979,fig.12,75,fig.16). MPRIA pottery was present at Little Waltham from c.250 BC but we do not know when it evolved from earlier styles. There are few groups transitional between EPRIA and MPRIA pottery (see above) and the c.350 BC date proposed here for the divide between the periods must be viewed as tentative and provisional.

An interesting component of Essex MPRIA pottery is the Little Waltham form 13 everted rim footring bowl. Petrological analysis indicates the presence of glauconite in some of them, and an origin in the Mucking-Chadwell area has been claimed (Drury 1978a,128; Hamilton 1988,76 with more details of the petrology). In fact the source is the Maidstone region (Thompson 1982,7,11-12 her Medway zone; see also Pollard 1988,31-2) and these pots represent a trade in vessels from Kent, north across the Thames (not the other way round). Confirmation comes from the incidence of form 13 north and south of the Thames. At Farningham (Kent), 30% of the pottery from Period I (after c.50 BC) is glauconite-tempered form 13 (without the sand-tempered copies found in Essex) (Couldrey 1984,50) and such high percentages are not replicated north of the river. In north Essex glauconite-tempered form 13 bowls are rare or absent; only sand-tempered versions are found. Glauconite was not reported from Wendens Ambo and only one sherd is present in a large assemblage of MPRIA pottery from Birchanger (Brown 1994,34), suggesting the Stansted region marks the north-west limit of its distribution.

The form 13 bowl is important because it is the earliest evidence for a significant proportion of the vessels in use in the county coming from a source elsewhere. Another instance of non-local pottery is the remarkable find at Heybridge of a Glastonbury ware bowl from the Shepton Mallet region of Somerset, the most easterly findspot for this ware in the country (Brown 1987a,31,fig.15 no.34,32; Peacock 1969,fig.2 group 2,46). Such wares are important because the mechanisms of their distribution facilitated imports of Roman table crockery before the Claudian conquest, and subsequently the widespread movement of pottery across the province that is so prominent a feature of the archaeological record for Roman Britain. Indeed it is in the MPRIA that one catches the first glimpse of trade with the Mediterranean world. C. R. Wallace tells me that Dressel 1a wine amphoras have been found in the 1993-94 excavations at Heybridge Elms Farm; such vessels are also present in the MPRIA Stansted village (see below).

MPRIA pottery of the kind represented at Little Waltham is found throughout the county. But along the Thames estuary, the composition of MPRIA assemblages more closely resembles those of Kent, than of districts further north. This is apparent from Ardale School, where Little Waltham form 13 was the most common vessel present in Area A. One in five of the pots at the same site is shell-tempered ware (Hamilton 1988,80-1) and this provides further evidence of links with Kent (where the fabric is also present). There is much to be said for regarding south Essex along the Thames as isolated from the rest of the county by its London Clay hinterland and being part of Kent instead (Jones and Jones 1975,137).

The concept of a *Mucking-Crayford* pottery style-zone for the MPRIA pottery of Essex and Kent is unfortunate because the Essex pots chosen to illustrate the style-zone are those from the south of the county with stamped and incised decoration, and the plainer wares from the rest of the county (although now acknowledged by Cunliffe as part of the zone) are omitted (Cunliffe 1978,fig.3:8,52, fig.A:24;1991,fig.4.9,89-90,fig.A:26). Decorated vessels are in any case apparently only a minority in a plain ware matrix. Nor does the term encompass the shell-tempered wares of the Thames estuary. The unsatisfactory definition of the term is unfortunate because it had the great merit of drawing attention to the links between Essex and Kent in the MPRIA.

Brown (1991b) has proposed the term *Mucking-Oldbury* for a MPRIA pottery style with flowing lines and vertical scored decoration. In Essex, the curvilinear decoration is found along the Thames, where it is said to be earlier than the crisper patterns of the so-called Mucking-Crayford style, although a patterned bowl from Suffolk dated c.25 BC-AD 25 compromises this chronology (Martin 1988,7-8, fig.24 no.157,49). The term has some validity provided its use is restricted to describing a decorative technique within the broader context of MPRIA ceramics and it is not elevated to the status of a pottery style-zone as such.

Middle Pre-Roman Iron Age Domestic Architecture

The standard domestic architecture of the Essex MPRIA was the round house (Drury 1978a,11-36,118-24). Around many such houses was a deep eaves-drip gully, the butt ends of which in particular can be prolific in finds. The replacement of this house type in the LPRIA by one that left little archaeological trace deprives us of much of the evidence that would otherwise come from these gullies and goes some way to account for the fact that the round house is redressing the traditional *imbalance* of evidence in favour of the Essex LPRIA.

Publication of the Mucking site atlas has made available for study the plans of some 110 round houses of Iron Age type (Clark 1993; Going 1993,19). At least 175 or so are now known for the county. Not all of course will be MPRIA, but it is difficult to avoid the feeling that this was a period of sustained population growth. Porches have been reported from some of the Mucking round houses (Jones and Jones 1975,142), and the site atlas now provides further details; Uphall Camp has also provided houses with porches of some architectural pretension (Greenwood 1989,87). Otherwise details of superstructures remain elusive but fired clay representing burnt daub continues to yield impressions of wattles. Scientific analysis of such burnt clay indicates organic compounds that confirm it was indeed daub (Major 1987b). Where chalk was available, the outer coat of house daub was sometimes a cream cob (Major 1988,97) and this explains the whitewash on daub from Wendens Ambo (Hodder 1982,8). The striking appearance of such round houses in the Essex landscape with their yellow thatched roofs and whitewashed walls may well be imagined.

Aspects of Middle Pre-Roman Iron Age Ritual and Religion

Isolated Rectangular Shrines The rectangular shrines at Little Waltham and Stansted are described below. Here attention is drawn to the rectangular post-built structure of c.4th century BC date which stood alone in the prehistoric landscape on Chelmsford Site Z. This too may have been a shrine, raising the possibility that ritual structures were not confined to villages (Drury 1980b,fig.3.2,54; 1988,fig.5,9,117,125).

The Cult of the Severed Head Not all human remains from archaeological contexts can be explained in terms of mortuary practice; this is particularly so of those sites with skulls. Several Iron Age sites in Essex have produced such material: part of a human skull was present in a MPRIA to LPRIA enclosure ditch at Stifford Clays (Luff 1988); another was buried outside a MPRIA round house at North Shoebury (Wymer and Brown 1995, 34, 129, pl. 14); at Birchanger, skull fragments were found in a MPRIA ditch (Medlycott 1994,28; Bedwin 1994), and part of the skull of a young man was found in a MPRIA pit at Wendens Ambo (Hodder 1982,40). The most interesting case comes from Harlow. There a pit at the temple site included the skull of a young adult, an iron spear blade and a bronze ring. Its British QC coin assigns it to the start of the LPRIA (France and Gobel 1985,23,fig.10B,fig.48 no.6,98; Dorrington and Legge 1985,123).

In southern England it is not uncommon to find fragments of human skulls on Iron Age sites. They cannot be accounted for simply as the relics of excarnated bodies because bones from other parts of the anatomy are not always present. They may instead have been trophies taken in war and put on display until their deliberate burial or inadvertent incorporation in midden deposits. The phenomenon is linked to the cult of the severed head among the Celts, rather than to funerary practice as such (Wilson 1981,147,162; Wait 1985,120) and the evidence from Essex shows that head hunting was practised there in the mid to late Iron Age, at least in the west and south of the county.

Middle Pre-Roman Iron Age Settlements
The only MPRIA settlement excavation published in full since 1978 is Wendens Ambo. This unenclosed hamlet lay on a fertile slope with different soils in the immediate vicinity: heavier boulder clay on the higher ground, and damp alluvial land below. In antiquity this presumably translated into a system of economic exploitation in which the lowest land was pasture for livestock, with arable immediately adjacent the farm, and the boulder clay woodlands managed for fuel, building materials and pigs. Two round houses were sited alongside an open-ended sub-rectangular compound. One had been replaced by two successor houses in much the same position. A welter of other features included grain storage pits with vertical sides. All four of the hearths found lay outside the houses. No doubt baking and cookery were done in the open whenever possible to reduce the risk of setting fire to the houses themselves. The distributions of different kinds of pottery and animal bone led to the identification of parts of the site where butchery and food preparation had been undertaken, as distinct from areas where refuse from meals had accumulated (Hodder 1982,4-10,24-9,64; Halstead 1982b,61-2; Halstead *et al.* 1978; 1982).

The most completely excavated MPRIA settlement since 1978 is the Airport Catering Site (ACS) at Stansted (Brooks 1987,45-6; 1989a; 1989b,6-7; 1993,47-50; Brooks and Bedwin 1989,8-11; Brooks and Wall 1994,22,fig.5.5). It began life *c.*75 BC as two round houses. By *c.*50 BC it had developed into a village of some six or seven round houses, defended by a ditch and rampart. The houses were positioned just inside the rampart. In the middle of the site was a square shrine. A dearth of crop processing waste shows that ACS consumed grain brought from elsewhere and it would seem that the village concentrated instead on livestock. Among the most important finds were a group of imported Italian wine amphoras of form Dressel 1. Typologically some are *at least* as early as *c.*75 BC and they represent some of the earliest such vessels from Essex. Another significant find was a hoard of potin coins buried in the gully of a round house (see below). ACS was occupied until the LPRIA when it was abandoned *c.*25 BC, but the sanctity of the village shrine was remembered in local folklore because it was the focus of ritual offerings on the eve of the Roman invasion and in the early Roman period.

Another site that was occupied permanently in the MPRIA was Asheldam Camp, where there was a granary in which cereals had been stored in oak barrels and pottery jars. But of course this need not mean that the defences were still maintained then (they were constructed in the EPRIA), and any MPRIA recuts of the ditch may have been obliterated by the medieval refurbishment of the camp (Bedwin 1991).

The most impressive of the MPRIA settlements in Essex was Uphall Camp, a defended site on gravel in Ilford on the east bank of the river Roding (Wilkinson 1979; Greenwood 1988; 1989; Merriman 1990,40-1,43). The defences were univallate, strengthened on the west by an additional bank. An area of some 24 ha was enclosed, to make it the largest earthwork of its kind in the county. At least ten round houses have been excavated in the interior. The largest had stake holes suggesting the partitioning of the interior into rooms; the same house had an impressive porchway entrance. Debris from smithying was found in the eaves-drip gully. Another round house had a narrow entrance facing the prevailing wind, presumably to create a well ventilated structure which may have been a granary, an interpretation supported by adjacent four-post structures (themselves traditionally regarded as grain stores), associated with charred cereals. Rectangular buildings may have been tool sheds or barns. Large penannular gullies with deep ditches were interpreted as livestock pens, rather than as houses. The alignment of houses hinted at roads in the settlement. It is not clear how much of the interior was occupied but excavation has indicated open spaces and one should not think of the camp as necessarily having a dense scatter of round houses. Class I potin coins were used and lost by the Uphall community. Pottery shows that the settlement was built in the MPRIA and the shell-tempered ware present suggests a date towards the end of the period.

At some point after its (apparent) construction in the late Bronze Age, the ditches of Chipping Hill Camp at Witham were recut (Rodwell 1993,19,106; Davison 1993,22; Flook and Bedwin 1993,27). Although occupation is attested in the MPRIA, the form it takes (dumps of material in the ditches) shows the defences were no longer maintained. The most interesting find was the skeleton of a dog, alongside which lay the skulls of a horse and a pig (Bedwin 1993,112). This can hardly be regarded as a midden of butchered bone or as the straightforward burial of animal carcasses. It exemplifies instead the phenomenon known as a *special animal bone deposit*. This rite was first recognised at Danebury (Hampshire) by Grant (1984,533-43; Grant *et al.* 1991,482). Its geographical distribution was researched by Wait (1985,123), who demonstrated a striking concentration in Wessex, with an extension north across the upper Thames. Witham is the first report of the rite in Iron Age (but not Roman) Essex and the most easterly in the whole country. A hint at how the practice may have reached the county comes from a Kimmeridge (Dorset) shale bowl from the same context. Such vessels are rare in Iron Age Essex (only four are known) and it is a significant find in its own right (Major 1993).

What does emerge from a survey of the MPRIA is the diversity of settlement morphology. There are small farmsteads or hamlets such as Wendens Ambo, sprawling and amorphous sites like Mucking, open villages such as Period II Little Waltham, and enclosed defended sites like the Stansted ACS village. Although many settlements are enclosed, it would be mistaken to think in terms of a general trend towards enclosure in the MPRIA because such sites are now known for the EPRIA (Turner 1982,5; Brown 1987b,90 *pace* Drury 1978b,74-5; 1980a,52;).

Aspects of Iron Age Craft Production

A miniature pot used as a crucible for glass or enamel was found in the ditch of a MPRIA sub-rectangular enclosure at Woodham Walter. What exactly was produced is not known, but beads are unlikely because they are so rare in Essex (Guido 1978). Dumps of charcoal in the enclosure ditch presumably relate to this industrial activity and show that it was undertaken over an extended period of time. Production came to an end c.50-25 BC after a calamitous fire and the site was abandoned (Buckley *et al.* 1987,7,10; Rodwell 1987,fig.15 no.13,22; Evans 1987).

Several non-ferrous metalworking finds of Iron Age date have now been reported from Mucking, although details of their chronology are not yet available. They include an intact crucible for melting bronze; fragments of four others were also recovered. Three clay moulds for bronze objects were present and an ingot mould that had been used for gold and silver. The sporadic character of these finds at Mucking brings home their rarity in the archaeological record generally (Bayley 1993). It is all the more remarkable therefore that a 1st century AD LPRIA crucible for copper-alloy came from limited excavations at Layer-de-la-Haye (Priddy 1984,134). Bronze working might also be attested at Southchurch, where bronze waste was found unstratified with EPRIA pottery (Rodwell 1977,fig.2 nos 1-3,247).

At Lofts Farm a settlement of some fifteen round houses established in the MPRIA was occupied until the early 1st century AD. A hoard of at least nineteen bronze items found just inside the eaves-drip gully of a round house there casts an interesting light on the weaponry, art and metalworking of the period. It included a decorated ring, straight lengths of U-shaped binding and six of the button studs in which such bindings terminated. The ring was complete but the bindings and terminals are small scrap items (Brown 1985). Stead (1993,20-1,24-6,30) has shown that the bindings and their button terminals come from hide-shaped shields, apparently the most common type of shield in southern England from c.100 BC. More of these bindings were found in the primary silt of a round-house gully at the Harlow temple site (Bartlett 1988a,9,12; 1988b,166).

The bronze ring, with its interlocking arcs, is the first instance from the county of metalwork with an identical motif to that on pottery (Grimes 1953,171 on this lacuna;

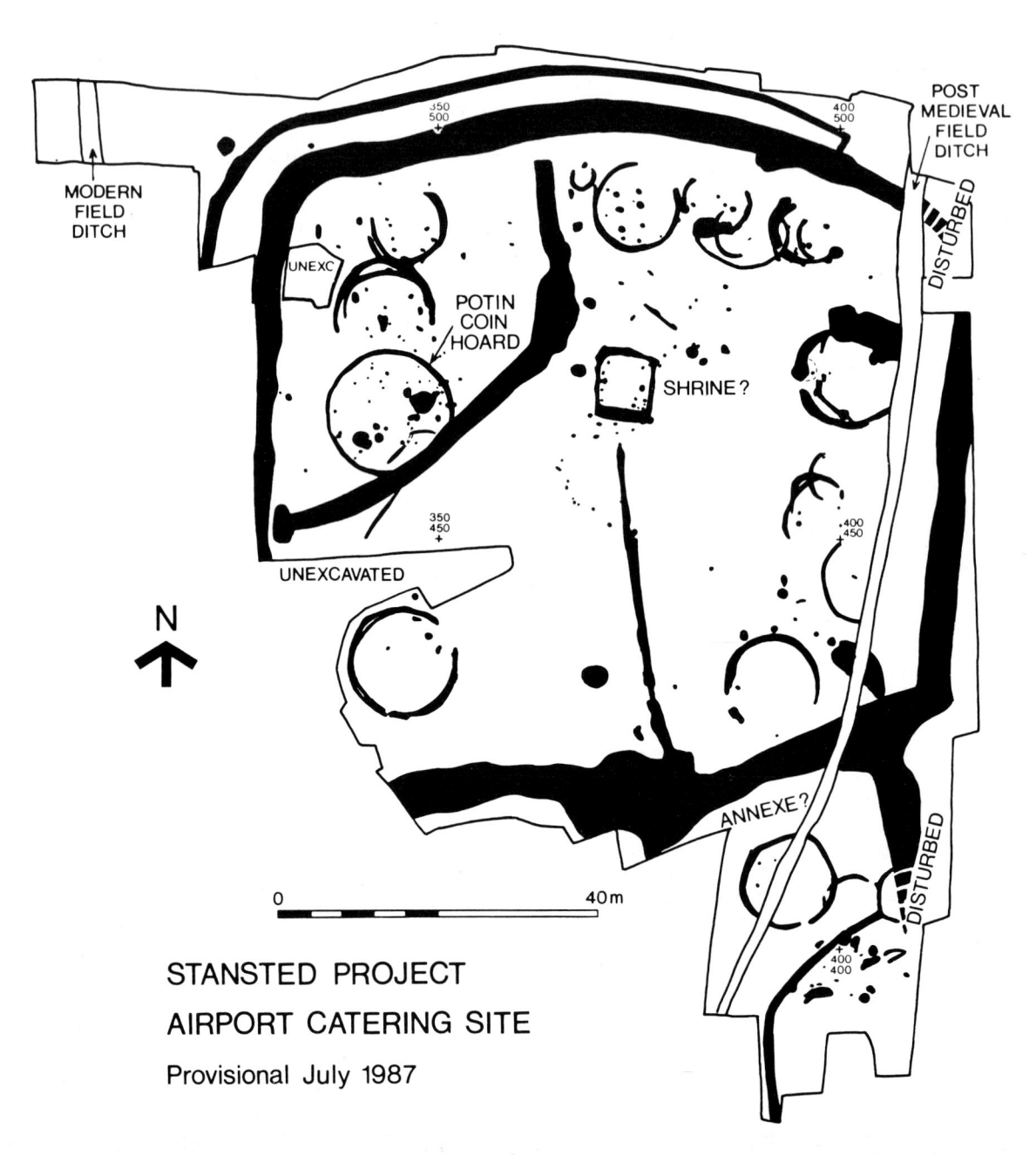

Fig.4 Plan of the MPRIA village at the Stansted Airport Catering Site

THE IRON AGE OF ESSEX

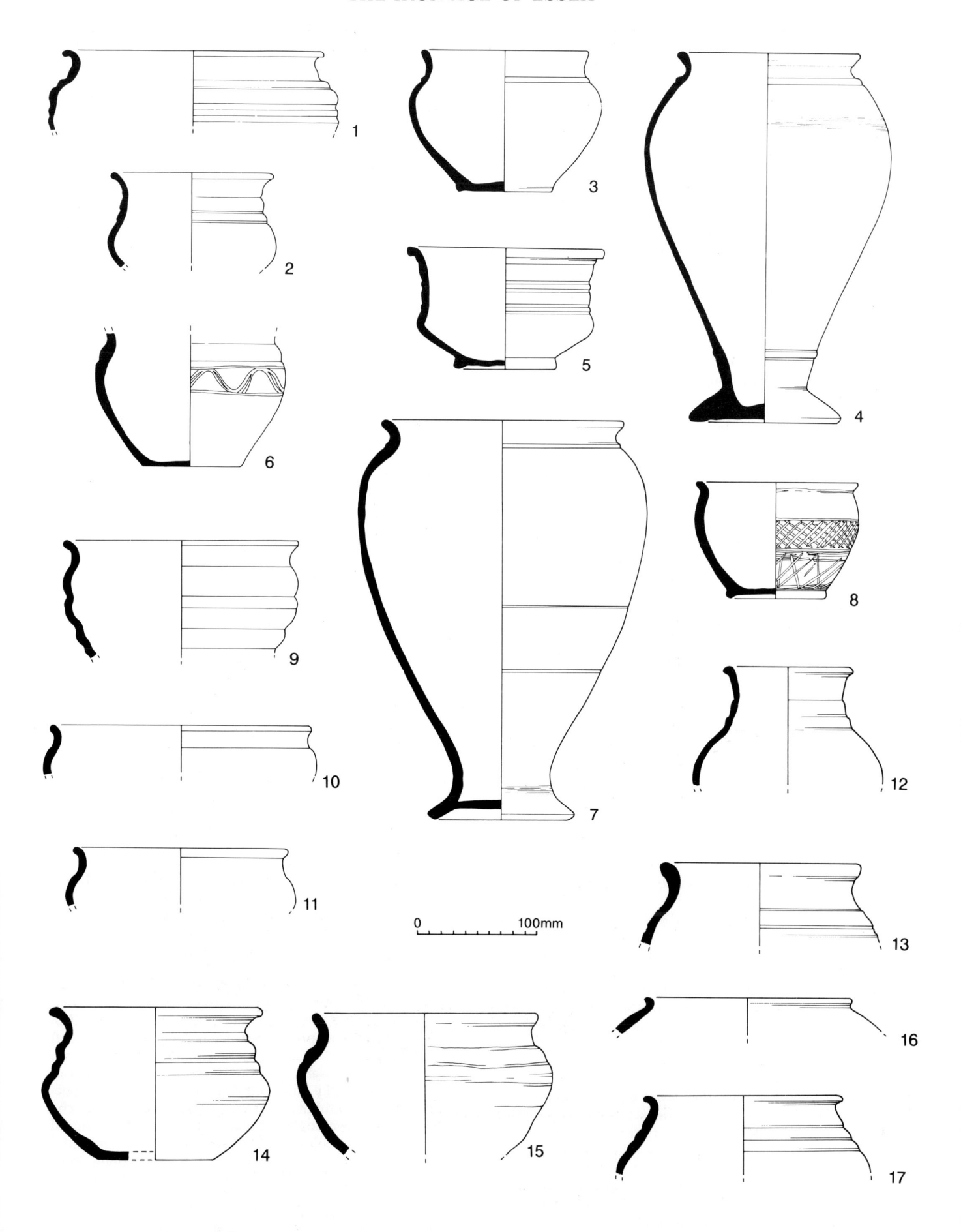

Fig.5 LPRIA Belgic pottery. Nos 1-2, Ardale School; nos 3-8 Maldon Hall Farm; nos 9-11, Woodham Walter; nos 12-17, Billericay Secondary School (after Wilkinson 1988, Lavender 1991, Buckley *et al.* 1987 and Rudling 1990)

Elsdon 1975,fig.5 nos 1-2,22-3 for the pottery). Just such decoration is present on a vessel from a pit beneath Red Hill 89 at Langenhoe dated c.50-25 BC on the basis of its association of MPRIA and LPRIA Belgic pottery (Reader 1908,28-9; Drury 1978a,131-3; Rodwell 1979,154; Thompson 1982,754-5; Jefferies and Barford 1990,36). It is felt that decorated pottery of this kind appears in Essex towards the end of the MPRIA, by c.100 BC (Elsdon 1989,30-8; Brown 1991b,165) and so the c.100-25 BC date suggested here for the ring offers independent dating evidence for the shield bindings that make up the rest of the hoard.

It is a remarkable reflection that the Lofts Farm hoard should be the only cache of bronze from the Essex Iron Age (apart from coin hoards). The modest weight of its individual items of scrap show that bronze in MPRIA Essex was a precious commodity, not to be wasted. No doubt the contents of the hoard were destined for recycling: it is in fact a distant echo of the great industrial hoards of the late Bronze Age with which we began.

This discussion of craft production would be incomplete without reference to the gully of a round house at Ardale School that produced worked flints. Some were demonstrably residual but there was sufficient evidence for Martingell (1988,72-3) to air the possibility - for the first time in Essex - of flint working in the Iron Age. She took as her starting point the flint artefacts from West Harling (Norfolk) (Clarke and Fell 1953,34-5) but they are apparently residual from the middle Bronze Age (Pryor 1987,100-1). However the seventeen flints from Ardale were associated with a concentration of MPRIA pottery and the assemblage does serve as a reminder that some flint may have been worked in the period.

One may end at Mucking, where iron working slag was found with flint-tempered pottery, presumably of EPRIA date (McDonnell 1993,33); the association is apparently the earliest tangible evidence for iron technology in the county.

The Introduction of Coinage
This is not the place to review the entire field of Iron Age numismatics and an attempt is made instead to highlight research and discoveries of direct relevance to the county.

Reference however should be made to the important paper by Allen (1976a), in which he explored the function of Celtic coinage. Haselgrove (1979,201-6; 1987,17-27) has a survey of the whole topic, with comprehensive bibliographies. Coinage was issued to make major payments for goods and services, especially as a reward for warrior retinues and to raise the supplies needed to wage war. The opportunity is taken here to draw attention to a significant text that has been overlooked in studies of the topic (Cassius Dio 54.21.28), where (for Gaul) the link between gold and silver resources and the ability to conduct warfare is demonstrated. The role of coinage in facilitating individuals with access to precious metals to extend their influence in society (by using it as a convenient form of treasure for gift exchange) played a part in the development of the monarchies and states attested in Britain by the end of the LPRIA. It is important to remember that in antiquity individuals could be wealthy enough to make significant private contributions towards the expenditure of the state, even in the Roman world (Augustus *Res Gestae*, 15-21; Brunt and Moore 1988,57-60). Once Iron Age coins had found their way into circulation, they were used as dowries, ransoms, compensation payments, temple offerings, tribute payments and inducements or political bribes. Coins were *not* minted to promote trade (although this is still claimed) and if any low value coins ever did act as a medium of exchange, it was only sporadically towards the end of the period and not even then as an act of policy by the issuers.

In Essex coinage was an innovation of the MPRIA, in the latter half of the 2nd century BC. Coins reported from the county since 1960 have been published by Haselgrove (1978; 1984; 1989b) and a list of the coin legends has been assembled by Mays (1992). Rodwell (1981) stressed the inherent biases in the discovery and recording of Iron Age coins in the county, so it is encouraging to see that an increasing number of them are being retrieved from excavated contexts. Most such are potin and bronze, but coins in the precious metals have been excavated from the Harlow temple, and it is further heartening to learn from M. Atkinson, Dr O. R. Bedwin and H. J. Major that a Gallo-Belgic B stater and a gold quarter-stater of Cunobelinus have been found in the 1993-94 excavations at Heybridge Elms Farm.

The most important developments for Essex have come in the field of potin, the first coinage to be issued in Britain (Haselgrove 1989a). Potin is a chill-cast high-tin bronze coinage which first appeared in Britain towards the end of the 2nd century BC in imitation of prototypes from Gaul. It ceased to be issued in the last decades BC, although it remained in circulation until the Roman period. There are fifteen types belonging to two chronological divisions: Types A-L (omitting I to avoid confusion with Class I in general) belong to the earlier Class I series, and Types M-P belong to the later Class II (Allen 1971,132-6 endorsed by Haselgrove 1989a,100-2). A useful adjunct to the Allen system is the classification developed by Van Arsdell (1986), based on changes in the casting technology behind the coins.

Initially potin coinage was most common in north Kent and south Essex, Surrey and the lower Thames. Traditionally the coinage has been seen as a Kent phenomenon but the growing number of finds north of the Thames has established Essex as part of its circulation zone. To begin with, it was only the Thames estuary regions of the county that saw its widespread use but towards the end of its history, potin circulated further north throughout much of the rest of Essex. Indeed Type P potins (typologically the last of the whole series) are more common in Essex than elsewhere. The Thameside distribution of potin is the numismatic counterpart of the ceramic links between Kent and Essex in the MPRIA (Haselgrove 1989a,116).

The start of this coinage is illustrated by the major hoard find of some 2,300 Class I coins from Corringham, the largest potin hoard from Britain. In the literature the findspot is given as Thurrock and I am grateful to R. W. Bartlett for pointing out that the hoard was in fact found further east, at Corringham. At least sixteen varieties of coin are present, each of which is illustrated by Van Arsdell as his Thurrock-type potins. He dated the find c.100-90 BC and saw it as a short-lived coinage issued in Essex, based on prototypes from Kent (Van Arsdell 1989,320-8 nos 1402-1 to 1442-1,pl.38). This has been questioned by Haselgrove, who puts the coins instead at the very start of the potin series minted in Britain. A specimen from Maiden Castle (Dorset) confirms the Haselgrove chronology and places the Corringham hoard in the late 2nd century BC (Haselgrove 1993a,36-8,pl.9 no.4; 1993b,412). Whether or not the Corringham coins were issued north of the Thames or in Kent, the find demonstrates the involvement of Essex in the potin phenomenon from the start (Northover 1992,261-2). The only other possible Class I potin hoard from the county is the Chipping Hill Camp cache of five coins (Rodwell 1993,105-6).

A later hoard was excavated at the Stansted ACS village (see above). It consists of fifty-one issues, most of which are Type M but with some which approach Types N or O (Haselgrove 1989a, M1/03-4 being Appendix 1b no.5; Northover 1994,262). The likelihood is that this Class II hoard was buried around the middle of the 1st century BC. Stansted is only the second Class II hoard known (there were none until 1978) and their existence refutes suggestions there was a difference in function between potins of Classes I and II on the grounds that it was only the former that was hoarded (Haselgrove 1979,207; 1989a,100; Fitzpatrick 1991a,150). Apart from Snettisham (Norfolk) (Clarke 1955), an exceptional case by any standards (Stead 1991), potin was never hoarded with gold or silver: it was not small change. However exactly potin functioned, it did so independently of the precious metal coinages which circulated at the same time in the same regions. It is possible that it operated at a lower social level, rather than that it fulfilled a different role to the other coinages.

Analyses of the alloys used in the Corringham and Stansted hoards cast an interesting light on the sources of their metals and show a major shift in the pattern of supply over time. Corringham used a source with a cobalt impurity located in south-west England which was exported overseas to the mainland of Europe. Some half a century later, the situation at Stansted was quite different. There the alloy had been imported from central or Alpine Europe (Northover 1992,261-3) and might explain an otherwise puzzling reference in Caesar (*De Bello Gallico* 5.12) to the import of bronze by the Britons.

The Impact of the Gallic Wars
The end of the Essex MPRIA coincides with the conquest of Gaul by C. Julius Caesar in 58-51 BC. The many Class I potin coin hoards hitherto thought to have been buried when he attacked Britain in 55 and 54 BC are now believed to predate the war (Haselgrove 1989a,108-10). But two hoards found since 1978 *can* be dated to the Gallic Wars because they consist exclusively of Gallo-Belgic E. The smaller is the 1992 discovery of two coins from West Bergholt, kindly shown me by D. W. Bradbury. The find exemplifies the tendency towards smaller hoards as the Iron Age progresses; the number of such hoards is greater than is generally realised (Haselgrove 1993a,50-1). The second is the much larger hoard of thirty-three unworn Gallo-Belgic E discovered at Southend in 1985 (Cowell et al. 1988,2,pls 1-2 nos 1-33; Priddy 1987,163).

Gallo-Belgic E staters were issued by a confederacy of Belgic states in Gaul to finance the war. It has been suggested they reached Britain as payment for mercenary warriors and provisions (Kent 1978,53,55,58; 1981,40 citing Caesar *De Bello Gallico* 4.20). Among Gallo-Belgic E there are six subvarieties; only the earliest are present in hoards from Britain, suggesting they may belong to the years immediately preceding the first attack of 55 BC. As the later subvarieties are less common, one suspects that the invasion mounted by Caesar was effective and dramatically reduced the subsequent involvement of Britons in the Gallic Wars. Such assistance moreover would have been inappropriate for the Trinovantes, who were now bound to Rome by treaty obligations.

The account of the Trinovantes in Caesar marks the entry of Essex into the realms of written history. Attempts have been made to relate imports of Italian wine in Dressel 1 amphoras to the treaty arrangements between Caesar and these people. But amphoras from the Stansted village and Heybridge show the trade began earlier (see above). Nor can we follow Peacock (as he himself now acknowledges) and see the territory of the tribe defined by rich graves of Welwyn-type with these wine jars (Caesar *De Bello Gallico* 5.20-1; Peacock 1971,161,175-8; 1984,39 for the retraction).

Reference may be made here to the celebrated statement in Caesar (*De Bello Gallico* 5.12) about the settlement of coastal parts of the country by immigrant Belgae before the Gallic Wars. Scholarship has fought itself to a standstill over the intractable problem of the archaeological identity of these immigrants and it is understandable that the topic has now been quietly dropped from the agenda. The last contribution to this debate with an Essex perspective was a valiant essay by Hawkes (1983,4-9).

The Late Pre-Roman Iron Age

Late Pre-Roman Iron Age Pottery
Essex ceramics in the LPRIA were dominated by the shell-tempered ware (STW) of the Thames estuary, and by the Belgic pottery found there and elsewhere in the county. Each is discussed in turn, with particular reference to the neglected topic of STW.

Belgic pottery This is the wheel-thrown and grog-tempered ware so common in Essex and neighbouring counties in the LPRIA and early Roman period. Its study is still dominated by the massive survey undertaken by Thompson (1982). Her typology and classification are difficult to apply in practice, but the gazetteer remains a mine of information. It was Thompson who insisted on the significance of grog temper as the diagnostic feature of this ware; attempts to subdivide the fabric are of limited value. Tests on pottery with various tempers have shown that grog gives the strongest pot, and sand the weakest (Shepard 1965,27,131-2). It is odd that sand replaced grog as the standard temper in Essex after AD 43; the disadvantage of abandoning grog was presumably disguised by the harder finish obtained in Roman kilns.

Drury (1978a,131,133) showed that Belgic pottery first appeared in Essex *c.*50-25 BC (at least at Little Waltham). There are now two major assemblages of pottery that elucidate the transition from MPRIA to Belgic ware. Both are large enough for the absence of imported Roman crockery to be significant, suggesting they are earlier than *c.*25 BC. The assemblages are those from ditch F350 at Kelvedon (Rodwell 1988,103-6,132-3) and ditch AF1 at Woodham Walter (Rodwell 1987,20-5,37-8). Similarities between them indicate they are contemporary and the evidence adduced to demonstrate a *c.*50-25 BC date for Kelvedon applies to both groups. There is no case for Belgic pottery before *c.*50 BC in Essex. It is reassuring that the pot in which the Southend Gallo-Belgic E coin hoard of the Gallic Wars had been hidden (see above) was a handmade flint-tempered MPRIA vessel.

There is no sense in which Belgic pottery developed from MPRIA ceramics: it is an intrusive and novel departure that soon displaced MPRIA wares throughout the county. Only at Wendens Ambo is there any sign of a chronological outlier: there a ditch (dated Roman in the report) produced MPRIA sherds - and no Belgic material - associated with an imported Roman *terra nigra* platter, suggesting that pre-Belgic ceramics may have lasted there until at least the late 1st century BC (Hodder 1982,10-11,32 nos 13-16 *pace* p.25 where pottery of MPRIA type is claimed to have lasted until AD 43).

Shell-Tempered Ware Essex STW takes its name from the abundant inclusions of crushed shell which give vessels a speckled white appearance. There is a description of the fabric in Green (1980,65). In acidic soils the shell has dissolved to give the surface a pitted (vesicular) appearance (Drury and Rodwell 1973,74 n.38). Scientific analysis has shown that the inclusions are the fossil shells present in the Woolwich Beds of the south of the county (Hamilton 1988,76). The same formation was exploited in Kent for the contemporary STW found there (Couldrey 1984,42). An additional source was presumably provided by the shell banks along the Thames estuary (Wilkinson 1988,126-7).

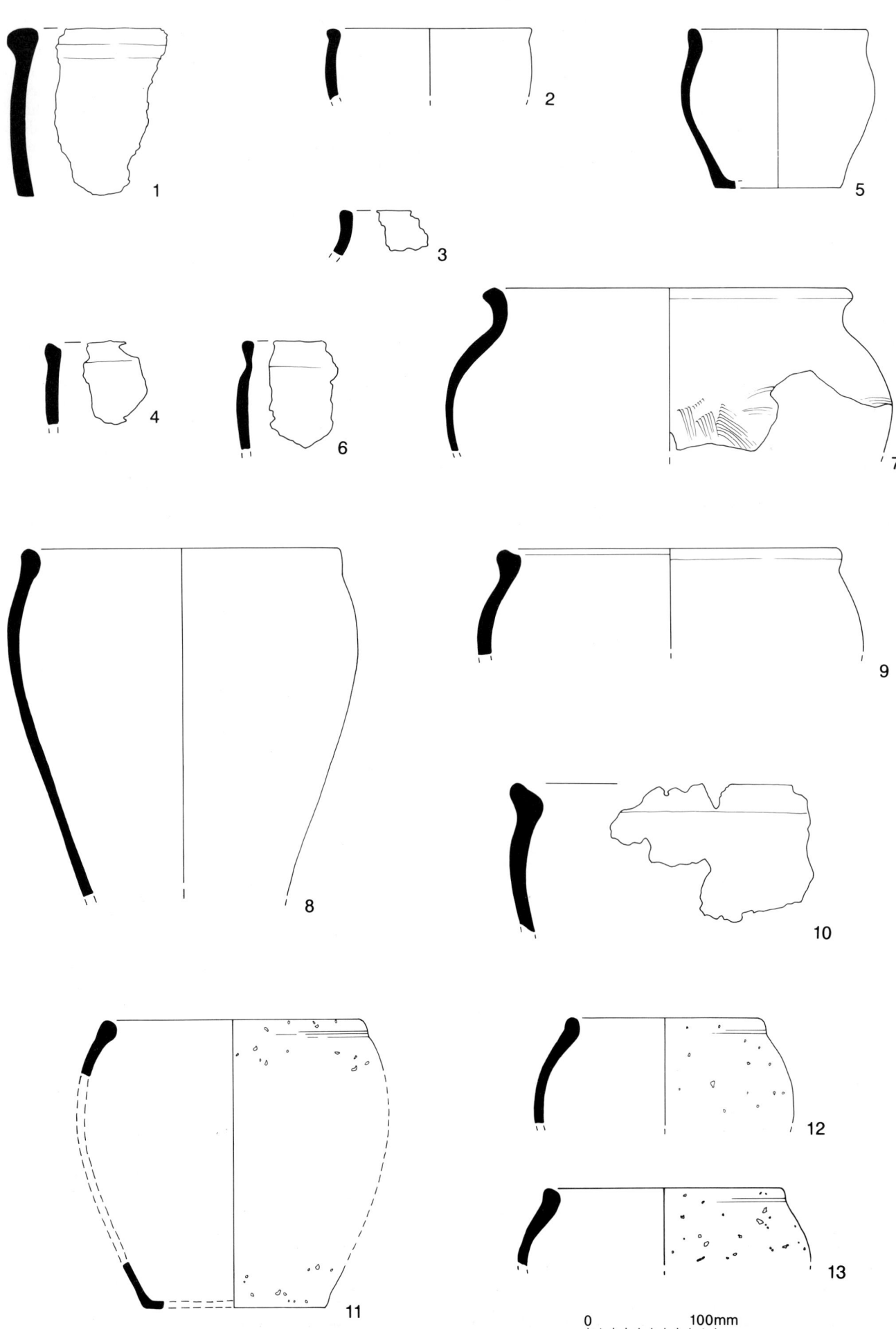

Fig.6 Shell-tempered ware. Nos 1-4, MPRIA Ardale School; nos 5-6 MPRIA to LPRIA Ardale School; nos 7-10, LPRIA Ardale School; nos 11-13 LPRIA Billericay Secondary School (after Wilkinson 1988 and Rudling 1990)

MPRIA vessels in STW are handmade, and the potters who continued to make this ware in the LPRIA were evidently reluctant to adopt the wheel because many of the pots were still made by traditional methods even then.

STW is found sporadically in the south of the county in the EPRIA, where it can be locally important (see above), but it is only apparently in later centuries that it is of widespread significance there. STW included forms current in the existing standard MPRIA repertoire, as represented by the vessels present at Little Waltham in other fabrics. Eventually the ware assumes more of a typological identity with distinctive forms not found in the sand or grog-tempered wares of MPRIA and LPRIA Essex. Since 1978 only limited amounts of STW have been published from the county (Hamilton 1988,76; Wilkinson 1988,75,80-6; Thompson 1988; Rudling 1990,28,30-1) and there is nothing comparable yet to the variety of forms represented across the Thames estuary from the farmstead at Farningham (Kent), occupied c.50 BC-AD 43 (Couldrey 1984 *passim*).

STW is found in the south of the county along the Thames estuary, in what Thompson (1982,7,9-11) called her Zone 2, a tract running from the Crouch estuary in the east to the Mar Dyke in the west. Some vessels were traded north to the rest of Essex but they are few and far between. Finds from Uphall Camp on the river Roding (Greenwood 1989,98) show that the zone can be extended west towards London. Similar pottery has been reported from north-west Kent (Thompson 1982,7; Couldrey 1984; Pollard 1988,31-3,40). In south Essex (as Thompson indicates), STW is a significant component of pottery assemblages from settlement sites (where it is found with Belgic pottery), although comprehensive quantification of this perception must await future work. Even where STW is most common, it is invariably Belgic pottery that was used for funerary vessels (Thompson 1988). STW becomes conspicuous at the end of the MPRIA and, for at least a brief period before the Belgic pottery tradition is established, it comprised most of the pottery in use. Three pits from Ardale School (one with a quoit-shaped Belgic pedestal base of the 1st century BC) each had pottery assemblages with over 80% STW (Wilkinson 1988,81).

The Essex STW phenomenon is familiar to archaeologists in the county but the dearth of significant published assemblages has conspired to achieve its neglect by the wider archaeological public elsewhere. The *floruit* of this ware starts at the end of the MPRIA and there is a real sense in which it is an outlier of MPRIA traditions at a time when the rest of the county adopted Belgic pottery and abandoned its existing ceramic identity. It is remarkable that this technologically backward ware should have survived at a time of such change, and one wonders if the tenacity of this insular and conservative tradition is giving us an insight into the tenor of the communities that made and used it. In the early Roman period, STW comes into its own when - as a more regularly wheel-made ceramic - it constitutes over half the pottery in assemblages from the south of the county as late as the Flavian period (Going 1987,10 fabric 30).

Late Pre-Roman Iron Age Funerary Practices
Until the LPRIA, funerary rituals in Essex left little or no discernible trace in the archaeological record. The earliest burials are an unaccompanied crouched inhumation in an EPRIA pit at North Shoebury and an infant burial in the butt end of a ditch (Wymer and Brown 1995, 129). These are the first examples from the county of a practice widespread in Wessex, with an extension north-east towards Norfolk, of burying a very few selected individuals in isolation (Whimster 1977,317-19; 1981,4-36). In the LPRIA there is a radical change in the picture, with the adoption of communal cemeteries where cremation and - to a lesser extent - inhumation were practised.

The Cremation Rite LPRIA cremation burials are so familiar a component of Essex archaeology that it is difficult to approach the topic with fresh eyes and a new perspective, but developments since 1978 have now made this possible.

What is apparently the earliest cremation in Essex comes from Harlow temple, where cremated human bone from Pit H was associated with pottery (nowhere illustrated or described in the report) called early Iron Age (France and Gobel 1985,21). N. R. Brown has pointed out to me that subsequent excavations on the site by R. W. Bartlett have suggested instead that Pit H was the central burial of a Bronze Age pond barrow. A more secure early example of Iron Age cremation is a Mucking burial in which the calcined bones were placed in a hand-made stamped omphalos bowl (Elsdon 1975,50,pl.3,fig.13 no.2, 73,78), associated with a corrugated Belgic pot (shown the writer in 1982). Otherwise the pottery associated with LPRIA cremations is invariably Belgic, and both cremation and Belgic pottery are innovations of the period c.50-25 BC.

It is clear that cremation represents the adoption of a rite from Gaul and the Rhineland (Stead and Rigby 1989,86) and these links find further expression in rectangular funerary enclosures. At Maldon Hall Farm, a small enclosure dated c.50-1 BC had three cremations; one included a silver Almgren 65 brooch and eight pots. Five more pits with steep sides and flat bottoms were devoid of surviving finds. Another pit had burnt flints, fired clay and sherds from a storage jar, but no cremated bones (Lavender 1991). On a settlement site this would be viewed as a typical domestic rubbish assemblage but its presence here on a funerary enclosure suggests it played some part in the rituals of Iron Age death and burial. There is in fact reason to think that some apparently straightforward midden deposits may instead be material carefully selected in accordance with some unfathomable rites of behaviour, even when found on settlement sites (Haselgrove 1993b,413; Hill 1994; 1995). Lavender (1991,209) also describes another funerary enclosure, from Mucking. At North Shoebury, a line of three cremation burials marked a settlement boundary. The central burial was placed within a small rectangular enclosure marked by slight gullies or palisade slots (Wymer and Brown 1995, 34-5, fig. 27). A remarkable addition to the funerary repertoire of the county are the square-ditched barrows containing 1st century BC cremations at Mucking (Going 1993,19-20).

The most exciting enclosures are those at Stanway, where funerals took place just outside the Colchester dyke system between the 1st century BC and the early Roman period (Crummy 1992; 1993; 1994,6-7). The grandest of the LPRIA graves lay in the centre of its enclosure and dated c.AD 20-30. There the deceased had been laid out in a mortuary chamber erected in a large pit, with the roof protruding above ground. The chamber was timber built, with the structural members nailed together. After an interval, the corpse was removed and cremated alongside the chamber; this set the roof on fire. When the funeral pyre had died out, cremated bones were collected and cast inside the remains of the chamber, along with broken pottery. As the superstructure collapsed, the pit was backfilled with more pottery sherds and cremated bone. At least twenty-four vessels were present, all of them imports from the Roman world. Elaborate funerary rituals like this had their origins in Belgic Gaul (Metzler *et al.* 1991) and reached their apogee in Britain with the c.AD 50 burial at Verulamium Folly Lane (Niblett 1992). Such graves at last allow us to see the Lexden Tumulus as something other than a freak of funerary practice (Laver 1927; Foster 1986 - note her prophetic suggestion that the tumulus had a timber mortuary chamber).

Some LPRIA cremations in Essex are unurned, even when pottery is present in the grave (Hull 1962,15 from Ardleigh) and the number has grown since 1978. The most significant single concentration comes from an unenclosed cemetery of thirty graves at Mucking. Many of these were unurned, or indeed accompanied by any grave goods at all (Going 1993,20). When cremations do have grave furniture, it is usually ceramic. An exception comes from the cemetery at the Stansted Airport Duckend Farm Site, where a cremation had carved bone cheek pieces from horse harness (Brooks and Havis 1991,2).

After the Stanway burials, the most significant new grave is the warrior burial from Great Braxted. This was a chance discovery made in 1982 and drawn to my attention by C. J. Going, who kindly made the finds available for study in advance of his report. The grave goods included an iron sword bent into a right angle, a plain bronze scabbard from a shorter weapon, three spears and an iron shield umbo (Stead 1985a,36,39; 1985b,44). There was also a bronze tankard handle and a bronze dish. Associated pottery included three pedestal urns with quoit-shaped bases, suggesting a date of c.50-1 BC for the grave. Bone does not usually survive in the acidic soil of the Great Braxted area, so it is not clear if this was an inhumation or cremation. Warrior burials are rare in southern Britain (Collis 1973; Whimster 1977,322-3; 1981,fig.50,134-7) and Great Braxted is the first instance from the county of this particular rite, if we discount the implications of the mail in the Lexden Tumulus (Laver 1927,pl.53 fig.3,pls 54-5,246,248; Foster 1986,82-7). The grave goods give us a glimpse of the armaments of an Essex warrior at a time when we know that warfare was endemic. The array of weaponry at Great Braxted brings to mind a comment by Allen (1958,55), who described the foot soldier on the coinage of Cunobelinus as "generally over-encumbered with gear" ! Perhaps too it is no coincidence that a graffito naming the great Celtic war god Teutatis was found nearby at Kelvedon, in a context dated c.AD 80-100 (Rodwell 1988,fig.77 no.1,127-8), or that warriors are depicted on a unique LPRIA pot from the same site (Rodwell 1974; 1988).

Cremations in Essex are found in an arc running along the border with Suffolk, south along the coast and up the Thames estuary. They are rare across an extensive tract of western central Essex within this arc (Whimster 1981,fig.52,153; Foster 1986,fig.44). Even in parts of the county where they are better represented, cremations can hardly be described as common and it is a widespread misconception to regard the rite as somehow the dominant funerary mode (*pace* Wait 1985,121). The modest size of the cemeteries reinforces this: only three cremations at both the Maldon Hall Farm and North Shoebury cemeteries, fourteen from the Stansted cemetery (some of which are early Roman) and thirty from Mucking. These are meagre figures compared with the 170 or so cremations from the (admittedly exceptional) 1st century BC cemetery of Westhampnett (West Sussex) (Fitzpatrick 1994). There is no reason to suppose that the introduction of cremation in the LPRIA meant the abandonment of those existing funerary rites that have left no trace in the archaeological record. Indeed the modest size of the Essex cemeteries compels one to consider the possibility that cremation was a rite confined to certain elements of society, perhaps initially refugees from the Gallic Wars and their aftermath. The contribution of a Gaulish refugee element is most apparent in warrior burials like Great Braxted (Whimster 1977,323; 1981,141,146). Cremation may not have become widespread until the early Roman period, when its ascendancy was confirmed by cremating Roman newcomers. This seems to have been the case at King Harry Lane (Hertfordshire), where the incidence of cremation increased towards AD 43 and where most of the graves were apparently post-conquest (Stead and Rigby 1989; Fitzpatrick 1991b,326).

Inhumation Cemeteries In those counties where cremation was practised in the century or so before AD 43, inhumations are occasionally present. At King Harry Lane (Hertfordshire) there were seventeen inhumations and 455 cremations in a cemetery dated c.AD 1-60 (Stead and Rigby 1989,80,204,207). The ratio of inhumation to cremation was about 1:30 and this may have been typical of neighbouring counties.

Since 1978 details of two inhumation cemeteries have emerged in Essex, on the north bank of the Thames at Mucking (Wilkinson 1988,58; Going 1993,19) and - only 8 km to the west - at Ardale School (Wilkinson 1988,37-8,58,fig.64 no.1; Thompson 1988). Both had much in common. Each consisted of only eight graves, lying outside a settlement perimeter ditch but not in an enclosure of its own. Few burials had grave goods. Apart from some scraps of burnt human bone in the upper fill of a grave at Ardale, there were no cremation burials in either cemetery. At Mucking the bodies were coffined, with legs flexed. No trace of coffins (or indeed of corpses) had survived at Ardale. There the floor of one grave had been turfed and another turf blanket apparently overlay the body. The Ardale cemetery was dated to the early 1st century AD but it is not yet clear when inhumation first appeared in the LPRIA.

Late Pre-Roman Iron Age Ritual and Temples

Ironwork Hoards and Their Significance Iron is rare in Essex in the Iron Age and only becomes common towards the end of the period, a pattern typical of much of the country (Manning 1972,239-40). The largest single find is the spectacular hoard of twenty-three artefacts from the Town Mead at Waltham Abbey (Fig. 7), a deposit recovered from a former course of the river Lea in 1967. Many of the tools illustrate the craft of the blacksmith, *par excellence* the tongs (the largest collection of their period from the country), and the anvils, hammers and poker. Carpentry tools are also represented. The find is dated c.25 BC-AD 43 on the basis of a sword fragment and linch pin. The riverine context of the find and the deliberate bending of so many of the tools leave no doubt that the hoard had been cast in the waters of the river Lea as a ritual offering (Manning 1972,231; Lang and Williams 1975,202 for a metallurgical examination of the sword; Manning 1980; 1985; Longworth 1985,59 no.77 and Merrifield 1987,pl.8 for photographs).

Ironwork hoards are also found on dry land contexts. The Waltham Abbey hoard itself reminds one of the three slices or pokers from Witham, a hoard of tools used by blacksmiths to manipulate fuel in the fire. So far from being grave goods from an inhumation cemetery, the Witham slices can more reasonably be seen as another hoard (Sealey 1985,103-4; Rodwell 1993,10,31-2,98,fig.51).

Another ironwork hoard was found at Springfield Lyons. There a LPRIA sword and its scabbard had been buried in a pit, central to the abandoned late Bronze Age enclosure; other ironwork present may have been a spear. The sword had been bent into an almost oval shape (Stead 1987).

N. R. Brown and C. J. Ingle tell me that a fourth ironwork hoard was excavated at Orsett "Cock" (Toller 1980 and Rodwell 1975 for the site). It consisted of six spears buried in the innermost ditch of a triple-ditched enclosure constructed on the eve of the Roman invasion. A seventh spear was found nearby in the adjacent ditch. The typological variety of the spears suggests a set belonging to an individual warrior. Coupled with its secure date, this

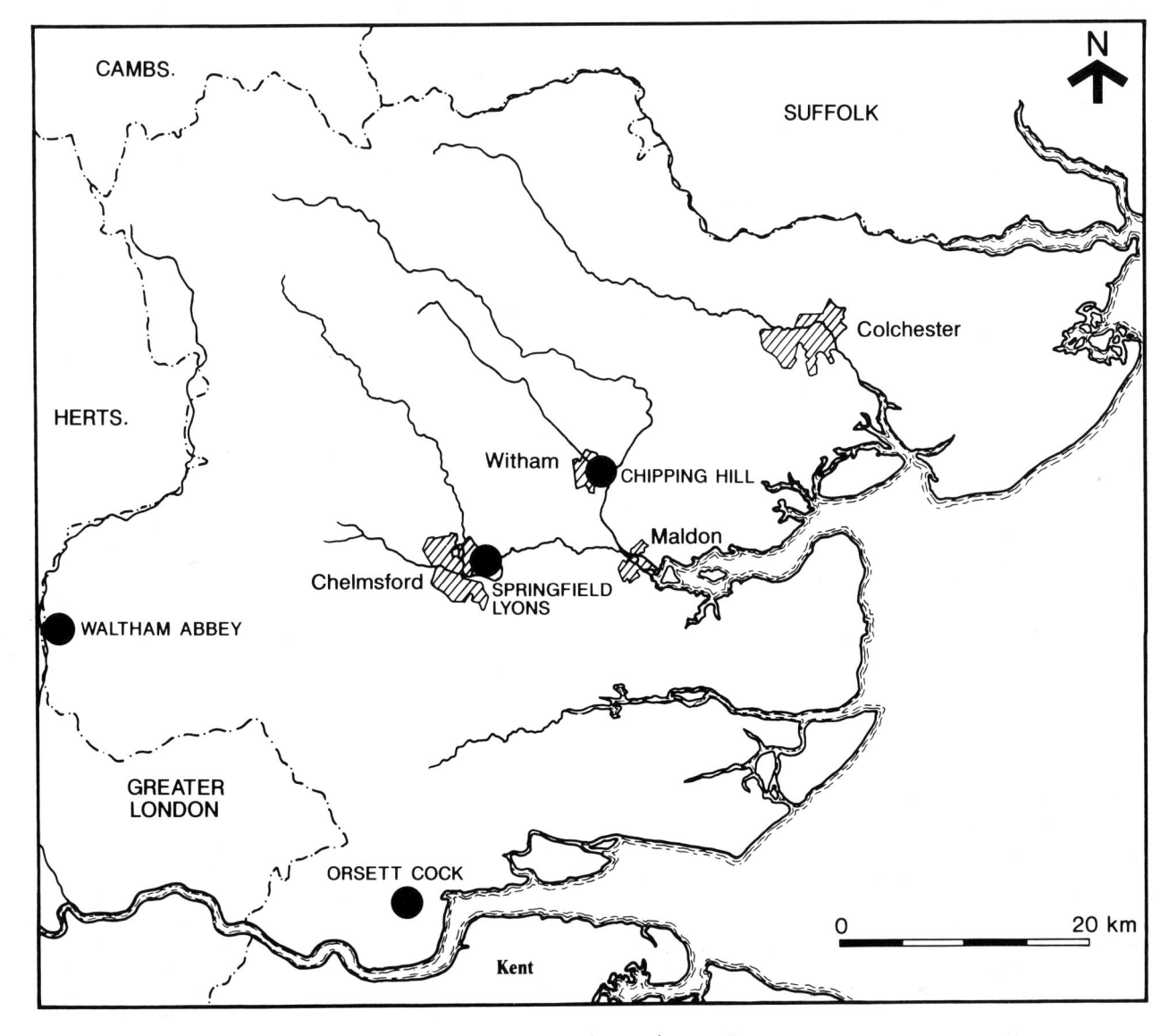

Fig. 7 Ironwork hoards in prehistoric Essex

range of form will make the published hoard an important fixed point in the archaeology of Iron Age weaponry.

The ironwork hoards of prehistoric Essex have been widely overlooked and the implications deserve examination. Haselgrove (1989d,6) and Hingley (1991,105) both wonder if the known distribution of the iron currency bars mentioned by Caesar (*De Bello Gallico* 5.12) had been influenced by regional patterns of hoarding. Their absence from Essex (where the hoarding of iron *was* practised) suggests not: it would seem that in this instance Caesar was not describing a feature of south-eastern England, and that currency bars were indeed a phenomenon confined to Wessex, the West Country and the south Midlands. The ritual character of the Waltham Abbey hoard from the river Lea is manifest: although this ceremonial deposition of metalwork in water is familiar to prehistorians, there has been some reluctance to concede this of ironwork hoards from other contexts, and so the Springfield Lyons cache with its bent sword is a timely reminder that there are indeed dry land ritual hoards of metalwork. One suspects the same of the spear hoard from the ditch of the Orsett enclosure, bearing in mind how the weapon was especially favoured for Iron Age deposition in the Thames (Fitzpatrick 1984,179-80), and that many of the currency bar hoards were buried in protective rituals at the perimeters of settlements (Hingley 1991,107,109-10). Waltham Abbey shows that ironworking tools were regarded as suitable for ceremonial discards and suggests that the apparent hoard of blacksmithing artefacts from Witham may likewise have been ritual.

Late Pre-Roman Iron Age Religious Activity at Ivy Chimneys The importance of water offerings in prehistory has already been noted. At Ivy Chimneys in Witham, a LPRIA palisade enclosed marshland on the site of the subsequent Roman temple and pond, an operation that looks like the erection of an enclosure around a wet place revered as holy (Turner 1982,4-6).

The Late Pre-Roman Iron Age Temple at Harlow The most striking evidence for the religious life of the period comes from Harlow. On a low hill south of the river Stort stood a round house which was the focus of cult offerings from c.50 BC until the Roman invasion and later. Pottery from the gully of this shrine is a mixture of MPRIA and Belgic wares.

R. W. Bartlett tells me that some 900 Iron Age coins have been recovered from a buried LPRIA and early Roman soil on the site. This is the largest tally from an *excavated* Iron Age sanctuary in Britain; many are in mint condition. The earliest are Gallo-Belgic E gold staters minted in the Gallic wars; most of the remainder are bronze issues of Cunobelinus. Coins of Tasciovanus and his associates are also present in quantity, showing the temple lay in territory that was Catuvellaunian, not Trinovantian. But the

Trinovantes cannot have been far away and the temple was evidently sited on the frontier, as were a significant number of other Iron Age shrines (Wait 1985,176; Bradley 1987,359-61). Pilgrims from further afield are attested by coins of the Iceni, Corieltauvi and Durotriges. The ritual deposition of coins at sacred sites is the clearest contextual archaeological evidence for the function of Celtic coins. Other offerings included brooches, iron tools, shield bindings and thin iron strips. Lamb was evidently in demand for sacrifice at Harlow because more than 80% of the beasts present in the faunal remains were lambs, slaughtered between six and nine months of age, in the autumn. A predilection for sheep is repeated at the Iron Age temple on Hayling Island (Hampshire) (Downey et al. 1980,294; King and Soffe 1994,115). The Roman conquest saw no immediate interruption of these rites and the hill remained a holy place until late antiquity (Allen 1965; 1968; 1969; France and Gobel 1985; Bartlett 1988a; 1988b; Haselgrove 1987,383-97; 1989c).

A fresh look at the 1970-71 excavations at Holbrooks (Conlon 1973), 500 m north-east of the Harlow temple, suggests the site did not represent workshops where artisans produced offerings for the nearby temple. Instead it too may have been a shrine where offerings were made and - to judge by the coin list - where activity began earlier than at the main temple. There is the exciting possibility that the Harlow complex is the first instance in Britain of the extensive rural sanctuaries known in Gaul (Fitzpatrick 1985,52; Haselgrove 1987,397-8).

Late Pre-Roman Iron Age Domestic Architecture
In the LPRIA the hitherto ubiquitous round house is replaced by structures of rectangular plan which leave less evidence in the ground because their construction was based on solid timber cills or other structural members which sometimes rested directly on the ground without foundations (Rodwell 1978). Understandably therefore, few rectangular houses of the LPRIA have been reported because they are so vulnerable to plough damage. Most of the recent evidence has come from Kelvedon. There a room 4 x 3 m wide was linked to another by a passageway 0.7 m wide. Another building - of unknown length - was 3.75 m wide (Eddy and Turner 1982,8-9). The most ambitious of the Kelvedon rectangular houses stood in an enclosure and was 21 m long and 5 m wide, with tapering ends (Rodwell 1988,15,20-1,132-3). But one building that should be removed from the corpus of Iron Age rectangular houses is a structure from Sheepen at Colchester, now recognised as a Roman architectural form complete with verandah (Hawkes and Hull 1947,89-91,pl.9 explained by Niblett 1985,24 *pace* Rodwell 1978,34,38).

The few round houses erected in the early Roman period have every appearance of marginal buildings that represented a quaint backward tradition kept alive by the more conservative elements in society (Drury 1978b,76). A building that bridges the gap between the classic MPRIA round house and those of Roman date was excavated at the Doucecroft site in Kelvedon. With a diameter of c.7 m, it is half the size of the largest houses at Little Waltham (Drury 1978a,14). The wall trench consisted of a series of discontinuous oval or rectangular pits with steep sides and flat bottoms. One presumes the spaces between the wall trenches were filled with wattle and daub. The inside of the house and the area immediately outside was cobbled with pebbles. A construction date in the early 1st century AD was suggested (Clarke 1988,21,fig.12,37).

What does need emphasis is the extent to which the round house tradition was supplanted in the LPRIA by rectangular architecture. In Roman Essex round houses are rare, but this is not the case with most of lowland Britain, where they remained common in rural areas throughout the 1st and 2nd centuries AD (Hingley 1989,31-5).

Late Pre-Roman Iron Age Overseas Trade
Trade between Britain and the Roman world intensified in the LPRIA and Essex was one of the regions in which this exchange was conspicuous (Sealey 1981). After Caesar, the imports of Italian wine already attested by the Dressel 1 amphoras at Stansted and Heybridge continued; Fitzpatrick (1985a,fig.4,324-5) has a gazetteer and map. These sturdy pots were well-suited to secondary use and this accounts for their presence in quantity on sites founded even after the c.10 BC terminal date of the form, as at Colchester Sheepen (Sealey 1985,101-8). This also goes some way to explain why such amphoras are seldom found in settlement contexts contemporary with the form, i.e. earlier than c.10 BC. A possible exception is a long rectangular house at Kelvedon (see above), occupied in the period c.50-1 BC. One of the sources of the wealth of this household may have been marine salt, to judge by the number of briquetage sherds there (Rodwell 1988,15,20-1,81-2,101,fig.84 no.156,132-3). The few LPRIA imports found on the Red Hills themselves show that the wealth generated by salt was seldom enjoyed where it was actually produced. Towards the end of the 1st century BC, Italian wine was joined in Essex by vintages from the Roman provinces: since 1978 it has emerged that Catalan wine from Roman Spain was imported. It is attested at Thaxted in the 1st century BC (Williams 1981,130; Sealey 1985,149) and at Colchester Stanway, in a grave dated c.AD 20-30.

A perplexing gap in the Essex LPRIA is the dearth of stratified settlement material with imported Roman crockery for the period centred on c.10 BC-AD 5, the years between the Lexden Tumulus and the foundation of the Colchester Sheepen site. Essex has nothing comparable to the Hertfordshire assemblages from Puckeridge-Braughing (Partridge 1980; 1981; Potter and Trow 1988). Belgic pottery cannot be so closely dated that we could identify deposits of that date without Roman imports; if they are absent, such contexts might easily escape recognition altogether. This interlude could be explained by the reign of Dubnovellaunos, a king whose coinage has negligible Roman influence and who (by implication) may have discouraged dealings with the Mediterranean world (Allen 1944,31; Haselgrove 1987,203).

But in the 1st century AD - in the reign of Cunobelinus - trade with Rome reached a new apogee. Nowhere is this more apparent than in the rich grave of c.AD 20-30 from Stanway (see above), which V. A. Rigby tells me has the largest collection of imported Iron Age pottery in the country (Crummy 1992,3). Since 1978 it has emerged that the sources of the table crockery imported by prehistoric Essex included an unlocated industry in central Gaul making flagons, platters and lid-seated jars (Tyers 1981; Rigby and Freestone 1983; 1986; Stead and Rigby 1989,117-21).

Important new evidence for how overseas trade was conducted takes the form of a ship on two bronze coins minted at Camulodunum early in the reign of Cunobelinus. The first was discovered at Canterbury (Muckleroy et al. 1978); another was retrieved from the river Colne at Colchester in 1980, at c.TL 988 261. Its ship is from a different die to that of the Canterbury coin (Pl.1) (McGrail 1990,43-5). The craft on these coins is a tall vessel with steep sides. There is a single mast and a steering oar. Its flat keel extends beyond the stem-post in a forefoot. A die-cutter at Colchester must have seen such craft on the river Colne. Ships of this kind correspond to those built by the Gauls on the Channel coast and described by Caesar seventy-five years earlier (*De Bello Gallico* 3.13-15 *pace* Marsden 1990,70-1). Evidently this tradition of naval architecture survived the Gallic Wars and continued to play a part in contact between Britain and the mainland of Europe; the flat bottoms of such ships will have made them well suited for the shallow waters of the Essex estuaries. There are no other merchant ships on coins of this period, in or beyond the Roman world (Casson 1975,15) and so the vessel on the coinage of Cunobelinus is of major significance for European maritime history.

Late Pre-Roman Iron Age Salt Production and the Coastline
The Red Hills of the modern Essex coastline and its hinterland were the mounds of red earth that mark the sites of Iron Age and Roman period salt extraction. Excavation shows the hills abound in fired clay equipment - briquetage - used for the evaporation of sea water to produce the salt.

A hill in operation from the LPRIA until the early Roman period was excavated by de Brisay (1978) at Peldon, Red Hill 117. A series of three clay lined tanks were presumably filled with sea water at high tide and served as reservoirs to fill the actual briquetage evaporation pans. Nearby was a hearth, which had seen service for a protracted length of time. Impressions in the wall showed it had taken the firebars that supported the evaporation pans. There was a dearth of other finds, but Belgic pottery showed the hill had been active before the Roman invasion. Four bronze coins of Cunobelinus - the first Iron Age coins from an Essex Red Hill - have been reported from another hill on the Blackwater estuary at Langenhoe (Sealey 1995,65,71,73).

The Red Hill phenomenon was reviewed by Rodwell (1979), who emphasised the differences in briquetage assemblages from the north of the county and from the Canvey Island region. But the most significant contribution to the whole topic is the magisterial survey by the *Colchester Archaeological Group* (Fawn et al. 1990), a worthy successor to the work of the Red Hills Exploration Committee of the early 20th century. This monograph gives details of over 300 Red Hills in the county. Although many are of Roman date, it is equally clear that many others have Iron Age origins and that the enigmatic process that generated the red earth itself was an innovation of the LPRIA. The number of Red Hills in some parts of the county is large enough to allow the outline of the coast in antiquity to be established. Just how different it could be is most immediately obvious in the Dengie peninsula where a line of hills stands several kilometres inland parallel to the modern shore. More Red Hills have been reported since the *Colchester Archaeological Group* survey (Eddy 1989).

In the Bronze and Iron Ages there was a marine transgression that prevented settlement on what is now the foreshore and its environs. But activity on the coastline is not only indicated by the Red Hills, but by wooden structures representing landing stages and trackways, as well as hurdle fences washed there from elsewhere by accident. The most striking Iron Age feature is a hurdle footbridge that spanned a creek in the Blackwater estuary at the Stumble (Wilkinson and Murphy 1995,132,150-2,164-5).

Late Pre-Roman Iron Age Art
Essex is not a county rich in decorated metalwork of Iron Age date and little has emerged in recent years to redress the situation, although what has come to light is not without interest.

From Bocking comes a horse brooch, the product of a workshop in the West of England; a copper-alloy bridle-bit from Fingringhoe represents another item of horse harness. Both may belong to the 1st century AD (Sealey 1991,1-3,6-8). A linch pin in Saffron Walden Museum may also be assigned to the end of the period (Major 1987a). The *two* mirrors from Rivenhall have been published (Lloyd-Morgan 1993), with scientific analyses of the alloys of others from the county (Northover 1993). Dr I. M. Stead and V. A. Rigby kindly drew my attention to another fragmentary mirror, found at Colchester in 1974 (but not acquired by the British Museum until 1986). It was a chance find at c.TM 002 244 in Hyderabad Barracks; nothing is known of its context or associations. The handle is remarkable for its Roman inspiration.

The most interesting addition to the art of the period is a unique stamped pottery bowl from Kelvedon, made on the eve of the Roman invasion. Around the rim ran a series of tiny rectangular panels decorated in relief, apparently showing a procession. The most complete panel shows a man on horseback holding a shield and shepherd's crook; the spiky hair on this and other figures from the pot is explained by the practice among the Gauls of treating the hair with lime (Powell 1980,65-6). This is of some interest because limed hair is apparently not attested on Iron Age coins from Britain (Allen 1958,55-6) and the Kelvedon warrior is apparently the clearest evidence of this practice in Britain. The prototypes of the Kelvedon bowl were presumably bronze vessels decorated with scenes in relief, but no such vessels survive from the Essex Iron Age and the Kelvedon bowl is a tantalizing glimpse of what has been lost (Rodwell 1974; 1988).

Late Pre-Roman Iron Age Coinage
In the last quarter of the 1st century BC the coins circulating in Essex included inscribed issues bearing the names of Tasciovanus, Addedomaros and Dubnovellaunos. Tasciovanus is regarded as king of the Hertfordshire Catuvellauni and his home territory only encroached on the eastern border of Essex, most conspicuously at the Harlow temple site; his temporary seizure of Camulodunum is described below. Addedomaros was apparently a contemporary of Tasciovanus and was followed by Dubnovellaunos. The inherent difficulties of establishing a precise chronology on the basis of the limited evidence available (Haselgrove 1993a,44) preclude a more detailed assessment of their relationships here and the lack of consensus among scholarship anyway makes discussion of the period difficult within the constraints of a review on this scale.

But the discoveries and research that will eventually unravel these difficulties continue to accumulate. Dr R. F. Bland and N. P. Wickenden tell me that a hoard of two gold staters of Addedomaros was discovered at TL 898 099 in Little Totham parish in 1993. Analytical work on the metallurgy of the coins holds out still more hope of progress. It has been established that the gold staters of Addedomaros are typically 39-41% gold, not much different to those of Tasciovanus although of a slightly higher weight (Cowell 1992,225). Knowledge of the composition of the coins is of particular significance when one turns to Dubnovellaunos, a king whose coins are found on both sides of the Thames estuary. Traditionally he has been seen as a dynast who conquered Essex from a homeland in north-east Kent (Allen 1944,23,30-2). Rodwell (1976,261-3) emphasised the differences between the Kent and Essex coins; he proposed two contemporaries bearing the same name, a challenging view that has divided informed opinion. But analytical work on the coinage shows an identical composition for the later debased issues of 39-40% gold on both sides of the Thames (Cowell 1992,230), suggesting that we are in fact dealing with only one Dubnovellaunos.

The Reign of Cunobelinus
The reign of Cunobelinus c.AD 10-40 was the culmination of Essex prehistory. His was a territorial state ruled by an hereditary monarchy with its own coinage, enjoying diplomatic and trading links with the Roman world.

But was he Trinovantian or Catuvellaunian? The crucial text is Cassius Dio (60.20.1), where the Roman invasion of Britain is described. P. J. Crummy invited E. W. Black to translate the passage with an eye to resolving the problem; the outcome establishes that Cunobelinus and his dynasty were Catuvellaunian: "*Plautius...first defeated Caratacus and then Togodumnus, the sons of Cunobelinus, since he himself was dead. When they had fled, he* [Plautius] *won over by agreement a section of the Bodounni whom they had ruled although they* [Caratacus and Togodumnus] *were Catuvellauni*" (Hawkes and Crummy 1995,173). As the gist of this translation is uncontroversial (Hind 1989,7) it is not immediately obvious why students of the period should have made the relationship between Cunobelinus and Tasciovanus such an intractable problem (*pace* Fitzpatrick 1985b,62). Coin legends in which Cunobelinus declares himself son of Tasciovanus, king of the Hertfordshire Catuvellauni, may indeed therefore be taken at face value. His reign saw the conquest of the Essex Trinovantes by the Catuvellauni; claims that Cunobelinus was Trinovantian may be discounted (*pace* Rodwell 1976,265-77; Kent 1978,56,58 n.11). The geographical distribution of his coin legends confirms this. Those proclaiming his descent from Tasciovanus are rare in east and south Essex; they concentrate instead in the more westerly parts of his kingdom, where Tasciovanus had ruled before him and where it was therefore appropriate to declare his ancestry. Such coins would have been an affront to the Trinovantes; among them, the coins of Cunobelinus usually omit any reference to his origins. This was one of the major conclusions of the report on the Harlow temple coins (Allen 1965,4; 1968,4). The picture has subsequently been confirmed by other sites - in Hertfordshire - where coins with the sole name Cunobelinus are outnumbered by those in which his father is named alongside him (Goodburn 1981,128; 1986,98; Haselgrove 1988,29).

The conquest of the Trinovantes marks the start of his reign. One says this because the earliest of the Cunobelinus gold staters - the rare *biga* series - are confined to Essex, with one example from the Cambridge region and a contemporary forgery from the Maidstone region of Kent (Allen 1975,3 n.1,13,16,19; Haselgrove 1984,131-2). The early silver and bronze coins have a similar, easterly distribution (Rodwell 1976,268,figs 32-4). When Cunobelinus came to power (let alone exactly how) is unclear; it is important to remember that the traditional date of c.AD 10 is only an estimate (Fitzpatrick 1986,36). From start to finish most of the coinage of this energetic figure was issued from Camulodunum; it is the only mint name to feature on his coins. Coin moulds from

Pl.1 Bronze coin of Cunobelinus with a ship found at Colchester. Scale: enlarged x 3.5 (Photograph: Colchester Museum)

Verulamium assigned to the reign of Cunobelinus show there was a mint there as well (Frere 1983,3,30-2) but it was subordinate to Camulodunum (no coin of Cunobelinus in any metal ever mentions Verulamium) and its output presumably concentrated on those types that name him the son of Tasciovanus (Allen 1968,4). Once Cunobelinus had secured a hold over the Trinovantes in Essex, he turned his attention west and united his new conquests with the old kingdom of his father. Thus ended a period of turmoil among the Catuvellauni that can be traced back to the last years of Tasciovanus, when a perplexing number of people issued coinages either in association with him (ANDOCO, DIAS and SEGO), or apparently independently (RUES) (Allen 1968,3-4; Van Arsdell 1989,21-3). Cunobelinus put an end to this confusion: with the possible exception of SEGO, these over-mighty subjects (if such they were), disappeared from the scene.

Territorial expansion followed elsewhere and it is clear from the distribution of his coins that the kingdom of Cunobelinus eventually covered much of south-eastern England (Sellwood 1984,figs 13.5-6). Research in East Anglia has been able to suggest where the divide between the Iceni and the Catuvellauni-Trinovantes was located (Martin 1988,68-72; Moore *et al.* 1988,12; Gregory 1991,200-1). At Burgh-by-Woodbridge (Suffolk), a c.AD 15-25 destruction horizon was followed by the replacement of the local pre-Belgic pottery traditions with wares drawn from Colchester, and one may be forgiven for linking this with territorial expansion driven by Cunobelinus (Martin 1988,72). The resources needed to trade with Rome were a factor behind this aggression (Haselgrove 1989d,15).

Coinage also sheds light on the organisation of the kingdom. Towards the end of his reign, Cunobelinus allowed his son Adminius to issue coins in Kent. This late experiment in devolution (if such it was) ended in tears with the flight of Adminius to Gaius in AD 39/40 (Allen 1976b; Nash 1982). Other subordinates or client kings (none is described as his son) feature fleetingly on the coinage of Cunobelinus in the legends SE, AGR and SOLIDV (Mays 1992). SE is found on the two bronze coins showing a ship (see above); one wonders if this is our last glimpse of the SEGO associated with Tasciovanus. The legend AGR found on a gold and a silver coin is still more obscure, but neither SE or AGR are mint names because both are found on coins issued at Camulodunum. The name SOLIDV found on a silver coin of Cunobelinus is also presumably the name of a person, rather than a mint. All these legends are rare and there is little sign that Cunobelinus readily and willingly shared power with others; attempts to see

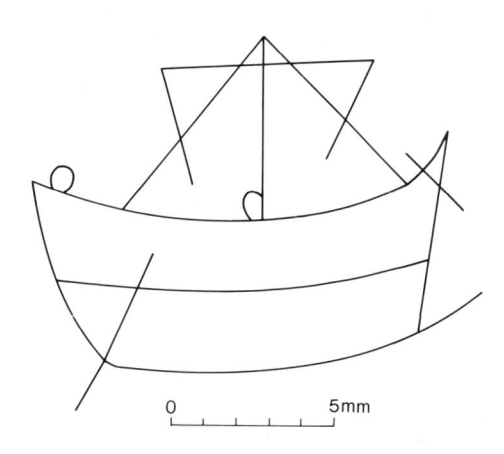

Fig.8 An interpretation of the ship on a bronze coin of Cunobelinus from Canterbury

him as some kind of paramount chief might be mistaken (*pace* Haselgrove 1989d,18).

It will be clear by now how important the numismatic evidence is as source material for the reign of Cunobelinus; any account of the coinage would be incomplete without a glance at some of the more technical research that underpins its study. Scheers (1992,34,pl.2 no.11) has identified new Roman numismatic prototypes for some of the types; the depiction of Neptune is of particular interest, because it was inspired by a type found on the coinage of Gaius and Claudius, allowing sharper definition of a demonstrably late element in the coinage. Nor has the metallurgy of the coins been neglected. Analysis shows that the content of the silver coins is generally as high as 96% silver (Northover 1992,255,257), but that in the gold coins there is typically only 41% gold. This gold standard of about 40% was reached in the late 1st century BC by his predecessors and maintained by Cunobelinus throughout his long reign (Cowell 1992,225-6,fig.9,232). His success (and that of his immediate predecessors) in keeping to this gold standard halted the progressive debasement to which the various Celtic coinages of Britain had been prone. It was a significant achievement, particularly in the light of the export of British gold and silver to the Roman world reported by Strabo (4.5.2), with all the repercussions these exports may have had on insular jewellery in the precious metals (Sealey 1979). The movement of gold and silver overseas in the LPRIA effectively rules out the possibility that imported Roman bullion and coinage was the source of the metal in the British coinages (*pace* Northover 1992,249,253,255,257; Haselgrove 1993a,45 n.57,61). There are few coin hoards of Cunobelinus but two have come to light since 1978. Five gold staters were found at Chippenham (Cambridgeshire) in 1981 (Burnett 1986,1,3) and Dr A. M. Burnett tells me that a hoard of 31 was discovered at Somerton (Suffolk) in 1990. The size of the latter hoard has prompted a fresh look at the comprehensive survey of the gold coinage by Allen (1975).

What eventually became the royal seat of Cunobelinus at Colchester is first recorded on some rare gold issues of Tasciovanus, struck early in his reign c.15 BC. A bronze coin of the same king with the legend *camlv*, discovered at Great Canfield, now shows that his coins with a Colchester mint mark were not confined to gold (Eddy and Priddy 1982,35,37). Another of his bronze coins, with the possible legend *camo* was excavated at Baldock (Hertfordshire) (Goodburn 1986,92 no.14,97). The rarity of these issues is a reminder that the seizure of Colchester by Tasciovanus was a short-lived episode of his reign (Allen 1944,15; Hawkes and Crummy 1995,92-3). Where the father failed, the son succeeded and under Cunobelinus the capital of the rejuvenated Catuvellauni was moved to Camulodunum. Its ascendancy may not be unconnected with the eclipse of the Braughing-Puckeridge (Hertfordshire) settlement in the 1st century AD (Haselgrove 1988,27). The archaeology of Camulodunum itself is now fully accessible in the monumental publication of the entire dyke system, a project anticipated fifty years ago (Hawkes and Crummy 1995).

Agriculture in Iron Age Essex

Livestock Husbandry

The acidic soil conditions of so many Iron Age sites in Essex have not lent themselves to the preservation of bone. Often only teeth have survived, and faunal reports can do little more than record the presence of the major domesticates: we are in no position to write a survey of Iron Age animal husbandry in the county. But three sites with substantial bone assemblages - Wendens Ambo, Nazeingbury and Birchanger - have been published since 1978. It emerged at MPRIA Wendens Ambo that although sheep outnumbered cattle, it was the latter that were the major source of meat (Halstead 1982a,49). What may have been a more typically mixed regime obtained at LPRIA Nazeingbury. There are details in Table 1 (Huggins 1979,108). Birchanger (Table 2) tells much the same story; the faunal remains came from MPRIA, LPRIA and early Roman contexts (Bedwin 1994).

cattle	horse	sheep	pig	deer	dog
19	5	20	5	1	1

Table 1. The Animal Population at Nazeingbury (quantified by minimum number of animals)

cattle	horse	sheep	pig	dog	bird
26.3 %	2 %	48.1 %	19 %	4.4 %	0.2 %

Table 2. The Animal Population at Birchanger (quantified by bone count by species)

The poverty of faunal remains makes the distribution map of triangular Iron Age loom weights prepared by Major (1983,fig.7) all the more useful because it indicates parts of the county where sheep management was important. There is a concentration in the Orsett region at the south, with many of the remaining loom weights lying on or near the coast as well, or at the heads of estuaries. Four more from Red Hill 147 at Great Wigborough reinforce the picture (Sealey 1995,69-71). The distribution has an uncanny affinity with the location of sheep pasture as reported in the Domesday survey (Darby 1971,fig.63) and there is a real possibility that the Essex salt marshes supported a significant sheep population in later prehistory (Wilkinson and Murphy 1995,165; Sealey 1995,71). Sheep were also kept on inland pastures and one notes the presence of a loom weight at Witham Chipping Hill, where half the animal bones from the same MPRIA context were sheep (Major 1993; Bedwin 1993,111).

Cereal Cultivation

A large dump of cereals from Rectory Road at Orsett consisted of spelt wheat. They had been stored in a circular pit - a reminder that not all grain in Essex was housed above ground in four-post granaries. Associated pottery was EPRIA (Wilkinson 1988,11,13 for the pit; Hamilton 1988,78,fig.68 nos 2 and 4-6 for the pottery; Murphy 1988,99-100 for the grain). Another EPRIA group from Orsett (from the causewayed camp site) had a quite different composition: there, barley outnumbered emmer wheat by about 4:1 (Barrett 1978,280,fig.40 nos 40-7 for the pottery; Hubbard 1978 for the grain). At Asheldham Camp, a MPRIA cache of the wheats spelt and emmer (mainly), and some barley, with oats and rye present in small quantities (as weeds ?) had a more mixed composition. Storage had been above ground in pottery jars and wooden barrels from a granary (Bedwin 1991,24 for the granary; Brown 1991a,28 for the pottery; Murphy 1991a for the grain and barrels). At MPRIA Wendens Ambo, wheat (1750 grains) was dominant, with barley significant (989 grains) and oats in a minority (72 grains) (Jones *et al.* 1982,50).

There are no significant finds of LPRIA grain but the briquetage of the Red Hills is tempered with vegetable matter and provides further source material for agricultural practice in Iron Age Essex. The temper itself is crop-processing waste from cereal cultivation and includes the occasional grain of corn (de Brisay 1978,54-5). The main cereal present is spelt, with some emmer and bread wheat, and with hulled barley and oats in a minority (Murphy 1991b,337; Wilkinson and Murphy 1995,180-1). The chaff and cereal waste taken to the Red Hills for temper may also have provided some of the fuel for the surface bonfire kilns in which briquetage was produced; one has a glimpse here of how these salterns were integrated with the agrarian economy behind the coastline.

The cultivation of grain in Iron Age Essex was hardly mentioned at the 1978 conference, so it is gratifying to note the data that has become available since then, although the diversity of the cereal caches described is such that it would be premature to attempt to identify regional patterns or chronological trends. Unravelling such trends may be more difficult than might appear at first because of the different roles of different cereals: it is quite possible that the grain deposits from EPRIA Orsett represent one for bread (the Rectory Road wheat) and another for malting (the causewayed camp barley).

Aspects of Farming Practice
An interesting light on farming practice has been cast by excavations at Birchanger. A number of EPRIA and MPRIA pits there had been filled with decaying organic matter covered by spreads of soil to keep down the smell and flies. Periodically they were dug out and the contents presumably used as manure; it seems reasonable to regard them as compost heaps (Medlycott 1994,28,figs 8-10,44).

The sea can be harvested as well as the land: LPRIA North Shoebury has furnished evidence for the gathering of oysters, mussels and cockles from the nearby coast (Wilkinson and Murphy 1986,192; Wymer and Brown 1995, 142).

Priorities for Future Work
The pace at which the Red Hills are disappearing is alarming but their destruction is not matched by any commensurate fieldwork programme and this should be rectified at the earliest opportunity. Attention should also be devoted to the archaeology of the opening centuries of the period and to the rectangular houses - with their settlements - found in the county on the eve of the Roman invasion.

Acknowledgements
I am indebted to the following for advice and help: M. Atkinson, R. W. Bartlett, Dr O. R. Bedwin, P. Bennett, P. J. Berridge, E. W. Black, H. Brooks, D. W. Bradbury, D. G. Buckley, Dr A. M. Burnett, J. P. C. Catton, P. J. Crummy, N. R. Brown, S. E. M. Dalloe, P. J. Drury, C. J. Going, Dr P. A. Greenwood, R. Havis, J. J. Heath, J. E. C. Herbert, C. J. Ingle, L. Pole, V. A. Rigby, Dr W. J. Rodwell, Dr I. M. Stead, R. D. Van Arsdell, C. R. Wallace, S. P. Wallis, N. P. Wickenden, M. J. Winter and Dr J. J. Wymer. Dr O. R. Bedwin and N. R. Brown made many helpful amendments to an early draft of this paper. I am grateful to Julia S. Grant for her help and companionship on site visits and to Dr A. P. Fitzpatrick for allowing me to read his MS on Iron Age cremation.

Bibliography
Adkins, P. C. *et al.* 1986. "Rook Hall". In D. A. Priddy (ed.) "Work of the Essex County Council Archaeology Section 1983-84" *Essex Archaeol. Hist.*, 16 for 1984-85, 94-9
Alexander, J. A. *et al.* 1979. "Ambresbury Banks, an Iron Age camp in Epping Forest, Essex" *Essex Archaeol. Hist.*, 10 for 1978, 189-205
Allen, D. F. 1944. "The Belgic dynasties of Britain and their coins" *Archaeologia*, 90, 1-46
Allen, D. F. 1958. "Belgic coins as illustrations of life in the late pre-Roman Iron Age of Britain" *Proc. Prehist. Soc.*, 24, 43-63
Allen, D. F. 1965. "Celtic coins from the Romano-British temple at Harlow, Essex" *Brit. Numis. J.*, 33 for 1964, 1-6
Allen, D. F. 1968. "Celtic coins from the Romano-British temple at Harlow" *Brit. Numis. J.*, 36 for 1967, 1-7
Allen, D. F. 1969. "Celtic coins from the Romano-British temple at Harlow" *Brit. Numis. J.*, 37 for 1968, 1-6
Allen, D. F. 1971. "British potin coins: a review". In D. Hill and M. Jesson (eds) *The Iron Age and Its Hill-Forts: Papers Presented to Sir Mortimer Wheeler*, 127-54. Southampton
Allen, D. F. 1975. "Cunobelin's gold" *Britannia*, 6, 1-19
Allen, D. F. 1976a. "Wealth, money and coinage in a Celtic society". In J. V. S. Megaw (ed.) *To Illustrate the Monuments: Essays on Archaeology Presented to Stuart Piggott*, 199-208. London
Allen, D. F. 1976b. "Did Adminius strike coins ?" *Britannia*, 7, 96-100
Andrews, D. D. & Priddy, D. A. 1990. "Sheering". In P. J. Gilman and A. Bennett (eds). "Work of the Essex County Council Archaeology Section, 1989" *Essex Archaeol. Hist.*, 21, 119
Barrett, J. C. 1978. "The EPRIA prehistoric pottery". In J. D. Hedges and D. G. Buckley. "Excavations at a Neolithic causewayed enclosure, Orsett, Essex, 1975" *Proc. Prehist. Soc.*, 44, 268-88
Barrett, J. C. 1980. "The pottery of the later Bronze Age in lowland England" *Proc. Prehist. Soc.*, 46, 297-319
Bartlett, R. W. 1988a. "Excavations at Harlow temple 1985-87" *Essex J.*, 23, 9-13
Bartlett, R. W. 1988b. "The Harlow Celtic temple" *Current Archaeol.*, 10, 163-6
Bayley, J. 1993. "Non-ferrous metalworking finds". In A. J. Clark *Excavations at Mucking. Vol.1: The Site Atlas. Excavations by Margaret and Tom Jones* (English Heritage Archaeological Report No.20), 34. London
Bedwin, O. R. 1991. "Asheldham Camp - an early Iron Age hill fort: the 1985 excavations" *Essex Archaeol. Hist.*, 22, 13-37
Bedwin, O. R. 1992. "Early Iron Age settlement at Maldon and the Maldon *burh*: excavations at Beacon Green 1987" *Essex Archaeol. Hist.*, 23, 10-24
Bedwin, O. R. 1993. "Animal bone". In W. J. Rodwell *The Origins and Early Development of Witham, Essex: a Study in Settlement and Fortification, Prehistoric to Medieval* (Oxbow Monograph No.26) Oxford, 111-12. Oxford
Bedwin, O. R. 1994. "Faunal remains. Human remains". In M. Medlycott, "Iron Age and Roman material from Birchanger, near Bishops Stortford; excavations at Woodside Industrial Park, 1992" *Essex Archaeol. Hist.*, 25, 43
Bradley, R. J. 1987. "Stages in the chronological development of hoards and votive deposits" *Proc. Prehist. Soc.*, 53, 351-62
Brooks, H. 1987. "The Stansted project: a report on the first year's work" *Essex J.*, 22, 43-6
Brooks, H. 1989a. "The Stansted temple" *Current Archaeol.*, 10, 322-5
Brooks, H. 1989b. "The Stansted project: a report on the second and third years' work" *Essex J.*, 24, 6-10
Brooks, H. 1993. "Fieldwalking and excavation at Stansted airport". In J. P. Gardiner (ed.) *Flatlands and Wetlands: Current Themes in East Anglian Archaeology* (East Anglian Archaeology Report No.50), 40-57. Norwich
Brooks, H. and Bedwin, O. R. 1989. *Archaeology at the Airport: the Stansted Archaeological Project 1985-89* Chelmsford
Brooks, H. and Wall, W. 1994. "The Stansted project: bashing the boulder clay in north west Essex". In M. Parker Pearson & R. T. Schadla-Hall (eds) *Looking at the Land. Archaeological Landscapes in Eastern England: Recent Work and Future Directions*, 20-3. Leicester
Brown, N. R. 1987a. "The prehistoric pottery". In N. P. Wickenden, "Prehistoric settlement and the Romano-British small town at Heybridge, Essex" *Essex Archaeol. Hist.*, 17 for 1986, 31-3
Brown, N. R. 1987b. "Hadleigh, Chapel Lane" *Essex Archaeol. Hist.*, 18, 88-91
Brown, N. R. 1988. "A late Bronze Age enclosure at Lofts Farm, Essex" *Proc. Prehist. Soc.*, 54, 249-302
Brown, N. R. 1991a. "Prehistoric pottery". In O. R. Bedwin. "Asheldham Camp - an early Iron Age hill fort: the 1985 excavations" *Essex Archaeol. Hist.*, 22, 27-8
Brown, N. R. 1991b. "Middle Iron Age decorated pottery around the Thames estuary" *Essex Archaeol. Hist.*, 22, 165-6
Brown, N. R. 1992. "Prehistoric pottery". In O. R. Bedwin. "Early Iron Age settlement at Maldon and the Maldon *burh*: excavations at Beacon Green 1987" *Essex Archaeol. Hist.*, 23, 15-18
Brown, N. R. 1994. "Early and middle Iron Age pottery". In M. Medlycott. "Iron Age and Roman material from Birchanger, near Bishops Stortford: excavations at Woodside Industrial Park, 1992" *Essex Archaeol. Hist.*, 25, 34-9
Brown, P. M. 1985. "The late Iron Age hoard from Lofts Farm" *Essex J.*, 20, 42-5
Brunt, P. A. and Moore, J. M. 1988. *Res Gestae Divi Augusti: the Achievements of the Divine Augustus* Oxford
Buckley, D. G. *et al.* 1987. *Excavations at Woodham Walter and an Assessment of Essex Enclosures* (East Anglian Archaeology Report No.33) Chelmsford

Burgess, C. B. 1979. "A find from Boyton, Suffolk, and the end of the Bronze Age in Britain and Ireland". In C. B. Burgess and D. G. Coombs (eds) *Bronze Age Hoards: Some Finds Old and New* (British Archaeological Reports, British Series No.67), 269-82. Oxford

Burgess, C. B. and Coombs, D. G. 1979. "Preface". In C. B. Burgess and D. G. Coombs (eds) *Bronze Age Hoards: Some Finds Old and New* (British Archaeological Reports, British Series No.67), i-vii. Oxford

Burnett, A. M. 1986. "Chippenham, near Ely, Cambs: 4 Roman aurei and 37 denarii to AD 41; and (?) 5 staters of Cunobelin". In A. M. Burnett and R. F. Bland (eds) *Coin Hoards from Roman Britain. Vol.VI* (British Museum Occasional Paper No.58), 1-3. London

Burnett, A.M. 1995. "Somerton, Suffolk, treasure trove", *Brit. Numis. J.*, 64, 127-8

Casson, L. 1975. "Ships on coins". In A. L. Ben-Eli (ed) *Ships and Parts of Ships on Ancient Coins*, 11-17. Haifa

Clark, A. J. 1993. *Excavations at Mucking. Vol.1: The Site Atlas. Excavations by Margaret and Tom Jones* (English Heritage Archaeological Report No.20) London

Clark, R. R. 1955. "The early Iron Age treasure from Snettisham, Norfolk" *Proc. Prehist. Soc.*, 20 for 1954, 27-86

Clark, J. G. D. and Fell, C. I. 1953. "The early Iron Age site at Micklemoor Hill, West Harling, Norfolk, and its pottery" *Proc. Prehist Soc.*, 19, 1-40

Clarke, C. P. 1988. "Late Iron Age enclosures at Kelvedon: excavations at the Doucecroft site 1985-86" *Essex Archaeol. Hist.*, 19, 15-39

Collis, J. R. 1973. "Burials with weapons in Iron Age Britain" *Germania*, 51, 121-33

Conlon, R. F. B. 1973. "Holbrooks - an Iron Age and Romano-British settlement" *Essex J.*, 8, 30-50

Couchman, C. R.(ed.) 1979. "Work of Essex County Council Archaeology Section 1977" *Essex Archaeol. Hist.*, 9 for 1977, 60-94

Couldrey, P. O. 1984. "The Iron Age pottery". In B. J. Philp *Excavations in the Darent Valley, Kent*, 38-70. Dover

Cowell, M. R. 1992. "An analytical survey of the British Celtic gold coinage". In M. R. Mays (ed.) *Celtic Coinage: Britain and Beyond. The Eleventh Oxford Symposium on Coinage and Monetary History* (British Archaeological Reports, British Series No.222), 207-33. Oxford

Cowell, M. R. et al. 1988. "Celtic coinage in Britain: new hoards and recent analyses" *Brit. Numis. J.*, 57 for 1987, 1-23

Crummy, P. J. 1992. "Royal graves" *Colchester Archaeol.*, 5, 1-5

Crummy, P. J. 1993. "Aristocratic graves at Colchester" *Current Archaeol.*, 132, 492-7

Crummy, P. J. 1994. "Late Iron Age and Roman Colchester". In J. M. Cooper (ed.) *The Victoria History of the Counties of England. Essex. Vol.9. The Borough of Colchester*, 2-18. Oxford

Cunliffe, B. W. 1968. "Early pre-Roman Iron Age communities in eastern England" *Antiq. J.*, 48, 175-91

Cunliffe, B. W. 1974. *Iron Age Communities in Britain* (first edition) London

Cunliffe, B. W. 1978. *Iron Age Communities in Britain* (second edition) London

Cunliffe, B. W. 1991. *Iron Age Communities in Britain* (third edition) London

Darby, H. C. 1971. *The Domesday Geography of Eastern England* (third edition) Cambridge

Davison, B. K. 1993. "The excavations of 1969 and 1971". In W. J. Rodwell *The Origins and Early Development of Witham, Essex: a Study in Settlement and Fortification, Prehistoric to Medieval* (Oxbow Monograph No.26), 19-22. Oxford

de Brisay, K. 1978. "The excavation of a Red Hill at Peldon, Essex, with notes on some other sites" *Antiq. J.*, 58, 31-60

Dorrington, E. J. and Legge, A. J. 1985. "The animal bones". In N. E. France and B. M. Gobel *The Romano-British Temple at Harlow*, 122-33. Gloucester

Downey, R. et al. 1980. "The Hayling Island temple and religious connections across the Channel". In W. J. Rodwell (ed.) *Temples, Churches and Religion in Roman Britain* (British Archaeological Reports, British Series No.77), 289-304. Oxford

Drury. P. J. 1978a *Excavations at Little Waltham* (Chelmsford Excavation Committee Report No.1 & Council for British Archaeology Research Report No.26) London

Drury, P. J. 1978b. "Little Waltham and pre-Belgic Iron Age settlement in Essex". In B. W. Cunliffe and T. Rowley (eds) *Lowland Iron Age Communities in Europe* (British Archaeological Reports, International Series No.48), 43-76. Oxford

Drury, P. J. 1980a. "The early and middle phases of the Iron Age in Essex". In D. G. Buckley (ed.) *Archaeology in Essex to AD 1500* (Council for British Archaeology Research Report No.34), 47-54. London

Drury, P. J. 1980b. "Non-classical religious buildings in Iron Age and Roman Britain: a review". In W. J. Rodwell *Temples, Churches and Religion in Roman Britain* (British Archaeological Reports, British Series No.77), 45-78. Oxford

Drury. P. J. 1988. *The Mansio and Other Sites in the South-Eastern Sector of Caesaromagus* (Chelmsford Archaeological Trust Report No.3.1 and Council for British Archaeology Research Report No.66) London

Drury, P. J. and Rodwell, W. J. 1973. "Excavations at Gun Hill, West Tilbury" *Trans Essex Archaeol. Soc.*, 5, 48-112

Drury, P. J. and Rodwell, W. J. 1978. "Investigations at Asheldham, Essex. An interim report on the church and the historic landscape" *Antiq. J.*, 58, 133-51

Eddy, M. R. 1989. "Red Hills at New Hall Farm, Little Wigborough" *Essex Archaeol. Hist.*, 20, 172

Eddy, M. R. and Priddy, D. A. (eds) 1982. "Work of the Essex County Council Archaeology Section, 1980" *Essex Archaeol. Hist.*, 13 for 1981, 32-47

Eddy, M. R. and Turner, C. E. 1982. *Kelvedon: the Origins and Development of a Roman Small Town* (Essex County Council Occasional Paper No.3) Chelmsford

Ehrenreich, R. M. 1985. *Trade, Technology and the Ironworking Community in the Iron Age of Southern Britain* (British Archaeological Reports, British Series No.144) Oxford

Elsdon, S. M. 1975. *Stamped Iron Age Pottery* (British Archaeological Reports No.10) Oxford

Elsdon, S. M. 1989. *Later Prehistoric Pottery in England and Wales* Princes Risborough

Evans, J. 1987. "Crucible analysis". In D. G. Buckley et al. *Excavations at Woodham Walter and an Assessment of Essex Enclosures* (East Anglian Archaeology Report No.33), 39-40. Chelmsford

Fawn, A. J. et al. 1990 *The Red Hills of Essex: Salt-Making in Antiquity* Colchester

Fitzpatrick, A. P. 1984. "The deposition of La Tène metalwork in watery contexts in southern England". In B. W. Cunliffe and D. Miles (eds) *Aspects of the Iron Age in Central Southern Britain* (University of Oxford Committee for Archaeology Monograph No.2), 178-90. Oxford

Fitzpatrick, A. P. 1985a. "The distribution of Dressel 1 amphorae in north-west Europe" *Oxford J. Archaeol.*, 4, 305-40

Fitzpatrick, A. P. 1985b. "The Celtic coins". In N. E. France and B. M. Gobel *The Romano-British Temple at Harlow, Essex*, 49-66. Gloucester

Fitzpatrick, A. P. 1986. "Camulodunum and the early occupation of south-east England. Some reconsiderations". In D. Planck and C. Unz (eds) *Kongress-Akten der Beitrage am Limes-Kongress in Aalen 1983*, 35-41. Stuttgart

Fitzpatrick, A. P. 1991a. "A hoard of Iron Age Class II potin coins from New Addington, Surrey" *Surrey Archaeol. Collect.*, 80 for 1990, 147-52

Fitzpatrick, A. P. 1991b. "Death in a material world: the late Iron Age and early Romano-British cemetery at King Harry Lane, St Albans, Hertfordshire" *Britannia*, 22, 323-7

Fitzpatrick, A. P. 1992. "The roles of Celtic coinage in south east England". In M. R. Mays (ed.) *Celtic Coinage: Britain and Beyond. The Eleventh Oxford Symposium on Coinage and Monetary History* (British Archaeological Reports, British Series No.222), 1-32. Oxford

Fitzpatrick, A. P. 1994. "The late Iron Age cremation cemetery at Westhampnett, West Sussex". In A. P. Fitzpatrick and E. L. Morris (eds) *The Iron Age in Wessex: Recent Work*, 108-12. Salisbury

Flook, R. and Bedwin, O. R. 1993. "The excavations of 1988". In W. J. Rodwell *The Origins and Early Development of Witham, Essex: a Study in Settlement and Fortification, Prehistoric to Medieval* (Oxbow Monograph No.26), 22-8. Oxford

Foster, J. A. A. 1986. *The Lexden Tumulus* (British Archaeological Reports, British Series No.156) Oxford

France, N. E. and Gobel, B. M. 1985. *The Romano-British Temple at Harlow, Essex* Gloucester

Frere, S. S. 1983. *Verulamium Excavations. Vol.2* (Reports of the Research Committee of the Society of Antiquaries of London No.41) London

Going, C. J. 1987. *The Mansio and Other Sites in the South-Eastern Sector of Caesaromagus: the Roman Pottery* (Chelmsford Archaeological Trust Report No.3.2 and Council for British Archaeology Research Report No.62) London

Going, C. J. 1993. "The Iron Age. The Roman period". In A. J. Clark *Excavations at Mucking. Vol.1: The Site Atlas. Excavations by Margaret and Tom Jones* (English Heritage Archaeological Report No.20), 19-21. London

Goodburn, R. 1981. "The Celtic coins". In C. R. Partridge *Skeleton Green: a Late Iron Age and Romano-British Site* (Britannia Monograph Series No.2), 121-9. London

Goodburn, R. 1986. "Celtic coins". In I. M. Stead and V. A. Rigby *Baldock: The Excavation of a Roman and Pre-Roman Settlement, 1968-72* (Britannia Monograph Series No.7), 89-99. London

Grant, A. 1984. "Animal husbandry". In B. W. Cunliffe *Danebury: an Iron Age hillfort in Hampshire. Vol.2. The Excavations, 1969-1978: the Finds* (Council for British Archaeology Research Report No.52), 496-548. London

Grant, A. et al. 1991. "Animal husbandry". In B. W. Cunliffe and C. Poole *Danebury: an Iron Age Hillfort in Hampshire. Vol.5. The Excavations 1979-1988: The Finds* (Council for British Archaeology Research Report No.73), 447-87. London

Green, C. M. 1980. "The Roman pottery". In D. M. Jones *Excavations at Billingsgate Buildings "Triangle", Lower Thames Street 1974* (London and Middlesex Archaeological Society, Special Paper No.4), 39-79. London

Green, M. J. 1992. "The iconography of Celtic coins". In M. R. Mays (ed.) *Celtic Coinage: Britain and Beyond. The Eleventh Oxford Symposium on Coinage and Monetary History* (British Archaeological Reports, British Series No.222), 151-63. Oxford

Greenwood, P. A. 1988. "Uphall Camp, Ilford" *Essex J.*, 23, 19-20

Greenwood, P. A. 1989. "Uphall camp, Ilford, Essex: an Iron Age fortification" *London Archaeol.*, 6, 94-101

Gregory, A. K. 1991. *Excavations in Thetford, 1980-1982, Fison Way* (East Anglian Archaeology Report No.53) Dereham

Grimes, W. F. 1953. "The La Tène art style in British early Iron Age pottery" *Proc. Prehist. Soc.*, 18 for 1952, 160-75

Grimes, W. F. and Close-Brooks, J. 1993. "The excavation of Caesar's Camp, Heathrow, Harmondsworth, Middlesex, 1944" *Proc. Prehist. Soc.*, 59, 303-60

Guido, M. 1978. *The Glass Beads of the Prehistoric and Roman periods in Britain and Ireland* (Reports of the Research Committee of the Society of Antiquaries of London No.35) London

Halstead, P. 1982a. "The animal bones". In I. A. Hodder *Wendens Ambo. The Excavations of an Iron Age and Romano-British Settlement* (The Archaeology of the M11. Vol.2), 44-9. London

Halstead, P. 1982b. "The economy". In I. A. Hodder *Wendens Ambo. The Excavations of an Iron Age and Romano-British Settlement* (The Archaeology of the M11. Vol.2), 61-3. London

Halstead, P. et al. 1978. "Behavioural archaeology and refuse patterns: a case study" *Norwegian Archaeol. Rev.*, 11, 118-31

Halstead, P. et al. 1982. "Within-site patterning: Iron Age". In I. A. Hodder *Wendens Ambo. The Excavations of an Iron Age and Romano-British Settlement* (The Archaeology of the M11. Vol.2), 55-8. London

Hamilton, S. 1988. "Fabric analysis of selected first millennium BC pottery types. Earlier first millennium BC pottery from Rectory Road and Baker Street" In A. J. Wilkinson *Archaeology and Environment in South Essex: Rescue Archaeology along the Grays By-Pass 1979/80* (East Anglian Archaeology Report No.42), 75-80. Chelmsford

Haselgrove, C. C. 1978. *Supplementary Gazetteer of Find-Spots of Celtic Coins in Britain, 1977* (University of London Institute of Archaeology Occasional Paper No.11a) London

Haselgrove, C. C. 1979. "The significance of coinage in pre-conquest Britain". In B. C. Burnham and H. B. Johnson (eds) *Invasion and Response: the Case of Roman Britain* (British Archaeological Reports, British Series No.73), 197-209. Oxford

Haselgrove, C. C. 1984. "Celtic coins found in Britain, 1977-82" *Bull. Inst. Archaeol. Univ. London*, 20 for 1983, 107-54

Haselgrove, C. C. 1987. *Iron Age Coinage in South-East England: the Archaeological Context* (British Archaeological Reports, British Series No.174) Oxford

Haselgrove, C. C. 1988. "Iron Age coins". In T. W. Potter and S. D. Trow *Puckeridge-Braughing, Hertfordshire. The Ermine Street Excavations 1971-72* (Hertfordshire Archaeology Vol.10), 21-9. Hertford

Haselgrove, C. C. 1989a. "The archaeology of British potin coinage" *Archaeol. J.*, 145 for 1988, 99-122

Haselgrove, C. C. 1989b. "Celtic coins found in Britain, 1982-7" *Bull. Inst. Archaeol. Univ. London*, 26, 1-77

Haselgrove, C. C. 1989c. "Iron Age coin deposition at Harlow temple, Essex" *Oxford J. Archaeol.*, 8, 73-88

Haselgrove, C. C. 1989d. "The later Iron Age in southern Britain and beyond". In M. Todd (ed.) *Research on Roman Britain 1960-89* (Britannia Monograph Series No.11), 1-18. London

Haselgrove, C. C. 1993a. "The development of British Iron Age coinage" *Numis. Chron.*, 153, 31-63

Haselgrove, C. C. 1993b. "Warfare, ritual and society in Iron Age Wessex" *Archaeol. J.*, 149 for 1992, 407-15

Havis, R. and Brooks, H. 1991. "The Stansted project - the fourth and fifth years' work" *Essex J.*, 26, 40-3

Hawkes, C. F. C. 1983. "Colchester before the Romans or who were our Belgae?" *Essex Archaeol. Hist.*, 14 for 1982, 3-14

Hawkes, C. F. C. and Crummy, P. J. 1995. *Camulodunum 2* (Colchester Archaeological Report No.11) Colchester

Hawkes, C. F. C. and Hull, M. R. 1947. *Camulodunum* (Reports of the Research Committee of the Society of Antiquaries of London No.14) London

Hill, J. D. 1994. "Why we should not take the data from Iron Age settlements for granted: recent studies of intra-settlement patterning". In A. P. Fitzpatrick and E. L. Morris (eds) *The Iron Age in Wessex: Recent Work*, 4-8. Salisbury

Hill, J. D. 1995. *Ritual and Rubbish in the Iron Age of Wessex: a Study on the Formation of a Specific Archaeological Record* (British Archaeological Reports, British Series No.242) Oxford

Hind, J. G. F. 1989. "The invasion of Britain in A.D. 43 - an alternative strategy for Aulus Plautius" *Britannia*, 20, 1-21

Hingley, R. 1989. *Rural Settlement in Roman Britain* London

Hingley, R. 1991. "Iron Age 'currency bars': the archaeological and social context" *Archaeol. J.*, 147 for 1990, 91-117

Hodder, I. A. 1982. *Wendens Ambo. The Excavations of an Iron Age and Romano-British Settlement* (The Archaeology of the M11. Vol.2) London

Hodson, F. R. 1962. "Some pottery from Eastbourne, the 'Marnians' and the pre-Roman Iron Age in southern England" *Proc. Prehist. Soc.*, 28, 140-55

Hubbard, R. N. L. B. 1978. "Carbonised seeds". In J. D. Hedges and D. G. Buckley. "Excavations at a Neolithic causewayed enclosure, Orsett, Essex, 1975" *Proc. Prehist. Soc.*, 44, 294-5

Huggins, P. J. 1979. "Excavation of Belgic and Romano-British farm with middle Saxon cemetery and churches at Nazeingbury, Essex, 1975-6" *Essex Archaeol. Hist.*, 10 for 1978, 29-117

Hull, M. R. 1962. "Additions to the museum" *Report of the Museum and Muniment Committee for the Period April 1st, 1956, to March 31st, 1962*, 7-55

Jefferies, R. S. and Barford, P. M. 1990. "The pottery of the Red Hills" and "Gazetter 3: pottery from Essex Red Hills". In A. J. Fawn et al. *The Red Hills of Essex: Salt-Making in Antiquity*, 35-6 and 73-8. Colchester

Jones, G. et al. 1982. "The carbonised seeds". In I. A. Hodder *Wendens Ambo. The Excavations of an Iron Age and Romano-British Settlement* (The Archaeology of the M11. Vol.2), 50-4. London

Jones, M. U. and Jones, W. T. 1975. "The crop-mark sites at Mucking, Essex, England". In R. Bruce-Mitford (ed.) *Recent Archaeological Excavations in Europe*, 133-87. London

Kent, J. P. C. 1978. "The London area in the late Iron Age: an interpretation of the earliest coins". In J. Bird et al. (eds) *Collectanea Londiniensia: Studies in London Archaeology and History Presented to Ralph Merrifield* (London and Middlesex Archaeological Society Special Paper No.2), 53-8. London

Kent, J. P. C. 1981. "The origins of coinage in Britain". In B. W. Cunliffe (ed.) *Coinage and Society in Britain and Gaul: Some Current Problems* (Council for British Archaeology Research Report No.38), 40-2. London

King, A. C. and Soffe, G. 1994. "The Iron Age and Roman temple on Hayling Island, Hampshire". In A. P. Fitzpatrick and E. L. Morris (eds) *The Iron Age in Wessex: Recent Work*, 114-16. Salisbury

Lang, J. and Williams, A. R. 1975. "The hardening of iron swords" *J. Archaeol. Sci.*, 2, 199-207

Lavender, N. J. 1991. "A late Iron Age burial enclosure at Maldon Hall Farm, Essex: excavations 1989" *Proc. Prehist. Soc.*, 57 (2), 203-9

Laver, P. G. 1927. "The excavation of a tumulus at Lexden, Colchester" *Archaeologia*, 76, 241-54

Lloyd-Morgan, G. 1993. "The Celtic mirrors". In W. J. and K. A. Rodwell *Rivenhall: Investigations of a Villa, Church and Village, 1950-1977. Vol.2. Specialist Studies and Index to Volumes 1 and 2* (Chelmsford Archaeological Trust Report No.4.2 and Council for British Archaeology Research Report No.80), 27-33. London

Longworth, I. H. 1985 *Prehistoric Britain* London

Luff, R-M. 1988. "The animal bones". In A. J. Wilkinson *Archaeology and Environment in South Essex: Rescue Archaeology along the Grays By-Pass 1979/80* (East Anglian Archaeology Report No.42), 99. Chelmsford

Major, H. J. 1987a. "A late Iron Age linchpin in Saffron Walden Museum" *Essex Archaeol. Hist.*, 18, 114

Major, H. J. 1987b. "Fired clay". In D. G. Buckley et al. *Excavations at Woodham Walter and an Assessment of Essex Enclosures* (East Anglian Archaeology Report No.33), 39. Chelmsford

Major, H. J. 1988. "Baked and fired clay objects". In A. J. Wilkinson *Archaeology and Environment in South Essex: Rescue Archaeology along the Grays By-Pass 1979/80* (East Anglian Archaeology Report No.42), 94-7. Chelmsford

Major, H. J. 1990. "Lead objects. Stone. Baked clay. Roman tile". In D. R. Rudling "Late Iron Age and Roman Billericay: excavations 1987" *Essex Archaeol. Hist.*, 21, 42-3

Major, H. J. 1993. "Shale bowl. Baked clay loomweight". In W. J. Rodwell *The Origins and Early Development of Witham, Essex: a Study in Settlement and Fortification, Prehistoric to Medieval* (Oxbow Monograph No.26), 111. Oxford

Manning, W. H. 1972. "Ironwork hoards in Iron Age and Roman Britain" *Britannia*, 3, 224-50

Manning, W. H. 1980. "Blacksmith's tools from Waltham Abbey, Essex". In W. A. Oddy (ed.) *Aspects of Early Metallurgy* (British Museum Occasional Paper No.17), 87-96. London

Manning, W. H. 1985 *Catalogue of the Romano-British Iron Tools, Fittings and Weapons in the British Museum* London

Marsden, P. 1990. "A re-assessment of Blackfriars I". In S. McGrail (ed.) *Maritime Celts, Frisians and Saxons: Papers Presented to a Conference at Oxford in November 1988* (Council for British Archaeology Research Report No.71), 66-74. London

Martin, E. A. 1988. *Burgh: Iron Age and Roman Enclosure* (East Anglian Archaeology Report No.40) Ipswich

Martingell, H. E. 1988. "The flint industry". In A. J. Wilkinson *Archaeology and Environment in South Essex: Rescue Archaeology along the Grays By-Pass 1979/80* (East Anglian Archaeology Report No.42), 70-3. Chelmsford

Mays, M. R. 1992. "Inscriptions on British Celtic coins" *Numis. Chron.*, 152, 57-82

McDonnell, J. G. 1993. "The slags and metallurgical residues". In A. J. Clark *Excavations at Mucking. Vol.1: The Site Atlas. Excavations by Margaret and Tom Jones* (English Heritage Archaeological Report No.20), 31-3. London

McGrail, S. 1990. "Boats and boatmanship in the late prehistoric southern North Sea and Channel region". In S. McGrail (ed.) *Maritime Celts, Frisians and Saxons: Papers Presented to a Conference at Oxford in November 1988* (Council for British Archaeology Research Report No.71), 32-48. London

Medlycott, M. 1994. "Iron Age and Roman material from Birchanger, near Bishops Stortford: excavations at Woodside Industrial Park, 1992" *Essex Archaeol. Hist.*, 25, 28-45

Merrifield, R. 1987. *The Archaeology of Ritual and Magic* London

Merriman, N. 1990. *Prehistoric London* London

Metzler, J. et al. 1991. *Clemency et les Tombes de l'Aristocratie en Gaule Belgique* (Dossiers d'Archéologie du Musée National d'Histoire et d'Art No.1) Luxembourg

Middleton, A. P. 1987. "Technological investigation of the coatings on some 'haematite-coated' pottery from southern England" *Archaeometry*, 29, 250-61

Moore, I. E. et al. 1988. *The Archaeology of Roman Suffolk* Ipswich

Muckleroy, K. et al. 1978. "A pre-Roman coin from Canterbury and the ship represented on it" *Proc. Prehist. Soc.*, 44, 439-44

Murphy, P. L. 1988. "Cereals and crop weeds". In A. J. Wilkinson *Archaeology and Environment in South Essex: Rescue Archaeology along the Grays By-Pass 1979/80* (East Anglian Archaeology Report No.42), 99-100. Chelmsford

Murphy, P. L. 1991a. "Cereals and crop weeds", In O. R. Bedwin. "Asheldham Camp - an early Iron Age hill fort: the 1985 excavations" *Essex Archaeol. Hist.*, 22, 31-5

Murphy, P. L. 1991b. "Early crop production and wild plant resources in the coastal area of Essex, England". In J. M. Renfrew (ed.) *New Light on Early Farming: Recent Developments in Palaeoethnobotany*, 329-48. Edinburgh

Nash, D. E. M. 1982. "Adminius did strike coins" *Oxford J. Archaeol.*, 1, 111-15

Needham, S. P. 1986. "The metalwork". In M. O'Connell *Petters Sports Field, Egham: Excavation of a Late Bronze Age/Early Iron Age Site* (Research Volume of the Surrey Archaeological Society No.10), 22-60. Guildford

Needham, S. P. 1990. *The Petters Late Bronze Age Metalwork: an Analytical Study of Thames Valley Metalworking in its Settlement Context* (British Museum Occasional Paper No.70) London

Niblett, B. R. K. 1985. *Sheepen: an Early Roman Industrial Site at Camulodunum* (Council for British Archaeology Research Report No.57) London

Niblett, B. R. K. 1992. "A Catuvellaunian chieftain's burial from St Albans" *Antiquity*, 66, 917-29

Northover, J. P. 1984. "Iron Age bronze metallurgy in central southern England". In B. W. Cunliffe and D. Miles (eds) *Aspects of the Iron Age in Central Southern Britain* (University of Oxford Committee for Archaeology Monograph No.2), 126-45. Oxford

Northover, J. P. 1992. "Materials issues in the Celtic coinage". In M. R. Mays (ed.) *Celtic Coinage: Britain and Beyond. The Eleventh Oxford Symposium on Coinage and Monetary History* (British Archaeological Reports, British Series No.222), 235-99. Oxford

Northover, J. P. 1993. "Analysis of Celtic mirror I from Rivenhall". In W. J. and K. A. Rodwell *Rivenhall: Investigations of a Villa, Church and Village, 1950-1977. Vol.2. Specialist Studies and Index to Volumes 1 and 2* (Chelmsford Archaeological Trust Report No.4.2 and Council for British Archaeology Research Report No.80), 33 and 35. London

Partridge, C. R. 1980. "Excavations at Puckeridge and Braughing 1975-79" *Hertfordshire Archaeol.*, 7 for 1979, 28-132

Partridge, C. R. 1981. *Skeleton Green: a Late Iron Age and Romano-British Site* (Britannia Monograph Series No.2) London

Peacock, D. P. S. 1969. "A contribution to the study of Glastonbury ware from south-western Britain" *Antiq. J.*, 49, 41-61

Peacock, D. P. S. 1971. "Roman amphorae in pre-Roman Britain". In D. Hill and M. Jesson (eds) *The Iron Age and Its Hill-Forts: Papers Presented to Sir Mortimer Wheeler*, 161-88. Southampton

Peacock, D. P. S. 1984. "Amphorae in Iron Age Britain: a reassessment". In S. Macready and F. H. Thompson (eds) *Cross-Channel Trade between Gaul and Britain in the Pre-Roman Iron Age* (Society of Antiquaries of London Occasional Paper, New Series No.4), 37-42. London

Pollard, R. J. 1988. *The Roman Pottery of Kent* (Monograph Series of the Kent Archaeological Society No.5) Maidstone

Potter, T. W. and Trow, S. D. 1988. *Puckeridge-Braughing, Hertfordshire. The Ermine Street Excavations 1971-72* (Hertfordshire Archaeology Vol.10) Hertford

Powell, T. G. E. 1980. *The Celts* London

Priddy, D. A. (ed.) 1984. "Work of Essex County Council Archaeology Section 1982" *Essex Archaeol. Hist.*, 15 for 1983, 119-55

Priddy, D. A. (ed.) 1987. "Excavations in Essex 1985" *Essex Archaeol. Hist.*, 17 for 1986, 156-65

Pryor, F. M. M. 1987. "The flints". In G. B. Dannell and J. P. Wild *Longthorpe II. The Military Works-Depot: an Episode in Landscape History* (Britannia Monograph Series No.8), 99-101. London

Reader, F. W. 1908. "Report of the Red Hills Excavation Committee 1906-7" *Proc. Soc. Antiq. London*, 22, 164-214

Rigby, V. A. and Freestone, I. C. 1986. "The petrology and typology of the earliest identified central Gaulish imports" *J. Roman Pottery Studies*, 1, 6-21

Rigby, V. A. and Freestone, I. C. 1983. "The flagons". In M. E. Farley. "A mirror burial from Dorton, Buckinghamshire" *Proc. Prehist.Soc.*, 49, 291-3

Rodwell, K. A. 1988. *The Prehistoric and Roman Settlement at Kelvedon, Essex* (Chelmsford Archaeological Trust Report No.6 and Council for British Archaeology Research Report No.63) London

Rodwell, W. J. 1973. "An unusual pottery bowl from Kelvedon, Essex" *Britannia*, 4, 265-7

Rodwell, W. J. 1975. "The Orsett. "Cock" cropmark site" *Essex Archaeol. Hist.*, 6 for 1974, 13-39

Rodwell, W. J. 1976. "Coinage, oppida, and the rise of Belgic power in south-eastern Britain". In B. W. Cunliffe and T. Rowley (eds) *Oppida: the Beginnings of Urbanisation in Barbarian Europe* (British Archaeological Reports, Supplementary Series No.11), 181-367. Oxford

Rodwell, W. J. 1977. "Some unrecorded archaeological discoveries in Essex, 1946-75" *Essex Archaeol Hist.*, 8 for 1976, 234-48

Rodwell, W. J. 1978. "Buildings and settlements in south-east Britain in the late Iron Age". In B. W. Cunliffe and T. Rowley (eds) *Lowland Iron Age Communities in Europe* (British Archaeological Reports, International Series No.48), 25-41. Oxford

Rodwell, W. J. 1979. "Iron Age and Roman salt-winning on the Essex coast". In B. C. Burnham and H. B. Johnson (eds) *Invasion and Response: the Case of Roman Britain* (British Archaeological Reports, British Series No.73), 133-75. Oxford

Rodwell, W. J. 1981. "Lost and found: the archaeology of find-spots of Celtic coins". In B. W. Cunliffe (ed.) *Coinage and Society in Britain and Gaul: Some Current Problems* (Council for British Archaeology Research Report No.38), 43-52. London

Rodwell, W. J. 1987. "The pottery and its implications". In D. G. Buckley et al. *Excavations at Woodham Walter and an Assessment of Essex Enclosures* (East Anglian Archaeology Report No.33), 20-39. Chelmsford

Rodwell, W. J. 1988. "The stamped vessel". In K. A. Rodwell *The Prehistoric and Roman Settlement at Kelvedon, Essex* (Chelmsford Archaeological Trust Report No.6 and Council for British Archaeology Research Report No.63), 107-10. London

Rodwell, W. J. 1993. *The Origins and Early Development of Witham, Essex: a Study in Settlement and Fortification, Prehistoric to Medieval* (Oxbow Monograph No.26) Oxford

Rudling, D. R. 1990. "Late Iron Age and Roman Billericay: excavations 1987" *Essex Archaeol. Hist.*, 21, 19-47

Scheers, S. 1992. "Celtic coin types in Britain and their Mediterranean origins". In M. R. Mays (ed.) *Celtic Coinage: Britain and Beyond. The Eleventh Oxford Symposium on Coinage and Monetary History* (British Archaeological Reports, British Series No.222), 33-46. Oxford

Sealey, P. R. 1979. "The later history of Icenian electrum torcs" *Proc. Prehist. Soc.*, 45, 165-78

Sealey, P. R. 1981. *Trade between Southern Britain and the Roman World in the Late Iron Age 54 BC to AD 43* (University of Bristol Doctoral Thesis)

Sealey, P. R. 1985. *Amphoras from the 1970 Excavations at Colchester Sheepen* (British Archaeological Reports, British Series No.142) Oxford

Sealey, P. R. 1988. "A Late Bronze Age hoard from Fingringhoe" *Essex Archaeol. Hist.*, 18 for 1987, 7-15

Sealey, P. R. 1991. "Some finds of the Bronze and Iron Ages in Essex" *Essex Archaeol. Hist.*, 22, 1-12

Sealey, P. R. 1995. "New light on the salt industry and Red Hills of prehistoric and Roman Essex" *Essex Archaeol. Hist.*, 26, 65-81

Sellwood, L. 1984. "Tribal boundaries viewed from the perspective of numismatic evidence". In B. W. Cunliffe and D. Miles (eds) *Aspects of the Iron Age in Central Southern Britain* (University of Oxford Committee for Archaeology Monograph No.2), 191-204. Oxford

Shepard, A. O. 1965. *Ceramics for the Archaeologist* Washington

Stead, I. M. 1985a. *The Battersea Shield* London

Stead, I. M. 1985b. *Celtic Art in Britain before the Roman Conquest* London

Stead, I. M. 1987. "La Tène sword". In D. G. Buckley and J. D. Hedges *The Bronze Age and Saxon Settlements at Springfield Lyons, Essex: an Interim Report* (Essex County Council Occasional Paper No.5), 13. Chelmsford

Stead, I. M. 1991. "The Snettisham treasure: excavations in 1990" *Antiquity*, 65, 447-64

Stead, I. M. 1993. "Many more Iron Age shields from Britain" *Antiq. J.*, 71 for 1991, 1-35

Stead, I. M. and Rigby, V. A. 1989. *Verulamium: the King Harry Lane Site* (English Heritage Archaeological Report No.12) London

Thomas, R. 1989. "The bronze-iron transition in southern England". In M. L. S. Sorensen and R. Thomas (eds) *The Bronze Age-Iron Age Transition in Europe* (British Archaeological Reports, International Series No.483), 263-86. Oxford

Thompson, I. M. 1982. *Grog-Tempered. "Belgic" Pottery of South-Eastern England* (British Archaeological Reports, British Series No.108) Oxford

Thompson, I. M. 1988. "Late Iron Age pottery from Ardale Area B". In A. J. Wilkinson *Archaeology and Environment in South Essex: Rescue Archaeology along the Grays By-Pass 1979/80* (East Anglian Archaeology Report No.42), 86-8. Chelmsford

Toller, H. S. 1980. "An interim report on the excavation of the Orsett 'Cock' enclosure, Essex: 1976-79" *Britannia*, 11, 35-42

Turner, B. R. G. 1982. *Ivy Chimneys, Witham: An Interim Report* (Essex County Council Occasional Paper No.2) Chelmsford

Turner, B. R. G. forthcoming *Excavations of an Iron Age Settlement and Roman Religious Complex at Ivy Chimneys, Witham, Essex 1978-83* (East Anglian Archaeology Report)

Tyers, P. A. 1981. "A note on the mica-dusted vessels". In C. R. Partridge *Skeleton Green: a Late Iron Age and Romano-British Site* (Britannia Monograph Series No.2), 102-3. London

Van Arsdell, R. D. 1986. "An industrial engineer (but no papyrus) in Celtic Britain" *Oxford J. Archaeol.*, 5, 205-21

Van Arsdell, R. D. 1989. *Celtic Coinage of Britain* London

Wait, G. A. 1985 *Ritual and Religion in Iron Age Britain* (British Archaeological Reports, British Series No.149) Oxford

Wallis, S. P. and Waughman, M. forthcoming *Archaeology and the Landscape in the Lower Blackwater Valley* (East Anglian Archaeology Report)

Ward Perkins, J. P. 1937. "Iron Age site in Essex" *Antiq. J.*, 17, 194-5

Whimster, R. 1977. "Iron Age burials in southern Britain" *Proc. Prehist. Soc.*, 43, 317-27

Whimster, R. 1981. *Burial Practices in Iron Age Britain* (British Archaeological Reports, British Series No.90) Oxford

Wilkinson, A. J. 1988. *Archaeology and Environment in South Essex: Rescue Archaeology along the Grays By-Pass 1979/80* (East Anglian Archaeology Report No.42) Chelmsford

Wilkinson, A. J. and Murphy, P. L. 1986. "Archaeological survey of an intertidal zone: the submerged landscape of the Essex coast, England" *J. Field Archaeol.*, 13, 177-94

Wilkinson, A. J. and Murphy, P. L. 1995 *Archaeology of the Essex Coast, Vol.1: the Hullbridge Survey* (East Anglian Archaeology Report No.71) Chelmsford

Wilkinson, P. M. 1979. "Uphall Camp" *Essex Archaeol. Hist.*, 10 for 1978, 220-1

Williams, D. F. 1981. "The Roman amphora trade with late Iron Age Britain". In H. Howard and E. L. Morris (eds) *Production and Distribution: a Ceramic Viewpoint* (British Archaeological Reports, International Series No.120), 123-32. Oxford

Wilson, C. E. 1981. "Burials within settlements in southern Britain during the pre-Roman Iron Age" *Bull. Inst. Archaeol. Univ. London*, 18, 127-69

Wymer, J. J. and Brown, N. R. 1995. *Excavations at North Shoebury: Settlement and Economy in South-East Essex 1500 B.C.-A.D.1500* (East Anglian Archaeology Report No.75) Chelmsford

Colchester: Publications between the Clacton and Writtle conferences

Philip Crummy*

Much has been published on Colchester since the Clacton conference in 1978 and more is imminent. Since two of these publications (Crummy 1994a and d) cover much the same ground that ought to be covered here, it is proposed instead to provide a summary of publications relating to Colchester which have appeared in print since 1978. It would not be realistic or practical to list every publication in which Colchester or material from it is mentioned or discussed, but it is hoped that all the main ones are included. A note in brackets has been added after every bibliographic entry where the title does not make clear the reason for its inclusion. In addition to listing most of the recent publications, the following pages also contain comments updating specific points in the original Colchester article (P. Crummy, 'Colchester between the Roman and Norman conquests', in *Archaeology in Essex to AD 1500* (ed. D. G. Buckley), 76-81, CBA Res Rep, 34) where subsequent advances make this necessary.

The first of the Essex conferences took place in the middle of an extraordinary phase of excavations in Colchester when sites were being dug on a scale and in numbers never before seen in the town. This period lasted from 1970 through to 1986 and was the result of a strategy for major town-centre redevelopment which was being promoted by the Colchester Borough Council at a time when there was a nationwide building boom. The key element was the construction in 1971 of an inner relief road through areas which were residential. This created new development sites along the side of the new road (such as the Butt Road police station site, Middleborough, and St Mary's car park at Balkerne Lane) and made the construction of the Lion Walk and Culver Street shopping precincts easier, with their underground service basements linked to the new road. Since the Clacton conference in 1978, we have seen the completion and publication of the Butt Road site (*CAR 9*), and the excavation and publication of Culver Street (*CAR 6*) amongst other sites.

While much work took place within and close to the walled town, there was no equivalent pressure on Iron Age Camulodunum and the dyke system. Professor Hawkes and myself have been co-operating on a monograph on Camulodunum and the dyke system since the late 1970s. He had worked intermittently on the book since that time, and had more or less completed his parts of it before his death in 1992. The book was published in 1995.

Descriptions of the structures, stratification, and associated deposits and features from all the town-centre excavations between 1971 and 1985 are being published in the *Colchester Archaeological Reports*. Most of the loose finds are being dealt with according to the type of find. Thus there are, or will be, monographs devoted to the following topics: Roman small finds (*CAR 2*), coins (*CAR 4*), post-Roman pottery (*CAR 7*), Roman glass (*CAR 8*), Roman pottery (*CAR 10*), and animal bone (*CAR 12*). *CAR 11* deals with the work since the early 1930s, relating to the late Iron age oppidum and its development in the Roman period. Accounts of finds such as mosaics, wall-plaster, tile and votive vessels which are closely linked to excavated structures and features, are included in the relevant structural reports.

Colchester Archaeological Reports (published and forthcoming)

CAR 1   Philip Crummy (1981), Aspects of Anglo-Saxon and Norman Colchester, CBA Res Rep, 39
CAR 2   Nina Crummy (1983), The Roman small finds from excavations in Colchester, 1971-9
CAR 3   Philip Crummy (1984), Excavations at Lion Walk, Balkerne Lane, and Middleborough, Colchester, Essex
CAR 4   Nina Crummy (ed, 1987), The coins from excavations in Colchester, 1971-9
CAR 5   Nina Crummy (1987), The post-Roman small finds from excavations in Colchester, 1971-85
CAR 6   Philip Crummy (1992), Excavations at Culver Street and miscellaneous sites 1971-85, Colchester, Essex
CAR 7   John Cotter (forthcoming), Post-Roman pottery from excavations in Colchester, 1971-85
CAR 8   H E M Cool and Jennifer Price (1995), Roman vessel glass from excavations in Colchester, 1971-85
CAR 9   Nina Crummy, Philip Crummy, and Carl Crossan (1993), Excavations of Roman and later cemeteries, churches and monastic sites in Colchester, 1971-88
CAR 10 Robin Symonds and Sue Wade (forthcoming), Roman pottery from excavations in Colchester, 1971-86
CAR 11 C. F. C. Hawkes and Philip Crummy (1995), Camulodunum II
CAR 12 Rosemary Luff (1993), Animal bones from excavations in Colchester, 1971-85

Iron Age and Roman Camulodunum

Recent years have seen some substantial publications concerned with the native settlement. Rosalind Niblett (1985) has published her large-scale excavation in 1970 of part of the Sheepen site, the subject of the original *Camulodunum* (C. F. C. Hawkes and M. R. Hull, 1947), and Paul Sealey (1985a) produced a study of amphoras which was an enlargement of his contribution (1985b) to the Sheepen report. Jennifer Foster published a thoughtful and exhaustive re-appraisal of the 1924 Lexden Tumulus excavation subsequently discussed by C. F. C. Hawkes (*CAR 11*). The cropmarks at Gosbecks were plotted at a large scale following the dry summers of the mid 1970s and the site proposed as the true centre of Camulodunum, rather than Sheepen (Crummy 1979a). Also at Gosbecks was the discovery of over 6,000 *antoniniani* in three pots (Davies 1983; Bland & Carradice 1986). It is probably no accident that the hoards date to c. 270-75, when the town defences were being up-graded during a period of provincial insecurity (*CAR 4*, 76).

The start date for the Sheepen site and the significance in this respect of the proportion of Dressel 1B amphoras from the site continue to be the subject of debate (Fitzpatrick 1984, 1985b; Sealey 1985a; Haselgrove 1987a and b), to which C. F. C. Hawkes has recently offered a response (*CAR 11*).

The political history of Camulodunum as originally outlined by D. F. Allen from coins (D. F. Allen, 'The Belgic dynasties of Britain and their coins', in *Archaeologia*, 90 (1944), 1-46; C. F. C. Hawkes and M. R. Hull, *Camulodunum* (1947, 5-7) has seen further review by C. C. Haselgrove (1987a and b), A. P. Fitzpatrick (1985a), Barry Cunliffe (1981), and R. D. Van Arsdell (1989) amongst others. (For an overview of the divergent views, see *CAR 11* and Crummy 1994d). R. D. Van Arsdell is the most radical in his approach, but in general his book has been poorly received by numismatists (eg Burnett 1989).

Excavations at Stanway in the early 1990s resulted in the discovery of a high status funerary site (Plate I) for a limited number of the native nobility between the late 1st century BC and c AD 60 (Crummy 1992, 1993a, and 1993b). The excavation is to continue.

---

* I am grateful to Paul Sealey for his help with problems in the bibliography.

Black, E. W. 1990a. 'Caesar's second invasion of Britain, Cassivellaunus and the Trinobantes, *Essex Archaeol Hist*, 21 (1990), 6-10

Black, E. W. 1990b. 'British chariotry and territorial *oppida*', in *Essex Archaeol Hist*, 21 (1990), 142-3

Bland, R. F. and Carradice, I. A. 1986. 'Three hoards from Olivers Orchard, Colchester', in A. M. Burnett & R. F. Bland (eds), *Coin hoards from Roman Britain*, 6, 65-118, British Museum Occasional Papers, 58

Brasier, M. D. 1986. 'Excavation at 147 Lexden Road, Colchester', in *Essex Archaeol Hist*, 16 (1984-5), 145-9

Burnett, Andrew. 1989. 'Celtic coinage, by R. D. Van Arsdell', in *Brit Numismatic J*, 59, 235-7

Crummy, Philip. 1979a. 'Crop marks at Gosbecks, Colchester', in *Aerial Archaeology*, 4, 77-82

——— 1992. 'Royal graves', in The *Colchester Archaeologist*, 5 (1991-2), 1-5 [Stanway excavation]

——— 1993a. 'Aristocratic graves at Colchester', in *Current Archaeology*, 132, 492-7 [Stanway excavation]

——— 1993b. 'Warrior burial', in The *Colchester Archaeologist*, 6 (1992-3), 1-5 [Stanway excavation]

——— 1994d. 'Late Iron Age and Roman Colchester', in *The Victoria History of the Counties of Essex*, 9: *The Borough of Colchester* (ed J. Cooper)

Cunliffe, Barry. 1981. 'Money and society in pre-Roman Britain', in *Coinage and society in Britain and Gaul*, 29-39 [The significance of the distribution of coins minted in Camulodunum]

Davies, G. M. R. 1983. 'The Olivers Orchard hoards', in *Col Archaeol Group Bull*, 26, 2-7

Eddy, M. R. and Davies, M. 1982. 'Great Canfield', 35-7, in 'Work of the Essex County Archaeological Section 1980', in *Essex Archaeol Hist*, 13 (1981), 32-47 [Tasciovanus coin with Camulodunum mint mark]

Fitzpatrick, A. P. 1984. 'Camulodunum and the early occupation of south-east England: some reconsiderations', in *Kongress-Akten der Beitrage am Limes-Kongress in Aalen 1983* (eds D. Planck & C. Unz), 35-41, Stuttgart

Fitzpatrick, A. P. 1985a. 'The Celtic coins', in *The Romano-British temple at Harlow*, (N. E. France & B. M. Gobel), West Essex Archaeological Group, 49-66 [Consideration of coins struck at Colchester]

Fitzpatrick, A. P. 1985b. 'The distribution of Dressel 1 amphorae in north-west Europe', in *Oxford J. Archaeol*, 4, 305-40 [Dressel 1B amphoras at Sheepen]

Foster, Jennifer. 1986. *The Lexden tumulus*, BAR British Series, 156

Haselgrove, C. C. 1987a. *Iron Age coinage in south-east England: the archaeological context*, BAR British Series, 174 [Consideration of coins struck at Colchester]

Haselgrove, C. C. 1987b. 'The archaeological content of Iron Age coin finds on major settlement sites in eastern England: Colchester and St Albans', in *Mélanges offerts au Docteur J-B Colbert de Beaulieu* (eds J Bousquet and P Naster), 483-96 [Consideration of coins struck at Colchester]

Hawkes, C. F. C. 1983. 'Colchester before the Romans, or who were our Belgae?' in *Essex Archaeol Hist*, 14 (1982), 3-14

Hull, M. R. and Hawkes, C. F. C. 1987. *Pre-Roman bow brooches*, BAR British Series, 168

Muckleroy, K. *et al.* 1978. 'A pre-Roman coin from Canterbury and the ship represented on it', in *Proc Prehist Soc*, 44, 439-44 [Coin of Cunobelin]

Niblett, Rosalind. 1985. *Sheepen: an early Roman industrial site at Camulodunum'*, CBA Res Rep, 57

Partridge, J. 1993a. 'The investigation of cropmarks at Church Lane, Stanway, Colchester, in *Essex Archaeol Hist*, 24 (1993), 214-8

Van Arsdell, R. D. 1989. *Celtic coinage of Britain* [Much about Camulodunum and the Trinovantes]

The development of Roman Colchester

In 1978, there was still the slim possibility that the fortress had not really existed and that what was thought to be the fortress was really the early colony. However, the subsequent Culver Street excavation confirmed beyond all reasonable doubt the existence, the plan, and the alignment of the fortress as postulated in 1977 (P. Crummy, 'The Roman fortress and the development of the *colonia*', *Britannia*, 8 (1977), 65-108) and in *CAR* 3, after the Lion Walk and Balkerne Lane excavations (Fig. 1). The discovery at Culver Street of a substantial early timber building (Building 83) under one of the east-west pre-Boudican colonial streets was critical. Such a situation was predictable from the original model following the Lion Walk

Plate I Reconstruction of the funerary enclosures at Stanway, Colchester (by P. Froste)

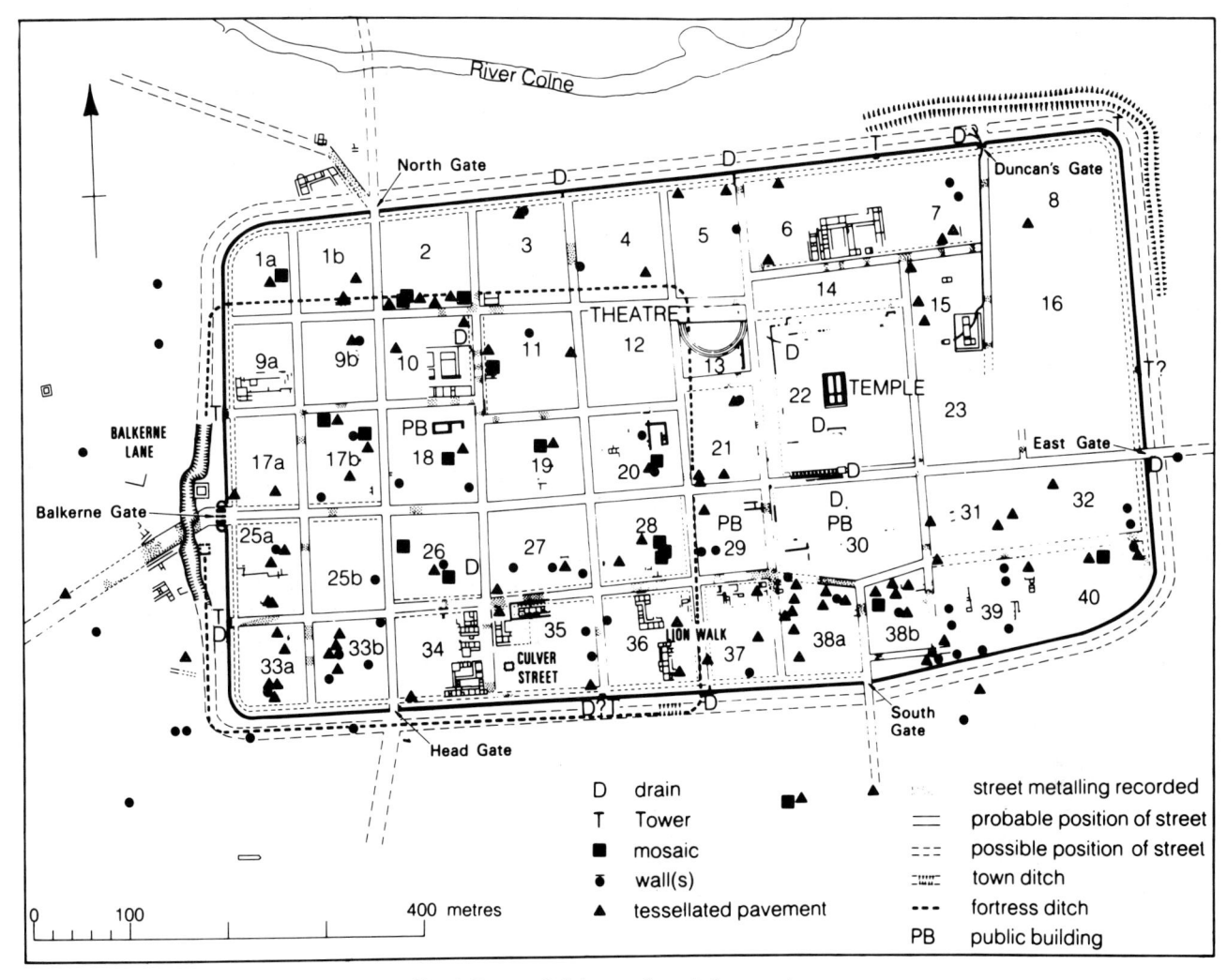

Fig. 1 Roman Colchester (late 3rd century)

excavations, and it provided confirmation of the major changes which took place to the eastern side of the fortress during its conversion to a town. The building was one of the probable tribunes' houses which lined the eastern side of the *via principalis* of the fortress. The Culver Street excavation also provided an opportunity to examine the centurions' quarters of the First Cohort (Crummy 1988, 1994a, 1994b, and CAR 6, esp 21-4), while concurrent work on the Gilberd School site allowed the first substantial examination of *contubernia* (CAR 6, 127-33).

The section through the defences at Culver Street led to a reassessment of the date of the wall. Its construction is now put at c 65-80, and is seen as a reaction to the Boudican destruction of the town. This means that the monumental arch at the Balkerne Gate can be dated to the foundation of the colony c 50 (CAR 6, 17-18, 62-4).

Since 1978, the Roman fortress has been shown to have been designed in multiples of fifty and a hundred Roman feet (*pedes Monetales* [CAR 3, 5, fig. 7]). The same principles have been demonstrated for buildings within the fortress (esp Crummy 1988 and 1994b).

The excavation and publication of the Roman church and large inhumation cemetery at Butt Road (CAR 9) has provided significant evidence of Christian burial practices, especially in the church (Plate II) and for family groupings in the burial area. The same publication also contains a summary and reassessment of the known burials and cemetery areas in Colchester. Dr D. Watts (1991) has considered the Butt Road site in a wider context, whilst Paul Drury (1984) has suggested that the Temple of Claudius may have been converted for Christian use (see Roman buildings below).

Carroll, K. K. 1979. 'The date of Boudicca's revolt', in *Britannia*, 10, 197-202 [AD 61 rather than 60]

Crummy, Philip. 1982a. 'The origins of some major Romano-British towns', in *Britannia*, 13, 125-34

——— 1985. 'Colchester: the mechanics of laying out a town', in *Roman urban topography in Britain and the western empire* (ed Francis Grew and Brian Hobley), 78-85, CBA Res Rep, 59

——— 1988. 'Colchester (Camulodunum/Colonia Victricensis)' in *Fortress into city* (ed Graham Webster), 24-41

——— 1994a. 'The development of Roman Colchester', in *Roman towns: the Wheeler inheritance, a review of 50 years' research*, 34-45, CBA Res Rep, 93

——— 1994b. 'Metrological analysis of Roman fortresses and towns in Britain', in *Roman towns: the Wheeler inheritance, a review of 50 years' research*, 111-19, CBA Res Rep, 93

——— 1994d. 'Iron Age and Roman Colchester', in *The Victoria History of the Counties of Essex, 9: The Borough of Colchester* (ed J. Cooper)

Davies, G. M. R. 1992. 'Prehistoric and Roman Colchester', in *The Colchester area* (ed N. J. G. Pounds), supplement to *Archaeol J*, 149 (1992), 7-11

Fuentes, N. 1988. 'The Trinovantes and the Antonine Itinerary', in *Essex J*, 23, 21-3 [Discusses the name of Colchester in the Roman period]

Jones, M. J. 1983. '*Coloniae* in Britain', in Roman urban defences in the west (eds J. Maloney and B. Hobley), 90-5, CBA Res Rep, 51 [Survey of the defences of the *coloniae* in Britain]

Walthew, C. V. 1988. 'Length-units in Roman military planning: Inchtuthil and Colchester', in *Oxford J Archaeol*, 7, 81-98

Watts, D. J. 1991. *Christians and pagans in Roman Britain*, Routledge [Butt Road cemetery and church]

Watts, D. J. 1993. 'An assessment of the evidence for Christianity at the Butt Road site', in CAR 9, 192-202

Plate II Reconstruction of the Butt Road Church, Colchester (by P. Froste)

Roman buildings

With the publication of the *CAR* reports, the opportunity has been taken to number the Roman and later buildings excavated wholly or partly since 1971 (*CAR* 3, Buildings 1-76; *CAR* 6, Buildings 77-138 and 141-70; *CAR* 9, Buildings 139-40; Shimmin and Carter forthcoming, Buildings 171-7; Shimmin 1994, Buildings 178-80; Benfield and Garrod 1992, Buildings 181-2).

The most important piece of work relating to the public buildings was the confirmation of the site of the theatre as predicted by M. R. Hull (Crummy 1982b). The Roman temples as a whole were surveyed in Crummy 1980; this includes a revised ground plan for the Temple of Claudius.

There has been some debate as to whether or not the construction of the Temple of Claudius could have started before AD 54, when Claudius died (Fishwick 1972 and 1991; Simpson 1993). This has some bearing on the date of the conversion of the redundant fortress into the colony, and thus the date for the end of our Period 1 and the start of Period 2 at the Lion Walk, Balkerne Lane and Culver Street sites. If the Temple was started before AD 54 (and thus presumably in c AD 50), then the date of AD 49/55 quoted everywhere (including all *CAR* reports) for these sites could be replaced simply by c 50 to imply the first few years of the colony. (The 49/55 date reflects the time assumed to be needed to level the legionary defences and construct the eastern extension of the street grid which was to incorporate the Temple of Claudius and its precinct (*CAR* 3, 8-9).)

The fate of the temple at the end of its life has also been the subject of some speculation. Paul Drury (1984) has argued that the front of the building was remodelled in a major way in the 4th century may be as part of its reuse for a Christian church. While such a change in function would not be surprising, the major structural alterations which Paul Drury suggests are not easy to accept on the basis of present evidence. It is hoped to test his hypothesis with a small excavation.

General

Barford, P. M. 1987. 'A fragment of Roman stucco from Colchester', in *Britannia*, 18, 273-4

Benfield, S. and Garrod, S. 1992. 'Two recently discovered Roman buildings at Colchester', in *Essex Archaeol Hist*, 23 (1992), 25-38

Black, E. W. 1992. 'A pre-Boudican bath-building at Colchester', in *Essex Archaeol Hist*, 23 (1992), 117-23

Crummy, Philip. 1980. 'The temples of Roman Colchester', in *Temples, churches and religion: recent research in Roman Britain* (ed Warwick Rodwell), 258-64

——— 1982b. 'The Roman theatre at Colchester', in *Britannia*, 13, 299-302; *CAR* 6, 367-8

Lockwood, F. D. and Tripp, D. P. 1985. 'Excavations at Crouched Friars, Colchester', in *Col Archaeol Group Bull*, 28, 27-40

Shimmin, D. 1994. 'Excavations at Osborne Street, Colchester', in *Essex Archaeol Hist*, 25, 46-59

Shimmin, D. and Carter, G. Forthcoming. 'Excavations at Angel Yard, High Street, Colchester, 1986 and 1989', in *Essex Archaeol Hist*

The Temple of Claudius

Drury, P. J. 1984. 'The temple of Claudius at Colchester reconsidered', in *Britannia*, 15, 7-50

Fishwick, D. 1972. '*Templum divo Claudio constitutum*', in *Britannia*, 3, 164-81

Fishwick, D. 1987. *The Imperial cult in the Latin West: studies in the ruler cult of the western provinces of the Roman Empire* (Études préliminaires aux religions orientales dans l'Émpire Romain, 108), Leiden

Fishwick, D. 1991. 'Seneca and the Temple of Divus Claudius', in *Britannia*, 22, 137-41

Simpson, C. J. 1993. 'Once again Claudius and the Temple at Colchester', in *Britannia*, 24, 1-6

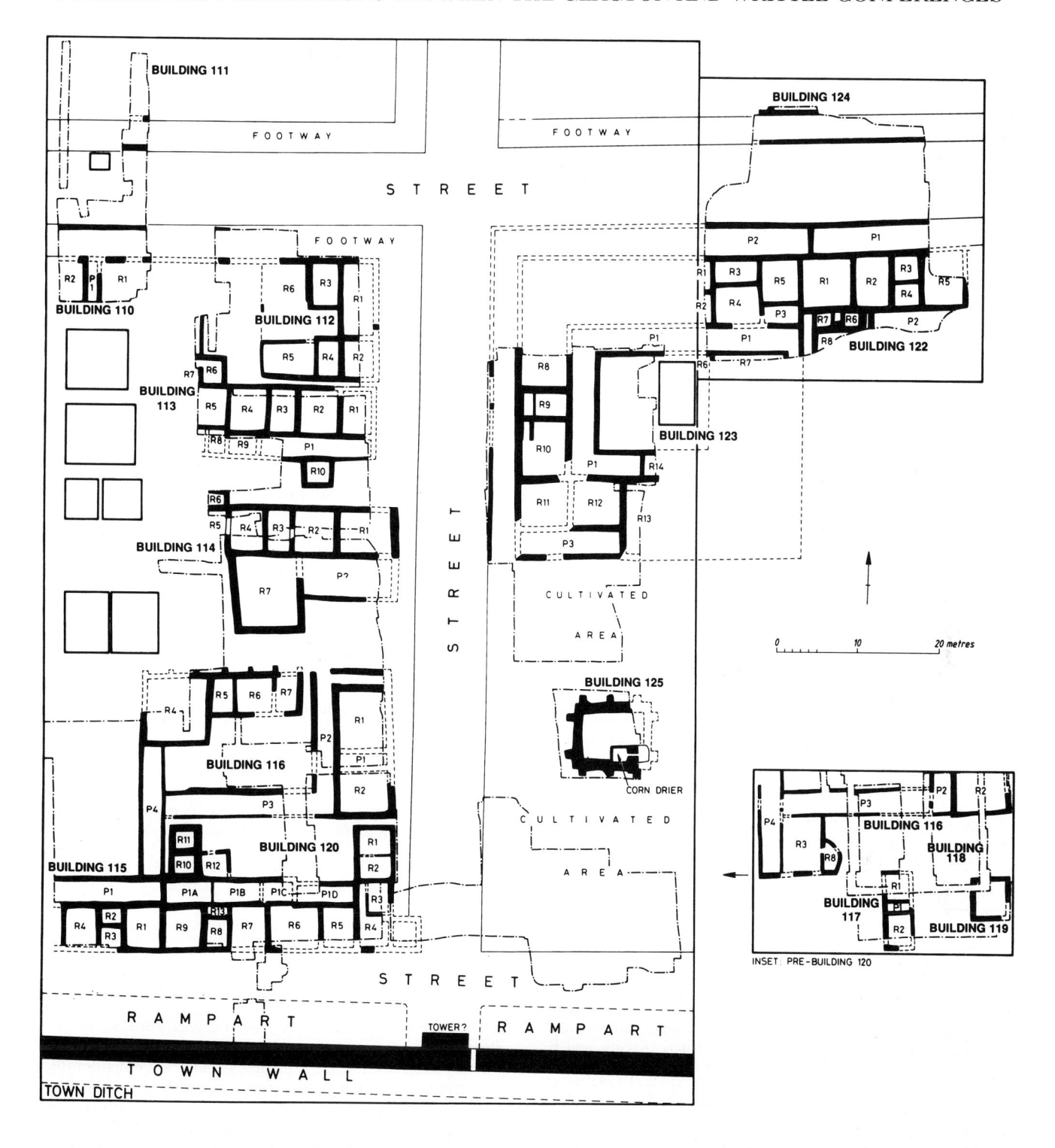

Fig. 2 Roman buildings in Colchester: the Culver Street site AD c 150/200 - c 275/325

The post-Roman period

Nothing has been found to conflict with the pattern of Anglo-Saxon occupation in Colchester as deduced in *CAR* 1 and summarised in the proceedings of the first Essex conference (P Crummy, 'Colchester between the Roman and Norman conquests', in *Archaeology in Essex to AD 1500* (ed. D. G. Buckley), 76-81). Excavations at Culver Street brought the known total of the town's sunken huts to three, with the discovery of a well-preserved building dated by finds including a bone comb to around the 7th century (*CAR* 6, 118-20). Evidence for middle and late Anglo-Saxon occupation continues to be sparse. The Angel Yard fronts on to the central part of the High Street and therefore is potentially a prime site for Middle and Late Anglo-Saxon occupation. Yet, like the Cups Hotel before it (*CAR* 6, 328, 333-5), the evidence for occupation of that date proved to be very meagre (Shimmin and Carter forthcoming). A sharp upwards swing in the population seems to have occurred in the late 10th century. Metcalf and Lean (1993) have provided a review of the Colchester mint which, for the first six years or so of starting c 991, was prolific in output.

The 1980s and late 1970s saw the publication of some of the most important medieval historical research into Colchester for many years. In particular Richard Britnell's book (1986a) deals with the economic history of mid to late medieval Colchester as gleaned principally from the borough records, while the latest VCH publication (edited by Janet Cooper) is a subsequent major piece of new research treating Colchester up to the present day.

Colchester Castle has been the focus of recent research. Paul Drury (1983) brought together various unpublished excavations in and around the castle and, together with the results of his own excavation in the keep, produced a dated sequence for the development of the keep and bailey. A ten-year programme for the repairing of the exterior of the keep was completed in 1993. Each stage of the work was preceded by detailed recording of the masonry at 1:20. Also during this time, an excavation was carried out on the site of the presumed chapel on the castle roof (Crummy 1988). None of this work is published, but there is a preliminary outline of some new ideas about the structural development of the castle and the dates involved (Crummy 1994c).

Anglo-Saxon finds
Ager, Barry. 1986. 'A cruciform brooch, said to be from Colchester', in *Essex Archaeol Hist*, 16 (1984-5), 149-50

Buckton, D. 1989. 'Late Anglo-Saxon or early Norman cloisonné enamel brooches', in *Medieval Archaeol*, 33, 153-5 [One example from Colchester]

Metcalf, D. M. and Lean, W. 1993. 'The battle of Maldon and the minting of Crux pennies in Essex: *post hoc propter hoc*', in *The battle of Maldon: fact and fiction* (ed J. Cooper) [The Saxo-Norman mint at Colchester]

Medieval history
Britnell, R. H. 1983. 'The oath book of Colchester and the Borough constitution, 1372-1404' in *Essex Archaeol Hist*, 14 (1982), 94-101

Britnell, R. H. 1986. *Growth and decline in Colchester, 1300-1525*, Cambridge

Britnell, R. H. 1987. 'Colchester courts and court records, 1310-1525', in *Essex Archaeol Hist*, 17 (1986), 133-40

Britnell, R. H. 1988. 'The fields and pastures of Colchester, 1280-1350', in *Essex Archaeol Hist*, 19 (1988), 159-65

Britnell, R. H. 1990. 'Bailiffs and burgesses in Colchester, 1400-1525', in *Essex Archaeol Hist*, 21 (1990), 103-109

Hart, C. R. 1993. 'Essex in the late tenth century', in *The battle of Maldon: fact and fiction* (ed J. Cooper), 171-204 [The formation of the Hundred of Colchester]

Martin, G. 1987. 'Book review: Growth and decline in Colchester, 1300-1525, by R. H. Britnell', in *Essex Archaeol Hist*, 17 (1986), 181

Stephenson, David. 1978. *The Book of Colchester*

Stephenson, David. 1986. 'Colchester: a smaller medieval English Jewry', in *Essex Archaeol Hist*, 16 (1984-5), 48-52

Colchester Castle
Crummy, Philip. 1988. 'The chapel on the roof', in *The Colchester Archaeologist*, 2, 1-3

— — — 1994c. 'The castle that Eudo built', in *The Colchester Archaeologist*, 7, 1-7

Drury, P. J. 1983. Aspects of the origins and development of Colchester Castle', in *Archaeol J*, 139 (1982), 302-419

Drury, P. J. 1990. 'Anglo-Saxon painted plaster excavated at Colchester Castle, Essex', in *Early medieval wall painting and painted sculpture in England* (eds S. Cather, D. Park and P. Williamson), 111-22, BAR British Series, 216

Partridge, J. 1993b. 'The excavation of a lift shaft at Colchester Castle, in *Essex Archaeol Hist*, 24 (1993), 234-6

Post-Roman general
Crummy, Philip. 1979b. The system of measurement used in town planning from the ninth to the thirteenth centuries', in *Anglo-Saxon studies in archaeology and history* (eds S. C. Hawkes, D. Brown, and J. Campbell), 149-64, BAR British Series, 72 [Possible planning at Colchester]

Fawn, A. J. 1984. 'A kiln at Olivers, Stanway', in *Col Archaeol Group Bull*, 27, 19-24 [Post-medieval brick kilns]

Fawn, A. J. 1985. 'A kiln at Olivers, 1985: second report', in *Col Archaeol Group Bull*, 28, 7-20 [Post-medieval brick kilns]

Roman and post-Roman small finds including coins
The three major groups of small Roman and post-Roman finds to be published since 1978 all relate to the town-centre excavations (*CAR 2* (Roman), *CAR 5* (post-Roman), *CAR 6*, 140-250 (Roman)). A substantial report on Colchester's clay pipes was prepared by Joy Hind and Nina Crummy (*CAR 5*, 47-66).

Also since 1978 there has been the publication of the section on pre-Roman brooches (Hull and Hawkes 1987) in Hull's major brooch corpus, although the bulk of it (the Roman section) is with the editor (Dr G. Simpson).

As regards coins, Robert Kenyon (1992), following his analysis of Roman coins from Culver Street and elsewhere in Britain, has suggested that there may have been a Claudian mint in Colchester, and Metcalf and Lean (1993) have published a re-appraisal of the Saxo-Norman mint in the town. (The latter and the Anglo-Saxon finds from the town are mentioned in the previous section.)

Bailey, D. M. 1988. *A catalogue of the lamps in the British Museum. III. Roman provincial lamps* [23 examples from Colchester]

Bennet, J. and Young, R. 1981. 'Some new and forgotten stamped skillets, and the date of P Cipius Polybius', in *Britannia*, 12, 37-44 [Three examples from Colchester]

Crummy, Nina. 1979. 'A chronology of bone pins', in *Britannia*, 10, 157-63 [Based on Colchester examples]

— — — 1981a. 'Bone-working at Colchester', in *Britannia*, 12, 277-85

— — — 1981b. 'An unusual brooch from Colchester', in *Britannia*, 12, 287-8

Davies, J. A. 1993. 'The study of coin finds from Romano-British towns', in *Roman Towns: the Wheeler Inheritance* (ed S. J. Greep), 123-33, CBA Res Rep, 93

Egan, G. 1989. 'Leaden seals for textiles - some archaeological evidence relating to fabrics and trade', in *Costume*, 23, 39-53 [Discussion of Colchester as a textile centre]

Galliou, Patrick. 1981. 'The eastern Gaulish brooches found in Britain', in *Britannia*, 12, 288-90 [One example from Colchester]

Hammerson, M. J. 1980. Romano-British imitations of the coinage of AD 330-48, thesis for degree of M. Phil, University of London [Draws on the hoard from the Cups Hotel site]

Henig, M. 1983. 'Two gold rings from Colchester', in *Essex Archaeol Hist*, 14 (1982), 153-5

Jackson, R. 1985. 'Cosmetic sets from late Iron Age and Roman Britain', in *Britannia*, 16, 165-92 [Many examples from Colchester - more than elsewhere]

Kenyon, R. 1992. 'The Claudian coins from Culver Street Phase 2 and the Gilberd School', in *CAR 6*, 295-307

Major, H. J. and Eddy, M. R. 1986. 'Four lead objects of possible Christian significance from East Anglia', in *Britannia*, 17, 355-8 [One example from the Balkerne Lane excavations at Colchester]

McPeake, J. C. and Moore, N. 1978 'A bronze skillet-handle from Chester', in *Britannia*, 9, 331-4 [Three examples from Colchester]

Wickenden, N. P. 1988. 'Some Roman military bronzes from the Trinovantian *civitas*', in *Military equipment and the identity of Roman soldiers: proceedings of the 4th military equipment conferences* (ed J. C. Coulston), 234-56, BAR International Series, 394

Pottery
Pottery is an area which continues to attract considerable attention and much publication. The major Roman project since 1978 has been the preparation for publication in corpus form of the pottery from the 1971-85 excavations in Colchester town centre (*CAR 10*). It is hoped that the report will appear in print in 1996. The equivalent volume for the post-Roman pottery (*CAR 7*) should follow later. Other major works concern the Sheepen amphoras referred to earlier (Sealey 1985a) and the Colchester kilns (Rodwell 1982) which is usefully supplemented by Swan 1984. The following list of publications is not exhaustive.

Crummy, P. and Terry, R. 1979. 'Seriation problems in urban archaeology, in *Pottery and the archaeologist* (ed. M. Millett), Institute of Archaeology, London, occasional publication, 4 [Based on pottery excavated in Colchester in the 1970s]

Hart, F. A. *et al.* 1987. 'An analytical study, using inductively coupled plasma (ICP) spectrometry, of samian and colour-coated wares from the Roman town of Colchester together with related continental samian wares', in *J Archaeol Sci*, 14, 577-98

Millett, Martin. 1987. 'Boudicca, the first Colchester Potters' shop, and the dating of Neronian samian', in *Britannia*, 18, 93-127

Niblett, Rosalind *et al.* 1985. 'The ceramics', in *Sheepen: an early Roman industrial site at Camulodunum*, 48-111, CBA Res Rep, 57

Rhodes, M. 1989. 'Roman pottery lost en route from the kiln site to the user - a gazetteer', in *J. Roman Pottery Studies*, 2, 44-8 [Details of the excavation in 1971 by G. M. R. Davies of the Second Pottery Shop at Colchester]

Rodwell, Warwick. 1982. 'The production and distribution of pottery and tiles in the territory of the Trinovantes', in *Essex Archaeol Hist*, 14 (1982), 15-76 [Review of the pottery kilns at Colchester]

Sealey, P. R. 1985a. *Amphoras from the 1970 excavations at Colchester, Sheepen*, BAR British Series, 142

Sealey, P. R. 1985b. 'The amphoras - summary and conclusions', in *Sheepen: an early Roman industrial site at Camulodunum* (Rosalind Niblett), 98-111, CBA Res Rep, 57

Sealey, P. R. and Davies, G. M. R. 1984. 'Falernian wine at Roman Colchester', in *Britannia*, 15, 250-4

Sealey, P. R. and Tyers, P. A. 1990. 'Olives from Roman Spain: a unique amphora find in British waters', *Antiq J*, 69 (1989), 53-72 [London 555 amphoras from the Culver Street site, Colchester, and from Fingringhoe]

Simpson, G. 1983. 'A revised dating for the Colchester samian kiln', in *Essex Archaeol Hist*, 14 (1982), 149-53

Storey, J. M. V. *et al.* 1989. 'A chemical investigation of 'Colchester' samian ware by means of inductively-coupled plasma emission spectrometry', in *J. Roman Pottery Studies*, 2, 33-43

Symonds, R. P. 1987a. 'Le problème gobelets ovoides sablés', in *Actes du Congrès de Caen 28-31 Mai 1987. Les céramiques Gallo-Romaines et Romano-Britanniques dans le Nord-Ouest de l'Empire: Place de la Normandie entre le Continent et les Iles Britanniques. Actualité des recherches céramiques en Gaule* (ed L. Rivet), 69-74 [Pottery made at Colchester]

Symonds, R. P. 1987b. 'La production de la sigillée à Colchester en Angleterre, et les liens avec les ateliers de la Gaule de l'Est: quelques résultats chimiques', in *Rev Archéol Est Centre-Est*, 38, 77-81

Symonds, R. P. 1990. 'The problem of rough-cast beakers and related colour-coated wares', in *J. Roman Pottery Studies*, 3, 1-17 [includes Colchester fine wares]

Symonds, R. P. and Wade, S. M. 1989. 'A remarkable jar found inside an amphora cremation chamber at Colchester', *J Roman Pottery Studies*, 2, 85-7

Symonds, R. P. and Wade, S. M. 1986. 'A large Central Gaulish glazed vessel with applied-moulded decoration from Colchester', in *J Roman Pottery Studies*, 1, 55-7

Swan, Vivien G, 1984. *The pottery kilns of Roman Britain*, 92-95, HMSO [Includes summary of those at Colchester]

Willis, S. H. 1990. 'Mould-decorated south Gaulish colour-coated cups from Fingringhoe Wick, Essex', in *J. Roman Pottery Studies*, 3, 30-4 [A riverside site downstream from the Roman town]

Bone, plant, and other organic remains

The main work on excavated animal bone is described in *CAR* 12 by Rosemary Luff, using some of the material incorporated in Luff 1982. Peter Murphy examined plant and other organic remains as part of his study of the environmental material from Culver Street and elsewhere, while Alison Locker undertook an equally informative analysis of the Roman and later fish bones (*CAR* 6, 273-8). Very little preserved wood and leather has been recovered in the absence of water-logged conditions, other than a small quantity from the Osborne Street site (Nina Crummy in Shimmin 1994). There has been some limited work on charcoal by Maisie Taylor (principally *CAR* 6, 284 and 289) and mineral-replaced wood by Jacqui Watson of the Ancients Monuments Laboratory at English Heritage (various objects in *CAR* 6 and 9).

Stephanie Pinter-Bellows completed a major report on the human remains from the Butt Road cemetery where she was able to provide some correlation between genetic characteristics and possible family plots detectable in the distributions of some graves (*CAR* 9, 7-8, 16-19, 32-3, 62-91).

Luff, Rosemary-Margaret. 1982. *A zooarchaeological study of the Roman north-western provinces*, BAR International Series, 137

Luff, Rosemary-Margaret. 1985. 'The Fauna', in *Sheepen: an early Roman industrial site at Camulodunum* (Rosalind Niblett), 143-9, CBA Res Rep, 59

Stirland, Ann. 1993. 'Analysis and description of the human remains from St John's Abbey Grounds and the Maldon Road site, 1971-2', in *CAR* 9, 289-90

Vessel glass

The Roman vessel glass from 1971-85 excavations has been published as *CAR* 8. A report on the medieval vessel glass from the excavations has been prepared by Rachel Tyson (1994).

Price, Jennifer, & Cool, H. E. M. 1991. 'The evidence for the production of glass in Roman Britain', in *Ateliers de verriers de l'antiquité à la période pré-industrielle* (eds Danièle Foy and Geneviève Sennequier) [Evidence for glass production at Colchester]

Niblett, Rosalind. 1985. 'The glass', in *Sheepen: an early Roman industrial site at Camulodunum*, 136-41, CBA Res Rep, 57

Tyson, Rachel. 1994. 'The medieval vessel glass from Colchester', Colchester Archaeological Trust Archive Report, place of eventual publication uncertain [Material excavated between 1971 and 1985]

The Roman Towns of Essex

N. P. Wickenden

Introduction

Just as the Clacton Conference of 1978 reviewed the progress made in the fifteen years since the publication of the Victoria County History of Essex volume 3, so the Writtle conference reviewed the fifteen years from 1978 to 1993. VCH Volume 3 was, of course, a milestone publication by Hull and Brinson in drawing together a century's worth of a millefiore of Late Iron Age and Roman excavations and findspots, and it justifiably remains a standard reference today.

Drury and Rodwell's *Settlements in the later Iron Age and Roman periods* in the Clacton proceedings (Drury and Rodwell 1980) drew on the massive increase in the number of excavations which had taken place in the later 1960s and first half of the 1970s as a result of the relentless pace of development seen at that time, and the resultant pressure of RESCUE and the emergence of professional field units. One such unit was Chelmsford Excavation Committee (later Chelmsford Archaeological Trust), founded in 1968 and which finally closed in 1988. A review of the work of this unit appears elsewhere in this volume (Wickenden, p192-8).

Units in those days were so frantic in their rescue bids that final publication was, sad to say, a luxury not then on offer. Thus, when Drury and Rodwell summarised the situation 15 years ago, they were still mainly working from interim reports. It helped, of course, that they were for the most part the site directors themselves. Their paper at the Clacton Conference followed on from their earlier papers in the 1975 British Archaeological Report *The Small Towns of Roman Britain* (Drury 1975; Rodwell 1975a), and Dunnett's *The Trinovantes* (1975).

Thus the overriding major advance in the past 15 years has been the emergence of the bulk of the final excavation reports, taking on average 16-20 years since the dates of the excavations[a]. The medieval sites of those days have, by comparison, not fared so well.

Much of what follows is, of course, the result of continuing work by the ECC Archaeology Section and various local societies in all of these towns, as well as publication of even earlier forays (eg the West Essex Archaeological Group's publication of the Harlow Temple: France and Gobel 1985).

Relatively little of what follows actually *changes* substantially the picture painted by Drury and Rodwell 15 years ago. Their distribution maps can be added to with a few new find spots; their research priorities remain almost unaltered, see below, p93-4[b]. The Chelmsford mansio may now be one of the most thoroughly examined examples of its genre, but there are still yawning gaps in our knowledge about how it operated. Recent work in other towns, such as Braintree and Great Dunmow, is failing to support the models and hypothetical town plans and road lines published in those final reports (Drury 1976; Wickenden 1988a; see below).

Nevertheless, advances have been made in many areas, both urban, thematic, such as Roman pottery typology and supply, Roman small find typology by function rather than material, and rural (Going, this volume). This paper briefly reviews the Iron Age origins of some towns, the early military landscape of Essex, Roman religion in the county, and then looks at parameters for defining a Roman town in Essex, and the associated evidence. In some instances I concentrate on Roman Chelmsford for my main evidence.

The Iron Age origins

It is possible to see many of the Romano-British small towns as mere developments of existing Late Iron Age farmsteads and hamlets. A fairly rich site is known at Great Chesterford, mainly from the Brambleshot Grove cemetery finds, notably a mirror, a bronze-bound bucket (Cunliffe 1978, pl 26b), shale vessels and Dressel 1 amphorae. Heybridge has been recognised as a port of some pretension in the late Iron Age (Wickenden 1987, 61-2). Another mirror comes from Billericay (Fox 1958, 96), and close by is the possible focus of a defended settlement at Norsey Wood. A strikingly high number of Late Iron Age cremations come from south of the town centre, along with potins and Cunobelin issues (Rudling 1990, 44-5). Even Chelmsford, for long thought to have been built on virgin land, now has a settlement of at least 9 roundhouses pre-dating its post-Boudican fort (see below).

The site of a Belgic *oppidum* was postulated at Braintree by Drury on the east side of the town below the Coggeshall Road (Drury 1976, 104-108, 121-123 and fig. 49). Recent work by the ECC Archaeology Section, however, identified the supposed bank at Mount House to be post medieval (Bedwin 1986). Excavations by the Brain Valley Archaeological Society have revealed the circular gullies from Iron Age round houses, and coins of Cunobelin and Addedomarus further to the south west on the Fountain and Boars Head sites (Priddy 1983, 163; Havis 1994, 61). A large ditched feature, full of Belgic pottery has also been found on the College House and 2-4 London Road sites[c]. It looks, therefore, as if the pre-Roman occupation must be looked for in this quarter at the expense of the *oppidum* (Burnham and Wacher 1990, 291). These sites also produced the earliest Roman occupation in the form of 1st-century timber buildings - surely no coincidence.

The early military landscape in Essex

The early 1980s saw disagreement between those, like the Rodwells, who postulated the presence of military forts in many of the small towns, based on the evidence of military-like defensive ditches and a handful of items of military equipment - and those, like Eddy, who adopted a minimalist approach (Drury and Rodwell 1980, 64-5; Eddy 1982). One can sympathise with both sides - a few pieces of military equipment are not indicative of a fort *per se* - nor are all ditches necessarily defending that fort.[d] On the other hand, there is a strategic logic in the placing of forts at key nodal geographical points in the county; and it is remarkable how little material evidence even known forts can leave behind.

---

[a]Saffron Walden, Bassett 1982; Saxon Heybridge, Drury and Wickenden 1982b; Roman Heybridge, Wickenden 1987; Kelvedon, K Rodwell 1988; Great Dunmow, Wickenden 1988; Chelmsford mansio, Drury 1988; Chelmsford temple, Wickenden 1992; Frontage sites in Chelmsford, Isserlin and Wickenden forthcoming.

[b]Since backed up by the publication of the ECC's Historic Towns in Essex in 1983 and Archaeology in Chelmsford: a Policy for the future (ECC Archaeology Section/Chelmsford Museums Service 1989, 3rd edition)

[c]I am grateful to Richard Havis for information.

[d]A ditch from Kelvedon was interpreted as coming from a military fort by the Rodwells (*Current Archaeology*, 45, 25-30). This was disputed by Eddy (Eddy 1982, *passim*). The final report restates the military case (K Rodwell 1988, 25-6, 135).

THE ROMAN TOWNS OF ESSEX

Today, on balance there is extremely little evidence for invasion-period military presence in Essex outside of the small 4-acre fort at Gosbecks and the legionary fortress on the ridge above the Colne at Colchester (Crummy 1988), though it can be safely postulated that the site at Fingringhoe must be a Claudian supply base (VCH 1963, 130-2).

In Colchester itself the barrack blocks of the fort built from about AD 44 have been revealed in large open-area excavations, notably Culver Street and the Gilberd School, and have recently been published along with a quantity of military metal and bone work (Crummy 1992).

Rodwell's postulated fort at Orsett Cock has since been proved by excavation to be a native Iron Age settlement with continuing occupation into the Roman period but with no question of any military involvement (Toller 1980, 41-2). The similar site at Hadleigh must thus similarly be discounted.

But of course, Trinovantian Essex was already heavily Romanised by the time of the invasion - the natives were friendly - as the material evidence shows: copper alloy patera and ewer sets known at Heybridge, Plesheybury, Rivenhall, Stanway and Stansted Airport, mirrors at Rivenhall and Billericay, wine amphorae, arretine at Camulodunum, Fingringhoe, Heybridge, Plesheybury, and Kelvedon. The apparent genuine lacuna of a Claudian military presence can thus be explained - there was no need for any further forts.

After the rebellion of Boudica there was a totally different situation, one where the Trinovantes were no longer trusted and needed supervision. The distribution of military metalwork is starting to reveal the pattern of deployment - however temporary - of Roman troops in the aftermath of the disaster at key nodal places on the road and river network in the county. It follows that it is no coincidence that some of those places subsequently grew into civilian market towns. Most of the Small Towns have revealed Late Pre-Roman Iron Age occupation, so that it is a matter of conjecture whether the Roman town is the natural result of continuation of occupation, or whether a phase of military occupation, detailed to supervise the Trinovantian settlements, provided the catalyst. The recent Treasure Trove hoard of early silver denarii, found close to the native site at Woodham Walter, may well be the savings of an officer sent to sort out a minor skirmish.[e]

Little can be made *per se* of single items of military equipment: a nielloed belt stiffener at Dunmow; an abraded strap end from Heybridge; a cuirass fitting at London Road, Braintree (*Essex Archaeology*, 2, p5); a couple of harness pendants and some shield binding from Kelvedon (Wickenden 1988b). Yet these are all places where some sort of military presence might be expected - Heybridge for instance was a major port from Iron Age times on, and must have been supervised and used by the Roman fleet.

Furthermore, a collection of military metalwork at Harlow (pendants, strap terminals, mounts and fasteners, and lobate hinge plates from lorica segmentata) may be put down to soldiers visiting a well-established religious site (or to the votive offering of military equipment by others), though material including a pilum head, a nielloed mount and 136 brooches also comes from the Holbrooks site on the south bank of the Stort at the crossing of the Braughing road, where a second temple has been postulated (*Current Archaeology*, 112, 163-6; France and Gobel 1985, *passim*; Wickenden 1988a, 243-4; Bartlett 1987a and pers comm). From excavations by the Rodwells at Beauchamps Farm, Wickford (1965-1971) come a fragment of a martingale, a trumpet mouthpiece and other finds (Wickenden 1988b). Further work there by Pauline Neild added an *as* of Tiberius, counterstamped TIB.IM, known to have been used on the Rhine frontier at Moguntiacum, whence came Legio XIV to take part in the Invasion (Couchman 1979, 41-50). There is also a length of military-type ditch at Wickford, and we can surely postulate a genuine military presence, possibly pre-Boudican, there.

Another genuine, probably post-Boudican, fort is at Great Chesterford - again a vital piece of strategic location, controlling the River Cam, Ermine Street, and the Icknield Way into East Anglia (Burnham and Wacher 1990, 138-142). It was also already a thriving settlement at the time of the Conquest. Finds include a trumpet mouthpiece, an early sword-chape from Vera Evison's excavations of the Saxon cemetery to the north, and two harness pendants discovered in 1987 800m south of the south gate of the town.[f] Outside the town, another harness pendant was also discovered in 1987, at Ashdon (Wickenden 1988a, 242 and pl 2).

The fort at Great Chesterford has been reduced in size since the discovery of its NE corner by Rodwell in 1972 (Rodwell 1972, 290-293; Eddy 1980, 42). That has been shown to be the corner of a possible eastern annexe, with the main eastern defensive line of the fort picked up in a trench in 1979 by the Chesterford Archaeology Group, comprising a double ditch, 4.5m wide x 1.3m deep with a counterscarp bank, and a timber-revetted rampart on a gravel base, 6m wide. The northern defences had previously been located by Brinson after the war, the western line is limited by the river, and the southern gate can be projected by extending the lines of the Roman roads. This gives a size now of 9.9ha, which still compares favourably with Longthorpe, for instance, at 10.3ha. It is still possible that an even earlier fort is lurking at Chesterford.

Chelmsford

The trouble is that military metalwork is virtually impossible to distinguish either side of AD60. At Chelmsford, a post-Boudican fort was postulated by Drury on the Godfreys site (Drury 1988, Site S), and the complete plan of the quadrilateral enclosure, with maximum dimensions of 101m x 66m, was subsequently recovered by the ECC Archaeology Section in 1987 (Wickenden 1991, 8). Further north, immediately south of the bridge over the rivers Can and Chelmer another fort has been located in excavations of the early to mid 1970s. The material evidence includes the bone hilt guard of a gladius handle, and the decorative hook of a bird-headed double-lobed pendant of a type found complete at Cirencester (Wickenden 1988a; Fig. 3). Work by Mike Bishop has suggested that these are an ethnic attribute of Thracian cavalry auxiliary, based on a study of their findspots and associated Thracian inscriptions;[g] There *is* Claudian samian from Chelmsford, but also a dearth of pre-Flavian coarse wares, and it was this discovery by Chris Going which helped dispel the idea of a Claudian fort there (Going 1987). The Claudian imitation *asses* from Chelmsford are also thought by Robert Kenyon to be later rather than earlier (pers comm).

---

[e] I am grateful to Dr Sealey for providing information on this hoard (Accession Number COLEM 1993. 19).

[f] Purchased by Saffron Walden Museum (Accesssion Number SAFWM 1988. 16-17

[g] Bishop 1987, 123-5. The bird-headed pendants have been found from Colchester, Cirencester, Gloucester Kingsholm, Wroxeter, and now Chelmsford. Apart from Chelmsford, all the other sites have also yielded evidence for Thracian military units.

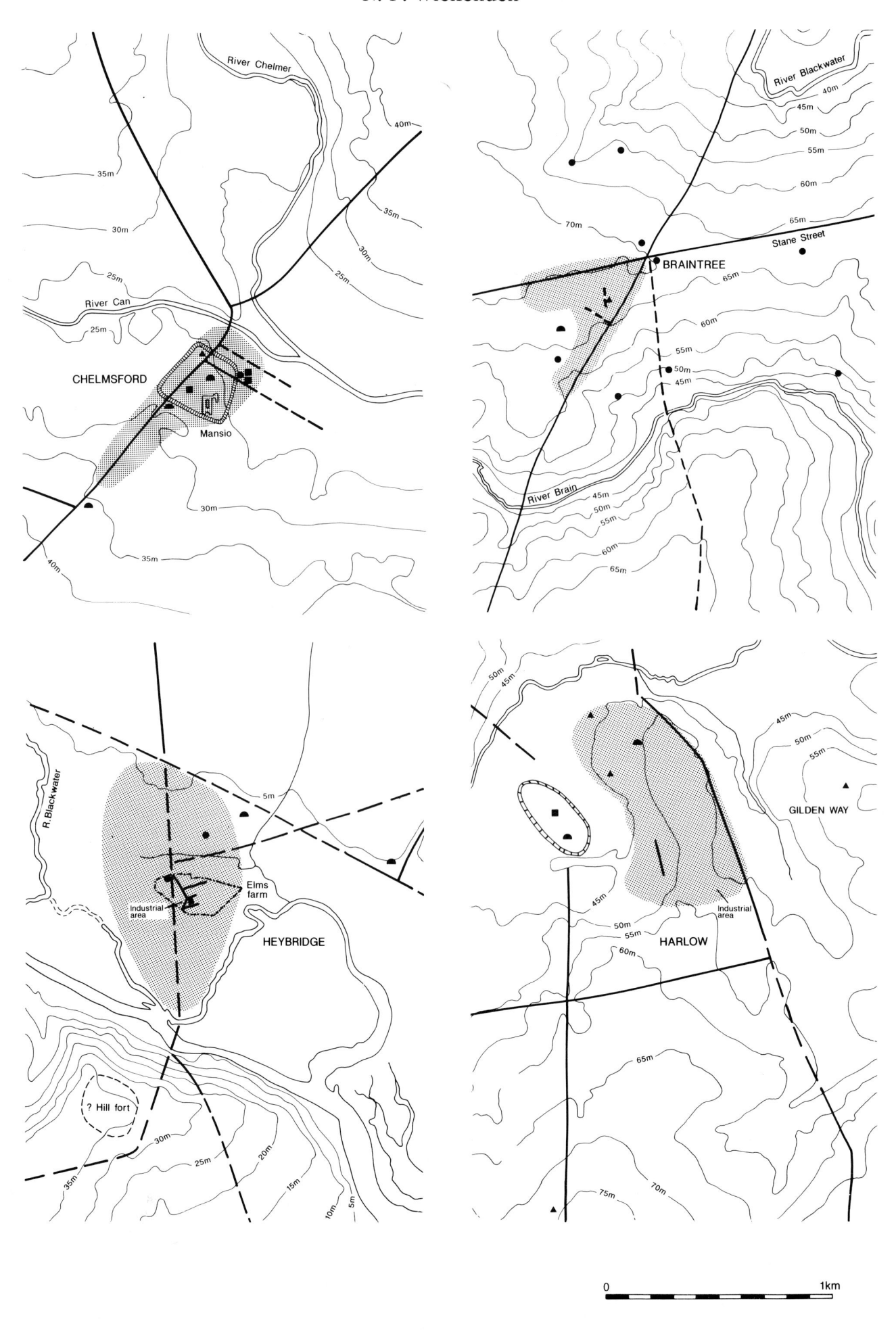

Fig. 1 The Roman 'Small Towns' of Essex (compare Rodwell 1975a, fig. 2)

THE ROMAN TOWNS OF ESSEX

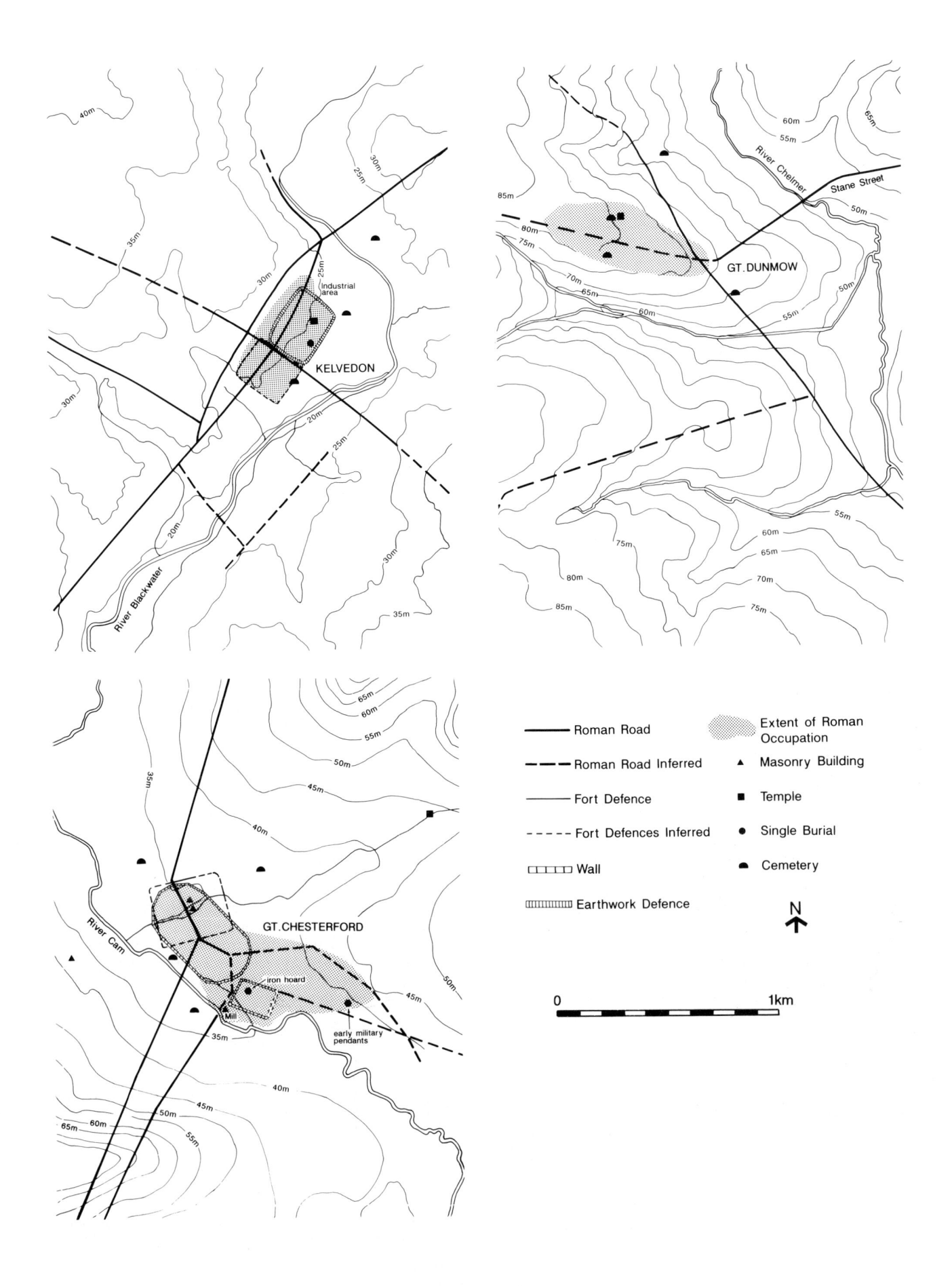

Fig. 2 The Roman 'Small Towns' of Essex

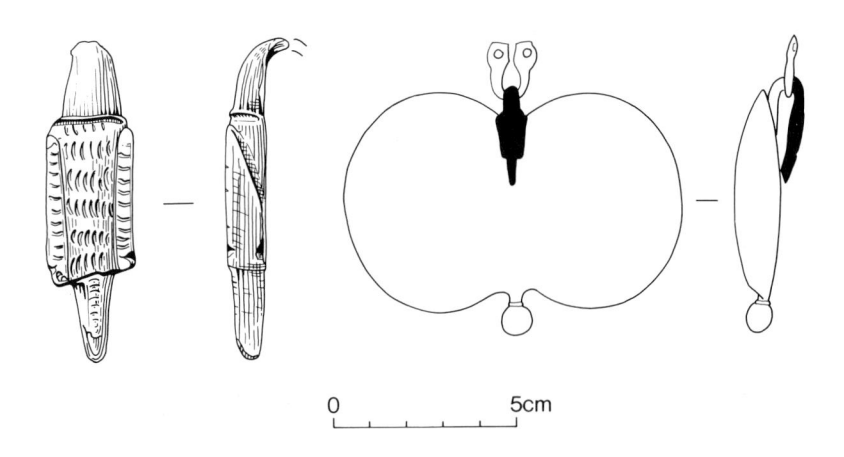

Fig. 3 Reconstruction of the bird-headed double-lobed pendant from Chelmsford

Structural evidence suggests that this northern fort superceded a small farmstead of at least 9 roundhouses on the site - though there is hardly a single scrap of Belgic pottery to accompany it. Slots for wooden beams, postholes and post-in-slot construction survive in just sufficient quantities to reconstruct the alignment and one main building (Fig. 4). There are also traces of an early, narrower road below the side road which leaves Moulsham Street east towards the port at Heybridge. There is no other indication of the size of the fort; Fig. 5 summarises the evidence for an early military landscape at Chelmsford: a northern fort; religious veneration outside to the north east, marked by early brooches, a decorated stud, apron strap and Claudian *as* copy; a *laconicum* outside to the south; and second fort or military compound further south still. The northern fort was probably very short-lived, perhaps no more than a few years, and the London-Colchester road alignment appears to have run straight across it, when finally gravelled c.AD65. One final observation - cutting one of the round-houses in the military levels was the deep burial of a young, apparently healthy male pig - a good luck sacrifice for legio XX? (Wickenden 1991, 8).

In briefly considering later military metalwork, there is a small collection of later Antonine equipment at Chelmsford, possibly indicating that the earthwork defences constructed there c.170 AD were the work of the military, as well as chapes and mounts from Gestingthorpe and High Easter (Drury 1988, fig. 63; Draper 1985, fig. 14. 98-100, fig. 15.114; Wickenden 1988b). The myth of the late Antonine fires sweeping through Roman towns in Essex must be finally put to rest. Some burnt samian is recorded, and some localised burnt deposits, but nothing on the scale that should be associated with major town fires, such as associated with Boudican deposits, and Antonine fires in London and Verulamium (Colin Wallace, pers comm).

Religion (Fig. 6)
Several different levels of religious practises in Roman Essex are apparent. On a private level, individuals owned personal items with religious significance, such as finger rings, decorated belt buckles or pipeclay figurines of Venus. An intaglio from Braintree found in 1983 in a late Roman pond depicts Asklepios and Hygeia, the first depiction of Asklepios in Britain, which might have belonged to a doctor or someone similar (Henig 1985, 241-2). From Harlow Temple comes a late Roman buckle plate engraved with a peacock pecking the fruit of a small tree, similar to a somewhat cruder strap end from Rivenhall, and both with obvious Christian significance (Bartlett 1987b; Fig. 7).

Some finds, such as the copper alloy Mother Goddess figure from the Dawes Heath villa, possibly part of a relief of *deae matres*, may also be personal possessions (Drury and Wickenden 1982, 242- 3). From Gestingthorpe come fragments of a clay mould for a classical male figurine, and an ivory casket fitting carved with a cupid (Draper 1985, fig. 38; p75, 80 and fig. 39.438). A copper alloy horse and rider figurine, found at Braintree in 1988, has been identified as a celticised Mars (H Major in Havis 1994, 44-6 and fig. 18).

As far as the pipeclay figurines are concerned, their exact significance is unclear, whether souvenir, portable deity or what. The two figurines in Chelmsford Museum, showing a boy holding fruit, have, however, been shown by Colin Wallace to be post-medieval.[h]

Objects for offering to deities at temple sites can be secular, such as fragments of bracelets or finger rings; or special, such as miniature axes[i], miniature iron spearheads from Harlow, or a bronze mounted ivory breast also from Harlow - the latter possibly an indication that the depositor had an illness or disease in that particular organ (Bartlett, pers comm).

Individuals could also display religious beliefs in graffiti on pottery, such as a TOUTATIS graffito on a grey ware jar from Kelvedon, a wheel graffito from Chelmsford, and Chi-Rho graffiti from Kelvedon and the Temple of Claudius at Colchester (Rodwell 1988, fig. 77; Wickenden 1992, fig. 58.8; Drury 1984, fig. 16.10).

Public religion was also organised at a 'municipal' level: most towns have revealed examples of Romano-Celtic temples, whether square, circular or octagonal. Many are built on long-lived religious sites often dating back to the Iron Age, as at Harlow. The octagonal temple at Chelmsford, built c AD 325, is the grand culmination of at least three centuries of veneration (Wickenden 1992). This started in

---

[h]The two pipeclay figurines were originally published as Roman by Jenkins (1978). Chelmsford and Essex Museum, Accession Numbers CHMER B18029, 18029A.

[i]Eg Draper 1985, Fig. 19. 145; a recent addition to the corpus of miniature axes was found at Tillingham. *Essex Archaeol. Hist.* 24 (1993), 220-1.

THE ROMAN TOWNS OF ESSEX

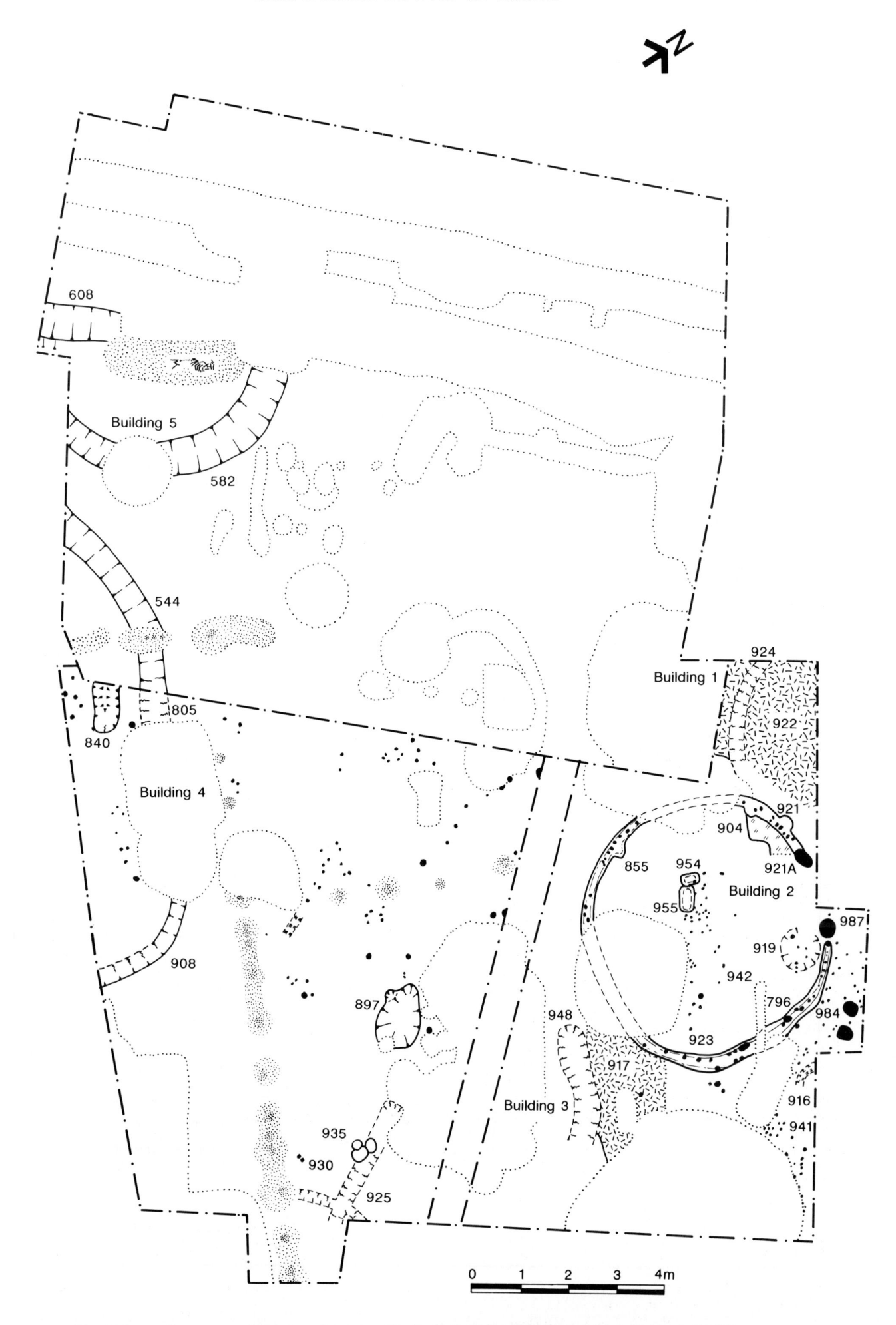

Fig. 4 The pre-Roman round-house settlement at Chelmsford, with early Roman military features stippled

the mid 1st century with a ditched enclosure, gravel path, and series of votive offerings of brooches, pieces of jewellery, an oddly decorated bar (Wickenden 1986), and a ceramic lamp chimney similar to one from Verulamium. This may have been used or even begun by the soldiers from the post-Boudican Fort. By the end of the 1st century AD, there was a two-celled apsidal temple or possible *schola* on the site, with masonry footings.[j] This was replaced in the Hadrianic period by another temple probably off the excavated site. Only ancillary corridor-like structures were found, perhaps indicating a much larger religious precinct with a number of constituent buildings, as at Pagans Hill. When the octagonal masonry temple was built, an area with lobed depressions, possibly a grove of trees, appears to have been dug up and filled in with masonry hardcore including painted wall plaster from an unknown source. One particularly remarkable find was a bone plaque carved with a person dressed in a toga, with either a strange coiffeur or possibly wearing a head dress (Wickenden 1986).

An analysis of the faunal remains from the temple site by Rosemary Luff suggested a possible specially bred herd of sheep in the 1st and 2nd centuries - based on the amount of calculus in the jaws, and a secondary foramen in the mandibles (Wickenden 1992, 120).

The corner of a second square Romano-Celtic temple has been tentatively identified at Chelmsford, inside the corner of the projected mansio precinct, close to the main London-Colchester Road, possibly for the private use of the guests of the mansio (Drury 1988, 134).

---

[j]The closest parallels for this apsidal building come from Neckarburken in Baden Wurttemberg in Germany, interpreted as a 'cult' building, either a mithraeum or a *schola* (Wickenden 1992, 128-129).

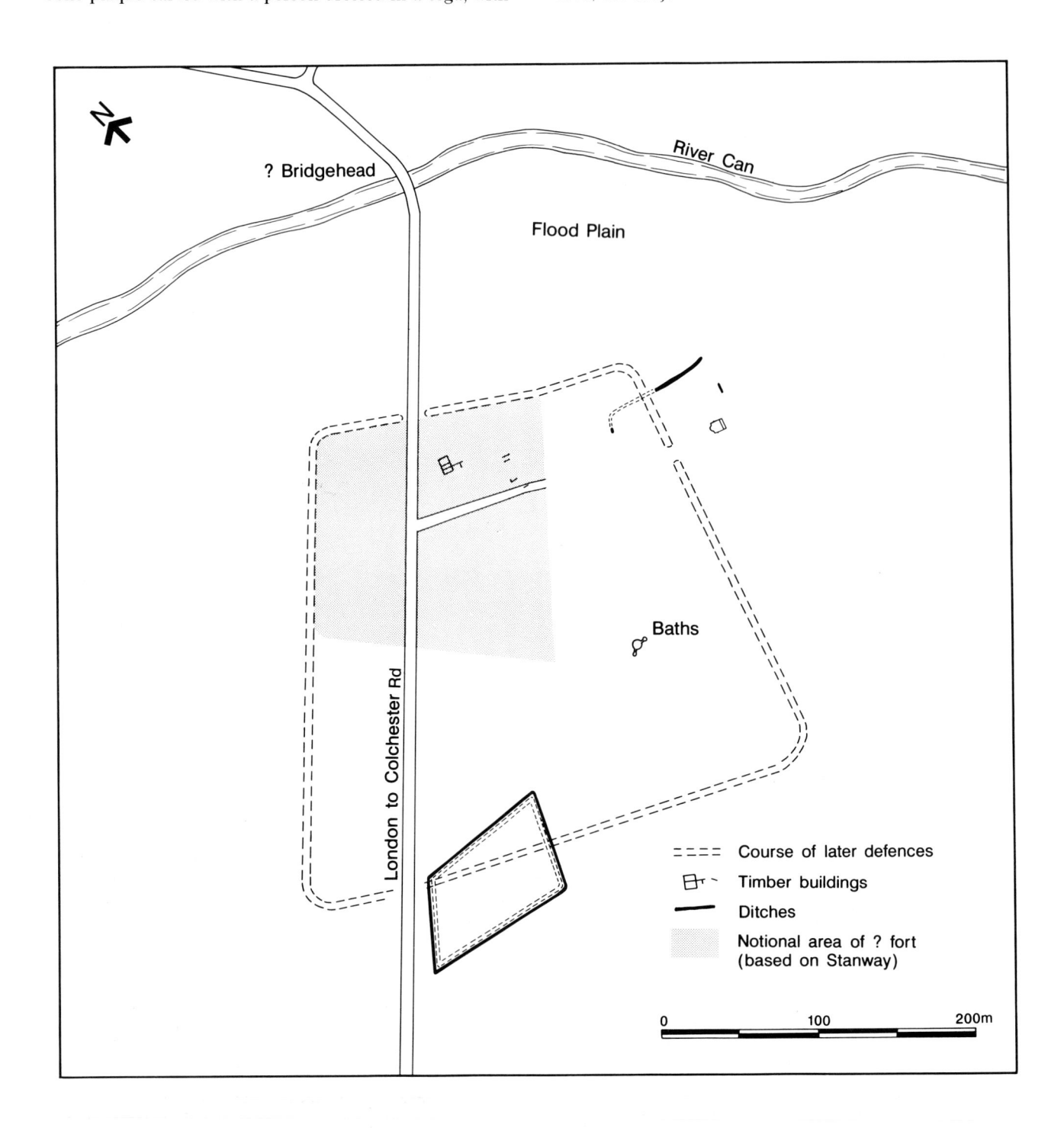

Fig. 5 The early military landscape at Chelmsford

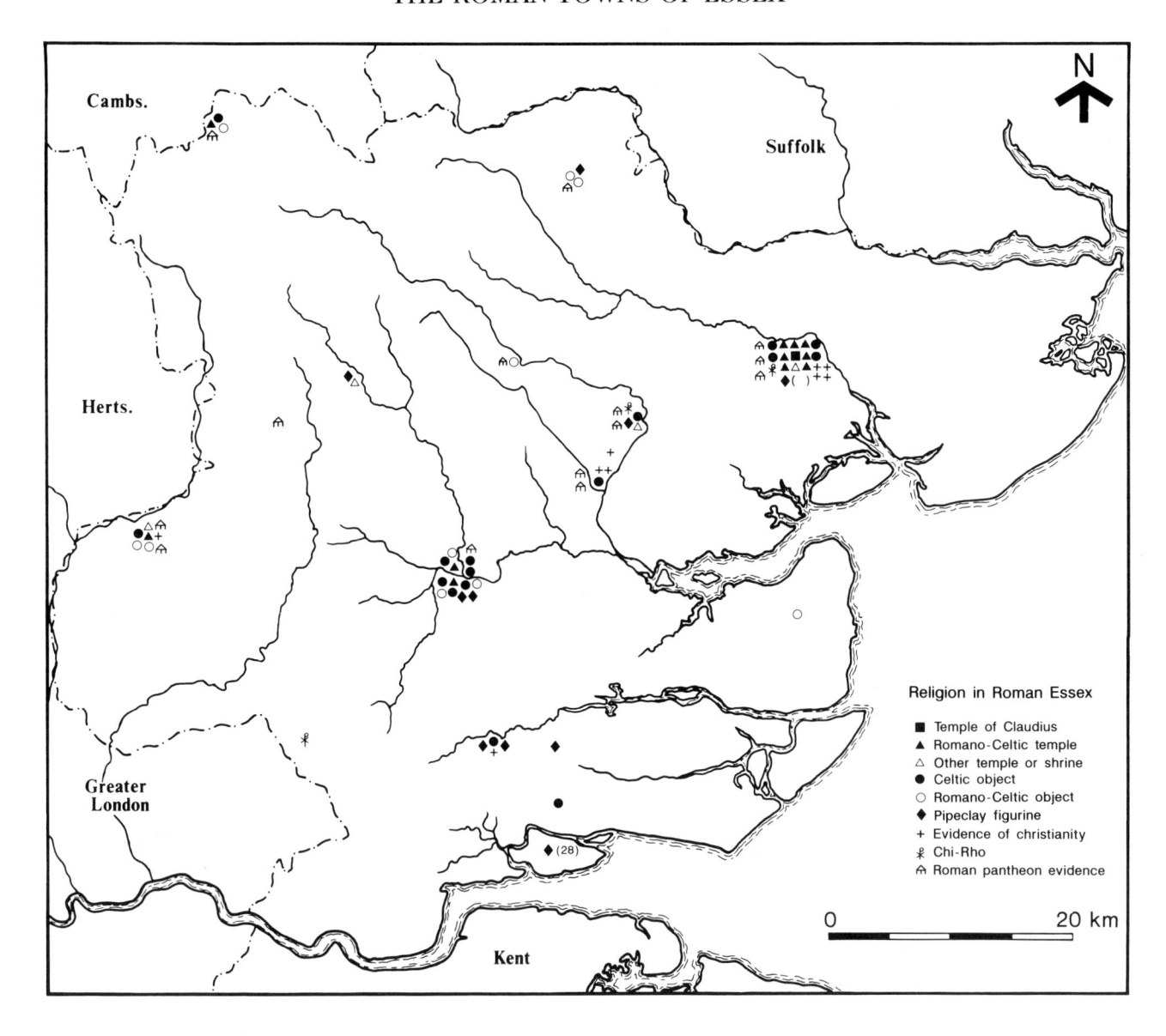

Fig. 6 Religion in Roman Essex

Elsewhere at Chelmsford is found the typical mix of Roman and Celtic religious evidence: a bronze cockerel figurine, an attribute of Mercury and possibly from a larger composite piece similar to one from Verulamium[k]; a gilded copper alloy plaque with a wheel (Drury 1988, fig. 66); and evidence for Epona worship in the form of a complete horse skeleton, 3-4 years old, from Lasts Garage, with its front hooves removed, but no other evidence for damage or disease (Wallis 1988). From near the mansio a well shaft was excavated, re-cut at least six times *above* the water line and filled with a strange assemblage of horse and cow skulls, cat and raven bones, and neonatal lambs. Further skulls had been hung on poles outside and lay smashed in a ditch (Drury 1988, Site AR).

At Kelvedon the excavations revealed a circular temple (Rodwell 1988, Fig. 42), and a lead defixio invoking Mercury and Virtue (*ibid*, 136; Henig 1984, 144). From a double square Romano-Celtic temple excavated at Great Chesterford in 1978 came a silver mask with lentoid eyes, bushy beard and a moustache (Henig 1984, 146).

At Great Dunmow a somewhat more rustic shrine has been published (Wickenden 1988). Reusing the site of an earlier Roman cremation cemetery, the shrine had two clear phases: one comprising a number of wear hollows, perhaps where wooden benches had been placed around the walls, and secondly at the end of the fourth century, when it was rebuilt on a trapezoidal plan on a raft of masonry incorporating a frame of wooden uprights. A number of sealed votive pits appear to initiate this, and can be dated to 350-360 on the coins present. Other votive finds include a pewter bowl with octagonal flange, and double-sided bone comb. Alongside the shrine was a gravel spread, possibly all that was left of a second building, or perhaps just a gravelled surface. Like Chelmsford, Witham and most other temples, it yielded a sizeable collection of fragments of jewellery, finger rings and bracelets, and a quantity of coins, up to and including the House of Theodosius. It recalls another gravel spread, with similar high proportions of coins and other finds outside the Cathedral at St Albans, excavated by the Biddles in the 1980s and interpreted as the site of a religious fair within the Roman cemetery where Alban was buried.

---

[k]Drury 1988, Fig. 63. 20. For the composite figurine from Verulamium see Henig 1984, 60-61. Another cockerel figurine from Great Canfield, Essex, was published by Drury & Wickenden 1982a (CHMER 1979. 513).

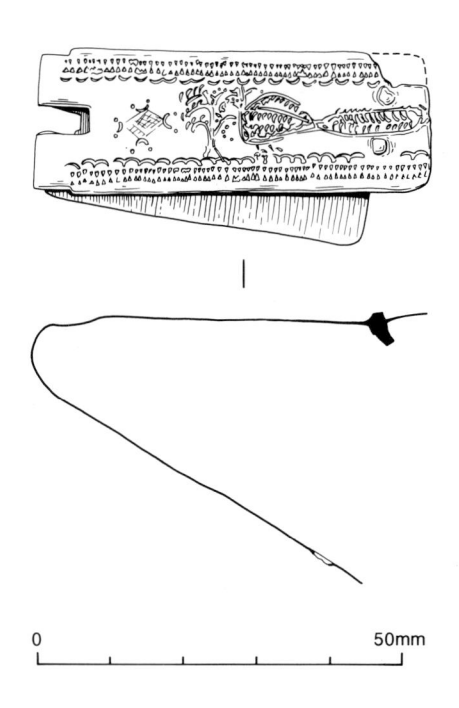

Fig. 7 Belt plate from Harlow engraved with the christian emblem of the peacock

In Colchester the earliest surviving Christian Church has been excavated (Crummy, Crummy and Crossan 1994), within the late Roman cemetery at Butt Road, and is now on public view. The building was first revealed in the 1840s, examined by Hull in 1935, Ros Dunnett in 1965, and eventually Philip Crummy from 1976 to 1979 and again in 1988. The church is 24.8m long x 7.4m wide with an apsidal east end, with an aisled nave and screened off eastern cell. The coin assemblage indicates construction around 320-340, surviving until c. AD 400.

The Temple complex at Ivy Chimney Witham (Fig. 8) was excavated in the late 1970s and early 1980s (Turner 1982). For its size it is remarkable in not appearing to lie within a Roman 'small town' as such, but just off the main road between Chelmsford and Kelvedon. It must thus have been a special place of pilgrimage, or site of a large religious fair, and the discovery of a pottery kiln could indicate a peripatetic potter setting up shop during a fair to make wares for the pilgrims.

The site was occupied in the pre-Roman Iron Age. In the early Roman period a timber temple was constructed within a temenos. In the 2nd-3rd centuries, a large pond was dug, fed by springs, and this became a dominant feature of the complex. In the later 3rd-early 4th century a major new timber Romano-Celtic temple was built, with a deep pit which may have held a large timber Jupiter column.

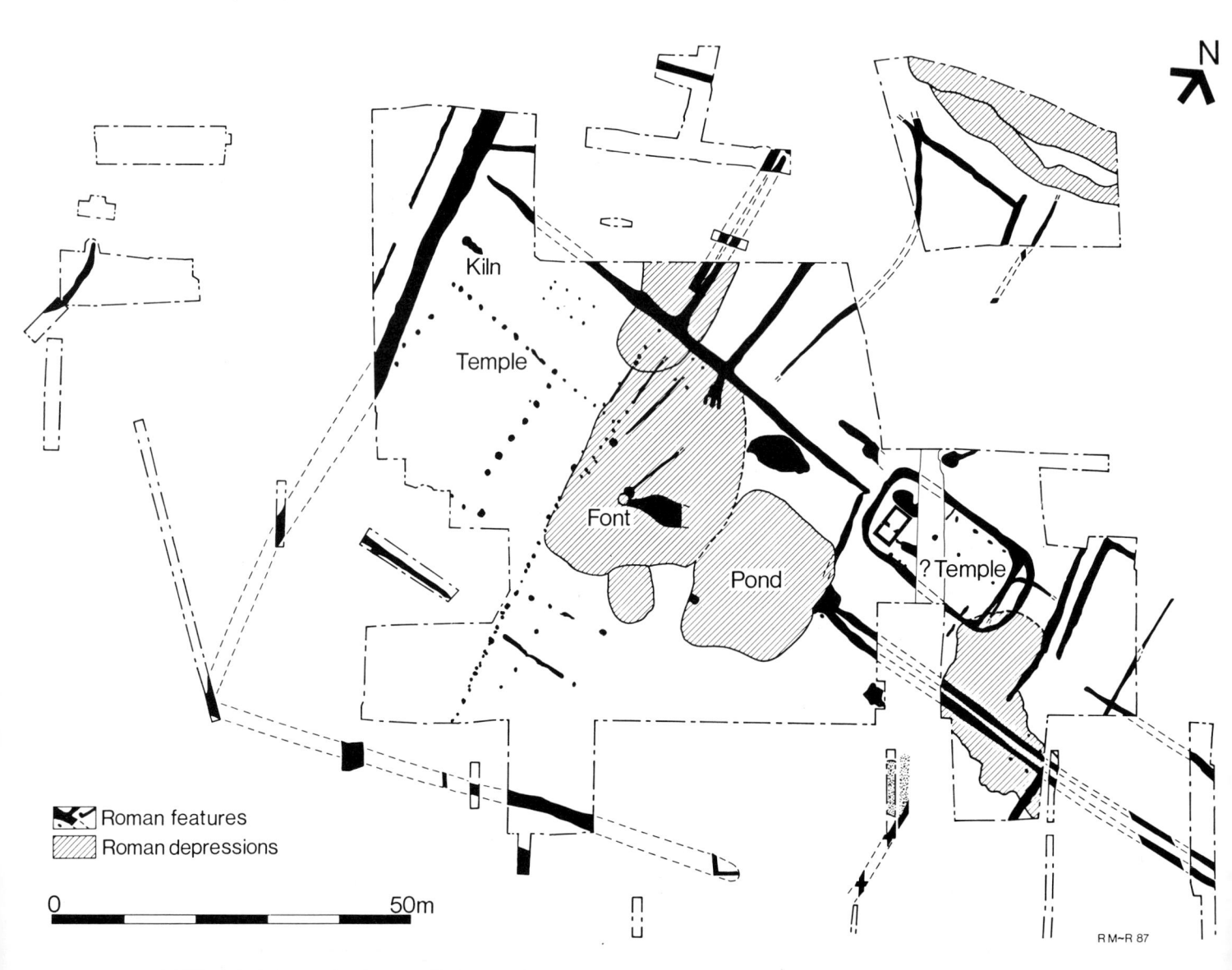

Fig. 8 Ivy Chimneys, Witham

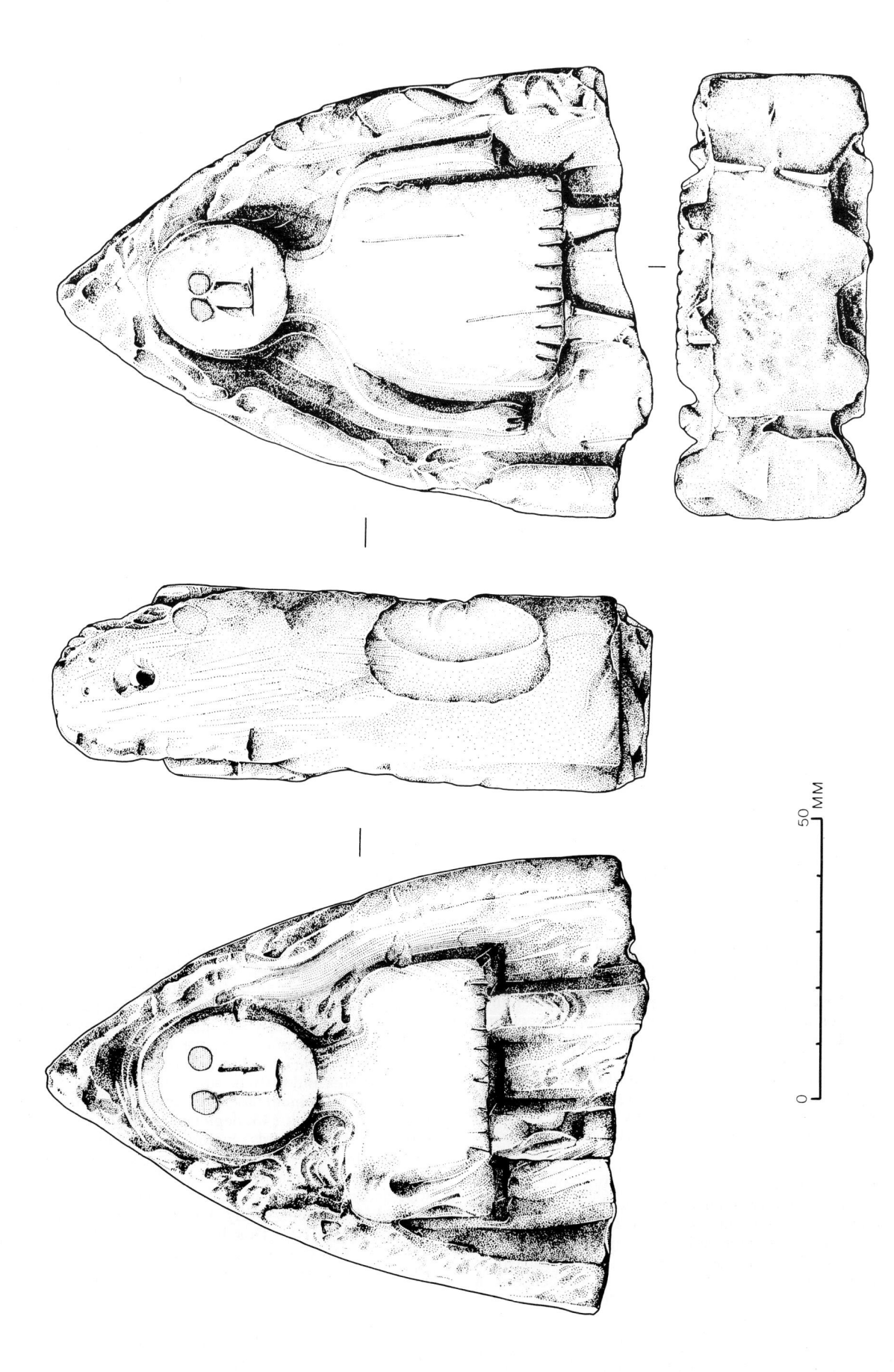

Fig. 9 Double-sided carved stone plaque from Witham

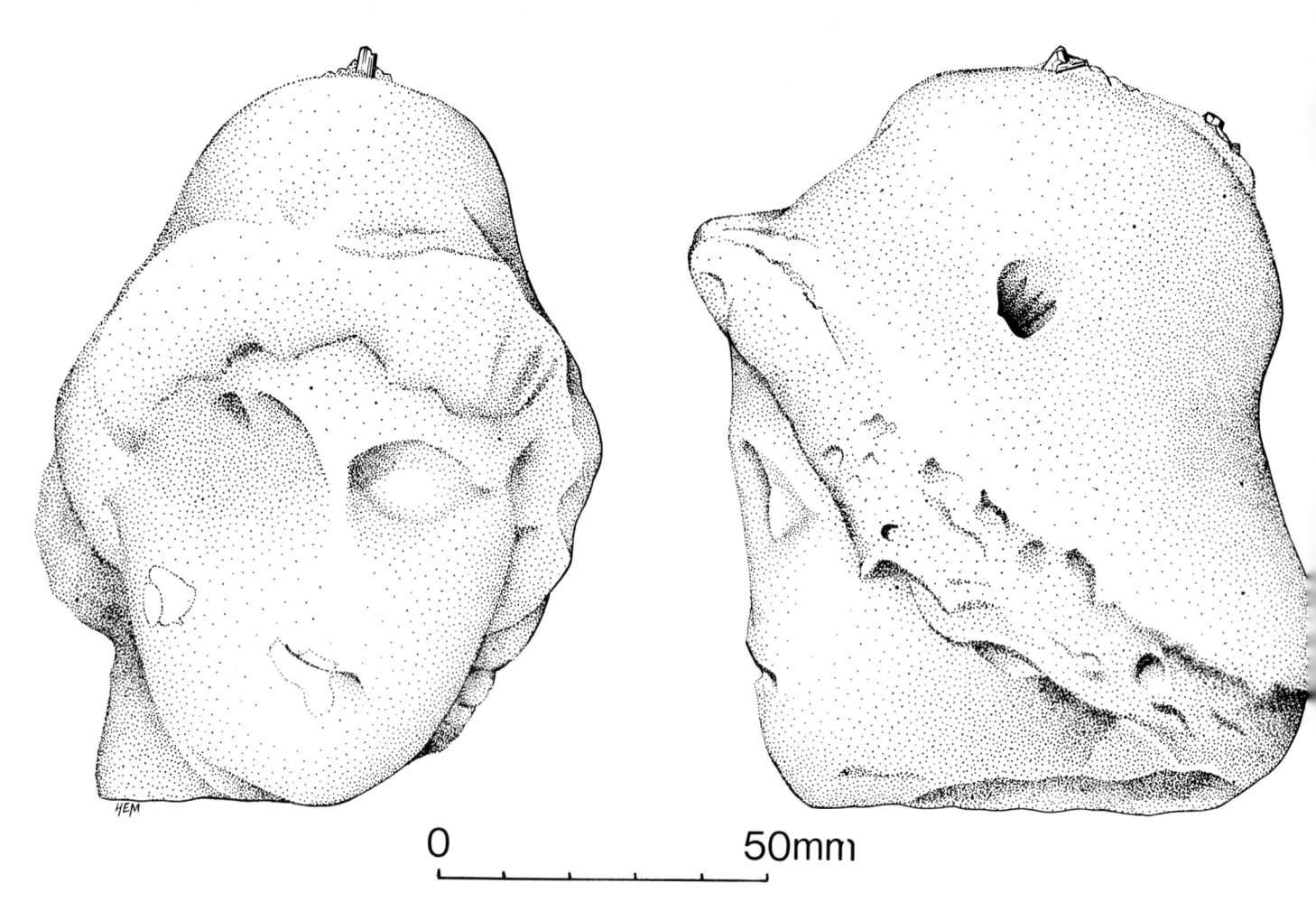

Fig. 10 Limestone head of Minerva from Harlow

By the mid 4th century, the temple was replaced on the far side of the pond by another large rectangular structure, and enclosed by a large continuous ditch with an apsidal end.

Throughout this time, the pond was clearly being used, in good Celtic tradition, as a place for the deposition of votive offerings: over 1000 coins, three hoards of Barbarous Radiates, a double-sided chalk figurine (Fig. 9) with drilled eyes filled with a white substance, copper alloy sheet defixios and other fragments of jewellery recalling Chelmsford and Dunmow, bronze letters from an inscription, a clay phallus possibly from statuary, and a collection of over 30 paleolithic hand axes, believed to have been the physical manifestation of Jupiter's thunderbolts. Letters from an inscription, and a palaeolithic axe were similarly found in the Kelvedon circular temple (Rodwell 1988, fig. 47 and p136).

Towards the end of the 4th century, Witham adopted christianity. A small two-cell stone chapel was built, and a baptismal tile font was constructed within the old pond. The font was later replaced by a large wooden box. Interestingly, whilst the old depressions were backfilled with midden material, and the old trees grubbed out, a brand new pond was dug in this phase. Publication of this important site is eagerly awaited.

Another probable place of pilgrimage, because of its size and quantity of offerings, is the Romano-Celtic temple at Harlow (France and Gobel 1985)[1]. Unlike Witham, Harlow does appear to lie within a Small Town, still rather shapeless, but slowly being made sense of by new excavations and watching briefs. Its *raison d'etre* must be the temple itself, and a likely second major temple in the Holbrooks area, but also the ford over the Stort and a junction of a number of minor roads. The main temple is situated on a gravel island in the Stort Valley, and is surrounded by a temenos ditch. Bartlett's excavations revealed its pre-Roman predecessor - a round house of the middle Iron Age, 13m in diameter, as well as a conquest-period circular post-holed building. 666 Celtic coins were found in the 1980s excavations, adding to a total of 232 known previously. The site was also visited, we assume, by the early military, since spearheads, miniature iron swords, fittings and pre-Flavian brooches have been found. Other finds include a remarkable assemblage of iron tools, ploughshares and fittings, suggesting possible offerings by smiths. Is it coincidence that the most popular coin of Cunobelin is Mack 248, depicting a smith God at his anvil. Other religious finds include an eroded warrior-god plaque, similar to that from Witham; a lead figure wearing a Phrygian cap; and a fragment of major statuary, otherwise sadly lacking from Essex, in the form of a somewhat eroded, helmeted, shelly Northants limestone head of Minerva (Fig. 10). This head is believed to have been defaced in antiquity, perhaps by marauding Christians (Bartlett 1987a).

The most important piece of work on the Temple of Claudius at Colchester was published by Drury in 1984. Drury pulled together the old excavations by Hull, Molly

---

[1] The ground plan of the temple was laid out in concrete slabs by the Harlow Development Corporation. This was discovered to be several metres out of true during Bartlett's excavations in the 1980s.

Cotton, Max Hebditch, Ros Niblett, and his own from 1977, to relate the level of the temple court to the podium for the first time. The Temple cannot in all reality have been completed by the time of the Boudican destruction, and must have required ritual cleansing in the aftermath, and substantial reconstruction. Further work was required following an Antonine Fire. A major change of form occurred in the 4th century with an apsidal-ended narrow structure built on a brick raft, resembling either a church or the great Audience Hall of Constantine at Trier. Drury argues that the Temple of the Imperial Cult was unlikely to have continued as such after the Edict of Milan in 313. Finally, the deposits of late Roman pottery, including quantities of fine wares, and Theodosian coinage, imply that the temple may have ended its days as a secure, defended compound.

Death and burial

The cemetery at Butt Road, Colchester has already been mentioned. 741 burials have been excavated; of these, 59 were aligned N-S, and yielded pottery and other grave goods, and can be considered to be a small, late pagan cemetery. Over these was superimposed a second, early 4th-century cemetery of tightly packed E-W aligned graves, many in nailed oak coffins. The assemblage included two decorated lead children's coffins, 6 double burial vaults, some bodies wrapped in shrouds, and some encased in gypsum. Although the christian traits of these are apparent, many were buried with grave goods, pottery and glass vessels, a jewellery box, hobnailed shoes, and wearing hairpins in their hair. One of the smallest and most stunning finds was a scrap of Chinese silk (Crummy, Crummy and Crossan 1994).

At Chelmsford, the cemeteries that appear to have lined Moulsham Street on the London side of the town, Broomfield Road, and presumably Springfield Road as well, are still little understood. However, the old cremation finds from the Oaklands Park, Elm Road area of Moulsham Street suggest a clustering around a possible T-junction with a newly recognised road which approximates to Writtle Road.

The discovery of a stone coffin immediately outside the town gate on the Godfreys Site, by contractors machine in 1987, may suggest a contraction of the town's southern suburbs by the early 4th century (*Essex Archaeology*, 7, p5). The burial was of a woman, presumably a wealthy VIP able to afford to transportation of a coffin quarried in Bedfordshire. Alongside the coffin was a second burial, of an individual burned on a pyre, and then interred rather than being totally cremated. This body was accompanied by a solid jet bangle and a tapering staff with transverse mouldings, and a hole drilled in the narrower end - still little understood but either a ceremonial spindle or a wand of office (*Essex Archaeology*, 9, p1). The finds recall the 1972 hoard of jet jewellery, also of the highest quality, from Hall Street, and further indicates trade connexions with York in the late Roman period (Henig and Wickenden 1988, 107-110). The two burials may well have rested in a wooden mausoleum, of which a few post-holes were also excavated.

Further stone coffins from Heybridge, a 19th century find, were published along with the pagan Saxon settlement in 1982, and summarised the coincidence of wealthy late Roman and early Saxon cemeteries in Essex, possibly explained as the owners of large *latifundiae* (Drury and Wickenden 1982, 34-5).

Cemeteries have also been published from Kelvedon, where four separate ones are known (Rodwell 1988, 136-7). In that excavated by the Rodwells, 60 inhumations and 35 cremations were found with the limits found on 3 sides. The statistics indicate a small family cemetery with a living population of 10-12 over a period of several hundred years (*ibid*, 50). Deeper vaults were also found. Another small family cemetery is known from Great Dunmow, this time a Flavian-late Antonine cremation cemetery in the Hertfordshire tradition, and Chris Going has identified that many of the vessels were deliberately killed at the time of burial, by stabbing flagons with a sharp stick, and snapping or even sawing off rim sections of platters (Going 1988a, fig. 20). The same can be seen on a cremation burial from Broomfield Road in Chelmsford[m].

In other towns, such as Harlow, the cemeteries have yet to be located properly. At Braintree the cemetery is located from past finds, but is under a housing estate; at Billericay there are a number of cremations, both LPRIA and Roman now known from recent excavations (Rudling 1990).

Urban traits

The major town of the Trinovantian civitas was, of course, Camulodunum, for which see Crummy, this volume. In comparison to Colchester, the Roman 'small towns' of Essex are extremely poor relations, yet most bear basic comparison with each other, and share characteristics, which will be examined below.

Bibliography
Two main syntheses on Roman towns in Britain have appeared since 1980; Roger Finch Smith's *Roadside Settlements in Lowland Britain* (1987) and Burnham and Wacher *The Small Towns of Roman Britain* (1990). Finch Smith's is a revised D Phil text, and does little more than summarise excavators' interim reports. Burnham and Wacher presents more useful, more up to date information, and new distribution maps and town plans, for Braintree, Harlow, and Great Chesterford. Chelmsford is not included: Wacher, instead, has revised it in his 2nd edition of *Towns of Roman Britain*, but it is fascinating to see people wrestling with trying to categorise *Caesaromagus* - Town, Small Town, or even Village (Hanley 1987, fig. 32). Other towns also get ignored by Burnham and Wacher: Kelvedon and Heybridge for instance, and possibly Dunmow, where publication in the 1980s might have warranted inclusion.

Wickford should no longer be thought of as a small town[n]. It is more probable that the site was rather a large sprawling villa and estate, defended for a time, and with evidence for a fire at the end of the second century. It does, however, share with the towns a Late Iron Age origin, on top of which was superimposed an early Roman military fort, evidenced by a length of ditch and numerous finds. Some 600 coins come from the excavations, including pre-Roman staters and potins, and it serves to highlight the confusion in status and form of what is a small *town* and what is, for example, a large country estate serving a large establishment.

What then is needed to call a settlement a Roman Small Town in Essex? First and foremost they are nearly always important points in the communication network - and this is their prime reason for their existence. They are situated at road junctions, near river crossings, and often have a ribbon-strip like development, such as Kelvedon, with little other planned internal structure. There are exceptions: Great Dunmow and Braintree clearly ignore the

---

[m]Found in 1962 and preserved in Chelmsford and Essex Museum (Accession numbers B18619-18622). The group comprises a well-scoured samian f18/31, a small plain greyware beaker, a Colchester buff flagon, and the base of a Romanising storage jar.

[n]The excavations of Warwick Rodwell from 1965 to 1971 have yet to be published. However, the site was written up by Chelmsford Archaeological Trust in the 1980s, and a typescript exists in Chelmsford and Essex Museum.

actual road junction as being the focus of the town centre, and appear to develop to one side.

Braintree, in particular, appears to have developed between Drury's Roads IV and VI (1976, figs 2-3), with a network of minor roads and alleys, and only expanded eastwards in the later 2nd and 3rd centuries. Drury's postulated road network, however, has not stood up to the scrutiny of numerous excavations and watching briefs, and Havis has published a revised plan (Havis 1994, fig. 29). He has simplified the staggered and complex road junction of Drury, and moved Stane Street further to the north, based on a re-interpretation of Drury's site as a ancillary road, and negative evidence further east. Negative evidence in long trenches at Tofts Garage and the Tabor High School also refute Drury's routes II and III.

Great Dunmow must be classified as a small town on the basis of its strategic position in the road network, but otherwise looks very rural; indeed nothing Roman has been found in fifteen recent watching briefs south of Stane Street. On the contrary, the area of the Junior School adjacent to the 1970-72 excavation is rich in Roman pottery (Wickenden 1988a, fig. 64; Havis, pers comm). Planned extensions to Redbond Lodge may provide a further opportunity for study. Again Going has produced a careful study of the villa network in the hinterland (Going 1988b).

Defences
When in times of trouble, the towns were often given defences (at least those that are named on the Antonine Itinerary are: *Camulodunum*, *Caesaromagus*, and *Canonium*). The septaria and tile wall at Colchester (four alternating courses of each) is now believed to have been built in the aftermath of the Boudican rebellion some time between 65 and 80 AD. The previous later dating was from the rampart, now realised to have been a later addition to the wall. Earlier reports of possible white washing of the wall exterior have been revised - this may now be a weathering effect (Crummy 1992, 64).

The circuit at Chelmsford is still only provisional, and requires further testing. It has been most fully recorded at the Godfreys Site by Drury in 1972 (Drury 1988, Site S), and again by the ECC Archaeology Section in 1987 when a third, previously unknown, parallel ditch was found (Wickenden 1991, fig. 29). The ditches were dug c.AD 170-75. It would appear that only the innermost ditch was first filled back in the early-mid 3rd century. The reason for its infilling was twofold - to release more land for building, but also to return part of the mansio precinct which had been cut off by the ditches. The middle ditch was filled in somewhat later in the mid 3rd century, again for the construction of a house (Building E). The outermost ditch contined to silt up throughout the remaining two centuries of Roman occupation, as probably did the northern defences. Thus the town does now appear to have retained some form of boundary in the later Roman period, though it is doubtful if this remained primarily defensive. What has yet to be explained is why the construction of the defences in the first place cut off the south-eastern corner of the mansio precinct, almost up to the walls of the mansio itself.

It has also been suggested that Great Dunmow may have had earthen defences, which may explain the subsequent total loss of Stane Street through the medieval town, and the replacement by a circuitous route to the north of High Street (Wickenden 1988a, 92).

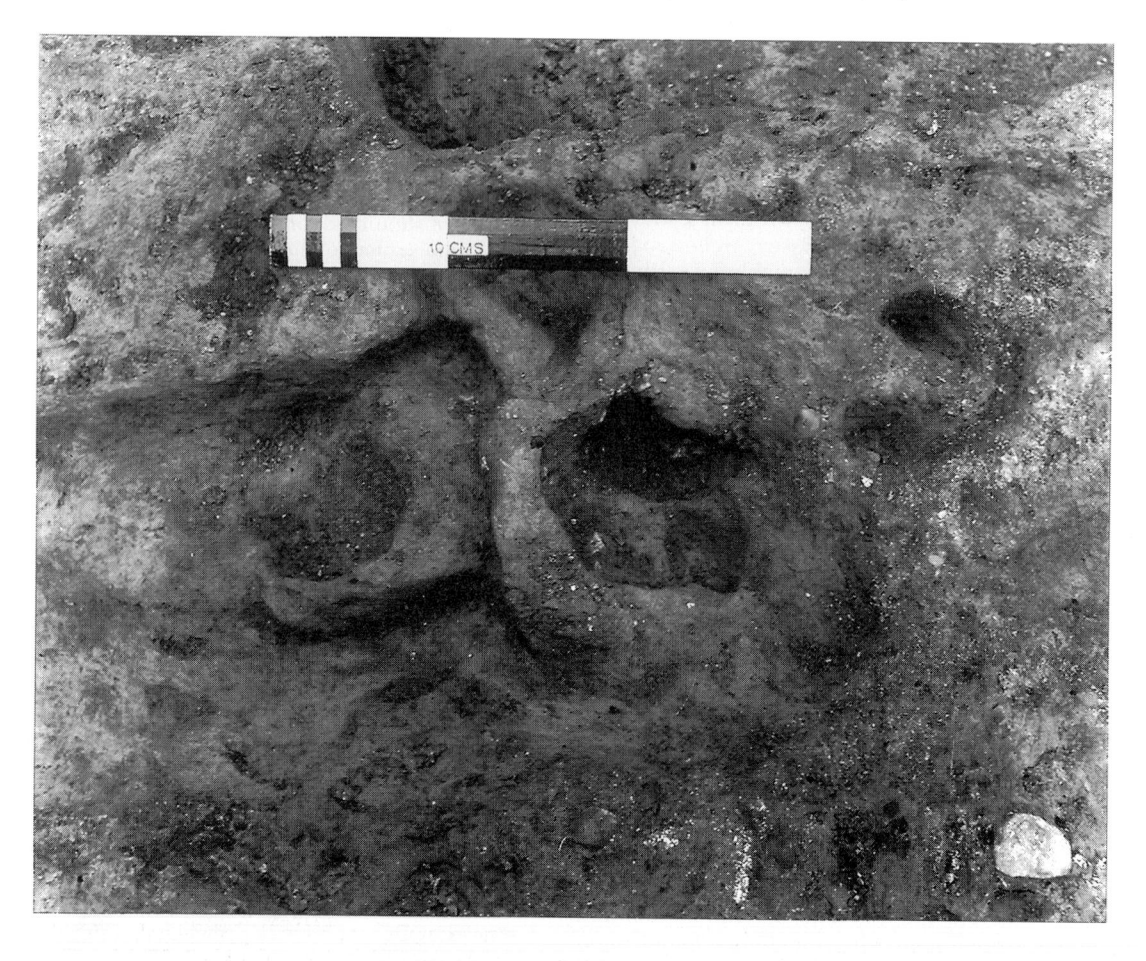

Fig. 11 Cattle footprints in a Moulsham Street verge at the Cramphorns site, Chelmsford

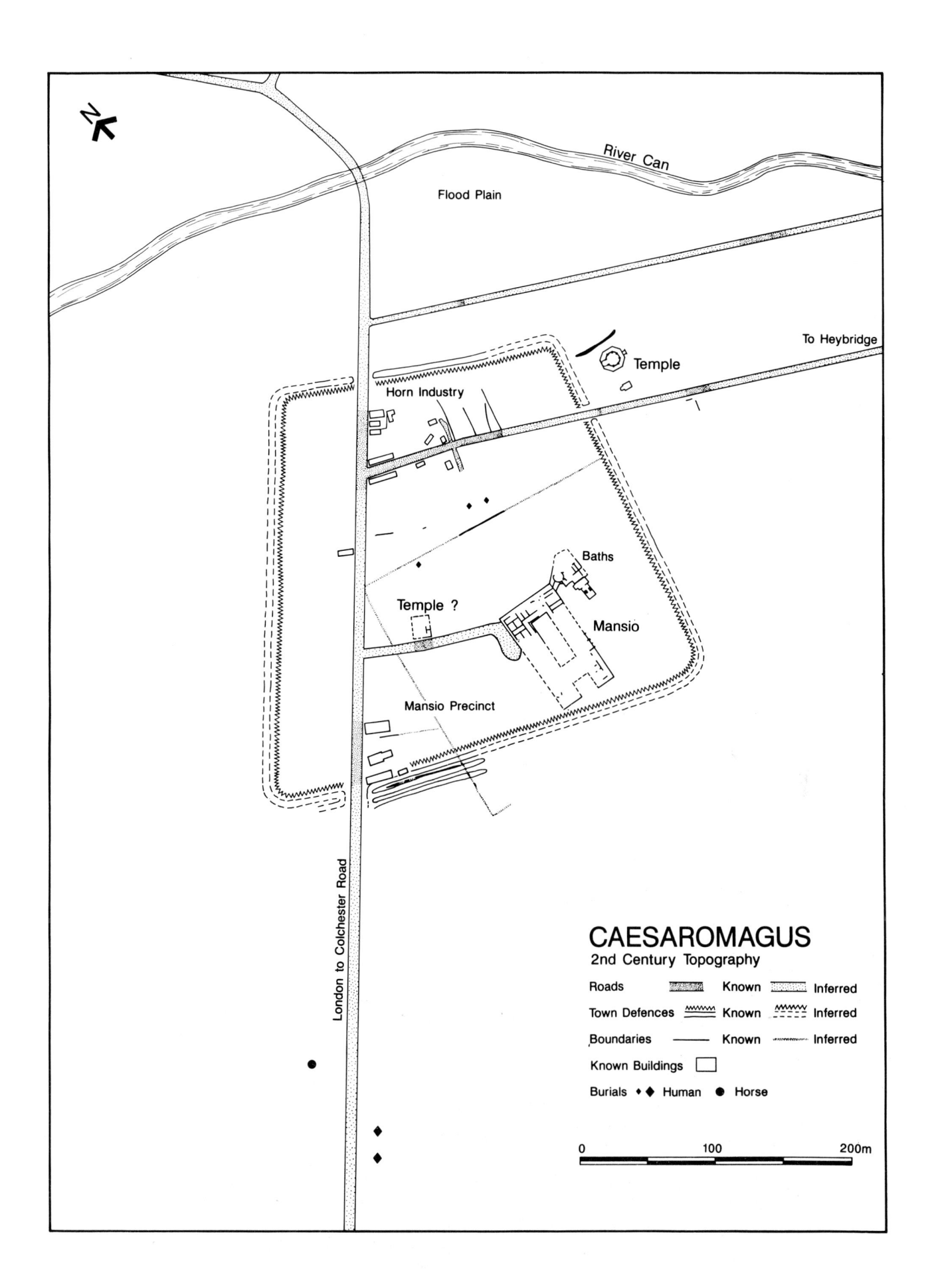

Fig. 12 *Caesaromagus*

THE CHELMSFORD MANSIO BATH HOUSE

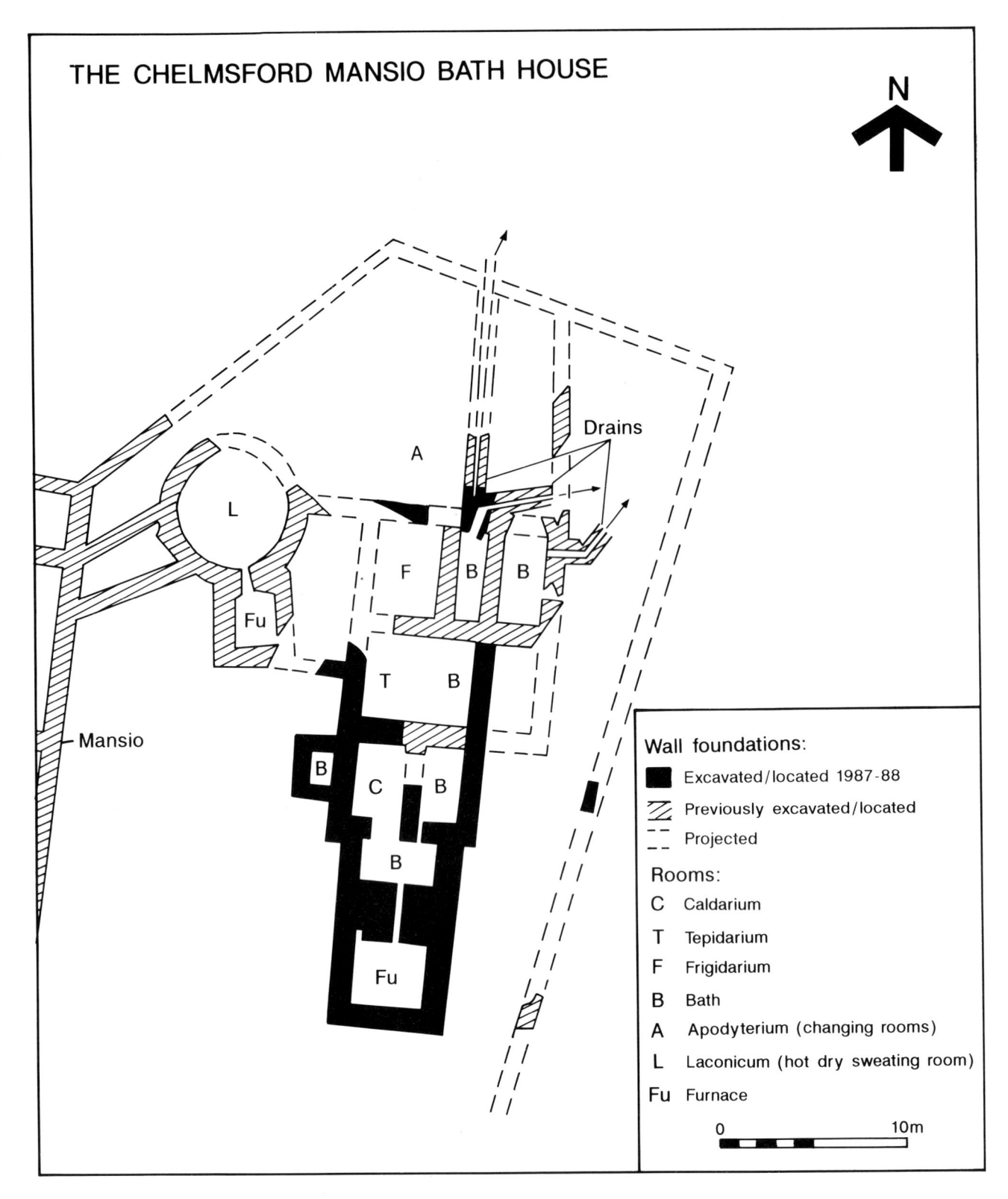

Wall foundations:
- Excavated/located 1987-88
- Previously excavated/located
- Projected

Rooms:
- C Caldarium
- T Tepidarium
- F Frigidarium
- B Bath
- A Apodyterium (changing rooms)
- L Laconicum (hot dry sweating room)
- Fu Furnace

Fig. 13 The Roman mansio bath-house at Chelmsford: excavations in 1987-88

Rural market centres

These settlements also served as market and artisan centres, just as they did in the medieval and post-medieval periods. They remained closely allied to the rural pursuits outside, and here differ from what we would think of as an urbanised place today. Large areas even in Roman Colchester have been shown at Culver Street to have remained quasi-rural, with the discovery of a large aisled barn (not a church as first reported), a granary and corn drying oven (Crummy 1992, 108-117). Cattle footprints have been found embedded in the soft verges of the London to Colchester road on the Cramphorns site at Chelmsford (Fig. 11; Rankov 1982, 370-1), where seasonal lambing and calving was also taking place, within the confines of the 'town'. Also at Chelmsford, a case can now be made for a large bone-processing plant in the north-eastern sector of the town, and one again wonders whether this might not be army-controlled. Cattle were brought in for slaughter and butchery, and their horns removed for the valuable outer ceratin, which unfortu-

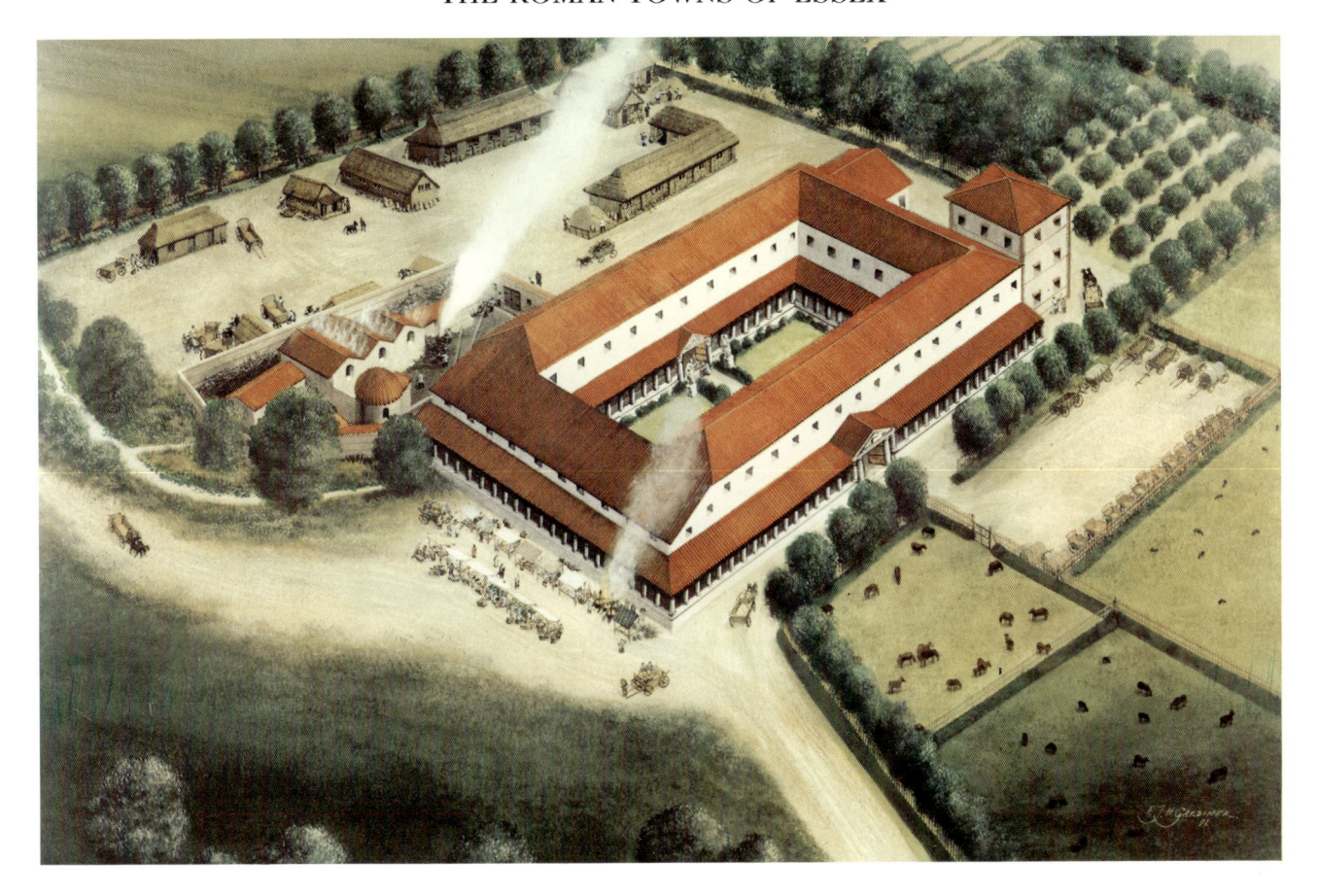

Fig. 14 Reconstruction of the Roman mansio at Chelmsford, c AD 160, drawn by Frank Gardiner

nately seldom survives in the archaeological record. After a period of smelly soaking in tanks, the horn core was discarded, being of no further use (Luff 1994).

Chelmsford (Fig. 12)

Chelmsford is now firmly identified as *Caesaromagus*, though the guessing goes on as to the reason for its enigmatically grand name. One new possibility is that Chelmsford was chosen to be the new tribal capital for the Trinovantes in the aftermath of the Boudican suppressing, and the army dispatched to build a fort with a view to laying out the infrastructure. For whatever reason Colchester was then rebuilt, possibly at the insistence of the still powerful native aristocracy who could not have contemplated a move away from Camulodunum, its stone walls were built and its former eminence regained. All this would have been at the expense of Chelmsford down the road, left with an important mansio complex in a crucial geographic position, with a wonderful name but little else.

Drury's excavations of the mansio appeared in print finally in 1988, though much has since been achieved by the ECC Archaeology Section, notably the location of the south-eastern corner at Grove Road (Drury 1988, 9), and the discovery that the eastern wall had been buttressed; and the excavations of the abattoir site of the bath-house which helped elucidate still further work done by Chancellor, Brinson, and Drury (Fig. 13; Allen 1988). The bath complex appears to have started with a free-standing masonry *laconicum*, built by the military; the main bath-house was added in the middle or even later 2nd century, that is after the mansio itself had been built, though a silted-up shallow marking-out trench shows that the baths had been originally planned. Four rooms were excavated: the furnace, hot bath, *caldarium* and *tepidarium*. A later plunge bath had been added to the *caldarium*. The furnace was later reduced in size to accommodate large water tanks on solid tile rafts, and a set of steps down into the furnace was found. By the 4th century, the walls were becoming damaged by heat but were not repaired, and the furnace became so clogged with soot and debris that it ended life as little more than a stoke hole. The *laconicum* suffered a catastrophic fire in the 3rd century, which appears to have damaged the east wing of the mansio which was partly re-roofed. More recent watching briefs at the 7th day Adventist Church produced Chelmsford's first evidence for a geometric patterned black and white stone mosaic, unfortunately too disturbed to lift (Patrick Allen, pers comm). Outside the bath-house itself, excavations have revealed the first evidence for the services - its yard and fuel store, in an open-sided shed with one load-bearing wall and lean-to roof (Fig. 14; Allen 1988).

The mansio at Chelmsford is likely to have developed from a military road station in the Trajanic and Hadrianic period, itself a successor to a post-Boudican fort and compound already discussed. Mansiones, in some guise or other, even if only an official means of requisitioning accommodation, must have existed in most towns in order to provide travellers with basic hospitality. A masonry mansio has been postulated at Heybridge (Wickenden 1987, 64), and roller-stamped box flue tiles have now been found on the outskirts of both Heybridge (P Brown, pers comm) and Braintree (Smoothy 1989, 20), where a substantial building and road have also been tentatively identified on the Brands site (Havis, pers comm). Again more exploratory work is needed. Because of the rarity of naturally occurring stone building materials in the county, any masonry buildings can be assumed to be important, and probably public or official.

One of the most valuable finds from Godfreys has been the uncovering of a complete building plot from along the Moulsham Street frontage, 35m wide and defined by shallow ditches, 59m and 76m long, either fenced or hedged (Fig. 15; Priddy 1988, 263). The plot contained a timber-framed house, a workshop with a massive central indus-

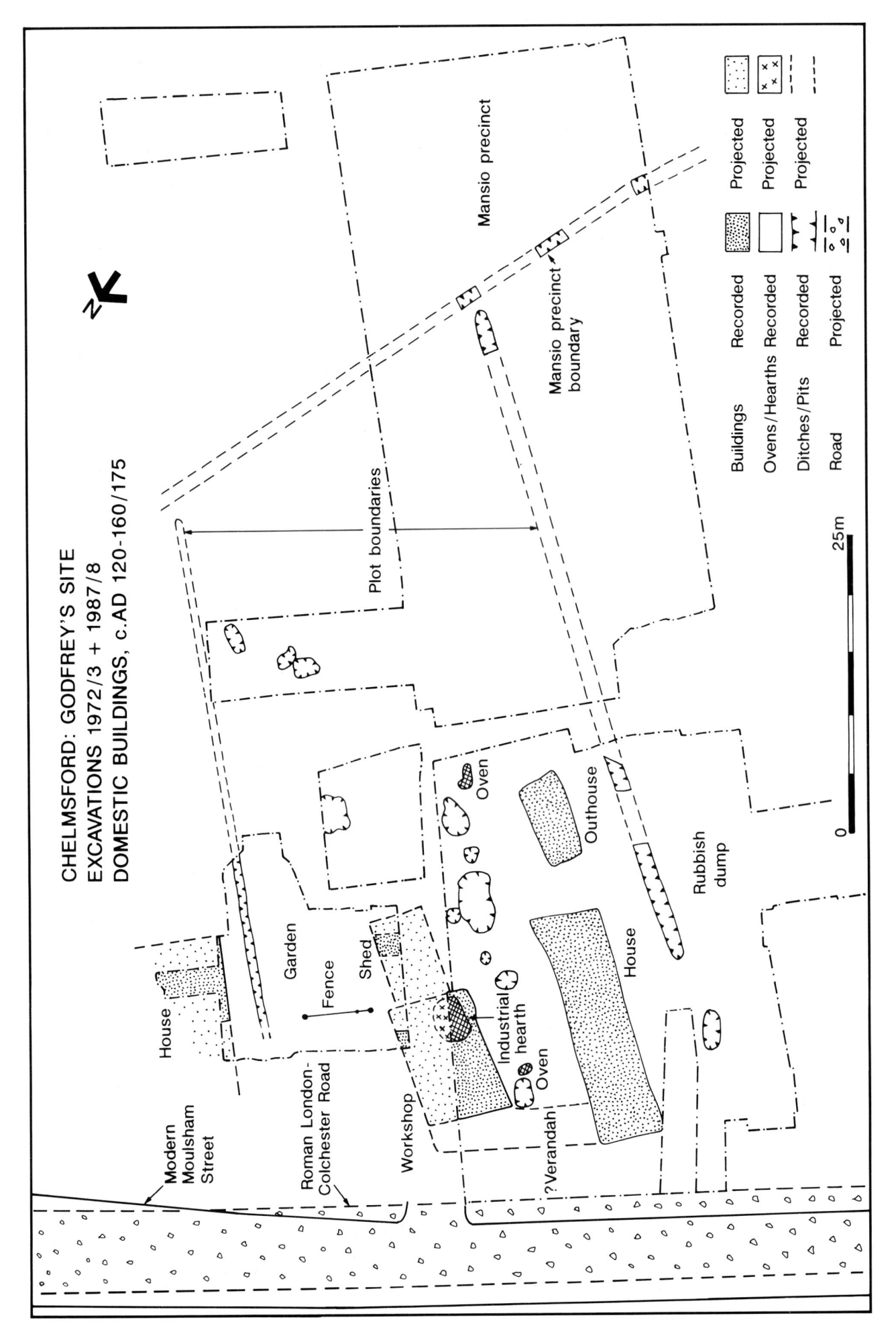

Fig. 15 A complete domestic building plot fronting the London to Colchester road at the Godfreys Site, Chelmsford

trial hearth some 3-4m across, a front verandah no doubt used as a shop, and rear ovens, privy, rubbish pits etc. At the back of the house was a second smaller room, well finished and probably a private room for the use of the landowner. The back of the plot is formed by its boundary ditch butting up against the mansio precinct ditch, itself dated pre-170 AD. To the north, the aisled house of the next plot along was found. To the south the plot was unoccupied until the defences were filled in and a building constructed. This burnt down c.AD 300 in a fire which consumed the buildings in the adjacent plots, and may have destroyed the wooden mausoleum in which the stone coffin lay. Remains of painted wall plaster, and three burnt window panes of the early Roman matt/glossy type were found in Building E. In the early 4th century, the fire damage was cleared and the buildings replaced by a potters shop - the kiln and Rettendon-type wares of which have been published by Going (1987, 73-8). By the later 4th century, the mansio and plot boundaries were no longer being respected. The buildings were replaced by a cattle stockade on the street frontage, with repair workshops behind, evidenced by a number of small smithying hearths and finds of broken knife blades etc. Evidence perhaps that domestic life in the later 4th century was breaking down, and the quasi-administrative and official operations of the mansio once again replacing them.

Elsewhere in the town a batch of 5 rectangular ovens were found at Cramphorns, presumably for bread making (Rankov 1982, 370-1). Another battery came from Cables Yard, with quantities of lava querns (Isserlin and Wickenden forthcoming).

Other towns have yielded similar industrial quarters: an iron working area at Braintree, with smithing slag from Brands, and College House, and a possible bloomery at Letchs Yard. Nothing similar came from Georges Yard. An iron and copper alloy quarter from Stafford House, Harlow; bone working industries at Colchester and Great Chesterford, from the Crown Orchard Site (Eddy 1981, 51-2).

There were also of course, potteries in the towns, but also outside in the hinterland as well, and some major production centres such as Rettendon and Hadham never grew to small town status, simply because they were not at a strategic communication nodal point. Going's study of the pottery from the mansio and other sites in the southeastern sector of Caesaromagus has been the one overrriding contribution in this field (1987). Elsewhere, the kiln at Buckenhams field at Billericay has been archaeomagnetically dated to the 1st century AD to 1 standard variation, which does not square with the product's stylistic date of the later 2nd century (Rudling 1990, 46). Very little is still known of the network of local tile kilns which must have existed to provide tiles for major buildings like mansiones, bath-houses and temples.

Durolitum

It is perhaps fitting at this point to consider the location of Durolitum, another known latin name, but still not conclusively located. Rodwell argued long ago for Chigwell (Rodwell 1975b, 93), and indeed the West Essex Archaeological Group did excavate a flint and tile built hypocausted bath suite with circular bath, window glass, tesserae etc dating to the late 4th century. But that is all. On the other hand, Fuentes has argued for Durolitum being at Romford, suggesting that the duro-element relates to an unknown fort (Fuentes 1986). He may well be right, although his list of Roman finds from Romford should not be taken at face value, since some have proved not to be Roman at all, and others have dubious provenances (Greenwood, pers comm). Dr Pamela Greenwood has, however, found the first genuine provenances of Roman cremation groups from Cotton Park Gardens in Romford.

Conclusion

Richard Reece's analogy of the British Roman town with a tender Mediterranean plant in foreign soil has much to recommend it: planted here, but never properly taking root, and eventually failing for lack of proper attention and feeding (Reece 1980, 78). This, however, assumes some sort of planned determination - many of the Trinovantian small towns more likely merely reflect a continuation of occupation from Late Iron Age antecedents, albeit with the catalyst of the Roman military, and newly acquired Roman trappings of civilisation.

In the later Roman period, we can see Reece's roots withering and dying in the East of Britain, much sooner than in the West, and well before the withdrawal of officialdom. Colchester, of course, was one of the *major* towns of the province - marked by a higher ratio of masonry buildings, stone walls, public baths and basilica, classical temple and theatre. But if it was still that important in the later 3rd century, why was its coastline not protected as part of the Saxon Shore ? Why were Chelmsford's defences not properly maintained nor made of stone, being the most crucial half way stage between London and Colchester? The answer might be that Colchester in the later Roman period was only a shadow of its former importance. The truth is that the bulk of Essex, the 'A12' and 'A120' routes were no longer crucial in late Roman Britain. What had replaced them was the sheep-rearing country around Great Chesterford in the west of the region, where alone in Essex, substantial investment was lavished on a stone wall circuit built as late as 390 AD (Going this volume, p95-107). We know from excavations at Chelmsford that the institutions such as the mansio were still operating in the later 4th century - and indeed a new Romano-Celtic temple was only built there in around AD 325, but the bath house furnaces were choking and no longer maintained. These are the daily motions of town life, where some reason for it still existed, rather than self-perpetuating town life *per se*.

Research priorities

I said at the beginning that Drury and Rodwell's research priorities (1980, 74) remain virtually intact, and so they do (Pre-Roman Braintree, military earthworks, town defences, and peripheral Saxon settlement to name a few). Much of the past fifteen years has been spent on writing up and publishing the excavations of the previous fifteen. With this backlog now almost clear, new ones have appeared; sites such as those at Braintree, excavated by a number of different bodies, such as Braintree Council and the MSC, are important for the proper undstanding of the small town at Braintree - and it is crucial that a proper post-excavation programme can be worked out to get these published.

Huge amounts of time and effort are now expended in the daily life of a post-PPG16 unit, with desk top evaluations in danger of clogging up the system. Large-scale excavations appear to be little more than a pipe dream at the moment, and most excavation is done in small pile and foundation trenches, encouraged by the English Heritage ethos to preserve at all cost. This ethos has become all-pervasive, and perhaps too blinkered. The exhortations of Drury and Rodwell in 1980 to concentrate on a small number of large sites, and disregard the inclination to go for small scale work whose results are at best poor value for money and at worst misleading, have largely been ignored.

Surely it cannot be coincidence that some of the best results have come from large-scale excavations, for instance Culver Street in Colchester and Godfreys in Chelmsford? That one latter site has yielded evidence for the post-Boudican quadrilateral enclosure, a third parallel defensive ditch, the excavation of a complete frontage plot, the line of the mansio precinct, and the stone coffin and jet burial - ironically enough found by contractors in one of the parts of the site left unexcavated; in fact virtually the entirety of all the major advancements to our knowledge from one large-scale excavation.

It is gratifying that, as I write, one of the most important large-scale excavations is underway in the heart of the small town at Heybridge. A 30-hectare site on agricultural land is being excavated with developer funding, and major English Heritage financial backing, and is promising to uncover a huge portion of the town, which we know to have been a Late Iron Age port, a Roman port, possibly complete with mansio, and an Early Saxon settlement. Chances like these will be rare in the later 1990s and the 21st century, and must be eagerly grasped, regardless of the costs. The results have proved themselves worthwhile time and time again.

Naturally it is important to continue with the small-scale excavations, especially where our knowledge is still lacking, and where the stratigraphy is sufficient to give us something - we need more information about Braintree, its Iron Age origins and the road network and line of Stane Street; the location of *Durolitum*; and what sort of a town Great Dunmow really was. At Chelmsford, possibly the most understood of the small towns, we still need more information on the round house settlement, the early military landscape, the defences, the mansio precinct area, the temple precinct, the town west of Moulsham Street, and the cemeteries outside.

Acknowledgements
It is of course very difficult to summarise 15 years of work in one short chapter and I apologise for any omissions or errors which remain my responsibility. I must thank, however, the following for discussions which have brought me as up to date as possible, and for correcting some of my own earlier impressions: Patrick Allen, Richard Bartlett, Ernest Black, Philip Crummy, Chris Going, Pamela Greenwood and Richard Havis.

Bibliography
Allen, P. 1988. 'Excavations of the mansio bath house, Chelmsford, 1987-1988', *Essex Journal*, Vol 23.2, 27-33
Bartlett, R. 1987a. *Harlow Temple excavations 1985-6, an interim report*, Harlow Mus Occas pap 1
Bartlett, R. 1987b. 'A Late Roman buckle from Harlow Temple, Essex', *Essex Archaeol Hist*, 18, 115-120
Bedwin, O. 1986. 'Excavations at Mount House, Braintree, 1984', *Essex Archaeol Hist*, 16, 28-39
Bishop, M. C. 1987. 'The evolution of certain features', in M. Dawson (ed), *Roman Military Equipment. The Accoutrements of War*, British Archaeol Rep, S336, 109-40
Bishop, M. C. 1989. 'Soldiers and military equipment in the towns of Roman Britain', in VA Maxfield and MJ Dobson (eds) *Roman Frontier Studies 1989*, Proceedings of the XVth International Congress of Roman Frontier Studies, 21- 27
Buckley, D. G. 1980 (ed). *Archaeology in Essex to AD1500*, CBA Res Rep, 34
Burnham, B. C. and Wacher, J. 1990. *The 'Small Towns' of Roman Britain*
Couchman, C. 1979. 'Work of Essex County Council Archaeology Section, 1978', *Essex Archaeol Hist*, 11, 32-77
Crummy, N. 1981. 'Bone working at Colchester', *Britannia*, 12, 277- 286
Crummy, N., Crummy, P. and Crossan, C. 1993. *Excavations of Roman and later cemeteries, churches and monastic sites in Colchester 1971-88*, Colchester Archaeological Report 9.
Crummy, P. 1988. 'Colchester', in *Fortress into City* (ed G. Webster), 24-47
Crummy, P. 1992. *Excavations at Culver Street, the Gilberd School, and other sites in Colchester, 1971-85*, Colchester Archaeol rep, 6
Cunliffe, B. W. 1978. *Iron Age Communities in Britain* (2nd edition)
Draper, J. 1985. *Excavations by Mr H. P. Cooper on the Roman Site at Hill farm, Gestingthorpe, Essex*, East Anglian Archaeol, 25
Drury, P. J. 1975. 'Roman Chelmsford - Caesaromagus', in Rodwell and Rowley 1975, 159-175
Drury, P. J. 1976. 'Braintree. Excavations and Research 1971-76', *Essex Archaeol Hist*, 8, 1-143
Drury, P. J. 1984. 'The Temple of Claudius at Colchester reconsidered', *Britannia*, 15, 7-50
Drury, P. J. 1988. *The Mansio and other sites in the south-eastern sector of Caesaromagus*, Chelmsford Archaeol Trust Rep 3.1, CBA Res Rep 66
Drury, P. J. and Rodwell, W. J. 1980. 'Settlement in the later Iron Age and Roman periods', in D. Buckley (ed) 1980, 59-75
Drury, P. J. and Wickenden, N. P. 1982a. 'Four Bronze Figurines from the Trinovantian *Civitas*', *Britannia*, 13, 239-243
Drury, P. J. and Wickenden, N. P. 1982b. 'An Early Saxon settlement within the Romano-British small town at Heybridge, Essex, *Medieval Archaeol*, 26, 1-40
Eddy, M. (ed) 1980. 'Work of the Essex County Council Archaeology Section, 1979', *Essex Archaeol Hist*, 12, 39-50
Eddy, M. (ed) 1981. 'Work of the Essex County Council Archaeology Section, 1980', *Essex Archaeol Hist*, 13, 32-47
Eddy, M. 1982. *Kelvedon. The origins and development of a Roman Small Town*, Essex County Council Occas Pap, 3
France, N. E. and Gobel, B. M. 1985. *The Romano-British Temple at Harlow*
Fuentes, N. 1986. 'Durolitum Found?', *Essex J*, 21.1, 18-21
Going, C. J. 1987. *The Mansio and other sites in the south-eastern sector of Caesaromagus: the Roman pottery*, Chelmsford Archaeol Trust rep 3.2, CBA Res Rep, 62
Going, C. J. 1988a. 'An archaeological gazetteer of Dunmow', in Wickenden 1988a, 80-85
Going, C. J. 1988b. 'The countryside around Great Dunmow', in Wickenden 1988a, 86-88
Hanley, R. 1987. *Villages in Roman Britain* (Shire Archaeology)
Havis, R. 1994. 'Roman Braintree: excavations 1984-90', *Essex Archaeol Hist*, 24, 22-68
Henig, M. 1984. *Religion in Roman Britain*
Henig, M. 1985. 'An inscribed intaglio', *Britannia*, 16, 241-2
Henig, M. and Wickenden, N. P. 1988. 'A hoard of jet and shale', in Drury 1988, 107-110
Luff, R. M. 1994. 'The conundrum of castration in the archaeological record: an interpretation of Roman cattle horn cores from Chelmsford, Essex', *International J. Osteoarchaeology* 4, 171-92.
Priddy, D. (ed). 1988. 'Excavations in Essex 1987', *Essex Archaeol Hist*, 19, 260-271
Rankov, B. 1982. 'Roman Britain in 1981', *Britannia*, 13, 328-422
Reece, R 1980 'Town and Country: the end of Roman Britain', *World Archaeol.* 12.1, 77-92
Rodwell, K. A. 1988. *The prehistoric and Roman settlement at Kelvedon, Essex*, Chelmsford Archaeol Trust Rep 6, CBA Res Rep, 63
Rodwell, W. J. 1973. 'The Roman Fort at Great Chesterford, Essex', *Britannia*, 3, 290-293
Rodwell, W. J. 1975a. 'Trinovantian towns and their settings', in Rodwell and Rowley 1975, 85-102
Rodwell, W. J. 1975b. 'Milestones, Civic territories and the Antonine itinerary', *Britannia*, 6, 76-101
Rodwell, W. J. 1976. 'Coinage, Oppida and the rise of Belgic power in south-eastern Britain', in Cunliffe, B. W. and Rowley, T. (eds), *Oppida in Barbarian Europe*, Brit Archaeol Rep, S11, 181-366
Rodwell, W. J. and Rodwell, K. A. 1986. *Rivenhall: investigations of a villa, church, and village, 1950-1977*, Chelmsford Archaeol Trust Rep 4.1, CBA Res Rep, 55
Rodwell, W. J. and Rowley, R. T. *The Small Towns of Roman Britain*, British Archaeol Rep, 15
Rudling, D. 1990. 'Late Iron Age and Roman Billericay', *Essex Archaeol Hist*, 21, 19-47
Smith, R. F. 1987. *Roadside Settlements in Lowland Roman Britain*, British Archaeol Rep, 157
Smoothy, M. 1989. 'A Roman site at Rayne, Essex: excavations 1987', *Essex Archaeol Hist*, 20, 1-29
Toller, H. S. 1980. 'Excavation of the Orsett 'Cock' enclosure, Essex', *Britannia*, 11, 35-42
Turner, B. R. G. 1982. *Ivy Chimneys, Witham. An Interim report*, Essex County Council Occas Pap 2
Wallis, S. 1988. 'On the outskirts of Roman Chelmsford: excavations at Lasts Garage 1987' *Essex Archaeol Hist*, 19, 40-46
Wickenden, N. P. 1986. 'A copper alloy votive bar and a carved bone plaque from Chelmsford, Essex', *Britannia*, 17, 348-51
Wickenden, N. P. 1988a. *Excavations at Great Dunmow, Essex*, Chelmsford Archaeol Trust Rep 7, East Anglian Archaeol, 41
Wickenden, N. P. 1988b. 'Some military bronzes from the Trinovantian civitas', in Coulston 1988, 234-256
Wickenden, N. P. 1991. *Caesaromagus* (Chelmsford Museums Service)
Wickenden, N. P. 1992. *The Temple and Other Sites in the north-eastern sector of Caesaromagus*, Chelmsford Archaeol Trust Rep 9, CBA Res Rep, 75

The Roman Countryside

C. J. Going

Introduction

By my reckoning this paper is part of the fifth synthesis embracing some or all of Roman Essex to be written this century. The first was the work of Francis Haverfield, who drafted notes for a planned Roman section in an early Victoria County History volume, a venture forestalled by his untimely death in 1919. Haverfield's papers, preserved still in the Ashmolean library, reveal Essex to be a *tabula rasa* in comparison with the data available today. The second study, published five years after the end of the First World War, covered only a part of the north-west of the county and was incidental to its main concern which centered on Cambridge (Fox 1923). During the twenties and thirties the county saw a slow increase in the pace of archaeological discovery, much of which was recorded by Rex Hull, then newly-arrived from the north of England. In a sustained outburst of energy Hull not only ran an important Museum but also organised with Christopher Hawkes the major excavation campaign at Sheepen (largely completed before the war but published in 1947). In addition he found time to visit the explorations of amateurs who at that time were beginning to carry out work in rural Essex, and to maintain records on countless incidental finds. While the first truly modern synthesis of Roman Essex was a lapidary sketch penned by Sir Ian Richmond in the front of VCH III (1963, 1-23), this relied much on the work of Hull and J G S Brinson who founded the Roman Essex Society. Indeed the volume's core was Rex Hull's formidable *Gazetteer* (1963, 35-203). Here, set forth parish by parish, are the careful records of sites and finds from site visits, builders' reports, and notes in the county journals amassed in over thirty years of devoted service to Essex archaeology, and meticulously recorded in voluminous files and six-inch maps kept in the Colchester and Essex Museum. For a generation now, all Romanists concerned with the county have begun with Rex Hull's Gazetteer.

During the nineteen sixties the pace of discovery quickened. Summaries of much of this new information were published by W J Rodwell and R Dunnett (1975a; 1975). Three years later, the work of the early-to mid seventies was presented in interim form by P J Drury and Rodwell (1980) at the 1978 Clacton conference. Fifteen years after, and a generation after the VCH Survey, another audit is due, for while many of the excavations and explorations presented in interim form at Clacton are now published, archaeological work has continued at an unslackened pace since the later seventies and this overview, like its predecessor, must draw as much on unpublished as on published data.

Communications

In the absence of specific projects devoted to this end, only comparatively slow progress has been made towards the elucidation of the Roman road network in the past fifteen years. Already by the 18th century John Horsley commented on the depredations of the plough on the county's ancient monuments and landscapes (1732, 331, 427-9). The Roman road network had long been fragmented and only a few trunk routes were known which survived as modern roads. Some 18th-century antiquaries (such as Dr Foote Gower) carried out fieldwork in the county, but the bulk of the work devoted to reconstituting the Roman road network in the county dates to the 20th century. Some of this work has not lasted well. In the early 1920's Miller Christy (1920; 1921) surveyed and published a large number of routes of which several have been contested since (Round 1923), while a number of roads claimed by the *Viatores*, who worked primarily in the south Midlands but who also pursued a number of routes up to the borders of the county, have also proved illusory (Simco 1984, 78-9). Most of these were omitted from the Ordnance Survey's first edition *Map of Roman Britain* (1924) and between its second (1928) edition and the third of 1956 it added only two, fragmentary road lengths near Colchester to the map. From the later 1950s on, however, increased fieldwork, usually by amateurs, resulted in some important extensions to the network. In north Essex, P C Dewhurst added materially to our knowledge of the *via Devana* (Margary 3) while fliers with the Colchester Archaeological Group extended knowledge of roads in the eastern part of the county. Significant work was undertaken elsewhere in Essex by Paul Drury and notably, Warwick Rodwell, who proposed a number of new routes in his paper on the Antonine Itinerary (Rodwell 1975b). The maps which accompany their site reports, also reproduced with minor modifications in the Clacton conference volume (Drury and Rodwell 1980, fig 24), summarise knowledge to the later 1970s.

Trunk Routes

Since then a number of further lengths of the trunk network, particularly valley routes, have been tentatively identified either from the ground or the air, and some have been tested by non-invasive means or sectioned. In the north-west of the county close to Great Chesterford, CUCAP images show a route crossing the Essex Cam from the town and heading northwards, probably towards the Icknield Way (Fig 1.A). Further south, bridging the Stort-Essex Cam gap, a north-south road has been discerned west of Saffron Walden, well preserved in Audley End park. Details of this route have been published by Bassett (1982, fig 3, Fig 1.B). East of Saffron Walden, a cross-country route has been pursued by Toller, who elucidated a length connecting Radwinter with Wixoe, a line pursued in its entirety by Charge (1986, fig 25, Fig 1.C). Charge traced its line east of Wixoe into Suffolk, and it is presumably to be linked with the road observed heading westwards from Long Melford. That a road ran along the opposite, Essex side of the river Stour here is now clear, as in 1976 the writer observed and photographed a parch mark of a road heading south westwards across the river Stour. Groundwork suggests that it continues westwards past Stoke by Clare, also in the direction of Wixoe (Fig 1.D). A spur from the Dunmow-Radwinter road (Margary 300) running south-westwards from Thaxted (Goddards Farm) in the direction of Elsenham was examined by Wacher (Goodburn 1978, 452, Fig 1.E).

Progress has also been made in the east of the county. West of Colchester, Oliver Rackham noted in Chalkney Wood the trace of a hollow way on the projected line of Margary 24, the celebrated *via Devana* which runs north-westwards from Colchester (Rackham 1980, figs 8.5, 15.6 and p 249). To the east of Chalkney Wood the alignment is preserved in hedgerows and a parish boundary, and it is also traceable in arable to the west of wood as the cropmarks of two side ditches aimed towards Halstead (Fig 1.F). While Charge has recently dismissed the *via Devana* as an antiquarian fancy (1986, 51-5), this evidence leaves little room to doubt that, while its name is recent, a major route did run north westwards from Colchester in the direction of Cambridge.

Further east, other roads have been noted in the Tendring district. Here the droughts of 1975-6 revealed a c. 10km long route linking Colchester with Mistley on the river Stour (Fig 1.G), and a spur road has been noted branch-

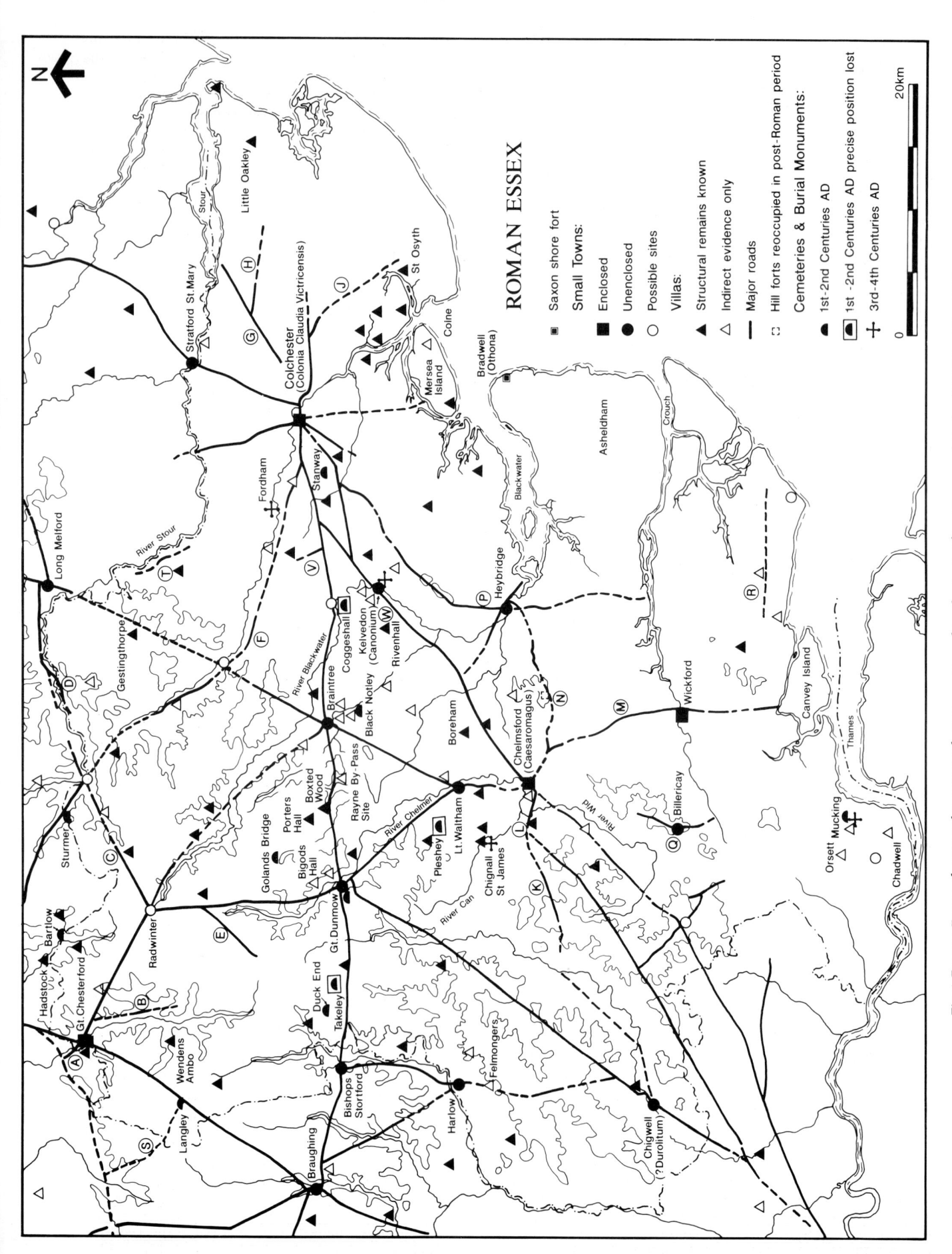

Fig 1 Roman Essex, showing the principal sites mentioned in the text. After Drury and Rodwell 1980, with additions

ing off this route. Initially this road (Fig 1.H) runs in the direction of Little Oakley, and thence, perhaps, in the direction of Harwich. To the south east of Colchester crop marks of stretches of a road alignment have been seen in the St Osyth area (Fig 1.J), suggesting that a route also ran towards the Essex coast somewhere west of Clacton, but its more southern course is quite unknown.

In central Essex, further roads have now been identified in the vicinity of Chelmsford. A route running between Chelmsford and Ongar to the west has been identified as a series of hedgebanks between Norton Heath and Horsfrith Park Farm (Fig 1.K). It appears to be a continuation of a short east-west length of road noted in Writtle (Fig 1.L), and probably met a route running northwards from Passingford Bridge (?*Durolitum*) somewhere near Ongar. The route was anticipated by Rodwell who suggested that it might be the course of Antonine *iter* V (Rodwell 1975b, fig 1 and pp 79, 93).

East and south of the London-Colchester road (Margary 2) matters are less clear. A road has been traced running south eastwards from Chelmsford towards Battlesbridge (Fig 1.M), but its course south of this place is not certain. A spur road probably branched off it in the vicinity of Danbury for Heybridge (Fig 1.N), where a number of fragmentary alignments have been noted (Wickenden 1986, fig 2). One of these (Fig 1.P), visible as a short length of crop mark near Langford, is a probable through route linking the site with Colchester. Further to the west, in the vicinity of Billericay, a linear feature aligned on Northey Wood and traceable northwards towards Stock (Fig 1.Q) probably marks the course of a road linking the settlement with Chelmsford. Further south, in Rochford hundred, Rippon has recently isolated a lengthy land boundary (1991, fig 6) which probably marks the course of an east-west road - one of the first to be reported from this part of the county (Fig 1.R).

Minor roads
While progress on the trunk network may be regarded as solid, if undramatic, our knowledge of the smaller routes, the numberless *diverticulae* which must have criss-crossed the county, remains woefully imperfect. In the north-east, a probable unromanised route appears to link the Braughing-Great Chesterford road (Margary 21b) with the Icknield Way near Royston (Fig 1.S,). It leaves the former road at the Langley tumulus (Hull 1963, 152). Since it is probable that this monument was sited at the junction formed by the two roads, the dating of the primary interment in it provides each with an Antonine *terminus ante quem*. Again in the north of the county crop marks of a small valley-side road photographed at Lamarsh (Fig 1.T) probably mark the course of a small through route.

Elsewhere, evidence is vanishingly slight. The Colchester Archaeological Group recently sectioned and confirmed a length of road (originally photographed as a parch mark by Ida McMaster) which ran northwards from Stane Street towards Great Tey (Fig 1.V), while at Rivenhall the villa approach road (Fig 1.W) was found in the bank of Cressing brook (Rodwell and Rodwell 1986, fig 15 and plate 13A-c). And here sure evidence gives out. For evidence of other roads we must make leaps in the gloom. If the numerous areas of landscape which have been claimed as ancient arable (see below) are, then a number of the spinal or axial boundaries belonging to them are certainly lanes and even through routes. Rodwell, for example, has identified one possible example in the Roding valley, which if it precedes Margary 30, dates to the inception of the Roman era (Rodwell 1978b, fig 11.9). At Gun Hill, the crop marks of a trackway running into a present day lane may date to the Roman period or earlier (Drury and Rodwell 1973, fig 1 and pl 2), and at Ardleigh too, crop marks suggest that what are clearly prehistoric or Romano-British droveways have an interesting congruence with some supposedly mediaeval lanes. It is safe to conclude that some roads and green lanes are of Roman, or even of prehistoric date, but none have yet been proved to be and each will have to be examined on a case by case basis.

Rural Settlements
If the roads are being progressively researched what of the network of settlements which they served? Early archaeological maps mask Roman Essex, and much of Roman Britain with a green tint denoting Wildwood (restored on a 'geological' basis), dotted here and there with villas and 'other substantial houses'. The 1924 OS Map depicted eighteen, of which perhaps six were the results of Neville's exertions in the previous century. Then, Essex could boast of some 22 other sites showing 'evidence of permanent settlement'. In the following decades the work in particular of M R Hull and J G S Brinson, with others such as H Cooper, J Lindsay and J P Smallwood began to increase this total, and by 1963 it was possible to adduce evidence for some sixty rural buildings. In the generation since, that figure has almost certainly doubled, even if the latest edition of the OS map, again adopting a minimalist stance, has cut us down to six 'villas' and 12 'substantial buildings'.

'Villas' and farmsteads
Our survey begins with sites of this class. Before looking at more recent finds we may review earlier explorations now published. Three principal excavations may be mentioned here: the first is that at Wendens Ambo, where a transect was excavated across an area to the east of the villa in advance of the construction of the M11 (Hodder 1982). This report allows the structure planned by Neville (Hull 1963, pl XXIXb) to be partially integrated into its agricultural setting and to be provided with a bath house and a corn drier. The site report includes an important assessment of the rural economy of the area by Paul Halstead (1982) which should be read in conjunction with T Williamson's study of nearby settlement densities (1984; 1986; 1990).

In central Essex, the Rivenhall excavations, begun by Brinson for the Roman Essex Society, and continued by the Rodwells, have also been published (Rodwell and Rodwell 1985; 1993). With its substantial study of the villa's landscape setting, the work will remain one of the most important contributions to villa studies in the county for some time to come.

Finally, the ill-known site at Gestingthorpe is now published (Draper 1985), having been provided with a more coherent ground plan by geophysical prospection which revealed traces on the site of two aisled buildings. The report managed to salvage much data from piecemeal excavations and is a tribute to the tenacity of the site owner, farmer Harold Cooper.

Since 1978 chance finds and fieldwalking exercises have added considerably to the number of potential sites: there are now indications, in the form of debris including tiles, flint scatters and tile *tesserae,* of 'permanent buildings' at (for example) Ashdon (Newham Hill); Birch (Gilman 1993, 197); Boreham; Chelmsford; Clavering (Chardwell Farm); Great Dunmow (Bigods Farm); Elsenham; Harlow (Felmongers; Gilden way); while examination of air photographs, excavation and other work at Rayne, Great Leighs, Toppesfield, and elswhere, has produced evidence of structures in the immediate vicinity. However villa plans, of which Frere noted a 'certain shortage' (1964, 257; 1985 1-2), remain rare, for only at a few of these sites (and others mentioned below) have excavations been carried out on any scale.

During this time some known villa sites were disturbed, necessitating examination and occasional excavation. A pipe-line cut across part of the villa at Little Hallingbury, and at Boxted Wood, Stebbing, in 1988 a reservoir constructed to the south east of the site disturbed ancilliary structures including a barn housing an animal-powered mill, and a small structure with its wooden sub floor joists clearly surviving as soilmarks (Bedwin 1989). The Hadstock villa (now in Linton parish, Cambridgeshire) has seen further work. Here the main range of the villa, originally explored by Neville, was clipped in 1990 by an Anglian Water pipeline. Rescue excavations revealed parts of the building and permitted something to be added to its overall plan (Hines and Ette 1993, fig 2). In an echo of more spectacular discoveries at such sites as Meonstoke in Hampshire (King and Potter 1990), what at first appeared to be a road or path proved on examination to be a fallen enclosure wall. Excavation and metal detector survey of the villa environs produced 112 coins, which outstrips any other villa in the region save for Gestingthorpe with its exceptional total of 544 coins.

Work has continued on some older discoveries. H J M Green's paced survey of the villa at Pleshey surfaced at the end of the 1970s and its plan may now be assessed. The evidence suggests that the structure bears a resemblance to the building at Chignall St James, possessing a central range with two deep side-wings set in a walled yard. In the east of the county, M Corbishley and Paul Barford have been working on his and the late Commander R A Farrands' old excavations at Little Oakley, of which a partial plan is now secured (Barford 1986, figs 2-3), while the long-lost records of the 1947 excavation at Boxted Wood, Stebbing, are being incorporated into the report on the 1988 excavation.

In the absence of a definitive publication of more than a few of these sites, it is impossible to present anything other than the broadest conclusions. Others apparently felt so too and during this period syntheses were rare. The last was a brief summary by Rodwell in 1978 which is essentially a rescencion of what was known at Clacton. In 1988, the writer published a small study of sites in the Great Dunmow region, considering in particular the setting of the villas in Stebbing parish in an effort to elucidate something of its parish boundaries, fully half of which seem to have existed as landscape features in the Roman period (Going 1988a). On the subject of Stebbing, the Porters Hall villa was recently cited as producing 'particularly impressive' evidence for industrial production beyond the needs of a local agricultural establishment (Branigan 1990, 47-8). This is a good example of the incestuous nature of much archaeological writing. The evidence cited by Branigan followed Dunnett (1975, 106-7), who got it from Hull (1963, 183), who got it in good faith from Campen the excavator, who imagined it.

Of the new sites explored, the Rayne by-pass site (Fig. 1), produced a substantial number of roller-stamped tiles and general structural debris suggesting a nearby villa (Smoothy 1989). Further south a building was found at Boreham and excavated by the Essex County Council. Its plan (Fig 2), is like that of building 4 at Wood Lane End, Hemel Hempstead (Neal 1983, 1984, fig 1). Both have ecclesiastical exemplars in the Eastern Empire, but the precise function of either structure is uncertain. The major villa at Chignall St James, photographed from the air by McMaster in 1975 was shortly afterwards the subject of excavations by the County Council which revealed much of the villa's *pars rustica,* together with a small later Roman inhumation cemetery (Clarke *in prep*).

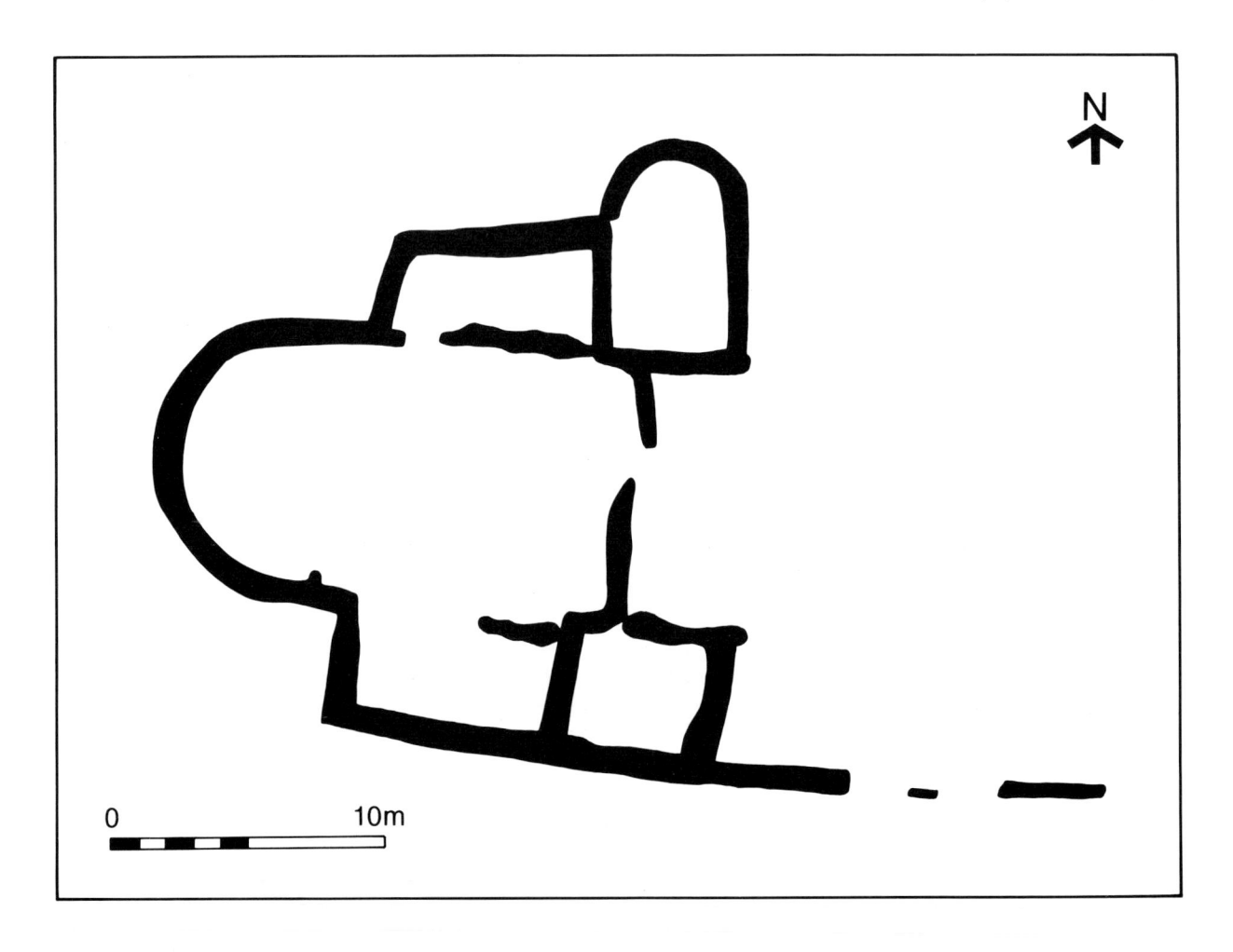

Fig 2 Roman apsed building at Bulls Lodge Quarry, Boreham

Fig 3 Farmstead at Mucking - the 'Double Ditched' enclosure. Roman period features shown open

We turn now to farmsteads. Of these perhaps the most important is at Mucking. 'DD Enc' - the so-called double-ditched enclosure (Fig 3), was once thought to be the outfield of an off-site villa, but it is clearly recognisable as a ditch-enclosed farmstead with an imposing two-leaf gateway and a range of internal buildings including a granary, central well, and an associated cemetery (Cemetery II). In its basic morphology, the site closely resembles the earlier phases of Barton Court Farm, Oxfordshire (Miles 1984). It is sites such as 'DD Enc' which are likely to be found right across the region, and a good parallel appears to have been recently discovered at Great Holts Farm, Boreham (Gilman 1993, 202).

The Mucking farmstead appears to have been destroyed by fire in the later second century AD, when debris from a principal building including over a tonne of daub (some roller-patterned), tools, and agricultural implements as well as domestic debris were dumped in the central well. The settlement appears not to have been rebuilt, and although the little cemetery appears to have continued in use as an ancestral burial ground into the 4th century, the enclosures and plots of the farm itself appear to have been turned over for agricultural uses. It is salutary to reflect that DD Enc, together with the Orsett 'Cock' site (Toller 1980; Carter forthcoming) are perhaps the sole examples of what was perhaps the most typical rural Roman settlement type in Essex to have been excavated on the scale necessary to elucidate with any confidence their layout, chronology, and morphological development. The results of the current work at Great Holts, near Boreham, will thus be of signal importance.

Of settlements classifiable as villages and hamlets, or small, isolated rural sites we know all too little. These sites, surely already evidenced in some numbers within the county Sites and Monuments Record as diffuse cropmark complexes in sensitive areas (Priddy and Buckley 1987), and elsewhere as, at most, thin scatters of pottery, have attracted almost no exploration and we remain as ignorant of these as ever.

Farm buildings

If our knowledge of formal domestic structures remains sparse, excavations have revealed more of the ancillary agricultural structures including barns. We may now add to Hadman's rather poor showing of Essex examples of the no-doubt once ubiquitous aisled barn (Hadman 1978, fig 61), structures at Gestingthorpe (from survey, Draper 1985, fig 6) and, probably, Pebmarsh (Smallwood 1964, fig 2, lower). However the aisled structure at Mucking (Fig 3; Mucking location 0650 1160), on occasion cited as Roman, is almost certainly medieval.

One class of structure which was scarcely known even nationally fifteen years ago is the water mill, of which many examples have recently come to light elsewhere in the Empire (eg Rakob 1993) and beyond it, in Ireland (Rynne 1992). Now examples are known in northern Britain (Simpson 1976), in Kent at Ickham (Young 1978), and in Northamptonshire (Frere 1991, 253 and fig 17). Fifteen years ago in Essex, only Great Chesterford had been identified as the site of a putative mill (on the evidence of the mill spindle in the Great Chesterford hoard: Manning 1972). Since then, however, R J Spain has revealed evidence of another at Ardleigh (Spain 1984, 111 and fig 6), while the Rodwells identified a site connected with the Rivenhall villa as a possible mill (Rodwell and Rodwell 1986, fig 29 site R2), bringing the total of known or suspected sites in Essex to three. With consciousness of the existence of these structures in the Roman era now heightened others will certainly be identified in Essex and elsewhere. Most will be on inland rivers but the existence of Roman tidal mills should not be overlooked.

Roman uses of water power appear to have been remarkably wide, and while the primary function of these sites may have been milling, the discovery of an asymmetrically burred ?trip hammer from Ickham (unpub), and the recovery of stone ?fulling troughs at the probable site of the Great Chesterford mill, suggests that these British sites performed a wide variety of jobs.

The Landscape

As the distribution maps started to fill up and evidence began to be amassed of expansion into the Boulder Clays as early as the Middle Iron Age, it became clear that these sites did not possess an outlook of unrelieved forest. Attention turned to the nature of the contemporary countryside. Haverfield tackled the problem in the early part of the century (Haverfield 1921), discerning in the parallelism of the Braintree-Gosfield road (Margary 33a), and the Leaden Roding to Dunmow road (Margary 30) the possible remains of the *kardines* of a *territorium* surrounding Colchester, a massive land-clearance covering perhaps a third of the county. The idea that much of rural Roman Essex was cleared or arranged in a major Colchester-based scheme endures: even quite recently the *via Devana* (Margary 24), spent some time pressed into service as another axis of the Haverfield system (Applebaum 1972), and the idea lives on, if in modified form, in the work of Professor Barri Jones, who in 1977 published the claim that two roads west of Colchester (Margary 32 and 320) were perhaps the principal axes of a massive land-allotment (Jones 1978; Mattingley and Jones 1990, fig 7.5).

None of these efforts to elucidate the principal axes of long vanished, planned landscapes have met with unqualified success, and perhaps in unconscious response, attempts were made to identify some exisiting landscapes, in some areas down to individual field boundaries, as ancient survivals. This work on 'relict landscapes', begun in Essex in the 19th century (Wilkinson 1988, 126-30 with refs), and advanced further with studies such as Margary's examination of Ripe in Sussex (1973, 73, with refs) and Applebaum's experiment with Great Wymondley in Cambridgeshire (1972, fig 10, 90-3) gave rise to the idea that it might be possible to reconstruct large fragments of ancient landscapes in Essex. At Little Waltham, Drury noted that some of the excavated features apparently continued beyond the excavation area as extant landscape features, and discerned in that part of the Chelmer valley the remnants of a reticulated field system parts of which appeared to pre-date the Chelmsford-Braintree Roman road (Drury 1978, fig 74). In a series of papers, Drury and Rodwell drew attention to the existence of similar rectilinear systems in central Essex and the Dengie peninsula (Rodwell 1978b; Drury and Rodwell 1978), while in West Essex Rodwell, perhaps influenced by Bonney's (1972) studies of earthwork boundaries in the Wiltshire region, drew attention to a series of apparently ancient boundaries in the Lea valley which, like the Chelmer system, appeared to be cut by a Roman road (Rodwell 1978b, fig 11.8).

Others quickly took up and expanded the approach: in the Saffron Walden area Bassett (1982, fig.3) observed similar patterns. Tom Williamson, then occupied with a massive fieldwalking programme in the Saffron Walden area (Williamson 1984), embraced the idea and went on to apply the same principles in the Scole-Dickleburgh region on the Norfolk-Suffolk border and elsewhere. Back in Essex, Wright (1981, 5) delineated similar systems in the Rochford area.

The reception to the hypothesis was mixed. Applebaum (1981) hailed it as a major breakthrough, but as it became clear that some of the initial claims had been over-optimistic more critical reaction set in. Fifteen years after, this contribution to landscape archaeology remains difficult to evaluate, largely because few proofs have been presented, which is hardly surprising in view of the massive work required to carry them out. Attempts have been made, however, and some regions (inevitably) have fared less well than others. Work such as that by Wilkinson on the Grays by-pass (1988, 126-30), and Rippon's study of the Rochford region (1991) allows us to conclude that while wholesale survival cannot be claimed without good archaeological grounds, some landscape survival has occurred, reaffirming the vital truism that landscapes are palimpsests.

Prior to this landscape work, Rodwell, in an echo of older concerns, explored the implications of mileage shortfalls in the Antonine *Itinerary* and postulated the existence of town 'zones' surrounding Colchester and Chelmsford (Rodwell 1975b): a study followed by Bassett, who discerned a *territorium* encircling Great Chesterford (Bassett 1989, fig 1.12), while as we have seen, Jones and Mattingley have published their evidence of cadastral planning west of Colchester (1991, fig 7.5). This has, however, been contested by I. McMaster (*pers comm*). Interestingly Crummy has isolated a series of crop marks of a regularly parcelled-out landscape south of Colchester, in the vicinity of the Roman river (1978, 33-5) which remains at the time of writing perhaps the most persuasive example of Roman land surveying yet known in Essex.

Most excavations have revealed what might be termed 'landscape fragments' - small slices, transects, edges, of the arable of villas, farms, or small towns. For example at Buildings Farm, Great Dunmow (Gilman 1993, 198), a series of ditched enclosures and fields has recently been exposed, but in the absence of an obvious settlement nucleus connected with them their relationship with the nearby small town remains unclear. Similarly at Great Lofts near Maldon, at Ardleigh, and indeed, at Stansted Airport itself where a major fieldalking programme was undertaken in the 1980s explorations have revealed similar agrarian landscapes: ditch-enclosed fields, droves and gores which affirm that the boulder clays were an increasingly used resource in the Roman era but provide us with little in the way of coherent, integrated plans embracing both field systems and settlements. For the present, just about the only site excavated on a scale sufficient to give us a coherent picture remains Mucking, where a 240,000m² excavation has provided us with a piece of total archaeology. Here it is possible to discern as many as eight significant landscapes, spanning the Mesolithic period to the 20th century. From the largely *ad hoc* landscapes of the prehistoric era, there developed in the Roman period enclosed ditch and field systems associated with at least one farmstead (for a simplified plan of its Roman features, see M U Jones 1978, fig 26.2). Like its predecessors, the Roman landscape at Mucking is a remarkably dynamic entity. First developing as an enclosed field system from the Iron Age enclosures such as RB I, gores, enclosures and pightles develop and fall out of use as a large farmstead develops in the later first century, its cemetery sited alongside the Iron Age burials on the slope. By the later third century these smaller enclosures have given way to larger fields which, in places at least, appear to have fallen into disrepair in the later 4th century. Interestingly, while there is good evidence for Romano-British utilisation of the late pre-Conquest landscape, with the exception of the east and west boundaries of Saxon Cemetery II and some banks which survived as earthworks, little of this Roman landscape survived *in use* in the Saxon period. The latter's enclosures and ditches prefigure its fully medieval successor.

Finally in this (over) compressed description of the physical landscape, we must turn to the work of environmentalists such as Oliver Rackham and Peter Murphy. It has recently become clear - and should have been obvious much earlier - that woodmanship has flourished in Britain for millennia: coppicing for example, is now abundantly apparent in the archaeological evidence from as early as the Bronze Age. Pollen diagrams and other work indicate clearly that by the Roman period trees were not the dominant vegetational cover save perhaps, for some regions of the county such as the London clays. Even here however, a significant fraction of it was probably managed woodland. While on vegetational grounds it may be possible to identify surviving modified climatic climax cover, proving the matter archaeologically is a more difficult matter. Elucidation of Roman woodland through fieldwork remains possible, however, and Rackham's suggestion (1980, 107) that the banks in Chalkney Wood which flank the hollow way on the line of Margary 24 may themselves be Roman (possible Roman wood banks have also been noted in Hertfordshire), raises exciting avenues of research.

As environmental sampling becomes more routine, data is beginning to transform our knowledge of the palaeobotanical landscape. Immediate (and more general) landscape conditions may be reflected in the environmental evidence. The evidence for crops has been reviewed by Murphy (this volume), and analyses have provided useful insights into the agricultural economies of sites at eg, Wendens Ambo, Stebbing/Boxted Wood (Murphy, in prep), Mucking, and in the Chelmsford region in the immediately post Roman period (Murphy *et al.* forthcoming). Important insights into the function of certain structures can result from samples analysis: data from corndriers at Wendens Ambo and Mucking in Essex and Chells and Foxholes Farm in Hertfordshire suggest these structures could equally have served as malting ovens, a function now successfully simulated at Butser (Partridge 1989, 16-18). Faunal analyses, too (Luff 1982; Dorrington and Legge 1985; King 1988) have thrown substantial light on pastoral practices in the region in the Roman era.

The Coast

The coast, with its vital agricultural resources, has continued to be the preserve of, in particular, the Colchester Archaeological Group, whose explorations of Red Hills and of salt winning gave rise to the successful 1974 conference (de Brisay and Evans 1974). In 1979 Rodwell published a brief synthesis which took the picture beyond Clacton, and in 1990 this survey was superceded by the publication by the Colchester archaeological group of a memorial volume to Kay de Brisay which brings the work up to date (Fawn *et al.* 1990). While this brings an impressive amount of data between one set of covers including a Gazetteer of currently known Red Hills (*ibid*, 48-67), one of the salient problems, the fate of the salt industry, remains controversial. On the face of it the evidence suggests that the Red Hills declined in economic importance after the Antonine period, eclipsed perhaps by inland sources such as the highly saline springs of the Cheshire/Droitwich region, which would have been at least as economical as the coastal salterns.

So, what of the later Roman era? Recently Richard Bradley, in a survey of saltern material in the Chichester harbour area (1992), noted the occurrence on some of later Roman pottery. In Essex certain Red Hills on the Blackwater and near Langenhoe have also produced later Roman evidence including coins. Sealey (1995) has accounted for the occurrence of this material, which for the most part appears to be unstratified by postulating that in the later Roman era the Red hills were not used for salt-winning but increasingly as temporary refuges and shelters by pastoralists using the salt marshes for grazing. Important in this context are some recent publications on coastal change which suggest that the lowering sea level trends observable in the early Roman period had been

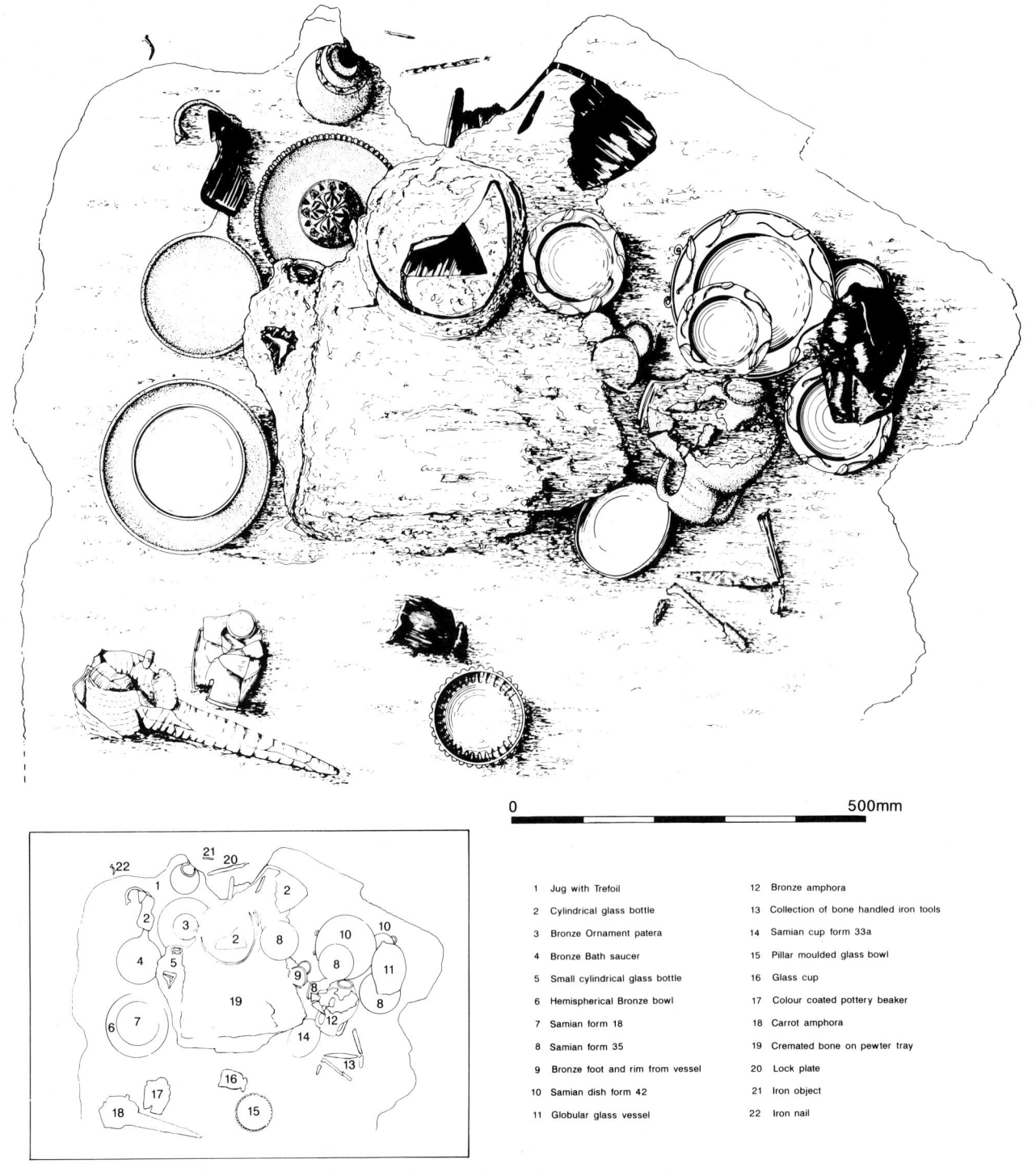

1	Jug with Trefoil	12	Bronze amphora
2	Cylindrical glass bottle	13	Collection of bone handled iron tools
3	Bronze Ornament patera	14	Samian cup form 33a
4	Bronze Bath saucer	15	Pillar moulded glass bowl
5	Small cylindrical glass bottle	16	Glass cup
6	Hemispherical Bronze bowl	17	Colour coated pottery beaker
7	Samian form 18	18	Carrot amphora
8	Samian form 35	19	Cremated bone on pewter tray
9	Bronze foot and rim from vessel	20	Lock plate
10	Samian dish form 42	21	Iron object
11	Globular glass vessel	22	Iron nail

Fig 4 Stansted. Boxed Hadrianic-Antonine cremation burial

checked and reversed by the 4th century. Clear evidence for diminished freshwater run off has been quantified nationally for the first time by the Waddeloves in their (1990) survey of highest astronomical tides (HAT). This data clearly indicates that there was a rise in sea level in the later Roman period which must have had an impact on Essex. In this context, the Hullbridge Basin Survey, which has thrown much light on the coastline of Roman Essex (Wilkinson and Murphy 1986) produced important data on the Crouch, where a jetty or trackway constructed across an extensive area of plainly ill-drained reedy marsh was carbon-dated to the second half of the 4th or the first half of the fifth century. If, like inland areas, the salt marshes were increasingly used for sheep ranching in the later Roman period, the use of small elevations such as the old 'Red Hills' as occasional refuges makes eminent sense (for an arresting image of the use of a similar mound in such a fashion see Grieve 1959, pl opp p 453).

Burials

Until recently rural Romano-British burials in Essex have been comparatively little reported or recorded. Some aspects of them had been studied by K Rodwell (1970), but they received comparatively brief attention at Clacton. During the past few years however, rural burials have been reported in some numbers and the more important finds are treated in Philpott's recent synthesis (1991). Standing at the beginning of the Roman era are the spectacular discoveries at Stanway discussed by Crummy (1993 and this volume). Scarcely less impressive burials of the later first and early second centuries (Fig 4) were found at Duck End during the recent Stansted project. These are comparable in their richness to those from the Bartlow Hills, while at Stebbing a number of richly-furnished Flavian burials were also excavated in the wake of plough damage (Goodburn 1978, 452). Metal detector users at Elsenham discovered a further important early burial which, happily, has been made available for archaeological study (Gilman 1992, 112). Less happily at Great Chesterford, a further rich burial which contained grave goods including a series of plaques decorated with enamel inlay was looted from within the scheduled ancient monument in 1988. In the south of the county, the Castle Point Archaeological Group excavated a number of cremations on Canvey Island, one of which contained one or more lead-glazed flagons. Discoveries of later Roman interments are much less common. Since Clacton, the only later Roman rural cemetery to be excavated was at Chignall St James. Among the burials were some decapitations. Noteworthy among the few grave goods recovered was a small glass palm cup. Other finds have come as the result of isolated discoveries: at Fordham, near Colchester, a stone coffin found in a complex of ditched enclosures observed as crop-marks was dated by its contents to the 3rd or 4th centuries AD (Davies 1984). Continued work on older excavations has thrown more light on rural funerary practices in the region: at Mucking, Roman cemeteries I and VI are primarily inhumation cemeteries of the later Roman period. Cemetery I, burial 19 appears to have been placed in a hedged plot, while as noted, Cemetery II (in DD Enc) produced burials dating down to the 4th century.

On the publication side there is much less to report. Interims or abbreviated summaries of some of the sites are in print or are included in recent works of synthesis but no final reports are published. Those which are, are connected with small towns rather than rural areas; for example the small 1st-2nd century cemetery at Redbond Lodge, Great Dunmow (Wickenden 1988), and the later Roman cemetery at Kelvedon, with its complex coffin fittings (K A Rodwell 1987, 26-52).

Crummy's discovery of a weapon grave at Stanway is a most welcome addition to the tiny number of such interments known. The Stanway burial, together with the later pre-Roman Iron Age weapon burial at Kelvedon (Going *in prep*) now provide us with a context for the poorly known box-burial from Little Walden, which was accompanied by a spear (Hull 1963, 195), and the enigmatic early inhumation from Toppesfield, which was accompanied by a sword, and a patera and ewer (Hull 1963, 192-3).

Many of these sites have produced evidence of funerary ritual. Grave goods showing signs of deliberate breakage have been noted at a number of sites, for example Great Dunmow (Going 1988b), Kelvedon (K Rodwell 1988, fig 88 Gr 74.b), Mucking, Skeleton Green, and elsewhere, and the occasional inclusion of sherds in grave fills has also been recognised as a ritual activity in these contexts. Other evidence of ritual, for example the provision of garlands, or of incense (recognised long ago at Bartlow Barrow II by Michael Faraday, and found more recently at Verulamium (Frere 1991, 260-1) must, however, await the examination of soil samples and deposits. At Stebbing/Golands Bridge, a deposit inside a *balsamarium* from burial 2 may be a spice, while burial 1 contained a cremated ?animal rib bone with a series of knife cuts suggesting a burnt offering. Some older finds may be of significance in this context: eighteenth century references to inscribed lead sheets found in pots buried at Great Chesterford are highly reminiscent of the messages to the dead supposedly written by the Gauls, one of which (in Gallic) was found recently in a burial on the plain of Larzac south of the celebrated Samian *atelier* of La Graufesenque.

Essex has an impressive number of funerary monuments, eg the Bartlow grave mounds at Ashdon (Hull 1963, 39-44), and lesser *tumuli* at Sturmer, Langley, East Mersea, and Takeley, and other tumulus-like monuments such as the 'wheel tomb' at Mersea, and *columbaria* at Pleshey, Coggeshall, and White Notley (Hull 1963 with refs). The Bartlow *tumuli* have not been much studied in recent years, although a find of a 4th-century pottery sherd on the flank of Barrow IV, the largest mound, suggests it may have been augmented after the principal burial, possibly well into the later Roman period. Rather neglected is the reference to the Takeley Street *tumulus* (Hull 1963, 185), which if accurately dated displaces the example from Knobs Crook, Dorset (Fowler 1965) as the earliest known from Roman-Britain. Of the other tomb discoveries, the long-lost 'vault' at Coggeshall (Hull 1963, 90) despite the somewhat Rosicrucian-tinged account of its contents may certainly be identified as a genuine find and the monument can now be located to the south of the town. Further data, in the form of an architect's plan, is now available on the *columbarium* at White Notley, excavated by M J Campen in the 1950's. This confirms that it contained three rather than four niches and shows three substantial masonry buttresses (the positions of which suggest a robbed out fourth) implying the existence of a tower-like superstructure with engaged pilasters in a (presumably rather rustic) echo of such works as '*La Conocchia*' at Santa Maria Capua Vetera (Toynbee 1971, pl 38). In the east of the county the burial vault located by Bryan Blake (1965) has been joined by a nearby second, found by Corbishley (in prep). Tombstones remain very rare: at Barking, parts of a funerary inscription - the first to be reported in Essex outside Colchester - were recovered during excavations, while just outside the county at Great Hallingbury, an (unpublished) fragment found unstratified in a field, depicts a (now headless) togate figure carved in semi-round, leaning against a leaf-encrusted pillar.

The development of rural Roman Essex: an overview

The initial impetus in rural development appears to have occurred about ten or fifteen years after the Boudican revolt, in the Flavian period, and it is to roughly this date bracket that a number of the villa sites overlooking the Colne estuary may be assigned. At about this time some proto-villas may have been constructed in other parts of the county, for example Rivenhall, but in Essex at least, and probably elsewhere as well, it is by and large during the second century that the villa system reached its apogee, with many rural Romanised structures being built in the Hadrianic, and most particularly, during the Antonine periods. Quite recently the conventional picture of later Roman Britain drawn by Romanists depicted these islands as a comparative haven (with minor outbreaks of unrest, eg in AD 367), but the veracity of this image (which was largely based on archaeological data from central rather than eastern England) is now increasingly questioned. In fact it was always contradicted by historical evidence (Salway 1982; Thompson 1991): from the time of the 'third-century decline' on, the archaeological evidence becomes diffuse, vague, and increasingly difficult to interpret. By the end of the 1970's, Reece (1980) advanced the view that the towns in the eastern part of the island had begun to decline well before the end of the Roman era. While this paper was ill-received at the time, the archaeological evidence in favour of this suggestion is steadily strengthening. Numismatic evidence certainly indicates a fall-off in coin use in the eastern part of the Province in the 4th century and data from towns such as Chelmsford, Colchester and Braintree (Wickenden this volume, Faulkner 1994) suggests shrinking settlement areas and widespread decline, if not dereliction, which is present too beyond the county borders at Cambridge,

Godmanchester and London (Burnham and Wacher 1991). Perhaps the most immediately obvious difference between towns in the east of the Province and Essex and those elsewhere, is in their defences. In the west many urban sites posessed walls by the 4th century. In the east, however, in the hinterland of the most exposed stretch of the *Litus Saxonicum*, few towns appear to have been similarly equipped.

If the towns are apparently in decline in the later Roman period what of the countryside? Despite the amount of excavation its scale has usually been small and in consequence there is still an appalling lack of data. There are, however, some pointers. These again highlight differences between the east and the west. While there is evidence for the creation in the later Roman period of new villas in the Cotswolds, the extension of others, and the installation of mosaic pavements, in the east evidence of late villa construction or enlargement is emphatically absent. Indeed in Essex the best we may currently hope for on many rural sites are coins of Periods XV and XVI or late pottery types such as Oxfordshire oxidised wares or 'late' shell-tempered pottery which suggest occupation after c. AD 360/75. The picture available for the few known farmsteads is perhaps even worse. Only really at Mucking, where a landscape of some size has been excavated and explored, is it possible to elucidate something of the later Roman countryside. How typical of other areas this site was is unclear, but the farmstead here appears not to have been rebuilt after a fire in the later second century but to have gone out of use and been reconverted to arable, while the field system surrounding it was remodelled into larger plots. As pottery of the post mid-4th century appears only in the upper levels of the ditches of this later landscape it seems likely that it went out of maintenance well before the end of the 4th century.

The kind of landscape changes seen at Mucking - the disappearance of on-site settlement in the later Roman era - and the remodelling of the field system may reflect wider changes. Elsewhere there is evidence of major changes in agricultural practices: examination of the dates of the few excavated field systems suggests extensive remodelling of land allotments, with field sizes being increased consistent both with more intensive, large-scale crop production and also the introduction of a major pastoral element in the agricultural regime (to an anonymous panegyrist of AD 305 Britain was a land of sheep). Similar evidence available from other sites, which suggests that in not a few regions of the county land which once had belonged to small farms had been incorporated into massive technologically advanced *latifundia* (as evidenced by the tools from the Worlington (Suff). and Great Chesterford ironwork hoards) while pockets of *agri deserti* were spreading, but for more detailed answers to these questions we must increasingly rely on palaeobotanical and faunal research.

It is clear that a complex interplay of agricultural, climatological, and other factors may have tipped the region into full-scale decline in the 4th century. One factor appears to have been disasters on the Continent requiring increased food exports. The massive scale of the problems on the Continent is clear both from archaeological and historical sources. For example, Brulet's remarkable image of settlement evidence during the Haut- and Bas Empires within and beyond the territory of the Menapii (Brulet 1991, fig 26.21) suggests widespread later Roman abandonment, presumably locating geographically part, at least, of the enormous Gallic tract (now estimated to be some 24,000 square miles in extent) recorded in Julian's celebrated letter to the Athenians (*Ep ad Ath*) as having ceased to be agriculturally productive in the wake of the incursions of the AD 360's. That Gallic towns endured equal privations is apparent from Libanius' funeral oration to Julian (*Lib Or* XVIII.35), which notes that at this time the inhabitants of some Gaulish towns not only stored food within their walls, but grew and harvested it there too - a situation at which the tower granary at Colchester presumably hints.

When it is recollected that at about this time parts of the Essex coast and the Fens were becoming wetter as rising sea levels significantly retarded freshwater run-off and freshwater marshes backed towards Cambridge, we may envisage not only population displacement but also the loss of grain-producing land, and it is possible to suggest that the food-producing sector of eastern Britain was verging on breakdown for much of the 4th century. Nor were the authorities quick to apply relief. Quite the contrary. Increased superindictions seem to have been causing problems as early as Constans' reign and may have been responsible for another revolt after the suppression of Magnentius. However that was settled, only five years later, in AD 359, Julian massively stepped up British food exports to Gaul. While it is unclear how large these exports had traditionally been, the enormous fleet size required to transport the extra suggests that for a time at least the British laboured under a much increased burden.

In the context of these problems we may reassess the role of the Roman settlement at Great Chesterford, which is apparently unusual even among walled towns in having been twice provided with defences. Eighteenth-century references clearly indicate that a substantial wall once enclosed much of the area between the existing mill and the present-day churchyard. This circuit was completely robbed-out by the seventeenth century, but it has been sectioned in a number of places, most recently in 1984. These suggest it is about the size of Horncastle (Field and Hurst 1983, fig 3). Its date is not entirely clear, but it was probably constructed between the later 3rd and the early 4th centuries AD. Some time after the mid-4th century however, it appears to have been replaced by a much larger enclosure to its north. The plan of this later *enciente* (which resembles the circuit at Reims) is taken straight off a *mensor's* drawing board and imposed on the landscape almost without modification. This is no fancy of the local *Curia*, but an official construction undertaken on orders at the highest level.

While the best historically attested context for undertaking such a work remains the years after 367 it is unwise to assign a construction of this kind to Theodosius on those grounds. However what is plain is that if, as Bartholomew (1984) and Thompson (1991) have argued, Theodosius had just been fighting on internal lines in this region his report to Valentinian, shorn of rhetoric, would have made it plain that not only were the eastern Provinces of the islands in a parlous state (perhaps significantly in this context at Burgh Castle and perhaps, Caistor by Yarmouth there are dislocations in the ceramics and coin lists which indicate disruptions in occupation in the 4th century), but that the principal route centres in the *litus* hinterland were effectively without defences. After three centuries the vital strategic significance of the town, which guarded the Icknield way between the Stort-Essex Cam gap, might have become clear once more. This and the need for an effective *annona* point justified the construction of the sole major fortification to be built in East Anglia in the later Roman period.

The end of Roman Essex
In portraying Roman Essex as having reached its apogee in the second century and then as experiencing a long decline I have drawn a more apocalyptic picture than the one presented in 1978 by Drury and Rodwell. While parts of the east *were* rich, indeed, wealthy, in the later Roman period, much of the region, materially at least, seems not to have been and at the end of the Roman era vanished almost with ease from the archaeological record. The

explanation for this would appear to be rooted in the proximity of the region to the continent and the probability that it was seen as a source of ready supply. Major changes in the later Roman agricultural regime in which large, technologically advanced *latifundia* practising large scale arable farming and cereal growing snuffed out the small farms of the first and second centuries. The importance of the region for livestock growing cannot be overestimated, and if Sealey (1995) and others are correct in their interpretation of the later Roman evidence from the Red Hills, the salt marshes were also increasingly used for pastoral ends (as in Gaul). In the Middle Ages, East Anglia and Essex grew rich from this type of farming and the wealth then generated is still visible, for much of it was ploughed back into the region by merchants and landowners as houses and churches. What happened to the fortunes of their Roman counterparts is less certain. Possibly the population had split into a small rich elite whose wealth was expressed in the (portable) hoards of plate such as those from Hoxne and Mildenhall, serviced by a tied Colonate of increasingly disaffected peasantry. Such a countryside, its towns in decline, its population thinning, may have been reverting by the Constaninian period to a way of life more akin to that of the later Iron Age.

By the end of the Roman period then, the overwhelming majority of the Romano-British population may have differed little from the Saxons in material terms. Archaeologically speaking, however, having become almost wholly aceramic, they were even less visible than the newcomers. The role of negative evidence has bedevilled thought about the end of Roman Britain for a very long time, but half a century ago R E M Wheeler (1935) noted the lack of 'Germanic' habitation evidence away from the Eastern littoral and postulated that within the triangle formed by London, Colchester and Verulamium, British power endured long after the collapse of Roman Britain. Wheeler's suggestion has recently (1982) received strong support in a survey of the Chiltern region by K Rutherford Davis. The conclusion of this underrated work was that a British hegemony did indeed survive in this region for a lengthy period after the end of the Roman era. Unfortunately Rutherford Davis omitted from his study west and north-west Essex, which properly belong with it. Indeed a newly strengthened Great Chesterford, blocking as it does access along the Icknield Way, is probably the key to its endurance. Recent work on the Cambridgeshire dykes (Welsh 1994,12) suggests that some originated at the end of the Roman era. It seems likely that the power of this British neighbour kept the kingdom of the *East Seaxe* a largely coastal entity until its collapse allowed Saxon hegemony to be carried in a concerted later-sixth century *landnam*, into present-day Hertfordshire, Middlesex and Surrey.

Conclusions

In recent years some Romanists have expressed dissatisfaction at the fact that the accumulation of information which has occurred since the last war has apparently answered so few questions, and that the research priorities initially set decades ago, and repeated by the Society for the Promotion of Roman Studies (SPRS 1985) have changed so little. Cunliffe (1984, 178), pungently likened the world of Romano-British studies to an 'airless room' in which an image of Britannia was venerated by acolytes. Cunliffe's views drew a mild riposte from Todd (1985), but a recent (1990) volume of research work in Roman Britain edited by the latter generated little enthusiasm and some reviewers (eg Scott 1990; Reece 1991) waxed caustic at the lack of progress. The problem is not unfamiliar. Many of the ideas about Roman Britain, and for that matter Roman Essex, were formed decades ago and are now reaching the end of their allotted span. The data stream continues as great as ever, yet we have reached intellectual slack water, as it were, and our questions seem impossible to answer. What are needed now are new hypotheses (eg Going 1992), for only then will the data make more sense and further progress become possible.

At a local level we may be more optimistic. Echoing Todd (1985) we can point to the past fifteen years as being ones of solid activity, largely devoted to unglamorous infrastructure work, to be sure, rather than to thinking at length about the meaning of it all. Yet the accumulation of data since 1978 has led to some profound changes in our perceptions of Roman Essex. We know more about the argicultural practices in the region, and we have a greater appreciation of the potential of palaeobotanical studies. Exploration of the coastline is beginning to produce important new data on the utilisation of the coast during the Roman era and after. The 'continuity' debate is being refined and refocussed, and when Mucking's complex site plan is finally unravelled, its evolving landscape will present us with a valuable paradigm of landscape evolution. As Reece and others pursue their work on Roman coinage context dating is being refined. Pottery too, is beginning to be used with more sensitivity. The Romano-Saxon pottery debate, of which many of the known examples are from Essex (W J Rodwell 1970) is now resolved: the ware is a late Roman pottery type (Gillam 1979; Roberts 1982) and Myres' valiant recent (1986) attempt to resurrect it is based on a piece of casuistry. 'Late' shell-tempered pottery is now known not to have endured much beyond the opening years of the fifth century (*contra* Lyne and Jefferies 1979). It remains, with Oxfordshire red wares, a useful tool for examining later 4th century AD settlement densities. Palaeobotanical data may play an increasingly important role in exploring ancient agricultural regimes. Grain samples allow us to examine crop types, and to identify plant remains, while dendrochronology will allow us to start to apply absolute dates where hitherto we have had no such precision.

The study of Roman Britain and Essex, while apparently static, is no such thing. It is just that this time is a period of stasis before the enormous amount of data (which dwarfs that of all prehistoric periods) retrieved in the latter half of this century is adequately synthesized. When this happens a new Roman Britain will emerge. That much of this data comes from Essex is to a substantial part due to the exertions in the middle decades of the century of Rex Hull, and later, Jack Brinson; in the sixties and seventies to Paul Drury and Warwick Rodwell, Rosalind Niblett and Philip Crummy and their successors, to members of amateur organisations such as the Colchester Archaeological Group, and the exceptional singleton investigator, and now, to staff archaeologists of the present-day Essex County Council Archaeology Section. The remaining years of the 20th century will, no doubt, see little slackening in the flow of information.

Bibliography

Applebaum S, 1972: 'Roman Britain' in H P R Finberg (Ed), *The Agrarian History of England and Wales.* Vol 1.2, AD 43-1042. 3-277.
1981: The Essex Achievement' *The Agrarian History Review* 29.1, 42-4.
Barford P, 1986: 'The Excavations and Fieldwork of R H Farrands 1950-1985'. *Colchester Archaeological Group Bulletin* 29, 3-15.
Bartholomew P, 1984: 'Fourth century Saxons'. *Britannia* 15,169-185.
Bassett S R, 1982: *Saffron Walden; excavations and research 1972-80.* Counc Brit Archaeol Rep 45.
1989: 'In search of the origins of the Anglo-Saxon Kingdoms' in S R Bassett (Ed) *The Origins of the Early Anglo Saxon Kingdoms. Studies in the Early History of Britain.* Leicester University Press, 3-27.
Bedwin O, 1989: Excavations at Boxted Wood, Stebbing Green. Essex County Council
Blake B, 1965: 'Roman Building at St Osyth'. *Trans Essex Arch Soc.* I.4 (3rd Ser), 259.
Bonney D J, 1972: 'Early boundaries in Wessex' in P J Fowler (Ed) *Archaeology and the Landscape,* 68-86.

Bowen H C & P J Fowler (eds) 1978: *Early Land Allotment.* BAR Brit Ser 48.

Branigan K, 1990: 'Specialisation in villa economies' in Branigan and Miles (eds), 42-50.

and D Miles 1990: *The Economies of Romano-British villas,* Sheffield.

Bradley R, 1992: 'Roman Salt production in Chichester Harbour: Rescue excavations at Chidham, West Sussex'. *Britannia* 23, 27-44.

de Brisay and K A Evans 1975: *Salt. The Study of An Ancient Industry,* Colch Arch Group.

Brulet R, 1991: 'Le Litus Saxonicum Continental', in V A Maxfield and M J Dobson (Eds) *Roman Frontier Studies 1989,* Univ of Exeter Press. 155-169.

Burnham B, & J Wacher 1991: *The Small Towns of Roman Britain,* Batsford.

Charge B, 1986: 'Roman Roads in Southern East Anglia - a reappraisal in the light of recent fieldwork'. *Journ Haverhill & Dist Arch Group* 4.2, 46-74.

Christy M, 1920: 'On Roman Roads in Essex', *Transactions of the Essex Archaeological Society* 15.3 (New Ser), 190-229.

Christy M, 1921: 'Roman Roads in Essex: An Addendum', *Transactions of the Essex Archaeological Society* 16.2 (New Ser), 127-30.

Crummy P, 1978: 'Crop marks at Gosbecks, Colchester'. *Aerial Archaeology* 4, 77-82.

1993: 'Aristocratic graves at Colchester' *Current Archaeology* 132, 492-7.

Cunliffe B, 1984: 'Images of Britannia'. *Antiquity* 58, 175-8

Draper J, 1985: Excavations at Hill Farm, Gestingthorpe. *East Anglian Archaeology* 25.

Davies G M R, 1984: Roman burials and a new villa site at Fordham'. *Colchester Archaeological Group Bulletin* 27, 32,44.

Dorrington E, & T Legge 1985: 'The animal bones' in N E France and B. Gobel, *The Romano-British temple at Harlow,* West Essex Archaeol. Group.

Drury P J, 1978: *Excavations at Little Waltham 1970-71.* CBA Res Rep 26.

and W J Rodwell 1973: 'Excavations at Gun Hill, West Tilbury' *Essex Arch. Hist.* 5, 48-112.

and W J Rodwell, 1978: 'Investigations at Ashledham, Essex: an interim Report on the church and the historic landscape'. *Antiq Journ* 58.1, 133-51.

and W J Rodwell, 1980: 'Settlement in the Later iron Age and Roman periods in D G Buckley (d) 1980, 59-75.

Dunnett R, 1975: *The Trinovantes,* Duckworth.

Ette J, & S Hines 1993: Excavations at Linton Roman Villa. Cambridgeshire County Council Archaeology Section Report Nr 88.

Faulkner N, 1994 'Later Roman Colchester' *Oxford Journal Archaeology* 13.1, 93-119.

Fawn A J, K A Evans, I McMaster and G M R Davies 1990: *The Red Hills of Essex,* Colchester Arch Group.

Field N, and H Hurst, 1983: Roman Horncastle' in *Lincs Hist and Arch* 18, 47-88.

Fox C, 1923: *The Archaeology of the Cambridge Region.* CUP.

Fowler P J, 1965: 'A Roman Barrow at Knobs Crook, Woodlands, Dorset'. *Antiq Journ* 45, 22-51.

Frere S S, 1964: Review of VCH III. *Antiq Journ* 44.2, 256-7

1985: Introduction, to Draper 1985, 1-2.

1991: 'Roman Britain in 1990, Pt I: Sites Explored. *Britannia* 22, 222-292.

Gillam J P, 1979: 'Romano-Saxon Pottery: an alternative explanation' in P J Casey (Ed), *The End of Roman Britain,* BAR Brit Ser 71, 103-18.

Gilman 1992: 'Archaeology in Essex 1991'. *Essex Arch and Hist* 23 98-113.

Gilman 1993: 'Archaeology in Essex 1992'. *Essex Arch and Hist* 24 195-210

Going C J, 1988a: 'The Countryside around Great Dunmow', in N P Wickenden, *Excavations at Great Dunmow, Essex: a Romano-British Small Town in the Trinovantian Civitas.* East Anglian Archaeology 41, 86-8.

1988b: 'Ritual', in N P Wickenden, 1988, 22-3.

1992: 'Economic long waves in the Roman Period? A Reconnaissance of the Romano-British Ceramic evidence'. *Oxford journal of Archaeology* 11.1, 93-117.

1993:'The Roman Period ' in A Clark, *Excavations at Mucking Vol 1; the site atlas,* 20-1. English Heritage.

Goodburn R, 1978: 'Roman Britain in 1977' *Britannia* 9, 430-71.

Grieve H, 1959: *The Great Tide. The story of the 1953 flood in Essex,* Essex County Council.

Hadman J, 1978: 'Aisled buildings in Roman Britain' in Todd (ed) 1978, 187-94.

Halstead P, 1978:'The Economy' in I Hodder, *Wendens Ambo. The Excavations of an Iron Age and Romano-Briish Settlement. The Archaeology of the M11. Vol II,* Passmore Edwards Museum. 61-63.

Haverfield F, 1921: 'Centuriation in Roman Essex', *Trans Essex Arch Soc.* 25.2, 115-125.

Hull M R, 1963: Gazetteer of Roman Essex, in *VCH III,* 35-203.

Hodder I 1982: The Archaeology of the M11, Vol 2: *Excavations at Wendens Ambo,* (London)

Horsley 1732: *Britannia Romana.*

Jones B, 1978: 'The Colchester and Ipswich aerial Survey' in *Aerial Archaeology* 1, 23-5.

Jones M U J, 1978: 'Rough Gound, Lechlade, and Mucking, Essex' in H C Bowen and P J Fowler (Eds) 1978, 171-4.

King A 1988: 'Commmentary on the Faunal remains' in T W Potter and S D Trow, Puckeridge-Braughing, Hertfordshire. The Ermine Street excavations 1971-2. *Hertfordshire Arch* 10, 154-6.

King A C and Potter T W, 1990: A new domestic building facade from Roman Britain. *Journal of Roman Archaeology* 12, 195-204

Luff R-M, 1982: *A Zooarchaeological Study of the Roman North Western provinces,* BAR Int Ser 137.

Lyne M A B & Jefferies R S, 1979: *The Alice Holt/Farnham Roman pottery industries,* CBA Res Rep 30.

Manning 1972: 'Iron work Hoards in Iron Age and Roman Britain', *Britannia* 3, 224-250.

Margary I, 1973: *Roman Roads in Britain,* (3rd Edn).

Mattingley H, & B Jones. 1990: *Atlas of Roman Britain.*

Miles D, 1984: *Barton Court Farm,* CBA Res Rep 50

Murphy P, in prep: Chelmsford by-pass palynological report.

Myres J N L, 1986: *The Saxon settlements.*

Neal D S, 1983: 'Unusual Buildings at Wood Lane End, Hemel Hempstead, Herts' *Britannia* 14, 73-86.

1984: 'A Sanctuary at Wood Lane End, Hemel Hempsted', *Britannia* 15, 193-215

Partridge C R, 1989: *Foxholes Farm: A Multi-Period gravel site,* Hertfordshire Arch Trust/Allan Sutton.

Philpott R, 1991: *Burial Practices in Roman Britain. A survey of grave treatment and furnishings, AD 43-410,* BAR Brit Ser 219.

Powell W R (Ed) 1963: *A History of the County of Essex. Volume III, Roman Essex.*

Priddy D, 1983: 'Excavations in Essex, 1982', in *Essex Archaeology and History* 15, 163-72

1985: 'Excavations in Essex, 1983-4', in *Essex Archaeology and History* 16, 123-39.

1986: 'Excavations in Essex, 1985', in *Essex Archaeology and History* 17, 156-65.

1987: 'Excavations in Essex, 1986', in *Essex Archaeology and History* 18, 104-13.

Priddy D and D G Buckley 1987: 'An Assessment of Excavated Enclosures in Essex Together with a Selection of Cropmark Sites', in D G Buckley and J D Hedges, *Excavations of a Crop Mark Enclosure Complex at Woodham Walter, Essex, 1976.* East Anglian Archaeology 33, 48-77.

Rackham O, 1980: *Ancient Woodland: its history, vegetation and uses in England,* Arnold.

1986: The History of the Countryside.

Rakob F, 1993: Der Neufund einer romischen Turbinenmuhle in Tunesien, *Antike Welt* 24 Hft 4, 286-7

Reece R, 1980: Town and country: the end of Roman Britain, *World Archaeology* 12.1, 77-92.

1987: *My Roman Britain,* Cotswold Books.

1991: Review of Todd *et al.* 1989, in *Arch Journ* 147, 445-7.

1991: 'Coins and villas' in Branigan and Miles (edd) 34-41.

Richmond I, 1963: Roman Essex, in W R Powell (Ed) A History of the County of Essex, *Victoria County History* 3, 1-24.

Rippon S, 1991: Early planned landscapes in South-east Essex. *Essex Archaeology and History* 22, 46-60.

Roberts W I, 1982: *Romano-Saxon Pottery,* BAR Brit Ser 106.

Rodwell K A, 1970: *Some Rich early Roman burials in S E England,* Inst Arch Lond Thesis.

1988 *The prehistoric and Roman settlement at Kelvedon, Essex,* CBA Res Rep 63.

Rodwell W J, 1970: Some Romano-Saxon Pottery from Essex. *Antiq Journ* 50, 262-76.

1975a: *Roman Essex,* Colchester Borough Council.

1975b: 'Milestones, Civic Territories, and the Antonine Itinerary' *Britannia* 6, 76-101.

1978a: 'Rivenhall and the emergence of first century villas in Northern Essex' in Todd (ed) 11-32.

1978b: 'Relict landscapes in Essex' in H C Bowen and P J Fowler (Eds) 1978, 89-98.

1979: 'Iron Age and Roman salt-winning on the Essex Coast' in B Burnham and J Wacher *Invasion and Response,* BAR Brit Ser 73, 133-75.

and K A Rodwell, 1986: *Rivenhall: investigations of a villa, church and village 1950-1977. Vol 1.* CBA Res Rep 55.

and K A Rodwell, 1993: *Rivenhall: investigations of a villa, church and village 1950-1977. Vol 2.* CBA Res Rep 80.

Round J H, 1923: 'The Roman Road from Colchester to Mersea' *Essex Arch Soc Trans.* 16.4, 273-76.

Rynne C, 1992: 'Milling in the 7th century -Europe's earliest Tide Mills' *Archaeology Ireland* Vol 6.2 (Nr 20), 22-24.

Rutherford-Davies B, 1982: *Britons and Saxons. The Chiltern Region 400-700*, Phillimore.

SPRS 1985: *Priorities for the Preservation and Excavation of Romano-British Sites*, Soc Proc Rom Studs.

Salway P, 1982: *Roman Britain*, Oxford.

Sealey P, 1995: 'New light on the salt industry and the Red Hills of prehistoric and Roman Essex', *Essex Archaeol. Hist*, 26, 65-81.

Scott E, 1990: 'Talking about their generation. Review of Todd (ed) 1989'. *Antiquity* 64.245, 953-6.

Simco A, 1984. *Roman Bedfordshire*.

Simpson G, 1976: *Watermills and Military Works on Hadrians Wall: Excavations in Northumberland 1907-13*.

Smallwood J P 1964: 'A Roman Settlement at Pebmarsh', *Trans Essex Arch Hist* 1.3 (3d Ser) 171-8.

Smoothy 1989: 'A Roman Rural site at Rayne, Essex: excavations 1987' *Essex Arch and Hist* 20, 1-29.

Spain R J, 1984: 'Romano-British Watermills', *Arch Cantiana* 100, 101-28.

Thompson E A, 1991: 'Ammianus Marcellinus and Britain', *Nottingham Mediaeval Papers* 34, 1-15.

Todd M, 1978: *Studies in the Romano-British Villa*, Leicester.
1985: 'Roman Britain' *Antiquity* 59.225, 49-50 (ed)
(ed) 1989: Research on Roman-Britain 1960-89. Brit Mono Ser 11.

Toller H, 1980: Excavations of the Orsett 'Cock' enclosure, Essex. *Britannia* 11, 35-42.

Toynbee J M C 1971: *Death and Burial in the Roman World*.

Viatores, The: 1964: *Roman Roads in the South-East Midlands*, Gollancz.

Waddelove A C, & E, 1990: 'Archaeology and research into sea level during the Roman Era: Towards a Methodology based on Highest Astronomical Tide'. *Britannia* 21, 253-66.

Welsh K, 1994: Excavations at Bran Ditch, 1993. An Interim Report. *Cambs County Council Archaeology Section Report* Nr 94.

Wickenden N P, 1986: 'Prehistoric Settlement and the Romano-British Small Town at Heybridge, Essex'. *Essex Arch and Hist* 17, 7-68.
1988: *Excavations at Great Dunmow, Essex: a Romano-British Small Town in the Trinovantian Civitas*, East Anglian Archaeology 41, 86-8.

Wilkinson T J, 1988: *Archaeology and Environment in South Essex: Rescue Archaeology along the Grays By-Pass, 1979/80*. East Anglian Archaeology 42.

Williamson T, 1984: 'The Roman Countryside. Settlement and agriculture in N W Essex' *Britannia* 15, 225-30.
1986: 'The Development of Settlement in North West Essex; the results of recent field survey'. *Essex Archaeology and History* 17, 120-33.
1990: 'Settlement, hierarchy and economy in Northwest Essex' in Branigan and Miles (eds) 73-82.

Wheeler R E M, 1935: *London and the Saxons*, London Mus Catalogues 6.

Wright A, 1981: *South East Essex in the Saxon Period*, Southend Museum and Southend on Sea Borough Counc Pub No 21.

Young C, 1975: 'Excavations at Ickham'. *Arch Cant* 91, 190-1.

Early Saxon Essex AD 400-700

by Susan Tyler

The first half of the fifth century witnessed the beginnings of Saxon settlement in Essex. Excavated sites show extremes of choice of site location and of size and duration of settlement demonstrating a somewhat 'ad hoc' rather than a programmed process of colonisation. Figure 1 shows the distribution of known Early Saxon sites. One cannot ignore the fact that excavated settlements in Essex are few and far between, however. Two factors are apparently significant in choice of settlement: most sites are along the river valleys; also previously cleared and settled land is reused. As will be examined in this paper, Saxon re-use of sites takes two forms: in the most obvious, actual standing structures are re-utilised (as at Lion Walk, Colchester); in other instances the site is simply re-used because it has been cleared by their predecessors (as at Mucking). The thorny problem of the relationship between the incoming Saxon settlers and the native Romano-British population will be addressed with recently published sites such as Mucking (where it is thought that the native population had deserted the site before the Saxons arrived) and Rivenhall villa (where it is thought that Saxons peacefully co-existed with the Romano-British) being examined. With Saxon cemetery sites, it is also common for prehistoric and later enclosure ditches to be re-used as cemetery boundaries (as at Springfield Lyons, Chelmsford).

Settlements

A small number of settlements (or in most cases small parts of settlements) have been excavated in the past fifteen years; most are sited on gravel terraces along the river valleys. Many have been excavated in advance of gravel extraction or road and housing construction. At Ardale School, North Stifford, part of a settlement and cemetery was excavated in advance of the construction of the Grays By-pass (Wilkinson 1988). The evidence for Saxon settlement comprised five definite, and one possible, sunken-featured buildings; cropmarks suggestive of two additional sunken-featured buildings were observed. The associated cemetery, dated by grave-goods to the sixth to eighth centuries AD was located within 100m of the settlement to the south-west. The graves were scattered within the east half of a first-century AD enclosure.

Two ring gullies appeared to be contemporary with the cemetery and may originally have surrounded cremations. The problem with analysing this site however, as with several others in Essex, is that it is evident that only a small part of the settlement and cemetery were excavated before destruction. Also on the Thames gravels at Orsett, Barrington's Farm, rescue excavations revealed six Saxon features (three sunken-featured buildings, two postholes and one ditch) yielding a total of 4.9kg of Saxon pottery of fifth to seventh-century date (Tyler 1987a). Again the evidence is frustratingly incomplete; these features obviously form part of substantial settlement: one sunken-featured building was excavated in 1968 (Rodwell 1975, 23-32) to the south-west and another four (or possibly five) to the west during 1976-79 (Toller 1980, 35-42; Carter forthcoming). Figure 2 shows the excavated sunken-featured buildings at Orsett and the substantial number of surrounding cropmark maculae, many of which were not excavated prior to their destruction by road building and gravel extraction. No doubt some maculae are geological, as found during the 1993 excavations (Milton 1987, 23), but many could represent Saxon sunken-featured buildings and associated pits. The appearance of such maculae on aerial photographs suggests that occupation at Orsett is part of a larger pattern, perhaps centred on Mucking, that spreads west and north-west across the terraces (Carter forthcoming). This fragmented picture of fifth to seventh-century settlement along the Thames gravel terraces has to some extent been offset by the publication of the results of the excavation of a large settlement at Mucking, Thurrock (Hamerow 1993), discussed later in this paper.

Elsewhere in Essex, rescue excavations of single or small groups of sunken-featured buildings have continued to add sites to the distribution map (Fig. 1). In the south of the county at Barling Hall, Barling Magna (Buckley in Couchman 1977, 60-7), Temple Farm, Sutton (Brown and Arscott in Priddy 1986, 163), and Great Wakering (Crowe, forthcoming), excavations revealed sunken-featured buildings with artefacts dating from the fifth century. Along the river Blackwater, a site at Hill Farm, Tolleshunt D'Arcy (Adkins in Priddy 1984, 135) produced two possible sunken-featured buildings dug into the upper fills of two Roman wells.

In the north-west of the county, rescue excavations, field-walking projects and metal-detectorists have also located some evidence for Saxon settlement in an area often written off as devoid of habitation (at least Germanic habitation) during the Early Saxon period. Excavations in advance of the expansion of Stansted airport in the late 1980s produced slight evidence of Saxon occupation on two sites (Brooks 1993, 40-57): at the Airport Social Club site, two pits produced a quantity of Saxon pottery belonging to the sixth and seventh centuries, whilst at Roundwood, three postholes contained pottery of the same date (this material was abraded which may indicate that it was deposited into later features). In addition, a programme of intensive fieldwalking identified further evidence of Saxon settlement in the form of at least five pottery scatters (Tyler, in prep., a; Havis, in prep.).

This evidence for sixth to seventh-century settlement in north-west Essex backs up the findings of an earlier field-walking programme which also found Saxon pottery indicating Saxon settlement particularly on the margins of the lighter clay and chalk soils of the valleys (Williamson 1986, 126-7). We therefore know that there was some settlement on at least the most agriculturally viable land from the sixth century onwards, but even intensive survey was 'not entirely successful in elucidating the development of settlement in the immediate post-Roman centuries' (Williamson 1986, 126). A metal-detector find of three fifth to sixth-century brooches suggests that there was an Early Saxon cemetery to the north of Harlow, situated in the valley of the River Lea (Tyler 1994). North-west Essex was not then devoid of Early Saxon settlement, but parts were no doubt heavily wooded and would have been avoided by Early Saxon settlers in favour of previously cleared land.

If we look at the excavated evidence it is still difficult to elucidate the precise relationship between the Saxon and Romano-British populations. At Lion Walk, Colchester, excavations during 1971-4 revealed two sunken-featured buildings and much Early Saxon pottery (Crummy 1981, 1-7). One of the buildings had been built up against the outside wall of a Roman house with its floor dug through the stokehole of a hypocaust and the other had been dug through a Roman tessellated pavement. Crummy interprets this as mid-fifth century Saxon settlement post-dating the collapse of Roman Colchester. The pottery from the hut fills suggests a fifth to sixth-century date for the building dug through the pavement and a slightly later date (sixth to seventh century) for the other hut. The siting of Early Saxon sunken-featured buildings apparently

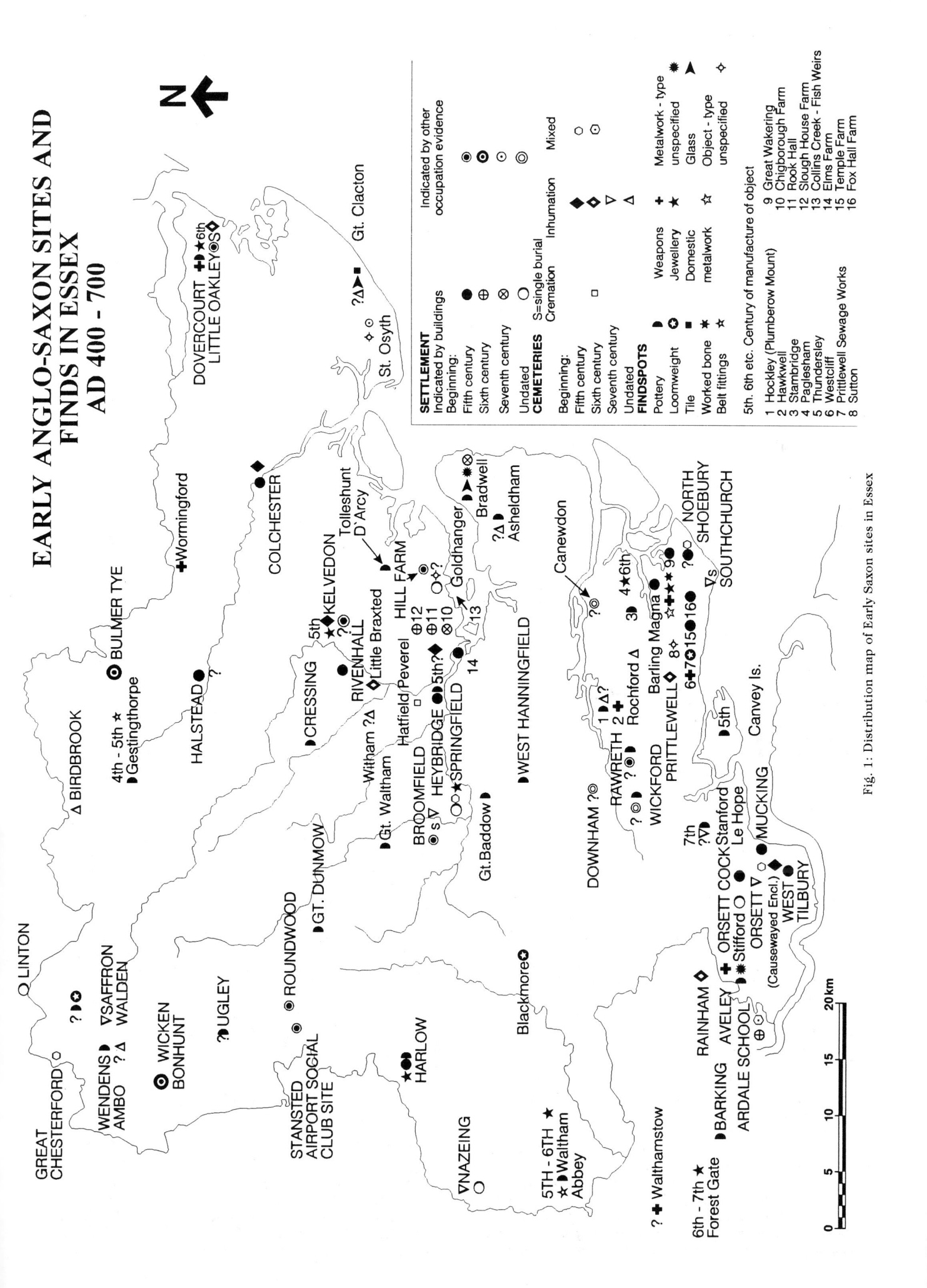

Fig. 1: Distribution map of Early Saxon sites in Essex

in the ruins of a large Roman town finds parallels on other sites as at Canterbury, in neighbouring Kent (Hawkes 1982, 64-78), although here the buildings were later (seventh to eighth century).

At Harlow Temple, Early Saxon occupation was recognised to the north of the site associated with an earth-fast post structure; it lay above Roman destruction levels and is seen as sub-Roman squatting on the site, possibly in the remains of a building (Bartlett, in prep.).

In contrast, at Heybridge, five sunken-featured buildings and a probable ground-level building excavated in 1972 are interpreted as contemporary with the late Roman town, and Drury and Wickenden (1982, 1-40) suggest that the Saxon settlers were involved either economically or militarily in its life. Recent excavations at Elms Farm, Heybridge, where a number of Saxon structures are evident, may shed new light on this interpretation (Clarke 1994).

The same problems of interpreting the archaeological evidence relating to the nature of Saxon and Romano-British co-existence is found on Roman villa sites. In Essex, excavated evidence shows that the first wave of Saxons settled on Roman villa sites at Little Oakley (Farrands 1958, 43-8; Barford, forthcoming) and at Rivenhall (Rodwell and Rodwell 1985, 68-77). At Little Oakley, 8kg of Early Saxon pottery was recognised, most coming from the upper fills of two Saxon pits excavated by R.H. Farrands in 1952 and 1958; the quantity of pottery and types of features encountered are suggestive of Saxon settlement on the site of the villa, but the nature of the occupation cannot be more closely defined. However, at another Roman villa site we have more definite evidence in the form of actual structures: a post-built hall and well are interpreted as of fifth-century date; Early Saxon finds included pottery and a fifth-century glass vessel. Rodwell and Rodwell (1985, 68-77) see the Early Saxons as not only building new structures but also occupying a disused Roman barn which in effect served as an aisled hall. They see the fifth-century settlers as being employed and housed on the villa estate, with the estate remaining under the control of its native proprietor. This re-use of, or simultaneous occupation with the Roman population of, villa estates is not confined to Essex; parallels can be found in Kent. At Darenth Roman villa, a seven-metre long post-built structure and four possible sunken-featured buildings containing pottery (tentatively dated to the fifth and sixth centuries) were concentrated in the south-west corner of the main villa complex; Philp (1984, 93) suggests a continuity of essential farming functions on villa-estates up until perhaps AD 450. We therefore have a growing body of evidence of fifth-century Saxon settlement on villa estates; which can be interpreted in two fundamentally different ways: one can either see the fifth-century Saxons as being in some way actively involved in the day to day maintenance of late Roman villa estates; or one can see their presence simply as opportunist re-use of land and in some cases actual structures.

Cemeteries

Few exclusively fifth-century cemeteries have been excavated in Essex. One such site at North Shoebury comprised eight inhumations and nine cremations, (excavated by D.G. Macleod of Southern Museum between 1971 and 1972). Grave-goods from the cemetery could all belong to the fifth century and include late Roman military buckles and belt fittings. The cemetery may have been the burial ground of a small community of 'laeti' (Saxon mercenaries and their families) who may have been given land nearly to cultivate in return for military assistance to the depleted Roman army (Tyler 1995).

At Mucking, Thurrock, the metalwork and coin evidence from some 203 sunken-featured buildings and 53 ground level buildings (Hamerow 1993, 8-21) suggests uninterrupted Saxon occupation from the first half of the fifth century to the beginning of the eighth - a shifting hamlet - unparalleled elsewhere in the country. This settlement is thought to have had an 'active' average population of c.100 with a minimum of ten posthole buildings and fourteen sunken-featured buildings standing at any one time (Hamerow 1993, 314). In addition, Mucking has two contemporary cemeteries, sited immediately adjacent to the settlement. The analysis of the Mucking excavations has made available a large corpus of structures and finds for comparison with other sites. Here 90 per cent of sunken-featured buildings were of the two-post variety and evidence suggests that the floor of the hollow served as the occupation surface. Hamerow (1993, 8) sees the ground-level buildings contributing little to the current state of research on such buildings, but Dixon (1993, 125-143) suggests that there is enough evidence to attribute the construction of the halls to the Romano-British population employed to do so by the Saxon immigrants. His evidence is that the halls are laid out using Roman measurements; for example the entrance width in all ten halls with clearly defined doorways is five Roman feet (pedes). He sees this as one of the few obvious manifestations of co-existence between the Saxon and Romano-British populations. It is clear that Mucking is fundamentally a community of farmers but the interpretation of the initial settlers being 'laeti' as proposed by the Jones's nearly twenty years ago (Jones and Jones 1975, 133-170) still holds good; Hamerow (1993, 14) sees the hypothesis as unproven as the archaeological evidence from the settlement is inconclusive.

While the coincidence of Romano-British and Anglo-Saxon settlement at Mucking and continuity of land use are clear, the existence of socio-economic continuity at a more profound level cannot be demonstrated. It seems that certain questions regarding the nature of the Saxon settlement at Mucking will remain open to interpretation; there is no doubt however, of the importance of the site to Saxon studies in Essex in that it presents a large corpus of comparanda for both structures and finds, in particular pottery: the identification of a broadly datable pottery sequence for the period is to be welcomed (Hamerow 1993, 22-59).

Known Early Saxon cemeteries are far more numerous than settlement sites; at only two sites; Ardale School and Mucking (both in Thurrock), can cemeteries unequivocally be associated with excavated settlements. At Mucking, the cemeteries lie next to and partly overlap each other. Other cemeteries are contiguous with structures but their coexistence is unproven, as at Springfield Lyons near Chelmsford. It may be, as demonstrated in the Darenth Valley, north-west Kent, that cemeteries and settlements were sited some distance from each other and that the Mucking model of adjacent cemeteries and settlement is not the norm (Tyler 1993, 71-81; Tyler, in prep b).

Springfield Lyons

The cemetery at Springfield (Fig 3; Buckley and Hedges 1987) is the largest to be excavated since investigations at Mucking in the 1970s recorded two cemeteries with a total of 468 cremations and 399 inhumations. An analysis of the cemetery (Tyler, in prep. c) shows it to consist of 143 cremation burials and 111 definite inhumations and a further 28 possible inhumations; a total of 282 burials. A Bronze Age enclosure ditch appears to have been utilised as the cemetery's northern boundary. The cremation burials were contemporary with the inhumations and in some parts of the cemetery both burial rites occurred alongside each other; however, some areas seem to have

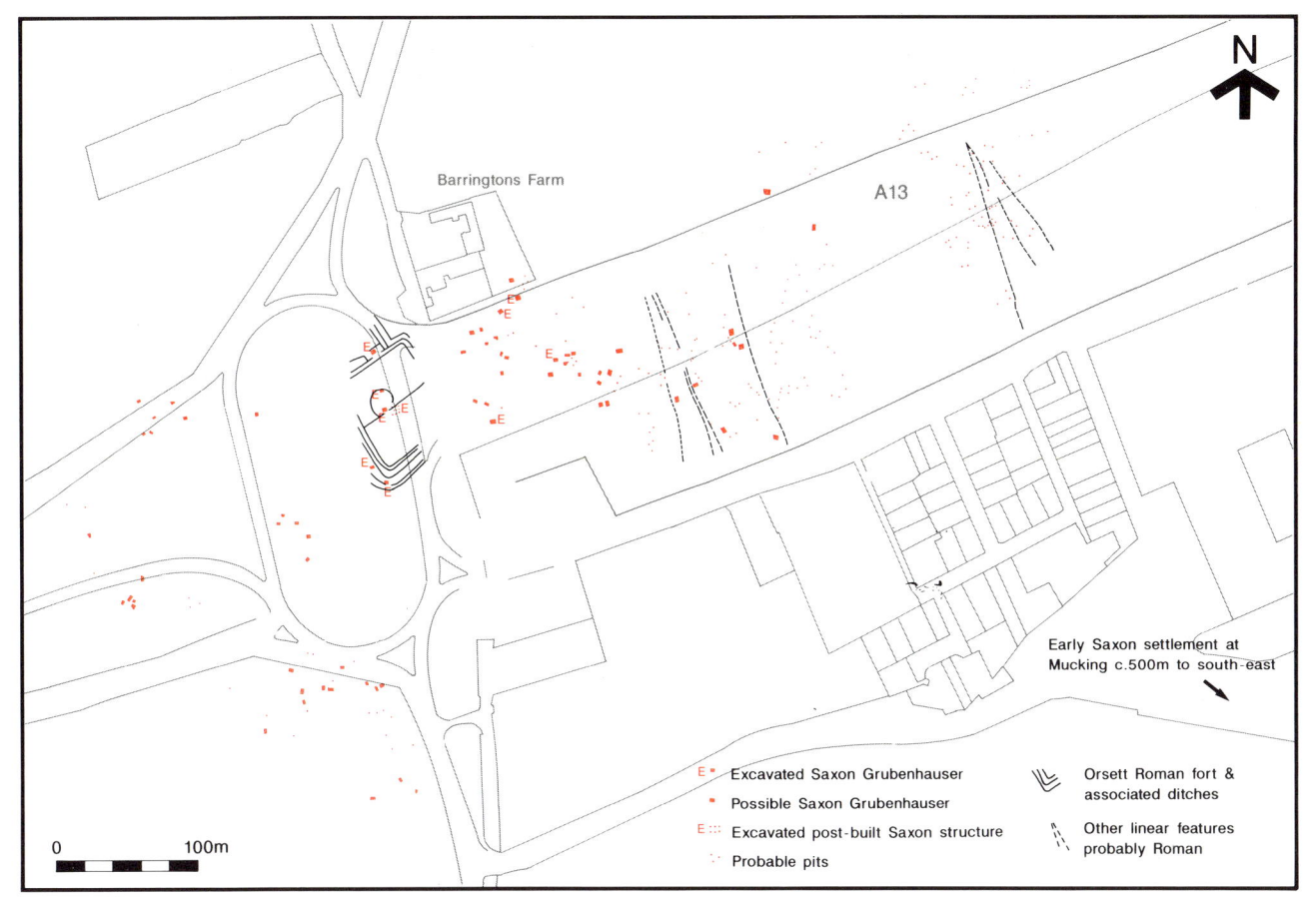

Fig. 2: Orsett, Thurrock: Early Saxon settlement

been exclusively for cremation burials and others for inhumations. Twenty-three cremation burials contained artefacts: beads; vessel glass; brooch fragments; tweezers and gaming counters, but few were closely datable. Thirty of the cremation urns were decorated and the general schemes of decoration (often incorporating bosses, stamps and incised lines) used indicate a date range beginning in the late fifth century and going on well into the sixth.

The inhumations were also mostly of sixth-century date. Forty-five inhumations contained grave-goods including: brooches, beads; buckles, knives; spears; shields; buckets and pots. The acid soil meant that little bone survived, but as at Mucking, in some graves body marks and coffin stains were visible. From the associated grave-goods, some 26 female graves and six male graves could be identified; the rest could not be sexed. A range of burial practices were present: inhumations were occasionally paired (sometimes two adults; sometimes an adult and a child). One inhumation (probably male) was surrounded by a ring ditch, outside which was a cluster of rich sixth-century female graves; two adjacent cremation burials also had a surrounding ring ditch; one pit contained a horse-head burial complete with iron bridle fittings. The grave-goods show affinities with those from both East Anglian cemeteries and those to the south, particularly north-western Kent. The garnet-inlaid buckle-plate and gilt copper alloy saucer brooches for example are types of object more commonly found south of the Thames and a study of parallels for the small-long brooches from the cemetery demonstrate strong links with the Lower Thames valley cemeteries both north and south of the Thames (Tyler 1987b, 18).

The settlement at Springfield has been dated to the Late Saxon period (Buckley and Hedges 1987, 25-8), whereas the cemetery belongs to the mid-fifth to early seventh centuries. The dating evidence for the Late Saxon settlement is, however, very sparse and far from conclusive. The settlement is labelled Late Saxon mainly by virtue of a handful of tenth and eleventh-century pottery recovered from the structures and further quantities (still relatively small amounts) from rubbish pits (Buckley and Hedges 1987, 25-8). Other finds of Late Saxon date are few, but included a fragment of lava quern or millstone and a silver penny of Aethelred II, dating to the last decade of the tenth century. An almost equal amount of much abraded Early Saxon pottery was recovered from the structures and rubbish pits, although some was from disturbed cremation urns.

Nonetheless, an argument can be made for assigning some of the structures to the Early Saxon period and seeing them as contemporary with the cemetery, though not necessarily domestic in function (Fig. 4). One structure (structure 'A'), in particular fits into a large gap in the cemetery; it is c.20m long and has a cremation burial at three of its four corners and an inhumation burial containing grave-goods, which interestingly included two iron keys, located directly outside one of its two entrances. It can be paralleled at Rookery Hill, Bishopstone, Sussex (Bell 1977) where a similar post-built structure (structure 37) had a burial immediately outside its entrance and was seen as clearly belonging within the fifth to seventh-century context of the settlement as a whole (Welch 1985, 22). There is a strong possibility therefore that the Springfield structure could belong to the same period and, thus, be contemporary with the cemetery. Perhaps one argument against this early dating is in the large size of the Springfield building; some 20m long; structure 37 at Bishopstone was only 10m long. Excavations at Chalton, Hampshire, however provide us with an example of an Early Saxon building with slightly bowed sides and a partition at one end with a total length of some 31m

(Welch 1985, 25-6). We can therefore find parallels amongst Early Saxon structures for Springfield structure 'A' and a fifth to seventh-century date for it is plausible making it contemporary with the surrounding cemetery. Other structures could also belong to the cemetery: structure 'B' had a deep foundation trench enclosing a rectangular area c.35 by 2.5m (Buckley and Hedges 1987, 27). Because the foundation trench is very substantial compared to the area enclosed, the superstructure may have been of more than one storey: a bell-tower is a possible interpretation. A post-and-slot building, structure 'C', abutted the east end of structure 'B' and they may have formed a single building; however, there is a slight offset in the alignment of the walls which makes the relationship unclear (Buckley and Hedges 1987, 27). A grave (feature 4860) inside structure 'C' dug alongside the northern wall of the building is no doubt contemporary with it. It is very tempting to interpret structures 'B' and 'C' as a focus building for the cemetery; given the pagan nature of the site, the term 'church' seems inappropriate, but it could certainly have been a place where pagan rites were performed. There is slight evidence that the cemetery was divided into areas: lines of stakeholes could be the remains of fences between different family groups.

Fig. 3: Springfield Lyons: Early Saxon burials

Fig. 4: Springfield Lyons: Anglo Saxon features

As with some of the grave-goods from the cemetery at Springfield Lyons, analysis of grave-goods from two other sites has illustrated links with Kent. Artefacts from an inhumation cemetery at Prittlewell, near Southend-on-Sea, have further illustrated contact with north-west Kent (Tyler 1988, 91-116). The excavation of sixteen certain and eleven possible inhumations produced a large number of weapons including seventeen spears and six swords; but they include a small group of distinctively Kentish material comprising a gold bracteate and gold pendant (Plate 1), garnet-inlaid gilt saucer brooches (Plate 2) and wheel-thrown pottery. These objects may indicate small-scale movement of people across the river Thames and/or increased trading links between Essex and Kent during the seventh century. This Kentish link was also demonstrated at Mucking where pottery stamps have been shown to be of the same design as those found on pottery from cemeteries located in the Darent valley and the Thames coastlands: in particular, links between Mucking and the Horton Kirby, Riseley and Northfleet cemeteries were identified (Briscoe in Tyler, in prep b; Briscoe in Hamerow 1993, 51).

Seventh to Eighth Century Settlement:

Evidence for Saxon settlement in Essex in the seventh to eighth centuries is not as abundant as the preceding two. Ring-ditch burials at Alresford in north-east Essex and Orsett, Thurrock could belong to this period. At Orsett, limited excavations designed to investigate a cropmark of a Neolithic causewayed enclosure (Hedges and Buckley 1985), revealed three ring ditches, two of which were excavated and found to contain single extended inhumation burials in east-west aligned pit graves. One grave contained a body stain, underlying which was a textile bag or wrapping containing objects which were probably thought to have amuletic or magical properties including a Kimmeridge shale or lignite bead and hanging-bowl fittings; these were probably slipped into the grave by those charged with her burial (Webster in Hedges and Buckley 1985, 9-14). At Alresford, rescue excavations in advance of gravel extraction revealed burials probably of Saxon date, comprising three ring ditches each with a central grave (Bedwin 1986). One of the graves showed an unusual burial rite not recognised elsewhere at present: a body placed in a grave in a winding sheet or onto a blanket with

Susan Tyler

Plate 1: Gold pendant from Prittlewell (Diameter 33 mm)

Saxon re-use of prehistoric sites

It can be very difficult and sometimes impossible to assess the percentage of prehistoric ditch and bank extant during the Early Saxon period. However, it is evident that on some sites ditches and banks did survive as such and were utilised during the fifth to eighth centuries as boundary ditches for cemeteries. At Springfield Lyons, the Late Bronze Age enclosure ditch forms the northern and to some extent the eastern boundary; a probable explanation is that the southern and western ditch circuits had become completely infilled by the fifth century. Because of the intensive arable farming that has taken place in Essex, ploughing has levelled the vast majority of prehistoric barrows; this has no doubt destroyed not only prehistoric burials, but also Saxon. In the north of Hertfordshire, several prehistoric barrows were found to have secondary Saxon interments: the Neolithic long barrow on Therfield Heath, excavated in 1855 by Nunn and in 1935 by Phillips (1935) contained several secondary burials, one with an Early Saxon spearhead.

It may well be that prehistoric barrows re-used by Early Saxons in Essex have now been completely plough-razed and any burials not dug down into the natural totally destroyed. Just as prehistoric monuments affected the siting and pattern of succeeding settlements and cemeteries, Saxon monuments appear to have influenced successive landscape features. At the Orsett cemetery, the burials are located close to the junction of a number of later field boundaries and the mounds may well have served as boundary markers for these (Hedges and Buckley 1985, 19-22).

Industrial sites

Early Saxon industrial sites are rare in Essex, but we do not have a growing body of information: as McDonnell states (in Hamerow 1993, 82-3) "the evidence emerging from Essex indicates that ironworking during the Anglo-Saxon period took place on a small scale to satisfy local needs using local ores - either 'bog ores' from waterine environments or ironstones from glacial deposits of clays

a wooden support for the head and a series of narrow wooden poles laid along the grave above the body.

At Chigborough Farm, Goldhanger, a large, boat-shaped structure was found which could be of Saxon date, although there was no artefactual evidence (Wallis and Waughman forthcoming). An eighth to tenth-century date was suggested by the excavator by virtue of the shape of the ground plan: bow-sided with rounded ends. Earlier excavations here had revealed a post-built hall with loomweights of seventh to ninth-century date packed into one post hole (Adkins and Adkins 1985, 44-56; Tyler in Priddy 1986, 147-8).

Plate 2: Pair of garnet-inlaid gilt saucer brooches from Prittlewell

114

or gravels". At Mucking, slag came from the fills of five sunken-featured buildings and three pits; the deposits represent ironworking residues and not *in situ* ironworking. Three major foci of activity were identified: around Grubenhaus 196; around Grubenhaus 202 and around Grubenhauser 44 and 45 all of sixth to seventh-century date. Both smithing and smelting slag were present, but the small amount (118kg) of slag blocks from the site do not indicate the presence of major iron smelting operations (McDonnell 1993, 82-3). At Broomfield Borrow Pit, close to the site of the seventh-century 'princely' burial, excavations in advance of gravel extraction (Gee in Priddy 1986, 144-7) revealed three oval pits, one of which contained several considerable lumps of iron-smithing slag and a number of small, amorphous pieces or iron. Pottery from the pits was of fifth to sixth-century date.

During the 1980s, to the north of the river Blackwater, excavations at Rook Hall, Little Totham (Adkins 1989, 262-3) and at nearby Slough House Farm, Great Totham (Wallis and Waughman forthcoming) have identified an extensive Early Saxon iron-working industry. At Rook Hall, six sunken-featured buildings and possibly at least one large post-built building were found in association with huge quantities of metalworking debris. The latter comprised slag, cinder, ore and tuyere fragments and was largely discarded in pits, but one feature had *in situ* tuyeres and a vitrified furnace wall, and is interpreted as a smelting furnace of the slag-tapping type. A pottery tuyere from this feature has been dated by thermoluminescence to AD 530+29. Quantities of grass-tempered pottery were recovered and included a substantial part of a whole pot.

Charcoal from the area gave a radiocarbon date of AD 607+61. One smithing hearth was within a sunken-featured building. At Rook Hall we therefore have an Early Saxon site with both iron-smelting and smithing taking place; there was also evidence for the ancillary processes of charcoal making and ore roasting. At Slough House Farm the main features comprised: a large pit containing metalworking debris and sixth century pottery; a second large pit, the fill of which had a high charcoal content; a large shallow pit with sixth-century pottery and slag; two timber-lined wells (one incorporating a hollowed oak trunk) both dated to the sixth to seventh centuries by dendrochronology (Wallis and Waughman forthcoming). The wells were over 250m apart, and indicate scattered occupation across the area. These two sites are important in illustrating that there was considerable industrial activity taking place in Early Saxon Essex, a fact hinted at by earlier finds at Mucking and other sites.

River surveys

Further evidence of Early Saxon occupation and utilisation of the river estuaries has been brought to light by surveys of the river valleys; in particular, the Hullbridge Survey (Wilkinson and Murphy 1995), which identified several wooden structures of Saxon date. At 'The Stumble', one of the most interesting was a wooden structure comprising a group of upright posts set in grey estuarine clay, a scatter of horizontal wood, smaller brushwood rods with two small interwoven areas. Finds from in and around the structure included fired clay (possible briquetage) and two sherds of pottery. The fire clay was tempered with salt-marsh plants and crop processing waste before it was partly fired. Unlike most other wooden structures in the area, this structure was not associated with the creek system; it was on marsh. The artefactual evidence implies domestic activity and the structure may have been a temporary shelter for occasional use by workers on the marsh engaged in salt-production, sheep-herding or other activities (Wilkinson and Murphy 1995). This particular structure belonged to the Late Saxon period, radiocarbon dated to AD 930, but one can envisage such shelters in use throughout the Saxon period. The same can be said for the fish-traps sited in river estuaries; fishing was no doubt an important part of the economy throughout the Anglo-Saxon period and several have been located.

One of the most substantial, first recorded by Ron Hall (1991) and subsequently by members of Essex County Council's Archaeology Section, is located at Collins Creek in the Blackwater Estuary and consists of many thousands of wooden posts 100-150mm in diameter set in parallel lines. The posts run for approximately one mile in an east-west direction; another row of posts runs off from this main alignment in a south-easterly direction for about half a mile. The gaps between the posts are infilled with interwoven brushwood/hurdle-like material. Two samples collected for radiocarbon dating gave dates of AD640-675 and AD 882-957. The site is still under investigation but current thought favours its interpretation as a series of fish-weirs.

In conclusion, since the last conference in 1978, considerable advances have been made in our understanding of the nature of Early Saxon settlement in Essex. This has come about through the analysis and publication of excavated sites such as Rivenhall and Mucking and by the re-analysis of material in museum collections, such as the Prittlewell material and most importantly by the identification investigation of previously unknown sites, the most notable being the cemetery and settlement at Springfield Lyons, the industrial sites at Rook Hall and Slough House Farm and the fish-traps and other wooden structures identified in river estuaries.

In the future, we need to address further the question of the relationship between the Romano-British population and the Saxon settlers. We need to identify and excavate as fully as possible more settlements, to provide data for comparison with the extensive site at Mucking, Thurrock. Recent fieldwalking projects have shown that Early Saxon sites can be identified by this method and further fieldwalking coupled with geophysical surveys could lead to the identification of more sites. Further surveys of intertidal zones could also yield more data on the Early Saxon economy; aerial photography is potentially the most useful tool in the initial recognition of sites such as the fish-weirs at Collins Creek. Cropmarks on aerial photographs do not always show Saxon features, as graves and sunken-floors and post-holes tend to be too shallow, but occasionally they do show clearly (as at Mucking) and this method of reconnaissance could reveal new sites in the future; particular attention should be given to potentially Saxon features in and around prehistoric monuments as it is evident that such sites are often re-used by Saxons as cemetery boundaries.

Bibliography

Adkins, P. 1984. 'Tolleshunt D'Arcy Hill Farm' in Priddy. D.(ed.), 'Excavations in Essex 1983-4' *Essex Archaeol. Hist.*, 16, 135

Adkins, K. P., and Adkins, P. C. 1985. 'Saxon loom weights and Roman pottery from Chigborough Farm, Little Totham', *Colch. Arch. Grp. Bull.* 28, 44-56

Adkins, P. 1989. 'Rook Hall : An extensive Anglo-Saxon iron working complex', *Current Archaeol.* 115, 262-3

Barford, P. M. Forthcoming. *Excavations at Little Oakley, Essex 1951-78 Roman Villa and Saxon Settlement*, E. Anglian Archaeol.

Bartlett, R. Forthcoming. Excavations at Harlow Temple, Latton

Bedwin, O. 1986. 'The Excavation of 3 Ring Ditches at Broomfield Quarry, Alresford, Essex, 1984, *Essex Archaeol. Hist.* 17, 69-81

Bell, M. G. 1977. 'Excavations at Bishopstone', *Sussex Archaeol. Collect.* 115

Briscoe, T. 1993. 'Pottery Stamps' in Hamerow, H., *Excavations at Mucking Volume: 2 the Anglo-Saxon settlement Excavations by MU Jones and WT Jones*, English Heritage Archaeol. Rep. no. 21, 45-51

Briscoe, T. in Tyler, S. in prep. 'The pottery stamps' in Three Anglo-Saxon Cemeteries of the Darenth valley, West Kent : Riseley and South Darenth, Horton Kirby and Charton Farm, Farningham

Brooks, H. 1993. 'Fieldwalking and excavations at Stansted Airport' in *Flatlands & Wetlands Current Themes in East Anglian Archaeology*, E. Anglian Archaeology 50, 40-57

Brown, N., and Arscott, R. 1986. 'Sutton, Temple Farm', in Priddy, D. (ed.), 'Excavations in Essex 1985', *Essex Archaeol. Hist.*, 17, 163

Buckley, D. G. 1977. 'Barling Hall, Barling Magna' in Couchman, C. (ed), 'Work of Essex County Council Archaeology Section 1977', *Essex Archaeol. Hist.*, 9, 60-7

Buckley, D. G. and Hedges, J. D. 1987. *The Bronze Age and Saxon Settlements at Springfield Lyons, Essex An Interim report*, Essex County Council Occ. Paper No. 5

Carter, G. A. Forthcoming. *Excavations at the Orsett 'Cock' Enclosure, Essex 1976*, E. Anglian Archaeol.

Clarke, P. 1994. Elms Farm, Heybridge, Essex: Project Design. ECC Field Archaeology Group

Crowe, K. Forthcoming. 'Excavations at Great Wakering', South East Essex Archaeology

Crummy, P. 1981. *Aspects of Anglo-Saxon and Norman Colchester* CBA Res. Rep. 39

Dixon, P. H. 1993. 'The Anglo-Saxon Settlement at Mucking : an interpretation', *Anglo-Saxon studies in Archaeology and History 6*, 125-47

Drury, P. J. and Wickenden, N. P. 1982. 'An Early Saxon Settlement within the Romano-British Small Town at Heybridge, Essex', *Med. Archaeol.* 26, 1-39

Farrands, R. H. 1958. 'Romano-British Villa at Little Oakley', *Colch. Arch. Group Bull.* 1, No. 4, 43- 5

Gee, M. 1986. 'Broomfield Borrow Pit' in Priddy, D. (ed.), 'Work of Essex County Council Archaeology Section 1985', *Essex Archaeol. Hist.* 16, 144-7

Hall, R. 1991. 'Preliminary Report of Findings of Timber Structures, Upper and Lower Collins Creeks'. Unpublished. Copy in ESMR.

Havis, R. in prep. Archive Report for Roundwood. Essex County Council

Hamerow, H. 1993. *Excavations at Mucking Volume 2: the Anglo-Saxon settlement Excavations by MU and WT Jones*, English Heritage Archaeol. Rep. no. 21

Hawkes, S. C. 1982. 'Anglo-Saxon Kent c.425-725' in Leach, P.E. (ed.) *Archaeology in Kent to AD 1500*, CBA Res. Rep. 48, 64-78

Hedges, J. D. and Buckley, D. G. 1985. 'Anglo-Saxon and later features excavated at Orsett, Essex, 1975', *Medieval Archaeol.* 29, 1-25

Jones, M. U. and Jones, W. T. 1975. 'The crop-mark sites at Mucking, Essex, England, in Bruce-Mitford, R. (ed.), *Recent Archaeological excavations in Europe*, 133-87

McDonnell, G. 1993. 'Slags and ironworking residues' in Hamerow, H., *Excavations at Mucking Volume 2: the Anglo-Saxon settlement*, English Heritage Archaeol. Rep. no. 21., 82-3

Milton, B. 1987 'Excavations at Barrington's Farm, Orsett Cock, Thurrock, Essex 1983', *Essex Archaeol. Hist.* 18, 16-33

Phillips, C. W. 1935. 'A Re-examination of the Therfield Heath long barrow, Royston, Hertfordshire', *Proc. Prehist. Soc.*, 1, 101-7

Philp, B. 1984. *Excavations in the Darent Valley, Kent*

Rodwell, W. J. 1975 'The Orsett "Cock" cropmark site, Essex', *Essex Archaeol Hist.* 6, 13-39

Rodwell, W. J. and Rodwell, K. A. 1985. *Rivenhall: investigations of a villa, church, and village, 1950-1977*, Chelmsford Archaeol. Trust Rep. 4.1, CBA Res. Rep. 55

Toller, H. 1980. 'An Interim Report on the Excavation of the Orsett 'Cock' Enclosure, Essex: 1976-79', *Britannia* 11, 35-42

Tyler, S. 1986. 'Goldhanger, note on loomweights from site 1 Chigborough Farm' in Priddy, D. (ed.) 'Work of the Essex County Council Archaeology Section 1985', *Essex Archaeol. Hist.* 17, 147-8

Tyler, S. 1987a. 'The Anglo-Saxon Pottery', in Milton, B., 'Excavations at Barrington's Farm, Orsett Cock, Thurrock, Essex 1983', *Essex Archaeol. Hist.*, 18, 28-31

Tyler, S. 1987b. 'The Early Saxon grave goods' in Buckley, D.G., and Hedges, J.D., *The Bronze Age and Saxon Settlements at Springfield Lyons, Essex An Interim Report*, Essex County Council Occ. Paper No. 5, 18-23

Tyler, S. 1988. 'The Anglo-Saxon cemetery at Prittlewell, Essex: an analysis of the grave goods', *Essex Archaeol. Hist.* 19, 91-116

Tyler, S. 1993. 'Anglo-Saxon settlement in the Darenth valley and environs', *Arch. Cant.* 90, 71- 81

Tyler, S. 1994. 'Three Anglo-Saxon brooches from Pishiobury', *Essex Archaeol. Hist.* 25, 248- 9

Tyler, S. 1995. 'The Early Saxon cemetery' in Wymer, J.J., and Brown, N.R., *Excavations at North Shoebury: Settlement and economy in South-East Essex*, E. Anglian Archaeol. 75, 46-52

Tyler, S. in prep a. 'Report on the Saxon pottery' in Excavations at Stansted Social Club Site. Essex County Council

Tyler, S. in prep. b. Three Anglo-Saxon cemeteries of the Darenth Valley, West Kent: Riseley and South Darenth, Horton Kirby and Charton Farm, Farningham

Tyler, S. in prep. c. Springfield Lyons Anglo-Saxon cemetery analysis

Wallis, S., and Waughman, M. Forthcoming. *Archaeology and the Landscape in the Lower Blackwater Valley*, E. Anglian Archaeol.

Webster, L. 1985. 'The Grave goods' in Hedges, J.D. and Buckley, D.G., 'Anglo-Saxon burials and later features at Orsett', *Medieval Archaeol.* 29, 9-14

Welch, M. G. 1985. 'Rural settlement patterns in the Early and Middle Anglo-Saxon periods', *Landscape History*, 7, 13-25

Williamson, T. 1986. 'The Development of Settlement in North West Essex: the results of a recent field survey, *Essex Archaeol. Hist.* 17, 120-32

Wilkinson, T. J. 1988. *Archaeology and Environment in South Essex: Rescue Archaeology along the Grays By-pass, 1979/80*, E. Anglian Archaeol. 42

Wilkinson, T. J., and Murphy, P. 1995. *The archaeology of the Essex Coast, volume 1: The Hullbridge Survey Project*, E. Anglian Archaeol. 71

Wymer, J. J., and Brown, N. R. 1995. *Excavations at North Shoebury: settlement and economy in south-east Essex*, E. Anglian Archaeol. 75

ESSEX c.700 - 1066

by Stephen Rippon

Introduction
This paper will consider Essex from c.700 to 1066. Though there is a wide range of evidence, and a number of important excavations on Middle to Late Saxon sites in the County, this is the first synthesis of the available material. Spatially, this paper will consider the old County of Essex, corresponding to the Late Saxon shire. London, the seat of the East Saxon Bishopric, will be referred to in passing, but its archaeology and history are adequately dealt with elsewhere (eg. Vince 1990).

The seventh century saw a number of important changes in Anglo-Saxon England including the crystallisation of stable kingdoms (Dumville 1989; Yorke 1990), increased social stratification reflected in the burial record (eg. Broomfield: Jones 1980, 89-90), and the gradual conversion to Christianity. There were also changes in the rural landscape, with fairly widespread evidence for a dislocation of settlement. The other chronological limit of this paper, the Norman conquest, was of great significance in terms of political history and landowning, but with regard to the wider landscape, forms a rather arbitrary division.

Firstly, this paper will identify the sources available for the period. Secondly, royal and other high status sites will be considered, including the emergence of early "central places", towns and the church. Thirdly, the impact of the Vikings will be questioned, and finally, the rural landscape will be examined and emphasised as the major area in which further research is required.

The Sources
The material available for this period though varied, is rather sparse compared to neighbouring areas such as Kent (eg. Brooks 1989; Everitt 1986) and East Anglia (eg. Newman 1992; Williamson 1993). Documentary sources such as the Anglo-Saxon Chronicle provide a skeleton political and ecclesiastical history, though there are no insular sources apart from a handful of charters (Bailey 1988; Dumville 1989; Hart 1993a; Yorke 1990). These are mainly late, most dating from the mid-tenth century, and lack detailed boundary descriptions (Hart 1971). Place-names should form an important source of information, though the main work (Reaney 1935) is now rather out of date, and apart from Margaret Gelling's (1976; 1988) work on the Mucking area, Essex lacks recent place-names scholarship (but see Gelling 1992 on Suffolk).

Archaeological sites of this period have proved difficult to locate, due to a lack of datable material culture. The conversion to Christianity meant that fewer grave goods were deposited, and scientific dating methods need to be more widely applied both on burials (eg. Huggins 1991a), occupation sites (eg. Gilman 1990, 132) and waterlogged wooden structures (eg. Crummy et al. 1982; Goodburn and Redknap 1988).

In Early Saxon Essex, sand-tempered pottery predominated, though during the seventh century, this was gradually replaced by grass-tempered wares (Cunningham 1982, 360; Hamerow 1987; 1993, 22-59). Cunningham (1982, 360) claims that the eighth and ninth centuries were largely aceramic in Essex, though the two sites usually cited as evidence for this are both churches (Asheldham: Drury and Rodwell 1978; Hadstock: Rodwell 1976a). In London (Redknap 1991, 356), Middlesex and Berkshire (Astill and Lobb 1989; Hodges 1981, Fig. 6.2; Vince 1984), grass-tempered pottery clearly continues into the ninth and possibly the tenth centuries, though with reduced importance. The same appears to be true of Essex. At Barking, it formed 77% (by weight) of the pottery from a Middle Saxon quarry pit, sealed by a building whose pottery assemblage contained just 46% grass-tempered ware (Redknap 1991, 356); a coin of 845-55 was associated with the upper levels of this building. A wooden mill-leat, dated by dendrochronology to 770, produced an assemblage of 32% grass-tempered ware (Redknap 1991, 356).

The occurrence of Middle Saxon pottery imported from Ipswich, whose production appears to have started c.650 and ceased c.850 (Wade 1988, 93), is rather more widespread in Essex than has been previously thought, though it is still rare to find more than a few sherds on any one site (Fig. 1; cf. Wade 1988, fig. 54). Interestingly, fieldwalking in north-west Essex yielded several sites with Ipswich Ware sherds (Williamson 1986), suggesting that here at least, it was in use even on rural settlements.

From the ninth century, pottery becomes more common with the appearance of "Saxo-Norman" wares. Barking has "Late Saxon Shelly Ware", derived from the Upper Thames Valley (Redknap 1991), while elsewhere in Essex St. Neots Ware from Cambridgeshire and locally produced St. Neots-type shell-tempered wares predominate. St. Neots Ware is generally thought to have been produced from the late ninth century (Rodwell and Rodwell 1993, 78), though its appearance in Essex cannot be closely dated (the occurrence of St. Neots and Thetford Ware in association with ninth-century coins at Witham (Cottrill 1934) is erroneous; Rodwell 1993a, 102). There are also some imports of Thetford and Thetford-type Ware, the latter possibly produced in Ipswich. In Colchester at least, its use may have ceased by the mid-eleventh century (Crummy 1981, 40). During both the Middle and Late Saxon period there are also a limited number of high status sites with imports from the continent (Fig. 1). Therefore, during our period, a near continuous pottery sequence exists, though such material remains rare and is only found in any quantity on high status sites.

In addition to pottery, there is a limited amount of metalwork from several sites, and also a range of coins. The final class of evidence for this period is that of standing buildings. Apart from the church at Greensted, the only surviving structures appear to be of stone. A number of Late Saxon churches are known while excavations at several churches have revealed Late Saxon predecessors, of which no evidence survives above ground (see below).

The East Saxon Kingdom and Royal Estates
For much of the period covered by this paper, the archaeology and history of Essex is dominated by sites with high status associations, particularly with the Crown, but also the church. A unified East Saxon kingdom probably emerged in the late sixth century out of a series of smaller territories such as the Rodings and Dengie (Bailey 1988, 34), not unlike the early estates identified in Kent (Everitt 1986, 75-9). In the seventh century, the kingdom probably extended as far as Middlesex and Surrey (Dumville 1989; Yorke 1990). Around 700, Middlesex, Surrey and London were lost to Mercia, and though Essex itself appears to have been subject to limited Mercian overlordship thereafter, it remained an independent kingdom until around 820 when it was incorporated into Wessex (Dumville 1989, 135).

Metcalf (1978; 1993, 21) has shown how eighth-century "Series S" sceattas were issued by the East Saxon kings, probably as an expression of independence from their political overlords. Coins of Mercia were copied, but the

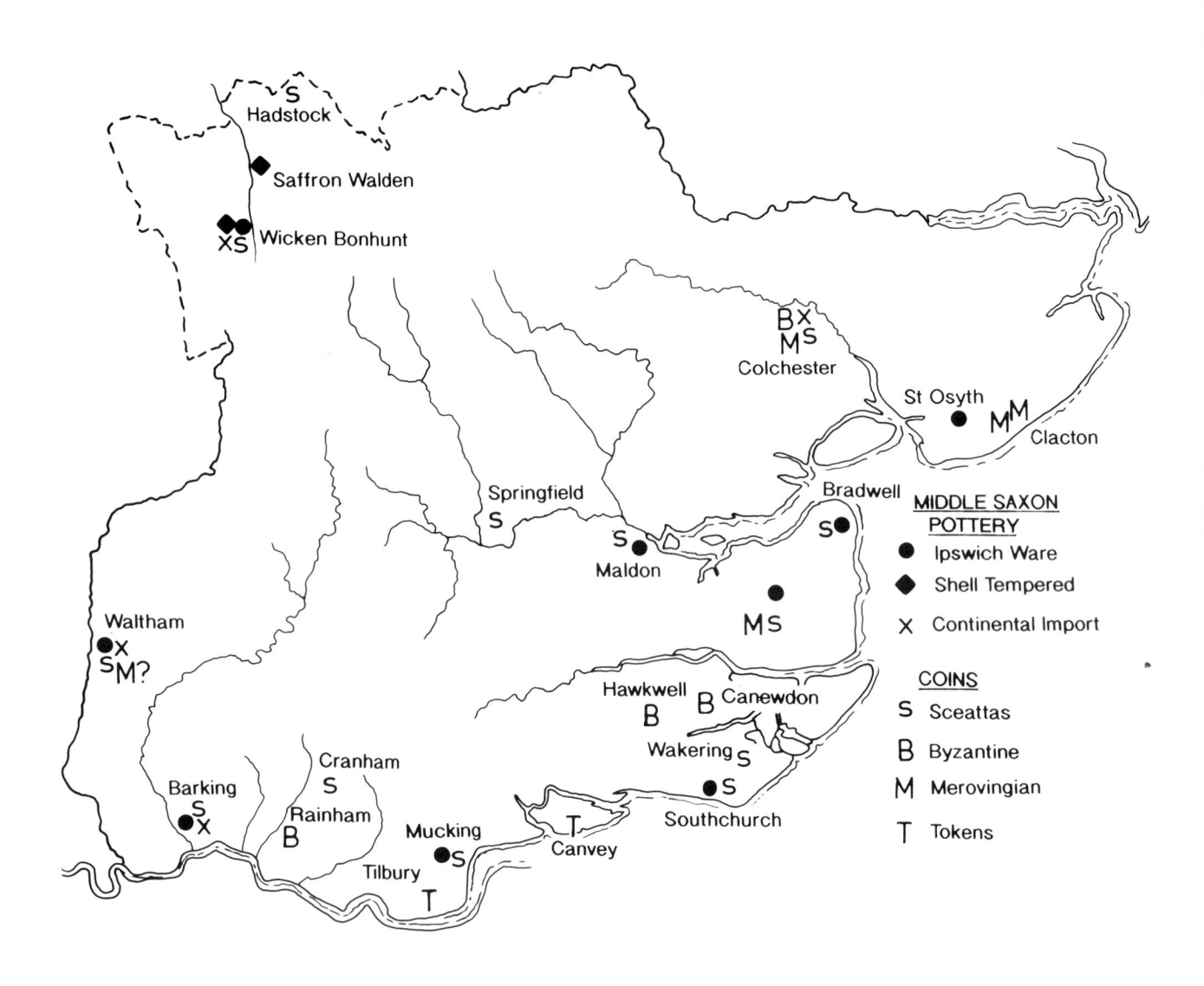

Fig.1 Middle Saxon Essex: Imported Material

king's head was replaced by a sphinx, perhaps recalling past classical glories of Colchester (Metcalf 1978; 1984, 34). Early eighth-century "Series B" sceattas may also be derived from Essex (Metcalf 1993, 94-104).

The kingdom would have been administered through a series of royal vills. The location of various possible *villae regales* can be postulated through documentary, place-name and archaeological evidence, though care must be taken to avoid regarding every "high status" settlement as a royal vill (Sawyer 1983, 283). Too much emphasis should not be placed upon back-projecting evidence from Domesday, as the 1086 survey lists the ancient royal demesne along with the holdings of Harold (Boyden 1986, 71).

The major Royal holdings of middle to late Saxon Essex are shown on figure 2 and listed in Table 1. This is not an attempt to provide a definitive guide to royal vills as some may have passed into secular or ecclesiastical hands without record. It clearly shows a correlation with major Roman sites, and Roman roads that must have survived throughout the period as they are still in use today. In central and northern Essex there also appears to be a correlation with Early Saxon cemeteries. This use by the Saxon elite of pre-existing monuments (also Springfield Lyons: Buckley and Hedges 1987), seen elsewhere in southern England (Harke 1994) must surely be some form of legitimisation. The same can be seen in the East Anglian Wuffing dynasty lineage which includes Caesar (Scull 1992, 14).

Many royal vills later became hundred centres possibly from the time of Edward the Elder (Boyden 1986, 178), while several saw the construction of *burhs* and went onto to become towns with market and mint functions (see below). Britnell (1978) has suggested that the right of holding hundredal markets may date to the Late Saxon period and these also show a strong correlation with royal centres, as do hundred moots (Christy 1928). Clearly, these royal vills were important "central places", with administrative, economic, and ecclesiastical functions which, if not in the same location, were at least in close proximity.

ESSEX c700-1066

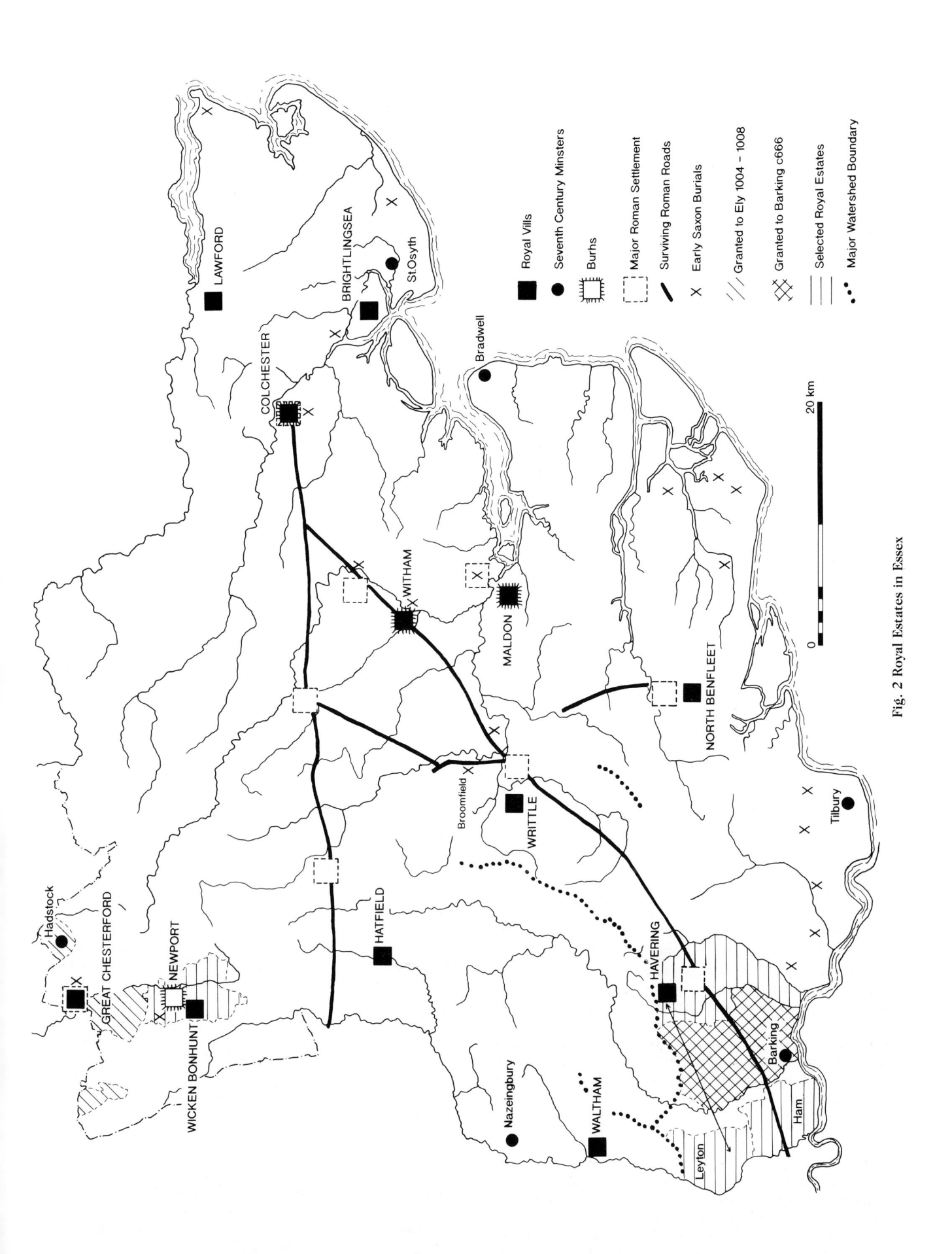

Fig. 2 Royal Estates in Essex

TABLE 1 : ROYAL VILLS

Royal Demesne (Domesday)	Roman Road	Roman Town	Pagan Cemetery	Hundred Moot	Hundred Market ?	Ferm ** Payments
Brightlingsea			Alresford			X
Chesterford		(Chesterford)	Chesterford			
Colchester	X	*Camulodunum*	Colchester	Lexden		
Lawford						X
Havering	X	*Durolitium*		Dagenham		
Hatfield					X	
Maldon		(Heybridge)	Heybridge			
N. Benfleet	X	(Wickford)				
Waltham				Waltham	X	
Witham	X	(Ivy Chimneys)*	L. Braxted	Witham		
Wicken/Newport		Wendens	Wendens		X	
Writtle	X	*Caesaromagus*	Broomfield, Springfield	Writtle	X	X

* Temple/Church site
**provisions to maintain the king's household

Each of the major sites will now be described in turn, demonstrating how a wide range of evidence is both necessary and desirable in order to understand the development of these centres.

Colchester

The former classical grandeur of Colchester provides an obvious location for a royal vill, its reuse legitimising East Saxon power. Tentative support for this hypothesis comes from the late seventh-century "Vanimundus" sceattas probably minted in Essex (Metcalf 1993, 80-1). They are copied from Merovingian coins, and a specimen from Colchester includes the letters "CA". It is intriguing to think that a particular Merovingian coin may have been selected for copying as it contained these two letters, actually referring to *Cabilonnum*, because they were the first two letters of *Camulodunum* (Metcalf 1993, 80-1).

Roman Colchester appears to have been virtually abandoned in the early fifth century, and the scatter of Early Saxon huts does not suggest any degree of continued urban life (Crummy 1981; 1984, 73-5; 1992, 118-20, 333). Several Roman extra-mural cemeteries saw continued burial in the fifth to seventh centuries (Crummy 1981, 6-21), though they may have served a wider areas than just the town itself.

There is almost no evidence for occupation between the eighth and ninth centuries (Crummy 1981, 23; 1992, 34), and the sparsity of Middle Saxon grass-tempered pottery and total absence of Ipswich Ware may suggest a genuine hiatus of occupation (the Ipswich Ware sherd shown by Wade 1988, fig. 54. is erroneous; Wade pers. comm.). Several east-west burials just to the west of the later castle may date to the Middle Saxon period (Drury 1982, 386), though no absolute dates have been determined; a Late Saxon date is quite plausible.

A potentially important site, called Old Heath derived from Old English for "old landing place" (Reaney 1935, 376-7), lies beside the River Colne around 3 km to the south east of the Roman town. A seventh-century Merovingian vessel has been discovered there (Crummy 1981, 21-2). Thus, the situation in Colchester may be similar to that in London, where a trading settlement lay outside the Roman walls, whereas the royal vill was inside (Hobley 1988, 73; Vince 1990).

Therefore, evidence for a *villa regalis* at Colchester in the eighth and ninth centuries is tentative. However, a royal vill was certainly established within the walls sometime after the early tenth century, in the area later occupied by the Norman castle (Drury 1982). In 916, Edward the Elder lay siege to Colchester, expelled the Danish army and established a *burh* (Crummy 1981, 24; Dodgson 1991). Morphological and metrical analysis of the field- and property-boundary pattern suggests that much of the intra-mural area was replanned using a module of four poles (22 yards) (Crummy 1981, 50-1). This event is undated, but the early tenth century is the obvious context (Crummy 1981, 72). Thetford Ware has been found in a number of sites within the intra-mural area, especially along the High Street, but only from the late tenth century, when Colchester also became a mint (Crummy 1981, 32-40, 70).

Maldon

The Roman small town at Heybridge declined in the fourth century, though fifth century occupation is testified by several Saxon "sunken-featured buildings" and pagan Saxon burials in the Roman cemetery (Drury and Wickenden 1982). In the Middle Saxon period, the focus of occupation appears to have shifted across the river, to the hill at Maldon. A sherd of Ipswich Ware from close to the later church (Webster and Cherry 1973, 140-1), and an early eighth-century sceatta (Rigold and Metcalf 1984, 257) are the earliest indications of occupation. The place-name "Maldon" means "hill marked by a cross" (Reaney 1935, 218), and Cooper (1993b, ix) has recently suggested that this might imply the presence of an early religious site, perhaps a minster in a royal vill.

In 912, Maldon was used as a forward base during the campaign of Edward the Elder, implying it was a royal estate, and during 916 Maldon was chosen as a site for a *burh* (Dodgson 1991, 170). A plausible location of this has recently been established (Bedwin 1992, 21), though there is little evidence for contemporary occupation within its defences (Webster and Cherry 1973, 140-1). Rather, tenth century and later occupation appears to have been focused just to the east, around the site of the medieval church and market place (Bedwin 1992, 21; Bennett and Gilman 1989, 151).

Witham

"Witham" was the site of another *burh*, constructed during King Edward's campaign of 912. The site of this *burh* has recently been considered in detail by Rodwell (1993a) in his excellent work on the landscape of Witham, and the arguments need not be repeated here. Suffice to say that a series of excavations have failed to produce any evidence for Late Saxon refortification of the Late Bronze Age/Iron Age hillfort at Chipping Hill and a more plausibe location is provided by a rectangular enclosure at "Burgate" in Rivenhall End or the D-shaped enclosure under the medieval new town of Witham (Rodwell and Rodwell 1986, 179-82; 1993, 176).

Either way, a remarkably similar sequence can be postulated to that at Maldon, with a royal estate centre, probable minster church and triangular market place (Rodwell 1993, Fig. 25, 67-71) adjacent to a substantial Roman site (the pagan temple and Christian church at Ivy Chimneys; Turner 1982), and a pagan Saxon cemetery at Little Braxted (Tyler 1992). Like Newport and possibly Horndon-on-the-Hill, Witham failed to develop into a true urban centre in the late Saxon period, until the creation of a twelfth-century "new town" (Rodwell 1993a, 87).

Wicken Bonhunt and Newport

The settlement excavated at Wicken Bonhunt was enclosed by a substantial ditch, and consisted of numerous timber-framed buildings beside an open area (Wade 1980). The material culture suggests a very high status settlement, with pottery imported from St. Neots, Ipswich and the continent. The bone assemblage showed a very high proportion of pig, which would also suggest high status consumption. An extensive cemetery lies close by (Atkinson 1993 and pers. comm.).

There is no known royal association with Wicken Bonhunt, but Rickling just to the south appears to be named after "Ricola", wife of the late sixth-century king Sledda of the East Saxons (Reaney 1935, 532), and it remained royal demesne until Domesday. A possible derivation of the neighbouring place-name Quendon is "Queens valley" (Reaney 1935, 53). The Royal connection is strengthened by the probable location of the Edwardian *burh* of "Wigingamere" at Newport, a parish that seems to have been carved out of Wicken and the neighbouring parish of Widdington (Haslam 1988, 29). The standing parish church at Newport is thirteenth century, but its cruciform plan may be suggestive of a former minster status (Rodwell and Rodwell 1977, 114). A link with Wicken Bonhunt is provided by a judgement, probably of the early twelfth century, stating that the chapel at Bonhunt formerly belonged to the church at Newport (Davis 1974, 17-18).

At Domesday, Newport paid 2 nights "ferm", the provisions to maintain the king's household, which suggests it was the last surviving element of a much larger royal estate (Round 1903, 31), one element of which appears to have been in Great Shelford, Cambridgeshire (Hart 1993a 13; Taylor 1974, 9). We can only speculate as to the other elements in this territory, though Rickling and Quendon form a physically discrete block of land assessed as 10 hides, and Wicken Bonhunt, Widdington, Newport and Wendens Ambo form another discrete unit of 30 hides.

Like Witham, Newport did not appear to have developed into a thriving town until the post-conquest period. There are no references to it having burgesses in Domesday, though its place-name does suggest a market (Reaney 1935, 531). The brief mint of "Nipeport" established under Edward the Confessor, traditionally located at Newport Pagnell, may have been at Newport in Essex (Boyden 1986, 260; Freeman 1985, 214-6).

Great Chesterford

Great Chesterford was held in 1066 by Earl Edgar, king Edward's nephew, while Little Chesterford was held by Queen Edith. The Royal estate was formerly more extensive, as Hadstock, Littlebury and Streetly Green were granted to Ely in the early eleventh century (Bentham 1771, 81; Hart 1971, Nos. 36, 41). Once again, this Royal vill was adjacent to an important Roman site which saw continued use in some form during the Early Saxon period. Saxon grass-tempered pottery is recorded from within the walled area (Rodwell 1976b, 238-9) and the northern Roman cemetery contains pagan Saxon burials (Evison 1969). The parish church lies on the edge of the southern cemetery, and its cruciform plan once again suggests a Saxon minster church (Rodwell 1980, 120).

Waltham Abbey

The place-name "Wealdham" is suggestive of a royal estate centre in a forest area (R. Huggins 1975), and recent excavations have revealed traces of a possible timber church associated with a burial radiocarbon dated to 560 ± 50 uncal. ad. (Huggins and Bascombe 1992, 334). A sceatta of c.715A.D. is recorded from just to the south (Huggins 1988a). Around the eighth century, the timber church was replaced by a stone structure (Huggins and Bascombe 1992) associated with a Middle Saxon settlement, indicated by finds including Ipswich Ware and continental pottery (Huggins 1970b; 1972; 1973; 1976; 1988a; 1988b; Musty 1978). Late Saxon occupation, including a possibly Norse-type turf-walled hall, also appears to have concentrated to the north of the church (Huggins 1988a, Fig. 1 with addition of 1992 site immediately to north of church in vicarage garden; Huggins pers. comm.). To the south of the church lies an enigmatic enclosure called "Eldeworth" (Huggins 1988b, Fig. 1). Dating of this is unclear, but does not preclude Late Saxon (Clarke *et al.* 1993).

Barking/Havering (Fig. 2)

Havering was another ancient royal manor at Domesday, including the vills of Romford and Hornchurch. It was assessed as ten hides, which seems rather low. The explanation is that the Havering hide was 480 acres, rather than the usual 120 (VCH Essex VII, 17); thus, Havering was in effect 40 hides. A variety of evidence suggests that much of the ancient Becontree Hundred, which included the later Havering Liberty, was formerly part of the royal estate. The 40 hide estate at Barking was granted by King Suidfred of Essex to Erkenwald c.666 (Hart 1971, No. 2), and thirty five hides were granted at Dagenham, Rainham and Ilford c.687 (Hart 1971, No. 4). Four hides and eight freemen in Leyton owed dues to the kings manor at Havering, and East and West Ham were royal land until 958 (Hart 1971, No. 15; VCH Essex VI, 8). When these various estates are plotted, they form a discrete block of territory covering the south-west corner of Essex, defined to the north by a major sinuous boundary which follows a watershed (Fig. 2).

Horndon-On-The-Hill

A Late Saxon mint was briefly established at Horndon, part of the royal policy of dispersing coin manufacture in a troubled time to ensure minimum disruption should any mint cease production (Eddy and Petchey 1983, 63; Freeman 1985; Metcalf and Lean 1993, 206). A large rectangular enclosure, c.800 m by 1500 m, can be defined by earthworks and the post-medieval field-boundary pattern, to the east of the High Street (Eddy 1980, 71-3). No excavations have been carried out within the enclosure, but Horndon's period as a mint is a plausible context for its construction.

The only other evidence for there having been a settlement here of urban character is a Domesday reference to "mansiones". Boyden (1986, 280) suggests these may be houses rather than hides. There are no known royal associations with Horndon, other than Domesday referring to several "invasions" against the king's property (Rumble 1983, 90). Recent excavations have produced a little tenth to eleventh-century pottery (Gilman 1992, 106; Wallis 1991), and a church is recorded in Domesday.

The Church

The development of the church in Essex was closely related to royal power. Two broad types of ecclesiastical institution emerged from the gradual seventh-century conversion; monasteries and minsters. We should not impose too rigid a division between the two, as documentary references can often be unclear as to what type of religious establishment existed (eg. White Notley: Taylor and Taylor 1965, 475). Sites may also have served as both monasteries and minsters at different times (eg. Hadstock: Rodwell 1976a).

Monastic sites were often characterised by their insularity, with coastal or riverside locations particularly favoured (Fig. 2). The early foundations were on royal lands, and concentrated around the periphery of the kingdom, a similar distribution to that in Kent (Brooks 1989, Fig. 4.2). At Barking, no evidence of the Saxon church itself has been discovered, but excavations in and around the precinct have revealed important evidence concerning the nature of this Middle to Late Saxon monastery. At the Barking Abbey Industrial Site, evidence of two buildings, wells and the leat of a mill have been excavated (MacGowan 1987). These and other excavations suggests a wealthy estate centre, scattered over a substantial area beside the River Roding, with evidence for iron, bronze and textile production. Most of the assemblage would fit happily with that from a contemporary trading port, with the exception of a small quantity of more specialised items such as styli, window glass and gold thread from woven braids, normally associated with monastic crafts (Redknap 1991, 359). Pottery was imported from Ipswich, North France/Belgium and the Rhineland with lava querns from the Eifel region (Redknap 1991, 359; 1992). The site's proximity to a tributary of the river Thames would certainly provide an ideal location for a port.

Barking appears to have been abandoned from c.870 to the early tenth century, though the community was certainly re-established by c.940 (MacGowan 1987, 35; Redknap 1991, 359). At Amberley Lane, part of an industrial complex has been excavated, including the base of a glass kiln, archaeomagnetically dated to 920±50; window, vessel and millifiore glass appear to have been produced (Gilman 1991, 150; K MacGowan pers. comm.). It is worth mentioning the contrast between the wealth of Barking, and austerity of other early monastic sites, such as Nazeingbury (Bascombe 1987; Huggins 1978).

The second type of ecclesiastical institution were minster churches, staffed by a group of priests who ministered to the local population (Blair 1988, 35; Morris 1989, 128-33). In the seventh and eighth centuries they were established by the Crown on its estates, and were often coterminous with the territory of the royal vill (Morris 1989, 128). One of the earliest such minsters in Essex was probably at Waltham Abbey (Huggins and Bascombe 1992).

From around the tenth century, secular lords began founding minster churches, while the final stage in the emergence of the medieval ecclesiastical structure of Essex was the fragmentation of the minster territories and provision of parish churches. The close correspondence of parish church and manorial hall in Essex is well known (Rodwell and Rodwell 1977, 92), and it is likely that many churches were initially built as estate chapels by the lord of the manor (eg. Ashingdon; Rodwell 1993b).

Unfortunately, the Essex Domesday paid little attention to churches; there are just 37 churches or priests recorded in Essex (Darby 1971, 257) compared to 345 in Suffolk (Rodwell 1980, 120). However, around Dunmow, a range of documentary and archaeological evidence suggests that out of 24 medieval parishes, 21 had churches by the mid-eleventh century (Rodwell and Rodwell 1977, 92). A similar density probably existed over most of the County, as where excavations have been on a fairly large scale, evidence of pre-Conquest structures are often found. At Cressing (Hope 1984), Rivenhall (Rodwell and Rodwell 1986) and West Bergholt (Turner 1984b), the remains of timber structures have been found under each of the Saxo-Norman stone churches. Another example may be Asheldham (Drury and Rodwell 1978), though recent excavations have cast doubt over the timber structure there (Andrews and Smoothy 1990). At Little Ilford, graves were cut by elements of a timber church probably of the eleventh century, replaced in stone during the mid-twelfth century (Redknap 1985). At Greensted, a timber church of the Saxon period actually survives to this day, though its dating is still uncertain (Christie et al. 1979).

Elsewhere, all that we can say is that the present medieval stone church was not the earliest on a site. For example, at Little Oakley (Corbishley 1984) and West Thurrock (Milton 1984) burials pre-date the early twelfth century stone churches. Taking documentary, architectural and archaeological evidence, we know of around 98 churches in Essex by the late eleventh century (Gilman 1989, 169-70; Redknap 1985; Rodwell 1980; Rodwell and Rodwell 1977; Taylor and Taylor 1965; Turner 1984a).

The Vikings

The Early Phase

In the late 860s, the Vikings began their conquest of eastern England, and during the 870s, East Anglia, Mercia and Essex fell (Crummy 1981, 92; Vince 1990, 18). Several Essex churches were destroyed in 870, such as St. Botolph's monastery at "Icanho" (possibly Hadstock : Rodwell 1976a, 69), and the Abbey at Barking (Hart 1993a, 117). There is certainly a hiatus in the occupation of Barking (Redknap 1991, 359), and the destruction of the excavated period 1 church at Hadstock may equate with this documented event, though there is no independent dating evidence (Rodwell 1976a, 70).

During the 880s the English recovered under Alfred and London was recaptured in 886, but the Vikings continued to be active in Essex, constructing encampments at Benfleet, Mersea, Shoebury and in the Lea Valley around 893/5 (Hart 1993a, 118, 501; Spurrell 1890). During the second decade of the tenth century, the English gradually recaptured Essex, building *burhs* at Witham in 912, Maldon in 916, and Newport in 917 (Bedwin 1992; Haslam 1988). Also in 917, the Danes were expelled from Colchester, and the fourth Essex *burh* established there (Crummy 1981). The only possible evidence for Danish activity at Colchester are "Viking Type" axe heads dredged from the River Colne, though they may actually date anywhere in the Late Saxon and Norman periods (Crummy 1981, 14). A "Viking Age" sword is recorded from Walthamstow (Richards 1991, 115), and a ninth-century "Danish-style throwing axe" from Asheldham (Laver 1930, 183-5).

Although Essex was part of Danelaw for several decades, there is in fact very little evidence for Viking settlement. A study of Domesday surnames in Colchester shows that Scandinavian names are no more significant that other ethnic groups (Crummy 1981, 24-5). Indeed, all the Anglo-Saxon Chronicle says is that Danes were expelled; it is unclear whether they ever established a permanent settlement or merely a temporary encampment.

There are a number of possible Scandinavian place-names in Essex, notably "thorpe", concentrating in the north east (Hart 1993a, Fig. 3.1). There are also supposed "Viking" burials in the west of the County at Saffron Walden (Bassett 1982, 13) and Waltham Abbey (Huggins 1988a), but these simply represent individuals buried with pieces of Scandinavian metalwork. The presence of these exchangeable artefacts, such as a pin from Wicken Bonhunt (Musty et al. 1973), and plate/mount from Waltham (Huggins 1984; 1988a, 145-7) need not imply that they were worn by Scandinavian settlers. However, the burial(s) from close to the churchyard at Leigh-on-Sea, supposedly found with a sword, horse and small hoard of late ninth-century coins, is suggestive of a Viking warrior (Biddle 1987).

This hoard was deposited c.895-900, and consisted of English coins (Biddle 1987; Blackburn 1989). It contrasts with a contemporary hoard from Ashdon, near Hadstock, that was comprised of predominantly Viking issues, possibly suggesting the far north-west corner of Essex fell within the Danish East Anglian sphere of monetary circulation (Blackburn 1989, 27). This repeats the pattern seen in the distribution of Middle Saxon pottery imported from Cambridgeshire (Fig. 1), in suggesting this area to economically look north not south.

The Second Phase
In the late tenth century, Essex once again became a battle ground, with conflicts at Maldon in 991 (Cooper 1993a; Hart 1993a, 533-543; Scragg 1991), and "Assandun", probably Ashdon not Ashingdon, in 1016 (Hart 1993a, 553-565; Rodwell 1993b). This period of Viking activity is not likely to have led to any folk settlement. However, at Waltham, King Canute's standard bearer Tovi is said to have had a hunting lodge (Huggins 1976, 75), and a hall claimed to be of a Norse tradition and dated on the basis of associated pottery to the late tenth/early eleventh century has been excavated just north of the church (Huggins 1976; cf. Graham-Campbell 1977). A burial was found nearby with a roughly contemporary metal plate of Late Saxon style; this may be the burial of "a member of Tovi's household, or a contemporary native with access to Viking equipment (Huggins 1984, 179).

Rural Settlement and the Landscape
By Domesday, Essex was extremely productive, and had a high density of population and ploughteams (Darby 1971; McDonald and Snooks 1985). Well organised estates certainly existed from the late seventh century, illustrated by the few early charters that survive for Essex (Hart 1971). The considerable resources that estate owners as early as c.700 could call upon is demonstrated by the Mersea causeway (Crummy et al. 1982) and other substantial timber structures possibly related to fishing in the Blackwater Estuary (Crump and Wallis 1992).

Estate Structure
The multiplicity of Domesday manors with the same name indicate that the mid-eleventh century estate structure had resulted from a long process of fragmentation. For example, there were seven Tolleshunts at Domesday. The place-name is interpreted as "*Toll's* spring" (Reaney 1935, 306). The two adjacent manors of Tollesbury also contain the personal-name "Toll", suggesting that together Tollesbury and Tolleshunt were part of one early territory. At Domesday these 12 manors amounted to 42 hides.

Another example of the fragmentation of an early estate is the Rodings (Bassett 1989b, Fig. 1.11), which had split into 16 manors by Domesday. In the medieval period these were grouped into 8 parishes. Therefore, we can postulate an original territory, which at Domesday was assessed at 29 hides, that subsequently fragmented into at least 16 units, several of which were combined when the parochial structure was imposed. Where the extent of Middle Saxon estates can be determine, it is notable that many tend to be around thirty to forty hides; Barking 40; Havering 40; Rodings 29; Tollesbury 42; Waltham Holy Cross 40; Wicken 40. These estates tend to be centred on settlements in river valleys, with their boundaries up on the watersheds (eg. Fig. 2).

Settlement Patterns
In the medieval period, the landscape typical of Midland England, with a nucleated village clustered around a church and manor surrounded by open fields, is largely absent from Essex. Instead, settlement was more dispersed, often occurring as loose nucleations in the valleys, with several other manors and small hamlets scattered throughout the rest of a parish, each with its own fields. Though the origins of this settlement pattern are obscure, they must lie in the Saxon period.

There are some signs of a settlement contraction in the fifth and sixth century including the abandonment of many Roman sites, especially at the more Romanized end of the settlement hierarchy such as villas. On some sites, this decay appears to have begun as early as the fourth century. Pollen analysis from the Mar Dyke shows a slight woodland or scrub regeneration in the extreme south of the County during the immediate post-Roman period (Wilkinson 1988), though other evidence from Essex (Murphy this volume) and the much greater volume of data from Norfolk and Suffolk show no major regeneration (Williamson 1993).

Extensive fieldwalking in Norfolk and Suffolk has shown that the heaviest clays were abandoned in the Early Saxon period, while in the valleys, Saxon settlements tend to occur close to Roman sites (Newman 1992; Scull 1992, 10). More limited work in north west Essex shows a similar picture (Brooks and Bedwin 1989; Brooks and Wall 1988, 12; Medlycott 1990; Williamson 1984; 1986). For example around Stansted and along the A120, Roman settlement was abundant in all areas (Fig. 3), but just one Early Saxon site was uncovered, through excavation not fieldwalking. However, considering Williamson had to fieldwalk areas in extreme detail and under ideal conditions in order to find the handful of Saxon sherds, it is not clear whether this is valid negative evidence.

In broad terms, settlement was expanding in the Middle to Late Saxon period. This is shown by "leah"/"feld"/"hyrst" place-names representing Late Saxon assarts (Gelling 1978, 119-23; Reaney 1935, 568). Woodland clearance was continuing, reflected in the large number of vills with less woodland in 1086 than 1066 (Round 1903, 379). The critical period in the evolution of the medieval settlement pattern appears to have been during this period of expansion.

Most Early Saxon sites appear to have been abandoned by the late seventh century; they lack Middle Saxon grass-tempered pottery and Ipswich Ware. However, it must be borne in mind that the former may not always have been distinguished from Early Saxon grass-tempered pottery, and the Ipswich Ware does not appear to have circulated widely in rural areas (Vince 1984, 433; Hamerow 1991, 14). At Mucking, the latest evidence for occupation comes from a small group of coins dated to c.685 and a sherd of Ipswich Ware (Hamerow 1991, 14; 1993, 5-6, 22), though a recent metal-detector find may indicate occupation continuing into the early eighth century; unfortunately the provenance of this find is unclear (H. Hamerow and M. Metcalf pers. comm.).

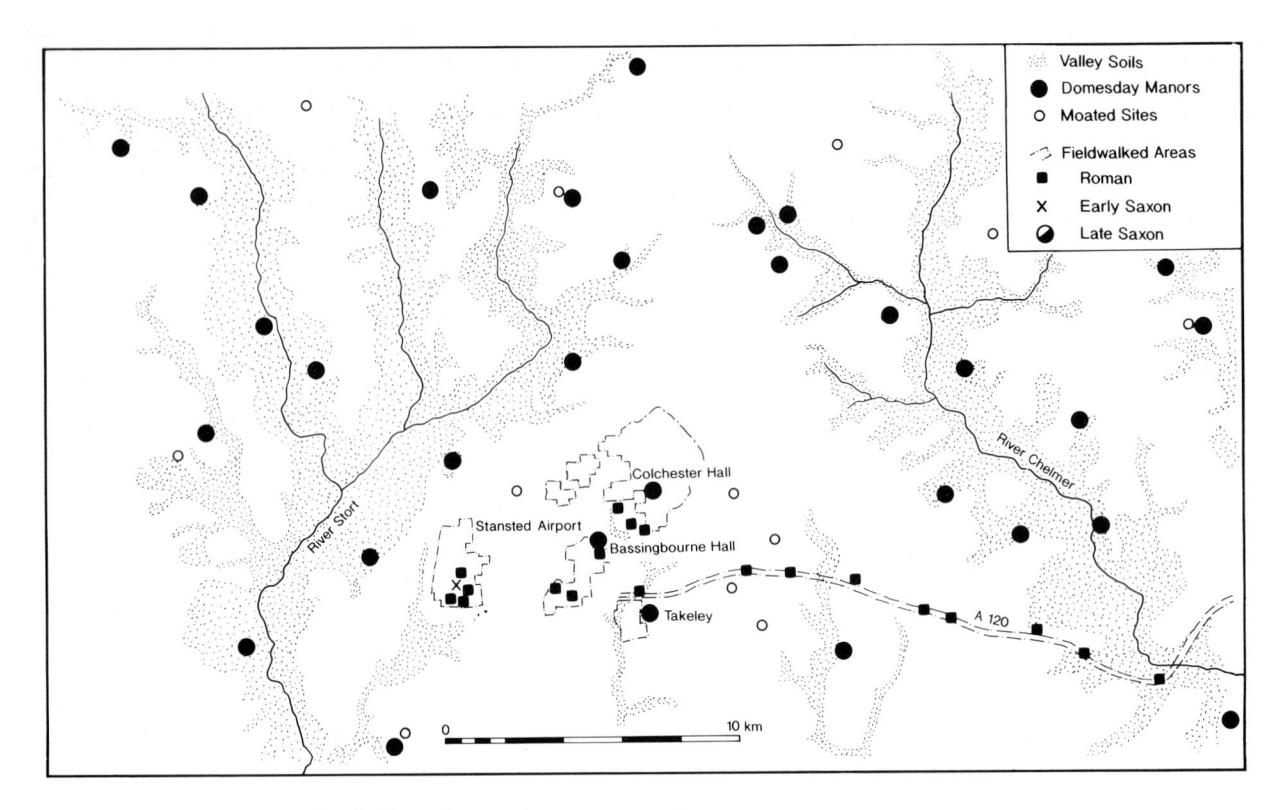

Fig. 3 The evolution of Late Saxon settlement around Stansted Airport

In Norfolk and Suffolk, extensive fieldwalking shows a shift in settlement during the Middle Saxon period, with Ipswich Ware tending to concentrate around later churches, rather than in the areas of Early Saxon occupation (Davison 1990; Newman 1988; 1992; Wade-Martins 1980). In north-west Essex, more limited fieldwalking suggests the same pattern (Williamson 1986, 125). Around Stansted, Domesday settlement was clearly concentrated in the river valleys, though several manors occurred on the edges of the interfluvial areas, such as Takeley, Colchester Hall and Bassingbourne Hall (Fig. 3). Whether these sites represent a recolonization of this area in the Late Saxon period (note the "leah" place-name), or whether there had in fact been near continuous, but virtually aceramic, occupation in the vicinity of these sites is impossible to determined; considering the scarcity of Early Saxon material from the Stansted excavations, the former is favoured.

Excavations have shown the Middle to Late Saxon origin of several church-hall complexes (eg. Asheldham: Drury and Rodwell 1978; Pentlow Hall: Andrews 1991; Rivenhall: Rodwell and Rodwell 1986). However, it is not always clear whether these ever formed the basis for nucleated settlements. At Little Holland, the church/hall complex certainly appears to have been isolated (Andrews and Brooks 1989), while at North Shoebury, extensive excavations around the church, have revealed a ditched enclosure (c.100 x 70 m) possibly dug as early as the eleventh century, but with no trace of an associated nucleated settlement (K. Crowe pers. comm.; Wymer and Brown 1995).

A number of other church/hall complexes have produced Late Saxon finds (eg. pottery - Danbury: Morris and Buckley 1978, 14; Great Chesterford: Brooks and Wallis 1991, 39-40; Little Waltham: Drury 1978, 136; Pentlow: Andrews 1991; Strethall: Williamson 1986, 127; Witham: Dunning 1962. Coins - Castle Hedingham: Priddy 1991; Kelvedon: Eddy 1982, 20; Takeley: Medlycott 1990, 79). However, it is not clear whether these finds relate to the hall itself, or a surrounding settlement as in Suffolk and Norfolk.

The largest scale excavation is at Springfield Lyons (Buckley and Hedges 1987, 24-31). The small amount of pottery is dated to the tenth and eleventh centuries, and other finds included Rhenish lava quern fragments and possible Rhenish pottery. This, along with the number, range and size of structures does suggest this was a fairly high status settlement (Buckley and Hedges 1987, 38). However, as there are so few sites with which to compare Springfield, even outside Essex (Astill and Lobb 1989, 88-90), we cannot be sure that this is not the material culture that we should expect on an ordinary rural settlement. One of the few lesser status settlements to be discovered in Essex is at Chignall St. James, where a single post-built structure was been excavated beside a ditched trackway; its function is unclear (Brooks 1992).

Rural Resources
Domesday records a wide range of non-agricultural resources which formed an integral part of the rural economy. Settlements show a marked tendency to occur on the margins of geological and topographical zones in order to exploit a variety of environments (eg. Fig. 3), with parishes including areas of both light and heavy soil. Long, sinuous lanes often traverse the whole parish, linking settlements in the centre with the variety of resources that existed.

One of the most important resources was pasture. In the Saxon period, grazing on coastal saltmarshes was a communal right, and settlements far inland had "pasture for sheep" on the Thames marshes (Round 1903, 369-70). By Domesday, coastal marshes were also used for boiling sea water to produce salt (Darby 1971, 246-7). Fisheries are recorded along the whole coast, and recent aerial photography has revealed the remains of wooden fish-weirs at several locations around the Essex coast, notably off Bradwell and Mersea Island (Clarke 1993; Crump and Wallis 1992). At Collins Creek, these fishweirs have yielded radiocarbon dates of 640-75 and 882-957 A.D. It is tempting to see these structures as associated with the early monastic foundation at Bradwell.

Essex was a relatively well-wooded county (Darby 1971). Like the coastal marshes, upland heaths and woods were exploited through intercommoning (Rackham 1986, 14; Rippon 1991, 58). Woodland was used for fuel, building timber and grazing pigs. The work of Rackham (1986; 1993) has clearly illustrated the importance of woodland as resource, and it should not be regarded as waste land waiting to be converted to arable. Deer parks were generally a post-Norman creation, but at Ongar at least, an enclosure to retain deer existed in the Late Saxon period (Cantor and Hatherley 1979, 71).

Landscape Management
The field-boundary pattern in parts of Essex possesses a high degree of regularity, indicating that large areas were planned out in a single episode (Rippon 1991, Fig. 1; also Bassett 1982, Fig. 3; Rodwell 1993a, Fig. 36; Williamson 1984, Figs. 6.3, 6.6). Many areas of this planned landscape were laid out during the late Iron Age or very early Roman period (eg. Little Waltham : Drury 1978, Fig. 74). The survival of these relict Roman field-systems suggests that the landscape must have been continuously exploited, for arable or pasture, so as to prevent the regeneration of woodland.

A particularly extensive regular landscape exists in the south east of the County, consisting of a series of planned field-systems (Rippon 1991, Figs 1, 6; Rackham 1986; Rodwell 1978). When these landscapes were laid out is not entirely clear, but south of Wickford at least, a Roman date again seems likely (Rippon 1991). However, at Shoebury, a radial arrangement of roads is certainly post-Roman, for they overlay a Roman field-system on an entirely different orientation. A *terminus ante-quem* is certainly provided by the insertion of the eleventh century manorial enclosure at Shoebury, while the late ninth-century Viking fortress may either have been inserted into an existing landscape, or have been used as the point from which to plan the landscape; the former appears more likely. Thus, there appears to have been a major reorganisation of landed resources in the Middle to Late Saxon period. Unlike the Midlands, this does not appear to have been associated with the nucleation of settlement.

Discussion
This paper has reviewed the diverse evidence for Middle to Late Saxon Essex. Though both archaeological and documentary evidence is sparse, an interdisciplinary approach has been able to illuminate a number of themes. The available source material makes high status centres and in particular the closely related royal and ecclesiastical sites most evident. These institutions controlled considerable resources, and were able to participate in foreign trade and industrial production.

During both the Middle and Late Saxon periods, the greatest trading centre in the region was undoubtedly London, but from c.700 this was under Mercian control. It is tempting to argue that the East Saxon kings continued to conduct foreign trade themselves possibly via Colchester, while the finds from Barking suggest that monasteries also had contacts with the continent. Certainly the distribution of imported material and early trade tokens suggests the Essex estuaries were important axis' of trade in the Middle Saxon period (Fig. 1; based on Archibald 1991; Bispham 1986; Burnett 1987, 182; Rigold 1975). It should be stressed that there are many similarities in the cultural histories of south Essex and north Kent (eg. Brown, Sealey and Tyler this volume), illustrating that in a period when water transport was so important, estuaries served as major thoroughfares not as boundaries. In trading terms, Essex appears to have been largely eclipsed by London and Ipswich by the Late Saxon period (Metcalf and Lean 1993, 208).

In Essex, the church never came to dominate the landscape. It was a major landowner, but the estates of even the major religious houses tended to be dispersed (eg. St. Paul's: Hart 1993a, 205-20). Another characteristic of Essex is the limited power of the lay aristocracy. The originally extensive Middle Saxon royal estates fragmented to an extreme level, and the royal demesne shrunk considerably, but few lay magnates built up large estates. By Domesday most landholders held just one manor (Boyden 1986, 173).

Therefore, even into the Late Saxon period, it was the royal centres that were all important. Their role in local government is reflected in the fact that many went on to become hundred centres, and their economic importance is reflected in their development into the hundred markets and towns. In the case of Colchester, it was the intramural area that developed, whereas at Maldon, Newport and Witham, settlements grew up outside the defences around triangular market places and adjacent churches.

Domesday records burgesses at Colchester and Maldon, suggesting sizeable urban populations and at both sites, and archaeological evidence suggests fairly extensive settlements from the late tenth century. Maldon is the oldest mint in Essex, sporadically producing coins from the reign of Aethelstan (924-39) and a mint was established at Colchester under Aethelred (978-1016) (Blackburn 1991, 162; Metcalf and Lean 1993). Other mints were briefly established at Horndon and possibly Newport, but along with Witham, these "proto-urban" centres never appear to have been successful.

Conclusion: The Future
Essex in the eleventh century had a very varied landscape, agriculturally rich and with an abundance of natural resources. It should be remembered that the landscape of even an area the size of Essex was extremely varied, and the ways in which each different environment was exploited will show subtle variations (eg. Kent: Everitt 1986, 43-68). The Boulder Clay and terrace gravels have seen a series of large scale excavations, and even though there is scope for much greater work here, we should not overlook other distinctive environments such as the London Clay basin.

The settlement pattern, estate structure and church hierarchy that formed the basis of the medieval landscape, all appear to have emerged in the Middle to Late Saxon period. Compared to other parts of south-east England, documentary sources and archaeological evidence in Essex is poor, but this should only serve to encourage new approaches in order to overcome the deficiencies in our data.

Certain themes need more attention, and conventional archaeology must take the leading role. Large scale excavations of carefully selected sites are essential to address a number of issues. The development of towns is poorly understood in this period, and particular attention should be paid to the "proto-urban" centres such as Witham, Newport and Horndon. A fundamental academic question with a bearing on both the urban and rural landscape of Essex is the impact of London. An enigmatic class of site that also deserves more attention are the large possibly manorial enclosures such as Horndon and Waltham. Another possible Saxon rectangular enclosure at Ongar (c.400 x 250 m) pre-dates the Norman castle (Eddy and Petchey 1983, Fig. 19.1). Another example of a private defensive work may be at Clavering, where a castle is possibly referred to in 1052 (Pewsey and Brooks 1993, 22; Round 1903, 345). We also need large scale investigation of several church-manor complexes and their environs, particularly to determine their relationship to the wider settlement pattern.

Essex has seen a considerable amount of church archaeology particularly in the 1970s, though there has been less research into the evolution of the ecclesiastical hierarchy as a whole. Important information continues to come from watching briefs, excavations (eg. Asheldham: Andrews and Smoothy 1990) and structural analysis (eg. Widdington: Gilman 1989, 169-70), but we must also consider documentary sources, place-names and dedications in order to identify the early hierarchy and the role of the church in the wider landscape.

However, it is in the countryside that most work needs to be done, in order to redress the bias towards high status sites. Here, the poor ceramic sequence means that we will never be able to trace the development of Saxon settlement in Essex as has been so successfully achieved in East Anglia (eg. Davison 1990; Newman 1992). This is why we need a new approach, one that is more interdisciplinary and holistic than current archaeological evaluations and excavation allows. In particular, we need to study the rural landscape as an entire system, rather than isolate individual components such as settlements and fields. Large-scale fieldwalking and selective excavation must play a part in understanding the genesis of the medieval settlement pattern. Such fieldwalking projects must take into account the poor visibility of Saxon pottery, and consider the approach adopted by Williamson (1986) of paying special attention to Roman and Saxo-Norman scatters, and church-hall complexes, in order to determine the presence or absence of Saxon occupation. Better relations with metal-detector users would also be beneficial, as recent survey results in south-east Suffolk have shown (Newman 1992).

There is a need for more palaeo-environmental research in this period, in order to understand changes in landscape exploitation. Pollen analysis in Norfolk and Suffolk has been very successful in illustrating the lack of forest regeneration in East Anglia, and indeed, indicating an expansion of arable in the Middle Saxon period (Williamson 1993, 110); similar data should be sought in Essex, particularly from valley peats.

Modern place-name scholarship has come a long way since Reaney's day, and a reassessment of Essex place-names is long overdue. This should concentrate not just on the chronology of settlement, but also its environmental/landscape context and tenurial relationships between settlements.

The technique that can bind all these other strands of evidence together, as well as providing invaluable information in itself, is the retrogressive analysis of the historic landscape, and especially field-boundary patterns. The value of this method has been shown in relation to planned landscapes (see above), but is equally appropriate in all other areas. A study of the whole of Essex would enable the surviving Roman field-systems to be quantified, and explanations for their distribution sought in terms of its relationship to the preceding and succeeding landscapes. These boundaries must, however, be subject to a programme of excavation to obtain dating evidence, as the Shoebury example has shown that not all regular landscapes need be Roman or earlier. Excavating boundaries still in use is pointless; rather, work should concentrate in areas where the regular landscape may have been abandoned relatively soon after its creation, and dating evidence should be undisturbed by later re-cutting. There is also a need for pollen analysis and extensive fieldwalking in areas with and without the survival of Roman field-systems, in order to examine whether this continuity in landuse is reflected in the settlement pattern. It is only through interdisciplinary studies of this kind, that the lack of direct evidence for the Middle to Later Saxon period will be overcome.

Acknowledgements

I wish to thank all the staff of the Essex County Council Archaeology Section for their help in my research, especially Mark Atkinson, Owen Bedwin, Nigel Brown, Helen Walker and Steve Wallis. Richard Britnell, Janet Cooper, Ken Crowe, Philip Crummy, Peter Huggins, Ken MacGowan, Michael Metcalf, Gustav Milne, Bernard Nurse, Mark Redknap, Keith Wade and Tom Williamson all kindly sent information. Finally, I would like to thank Dr. Grenville Astill (University of Reading), for his comments on this paper.

Bibliography

Andrews, D. (1991) "Pentlow Hall", *E.A.H.* 22, 176-80.

Andrews, D. and Brooks, H. (1989) "An Essex Dunwich: The Lost Church at Little Holland Hall", *E.A.H.* 20, 74-83.

Andrews, D. and Smoothy, M. (1990) "Asheldham Church Revisited", *E.A.H.* 21, 146-151.

Archibald, M. (1991) "Aspects of Saxon and Norman London: Lead Objects With Official Coin Types", in Vince, A.G. ed. *Aspects of Saxon and Norman London Vol. 2: Finds and Environmental Evidence.* London and Middlesex Archaeol. Soc. Special Paper 12, 279-36.

Astill, G.G. and Lobb, S.J. (1989) "Excavation of Prehistoric, Roman and Saxon Deposits at Wraysbury, Berkshire", *Arch. J.* 146, 68-134.

Atkinson, M. (1993) "Archaeological Evaluation of the Proposed M11 Widening Scheme", *Essex Archaeology and History News* July 1993, 12-14.

Bailey, K. (1988) "East Saxon Kings – Some Further Observations", *Essex Journal* 23(2), 34-40.

Bascombe, K. (1987) "Two Charters of King Suebred of Essex", in Neale, K. ed. *An Essex Tribute: Essays Presented to Frederick G. Emmison.* Leopard's Head Press, London.

Bassett, S. (1982) *Saffron Walden: Excavation and Research 1972-80.* Chelmsford Archaeol. Trust Rep. 2, C.B.A. Res. Report 45, London.

Bassett, S. (1989a) *The Origins of the Anglo-Saxon Kingdoms.* University Press, Leicester.

Bassett, S. (1989b) "In Search of the Origins of Anglo-Saxon Kingdoms", in Bassett, S. 1989a, 3-27.

Bennett, A. and Gilman, P. (1989) "Work of the Essex County Council Archaeology Section 1988", *E.A.H.* 20, 147-156.

Bedwin, O. (1986) "The Excavation of Three Ring Ditches at Broomfield Plantation Quarry, Alresford, Essex, 1984", *E.A.H.* 69-81.

Bedwin, O. (1992) "Early Iron Age Settlement at Maldon and the Maldon "Burh": Excavations at Beacon Green, 1987", *E.A.H.* 23, 10-24.

Bentham, J. (1771) *The History and Antiquities of the Conventual and Cathedral of Ely.* Cambridge.

Biddle, M. (1987) "The Hook Norton Hoard of 1848: A Viking Burial From Oxfordshire?", *Oxoniensis* 52, 186-95.

Bispham, J. (1986) "Recent Metal Detector Finds from Essex and Lincolnshire", *Br. Num. J.* 56, 183-5.

Blackburn, M. (1989) "The Ashdon (Essex) Hoard and the Currency of the Southern "Danelaw in the Late Ninth Century", *Br. Num. J.* 59, 13-38.

Blackburn, M. (1991) "Aethelred's Coinage and the Payment of Tribute", in Scragg, D. ed. 1991, 157-169.

Blair, J. (1988) "Minster Churches in the Landscape", in Hooke. D. ed. *Anglo-Saxon Settlements,* 35-58. Blackwell, Oxford.

Boyden, P. (1986) *A Study in the Structure of Landholding and Administration in Essex in the Late Saxon Period.* Unpublished PhD Thesis, Westfield College, London.

Britnell, R.H. (1978) "English Markets and Royal Administration Before 1200", *Econ. Hist. Rev.* XXXI, 183-96.

Brooks, H. (1992) "Two Rural Medieval Sites in Chignall St. James: Excavations in 1989", *E.A.H.* 23, 39-50.

Brooks, H. and Bedwin, O. (1989) *Archaeology at the Airport: The Stansted Archaeological Project 1985-89.* Essex County Council Archaeology Section/English Heritage, Chelmsford.

Brooks, H. and Wall, W. (1988) *The Stansted Project: Fieldwalking and Excavations At Stansted Airport. Second Interim Report.* Essex County Council Archaeology Section, Chelmsford.

Brooks, H. and Wallis, S. (1991) "Recent Archaeological Work in Great Chesterford", *E.A.H.* 22, 38-45.

Brooks, N. (1989) "The Creation and Early Structure of the Kingdom of Kent", in Bassett, S. ed. 1989a, 55-74.

Buckley, D.G. ed. (1980) *Archaeology in Essex to AD 1500.* C.B.A. Res. Rep. 34, London.

Buckley, D.G. and Hedges, J.D. (1987) *The Bronze Age and Saxon Settlements at Springfield Lyons, Essex: An Interim Report.* Essex County Council Archaeology Section Occasional Paper 5, Chelmsford.

Burnett, S. (1987) "A Provencal Solidus from Hawkwell, Essex", *Num. Chr.* 147, 182-3.

Cantor, L.M. and Hatherley, J. (1979) "The Medieval Parks of England", *Geography* 64, 71-85.

Christie, H., Olsen, O. and Taylor, H.M. (1979) "The Wooden Church of St. Andrew at Greensted, Essex", *Antiq. J.* LIX, 92-112.

Christy, M. (1928) "The Essex Hundred Moots : An Attempt to Identify Their Meeting Places", *T.E.A.S.* XVIII 172-198.

Clarke, C.P. (1993) "Collins Creek", *E.A.H.* 24, 209.

Clarke, C.P., Gardiner, M.F. and Huggins, P.J. (1993) "Excavations at Church Street, Waltham Abbey 1976-87: Urban Development and Prehistoric Evidence", *E.A.H.* 24, 69-113.

Cooper, J. ed. (1993a) *The Battle of Maldon: Fiction and Fact.* Hambledon Press, London.

Cooper, J. (1993b) "Introduction", in Cooper, J. ed. 1993a, ix-xi.

Corbishley, M. (1984) "Excavations at St. Mary's Church. Little Oakley, Essex 1977", in Turner, R. ed. 1984a, 15-27.

Cottrill, F. (1934)" A Trial Excavation at Witham, Essex", *Antiq. J.* XIV, 190-1.

Crummy, P. (1981) *Saxon and Norman Colchester.* Colchester Archaeological Reports 1.

Crummy, P. (1984) *Excavations at Lion Walk, Balkerne Gate, and Middleborough, Colchester, Essex Colchester 1971-85.* Colchester Archaeological Reports 3.

Crummy, P. (1992) *Excavations at Culver Street, the Gilbert School, and Other Sites in Colchester 1971-85.* Colchester Archaeological Reports 6.

Crummy, P., Hillam, J. and Crossan, C. (1982) "Mersea Island: The Anglo-Saxon Causeway", *E.A.H.* 14, 71-86.

Crump, B. and Wallis, S (1992) "Kiddles", *Essex Journal* 27(2), 38-42.

Cunningham, C.M. (1982) "Medieval and Post Medieval Pottery", in Drury, P.J. "Aspects of the Origins and Development of Colchester Castle", *Arch. J.* 139, 302-419.

Darby, H.C. (1971) "The Domesday Geography of Essex", in *The Domesday Geography of Eastern England.* University Press, Cambridge.

Davis., R.C.H. (1974) "The College of St. Martin-le-Grand and the Anarchy, 1135-54". *London Topographical Record* XXIII.

Davison, A. (1990) *The Evolution of Settlement in Three Parishes in South East Norfolk,* East Anglian Archaeology 49.

Dodgson, J.M. (1991) "The Site of the Battle of Maldon", in Scragg, D. ed. 1991, 170-179.

Drury, P.J. (1976) "Braintree: Excavations and Research 1971-76", *E.A.H.* 8, 1-143.

Drury, P.J. (1978) *Excavations at Little Waltham 1970-1.* Chelmsford Archaeol. Trust Rep. 1.; C.B.A. Res. Rep. 26, London.

Drury, P.J. (1982) "Aspects of the Origins and Development of Colchester Castle", *Arch. J.* 139, 302-419.

Drury, P. and Rodwell, W.J. (1978) "Investigations at Asheldham Essex: An Interim Report on the Church and the Historic Landscape", *Antiq. J.* 58, 133-51.

Drury, P. and Wickenden, N. (1982) "An Early Anglo-Saxon Settlement Within The Romano-British "Small Town" at Heybridge, Essex", *Med. Arch.* 26, 1-40.

Dumville, D. (1989) "Essex, Middle Anglia and the Expansion of Mercia in the South East Midlands", in Bassett, S. ed. 1989a, 123-40.

Dunning, G.C. (1962) "Saxon and Norman Pottery From Colchester Castle Park", *Antiq. J.* XLII, 62-7.

Eddy, M.R. (1980) "The Work of the Essex County Council Archaeology Section 1979", *E.A.H.* 12, 51-8.

Eddy, M.R. (1982) *Kelvedon The Origins and Development of a Roman Small Town.* Essex County Council Archaeology Section Occasional Paper 3, Chelmsford.

Eddy, M.R. and Petchey, M.R. (1983) *Historic Towns in Essex: An Archaeological Survey.* Essex County Council, Chelmsford.

Everitt, A. (1986) *Continuity and Colonisation: The Evolution of Kentish Settlement.* Leicester University Press.

Evison, V.I. (1969) "Five Anglo-Saxon Inhumation Graves Containing Pots at Great Chesterford, Essex", *R.O.B.* 19, 157-74.

Freeman, A. (1985) *The Moneyer and the Mint in the Reign of Edward the Confessor.* B.A.R. British Series 145, Oxford.

Gelling, M. (1976) "The Place-Names of the Mucking Area", *Panorama* 19, 7-20.

Gelling, M. (1988) *Signposts to the Past.* Second Edition. Phillimore, Chichester.

Gelling, M. (1992) "A Chronology for Suffolk Place-Names", in Carver, M.O.H. ed. *The Age of Sutton Ho* , 53-64. Boydell Press, Woodbridge.

Gilman, P. (1989) "Excavations in Essex, 1988", *E.A.H.* 20, 157-71.

Gilman, P. (1990) "Excavations in Essex 1989", *E.A.H.* 21, 126-39.

Gilman, P. (1991) "Archaeology in Essex, 1990", *E.A.H.* 22, 148-161.

Gilman, P. (1992) "Archaeology in Essex, 1991", *E.A.H.* 23, 98-113.

Goodburn, D. and Redknap, M. (1988) "Replicas and Wrecks From the Lower Thames Area", *London Archaeologist* 6(1), 7-10, 19-23.

Graham-Campbell, J. (1977) "Weston British, Irish and Later Anglo-Saxon", *Arch. J.* 134, 418-35.

Hamerow, H. (1987) "Anglo-Saxon Settlement, Pottery and Spatial Development at Mucking, Essex", *R.O.B.* 37, 245-73.

Hamerow, H. (1991) "Settlement Mobility and the "Middle Saxon Shift": Rural Settlements and Settlement Patterns in Anglo-Saxon England", *Anglo-Saxon England* 20, 1-17.

Hamerow, H. (1993) *Excavations at Mucking Volume 2: The Anglo-Saxon Settlement.* English Heritage Archaeological Report 21, London.

Harke, H. (1994) "The Location of the Anglo-Saxon Barrow at Lowbury Hill", in Fulford, M. and Rippon, S. "Lowbury Hill, Oxfordshire: A Re-investigation", *Archaeol. J.* 151, 158-211.

Hart, C. (1971) *The Early Charters of Essex.* Department of English Local History Occasional Papers, First Series 10 (Revised Edition). University Press, Leicester.

Hart, C. (1993a) *The Danelaw.* Hambledon Press, London.

Hart, C. (1993b) "Essex in the Late Tenth Century", in Cooper, J. 1993a, 171-204.

Haslam, J. (1988) "The Anglo-Saxon Burh at *Wiginamere*", *Landscape History* 10, 25-36.

Hobley, B. (1988) "Ludenwic and Ludenburh: Two Cities Rediscovered", in Hodges, R. and Hobley, B. ed. *The Rebirth of Towns in the West AD700-1050,* 69-82. C.B.A. Res. Rep. 68, London.

Hodges, R. (1981) *The Hamwih Pottery: The Local and Imported Wares From 30 Years of Excavations at Middle Saxon Southampton and Their European Context.* C.B.A. Res. Rep. 37, London.

Hope, J.H. (1984) "Excavations at All Saints Church, Cressing, Essex, 1979", in Turner, R. 1984a, 28-42.

Huggins, P.J. (1970a) "Excavations at Sewardstone Street, Waltham Abbey, Essex, 1966", *Post Med. Arch.* 3, 47-99.

Huggins, P.J. (1970b) "Waltham Abbey: Monastic Site and Prehistoric Evidence", *T.E.A.S. Third Series* II(3), 216-66.

Huggins, P.J. (1972) "Monastic Grange and Outer Close Excavations, Waltham Abbey, Essex 1970-2", *E.A.H.* 4, 30-127.

Huggins, P.J. (1973) "Excavation of Monastic Forge and Saxo-Norman Enclosure, Waltham Abbey, Essex, 1972-3", *E.A.H.* 5, 127-84.

Huggins, P.J. (1976) "Excavation of an Eleventh Century Viking Hall and Fourteenth Century Rooms at Waltham Abbey, Essex, 1969-71", *Med. Arch.* 20, 75-133.

Huggins, P.J. (1978) "Excavations of Belgic and Romano-British Farm with Middle Saxon Cemetery and Churches at Nazeingbury, Essex, 1975-6", *E.A.H.* 10, 29-117.

Huggins, P.J. (1976) "The Excavation of an Eleventh Century Viking Hall and Fourteenth Century Rooms at Waltham Abbey, Essex, 1969-71", *Med. Arch.* XX, 75-133.

Huggins, P.J. (1984) "A Note on a Viking Style Plate From Waltham Abbey, Essex, and its Implication for a Disputed Late-Viking Building", *Arch. J.* 141, 175-81.

Huggins, P.J. (1988a) "Excavations on the North Side of Sun Street, Waltham Abbey, Essex 1974-5: Saxon Burials, Precinct Wall, and South East Transept", *E.A.H.* 19, 117-53.

Huggins, P.J. (1988b) "Excavation at Market Place, Waltham Abbey, Essex 1981: The Moot Hall and Romano-British Occupation", *E.A.H.* 19, 196-214.

Huggins, P.J. (1989) "Excavations of the Collegiate and Augustinian Churches, Waltham Abbey, Essex, 1984-7", *Arch. J.* 146, 476-537.

Huggins, P. (1991a) "Waltham Abbey", *Current Archaeology* 125, 224-6.

Huggins, P. (1991b) "First Steps Towards the Minster Parish of London", *London Archaeologist* 6(11), 292-300.

Huggins, P.J. and Bascombe, K.N. (1992) "Excavations at Waltham Abbey, Essex, 1985-91: Three Pre-Conquest Churches and Norman Evidence", *Arch. J.* 149, 282-343.

Huggins, R.M. (1975) "The Significance of the Place-Name Wealdham", *Med. Arch.* XIX, 198-201.

Jones, W.T. (1980) "Early Saxon Cemeteries in Essex", in Buckley, D.G. ed. 1980, 87-95.

Laver, P.G. (1930) "*Sunecastre*, or the Camp of Asheldham", *T.E.A.S.* N.S. XIX., 180-5

MacGowan, K. (1987) "Saxon Timber Structures From The Barking Abbey Excavations 1985-6", *Essex Journal* 22, 35-8.

McDonald, J. and Snooks, G.D. (1985) "The Determinants of Manorial Income in Domesday England", *J. Econ. Hist.* XLV, 541-56.

Medlycott, M. (1990) *The Archaeological Survey of the A120 Trunk Road: Fieldwalking Report 1990.* Essex County Council Archaeology Section, Chelmsford.

Medlycott, M.(1992) *A120 Trunk Road: Archaeological Evaluations, 1991-2.* Essex County Council Archaeology Section, Chelmsford.

Metcalf, D.M. (1978) "Twelve Notes on Sceatta Finds", *Br. Num. J.* 46, 1-18.

Metcalf, D.M. (1984) "Monetary Circulation in Southern England in the First half of the Eighth Century", in Hill, D. and Metcalf, D.M. ed. *Sceattas in England and on the Continent.* B.A.R. British Series 128. Oxford.

Metcalf, D.M. (1993) *Thrymsas and Sceattas in the Ashmolean Museum Oxford. Volume 1.* Royal Numismatic Society and Ashmolean Museum, London.

Metcalf, D.M. and Lean, W. (1993) "The Battle of Maldon and the Minting of Crux Pennies in Essex": Post Hoc Propter Hoc?; in Cooper, J. 1993a, 205-224.

Milton, B. (1984) "Excavations at St. Clement's Church, West Thurrock, Essex, 1979", in Turner, R. 1984a, 1-14.

Morris, R. (1989) *Churches in the landscape*, London: Dent

Morris, S. and Buckley, D.G. (1978) "Excavations at Danbury Camp, Essex", *E.A.H.* 10, 1-28.

Musty, A.E.S. (1978) "Exploratory Excavation Within the Monastic Precinct, Waltham Abbey, 1972", *E.A.H.* 10, 127-73.

Musty, J. Wade, K., and Rogerson, A. (1973) "A Viking Pin and Inlaid Knife From Bonhunt Farm, Wicken Bonhunt, Essex", *Antiq. J.* 53, 289.

Newman, J. (1988) "East Anglia Kingdom Survey: Interim Report on the South East Suffolk Pilot Field Survey", *Bull. Sutton Hoo, Res. Comm.* 5, 10-12.

Newman, J. (1992) "The Late Roman and Anglo-Saxon Settlement Pattern in the Sandlings of Suffolk", in Carver, M.O.H. ed. *The Age of Sutton Hoo*, 25-38. Boydell Press, Woodbridge.

Pewsey, S. and Brooks, A. (1993) *East Saxon Heritage: An Essex Gazetteer.* Alan Sutton, Stroud.

Priddy, D. (1991) "Medieval Pottery From Maplecroft, Sudbury Road, Castle Hedingham", *E.A.H.* 22, 174-6.

Rackham, O. (1986) *The Woods of South East Essex.* Rochford District Council, Rochford.

Rackham, O. (1993) *Trees and Woodland in the British Landscape.* Second Edition. Dent, London

Reaney, P.H. (1935) *The Place Names of Essex.* English Place Names Society XII, Cambridge.

Redknap, M. (1985) "Little Ilford, St. Mary the Virgin, 1984", *London Archaeologist* 5(2), 31-7.

Redknap, M. (1991) "The Saxon Pottery From Barking: Part 1, Local Wares", *London Archaeologist* 6(13), 353-360.

Redknap, M. (1992) "The Saxon Pottery From Barking: Part 2, the Continental Imports", *London Archaeologist* 6(14), 378-381.

Richards, J.D. (1991) *Viking Age England.* Batsford/English Heritage, London.

Rigold, S.E. (1975) "The Sutton Hoo Gold Coins in the Light of the Contemporary Background of Coinage on England", in Bruce-Mitford, B.M. *The Sutton Hoo Ship Burial, Vol. I.,* 633-77. British Museum, London.

Rigold, S.E. and Metcalf, D.M. (1984) "A Revised Check List of English Finds of Sceattas", in Hill, D. and Metcalf, D.M. ed. *Sceattas in England and on the Continent.* B.A.R. British Series 128, 245-68. Oxford.

Rippon, S. (1991) "Early Planned Landscapes in South East Essex", *E.A.H.* 22, 46-60.

Rodwell, K. (1987) *The Prehistoric and Roman Settlement at Kelvedon, Essex.* Chelmsford Archaeol. Trust. Rep. 6 / C.B.A. Res. Rep. 63, London.

Rodwell, W.J. (1976a) "The Archaeological Investigation of Hadstock Church, Essex", *Antiq. J.* 56, 55-71.

Rodwell, W.J. (1976b) "Some Unrecorded Archaeological Discoveries in Essex 1946-75", *E.A.H.* 8, 274-48.

Rodwell, W.J. (1978) "Relict Landscapes in Essex", in Bowen, H.C. and Fowler, P.J. ed. *Early Land Allotment in the British Isles.* B.A.R. Br. Series. 48, 89-98. Oxford.

Rodwell, W.J. (1980) "Ecclesiastical Sites and Structures in Essex", in Buckley, D.G ed. 1980, 118-22.

Rodwell, W. (1993a) *The Origins and Early Development of Witham, Essex: A Study in Settlement and Fortification, Prehistoric to Medieval.* Oxbow Monograph, 26, Oxford.

Rodwell, W. (1993b) "The Battle of Assandun and its Memorial Church: A Reappraisal", in Cooper ed. 1993a, 127-158.

Rodwell, W.J. and Rodwell, K.A. (1977) *Historic Churches: A Wasting Asset.* C.B.A. Res. Rep. 19, London.

Rodwell, W.J. and Rodwell, K.A. (1986) *Rivenhall : Investigations of a Villa, Church and Village, 1950-1977.* Chelmsford Archaeol. Trust. Rep. 4.1; C.B.A. Res. Rep. 55, London.

Rodwell, W.J. and Rodwell, K.A. (1993) *Rivenhall: Investigations of a Villa, Church and Village, 1950-1977. Volume 2: Specialist Studies.* Chelmsford Archaeol. Trust. Rep. 4.2; C.B.A. Res. Rep. 80, London.

Round, H. (1903) The Domesday Book. *V.C.H. Essex*, Vol. 1, 333-578.

Rumble, A. (1983) *Domesday Book.* Phillimore, Chichester.

Sawyer, P. (1983) "The Royal 'Tun' in Pre-Conquest England", in Wormald, P. ed. *Ideal and Reality in Frankish and Anglo-Saxon Society: Studies Presented to J.M. Wallace-Hadrill.* Blackwells, Oxford.

Scragg, D. ed. (1991) *The Battle of Maldon A.D. 991.* Blackwell/The Manchester Centre for Anglo-Saxon Studies.

Scull, C. (1992) "Before Sutton Hoo: Structures of Power and Society in Early East Anglia", in Carver, M.O.H. ed. *The Age of Sutton Hoo*, 3-23. Boydell Press, Woodbridge.

Spurrell, F. (1890) "Haestons Camps at Shoebury and Benfleet", *Essex Naturalist* iv, 150-3.

Taylor, C.C. (1974) *Domesday to Dormitory: The History of the Landscape of Great Shelford.*

Taylor, H.M. and Taylor, J. (1965) *Anglo-Saxon Architecture.* University Press, Cambridge.

Turner, R. (1982) *Ivy Chimneys, Witham: An Interim Report.* Essex County Council Archaeology Section Occasional Paper 2, Chelmsford.

Turner, R. ed (1984a) *Four Church Excavations in Essex.* Essex County Council (Archaeology Section) Occasional Paper 4, Chelmsford.

Turner, R. (1984b) "Excavations at St. Mary's Church West Bergholt, Essex, 1978", in Turner, R. 1984a, 43-63.

Tyler, S. (1992) "Anglo-Saxon Metalwork from Little Braxted", *E.A.H.* 23, 126-30.

V.C.H. Essex VI (1973) *The Becontree Hundred.* Institute of Historical Research, University of London.

V.C.H. Essex VII (1978) *Liberty of Havering-Atte-Bower.* Institute of Historical Research, University of London.

Vince, A. (1984) "New Light on Saxon Pottery From the London Area", *London Archaeologist* 4(16), 431-9.

Vince, A. (1990) *Saxon London: An Archaeological Investigation.* Seaby, London.

Wade, K. (1980) "A Settlement Site at Bonhunt Farm, Wicken Bonhunt, Essex", in Buckley, D.G. ed 1980, 96-102.

Wade, K. (1988) "Ipswich". in Hodges, R. and Hobley, B. eds. *The Rebirth of Towns in the West AD 700-1050.* C.B.A. Res. Rep. 68, London.

Wade-Martins, P. (1980) "Village Sites in the Launditch Hundred", *East Anglian Archaeology* 10.

Wallis, S. (1991) *Mill Lane/High Road Corner, Horndon-On-The-Hill. Archive Report.* Essex County Council Archaeology Section, Chelmsford.

Webster, C.E. and Cherry, J. (1973) "Medieval Britain in 1972", *Med. Arch.* XVII, 138-88.

Wilkinson, T. (1988) *Archaeology and the Environment in South East Essex: Rescue Archaeology Along the Grays Bypass 1979/80.* East Anglian Archaeology 42.

Williamson, T. (1984) *Roman and Medieval Settlement in North West Essex.* Unpublished Thesis, Cambridge.

Williamson, T. (1986) "The Development of Settlement in North West Essex: The Results of a Recent Field Survey", *E.A.H.* 17, 120-32.

Williamson, T. (1993) *The Origins of Norfolk.* University Press, Manchester.

Wymer, J.J. and Brown, N.R. (1995) *North Shoebury: Settlement and Economy in South-East Essex 1500BC-AD1500*, E. Anglian Archaeol. 75

Yorke, B. (1990) *Kings and Kingdoms of Early Anglo-Saxon England.* Seaby, London.

Medieval Essex

Jennifer C. Ward

The fifteen years since the archaeology conference held in 1978 have seen a steady stream of work in archaeology and local history. Inevitably, some areas have been better served than others; in some cases, progress has continued along lines already laid down in 1978, in others new questions are being asked. In this paper I shall look at the principal areas of change within the period c.1066-1500, with particular reference to rural and urban settlement and church archaeology. We have become increasingly aware in recent years of the extent of continuity with earlier periods; however, after 1066, there were significant changes in exploitation of the land, the growth of towns and the development of monasticism. Compared with the earlier periods, there is far more documentation, especially after c.1200, but archaeological finds are crucial to the understanding of many aspects of medieval society.

The impact of the Normans on the county, as seen in their castles and churches, is more visually dramatic than their numbers warrant. It has been calculated that there were about 300 of the French aristocracy in the county in 1086, compared with a rural population of about 14,000 families and 600 burgesses (townspeople) in Colchester and Maldon (Powell 1990, 3). Norman control is best epitomised by Colchester castle, begun c.1076, which has been the subject of archaeological investigation in the 1980s (Drury 1982, 398-9; Davies 1991, 63- 4). The 1988 excavation in the south-east corner at second floor level has probably revealed the outer walls of the Norman chapel, while the complete record of the external fabric has been a major aid in interpreting the original construction. At the time when it was erected the Anglo-Saxons of Essex would have been left in no doubt as to the power of their new lords.

The estates granted by William the Conqueror to his followers provide a framework for landholding which in several cases persisted throughout the Middle Ages. Certainly there were changes among the families who held these estates, as a result of forfeiture, failure of direct heirs, marriage, and royal grants. However the estate itself often remained remarkably intact. To take the most notable example, the de Vere earls of Oxford of Castle Hedingham proved to be remarkable survivors throughout the Middle Ages and beyond. The continued significance of lordship explains why castle sites remained important well beyond the Norman period. This does not apply so much to Colchester castle which was not a baronial residence and was primarily used as a prison from the fourteenth century (Drury 1982, 302). Yet at castle-residences, building is found throughout the Middle Ages as fashions and the status of the family changed. Over the past fifteen years, work has been done at Pleshey, and at Rayleigh where the outer bailey may be an addition of c.1200, while fourteenth and fifteenth-century work has been found at Writtle (Milton and Walker 1987, 39-44; Priddy 1988, 166-75; Ecclestone and Reidy 1992, 110). The example of Writtle makes it clear that the elite did not necessarily live in castles, as is also shown by the twelfth-century great hall and chapel at Harlowbury (Bartlett 1986, 31-5). Opportunities to excavate on these sites have to be taken when and where they arise, and we could still learn a lot more, especially about the later Middle Ages. Building accounts show that work was going on at places where the present building is of far less significance, as at Great Bardfield Hall (Ward 1992, 55).

The great Norman lords granted lands to their own followers in return for knight service, and some of these families were again remarkable survivors, being found as knights and county gentry in the thirteenth and fourteenth centuries. Others came into the gentry through marriage, purchase of land, and service to barons or Churchmen or at the royal court. Relatively little is known about the residences and lifestyle of these men in the twelfth century, although the mottes found at Elmdon and Bulmer may provide a clue (Milton and Priddy 1984-5, 116-18). We are far better informed about the period after 1200 through the work done by archaeologists and architectural historians on moated sites and timber-framed buildings. The excavation at Southchurch Hall gives a good idea of a manorial centre c.1300 (Jackson 1987, 34-8). Recent work on fifteenth-century brick building has thrown new light on the aspirations of the families responsible for houses like Faulkbourne Hall (Smith 1985, 8, 18).

It was only the Anglo-Saxon aristocracy that was swept away after 1066. Elsewhere there is continuity, with both inhabitants and their settlements. It is in connection with rural settlement that investigation is most needed, and as yet relatively little has been done. Local studies based on documentation, maps and fieldwork add greatly to our knowledge of settlement as James Kemble has shown in his study of the boundaries of Ingatestone and Fryerning (Kemble 1993, 14-17). Some excavation has been carried out, as at Roxwell quarry in Chignall St James (Brooks 1992, 39-50) and at Stansted (Brooks 1987, 43-6; Brooks 1989, 7-9). Fieldwalking and field surveys are especially important as the amount of topographical information in manorial documents is limited, and, although the Walker, Chapman and Andre and early Ordnance Survey and tithe maps are useful, they inevitably reflect a later situation.

Settlement in the Middle Ages was anything but static; villages, hamlets and farmsteads grew, declined, and moved. The Normans came into a county which was already agriculturally developed and well settled. There was certainly potential for expansion but most villages received a mention in Domesday Book. The pattern of dispersed rural settlement with a variety of settlement types was well established. We find nucleated and polyfocal villages, hamlets and farmsteads. This has been brought out by Tom Williamson's field survey of the development of settlement in north-west Essex, an area of boulder clay, dissected by the valleys of the River Cam and its tributaries (Williamson 1986, 120-32). Hamlets and villages are situated on the valley floors and margins, with hamlets and farmsteads on the clay interfluves away from the major valleys. This type of field survey is an urgent priority for other areas of the county.

Domesday Book provides an insight into the pattern of settlement in 1066-86 especially as for Essex it often mentions hamlets as well as the main villages; this may well be due to the inclusion of Essex in the more detailed Little Domesday, and also to the pattern of landholding, with many villages being divided between several lords, each with his own manor. It is therefore possible to plot many manors on the ground, often with the aid of later documentation and maps. The question however arises as to whether the peasants belonging to a particular manor would be living near the centre of the manor, or whether the peasants of a village divided into three or four manors would be living altogether. Domesday does not provide an answer to this question, but there are signs that manors could well be differentiated on the ground. Work done in Cambridgeshire indicates that manors with lord and peasants can be distinguished within a village (Taylor 1977, 190-2), and evidence from the Walker Essex maps shows that peasant housing in the sixteenth century was still to be found round the manor house, as at Widford and Little

Leighs (Edwards and Newton 1984, plates 8, 19). This idea of a manor complex needs to be tested by fieldwork, but it is possible that by using Domesday likely foci of settlement can be identified. Thus at Matching there may well have been at least three foci, round Matching Hall and the church with the estates of Robert Gernon and Edmund son of Algot, Housham Hall which belonged to the honour of William de Warenne, and Brent Hall of which Geoffrey de Mandeville's small estate may have been part. These settlements would have been small; at Housham Hall in 1086 there were ten villeins, three bordars and one serf (VCH 8 1983, 198; *Domesday Book 2* 1783, fols 20b, 60a, 64a, 93b).

Essex was heavily wooded in 1086 and extensive assarting took place in the twelfth and thirteenth centuries, resulting in the expansion of existing settlements and the growth of new ones. This was due to the rise in the population of England which virtually doubled between the eleventh and early fourteenth centuries, reaching between five and six million by 1340. For north-west Essex, Williamson has shown that colonisation resulted in the growth of polyfocal villages, as at Strethall, Chrishall and Elmdon, and in new settlements such as the one next to High Wood in Elmdon.

More fieldwork is needed to establish the extent of the expansion, possibly on the lines of what has been carried out in East Anglia (Wade-Martins 1989, 149-65). Here investigation in the field found that settlement round greens was very unusual before the twelfth century and that the earliest pottery round the greens dated from c.1100. It was also rare to find churches on greens. Greens are frequently found in Essex; in Matching parish small settlements grew up at Carter's Green, Matching Tye and Newman's End, and the main village came to be located at Matching Green. Greens are to be found round Thaxted and Stebbing, and many other places. According to Reaney, *The Place-Names of Essex*, the names of greens are mostly first found in the thirteenth or fourteenth centuries, but too much cannot be made of this in view of the sparser documentation for the twelfth century. Field surveys might well provide the answer to the date of settlement.

There are many possible reasons for the varied pattern of settlement of the twelfth and thirteenth centuries. Where there was nucleated settlement, it is possible that lords were responsible for its development. In some cases this was clearly the case, as at Pleshey and Brook Walden, where settlements grew up round a castle or abbey. The creation of a market, often found in the thirteenth century, may have encouraged nucleation at a place where business was likely to prosper, as at Ingatestone. Housing built on common land might develop into the main part of the village; this may have been the case at Ingrave (Fig. 1) where growth was possibly fostered by traffic along the road to Tilbury. The creation of parks may have affected settlement; over one hundred parks are known to have been created in Essex between the twelfth and fifteenth centuries (Cantor 1983, 29-31). Areas of dispersed settlement may have been the result of weak manorial development; the preponderance of sokemen in north Essex in Domesday can be taken as a sign of this.

What is clear from recent investigations is the extent to which lords were exploiting the land in the thirteenth century. This was an age of inflation, particularly serious under King John (1199-1216), and lords exploited their manors directly under the supervision of their own officials instead of leasing them out as was the earlier and later pattern. Here the work which has been done on tim-

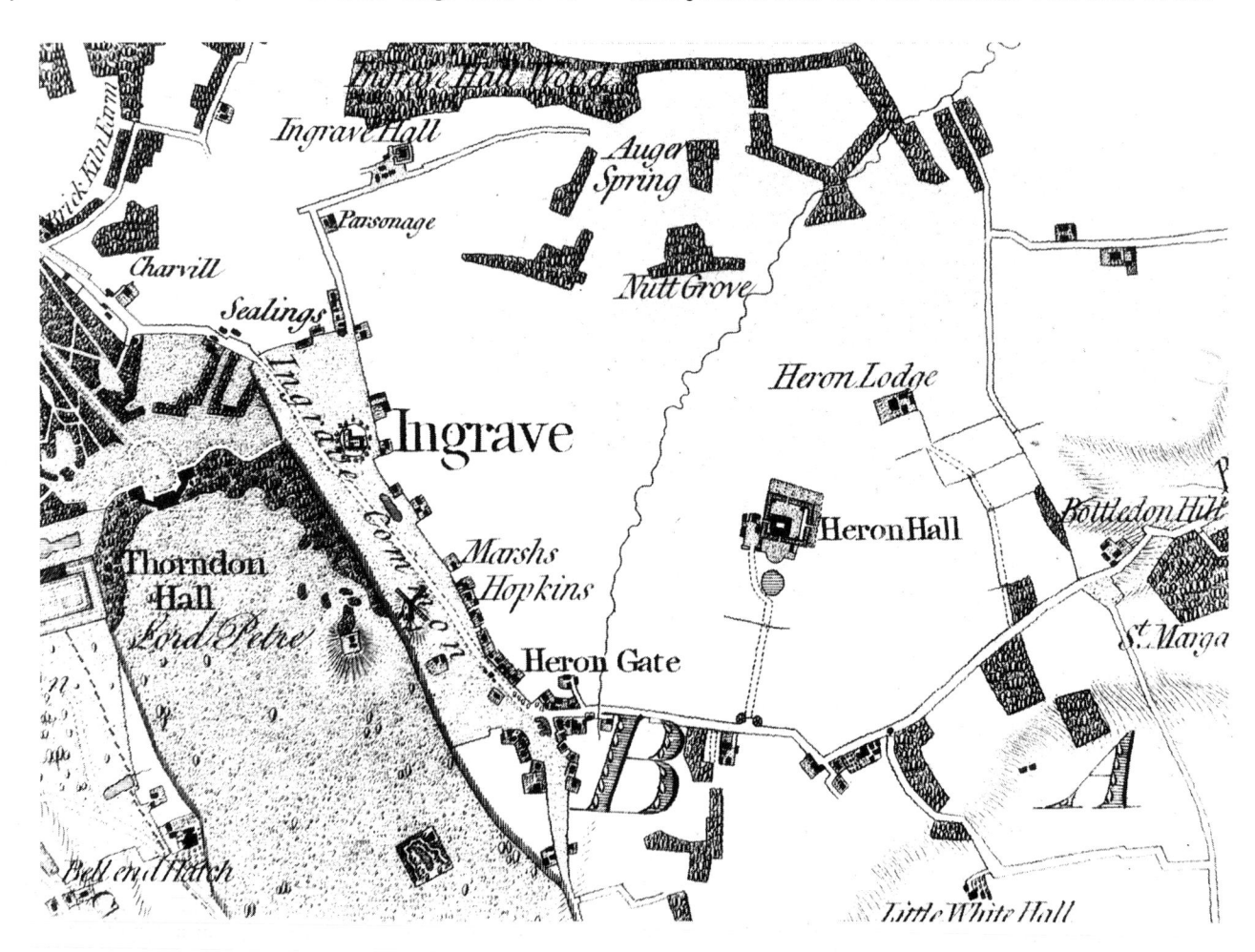

Fig. 1 Ingrave according to the Chapman and Andre Map of Essex, 1777, showing housing development on Ingrave Common along the road to Tilbury and away from Ingrave Hall

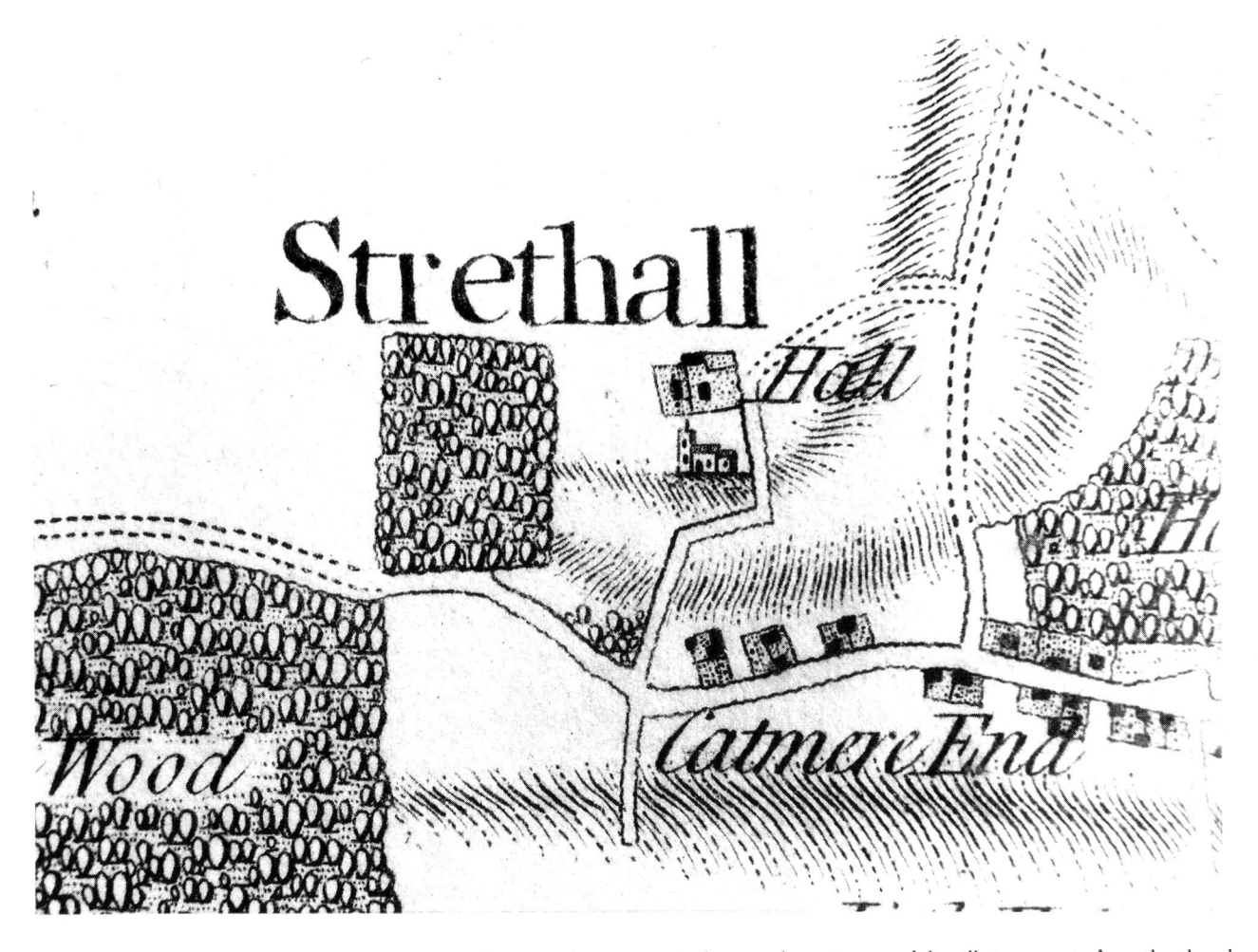

Fig. 2 Strethall according to the Chapman and Andre Map of Essex, 1777, showing the main part of the village separate from the church and hall due to late medieval shrinkage

ber-framed buildings has given us a much better knowledge of manorial complexes, while the barns at Coggeshall and Cressing emphasise the importance to lords of grain production, both for domestic consumption and for sale (Stenning 1993, 51-75). Animal husbandry was also important. The importance of sheep pasture on the marshes has long been known, but investigation of the sea-walls at Foulness has provided a better understanding of marshland reclamation and its problems. The discovery of kiddles (fish-traps) off Mersea Island and Bradwell-on-Sea has pointed to another area of manorial profit (Crump 1990, 31-3; Crump 1992, 38-42).

The famines of 1315-17, the Black Death of 1348-9 and subsequent plagues meant that population dropped substantially and only began to rise again in the 1520s. This was likely to have a long-term effect on settlement. The number of deserted villages in Essex is less than in neighbouring counties, yet we know from work done by L.Poos on late medieval population that Essex suffered a high level of mortality (Poos 1991, 96-103). Recent fieldwork has pointed to widespread shrinkage of villages and hamlets and the disappearance of farms. At Horsham Hall in Helions Bumpstead, a system of hollow-ways and platforms indicates settlement but it is not known when it was deserted (Charge 1984-5, 131-2). Williamson has shown that a number of sites in north-west Essex were abandoned in the fourteenth or fifteenth century, and that other places shrank; Strethall lost its loose nucleation and now has two clusters of houses, one next to the church and one to the south (Fig. 2). At Belchamp St Paul (Fig. 3) ribbon development along Church Street disappeared, and the modern centre of the village is separate from the church (Wallis 1991, 154). Erosion by the sea also has to be taken into account in the later Middle Ages; this may have been the fate of a village at Little Holland (Andrews and Brooks 1989, 74). It is likely that as more fieldwork is done more shrunken sites will appear; taxation records of 1428 list thirty-seven Essex parishes with less than ten inhabitants (*Feudal Aids*, 2, 183); there were approximately four hundred ancient parishes in the county.

Sites which have been excavated show farmsteads going out of use in the later Middle Ages. A farmstead at North Ockendon which possibly grew up as a result of assarting may well have gone out of use by 1500 (Wilkinson 1988, 67-8). On the Round Wood site at Stansted three timber structures of the twelfth and thirteenth centuries went out of use in the fourteenth (Brooks 1989, 7). The same can be said of the isolated rural settlement at the Molehill Green site (Brooks 1987, 45). Too much however should not be made of single structures which may have been in bad repair and been rebuilt on a different site.

It is probably too early as yet to reach a synthesis on late medieval desertion. What will be interesting to look out for is variation within the county. It may well be that industrial expansion, notably the growth of the cloth industry, and trade with London and elsewhere enabled some communities to grow while others shrank (McIntosh 1986, 136-78; Campbell *et al.* 1993).

The investigation of rural settlement needs to be treated as the main priority in the next few years. In comparison far more is known about medieval towns. Yet we need to know more about the relationships between villages and towns and get a better knowledge of medieval communications. The existence of good communications can explain whether a place was likely to prosper or decline.

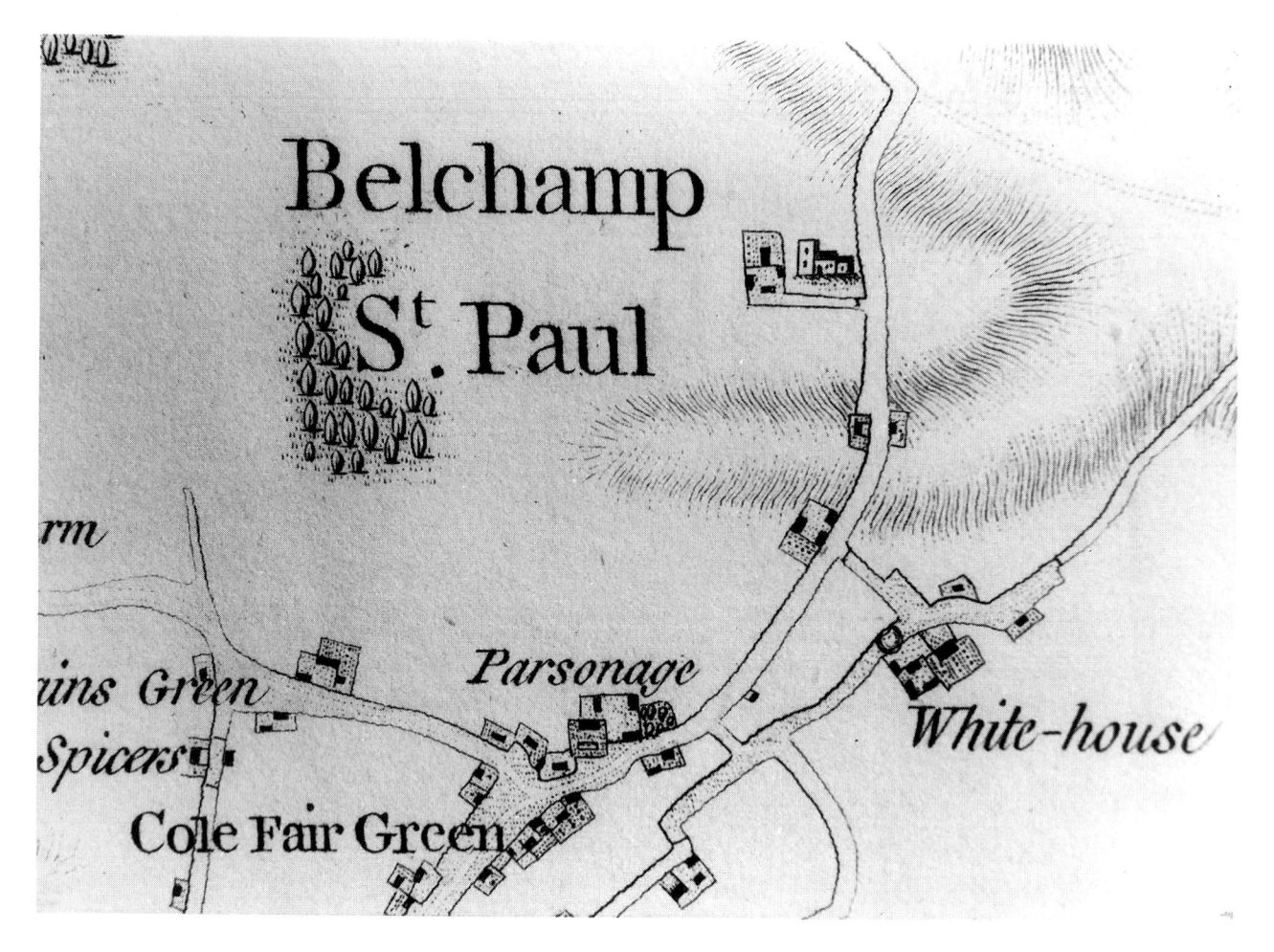

Fig. 3 Belchamp St. Paul according to the Chapman and Andre Map of Essex, 1777, showing the church isolated from the main part of the village due to late medieval shrinkage

As trade, towns, industry, and travel grew from the twelfth century, so communications became more important, and it is likely that historians have underestimated the amount of traffic on roads in the medieval period. Certainly water transport was cheaper, and the coast and rivers saw an increase of business, but a large part of the county was reliant on roads and in some cases roads were used in preference to water. Some roads were deliberately realigned to take them through new markets, and the building of bridges could have a marked effect on the local economy, as at Chelmsford c.1200 and at Stratford with the Bow and Channelsea bridges about a hundred years before. Roman roads continued to be used with some realignments, but what happened in parts of the county without Roman roads, as in the area between Horndon-on-the-Hill and Rainham where markets proliferated in the thirteenth century (Ward 1987, 104)? Were new roads and bridges developed in this area, or did it rely mainly on the Thames and to some extent remain cut off from the rest of the county? To find the answers to these questions, we again need a combination of use of documents, maps and field survey; references to roads in charters, and accounts of movement in household accounts have to be combined with topography and possibly excavation.

The growth of markets and towns is testified all over Europe in the twelfth and thirteenth centuries and the investigation of towns was well under way in 1978. This is a subject where work is ongoing in both historical (Britnell 1986; Grieve 1988) and archaeological terms. Our knowledge of both Colchester and Chelmsford is expanding, but what is of particular importance is the way in which archaeology is building up our knowledge of the topography, buildings and activities of the small towns of the county; this is an area on which relatively little work has been done until recently. At Waltham Abbey the market-place was first mentioned c.1235, and the Moot Hall was built there c.1250 to house the hundred and probably also the manor courts (Huggins et al. 1988b, 196-214). There is thirteenth-century evidence of the market on the north side of Market Street in Old Harlow and the discovery of Harlow ware pottery is probably an indication of local activity; this ties in with the grant of a market charter in 1218 to the abbey of Bury St Edmunds, and it is significant that the market was sited half a mile to the southeast of Harlowbury, by the junction of the London-Norwich and Hertford-Dunmow roads (Andrews 1991, 101-14). A similar shift in settlement because of the growth of a market has been indicated at Coggeshall (Godbold and Andrews 1992, 159-61).

Medieval towns underwent change, in fortune as well as topography, and it is important to discover whether there was shrinkage and economic decline at the end of the Middle Ages. This is an ongoing debate in historical circles. For a small town to flourish it is generally agreed that it needed a wide range of crafts and trades which would meet the needs of the surrounding area. Sometimes these are listed in rentals or mentioned incidentally in court rolls. Hatfield Broad Oak according to a 1328 rental had several smiths, tailors, cooks, brewers, and butchers, together with a carpenter, hatter, glover and draper; there was a bakery, tannery and wine-shop (Essex Record Office, D/DBa M10). Such information is relatively rare and therefore archaeological finds connected with the cloth, leather, pottery and metal crafts (including cutlery) are of inestimable value in charting the activities of townsmen and their fortunes.

In addition it is vital to trace the patterns of internal trade, and in view of the scarceness of documentation for some crafts, artefacts become invaluable. Pottery rarely appears in documents, but the investigation of pottery distribution can indicate lines of trade, as has been shown with a recent study of Scarborough ware (Cunningham and Farmer 1983, 54-67). Although there is considerable documentation on the cloth industry, much of it is concerned with taxation and customs duties, and there is little on distribution. The government never saw fit to put a tax on leather and therefore documentation is minimal even though it may well have been the most important industry in many places. There is however a difficulty here on the archaeological side because of the problems of survival of organic material.

Three sites in particular have provided some of the answers on the activities and fortunes of small towns, much of the work being done by Steven Bassett and David Andrews. On the industrial side, David Andrews has added to the work of Ken Newton (1960) on the cutlery industry at Thaxted (Andrews 1989a, 110-19). The site in Weaverhead Lane, with its boneworking waste, shows that the Thaxted cutlers were mainly engaged in putting bone handles on knives. The material mainly dates from the fifteenth century, and this part of the town contracted by the sixteenth century when it is known from other evidence that the industry was in decline.

Some of the most interesting urban research of the 1980s has been carried out at Harwich (Milton 1984-5, 23-7; Andrews et al. 1990, 57-91). Among the excavations and watching briefs, the Methodist chapel site in Church Street showed at least three phases of building and 'one of the best stratified assemblages known from the county' of pottery, with a wide range of imports. The town's thirteenth and fourteenth-century archaeological deposits are well preserved, and this was a time when the level in the town rose by up to 1.4 metres. This has been interpreted as a possible indication of dynamic activity, especially when it is linked to the three building phases and the intensive use of the areas behind for outbuildings. This interpretation is borne out by the vigorous lordship of the earls of Norfolk, not only in securing charters, but at one point compelling ships bound for Ipswich to put in at Harwich. Moreover, Harwich was an important base of operations early in the Hundred Years War. It is probable that the town was replanned c.1300 with a layout of parallel streets (West, Church and King's Head Streets), and at this time the sites in Church Street show that sand or clay was dumped to raise the level. The pottery shows a range of trading contacts in the thirteenth century, with London-type ware in the early to mid-thirteenth century, followed by Hedingham and Scarborough ware. Imports of Saintonge ware from south-west France were coming in c.1300, and German ware at the end of the Middle Ages.

At Saffron Walden work on the town in the twelfth and thirteenth centuries has shown that it was laid out in two phases (Bassett 1982a, 15-27). The early twelfth-century planned layout round Bury Hill, with High, Castle and Church Streets, has to be distinguished from the thirteenth-century layout to the south. This second phase should probably be associated with the Bohuns who succeeded to the earldom of Essex after the death of William de Mandeville in 1227, and may be associated with Earl Humphrey's charter to the burgesses which has to be dated to c.1300 rather than 1236 (Ward 1986). In any case it proved to be too ambitious and was not developed by the medieval burgesses. It would be interesting to know more about the fortunes of the town in the later Middle Ages; the scale of buildings, notably the church, and the references to a wide variety of trades in the court rolls after 1381 make it possible that we are dealing with a flourishing and prosperous small town at the end of the Middle Ages (Cromarty 1967, 104-14, 122-39, 181-6).

The work which is being done in urban archaeology underlines the importance of presenting as full a picture as possible of the life of people in the Middle Ages. A similar comment can be made on church archaeology which in the last fifteen years has built on the foundations laid at Rivenhall, Asheldham and Hadstock, and increased our knowledge of both religious houses and parish churches. The great increase in the number of religious houses in the county, mainly in the twelfth century, means that they were a significant part of the medieval landscape and study of their physical remains is vital in understanding medieval society, not only at the time of foundation but through to the Dissolution in 1536-40. In 1978 Warwick Rodwell stressed the importance of the work done at Waltham Abbey partly because of the findings for the Anglo-Saxon period and also because of the investigation of the monastic complex as a whole. This need to put the site in context remains important and not only for church archaeology. Further work at Waltham Abbey and the publication of pre-1978 excavations has added much to our understanding of monastic life. In addition to information about the monastic buildings (Musty et al. 1978, 127-73), more is now known about the work done on the church in the twelfth and thirteenth centuries, and about the line of the precinct wall, built c.1370 (Huggins et al. 1988a, 117-53). Industrial activities may have included the manufacture of vellum and parchment. Information of a different kind came from the analysis of seeds from a Waltham Abbey pit, notably black henbane and hemlock, possibly used as painkillers and throwing light on the medical knowledge a monastic house would possess (Moffat 1987, 121-4). Taking all the information together, we now know a considerable amount about the monastic complex and its activities over the whole of the Middle Ages.

Information about monastic life and death has resulted from excavations at Stratford Langthorne, founded by William de Montfichet in 1134. As a result of the discovery of burials by British Rail engineers in 1983, part of the monastic cemetery was excavated, and the north-east wall of the chancel and the north transept of the abbey church were discovered. Comparison of the excavations with documentary material shows that the cloisters and infirmary lay to the north of the church (Watson 1989, 33-7). The 128 skeletons excavated have been analysed and throw an interesting light on monastic lifestyle (Stuart-Macadam 1986, 67-71). It can be assumed that we are dealing with the monks' cemetery; 99% of the individuals who could be sexed were male. Only eight died under the age of eighteen, a reminder that the Cistercians, to whose order the abbey belonged, did not accept child oblates; in any case the general trend by c.1200 was for novices to be in their late teens. Sixty died over the age of thirty-five; no one lived over the age of fifty-five. Diet was adequate since there was no evidence for scurvy and rickets. Osteoarthritis was common, but there was little sign that the inmates engaged in heavy manual work. There was very little evidence of physical injury, although one man died of wounds inflicted by a weapon. Here there appears to be an insoluble mystery.

Ideally monastic sites need to be put in context and archaeological discoveries used to fill out the life of the inmates. This however is not always possible, and in some cases the discovery and layout of a site represents a major advance. This applies to a number of religious houses examined over the last fifteen years. Excavations at Cressing between 1978 and 1981 revealed the chapel (Hope 1987, 67-71), and excavations on the site are continuing (Andrews 1993). At St Botolph's, Colchester, the square east end of the church and the south transept have been discovered (Davies 1991, 65; Crossan 1992, 103).

Standing remains have been surveyed at Tilty (Andrews and Gilman 1992, 152-7). The Audley End courtyard garden excavation has revealed remains of the layout of Walden abbey, founded by Geoffrey de Mandeville as a Benedictine house c.1140 (Cunningham 1988, 266-8). The monastic cloister lay beneath the courtyard. Some of the buildings including the chapter-house were located, as were parts of the church, part of the tiled floor of the nave surviving *in situ*. Some idea of the size of the abbey church can be gauged from the foundations of the chancel which was more than twenty-eight metres long.

It is particularly interesting that the last fifteen years have seen some increase of knowledge of both friaries and hospitals. Being smaller and poorer foundations, these have not attracted so much attention, although both fulfilled an important role in the medieval world. Documentation tends to be more sparse, although Ray Powell has recently shown what can be done from documents in the case of the hospitals at East and West Tilbury (Powell 1988, 154-8). Hospitals can be difficult to locate, as in the instance of Brook Street hospital at Brentwood (Godbold 1990, 151-4). Likewise the whereabouts of the buildings of St Leonard's hospital at Newport remain a mystery, although more is now known of its documentary history, and the finds of moulded stonework show that the early thirteenth-century buildings were probably elaborate (Andrews and Nurse 1989, 84-91). One hospital which can be located is Colchester's medieval leper hospital in the churchyard of St Mary Magdalen (Crossan 1990, 129). Two hospital buildings have been found, one of them possibly the hospital's original chapel which was enlarged c.1200 to form the first parish church of St Mary Magdalen. Among the burials in the church was one containing a pewter chalice, probably the grave of a master of the hospital. Among the excavations carried out at Maldon, the site of the Carmelite friary, founded in 1293, has been discovered; the 1991 excavations revealed the north and east sides of the cloister, with burials set into the cloister floor, and possibly part of the church (Bryant 1991, 155-6; Bryant and Isserlin 1992, 106-7).

In dealing with religious houses, as with other areas of research, it is important for documentary and archaeological work to go hand in hand. The archaeology can do much to set the site in its social context, as the work at Waltham Abbey and Stratford Langthorne shows. Work is bound to be piecemeal as sites become available. It is important that we maintain our concern with the overall development of the site throughout its history, with the people who lived there and the activities which went on. An overall synthesis for the county will also be needed in order to see how the individual sites fit into a larger whole.

Parish church archaeoloogy is now regarded as a vital subject of investigation, and it may well become an even greater priority over the next decade, partly because of changes in liturgical and social uses of the church, but more because of financial difficulties which may lead to an increasing number of churches becoming redundant. It is important that attention is not confined to traditional parish churches, but extended to nonconformist chapels and Roman Catholic churches as well. Considerations of time and expense mean that it will rarely be possible to make a full examination of fabric and fittings, but recent work has shown that information can be gleaned from a more cursory examination. Whatever type of investigation is undertaken, it remains important to see the church as part of the local settlement and landscape and also in a broader context if matters such as pilgrimage and cultural influences are being considered.

The fullest building information is gained from excavation and a thorough examination of the fabric. Recent excavation revealed the early twelfth-century circular nave at St Clement's church in West Thurrock (Harrold 1991, 4-6). Sheltered housing development in the grounds of Little Holland Hall enabled the site of the church to be excavated in order to recover the ground plan; four building phases were identified and in spite of problems over dating it appears that an eleventh to twelfth-century church was enlarged twice by the fourteenth century (Andrews and Brooks 1989, 74-83).

The case of Bradfield church near Manningtree (Barford 1991, 173-4) shows that a less thorough examination can still produce valuable results. The stripping of external rendering and some internal plaster revealed new details of the church's architectural history; the porch which had been thought to be fourteenth century turned out to be largely a nineteenth century brick rebuilding with the medieval stone mouldings reset, and the east wall of the chancel only had 1-1.4 metres of its earliest stonework standing, the early work being replaced by post- medieval brick.

Although the investigation of structure is undoubtedly important, the study of individual details is equally significant for the light thrown on liturgy and ritual, cults, cultural influences, and ecclesiastical patronage. All these are areas of growing interest at present. The restoration of the twelfth-century wall paintings at Copford and the discovery of new paintings make it possible to assess artistic influences, learn more of contemporary costume, and get an idea of what twelfth-century people knew of the Bible. Inevitably, puzzles remain; why was the rare painting of the raising of Jairus' daughter included? The redecoration of the church at Great Burstead revealed traces of fourteenth-century paintings in the south aisle and south chapel which apparently dated from the same time as the construction of the aisle; subjects included the Virgin Mary and St Michael, and also St Christopher (Andrews 1989b, 150). Here were three of the most popular saints of the late medieval world. Sculptures have rarely survived, but the discovery at Waltham Abbey of a damaged statue of the Madonna and Child, dated to c.1380, underlines the importance of the cult of the Virgin Mary at that time, and the statue may well be associated with a local gild (Huggins *et al.* 1988a, 142-3; Dean 1993, 51-5). We need to know a lot more about liturgical change, and a combination of documentary and archaeological work is again called for.

A great deal has been achieved in the past fifteen years, and this paper has had to be selective. Looking ahead, the main priority for the medieval period must be to gain a greater understanding of rural settlement. More work can still be done in the urban and ecclesiastical fields, and here the concerns are ongoing, although it is important to be aware of change over time and of the need to reconstruct people's lives and environment. The years from 1066 to 1500 were a time of substantial change and swings of fortune. Much work can be done on a local basis adopting a multidisciplinary approach and combining documentary research and fieldwork. At the same time there will be a need for wider surveys so that county developments can be seen in perspective. All this calls for interdisciplinary work by historians, archaeologists and others; we shall need our magnifying glasses and walking boots, and the prospects for future discoveries are exciting.

References

Andrews, D., 1989a 'A late medieval cutlery manufacturing site at Weaverhead Lane, Thaxted', *Essex Archaeology and History* 20, 110-19.

Andrews, D., 1989b 'Great Burstead, church of St Mary Magdalen', in A. Bennett and P. Gilman (ed.) 'Work of the Essex County Council Archaeology Section, 1988', *Essex Archaeology and History* 20, 150.

Andrews, D., 1991 'An archaeological sequence at the edge of Harlow market-place', *Essex Archaeology and History* 22, 101-14.

Andrews, D. ed., 1993 *Cressing Temple. A Templar and Hospitaller Manor in Essex*, Essex County Council

Andrews, D., and Boutwood, J., 1984-5 'Coggeshall Barn, Discoveries 1983-4', *Essex Archaeology and History* 16, 150-3.

Andrews, D., and Brooks, H., 1989 'An Essex Dunwich: the lost church at Little Holland Hall', *Essex Archaeology and History* 20, 74-83.

Andrews, D., and Nurse, B., 1989 'The hospital of St Leonard's at Newport', *Essex Archaeology and History* 20, 84-91.

Andrews, D., Milton, B., and Walker, H., 1990 'Harwich: its archaeological potential as revealed in excavations at George Street and Church Street', *Essex Archaeology and History* 21, 57-91.

Andrews, D., and Gilman, P.J., 1992 'Tilty abbey: a note on the surviving remains', *Essex Archaeology and History* 23, 152-7.

Barford, P., 1991 'Bradfield St Lawrence's church', *Essex Archaeology and History* 22, 173-4.

Bartlett, R., 1986 'Excavations at Harlowbury manor and chapel, Old Harlow, Essex', *Essex Journal* 21, 31-5.

Bassett, S.R., 1982a *Saffron Walden to AD 1300*, Council for British Archaeology

Bassett, S.R., 1982b *Saffron Walden: excavations and research 1972-80*, Chelmsford Archaeological Trust Report 2, CBA Research Report 45.

Britnell, R.H., 1986 *Growth and decline in Colchester, 1300-1525*, Cambridge

Brooks, H., 1987 'The Stansted Project: a report on the first year's work', *Essex Journal* 22, 43-7.

Brooks, H., 1989 'The Stansted Project: a report on the second and third years' work', *Essex Journal* 24, 6-10.

Brooks, H., 1992 'Two rural medieval sites in Chignall St James: excavations 1989', *Essex Archaeology and History* 23, 39-50.

Bryant, S., 1991 'Maldon friary', in P.J. Gilman (ed.), 'Excavations in Essex 1990', *Essex Archaeology and History* 22, 155-6.

Bryant, S., and Isserlin, R., 1992 'Maldon friary', in P.J. Gilman (ed.), 'Archaeology in Essex 1991', *Essex Archaeology and History* 23, 106-7.

Campbell, B.M.S., Galloway, J.A., Keene, D., and Murphy, M., 1993 *A medieval capital and its grain supply: agrarian production and distribution in the London region c.1300*, Historical Geography Research Series No30.

Cantor, L., 1983 *The medieval parks of England. A gazetteer*, Loughborough.

Charge, B., 1984-5 'Moated sites survey: north-west Essex', in D. Priddy (ed.), 'Excavations in Essex, 1983-4', *Essex Archaeology and History* 16, 131-2.

Cromarty, D., 1967 'Chepyng Walden 1381-1420: a study from the court rolls', *Essex Journal* 2, 104-13, 122-39, 181-6.

Crossan, C., 1990 'Colchester, St Mary Magdalen's churchyard', in P.J. Gilman (ed.), 'Excavations in Essex 1989', *Essex Archaeology and History* 21, 129.

Crossan, C., 1992 'Colchester, St Botolph's priory church', in P.J. Gilman (ed.), 'Archaeology in Essex 1991', *Essex Archaeology and History* 23, 103.

Crummy, P., 1981 *Aspects of Anglo-Saxon and Norman Colchester*, Colchester Archaeological Report 1, CBA Research Report 39.

Crump, R.W., 1990 'The embanking of Foulness', *Essex Journal* 25, 31-3.

Crump, R.W., and Wallis, S., 1992 'Kiddles and the Foulness fishing industry', *Essex Journal* 27, 38-42.

Cunningham, C.M., 1988 'Saffron Walden, Audley End', in D. Priddy (ed.), 'Excavations in Essex 1987', *Essex Archaeology and History* 19, 266-8.

Cunningham, C.M., Farmer, P.G., and Farmer, N.C., 1983 'A Horse and Rider Aquamanile from Harwich, and the significance of Scarborough ware in Essex', *Essex Archaeology and History* 15, 54-67.

Davies, M., 1991 'Current archaeological opportunities in Colchester', *Essex Journal* 26, 63-6.

Dean, D., 1993 'The medieval gilds of Waltham Holy Cross', *Essex Journal* 28, 51-55.

Domesday Book, 1783-1816 *Liber censualis vocatus Domesday Book*, ed. A. Farley and H. Ellis, 4 volumes, London.

Drury, P.J., 1982 'Aspects of the origin and development of Colchester castle', *Archaeological Journal* 139, 302-419.

Ecclestone, J., and Reidy, K., 1992 'Writtle, Agricultural College', in P.J. Gilman (ed.), 'Archaeology in Essex 1991', *Essex Archaeology and History* 23, 110.

Edwards, A.C., and Newton, K.C., 1984 *The Walkers of Hanningfield: surveyors and mapmakers extraordinary*, London

Feudal Aids Inquisitions and Assessments relating to Feudal Aids, 6 volumes, London, 1899-1921.

Godbold, S., 1990 'The site of the medieval hospital at Brook Street, Brentwood', *Essex Archaeology and History* 21, 151-4.

Grieve, H., 1988 *The Sleepers and the Shadows. Chelmsford: a town, its people and its past*, Essex Record Office Publication No100.

Havis, R., and Brooks, H., 1991 'The Stansted Project: the fourth and fifth years' work', *Essex Journal* 26, 40-2.

Harrold, C., 1991 'West Thurrock church restored to life', *Essex Journal* 26, 4-6.

Hope, J.H., 1986 and 1987 'The Knights Templar and excavations at the Cressing Temple, 1978-81', *Essex Journal* 21, 31-5; 22, 67-71.

Huggins, P.J., et al, 1988a (with contributions by K.N. Bascombe, R.M. Huggins and G. Putnam) 'Excavations on the north side of Sun Street, Waltham Abbey, Essex 1974-75: Saxon burials, precinct wall and south-east transept', *Essex Archaeology and History* 19, 117-53.

Huggins, P.J., et al, 1988b (with contributions by K.N. Bascombe and R.M. Huggins) 'Excavations in the market place, Waltham Abbey, Essex 1981: the moot hall and Romano-British occupation', *Essex Archaeology and History* 19, 196-214.

Jackson, J.R., 1987 'Excavations at Southchurch Hall. An interim report', *Essex Archaeology and History* 18, 34-8.

Kemble, J., 1993 'The history and archaeology of boundary changes in an Essex parish', *Essex Journal* 28, 14-17.

McIntosh, M.K., 1986 *Autonomy and Community. The royal manor of Havering, 1200-1500*, Cambridge.

Milton, B.H., 1984-5 'Excavations at the White Hart Hotel, George Street, Harwich, 1979', *Essex Archaeology and History* 16, 23-7.

Milton, B., and Priddy, D., 1984-5 'Surveys of two small earthwork castles at Elmdon and Bulmer', in D. Priddy (ed.), 'Work of the Essex County Council Archaeology Section 1983-4', *Essex Archaeology and History* 16, 116-18.

Milton, B., and Walker, H., 1987 'Excavations at Bellingham Lane, Rayleigh, Essex', *Essex Archaeology and History* 18, 39-44.

Moffat, B., 1987 'A curious assemblage of seeds from Waltham Abbey', *Essex Archaeology and History* 18, 121-3.

Musty, A.E.S., 1978 'Exploratory excavation within the monastic precinct, Waltham Abbey, 1972', *Essex Archaeology and History* 10, 127-73.

Newton, K.C., 1960 *Thaxted in the fourteenth century*, Essex Record Office Publication No33.

Poos, L.R., 1991 *A rural society after the Black Death: Essex 1350-1525*, Cambridge.

Powell, W.R., 1988 'The medieval hospitals at East and West Tilbury and Henry VIII's forts', *Essex Archaeology and History* 19, 154-8.

Powell, W.R., 1990 *Essex in Domesday Book*, Essex Record Office Publication No103.

Priddy, D., 1988 'Pleshey castle - the northern bailey: excavations at the village hall site 1987', *Essex Archaeology and History* 19, 166-75.

Reaney, P.H., 1935 *The Place-Names of Essex*, English Place-Name Society 12, Cambridge.

Smith, T.P., 1985 *The medieval brickmaking industry in England 1400-1450*, BAR British Series, 138.

Stenning, D., 1993 'The Barley Barn, the Wheat Barn, and the early development of barns in south-east England', in D. Andrews (ed.), *Cressing Temple. A Templar and Hospitaller manor in Essex*, Essex County Council, 51-75.

Stuart-Macadam, P., 1986 'Health and disease in the monks of Stratford Langthorne abbey', *Essex Journal* 21, 67-71.

Taylor, C.C., 1977 'Polyfocal settlement and the English village', *Medieval Archaeology* 21, 189-93.

VCH 8, 1983 *The Victoria History of the County of Essex* 8, ed. W.R. Powell, London.

Wade-Martins, P., 1989 'The archaeology of medieval rural settlement in East Anglia', in *The rural settlements of medieval England*, ed. M. Aston, D. Austin and C. Dyer, Oxford, 149-65.

Wallis, S., 1991 'Halstead area mains replacement: Belchamp St Paul, Church Street', in P.J. Gilman (ed.), 'Excavations in Essex 1990', *Essex Archaeology and History* 22, 154.

Ward, J.C., 1986 *The De Bohun charter of Saffron Walden*, Saffron Walden Historical Society.

Ward, J.C., 1987 '"Richer in land than in inhabitants." South Essex in the Middle Ages, c.1066-c.1340', in *An Essex Tribute. Essays presented to Frederick G. Emmison*, ed. K. Neale, London, 97-108.

Ward, J.C., 1992 'Elizabeth de Burgh and Great Bardfield in the fourteenth century', in *Essex Heritage. Essays presented to Sir William Addison*, ed. K. Neale, Oxford, 47-60.

Watson, M., 1989 'Stratford Langthorne abbey restored', *Essex Journal* 24, 33-7.

Weaver, L.T., 1975 *The Harwich story*, Harwich.

Wilkinson, T.J., 1988 *Archaeology and environment in south Essex: rescue archaeology along the Grays by-pass, 1979-80*, East Anglian Archaeology 42.

Williamson, T., 1986 'The development of settlement in north-west Essex. The results of a recent field survey', *Essex Archaeology and History* 17, 120-32.

Standing Timber-framed Buildings

by D. F. Stenning

Introduction

The problem of relating the traces of structures found as a result of archaeological investigation and existing standing structures presents many difficulties. Frequently digging reveals suggestions of plan forms together with supposed 'post-holes' and other mysterious irregularities. The difficulties are exacerbated by the fact that few pre-1300 buildings survive above ground and that archaeology will also reveal traces of later, poorly-built structures that, again, have failed to survive intact. The late thirteenth-century wing at Tiptofts, Wimbish, has a number of interesting peculiarities and it seems possible that this may be a surviving building that was originally constructed with earth-fast posts. If this could be proved, it might provide clues for the identification of other surviving examples.

At what date earth-fast construction was superseded by structures with ground cills remains in doubt. Excavations in London have revealed some clues which may be relevant in a wider context (Milne 1992). It is of course possible that earth-fast construction remained in use; utilitarian structures and buildings such as the 18th-century cart lodge at Colville Hall, White Roding, suggest that this may well be the case (Meeson and Welch 1993).

Unfortunately, it is the lowest parts of a timber building that suffer the greatest decay and evidence for earth-fast construction will often have been lost in this way.

Interpretation of plan forms can again be hazardous in that minor internal partitions can leave firm evidence whilst the external envelope may have been frequently remade.

With all this in view, the author has decided not to confront these problems directly, but to examine various aspects of early building, including local schools of carpentry, the spread of particular carpentry techniques and building typology viewed in terms of distribution.

All these aspects may have some bearing, if somewhat indirect, on the interpretation of archaeological evidence and at least provide some possible lines of enquiry.

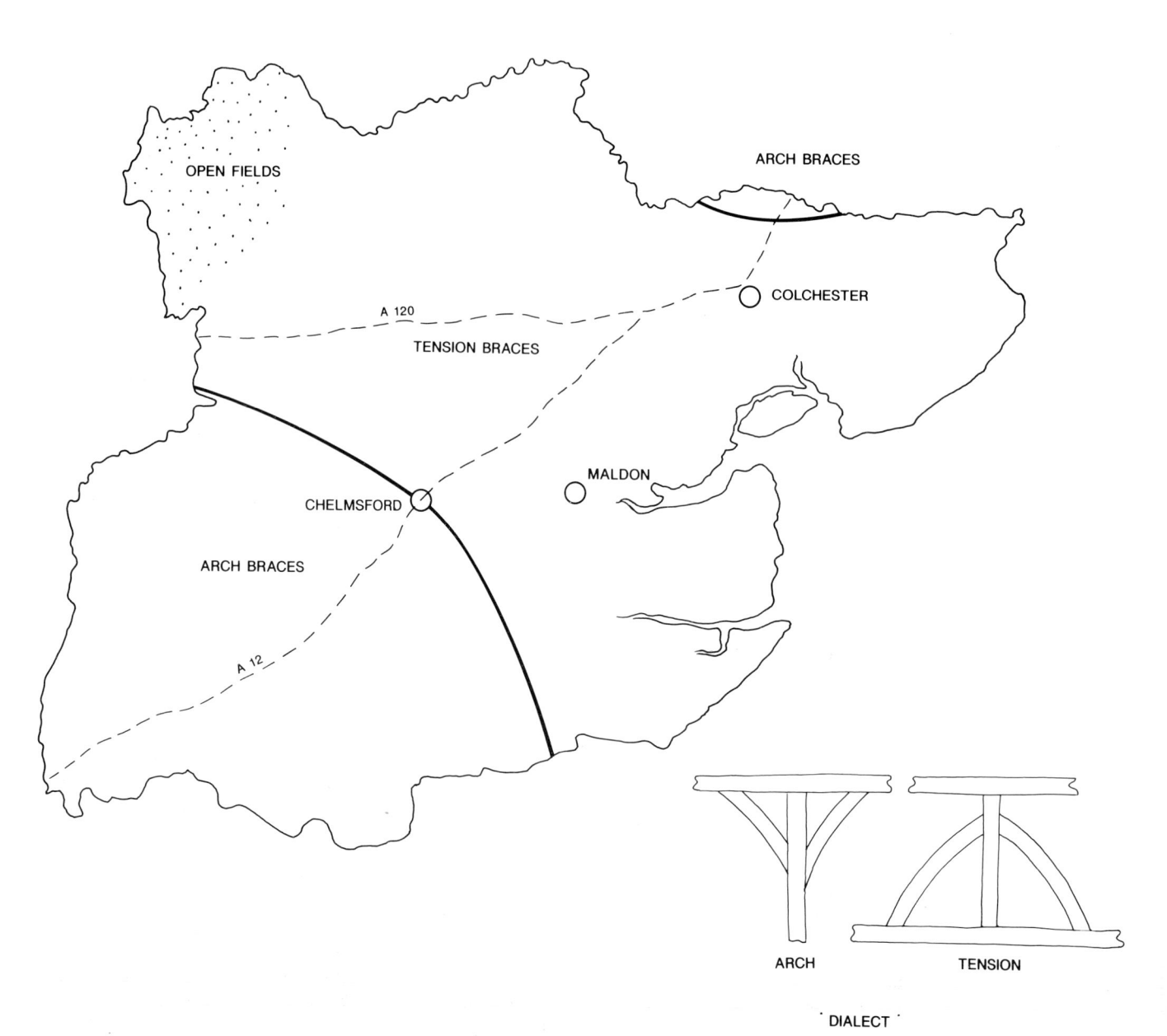

Fig. 1 Distribution of local carpentry styles in Essex

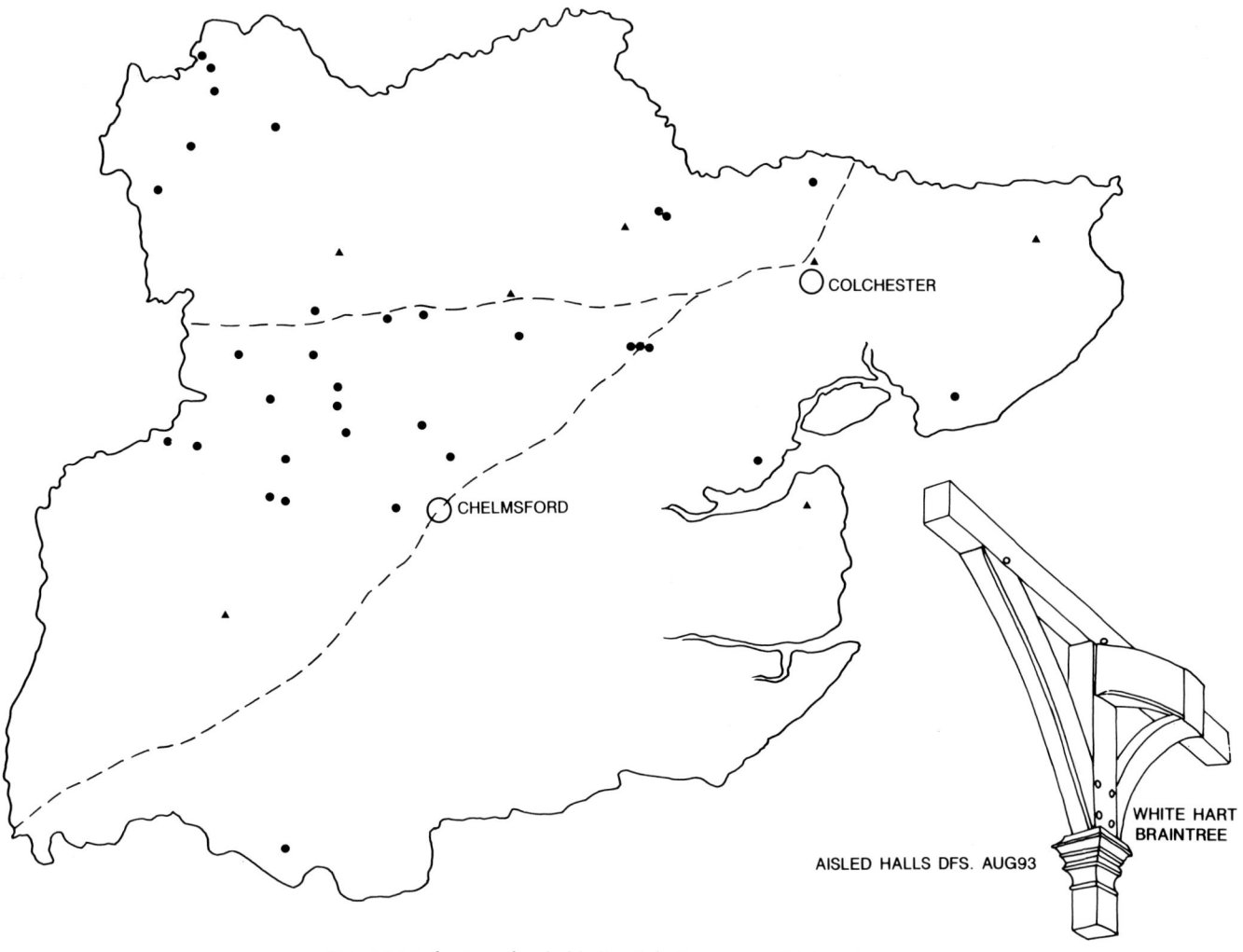

Fig. 2 Distribution of aisled halls (definite and possible) in Essex

Local Carpentry Styles in Essex

When viewed nationally, timber-framed buildings are seen to be extremely variable, both in typology and even more in terms of carpentry technique. This has long intrigued investigators and the expression 'local dialect' has recently been coined to describe this phenomenen (Harris 1989). If we could understand why this is the case and perhaps the processes by which this variety evolved, then we may well have a clearer understanding of past social and economic factors.

In Essex, pinning down the elements that represent local variety is a tricky problem, as the differences are always subtle and can only be recognised after prolonged study of numerous examples. However, an attempt can now be made to suggest the overall pattern and, no doubt, further study will help to clarify the picture. In general it would seem that differences in the way timbers are arranged and distributed is the key factor and that, except in special circumstances, building typology is somewhat secondary and can take less regard to local style.

The author contends that a substantial part of central/north Essex demonstrates a consistent carpentry style which shows signs of a consistent development throughout the medieval period (Fig. 1). As this is the predominant Essex style, it provides a useful yardstick by which to gauge the variables found elsewhere. A noticeable feature of this style is the use of 'tension' wall bracing, where the brace curves *down* from post to a lower horizontal member. It is generally thought that tension bracing represents a later and more advanced form of construction and it can be seen that this advance took place very early in this area (pre-1300) and this may have been due to a lack of building stone and the need to evolve a truly timber-framed technique.

Within this large area, the two oldest urban settlements, Colchester and Maldon, do seem to have retained a certain individuality. In Colchester, in particular, evolution of technique seems to be somewhat slower than in the rural hinterland and jowless posts continued in use long after jowles became normal in all other areas. It may well be that within the confines of an urban community, trade practices were more effectively controlled, resulting in a curious, conservative prolongation of techniques.

The second major area that can be identified is the south-western quarter of the county. Technique here is somewhat variable with much building in the towns (Billericay, Brentwood) following the central-north Essex Type. However, arch-bracing can also be found in buildings of all periods together with some 'exotic' detail. Arch-bracing, where the wall brace *rises* from wall post to an upper, horizontal, member is the type considered archaic, representing a phase when wall posts were earth-fast and all horizontal members were raised well above the ground. It seems likely in the circumstances that this arched-brace style relects the influence of nearby London, and that other exotic elements also reflect the long-lost practices of that City. It is interesting to note that buildings of the north Kent shore and of suburban Surrey often exhibit arch-bracing and thus the influence of London may have spread all around its rural hinterland.

The north-western fringes of Essex also illustrate a further variation, but here complicated by variations in typology. This part of the county, where open fields divided into strips, existed until recently, has nucleated villages asociated with this medieval form of agriculture. Generally this is reflected in the carpentry, in as much as there is a concentration of small dwellings, of poor or reused timber, apparently reflecting the limited status and means of the 'croft' holders. arch-bracing being found in a number of better-quality buildings. The small size of dwellings seems to have dictated the early use of the side-purlin roof to gain more headroom over low, in-line hall houses. Gables are invariably used, whereas over the rest of the county, cross-wings tend to have hipped rear slopes. Window positions also differ and are frequently found in the middle of a wall, rather than tucked up against a principal post, as is normal elsewhere. Crown posts, where used, have down bracing to the tie beams - a particularly archaic feature. It is suggested that the north-western fringes of Essex form part of a wider area of technique, perhaps related to West Suffolk, South Cambridgeshire and north-eastern Hertfordshire.

The fourth area of technique is physically very small and represents the north-eastern fringe, to the north and north-east of Colchester. This area belongs with south-east Suffolk, and demonstrates a hybrid form of arch-bracing, where the braces are often long and attenuated and clearly reminiscent of tension brace curvature. The villages of Dedham and Stoke-by-Nayland represent this type but examples are generally of a late date.

Whilst all this seems to represent the overall picture, certain other phenomenen ought to be noted. The entire northern fringes of the county, perhaps as far south as Braintree, were influenced by the culture and economics of the textile industry. This took the form of a particular decorative style, which can best be seen in Lavenham and was applied to many buildings, irrespective of the underlying structural technique. Noteworthy features are the use of 'brattishing' (carved cresting) and a form of capital with a cusped soffit that can be found throughout this zone.

A more general phenomenon seems to be that arch-bracing gained wider favour in the mid to late 16th century and was occasionally used where tension bracing had previously been the general norm.

Fig. 3 Distribution of raised aisled halls in Essex and Suffolk

STANDING TIMBER-FRAMED BUILDINGS

Typological Distribution Maps
Distribution maps of some of the well-known building types are presented in Figs 2 to 5. (The reader should bear in mind that such maps may on occasion reflect detailed study in a particular area rather than objective reality).

The Aisled Hall (Fig. 2)
The aisled hall was the usual format for large or medium sized houses up to c. 1400. Such houses had a central 'nave' and two or, less commonly, one aisle to provide a compact communal living area, in the centre of the plan.

Aisled variants such as the base-cruck hall or the raised aisled hall (see later) were rare in Essex and examples are included, undifferentiated, on the map. The real difficulty here is to determine whether a fragmentary aisled building was built as a house or a barn as the two were always somewhat similar as to their overall structure. In those cases where doubts exist, the buildings are marked with a triangle, rather than a circle, on the map.

The thirteenth-century aisled halls of Essex and Suffolk make an interesting group (Fig. 3, Fig. 6A [Fyfield Hall]). Comparisons suggest considerable uniformity, the differences being as variations on a theme. All use straight timbers, passing braces and simple, but effective, triangulation. As first constructed, they were of 'in-line' design, with all of the accommodation under one large roof. They clearly represent pure timber-framing solutions of a type that evolved in response to a total lack of building stone. Certain aspects of the technique can be found scattered elsewhere in England, but the origin of this approach surely lies in East Anglia.

In later aisled halls, the passing braces become less and less evident and timbers of curved profile are gradually introduced. The crown post arrives late in the 13th century (from France?) and is tentatively combined with a passing brace system (Edgars Farm, Stowmarket, Suffolk; Fig. 6B). It seems possible that the early popularity of the crown post, and perhaps also that of the Queen post, lies in the ease by which it can be incorporated into the pre-existing concept.

Raised Aisled Halls (Fig. 3)
Raised aisled halls differ from the conventional aisled hall in that the arcade posts, instead of standing on the ground, are perched on a large transverse beam which straddles the hall.

Whilst the advantage of this concept lies in providing an unencumbered floor area, it might well have arisen as a quite separate solution to the conventional aisled hall and its dissemination may have been due to a few widely distributed and influential examples. The oldest example known to the author is in a conventual building at Wherwell in Hampshire, where the existence of notched-lap joints suggests a thirteenth-century date. Wherwell Priory is a stone-walled building and the raised aisle approach may thus have stone walling origins.

As can be seen from the distribution map, the largest concentrations are to be found in a north/south band across central/east Suffolk (Fig. 3).

In this part of Suffolk, the idea of a roof structure, supported on two vertical posts, became the established con-

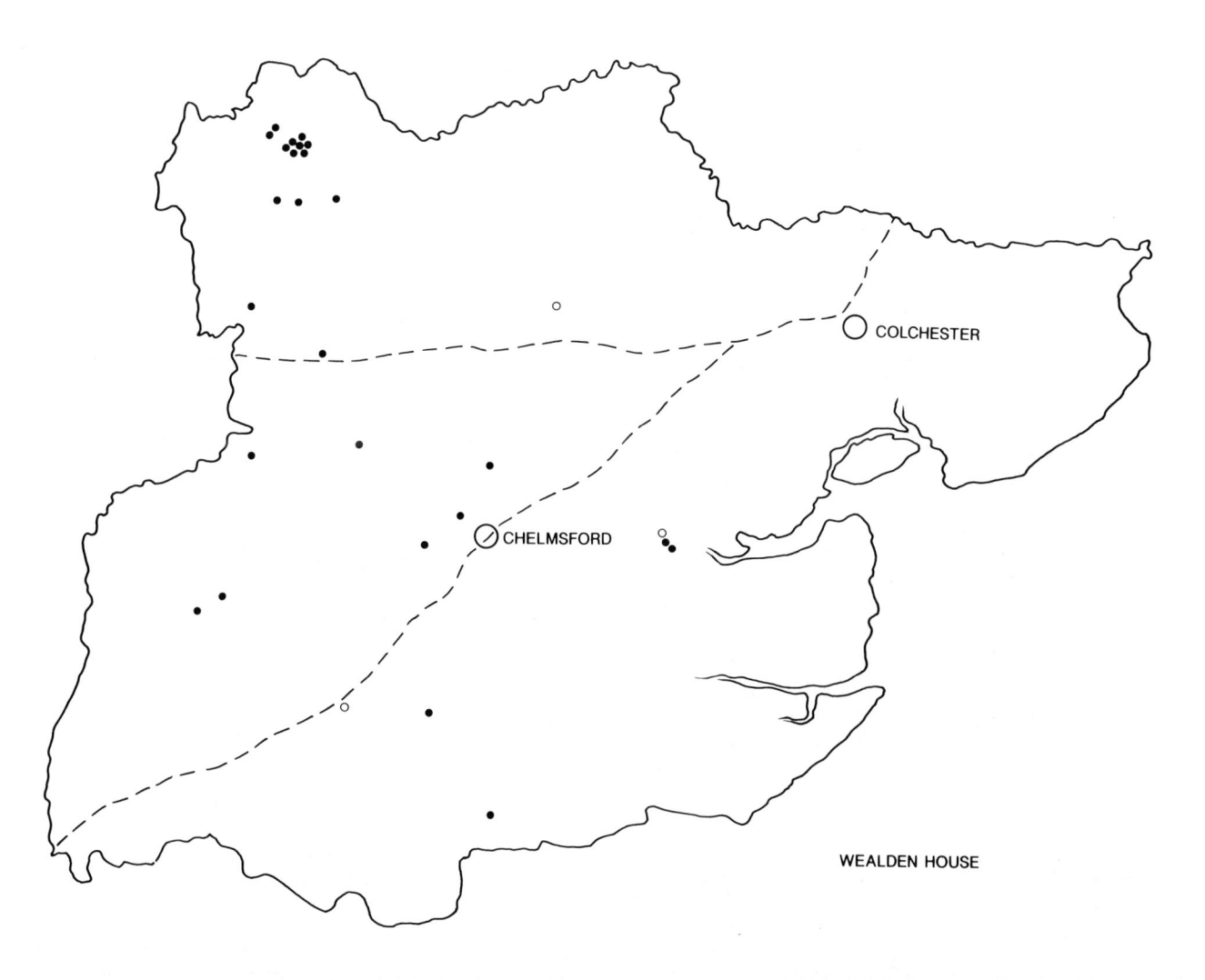

Fig. 4 Distribution of Wealden houses (definite and possible) in Essex

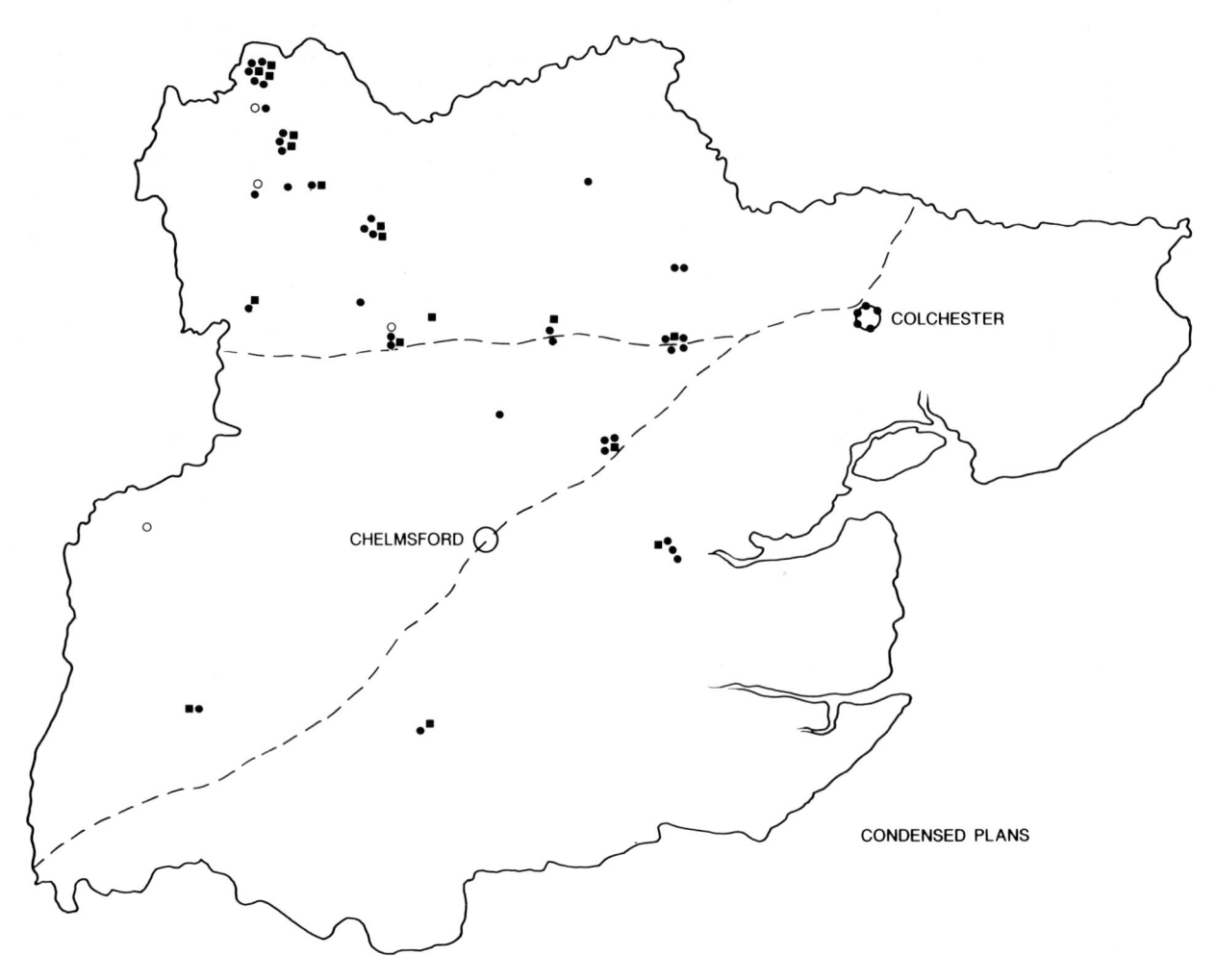

Fig. 5 Distribution of houses with 'condensed plans' in Essex

vention and later roofs made wide use of Queen posts, and examples can be seen over sixteenth-century brick barns. It is quite possible that the idea took its definitive forms in the Suffolk/Norfolk border area, perhaps in association with a Monastic house. (The only known example, in Essex, of a Queen-post roof, of this special kind, is in a sixteenth-century brick barn of Saffron Walden Abbey).

The raised aisle concept seems to have reached its most developed form and highest level of sophistication in two closely related examples. Lodge Farm, Denton (Norfolk) [Fig. 6C] and Church Farm, Fressingfield (Suffolk) are only a few miles apart, are both of the fourteenth-century and represent two stages in the process of the development. In both cases the 'aisle' walls are high, allowing room for large windows, and the straddling beam is mounted at about mid-wall height. Both roofs incorporate ashlar and soulace pieces, which may well be left-overs from an earlier, masonry walled prototype.

Compared with Suffolk, raised aisled halls are relatively few and far between in Essex. Of the six known examples, two were conventional aisled halls, later converted to the raised aisle type, and one was a 'base-cruck' hall, also later converted. (Conversions are marked with black squares on map).

Subtle differences suggests that, like other building types, the raised aisle concept was slightly reinterpreted to incorporate elements of the local carpentry tradition (Fig. 6D). Durham House, Great Bardfield in an interesting structure, where it appears that the visual attributes of the type were incorporated within a large box-like hall and were later modified to resemble a pseudo-hammerbeam roof. Similarly, the ornate low beams of 'The Borough', Thaxted and 'Prouds' also in Thaxted (Stenning and Wadhams 1986) may be variants on the theme.

Present knowledge suggests that examples of the raised aisled hall are limited to the south-east with a structure at Merton College, Oxford as the most westerly surviving example (Hewett 1980).

Wealden Houses (Figs 4 and 6E [Clavering])
The Wealden House, which is a hybrid form between the in-line type and a house with two jettied cross-wings, is found in large numbers in Kent and Sussex. Such was its popularity in the fifteenth and sixteenth-centuries that Wealdens can be found scattered throughout lowland England. Figure 4 shows the distribution of the 28 known examples in Essex and three possibles where the evidence is inconclusive. The map indicates a scattered pattern in the southern part of Essex and a dense accumulation in the north-west. The southern pattern probably represents the occasional adoption of an appropriate building type and no clear pattern of influence is apparent. However, in the north-west, the Wealden is, more often than not, a small, compact unit that was convenient to build in terraces. Many incorporate shops and the majority of 'export' Wealdens, outside Kent or Sussex, are of this type. In Essex, about half the examples are in 'urban' areas and the majority of the north-western examples are in this category.

There is little evidence to suggest that Wealdens were built by carpenters from Kent or Sussex and their carpentry usually displays local characteristics. However, one

STANDING TIMBER-FRAMED BUILDINGS

Wealden in Bridge End, Saffron Walden, has a crown-post roof of the type found in profusion in the Tenterden area.

Stud and plank, high-end partitions are another Kentish feature and the only known Essex examples are in the Saffron Walden environs. On this basis it does seem possible to envisage the spread of a few select architectural features up the important London to Cambridge Road.

The Condensed Plan (Fig. 5)

The house with a 'condensed plan' is one where the service cross-passage and/or the owners bench are slid under the storied end accommodation rather than forming part of the open hall (Fig. 6F [Stansted]). By this means the frontage width is reduced, without encroaching on the communal space of the hall. On the map (Fig. 5), recessed benches are represented by a black square and the more numerous, intruded cross-passages by a black circle. Hollow circles represent 'possible' examples where the evidence is incomplete. Some houses employ both devices and these examples are depicted with both a square and a circle. Both concepts can be found elsewhere in England, but are relatively rare and Essex seems to have the greatest concentration. Such house types are invariably found in 'urban' situations where the narrow frontage width was most advantageous, and evidence, at present, suggests considerable popularity in the towns and villages of northern Essex. It is possible that further survey work will reveal more southern examples as the type can be difficult to detect. Again, the great concentration, in the northwest, is particularly interesting as they form a common component of the little, late medieval houses of the nucleated, open-field villages. As can be seen, this typological study seems to take little heed of the 'local carpentry styles' aspect, considered earlier. The condensed plan can be found with open-hall houses or the later long-wall-jetty houses, with continuous first floor and is commonly found as a constituent of Wealden Houses.

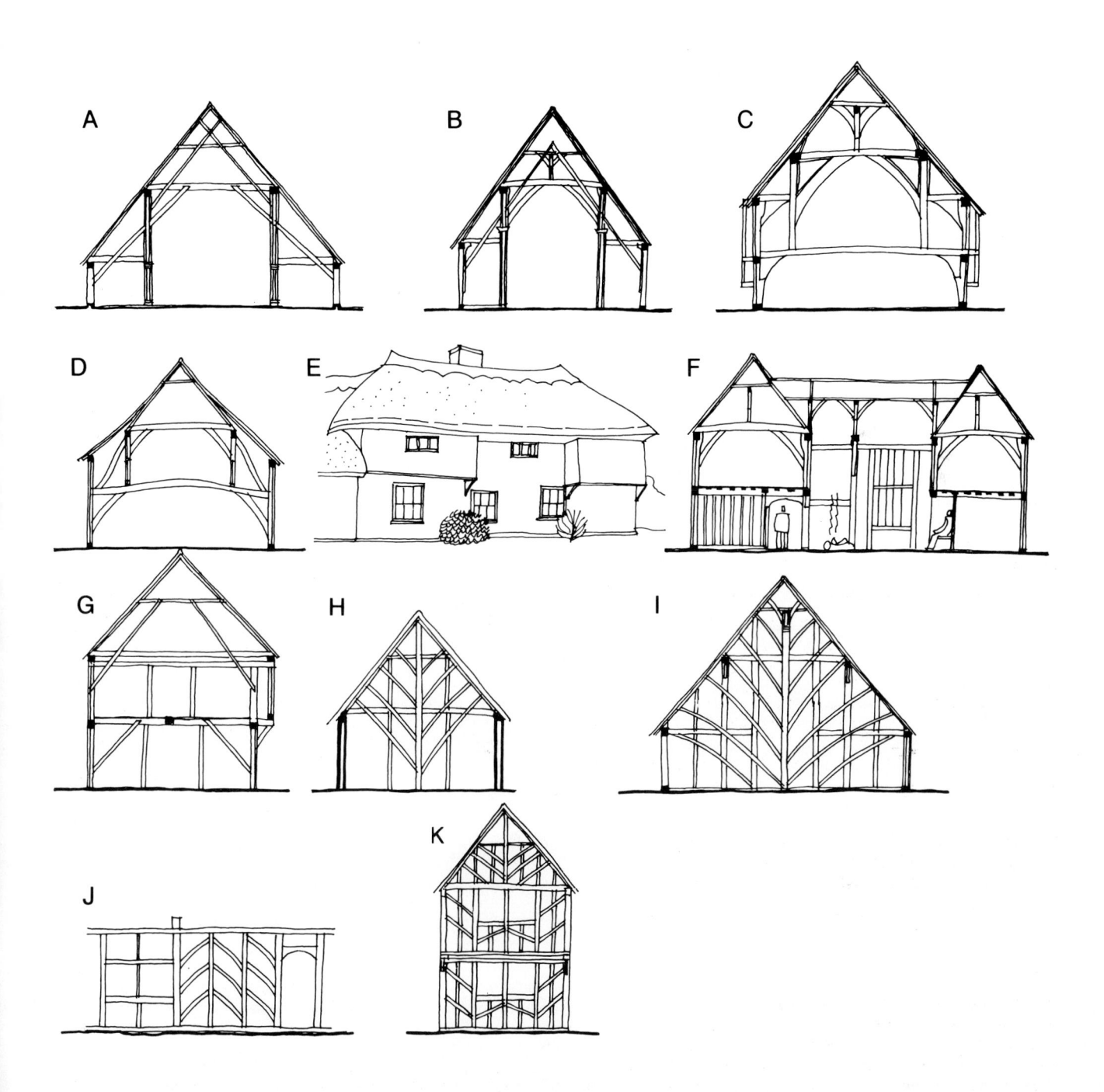

Fig. 6 Sketches of timber-frame variants mentioned in the text

Later Developments in Framing Technique
From the foregoing it can be concluded that building style and typology are not necessarily closely linked, although in certain situations (north/west Essex) special circumstances might suggest otherwise. It seems possible to put forward a case for suggesting that very early surviving carpentry was less subject to local variations than that which followed. This may in part be due to the higher survival rate of status buildings which may reflect the wider interests of their carpenters and patrons.

Mr Philip Aitkens has examined the remains of two, apparently thirteenth-century buildings within the grid-planned town of Bury St Edmunds (Fig. 6G); (Aitkens, forthcoming). Both are two-storeyed, with jetties to the street and have carpentry technique reminiscent of the early aisled halls. The building at Nos. 30/32 Kings Street, Kings Lynn (Norfolk) is again somewhat similar and shows adaptation of a passing-brace, notched-lap technique to an urban situation. It therefore seems probable that the type was once common throughout the towns of East Anglia, but the greater commercial pressures, in these situations, have brought about their demise.

Observation also suggests that certain, particular, architectural devices enjoyed a wider sphere of influence. A small number of early Norfolk buildings show a tendency to employ a fan-like arrangement of arch braces on internal trusses. A development of this idea, with curved bracing, is to be found on the high end truss of Church Farm, Fressingfield (Suffolk) (Fig. 6H); and Lodge Farm, Denton (Norfolk) shows a developed version of the same idea. The same fan-like arrangement can then be seen decorating the gable ends of a number of contemporary cross-wings in Suffolk and Essex (Baythorne Hall, Baythorne End, Essex) where it begins to become combined with recently introduced tension braces. It would seem that the next step in the process was to change the fan pattern into a chevron-like arrangement with alternating ups and downs in adjacent, infill, panels. This type can be found widespread in East Anglia, from the Priory Gatehouse at Little Walsingham (Norfolk), the flank walls of Church Farm, Fressingfield (Suffolk), the end walls of Little Wymondley, Bury (Herts.) to the flanks of the Mayor's Parlour, South Street, Rochford (Fig. 6I). Both fan and chevron can be found together (Little Wool Hall, Lavenham, Suffolk; Fig. 6J) emphasising that they were both, more or less, contemporary ideas.

By the mid fourteenth-century, the type loses popularity and tension bracing takes over in those areas where it was to become the prevalent fashion. This short period of richly decorated framing, in East Anglia, is of interest in itself, and may conceivably have influenced the much later decorative patterns of the West of England.

Bibliography
Milne, G. 1992. *Timber Building Techniques in London c. 900-1400 and Related Material*, London and Middlesex Archaeol. Soc. Special Paper 15
Meeson, R. A. and Welch, C. M. 1993. 'Earthfast posts', *Vernacular Architecture Journal*, 24
Harris, R. 1989. *V.A.G. Newsletter* 16
Stenning, D. F. and Wadhams, M. C. 1986. *Historic Building Studies* No. 1 Essex County Council
Hewett, C. A. 1980. *English Historic Carpentry*, Phillimore

Essex Record Office sources for medieval archaeology

Janet Smith

"What history needs is not more books, but more boots." In the years since the historian R. H. Tawney gave that much - quoted advice to his students, a whole generation of historians, both professional and amateur, inspired by W. G. Hoskins and his successors, has left the comfort of the libraries and archives to test out their reconstructions of the past by walking the landscape of their chosen field of study, examining the evidence on the ground -sometimes with startling results.

Archaeologists, of course, do not need to be convinced of the value of field work. As an archivist, what I want to do is to suggest that archaeologists of the medieval (and post-medieval) period ought to put that same process into operation in reverse; in other words, that they should remove their boots from time to time to venture into the local record office where there is a wealth of documentary evidence which is invaluable for the interpretation of archaeological findings; sometimes, too, it can lead to the discovery of sites. The purpose of this short paper is to draw attention to the kind of documentation available in the Essex Record Office and to highlight some of the pleasures and the pitfalls involved in using it.

Local history and archaeology are both aspects of the study of the past and they need to be closely linked. The archaeologist will not want merely to identify sites, to investigate and record them, but also to interpret the findings, placing them in the wider context of the landscape and the history of man's activities in that area. To do that, the archaeologist needs to turn to whatever documentary evidence is available. Similarly, the local historian needs the evidence of the archaeologist and the fieldworker in order to explain and interpret the documents in the light of what can be seen on the ground.

An early example in Essex of the useful results that can arise from bringing together documentary evidence and archaeological excavation involved Dr. Jennifer Ward in what must have been almost her first research into Essex history.[1] In the 1950s she studied the history of Old Thorndon Hall, using the surviving 16th-century accounts of its rebuilding by Sir John Petre, work which transformed a small moated manor house of the 15th century into an impressive brick Elizabethan mansion with a wealth of chimneys, towers and gables. The house no longer exists for it was pulled down in the 18th century when the new Hall was built on a different site. Shortly after Dr. Ward's study was completed the Thorndon Hall Excavation Group was formed to excavate the site of the old Hall and the evidence of the 16th-century building accounts and later plans of the house were used to help the excavations. While the documentary evidence helped to assist and certainly to explain the findings this was not always the case. The excavated foundations did not always relate closely to some 18th-century plans of the house and it eventually became clear that those plans proposed changes that were never carried out. Map evidence needs to be used with care, as will become apparent.

The survival of documentary evidence cannot be taken for granted. Very little written material survives for the period before Domesday; students of the Saxon period are restricted to a handful of monastic chronicles and a scattering of deeds and charters. As time goes on, the amount of available material steadily increases until we reach the present century when the archivist's pre-occupation is deciding what to select for permanent preservation and what to destroy, because the quantity of written records is overwhelming. The range of historical documents likely to be of interest to the archaeologist and the fieldworker is a wide one. Almost any document might prove useful; every source relating to a particular area can help to fill out the picture. This paper can do no more than draw attention to a selection of documents in the Essex Record Office which are most likely to be useful in throwing light on the problems of medieval archaeology. It will not concentrate solely on medieval records, because documents and maps from the post-medieval period will also help to re- construct the medieval landscape. The classes of documents referred to can be found in most county record offices, although each office will have different strengths and weaknesses in its collections.

Before you begin your research you need to decide how much time you are prepared to spend on documentary work. If it is done thoroughly, you can expect to spend as much time in the record office as you do in the field. Although the documentary research and the fieldwork ought to go hand in hand, the fieldwork will usually have to take priority. If the archivists do their job properly the documents will still be there in ten or twenty years' time - the site may not. When you come to use the documents you need to be aware of some of the problems you will encounter. The first and most obvious one for anyone interested in the medieval period is the difficulty of reading the documents. Most medieval records were kept in Latin, occasionally in Norman-French; legal records of all sorts continued to be written in Latin until 1733, with the exception of the Commonwealth period. Even when the documents are in English from the 16th century onwards, the handwriting may be difficult. Medieval handwriting is perhaps the most difficult of all, but some study of palaeography will also be necessary to read documents of the 16th and 17th centuries; after about 1650 there should be no difficulty at all. If you decide to come to grips with palaeography and with medieval Latin, help is available; the extra-mural departments of London, Cambridge and now Essex all offer courses and so does the Essex Record Office. Some sources will be available in print, fully transcribed or calendared and translated into English, but while this is particularly true of the calendars, lists and indexes of state records published by the Public Record Office in London, local records usually have to be consulted in the original. Occasionally enthusiastic individuals or local history groups have produced transcripts or translations of some records relating to their own area, but without an army of volunteers to undertake this the many hundreds of medieval records in our collections will be inaccessible to all but the most enthusiastic and dedicated amateur.

Having decided to turn to the documentary evidence, where does the medieval archaeologist start? A visit to the record office, preferably by appointment, leads you to the indexes and then to the catalogues describing the documents in detail, so that you can select and order what you wish to study. Assuming that you are investigating a particular site, the parish index will direct you to specific collections of documents relating to that area and, for the medieval period, the major source of information will be the manorial records. The manor was the basic unit of land administration and this could range in size from a few acres to many square miles. It is important to remember that the boundaries of a manor were not necessarily, or even usually, co-terminous with parish boundaries; a parish could contain one or several manors and as time went on new manors could be created or existing manors merged together.

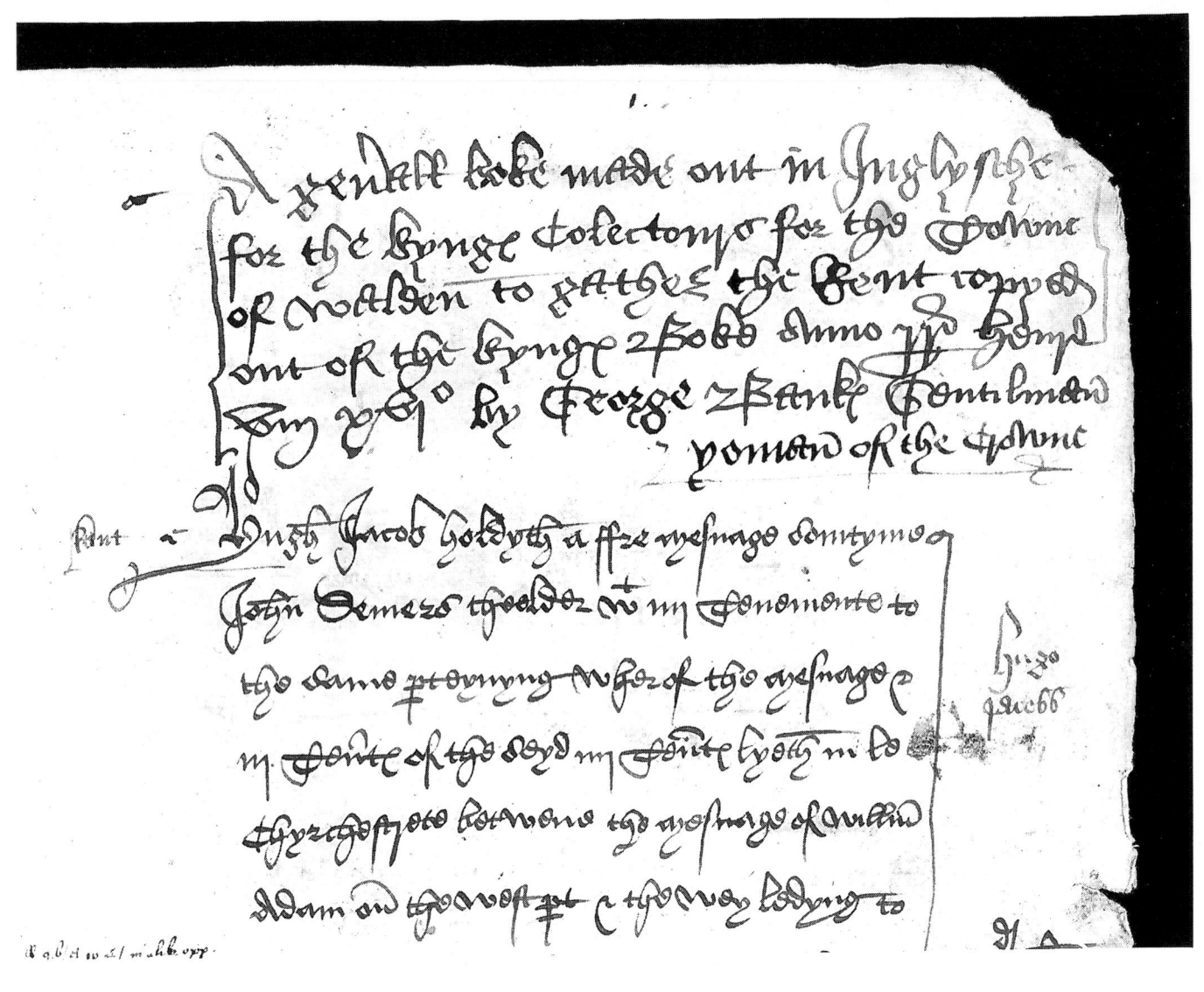

Plate 1 A rental of the Manor of Walden, 1524, 'made out in Inglysche', gives full details of property abuttals

The records of the manors include general records of estate management - rentals, surveys and accounts, for example, as well as the records of the manor court where the lord of the manor exercised his jurisdiction over his tenants.

The surveys and the related documents, if they survive, may be the most helpful to the archaeologist, since they are fairly straightforward descriptions of the property. These survive from the 13th century, one of the earliest for Essex being the Ingatestone survey of 1275 which appears to be part of a much larger survey of all the estates of Barking Abbey; much of the larger survey is now lost.[2] Unfortunately, the number of surviving medieval surveys is small, but many more survive for the 16th and 17th centuries and these can be used successfully to reconstruct the medieval landscape. Often, the earliest surveys describe only the demesne lands, that is the part of the manor farmed by the lord himself rather than his tenants, but later documents, usually called 'extents', included valuations of the whole of the manor. A more detailed later medieval survey was the 'terrier', where the description follows a topographical arrangement, giving as much attention to land held by tenants as well as to the demesne. Another, related, document is the 'rental' which lists each parcel of land and the income which was due from it to the lord of the manor.

Such documents can contain descriptions of fishponds, mills, woods, parks, perhaps even a detailed description of the manor house, and they may be of great value to the archaeologist in identifying and interpreting sites. However, when using documents, always be aware of their limitations. These were not surveys in the modern sense; the land was not accurately measured. Like many medieval documents their purpose was tenurial: they are a record of obligations by the tenants to the lord, a record of services or dues owed. Where measurements are given they may be customary measurements, compiled from statements made by jurors, and not actual measurements of surface area. A further problem is that they do not always give abuttals; sometimes the parcels of land may be listed in the order in which they lay, but often they are listed by type of tenure; that is, freehold or copyhold tenures are grouped together. This makes it more difficult to build up a map from the information in the survey, but used together with later maps and other evidence it may still be possible.

If your aim is to reconstruct the medieval field system, an enormous amount can be achieved if a field book survives for the manor under study. A field (or drag) book describes the holdings furlong by furlong, listing in order the number of lands (or plough ridges) held by each owner; it may also give their size, usually in acres and roods, but remember that these are conventional terms and not statute acres.

Where a series of these records survive for a single manor an accurate and detailed picture of the medieval field pattern can be built up. For example, the field system of Saffron Walden was studied by Dorothy Cromarty using a survey made in 1400, now in Cambridge University Library (a copy is in the Essex Record Office)[3] supplemented by the following records in the Audley End estate papers:

1) a 'Survey of the lands of the Parsonage of Walden' which is thought to have been written in 1575 but appears to be a copy of a much earlier manuscript. This is a very detailed terrier, listing the lands topographically, with their measurements.[4]

2) a rental of 1524 which gives the full abuttals of the property described. The heading declares it to be 'A general boke made out in Inglysche for the Kinges Colectorys for the Town of Walden to gather the Rentes copyed out of the Kynges Booke... by George Bankes Gentleman yoman of the Crown' (Plate 1).[5]

3) a field book c.1600 which lists the holdings of the manor furlong by furlong; written in English (Plate 2).[6]

4) a survey of similar date (c.1600) listed by tenure not topographically; written in Latin.[7]

There are several other Saffron Walden surveys of the early 17th century so the total amount of documentary evidence for this area is impressive, largely because these lands were once part of the estate of the Benedictine Abbey of Walden and then, after its dissolution in 1537, they became part of the great Audley End estate. Documents always have the best chance of survival in these circumstances, where ownership lay with institutions like the Church or the Crown or with other great estates which ensured continuous ownership and centralised record-keeping. Manors in private ownership which passed from hand to hand may not have such good series of records, but, even if rentals and surveys are scarce, there will usually be at least some court rolls or accounts, which will also yield useful information for the archaeologist.

The court rolls are usually the best preserved records of the manor. As a description it is somewhat misleading, since from the 17th century onwards many stewards preferred to record the proceedings of the manor courts in bound volumes rather than in membranes stitched and rolled together. Nevertheless, for centuries they were kept as rolls. The membranes can be several feet in length; some are in shorter lengths stitched at the head, others are stitched in a continuous roll, which can lead to certain practical problems when studying them.

All lords of the manor enjoyed the privilege of holding a court to which the tenants of the manor, both free and copyhold, could be summoned. The courts administered the customs of the manor and much of its business will only be of marginal interest to the archaeologist. Nevertheless, both in the court rolls themselves and in the bailiffs' account rolls for the manor, there may be fines for assarts and for offences involving parks, woods or rabbit warrens; there may be grants of waste and licences to build on them and tenants could be presented and fined for erecting dwellings without licence or for allowing them to fall into disrepair. The court rolls will record the changing ownership of copyhold land; while free tenants had the right to dispose of their property without permission, copyhold tenants could only do so with the consent of the lord of the manor. If a tenant died, his heir would appear before the court to be admitted as the new owner; purchases and exchanges could only be transacted by 'surrendering' the property into the hands of the lord and 'admitting' the new tenant to the property in open court. The court rolls are therefore a vital record of land ownership and they provide essential information about surnames which may link with the names of scattered settlements.

Manorial accounts will also provide evidence for the economic activity of the manor; they may refer to repairs to watermills, windmills, warrens, woodlands, building works, and the sales of produce. A good run of court rolls and account rolls, which survive in large numbers for many Essex manors, provides a contemporary account of the economic and social life of the manor which will enable the researcher to monitor changes and to follow the fortunes of individual settlements.

While the court rolls are the prime source of evidence for the ownership and transfer of copyhold property, freehold tenants had fewer obligations to their overlord and were able to convey their land by deed or gift. The Essex Record Office, like all other record offices, holds a vast quantity of charters and title deeds dating from the 12th century to the present day. There are many different types - feoffment, lease and release, bargain and sale, final concord - and this is not the place to explain these terms. All medieval deeds and charters, and later ones too, deserve analysis by the archaeologist. They can provide information about almost everything in the medieval landscape: tenements in villages and towns may be described with their abuttals and sometimes their sizes; there may be agreements about mills and fishponds, woods and parks;

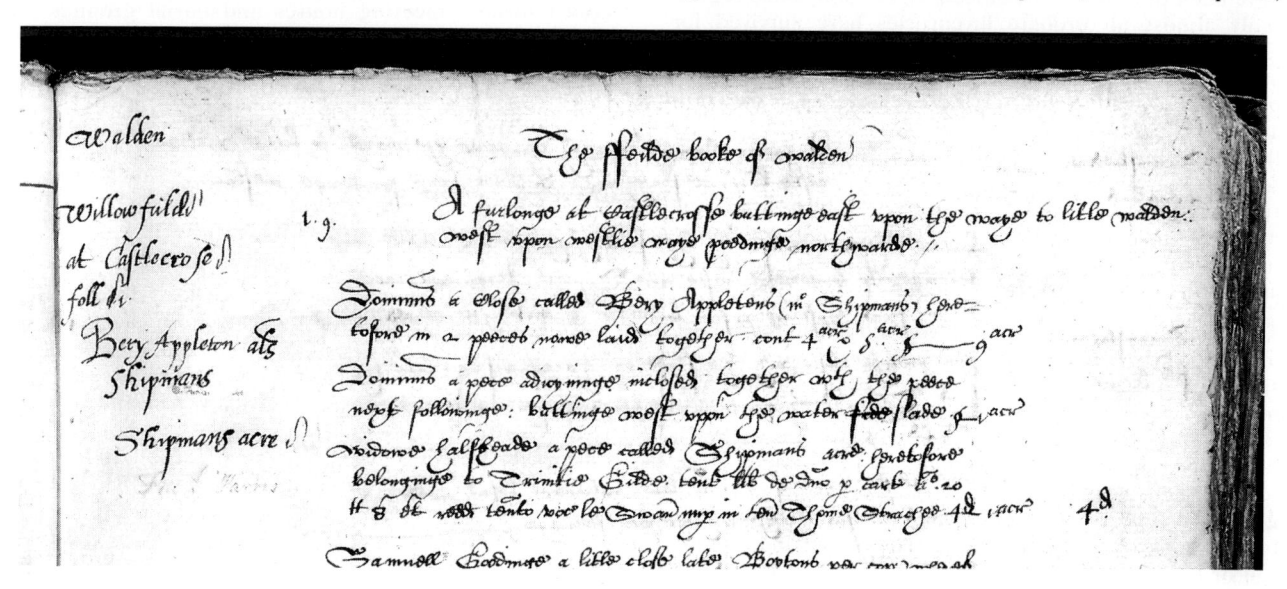

Plate 2 This field book of c.1600 is a detailed terrier of all holdings on the manor arranged topographically, furlong by furlong

the way in which physical features of the landscape are described can help to fix the line of roads and tracks; they sometimes contain useful descriptions of archaeological sites: of a mansion house, or a mill. Above all, they are a treasure trove of information about field names and provide clues to the field pattern, enclosures by hedges or ditches, the amalgamation and partition of properties and the existence and possible dating of dwellings and other buildings.

Like all documents, they have their drawbacks. Sometimes the property is only vaguely described - "all my lands and tenements in Cressing" - because the information was so well-known that it did not need to be stated. But where they do specify the property by giving the abuttals it is sometimes possible to identify its position. The phrase 'newly built' relating to a property may seem vital evidence for dating it, but unless a deed of the same site exists for a slightly earlier date making no reference to a building on the same property, beware. The phrase 'newly built' could be repeated again and again as the description of the property was copied out *verbatim* on later deeds of transfer. Title deeds may also contain legal coventions which were not intended as literal descriptions; the phrase "my freehold messuage with all the barns, stables and other buildings" does not necessarily imply that such outbuildings existed. Some documents contain exaggerated or inaccurate descriptions of property; they record fictitious legal actions whose purpose was merely to break an entail or to ensure that the transaction was recorded in the central courts. For this purpose a precise description was not necessary.

When it comes to the reconstruction of individual dwellings, surviving wills and inventories are a major source of information, but only for the larger mansions, owned by major landowners, are you likely to find lengthy and detailed inventories or valuations. Both Ingatestone Hall and Thorndon Hall, owned by the Petres, can be studied in detail in this way because several inventories survive for both, dating from the late 16th and 17th centuries; they list the furnishing and fittings room by room, which makes it possible to reconstruct the original room plan with some degree of accuracy.[8] The other source of similar information for humbler dwellings is the probate inventory compiled for valuation purposes after the death of a property-owner; again, these were usually drawn up on a room by room basis, including all the outbuildings and even crops in the field. Usually these inventories were filed with the original wills, where a will existed; this could not have been the case in the diocese of London, since regrettably almost no probate inventories have survived for Essex. The only exception is the Peculiar of Writtle, one area which lay outside the Bishop's jurisdiction, which preserved a small collection of inventories for the 17th and 18th centuries, now in the Essex Record Office.[9] Disappointing though this may be, the original wills themselves, which survive in large numbers from the 15th century, sometimes contain considerable detail about the property being bequeathed; some almost amount to house inventories and they are well worth searching. Most wills, apart from the earliest, are in English.

The one form of evidence which you will not find available for the medieval period is the most visual and, at first sight, the easiest to use: the map. Although the art of map-making is an ancient one it was not until the second half of the 16th century that cartography as we know it developed. There was what amounts to a revolution in cartography in the first years of the reign of Elizabeth I when geometrical methods of estate survey began to replace the techniques of the simple land measurer carrying a perch rod or knotted cord. Medieval land surveying, as we have seen, involved a written survey and a valuation rather than exact measurement. When accurate maps first appeared in the 16th century they were intended to supplement and to illustrate the written survey, not to replace it. Some of the earliest maps in the record office are contained in bound volumes of surveys where the maps are clearly meant to help the written description of particularly complex geography. Dating from that period onwards there is a vast collection of maps, printed and published maps and manuscript estate maps, which is available to the archaeologist and the local historian. Again, though, care is needed to interpret the evidence.

Everyone is familiar with the maps produced by the Ordnance Survey. Great Britain is the best mapped country in the world, thanks to this great map-making institution, and little needs to be said about these. Every fieldworker begins by studying the large scale plans produced at a scale of either 6in to the mile or 25in to the mile from the 1870s onwards and for towns with a population of over 4,000 plans at a scale of 120in (10ft) to the mile were drawn up in the 1870s. These maps record the landscape in meticulous detail and they are a vital source of evidence for field boundaries and settlement patterns. Sometimes antiquities are marked, but even when they are not, perhaps because their existence was not recognised when the map was made, they can be identified by deduction. A right-angled pond may turn out to be part of a medieval moated site, although it may be nothing of the sort. Continuous hedgelines forming large enclosures, together with place-name evidence, may suggest the location of a medieval deer park. The earlier, smaller scale editions of the Ordnance Survey are less well known. The first edition for Essex at a scale of 1 inch to the mile was published in 1805; this was not perfectly accurate and repeated the mistakes of some earlier map-makers, but the revised edition of 1844 is the first definitive survey. Both can be consulted in the Essex Record Office and both are worth studying; occasionally antiquities are marked on the earlier editions, recording information supplied by local knowledge, and they then disappear from later maps. These early editions are particularly valuable since they show the county just before the rapid growth in population, the spread of industrialisation and the coming of the railways began to transform its appearance.

The only really reliable map published in large scale before the 19th century is Chapman and André's map of Essex, surveyed in 1772-4 and published in 1777. This was drawn at a scale of 2 inches to the mile and it is detailed enough to show almost every building in the county outside the urban areas; each is shown by a block plan, with a perspective view sketch of all the churches. Some inns, nonconformist meeting houses and burial grounds are marked, there are signs for watermills and windmills - post mills and tower mills are distinguished. Some moats, 'ancient entrenchments' and other features of archaeological interest are included too, as are the forests, woods, coppices, paled parks, commons, heaths, greens and roadside wastes. Dr. F. G. Emmison, the first County Archivist of Essex, checked the detail of this map against contemporary estate plans and came to the conclusion that it is remarkably accurate.

The same cannot be said for many earlier printed county maps. While some were the result of fairly accurate surveys, many others plagiarised earlier work and copied maps which were already out of date at the time of reprinting. Many features are untrustworthy and even fictitious. The earliest county map was the work of Christopher Saxton who surveyed all the English and Welsh counties and produced his atlas in 1579. This map shows waterways, but no roads. Next came John Norden's *Map and Description of Essex* in 1594; this was unpublished for 250 years, but 4 of his manuscript copies survive, one in the Essex Record Office.[10] The next county map by John Speed, published in 1610, was based on Norden's; both show the road system and Speed also added a detailed plan of Colchester, the earliest extant plan of the town. After this, all published county maps were basically reprints of Saxton or Speed and no new survey was made until Ogilby and Morgan published their map in 1678; this in its turn was the basis for more plagiarism until the Chapman and André era.

The scale of these maps is of course too small for detailed fieldwork. They provide no more than a general indication of the relative position of towns, villages and country houses and the general route of major roads. They were of no practical use to the contemporary traveller (or the modern achaeologist) with the exception of Ogilby's road maps published in 1675. These show the principal roads in ribbon form, marking all the most useful roadside features and road junctions; it indicates churches, mills, woods and parks and other instantly recognisable landmarks, and may be of some value to the archaeologist if one of Ogilby's roads happens to pass through the area under survey.

To some extent the interest and usefulness of any of these published maps depends on the personality of the map-maker. Their interests and preferences influenced their choice of features. Some, like Speed, were antiquarians interested in identifying historical features; others, like John Rocque who was originally a landscape gardener, were more interested in recording parks, plantations and other aspects of land use and paid little attention to archaeological features. Sadly, Isaac Taylor, a keen amateur archaeologist, did not work in Essex. His county maps, like the one for Dorset in 1765, provide the fullest record of field antiquities before the Ordnance Survey. Chapman and André, though comparable in many ways, did not have the same interest.

The best, of course, has been left almost until last. The most attractive and also the most useful, because of the scale at which they were drawn, are the manuscript estate maps, compiled by a gradually emerging profession, the land surveyors, for private owners of estates. The Essex Record Office has one of the finest collections of estate maps to be found in any county record office, dating from the latter part of the 16th century to the mid-19th century (when they were superseded by the O.S. maps). These estate maps give us a uniquely detailed topographical picture which is often difficult and sometimes impossible to find elsewhere. The land surveyor working with pair of dividers, a plane table or theodolite and quill pen recorded the countryside more effectively than any written record, however detailed. A composite list of the features to be found on estate maps would, in the words of J.B. Harley, amount to a complete inventory of the rural landscape.[11] Like their predecessors the manorial surveys, though, they were tenurial, intended to record ownership, tenancy, farm sizes and, often, valuations. The surveyors were selective, only recording features that were relevant to the purpose of the map, in other words the assets of the commissioning landowner. Nevertheless they are rich in detail, sometimes depicting land use -arable, meadow, pasture, crops in rotation, woods, marsh, orchards, gar-

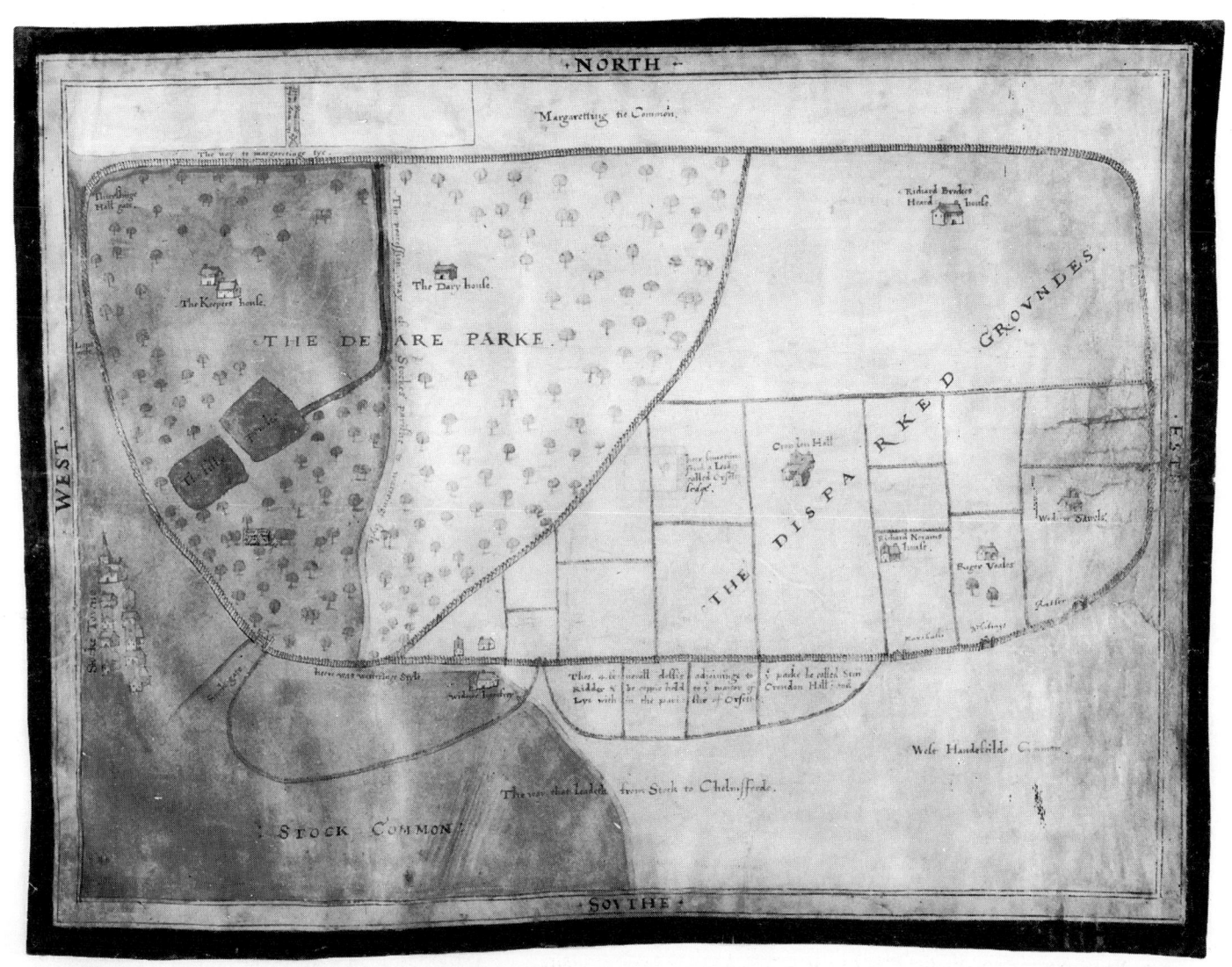

Plate 3 A map of Stock c.1575 shows evidence of disparking and of the former site of a vanished building, Orsett Lodge

dens, fishponds, vineyards, parklands. Where they incorporate a village settlement they may show not only the overall layout of the development but block plans of the larger buildings, even occasionally drawn to scale. They provide evidence for the sites of rural industries: forges, furnaces, lime kilns, chalk pits, tanyards and saltings.

Since many of the early land surveyors in Essex and elsewhere were schoolmasters and educated men, they were well informed about antiquity as well as the age they lived in and they sometimes recorded the sites of vanished buildings and other earthworks. A map of Stock c. 1575 shows quite clearly that the disparking of Crondon Park had already begun (Plate 3).[12] It also records a vanished building: "here sometime stood a lodge called Orsett Lodge" and one small detail is a wayside cross at the junction of the roads to the north of the park. A map of Chignall dated 1599 shows the moated site of a house which had disappeared before the map was made and clearly gives the name of the house as Beaumont Moates (Plate 4).[13] This name was later corrupted to Beaumont Otes and even Reaneys *Place Names of Essex* only gives the latter form.

Estate maps have to be used with care. One historian has called them 'a dangerous type of evidence', and you certainly need to question their reliability, just as you would any other documentation. Surveyors were not equally competent; some early map-makers were tradesmen or artists rather than scientific surveyors and the results of their work may bear little resemblance to the property described. A map of the parish of Messing dated 1650 is a case in point; it is crudely drawn and largely inaccurate, and the fields are out of proportion.[14]

Some map-makers, though, can be trusted without much doubt. Kenneth Newton, a former County Archivist, and Gus Edwards have shown beyond a doubt that the late 16th and early 17th-century maps produced by John Walker senior and John Walker junior were the result of precise survey and accurate measurement, even down to the scale and the smallest detail of the buildings shown.[15] They did not show buildings in normal perspective as some map-makers did; they drew front elevations with the baselines always in their correct positions. This may look odd, but it meant, for example, that a whole street could be shown in accurate profile. Ken Newton used the Walker plan of Ingatestone High Street together with a written survey of 1556 to reconstruct the village and its inhabitants;[16] Hilda Grieve, using Walker's plan of Chelmsford of 1591 and its accompanying survey, plus earlier surveys, title deeds, court rolls and accounts, was able to build up a series of complete street directories for the town from the 14th to the 16th century.[17] The Walker sketch of Old Thorndon Hall was vital evidence, alongside the building accounts and the archaeological excavation work, in identifying and reconstructing the Elizabethan house, as referred to earlier.[18] Nevertheless, even when using a Walker map, you need to beware. Their map of Housham Hall, Matching, in 1609 shows a meadow called Foreburie, but there is no indication of the ruins of a chapel there, even though the ruins still existed in Morant's day.[19] The land surveyors' purpose was a practical one; they were not

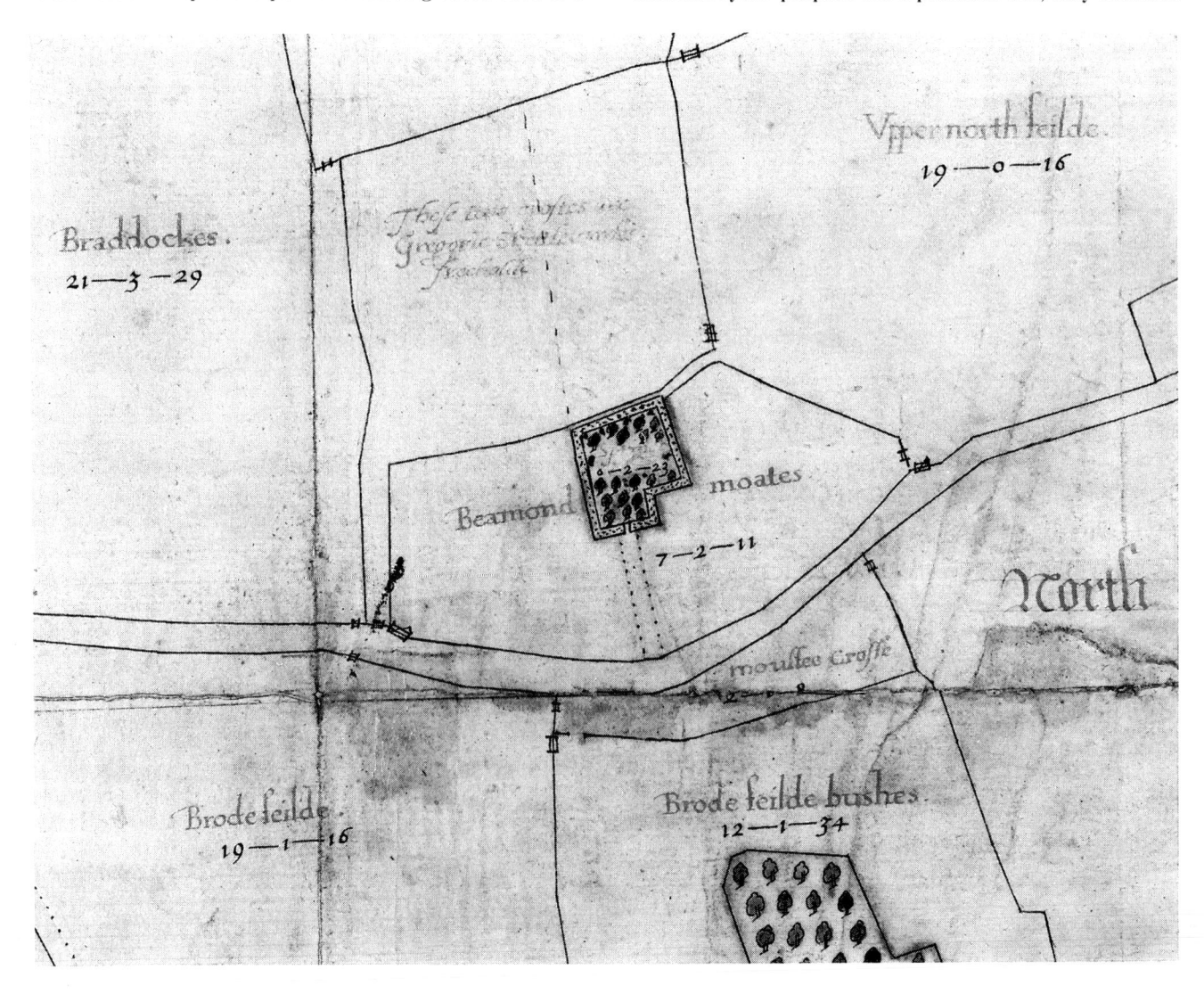

Plate 4 A map of 1599 showing a moated site provides clear evidence that the name Beamont Otes is a corruption of 'Beamont Moates'

archaeologists surveying antiquities and to argue from negative evidence in maps is dangerous.

No reference has been made so far to enclosure. Since Essex is what Oliver Rackham describes as ancient countryside, the result of piecemeal growth and the development of centuries, most enclosure took place long before the age of mapping, and long before the time of parliamentary enclosure.[20] Only in a few places, particularly in the north west of the county, was an open field system in operation, as can be seen from a series of estate maps of the Audley End estate in the Saffron Walden and Chesterford area.[21] Most of the enclosure which took place by Act of Parliament in this county was enclosure of commons and waste, but one exception is illustrated by a pair of enclosure maps from the parish of Langley. Rather unusually, two maps were drawn, one showing the strips in the open fields before enclosure, the other showing the closes after enclosure.[22]

Of more use, generally, than the enclosure maps for Essex are the tithe maps. These were drawn up for most parishes, following the Tithe Commutation Act of 1836; their purpose was to show all land on which tithes were paid and an accompanying award provides a complete schedule of owners and occupiers, plot numbers, field names, land use and, the purpose of the exercise, the amount of tithe rent which was to be paid in future. These maps, drawn up between 1836 and about 1850, are often the only maps to cover an entire parish before the date of the Ordnance Survey large-scale plans. Sealed by the Tithe Commissioners, they can be used for legal purposes, particularly as evidence for rights of way; like enclosure maps they are a prime source of evidence for field names, which can provide clues to earlier land use. Nevertheless, once again they need to be used with caution. Their purpose was a limited one, to indicate titheable land only; urban areas are usually blank because tithe payments had been extinguished long before; they were concerned with ownership, occupation and land use, but not with recording landscape features. Like estate maps, too, they vary in accuracy depending on the skill of the surveyor; some were not original surveys but copies of earlier parish maps drawn up for rating purposes.

Maps, therefore, of whatever kind, need to be evaluated carefully. Always ask how and by whom the map was made, since this is a crucial factor in its reliability. Look for ways of testing the accuracy of the map; try to test its scale, its distortion or orientation. Above all, do not use maps in isolation. Use them to complement other classes of evidence. Maps seldom tell you the whole story; they are merely one link in a chain of evidence which could include field work, aerial photography, and written documents.

This short account of documentary evidence available in the Essex Record Office has not even touched upon the 19th-century sources such as sale catalogues, directories and printed histories, nor has it discussed Essex records which are held in other repositories. Institutions like the colleges of Oxford and Cambridge held Essex estates, and their records will be found in College or University Libraries. Church estates, like those of the Dean and Chapter of St. Paul's, will have their own archives in St. Paul's Cathedral Library and elsewhere. Above all, there are the records in the Public Record Office in London. At no time since 1066 have local communities been entirely free from central control and so any study of a community must make use of documents created both centrally and locally. The records in local custody are only a small part of the whole, particularly for the medieval period. Central government records include grants of privileges, records of land transfer, Inquisitions Post Mortem, lay subsidies and other records of national taxation and records of the administration of justice. It is sufficient to say here that many of the printed calendars of these records and all of the Lists and Indexes which have been published can be consulted in the Essex Record Office.

Documentary research is an invaluable tool for the medieval archaeologist and in the Essex Record Office the fieldworker in Essex has a rich resource which few other counties can rival. There may be problems involved in using original records. Studying them is time-consuming; there are difficulties of language or of handwriting, problems caused by the erratic survival of evidence and, above all, problems of interpretation. Nevertheless, they can be of vital importance in finding sites, in identifying and explaining sites and in dating sites. The local record office is a resource that should not be overlooked by the archaeologist.

References
Unless otherwise stated, references are to documents in the Essex Record Office.
1. Ward, J. *The History of Old Thorndon Hall* and Marshall, K. *Excavations at Old Thorndon Hall, 1957-59.* Essex Record Office Publication No. 61 (1972)
2. D/DP M150
3. Cromarty, D. *The Fields of Saffron Walden in 1400.* Essex Record Office Publication No. 43 (1966); Cambridge University Library MS. Add. 7090; T/A 63
4. D/DBy M143
5. D/DBy M32
6. D/DBy M39
7. D/DBy M74
8. D/DP F205-231
9. D/APw P4
10. D/DMs P1
11. Harley, J. B. *Maps for the Local Historian. A Guide to British Sources.* British Association for Local History (1972)
12. D/DP P2
13. D/DP P6
14. D/DH P1
15. Edward's, A. C. and Newton, K. C. *The Walkers of Hanningfield.* Buckland (1984)
16. Edwards, A. C. and Newton, K. C. *op. cit.*
17. Grieve, H. E. P. *The Sleepers and the Shadows Vol. I The Medieval and Tudor Story.* Essex Record Office Publication No. 100 (1988)
18. Ward, J. and Marshall, K. *op. cit.*
19. D/DU 25
20. Rackham, O. *Trees and Woodlands in the British Landscape* (1976)
21. D/DQy 11-14, D/DU 120, T/M 123-124
22. Q/RDc 41

Post-medieval Essex

Paul Everson

This contribution to the conference came with a disclaimer which remains true of the published offering. It does not attempt any overall conspectus of the post-medieval period in Essex such as the organisers have urged as an objective on contributors for their several periods. Instead what it offers is a brief account of three or four individual pieces of non-excavational fieldwork that happen to have been undertaken by staff of the Royal Commission on the Historical Monuments of England from Keele over recent years in Essex, each for rather different reasons. If its content, therefore, seems more appropriate to a title reading 'Some recent examples of post-medieval fieldwork done by the RCHME in Essex plus asides on related matters', that is probably accurate, but it is done with the connivance, indeed with the urgent encouragement, of the conference organisers. Since a post-medieval chapter was absent altogether from the parallel conference 15 years ago and from its resultant publication (Buckley 1980), and because no overview is apparently possible, what we can at least hope to do is to focus attention on the period and to stimulate interest in its undoubted potential for archaeological fieldwork of various sorts.

As a consequence of this limited objective, of the nine thematic categories under which work is reported in the national period journal *Post-Medieval Archaeology* - namely ecclesiastical buildings; military and naval earthworks and structures; towns and corporate buildings; villages; manors, country houses and associated works; farms and small domestic buildings; industry; communications; sports and amusements - the paper that follows refers to only two or three in a pigeon-holed way, though it perhaps points to other aspects that may cross categories or not be so readily categorised. It also concentrates on topographical field survey as a primary technique at the expense of excavation, for example, or structural recording or geophysical survey or finds analysis, despite the contributions these have made (eg Drury 1975; Rodwell and Rodwell 1986, 152ff) or are capable of making to knowledge of this period.

It is undoubtedly the case that there is no lack of information and informed research in many specialist topics within the post-medieval and early modern periods in Essex, in a way that is characteristic, too, in industrial archaeology. Much of this is very locally based, and local publications available in Chelmsford central library are a rich source inadequately tapped here. Not least of these topics is the study of military remains, in which Essex has an enviably rich and varied surviving heritage complementing that of Kent on the other side of the Thames estuary (Kent 1988, 55-90). Coastal defenceworks have evidently and not surprisingly taken pride of place, and pre-eminently Tilbury Fort and the chain of Martello towers. Recent work by the County Council's archaeological section falls into that pattern, in planning part of a 16th-century fort at East Mersea in 1992 (Essex County Council, Field Archaeology booklet, 8) or in excavating in 1990 and 1991 a D-shaped coastal gun battery of the Napoleonic era in connexion with the Dovercourt by-pass at Harwich and subsequently arranging its display (Gilman 1992, 104-5). Remarkable voluntary effort, too, has gone into the study and restoration of the Harwich redoubt and of Coalhouse Fort at East Tilbury. RCHME staff from Keele were intrigued, therefore, in routine fieldwork inland near Chelmsford that was led by Ordnance Survey requirements in 1988 to come across the fragmentary earthwork remains of a defensive field line of the Napoleonic period. These remains lay at Widford (on Chelmsford Golf Course) and on Galleywood Common, south of Chelmsford. They originated in a scheme of 1803 consisting of two 'field-forts' at Widford and Galleywood linked by an arching bastion trace and designed overall as a fortified artillery position 3.4 km long to combat an anticipated enemy advance on London in the event of a successful landing on the Essex coast by the French (Figure 1). The best of the earthwork survivals comprise a fragment of the rampart and ditch of the Galleywood fort at the southern end of the line and an outwork gun battery, akin in plan to a blunt arrowhead, sited some 40-50m south-east of it (Figure 2). Remarkably, given the intensity of modern land-use that includes an early racecourse and surface quarrying and given the loose earthen construction, details including the banquette, counterscarp and ramped gun platforms survive in a recognisable state to show, for example, that the ordnance was intended to be deployed *en barbette*.

Artillery including 20 x 24 pounders and 6 x 8" howitzers is documented in connexion with the garrison at Chelmsford, though it is not clear whether the line would in the event have been equipped with these or lighter field pieces as normal (Duffy 1975, 83-85). In practice, it is unlikely that the position was ever manned or gunned, since it was designed to fulfil a tactical role for which the occasion never arose, rather than a strategic one. By 1808 with the extension of the chain of Martello Towers to include the Essex coast, British defensive strategy had moved away from plans to defeat the French once they landed to one of coastal defence. Already by 1813 the defences at Chelmsford were being dismantled and materials sold off, and 1815 brought the end of the war and the dispersal of the remaining ordnance.

What is remarkable in this case is that these fieldworks are not brick and stone military architecture, but completely earthwork and timber constructions, in intention of a wholly temporary nature. For that reason alone they are rare and surprising survivals in lowland England. In the case of Civil War remains at Newark-on-Trent, it is said to have been fear of the plague that caused the half-hearted levelling of the Royalist fortifications and Parliamentary siege lines and promoted their remarkable survival (RCHME 1964): at Chelmsford, location on common land was a critical factor in ensuring a differential survival in contrast to the greater part of the line that was returned shortly to farmland. But also such military fieldworks were typically erected by an army on campaign and almost by definition therefore any erected by the British army are likely to be on foreign soil. The best analogies lie in documented fieldworks of Wellington's Peninsular campaigns, and particularly the Lines of Torres Vedras created in 1809 to defend Lisbon (Oman 1908, 419-436; Glover 1974, 140-143). Elsewhere in the country, however, contemporary military features are certainly identifiable in fragile earthwork form, including features as slight as field kitchens (Butler 1967, 122; NMR SU 86 NE 2) or, for example, a camp for Napoleonic prisoners-of-war at Norman Cross near Peterborough, where the field remains are illuminated by the description of a literary eye-witness (Phillips and Barratt 1984-85; Borrow 1851, ch 4) or again the redoubts and other fieldworks, perhaps practice works, recorded by RCHME within Crowthorne Wood near Bracknell in Berkshire (NMR SU 86 SE 11; SU 86 NE 17). So the potential may be greater than one might anticipate.

Of greater impact on the landscape and a notable feature of the post-medieval period in Essex as elsewhere in England is the creation of emparked country houses.

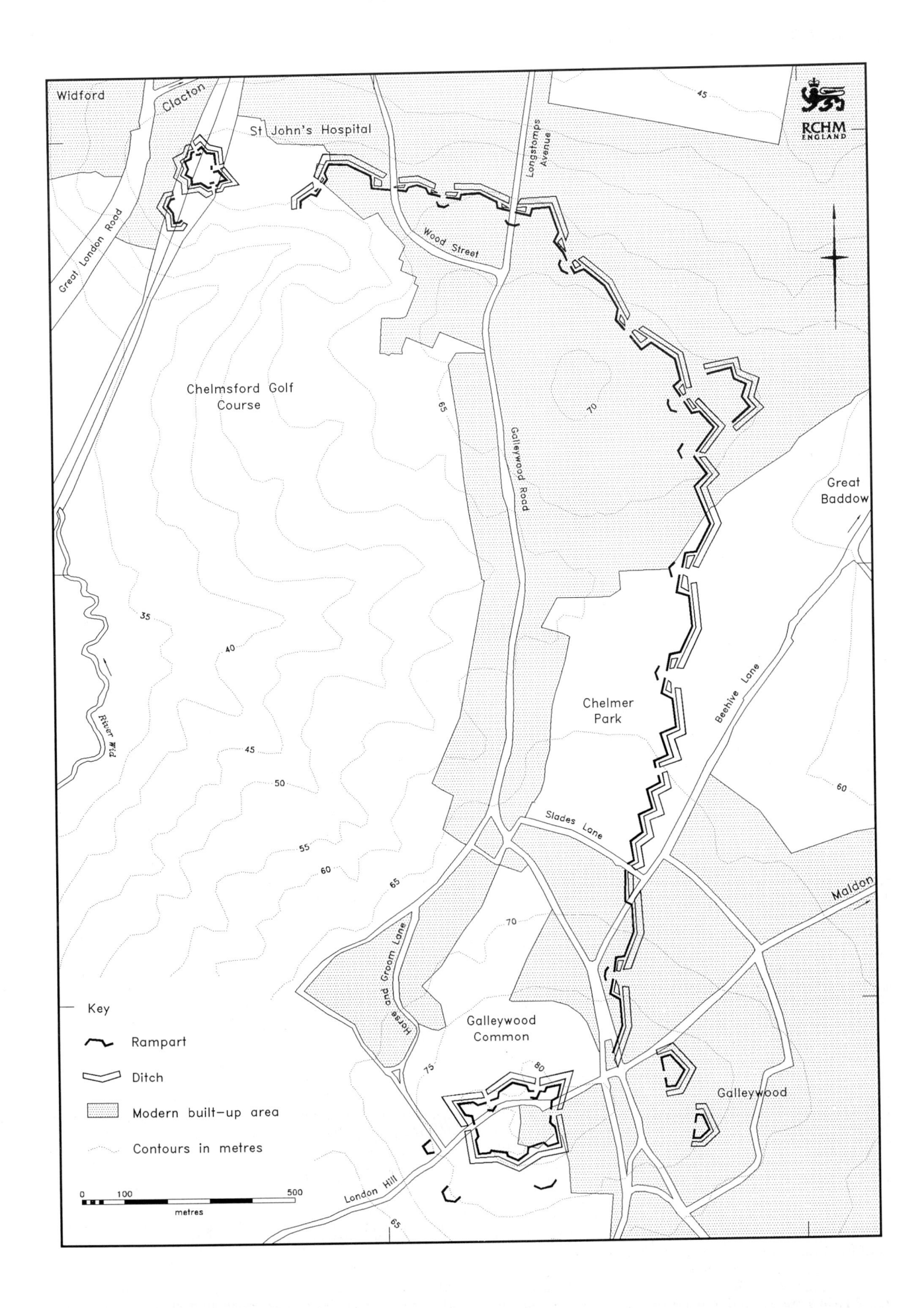

Fig. 1 Napoleonic field line near Chelmsford, location diagram (RCHME, ©Crown Copyright)

With an example like Audley End to point to in this county, it should be no surprise to be reminded that a number of these originate in the post-Dissolution conversion of monastic buildings. But it is certain that many more former monastic sites experienced a post-medieval phase of use, even if that is not now obvious in their surviving physical form as earthworks, buried site or site on public display. In the East Midlands and elsewhere, fieldwork experience has shown that it is very much the exception for a monastic site not to have had a post-Dissolution secular successor, even if that house lasted only 50 or 100 years. In Lincolnshire particularly, where monastic sites are quite commonly marked by good surviving earthworks and little else, those earthworks through recent detailed archaeological survey have typically proved to be wholly or in some significant part the remains of a post-Dissolution house and its formal gardens, overlying and modifying the monastic remains (Everson, Taylor and Dunn 1991, Barlings, Nun Coton, Stainfield); NMR TF 16 NW 3 (Tupholme); NMR TF 16 SE 4 (Kirkstead)). In Essex, Lord Rich's mansion on the site of the Augustinian house at Leez Priory is an instructive case in point; for though much in fact survives it went some way down the road to total demolition in the mid 18th century and in Pevsner's significant words 'the foundations of the 16th-century house can easily be confused with those of the medieval buildings' (Pevsner 1964, 265-7) - perhaps because the one incorporated or modified the other. At Cressing

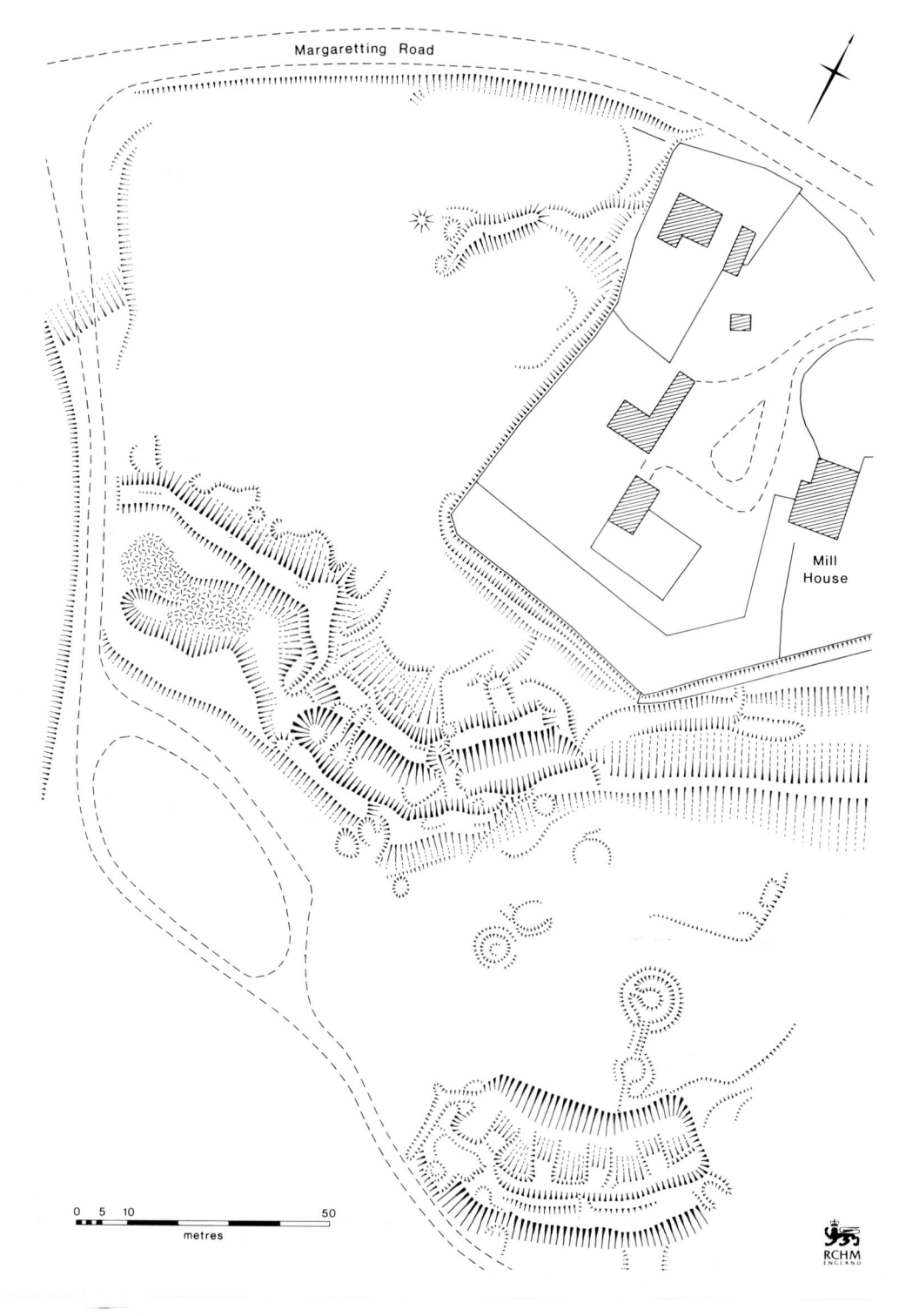

Fig. 2 Field survey of earthwork remains of Galleywood fort and outwork gun battery on Galleywood Common; scale 1: 1250 (RCHME, ©Crown Copyright)

Temple excavations by the County Council Archaeology Section have not only extended knowledge of the lost post-Dissolution house of the Smyths and Nevills there, but have also investigated the formal garden that goes with it (Andrews 1993). Even at an earthwork site like that of the Cistercian house of Tilty, where interpretation of the physical remains has hitherto focused entirely on the site as a medieval monastery, ancillary indications suggest that it ought to have a secular post-Dissolution aspect which might explain some of the perceived anomalies of layout (Andrews and Gilman 1992).

Waltham Abbey, too, falls within this pattern, but perhaps with some complicating factors. Certainly by the end of the 16th century, Sir Edward Denny had built Abbey House on part of the monastic site (VCH 1966,157-8; ERO T/M 125; Huggins 1972). Nothing obviously remains, though it was not demolished until c1770, except scraps of foundations in modern flower beds and the curiously unexplained survival of the medieval vaulted passage sometimes known as the 'Potato Cellar' (VCH 1966, 172). Also the rectangular brick-walled compartments to the E and the 'moated' water feature that they contain, which are presumably the residue of the formal gardens that would be the expected concomitant of such a residence, and which were certainly a noted feature in the early 18th century (Farmer 1735, 159). The chronology of this development may have been influenced by the King's direct interest in Waltham Abbey, which saw him create a walled hunting park there, E and N of the monastery, about 1541 (VCH 1966, 154, 157, 158; ERO T/M 125), when, too, there were royal stables at Waltham perpetuating medieval arrangements (VCH 1966, 167). Where precisely the contemplated royal house at Waltham-in-the-Forest, fashionably designed with almost mirror-image king's and queen's sides (Colvin et al. 1982, 14-15), was intended to be located is not known, but perhaps on the monastic site conveniently adjacent to the park, within which the Denny family as keepers occupied the house at Dallaunce before their final move to Abbey House. In practice the grand design was not built, and the assertion of established parochial usage kept the western nave of the abbey church standing and in use when the rest was demolished (VCH 1966, 172- 3).

Whether this post-Dissolution phase is approached by field survey, geophysics or excavation it is not a negligible part of the history of any monastic site. Indeed, the sites of short-lived post-Dissolution country mansions are one of the prime contexts in which one might expect to seek new information about lost great houses as well as surviving field remains of post-medieval formal gardens as a site type that has newly and increasingly been attracting archaeological attention (Egan 1988, 216-8 for excavated gardens at Audley End, in practice restored and replanted for display as they were in the 1830s; Brown 1991).

A related matter is the reuse of monastic buildings, whether something as grand as the western nave at Waltham, the conversion of the *capella ante portas* of the Cistercian house at Tilty to parochial use, or the curiously selective truncated survival of the S chancel aisle or Lady Chapel at Little Dunmow, presumably also preserved through established parochial rights in the priory church. For all the natural concentration on the survival of fine medieval architectural detailing, the event and process is a post-medieval one and likely to be accompanied by relevant physical evidence. Indeed to generalise rather grandly for the sake of making a point, the survival of any medieval monastic buildings in a county like Essex demands that there has been a positive post-medieval process, as is clearly the case, for example, with the monastic gatehouse at St Osyth in the context of Lord Darcy's mid 16th-century mansion there. That process is likely to be worthy of archaeological study in its own right, and is additionally liable to contribute to a better understanding of the original.

Not a successor to a monastery but one of the greatest country houses in the historic county, though it now lies within Greater London, was at Wanstead Park, and it may stand for the potential interest of many others.

There, Wanstead House, the great Palladian mansion designed by Colen Campbell and begun in 1715 for Sir Richard Child, later Earl of Tylney and Castlemaine, is reckoned by Pevsner (1965, 411-412) to have been the earliest pure Palladian building in England and has a commensurate importance in architectural studies (Harris 1985, 114-117). It was demolished between 1823 and 1825, and the remains of the stable court are now occupied by Wanstead Golf Club. It had in turn replaced a late 16th- and 17th-century house formerly owned by the Earl of Leicester, and the scene of royal visits of Elizabeth, James I and Charles I, with masques and the like entertainments, which itself developed an earlier royal residence (Colvin et al. 1982, 282-3). Sir Josiah Child, chairman of the East India Company, bought the house in 1667 and carried out garden work at 'prodigious cost'. After his death, this was further elaborated in several phases by Sir Richard Child at evidently even greater expenditure - £100,000 for the house and the same again on the garden are figures quoted - to create gardens and a setting for the house that are best known to us from John Rocque's plan and engravings of 1735, and were reckoned 'the finest Gardens in the World' and a wonder of their age.

The site of the house is now a hazard in the golf course (Figure 3). But a remarkably high proportion of the structure and details of these gardens survive as earthwork features in the landscape, together with modifications of the later 18th and early 19th centuries. They include the entrance gate piers, the octagonal Basin massively dammed against the slope, terraced parterres on the axis E and W of the house and the foundations of the Orangery, the axial vista eastwards down into the Roding valley and continued by the raised water sheet known as the Strait, two earthen amphitheatres and two mounts, and the island Fort within the lakes. The early 18th-century remains are the prime example in England of what John Harris has termed 'the Artinatural Style' of formal gardens (Harris 1986). Perhaps the most striking of the later modifications is the formal criss-cross parterre marked to the W of the house by low earthworks (Figure 3) that was added by Humphry Repton.

Yet these remains had not been recorded archaeologically or (at least in the National Monuments Record) been deemed to be a monument for archaeological record purposes. The opportunity for RCHME fieldwork arose in the winter of 1989-90, when the City of London Corporation commissioned a survey of this historic landscape as the basis for formulating a management strategy for the part of the site held in public hands, following a period of degeneration of the parkland after severe losses through Dutch elm disease, sycamore and scrub invasion, and latterly storm damage. The survey task was in itself a large and technically awkward one, which RCHME staff carried through at a scale of 1:1250 to integrate with Ordnance Survey basic scale mapping here. But more importantly the archaeological survey worked closely with John Phibbs of the Debois Landscape Survey Group, who had secured the City of London's contract to provide an analysis of the development of this garden landscape and proposals for its renewed management. By agreement RCHME supplied a metrically secure and archaeologically well-observed plan that included plan-positioning of significant trees and the Debois team contributed identification and interpretation of this residual planting together with an exhaustive level of documentary, cartographical and illustrative research far beyond that which RCHME could itself

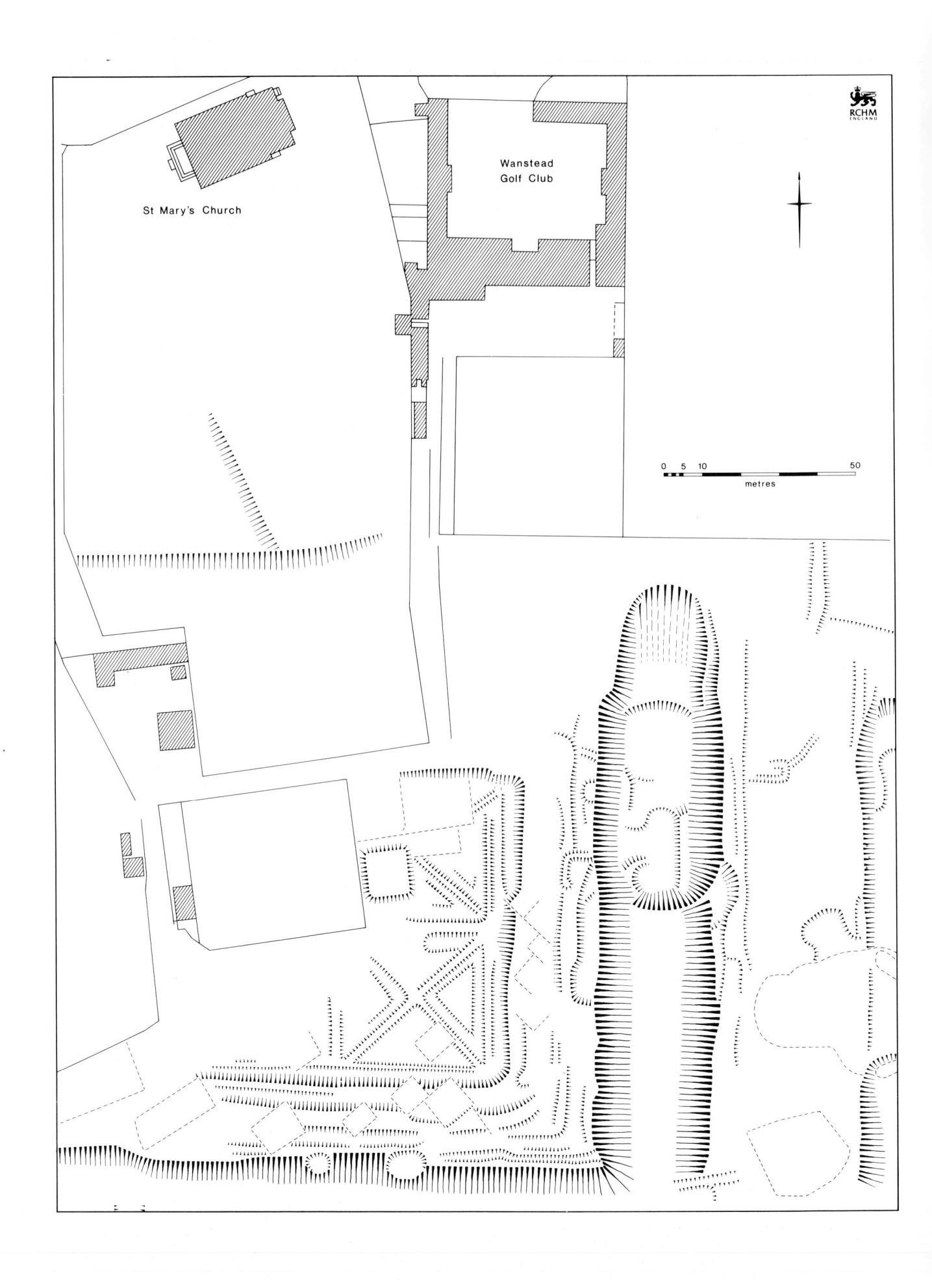

Fig. 3 Extract from field survey of Wanstead Park, site of Wanstead House and parterres; scale 1: 1250 (RCHME, ©Crown Copyright)

undertake. The combination of specialist skills exhibited here was essential to the specific short-term objectives of the survey task, but it was also of great benefit to the authority and detail of the survey product that became available for public deposit in the National Monuments Record (NMR TQ 48 NW 12 and 13).

At Wanstead Park it happened that little field evidence survived of the landscape that pre-dated the creation of the country house and its emparked setting. But this is not typical, for creation of parkland can have the effect of fossilising as archaeologically detectable traces the landscape it replaces, thereby allowing some understanding of the physical impact of that creation of an exclusive zone. Just such evidence has certainly been recorded in work by the Debois Group at Hylands near Chelmsford. Beyond that again, it has been suggested that the form in which traces of an earlier landscape survived in parkland, and perhaps were even enhanced or re-created, reflects an attitude or aesthetic in the design of parks and gardens which can most clearly be perceived in the field evidence. This is what Oliver Rackham and John Phibbs have called 'the pseudo-medieval landscape', citing principally East Anglian examples such as Blickling in Norfolk, Ickworth in Suffolk and Woodhall in Hertfordshire (Rackham 1986, 129; Phibbs 1991).

Also at Wanstead Park, and quite typically, the nearby church was affected by the developments of house and gardens. There St Mary's was rebuilt in 1787-1790 within the grounds of the house, formed an appropriate feature, and provided a setting for a monument to Sir Josiah Child (died 1699) of stunning magnificence, but the rebuilding was on or close to the site of the earlier church (Pevsner 1965, 412-3, pls 30b, 40). A contrast is provided by the church of St Michael at Woodham Walter near Maldon. Here a large-scale RCHME survey was directed at what had previously been categorised simply as a moated site but is in practice an elaborate country residence of the Radcliffe family, from 1525 Viscounts Fitzwalter and from 1542 earls of Sussex. The buttressed and turreted brick foundations of the house and surviving diaper-work perhaps suggest an early 16th-century date: it was certainly a sufficiently grand place to play host to the Lady Mary in 1550 on an occasion of her planned flight to the Continent by boat from Maldon. The earthworks demonstrate an impressively contrived access and extensive formal gardens (Everson 1991, 15; NMR TL 80 NW 15). But this elaboration of scale evidently superseded an earlier settlement or manorial complex and medieval church, with the result that the latter was displaced. Its former presence was attested by the material evidence of later medieval moulded stonework re-used in the core of the house's NW tower and of fragments of medieval grave cover ploughed from the adjacent field to add to surface finds, local tradition and perhaps aerial photographic evidence that point to the probable location of that church (Ainsworth *et al.* 1991). The extant church of St Michael at Woodham Walter is the mid 16th-century replacement, sited a third of a mile away to the NW where it either joined to or has subsequently been joined by a group of houses to form a settlement nucleus that is now the village of Woodham Walter. In this case, however, dynamic change in this post-medieval landscape did not stop there. For in 1573 the 2nd Earl of Sussex was granted the even grander house of New Hall at Boreham by Elizabeth I, with the probable short-term result that Woodham Walter Hall declined in residential use and in the longer term was demolished c1700. In the wider local landscape, non-residence also led by the early 17th century to disparking of the deer park anciently belonging to the manor and its conversion to farming use, as one element in that continuing pattern of piecemeal changing land-use that Jennifer Ward describes elsewhere in this volume.

Here, perhaps, are glimpses of what post-medieval archaeology *qua* landscape history can be about; that is not simply collecting pigeon-holed archaeological items of the period but developing an understanding of interconnected changes, of which the social and economic background and causes may also be perceived both in some detail and through a varied combination of sources that may not in themselves typically be thought of as archaeological.

Recent archaeologically-based rural parish studies (eg Rodwell and Rodwell 1986, 182-6; Andrews 1993, 25-35) evidently reveal a picture of diverse but generally small-scale change, like the conversion of the deer-park at Woodham Walter, running through the post-medieval period. This tallies with the simplified view of contemporary writers that Essex was an enclosed county by the 16th and 17th centuries, and with more complex modern assessment that in those sub-regions of the county that had had regimes of mixed husbandry remaining common fields were fast disappearing by then, while in wood pasture areas they had probably never existed (Thirsk 1967, 6-7, 53-55). An impression is easily formed of an old, rather static landscape. Yet Professor McIntosh's study of the manor and liberty of Havering through the 16th and into the 17th century reveals a doubling of population through that period and an agrarian economy ever more strongly orientated to supply the London market - 'a community transformed' as she characterises it (McIntosh 1991). CA Hewett, too, using principally examples from Essex has provisionally allied the development of a new pattern of timber-framed house with changing social conditions through the later part of the same period (Hewett 1973). These studies suggest challenges to archaeology and opportunities further to illuminate such changes from built, artefactual and landscape evidence. One particular area of extensive change was undoubtedly the increasingly systematic walling and inning of the coastal marshlands, consolidating and extending the reclamation of the medieval period and creating, as former grazing became suitable for the plough, different conditions for settlement and land-use (Grieve 1959, esp 14-34). Actual or virtual islands such as Canvey and Foulness came to lose their separateness, the former through the efforts of Dutch 'adventurers' in the early 17th century that led to a sequence of social and land-use changes culminating in modern sub-urban and industrial development (Cracknell 1959).

Finally I turn to the evidence from RCHME fieldwork of just one of the manufacturing industries of the county that became established in the post-medieval period and that gives a lead into the realms of industrial archaeology which John Boyes tackles separately. That is, gunpowder or black powder production at what became the Royal Gunpowder Factory at Waltham Abbey. This site, known in modern land-use as the RARDE North Site, extends to some 80ha lying along the River Lea on the county boundary with Hertfordshire, north of the E-W causeway crossing the valley here as Highbridge Street. It was another site which, despite its size and complexity, was represented in formal archaeological record systems only by notice of two small-scale excavations (Cherry 1973, 104; Cherry 1974, 132), in part no doubt because of its secure status and restricted access. A reconnaissance visit by RCHME and English Heritage staff in September 1992 encountered a bewildering complexity and quantity of field remains as earthworks, ruined or standing structures, about which information was rudimentary or non-existent. Fieldwork was resourced and carried through a survey of the site from January to March 1993, and the results were subsequently processed and written up as a typescript report for deposit in the NMR, but which is available to interested parties (RCHME 1994). Behind the report lies a large supporting archive deposit.

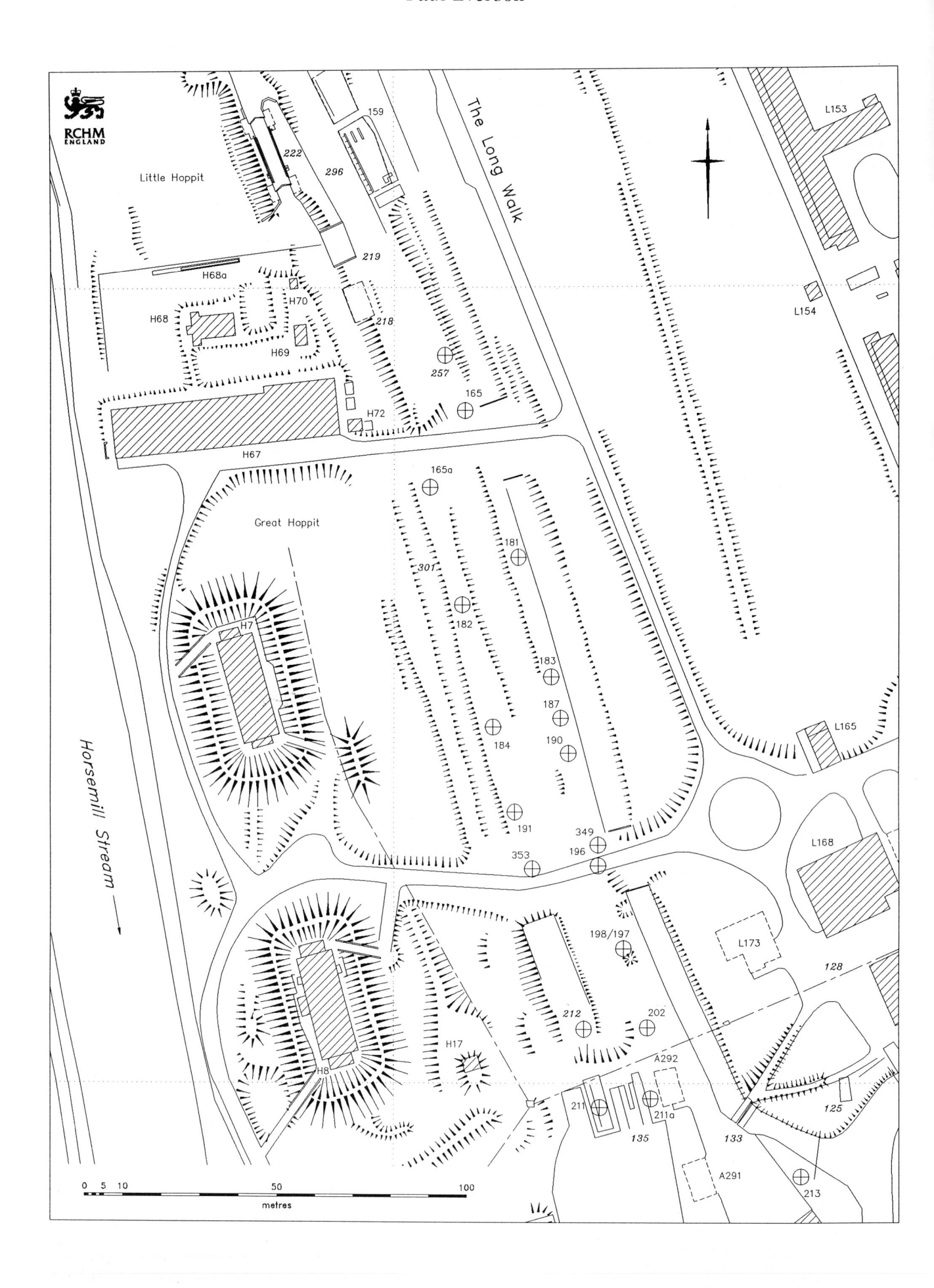

Fig. 4 Extract from field survey of Waltham Abbey Royal Gunpowder Factory, Millhead area; scale 1: 1250 (RCHME, ©Crown Copyright)

POST-MEDIEVAL ESSEX

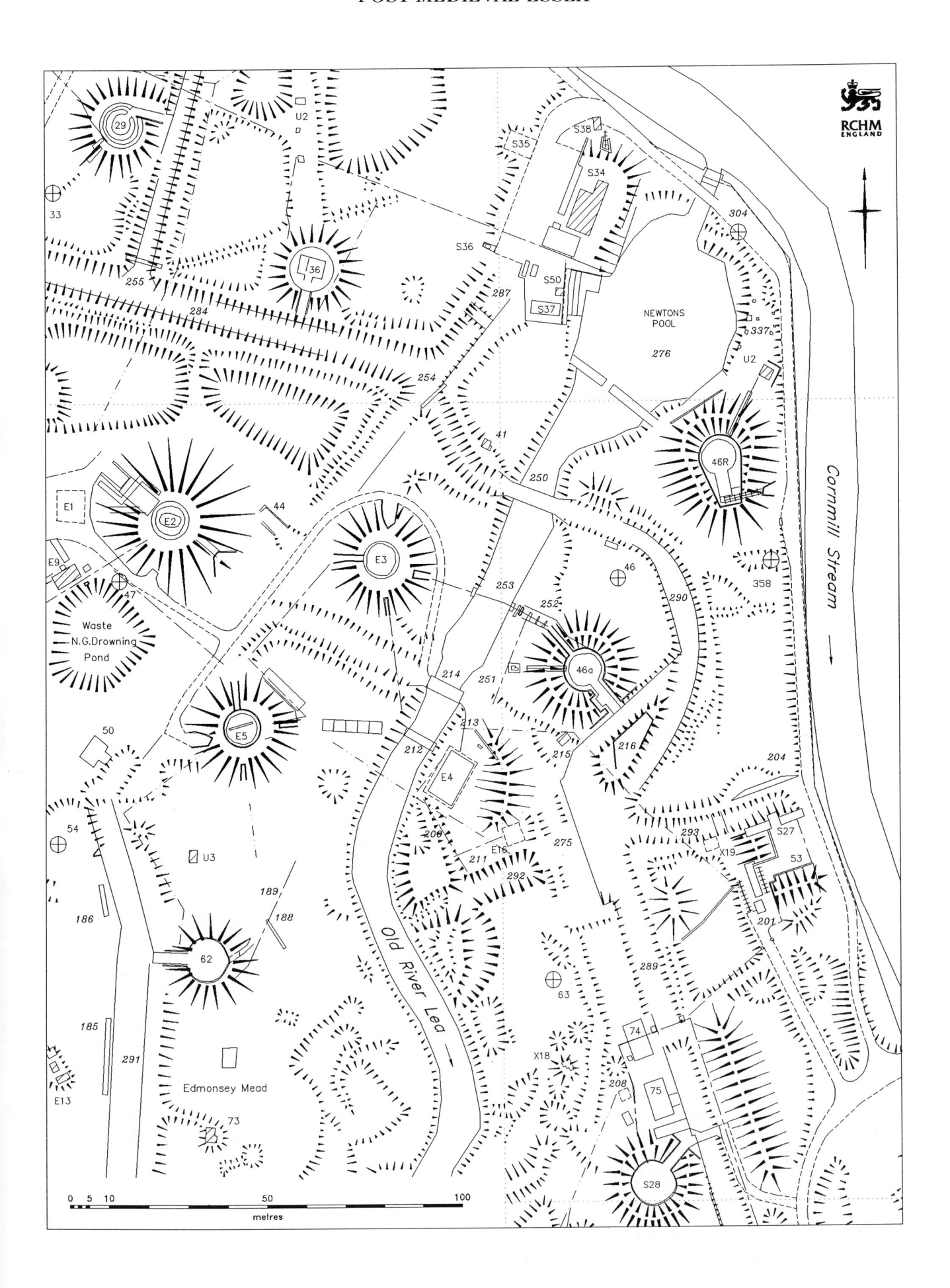

Fig. 5 Extract from field survey of Waltham Abbey Royal Gunpowder Factory, nitroglycerine factory; scale 1: 1250 (RCHME, ©Crown Copyright)

The practical context of this work was the closure of the former government research establishment in 1991 and moves to find a beneficial re-use for the site. This might have brought with it land-use changes potentially detrimental to the archaeological content of the site. In consequence, RCHME's survey programme had an agreed dual function - on the one hand to record a monument and series of constructions that are undoubtedly outstanding within the field of the production of gunpowder and high explosives, and on the other to provide English Heritage with basic information about location, function and importance of visible remains and buried features, upon which decisions about statutory protection might be based. To meet these needs, the immediate product of the survey programme were an original surveyed plan of the whole site at 1:1000 scale, descriptions of all buildings, structures and earthwork features, and a field photographic record of all buildings and structures. This has been supplemented by architectural survey of selected buildings and by RCHME professional photographic coverage of selected features. In addition, supporting research has sought out and extracted information from archive deposits at MoD Chessington, catalogued and uncatalogued deposits in the PRO, and at Epping Forest District Museum, and from contemporary manuals and technical sources. Although some systematic recording of gunpowder production facilities has taken place previously elsewhere, it has not been on this scale and complexity of processes: while in the realm of chemical explosives that succeeded gunpowder this was no less than a pioneering exercise.

Gunpowder production at Waltham Abbey is said to begin in the later 16th century, probably re-using or converting existing watermills but not certainly on this site. Production here was more certainly under way by the mid 17th century. When a first glimpse of it is available in Farmer's engraving of 1735 it was clearly already a complex factory-like process, based in a series of specialist buildings presumably involving substantial capital investment and for the greater part exploiting water power from a long header leat latterly known as Millhead. This leat and the early core of the site is identifiable as well-preserved earthwork and buried remains (Figure 4). The platforms on either side of it on which successive mills sat until the last superstructures were pulled down in the 1950s and the foundations were covered by a foot of soil may be expected to contain several metres of buried stratigraphy and consequent high archaeological potential. This has been confirmed by both formal excavation, revealing four or five phases of structures, and by recent casual intrusions. Significant technological change is likely to be represented, perhaps with waterlogged remains. It is here, among other potential, that mills to the designs of the engineer John Smeaton are believed to have been constructed.

In 1787 the factory was bought from private ownership by the state. In the short term and for the duration of the Napoleonic Wars it underwent a period of expansion and innovation. Then from the middle of the 19th century there began further sustained expansion and elaboration that spread the production facilities over the wider site as safety legislation, good practice and utilisation of power sources other than water increasingly allowed. These facilities were linked by an increasingly complex system of leats and canals providing an internal transportation network employing powder barges. The principal impetus for these developments appears to have been the needs of new large-bore guns, in respect both of the quantity of their requirements and of improved combustion from moulded powders.

A very full range of gunpowder processing facilities survive or can be identified on site, among them specialised types to meet the particular military needs. Some are buried features with excellent archaeological preservation, as above. Others are standing structures, which exceptionally have machinery still *in situ*. One example is a water-driven press house and hydraulic press, which seems to preserve an early form of hydraulic power system that predates the application of hydraulic power on site. Another is the group of steam-driven incorporating mills. In their scale and production capacity they may not be paralleled elsewhere, and, in that they were built successively over a period of years between 1857 and 1889 they exhibit a sustained and cumulative commitment to increased output. The survival practically intact of their underdriven power systems is an enormous bonus: for the system is known on paper and was an important development in other industries too, like textiles, but surviving examples are extremely rare in any context, the best probably being at Shirley's Bone Mill at Etruria in Staffordshire (Green *et al.* 1986). The network of moulding houses employing remote hydraulic power reflect the specialist production of moulded powders.

Though it goes rather beyond this paper's brief, from the 1860s onwards the RGPF began to develop and produce a range of chemical-based high explosives and propellants, principally cordite and its constituents, gun cotton and nitroglycerine. By the early 20th century these came to replace black powder and were in production alongside new developments such as tetryl, TNT and RDX until the end of the Second World War. The field remains of these activities (Figure 5) are probably as important, as rare and complete survivals of an early chemical industrial complex devoted to military ends, as the remains of the older gunpowder production. Certainly the 300-year continuum from one to the other, and continuous development of new processes and technologies, gives Waltham Abbey North Site an additional and probably international importance. As so often in post-medieval archaeology, too, it is the combination of standing and buried features, allied to the complex and remarkably complete field evidence for the various levels of infra-structure - transportation, power and communication - and supported by what in this case are enormous quantities of archival material in the form of technical manuals, historic mapping, drawings and early photography that gives the site at Waltham Abbey its exceptional standing. The combination allows a refined level of analysis and understanding of the field remains themselves, and offers a platform for studies by others than RCHME in a wide variety of directions.

The RGPF at Waltham Abbey brings this paper full circle to the military remains where it began. For the location and arrangement of the site were such as to allow the explosive products of the factory to be shipped by barge down the Lea onto the Thames and on, for example, to Woolwich or to the great magazines at Purfleet for distribution then to military installations. The conference organisers sought a statement of research priorities from each contributor. Perhaps the post-medieval period is a case rather for a research philosophy that this illustrates; namely the desirability, the opportunity and the excitement of seeking an integrated rather than a compartmentalised view of the landscape and the society, of which the field monuments and archaeological evidence form individual elements. In short, to implement the objectives eloquently and perceptively set out for the late Bronze Age in Essex by Richard Bradley, only in the post-medieval period with some assurance that the information is to hand to do so successfully.

Acknowledgments

All illustrations were prepared for publication by PM Sinton. The original fieldwork in each case was by staff of the RCHME Keele office, and specifically Fig. 2 by S Ainsworth and HM Jecock, Fig. 3 by WD Cocroft and WR

Wilson-North, and Figs. 4 and 5 by a team led by WD Cocroft. Original field records and processed results are deposited and on public access in the National Monuments Record, National Monuments Record Centre, Kemble Drive, Swindon SN2 2GZ; telephone 01793 414700, fax 01793 414707.

Bibliography and References

Ainsworth, S et al. 1991 'A fragmentary medieval grave cover and the site of Woodham Walter church', *Essex Archaeology and History*, 22, 170-173

Andrews, DD 1993 *Cressing Temple. A Templar and Hospitaller Manor in Essex*, Essex County Council

Andrews, DD and Gilman, P 1992 'Tilty Abbey: a note on the surviving remains', *Essex Archaeology and History*, 23, 152-7

Borrow, G 1851 *Lavengro*, London: John Murray 1900 edition

Brown, AE *(ed)* 1991 *Garden Archaeology*, London: CBA Research Report 78

Buckley, DG *(ed)* 1980 *Archaeology in Essex to A.D. 1500*, London: CBA Research Report 34

Butler, LAS 1967 'Post-Medieval Archaeology in Periodical Literature, 1966', *Post-Medieval Archaeology*, 1, 121-129

Cherry, J 1973 'Post-Medieval Britain in 1972', *Post-Medieval Archaeology*, 7, 100-117

Cherry, J 1974 'Post-Medieval Britain in 1973', *Post-Medieval Archaeology*, 8, 120-136

Colvin, H et al. 1982 *History of the King's Works Vol IV 1485-1660 (Part II)*, HMSO

Cracknell, BE 1959 *Canvey Island: the history of a marshland community*, Department of English Local History Occasional Papers no 12, Leicester University Press

Drury, PJ 1975 'Post-medieval brick and tile kilns at Runsell Green, Danbury, Essex', *Post-Medieval Archaeology*, 9, 203-211

Duffy, C 1975 *Fire and Stone. The science of fortress warfare, 1660-1860*, Newton Abbot: David and Charles

Egan, G 1988 'Post-Medieval Britain in 1987', *Post-Medieval Archaeology*, 22, 189-231

ERO Essex Record Office

Everson, P 1991 'Field survey and garden earthworks' in Brown 1991, 6-19

Everson, PL, Taylor, CC and Dunn, CJ 1991 *Change and Continuity. Rural settlement in North-West Lincolnshire*, London: HMSO

Farmer, J 1735 The *history of the ancient town and once famous Abbey of Waltham... Essex*, London

Gilman, P 1992 'Archaeology in Essex 1991', *Essex Archaeology and History*, 23, 98-113

Glover, M 1974 *The Peninsular War 1807-1814*, Newton Abbot: David and Charles

Green, T et al. 1986 'Jesse Shirley's Etruscan Bone and Flint Mill, Stoke-on-Trent', *Industrial Archaeology Review*, IX no 1, 57-70

Grieve, H 1959 *The Great Tide: the story of the 1953 flood disaster in Essex*, Chelmsford: Essex County Council

Harris, J 1985 *The Architect and the British Country House 1620-1920*, Washington: the AIA Press

Harris, J 1986 'The Artinatural Style' in C Hind ed, *The Rococco in England. A symposium*, London: Victoria and Albert Museum, 8-20

Hewett, CA 1973 'The Development of the Post-Medieval House', *Post-Medieval Archaeology*, 7, 60-78

Huggins, P 1972 'Monastic Grange and Outer Close Excavations, Waltham Abbey, Essex, 1970-1972', *Essex Archaeology and History*, 4, 30-127

Kent, P 1988 *Fortifications of East Anglia*

McIntosh, MK 1991 *A Community Transformed. The Manor and Liberty of Havering, 1500-1620*, Cambridge Studies in Population, Economy and Society in Past Time 16: CUP

NMR National Monuments Record

Oman, C 1908 *A History of the Peninsular War. Vol III Sept 1809 - Dec 1810*, Oxford: Clarendon Press

Pevsner, N 1965 *The Buildings of England. Essex* (2nd edition revised E Radcliffe), Harmondsworth

Phibbs, JL 1991 'The archaeology of parks' in Brown 1991, 118-122

Phillips, A and Barratt, G 1984-85 'Norman Cross Camp, Yaxley', *RCHME Annual Review 1984-85*, London

Rackham, O 1986 *The History of the Countryside*, London: Dent

RCHME 1964 *Newark on Trent. The Civil War Siegeworks*, HMSO

RCHME 1994 *Royal Gunpowder Factory, Waltham Abbey, Essex. An RCHME survey 1993*, Swindon

Rodwell, WJ and Rodwell, KA 1986 *Rivenhall: investigations of a villa, church and village, 1950-1977*, London: Chelmsford Archaeological Trust Report 4/ CBA Research Report 55

Thirsk, J *(ed)* 1967 *The Agrarian History of England and Wales vol IV 1500-1640*, CUP

VCH 1966 *A History of the County of Essex, Vol V*, ed WR Powell, OUP

Industrial Archaeology in Essex

John H. Boyes

As it is unusual to include a paper with the title 'Industrial Archaeology' in a publication based on a major Conference considering the archaeology of Essex from Palaeolithic times, it is perhaps pertinent to examine briefly what constitutes Industrial Archaeology, what relationship it has to the main discipline of archaeology, and how it relates to the county of Essex.

David Cranstone writing in the *Industrial Archaeology Review*[1] said 'The discipline of archaeology has developed over a period of some 150 years, though for much of this period its focus in Britain has been very much on the Prehistoric and Roman periods; only recently has our industrial heritage been recognised as a proper (indeed crucial) field for the deployment of fully-developed archaeological methodology, and this recognition is still not universal within the archaeological world. In mirror image of this situation, the discipline of Industrial Archaeology has grown up with (until recently) a disappointingly limited input from archaeology, and a limited understanding of, and the need for, archaeological approaches to industrial sites.'

In similar vein, the Government White Paper *This Common Inheritance*[2] includes the following general and all-inclusive comment, 'Buildings, Towns, Monuments and other Historic Sites give us a sense of place. They remind us of our past and how our forebears lived and how our culture and society have developed. They provide the context for new buildings and for changes in our own way of life. They teach us lessons for the future.'

This broad statement is restated and qualified in a later paragraph entitled 'Industrial Heritage' wherein we are reminded that 'This aspect of our National History, ie. industry, is not as fully commemorated or as widely appreciated as it deserves to be. Britain pioneered and applied many of the technologies on which 19th and 20th-century development was based all over the world. The archaeology of the period is a vital resource for understanding these developments, many of which are not recorded in written or pictorial form.'

Based on these premises, the Association for Industrial Archaeology has defined the scope of industrial archaeology as 'A period study embracing the tangible evidence of social, economic and technological development in the period since industrialization.'[3] But to me that definition is too restrictive. Certainly the point is made; 'Unlike earlier periods of archaeology at least the elite were literate in the industrial period and many aspects of society - patterns of government, religious allegiance, domestic and foreign policy, patterns of trade - are better arrived at by documentary rather than archaeological methods. The special value of archaeological evidence lies in determining the living and working conditions of ordinary people, since literacy was not generally a feature of working class society until the late 19th century.'[4]

That may be so within the parameters of post-industrial revolution progress, but industrial development is not something that happened *de novo* in the late 17th or early 18th century - it is a continuum, the origins of which go back to earliest man - or for instance to the neolithic axe factories on Stickle Pike in the Langdale Pikes in the Lake District and to the Roman and Saxon methods of spinning and weaving which are themselves aspects of the popular conception of archaeology. The superb production of the Colchester Archaeological Group *The Red Hills of Essex* is an excellent example of industrial archaeology in this early period.

Although there is reference to the archaeology of industry in a paper in 1878 on 'The Archaeology of the West Cumberland Coal Trade' read before the Cumberland and Westmorland Antiquarian and Archaeological Society, the term did not enter common usage until the 1950s when there occurred the growing recognition of the importance of industrial remains as a factor in modern historical interpretation.

My personal view of industrial archaeology is that it is the study and interpretation of man's economic and technological development throughout history as revealed in physical remains such as buildings, earthworks, artefacts and similar evidence. It thus includes features which have been investigated as part of the natural evolution of archaeology and extends to modern times so that industrial archaeology and industrial history converge just as classical archaeology and early history converge to allow the emergence of a more rounded and three-dimensional picture of man's place in any given period.

Generally speaking, in the past, industrial change occurred over long periods but as we move nearer to our own time, change has become steadily more rapid. As an example from personal experience, I remember having demonstrated to me in the early 1940s one of the first electron microscopes in the research laboratories of Metropolitan-Vickers in Manchester - the latest thing in high technology. Forty years later I was shown the very same piece of equipment being proudly displayed for the first time in a new gallery in the Science Museum. A fragment of the history of industry and technology within half my own lifetime.

And as archaeology provides a guide to man's evolution and technology throughout the world, so it must be recognised that, despite Britain's pioneer work in industrial development, particularly in the 18th and 19th centuries, industrial archaeology is an international, not a national or local, study and that often a world perspective is necessary if adequate evaluation of sites, monuments and landscapes is to be achieved. But as in any structure it is the bricks which create the overall design so it is necessary to examine the bricks which are to be found in the local approach; and the bricks we need to investigate urgently are the contributions of Essex to the complex whole and to assess the evidence which they can provide.

It has become established practice in an overview of the industrial archaeological field to group aspects of investigation under major headings though this grouping does not imply any degree of priority. These headings are:-

1. Power supplies - Animal, Wind, Water, Steam, Internal Combustion, Electricity and Nuclear Power.

2. Mining and quarrying.

3. Manufacturing. The whole range of production and service industry.

4. Public Utilities - Water, Gas, Electricity, etc.

5. Transport - Roads and Bridges, Waterways, Railways, Ports and Shipping.

---

[1]Excavation: The Role of Archaeology. David Cranstone. Industrial Archaeology Review. Vol XIV. No 2. p.119. Spring 1992.

[2]Government White Paper. Com 1200 of 1990.

[3]Industrial Archaeology: Working for the Future. Marilyn Palmer. I A Review. Vol XI. No 1. p.18 para 2.1. Autumn 1991.

[4]Ibid. para 2.2.

INDUSTRIAL ARCHAEOLOGY IN ESSEX

Plate 1 Harwich Dockyard Crane

But before studying the above headings in the post industrial revolution period - a matter of 250 years - it is advisable to look back to post-Saxon times and raise questions about medieval Essex which perhaps have not received as much attention from archaeologists as have earlier periods. Immediately we are faced with three problems. The first is the time span between the Norman Conquest in 1066 and the threshold of the industrial revolution in say 1700 - a span of 650 years, is equivalent to the time between the reign of Edward III and the present day and it is notorious that as time recedes so it becomes telescoped. The second problem arises directly from the first and that is that up to comparatively recent times historians, with a few notable exceptions, have concentrated, when dealing with national history, on the political and constitutional scene and on the power struggles with foreign states, while on the local level they have looked at manorial descents, land tenure and the dramatic civil disturbances such as the internecine struggles of the barons, though investigations into the Peasants Revolt have highlighted some of the economic problems arising after the Black Death. But in the period under review there were more than 20 generations of people living their day-to-day lives. The third problem again arises from the time span. Archaeology has provided answers for many questions prior to the Norman Conquest and documentary evidence is available in ever-increasing quantities for the past 250 years but for this long medieval period, apart from the political and military scene, evidence is relatively scant - partly because of the general illiteracy of the ordinary people, partly because of the absence of printing before 1476, and partly because of the ravages of time in destroying a great deal of material which was generated. But out of the surviving material much research has been done and today we are beginning to see the sort of life lived outside the castle, the monastery and the church; and that regular trade and industry was carried on, that technical innovation took place and that economic development at the local level occurred. Yet it is so easy to be bemused by dramatic events that we fail to ask ourselves questions such as : how was the stone quarried and transported for building castles, churches and monasteries in areas where no stone existed, eg. Castle Hedingham, Tilty Abbey, Coggeshall Abbey, etc? Who were the masons, carpenters and others involved in such building activities? Where was the cloth made for the rich robes we can see in illustrations and who made it? How was the technology of loom construction developed and how were the dyestuffs prepared? From where did the iron and steel come for use in a county like Essex devoid of natural ores? And so on. There are facile answers to many of these sorts of questions but a great deal of research embodying background technical knowledge is still required.

All these things were part of the development of Essex during those 650 years and yet adequate answers are often not forthcoming. Many of these things entered into the lives of ordinary people yet we are told very little about them. A common statement is that the people lived a self-sufficient economy and while that is true up to a point, it is certainly not the whole truth. So what can be said about Essex using the sub-divisions already mentioned?

Power

Animal Power By animal power I include both human and animal energy for driving machinery as opposed to animal power for transport purposes or haulage as in ploughing and associated activities in agriculture. Probably the best-known example in Essex and one that has been extensively studied is the dockyard crane at Harwich (Plate 1). Dating from 1667, it was removed to its present site in 1930 when the naval dockyard was closed. When it was erected it was in conformity with current technology, and the wharves on the Thames and other rivers serving sea-going vessels were lined with such cranes. It is thus an important survival reminding us of how men walking inside a large drum could provide the power for raising heavy loads. Berdon Priory and Gosfield Hall both have donkey wheels, where a donkey walked inside the drum, for water raising. It is unlikely that any new lifting devices of this type will be discovered in Essex.

Other animal powered machines were used on farms for driving barn machinery and examples of these may still survive in barns in Essex. The remains of one at Doggets Farm, Rochford, where a horse was harnessed to a large overhead wheel and in walking round in a circle under the wheel turned the wheel which through gearing drove barn machinery. Such wheels were still being made in the 19th and early 20th centuries. This equipment was generally less costly to install than windmills or watermills and was independent of the vagaries of wind and the availability of water.

Water Power In Domesday Book over 200 mills are recorded in Essex. Unfortunately the kind of mills they were is not stated. Only one thing can be said and that is that there were no windmills. It is probable that many of them were watermills but it is possible that there were a number of horsemills of a primitive type as mentioned in the foregoing paragraph. Some also may have been large hand-operated querns. But the very existence of these mills implies that there was a group of craftsmen with technical knowledge capable of dealing with mechanical problems who could pass on their skills from generation to generation. It also implies that there were also the facilities of trade in purchasing millstones and transporting them. It is one thing to fashion the structural components and gearing of a mill out of local timber but there is no local quarry from where millstones could be obtained. There is good reason to suppose that the millstones used in the Domesday watermills would have been brought from the Eifel region and the area around Cologne, a journey down the Rhine and across the North Sea to London or wharves on the Essex coast.

A comprehensive study of Essex watermills has yet to be made, but Hervey Benham's book 'Some Essex Watermills' covers the eastern part of the county so far as existing and recent watermills are concerned.[5] Further information is given for parts of western Essex in Volume II of 'Watermills of the London Countryside'[6] which covers the Lea, Roding, Chelmer and South Essex. I am sure that there are many more sites to be found, especially those of the medieval period, which were used for fulling as well as for corn and grist milling. I have identified over 100 sites in the Lea Basin, though that includes parts of Hertfordshire and Bedfordshire. Old estate maps are useful for identifying a site, as at Little Canfield in 1590, but so far as I am aware no archaeological investigation has yet taken place. The Essex Mills Group is actively concerned about the future of both water and windmill sites.

Although watermills were usually found on rivers and streams, there have been many sites round the coast where the mills relied on tidal power. Essex has had its quota of these mills, including what was the largest tide mill in the country at Three Mills Bromley-by-Bow, West Ham, on the tidal reach of the river Lea. Another which has recently been restored is on a creek off the Colne at Thorrington. Several other places on the coast, including Saint Osyth, are known to have had tide mills and investigation of suitable sites might reveal useful technical evidence.

Wind Power Windmills came to England at the end of the 12th century and Essex was in the forefront of this new technology, for the first authentic record of a mill in Essex is at Henham in 1202 yet within the next century at least 50 new sites were recorded and this steady growth continues up to the time of the Black Death. There was then a lull in building but by a century later the growth restarted and continued into the 19th century. The earliest account for building a mill in Essex is in 1299 and once again we see that the building was not a local affair but involved purchase and transport as well as negotiation - organisation beyond a DIY domestic job.

An extensive survey of Essex windmills, their history and technology, was achieved by the late K G Farries[7] and was published in five volumes in the 1980s. While it is undoubtedly the definitive work on the subject, there is still research to be carried out when the opportunity occurs of investigating the many mounds which have been described as mill mounds, though no documentary or above-ground evidence survives. Ken Farries has a chapter entitled 'The First 500 Years' and includes a list of documentary references dating from 1202 at Henham to 1349 at White Roding together with 39 mill mounds which are known to have had mills sited on them. Others have no other clue beyond the name Mill Hill or Mill Field e.g. Elmdon and Abbess Roding. Other parishes where it is known that mills have stood have not had the exact sites pin-pointed by ground investigation.

While the majority of windmills have been used for corn and grist grinding, there are instances in Essex of what became common practice in the Fens of the use of wind power for drainage purposes. There was a windpump at Tollesbury which collapsed in 1914 and the remains were still visible in 1971. Another at East Tilbury just over ¼ mile east of Gobions Farm drove an Archimedean screw for lifting the water from a lower to a higher level. As the use of Archimedean screws for this purpose was not uncommon in Holland, one wonders whether the same Dutch influence which was evident on Canvey Island also applied here. Unfortunately it was pulled down about the beginning of the Second World War, but identifiable remains survived until 1976.

Steam Power At one time as indicated by personal recollection and documentary sources, there were many steam engines working in Essex both in industry and agriculture but the majority have been scrapped either in favour of electricity or because the undertakings using them had closed down. A few examples have been preserved such as the very early 1845 Woolf Compound Beam engine at Beeleigh Mills together with its associated elephant boiler; and the much later 1931 inverted triple expansion pumping engine by the Lilleshall Company preserved by the Essex Water Company at Langford waterworks near Maldon (Plate 2). Excellent records of Essex engines have been compiled by the International Stationary Steam Engine Society and similar organisations. It is, however, often possible to identify positions of the larger steam engines by the massive and solid construction of their foundations in otherwise derelict buildings. Colin Bowden has done a great service to archaeology in his paper 'The Stationary Steam Engine : A Critical Bibliography' in which he expresses the hope 'that the references listed ..... will provide sufficient material to enable the industrial archaeologist to make an informed assessment of any engine and/or engine site, and to put it into its technological and historical context.'[8]

---

[5] Some Essex Watermills. Hervey Benham. 1976. Essex County Newspapers Ltd.

[6] Watermills of the London Countryside. Kenneth C Reid, ARIBA. 1989. Charles Skilton Ltd.

[7] Essex Windmills. Millers and Millwrights. Five volumes. K Farries. 1981-88. Charles Skilton Ltd.

[8] The Stationary Steam Engine: A Critical Bibliography. Colin Bowden. I A Review. Vol XV. No 2. p.177. Spring 1993

Plate 2 Inverted triple expansion pumping engine at Langford waterworks

Internal Combustion Engines It is now over 100 years since the principle of a practical internal combustion engine was first established and there have been several generations of developing types since then. At first fuel was principally coal gas, but later liquid fuels such as petrol, paraffin and diesel oils were used. Many such engines were used on farms but they were also to be found powering small factories and similar premises. On a destroyed site the presence of polluted earth may often indicate the type of engine which was installed.

Electric Power Electricity will be dealt with more fully under manufacture and public utilities but as this source of power has been available for over 100 years it is possible that the remains of old installations may be found in derelict buildings. Such remains can be of interest and importance.

Mining and Quarrying

Essex is not a mining county with extensive coal and iron ore deposits, and in the absence of major building stone there has been limited quarrying apart from chalk and gravel extraction. Chalk extraction with its courses of flints has wrought changes in the landscape both as major quarries as at Purfleet and Thurrock; and minor chalk pits particularly in the chalk beds in the north of the county. But little evidence remains of the methods adopted during the working years apart from the Thurrock deneholes, though examination of abandoned spoil heaps may reveal discarded tools and other artefacts. Abandoned chalk quarries have usually become havens for chalk-loving plants but they have also become repositories for equipment ignored by the scrap merchant. I am not aware of whether there has been any comprehensive survey of lime kiln sites in the county but in view of the importance of lime as a fertilizer there ought to be structural evidence remaining of the kilns themselves. Of course Purfleet was the main source of lime for the county and the roads from there carried vast quantities apart from the equally vast amounts which were transported partly by the first railway in Essex down to the wharves on the Thames from which it was shipped to more distant customers. One clue is given by the trade token issued by Samuel Irons of Purfleet in 1669 which illustrates a contemporary limekiln. As an aside I would point out that 17th and 18th-century trade tokens are a very useful aid in the study of industrial archaeology both from the names of the issuers and from the designs with industrial associations which they often bear.

The use of flint as a building material was, of course, important though it clearly had its limitations. But an ancillary activity was the calcining of flint for use in the pottery industry. This took place at West Thurrock and the calcined flint was then transported to Stoke-on-Trent and the Potteries. When the local supply diminished, flints from Normandy were imported and this led to a unique structure being erected on the bank of the Thames which will be mentioned later.

Allied to quarrying is sand and gravel extraction. Because of the nature of the geological deposits in Essex, the county has held the premier position for many years among English counties for the supply of sand and gravel, but the main surviving evidence is provided by the flooded gravel pits of which there are extensive examples in the Lea Valley.

The Essex clays in various parts of the county have been the raw material over the centuries for the brick making industry. Once the suitable clays had been exhausted from the local pits, adjacent to where the bricks were made and subsequently used, the brickfields have been redeveloped usually as housing estates and all trace of the industry has been lost. Originally the bricks would have been burnt in clamps and it was only later that kilns were erected. At first the kilns would have been single chamber Newcastle kilns, and only progressively after 1858 would have Hoffmann and Belgian top-fired kilns been introduced on the more sophisticated and extensively worked sites. In the 1960s, there were some Newcastle kilns still standing near Birchanger on the Hertfordshire border but these have all gone without, so far as I know, any record being made. A bottle kiln survives at Marks Tey at the old tile works. The influence of the Little Thurrock brickfields can be seen in the line of the rear of the houses in Clarence Road, Grays which was the line of the railway from the brickfields to Grays wharf.

Manufacturing

Cutlery Although Essex has no iron ore deposits nor an iron and steel industry, there was in the Middle Ages a cutlery industry in Thaxted and future archaeological investigation may yet throw light on some of the problems associated with it. It obviously had a place in the economic development of Essex yet because of its decline by the end of the medieval period it cannot have had any lasting effect. The fact that it was there is an indication of the growth of industry and technology at that period, yet economically there seems to be no more reason why it should have developed in Thaxted rather than in Braintree or Witham. It is also unclear when it started in Thaxted, but just prior to the Peasants' Revolt there were, according to the Poll Tax return of 1381, no less than 79 cutlers, 4 sheathers, 2 goldsmiths, and 11 smiths working in this 14th-century industrial town. The archaeological evidence of their trade is slight[9], yet there is the Guildhall - a monument to their wealth - and the name Cutlers Green is mentioned in 1581. Traces of their forges have been found

---

[9] D D Andrews, 'A late medieval cutlery manufacturing site at Weaverhead Lane, Thaxted', *Essex Archaeol. Hist.* 20 (1989), 110-9.

in the past and any archaeological excavation in Thaxted should always bear the possibility of traces in mind. But from where did they get their steel and to whom did they supply their wares - for there is no steel in Essex and 79 cutlers surely served more than local needs? I had assumed, without any evidence, that the steel had probably been imported from Sweden, via the Harwich area and along the Stour valley, and that it found its way to Thaxted because of the presence of plenty of wood for fuel. Sweden has had a long and successful steel industry and it is known that they exported steel. But I began to have grave doubts about this theory when I discovered another record which, while not referring to Thaxted, may have a bearing on the matter. In 1318 an English ship was seized allegedly by or through the influence of certain German Hanse merchants and the owner, because he could get no satisfaction from these merchants, in retaliation seized some of their goods in London. These goods included 60 barrels of steel at 60 shillings a barrel belonging to three merchants of Dortmund in the Ruhr area of Germany. It is known that steel from Solingen, which is not far from Dortmund, was being made, possibly in the middle of the twelfth century and certainly by the thirteenth century. The highest grades of this steel were regarded as the finest steel in the world for swords and cutlery. It was also used by armourers. This also may provide a tenuous link for Ken Newton, the late County Archivist, who spent some time researching Thaxted history, once told me that he thought that the Thaxted cutlery industry may have included the manufacture of armour, but he gave me no reference for this.

So here are barrels of steel, which was probably blade steel, being imported from Dortmund into London; and the only 14th-century cutlery centre near London was Thaxted. In 1336 Edward III passed a law forbidding the export of sheep's wool to Flanders in order to stimulate the local cloth manufacturing industry. Was Thaxted then a focal point in the developing East Anglian cloth industry, firstly in the manufacture of shears for clipping the fleeces from the animals, and then later in the manufacture of shearing knives for cutting the nap of the finished cloth? If not, where were the tools for the trade made?

Textiles The major industry in Essex in the past has been textiles but as this for much of its heyday was domestic industry, few physical remains survive, though its importance can be judged from associated buildings and their architecture such as Paycocke's House at Coggeshall and elsewhere. The history of the industry has been extensively covered but I would again mention the use of trade tokens, such as the Tayspells of Colchester with their differentiated merchant's marks, or those of Dedham or Coggeshall to act as guides for further archaeological research.

Perhaps even more striking is the gentrification of an old textile town such as Dedham where redevelopment can obscure its origins. As one walks along the road in front of the church one sees houses which are clearly of the 17th and 18th centuries representing an affluent community with no evidence of industry, but behind the frontages the houses run at right angles to the street and I suggest that these buildings were associated with the individual wealth, which was also responsible for the construction of the 15th-century church tower where the marks of Thomas and John Webbe are displayed. One large textile firm about which not too much is known is now impossible to investigate archaeologically as its site lies beneath the waters of King George's Reservoir at Sewardstone in the Lea Valley. A very old photograph shows a waterwheel which could have been one of the largest in Essex.

In the manufacture of woollen cloth, one of the important finishing processes is that known as fulling. Originally the process was to tread the cloth in a tub of water and fullers earth. At Sens, south-east of Paris, there is a Gallo-Roman tombstone showing a fuller at work and despite technical improvements this practice has continued in remote areas right up to modern times. The purpose was to release the residual grease from the cloth and to shrink the cloth by one-fifth to half its original size in a compact texture by felting it and thus inextricably entangling the fibres so that the weaving pattern became invisible. This provided a harder-wearing and more water-resistant fabric.

Pounding with a club eventually superseded the treading process and then some unknown genius sometime in the late twelfth century conceived the idea of using two clubs linked to a waterwheel to provide a mechanical process. This was probably the first mechanically operated machine other than a corn mill. The earliest reference to one of these fulling mills in England is in 1185 in Yorkshire. As far as I am aware, the first one recorded in Essex was at Lawford in 1286, but from other evidence it is more than probable that one was set up at Witham in 1185 by the Templars and which was known to be derelict by 1308. So Essex could have been in the forefront of this new technology. Complaint was made in 1298 that the weavers of London were sending their cloths out to the fulling mills of Stratford instead of being fulled under foot in London. Where were the Essex fulling mills? Chapman and André on their map marked fourteen in 1777, so their sites are known but there must have been many others, some of which were later converted to corn mills following the decline of the textile trade; other sites will no doubt be found during field research along the stream and river valleys.

Chemical Processes Although the production of salt from sea water was probably the first chemical production to be introduced into Essex - and with different technology is still continued today in Maldon - it is essentially an extraction process, rather than one involving chemical reactions. Such a process is exemplified by that already described by Paul Everson in this volume, the manufacture of gunpowder. Essex not only had the Waltham Abbey site which is being fully surveyed and recorded, (and advantage is being taken to obtain oral evidence from ex-employees to fill in gaps which neither archaeological investigation nor documentary records are able to complete), but it had other sites in the Lea valley most of which have succumbed to redevelopment.

The practice of taking oral evidence to supplement field recording should also be followed in relation to the oil refineries on Thames-side at Shellhaven and Holehaven, as first-generation practices disappear and old plant is replaced by new technology. When oil refining commenced on Thames-side, the oil was brought in in barrels and the old handling equipment has been replaced by the pipelines discharging the bulk tankers. It is possible that some of the earlier processing structures still remain. The company archives may hold some of the plant but it is important that technical details are not lost or destroyed. Future archaeological investigation will never be able to create the information that is available today, but future generations may wish to know as much about the present as we are seeking to learn about the remote past. What is important to remember is that although chemical processes occurred in the past they were from experience and not professional and controlled chemical analysis.

But there is one chemical process which does leave archaeological evidence. Animal skins were probably the earliest form of clothing worn by man and gradually there evolved the process of treating them to make them more acceptable. So leather was produced. Essentially leather is the middle layer of the skin after the outer hair or wool has been scraped off and the inner layer of fat and flesh removed. The middle layer is then cured by tanning, by being soaked in pits of water and oak chips so that the

INDUSTRIAL ARCHAEOLOGY IN ESSEX

Plate 3 Wooden cooling towers of Walthamstow Electricity power station (taken 30 June 1968). Now demolished

hide is converted into leather. Such pits are occasionally found in relation to farms, generally in early periods, but later because of the offensive nature of the work and the length of time required to treat the skins, separate tanneries were established. They, too, created problems because they polluted the water supply.

Engineering The evolution of engineering in Essex has depended upon the availability of tools. For centuries the blacksmith's smithy was the target for everyone who wanted metalworking done and so most villages had a smithy. From these came many of the men who later founded forges which developed into engineering works, like Hunt's of Earls Colne. These great undertakings should also be recorded as the buildings themselves often emphasised the work they did. But the great contribution of Essex industry in the engineering field was in electrical equipment. Crompton-Parkinsons, Marconi, and English Electric, all in Chelmsford, provided an industrial revolution in themselves and it is sad that so much of their pioneer work has gone out of the county. The buildings only tell part of the story and once those have gone there will be little left to reflect their importance - just as in the case of Ransome, Hoffman and Pollard, whose ball-bearings were sent world-wide.

Food Processes With its background of agriculture, Essex necessarily had food processing industries and because of their specialised products the buildings reflected their work. For instance, the Dunmow Flitch Bacon factory was very different from the Dunmow Brewery, now gone, but the latter was proud enough to have its date of construction in brick on its boiler chimney. Then, too, are the jam factories at Elsenham and Tiptree. How much record is there of these or of the village bakehouses like the one which partnered the long-since demolished Bovinger windmill?

Public Utilities

Gas With the conversion from coal gas to North Sea gas as the main supply to the county in the 1960s, all the coal gas plants were demolished including the largest gas works in the world at Beckton and although the standard process has been well recorded the individual idiosyncracies of the plants have been lost. Just fragments remain like the small building at the entrance to what was Saffron Walden gasworks.

Electricity Modernisation has taken its toll even though large power stations are structures erected within the memory of many of the older generation. Walthamstow Power Station, whose wooden cooling towers (Plate 3) dominated the centre of Walthamstow until the early 1960s, has gone and even Bradwell Nuclear Station is reaching its terminal date, after a life of about 30 years. Occasionally discoveries are made. A moth-balled duplicate switchroom at Barking Power Station was recently re-opened to find a complete 1930s switchboard; so research is required to ensure that nothing is overlooked in completing the full story of even modern industry.

Water The constantly rising demand for water has required new ideas in providing an adequate supply including the transfer of water to Essex from Denver Sluice in Norfolk, but there are still many examples of earlier sources including wells, pumps, water towers and reservoirs. Several pumps are either unique as at Earls Colne or are rare examples of a once common type like the wheel pump at Steeple. Again, recording is of vital importance.

Transport

Roads The road pattern of today is quite different from what it was 50 years ago and even more different from its pattern 500 years ago. Quite apart from the creation of motorways and the consequential diversions to adjacent roads there have been major improvements to cater for the needs of increased traffic over the years, as, for instance, the creation of the Epping New Road by-passing Loughton and Buckhurst Hill in the 1830s. Today, in some places, it is difficult to trace the course of an old road except by the line of hedges. Toll houses and milestones are clues but even milestones are not always what they seem, as the cast iron front of the milestone at Mountnessing hides the original stone on the Harwich road with the mileage given in Roman numerals.

Bridges These have been the subject of local parish and county interest over the centuries and today, with the constant need for strengthening them to cope with European loadings, original designs can easily be lost. A complete survey of the present state is essential.

Waterways The architecture associated with waterways has been well recorded and there is a strong public interest in their use and preservation.

Railways Essex had its first passenger railway over 150 years ago and since then there have been both national and local societies which have closely studied the history and development of the lines so that this subject is probably better served in the industrial archaeology field than any other.

Ports and Shipping Despite the long coastline of Essex and the interest which authors like Hervey Benham have taken in Essex coastal shipping, there is still a great deal of research to be done into the operations of the lesser creeks and wharves. But there is one structure that merits recognition. It is, as far as I am aware, the only set of gravity staithes in the south of England, though working in the opposite mode to those on the north-east coast. I referred earlier to the import of Normandy flints, though other minerals were imported in the same way. Cargo vessels moored at the end of this structure which extended into deep water in the Thames at West Thurrock (Plate 4). The minerals were grabbed from the hold and dropped into a holding hopper. Carried on the structure were two lines of rails which join to form a single track running to the end of the staithe. One line is higher than the other and slopes gently down to the single track while the other slopes in the reverse direction. A train of wagons was pushed on to the elevated track and braked. One wagon at a time was detached and under gravity ran to the end of the line and again braked. There it was loaded with the mineral from the hopper. The brake was released and the loaded wagon ran down the lower line. The process was then repeated until all the wagons were loaded and then the locomotive returned the train to the flint works.

The Future

There is clearly a great deal of interest in Essex industrial archaeology as is shown by the amount of research and published results by the various local historical and archaeological societies. Regrettably there is no specific county society collating the information produced. So far as the CBA Industrial Archaeological panels are concerned Essex is part of the East of England panel and joins with Norfolk, Suffolk and Cambridgeshire, each of which has its County Industrial Archaeological Society. Although attempts have been made in the past to form an Essex Industrial Archaeological Society they have not come to fruition.

The subject is not entirely neglected, for there is an Essex Mills Group which specialises in wind and watermills and from whom technical expertise in identifying artefacts and remains can always be obtained; and there are county branches of national societies studying railways and canals. But there is much to be done in the way of active recording. This is essential for buildings and sites can disappear overnight as was the case with Great Bardfield

Plate 4 Aerial view of the gravity staithes used by Thurrock Chalk and Whiting Co., and Lafarge Aluminous Cement Co. (taken 9 October 1970)

watermill destroyed by fire in 1993 and in this era of rapid change even modern factories can come and go in a few years.

To revert to my earlier metaphor, the bricks are there and more are being fabricated but the county needs an architectural group to use these bricks to design a structure which will place Essex in its rightful setting in the landscape of industrial archaeology. Such a group must not only be aware of archaeological methodology but should also be trained in measuring standing buildings, comprehending machinery and understanding process technology as well as undertaking documentary research. Industrial archaeology has as great a need of a broad spread of specialisations as archaeology but inevitably some of the essential specialisations will be very different.

Addendum: With regard to R. Hunt and Co. Ltd. of Earls Colne, a full survey and record of the premises was made by E.C.C. Planning Department, following the closure of the works.

Environmental Archaeology

Peter Murphy

Introduction
It is instructive to re-read Allen and Sturdy's (1980) introduction to the 'Environmental Background' of Essex in the review of 'Archaeology in Essex to AD 1500' (Buckley 1980), which represents the most recent synthetic paper on the topic. They draw information from the fields of Quaternary Geology and Palaeoecology, Palaeoclimatology, Soil Science and Geomorphology, but very little information from archaeological sites. Whilst the data to which they refer underpin our understanding of the development of the Essex landscape it is now possible to supplement this with results from studies in the Environmental Archaeology of sites excavated since 1980 by the Archaeology Section of Essex County Council (Fig. 1). Rather than thinking of an 'Environmental Background' we now have abundant data illustrating the dynamic interaction between people and their physical and biological environment. Furthermore an extensive series of radiocarbon determinations now provides an objective chronology for the Flandrian.

In the present paper it is unnecessary to reiterate Allen and Sturdy's account of the Pleistocene and Holocene Geology of the county, nor their description of soils and landscape regions, to which the reader is referred. It seems more appropriate to give a chronological account of landscape change, sub-divided for convenience by conventional archaeological periods but related to the radiocarbon chronology. By this means it is hoped to give an up-dated account of the changing Essex landscape and to highlight gaps in our knowledge, which should form the focus for future research priorities. The locations of sites mentioned in this paper are shown in Fig. 1. These are all sites which have produced significant results: small-scale analyses or assessments of samples from other sites which have produced sparse or inconclusive results will not be considered here.

Palaeolithic
Pleistocene deposits in Essex have been extensively investigated by Quaternary palaeoecologists and archaeologists over many years, and have formed the subject of several classic studies. A Cromerian palaeosol formed on the Kesgrave Sands and Gravels is known to occur widely (Rose et al. 1976; Rose and Allen 1977). This soil shows evidence of periglacial disturbance of Anglian date; and Anglian Chalky Boulder Clay covers much of the northern half of the county. Turner (1970) has described a complete vegetational record from lake sediments of the succeeding Hoxnian interglacial at Marks Tey. At Clacton, Late Anglian and Hoxnian gravels and marls have yielded faunal remains, pollen data and a Clactonian flint industry (Singer et al. 1973). The Clacton channel deposits have recently been re-investigated by Bridgland et al. (1992), who were able to confirm their Hoxnian age and Thames-Medway origin besides obtaining samples for micro-fossil analysis.

Some recent studies in Essex, and to the north in Suffolk, have resulted in significant revisions of Pleistocene chronostratigraphy and the relationship of human artefacts to it. In Suffolk, a pre-Anglian ('Cromerian Complex') river system flowing eastwards from the Midlands has been defined. Artefacts have been recorded from several sites, including Warren Hill and High Lodge, Mildenhall, establishing a human presence prior to the Anglian glaciation (Ashton et al. 1992; Wymer et al. 1991). In Essex, Bridgland (1994) has presented a revised account of the Pleistocene of the Thames terraces, relating them to oxygen isotope stages established from deep-sea cores and to other dating evidence including amino-acid epimerisation.

The distribution of artefacts in other Middle to Upper Pleistocene deposits is reviewed by Wymer (1980 and this volume). However, although the time-span of human activity in the region has now been extended, information on early hunter-gatherers still comes largely from artefacts in secondary, derived contexts.

Priorities for future work
Clearly studies of Pleistocene organic sediments are likely to yield additional palaeoecological information, but in the main these would be the preserve of Quaternary Geologists and Palaeoecologists. From an archaeological viewpoint the top priority must be the identification and investigation of *in situ* sites where there is a prospect of retrieving faunal and botanical remains directly related to human activity.

Late Upper Palaeolithic to Mesolithic

Vegetation and Landscape
At Enfield Lock in the Lea Valley the base of an organic mud has recently been dated to 9546 ± 56 BP (UB 3350). Pollen analysis indicates an open environment at the base of this sediment, dominated by sedges with some pollen of Late Glacial species such as dwarf birch (*Betula nana*) and willow (*Salix herbacea*). Above this, there is evidence for the development of birch-pine woodland and then pine-hazel-elm woods with oak and alder as later colonists by about 8500-7000 BP (Chambers and Mighall 1990). Late Glacial and Early Flandrian sediments are known from other sites in the Lea Valley. The significance of the correlation between charcoal-rich deposits and vegetational changes at Enfield Lock and other sites in the valleys of the Thames tributaries has been reviewed by Lewis, Wiltshire and MacPhail (1992).

Pollen evidence for the composition of later Flandrian woodland has come from the valley of the Mar Dyke, the Thames estuary and Bradwell-on-Sea (Scaife 1988; Devoy 1979; Evans 1995). At Bradwell a basal peat under marine sediments, dated to 6670 ± 130 BP (HAR 9643), produced a pollen assemblage indicative of deciduous woodland dominated by *Tilia* (lime). In the Mar Dyke, Zone MD:1 is dated from 5740 ± 120 BP (HAR 4522): woodland was of *Quercus* (oak), *Tilia* and *Corylus* (hazel) with *Alnus* (alder).

Together these sites illustrate a change from early post-glacial open landscapes with mainly herbaceous vegetation through to climax deciduous forest over a period of some 4000 years. This dramatic, if slow, environmental change clearly necessitated long-term changes in hunter-gatherer economies.

Coasts
During the Early Flandrian, relative sea-level rose rapidly, submerging large areas of the southern North Sea basin. Around 9500-9000 BP sea level was about 45m below that of today (Ludwig et al. 1981) and between 8500 and 7000 BP MHW rose from -25.5m OD to -8.9m OD (Devoy 1979). To speak of a coastline for the long period here under consideration would be misleading, but some major topographic features are distinguishable. On the basis of reflective seismic profiling (D'Olier 1981) it seems that

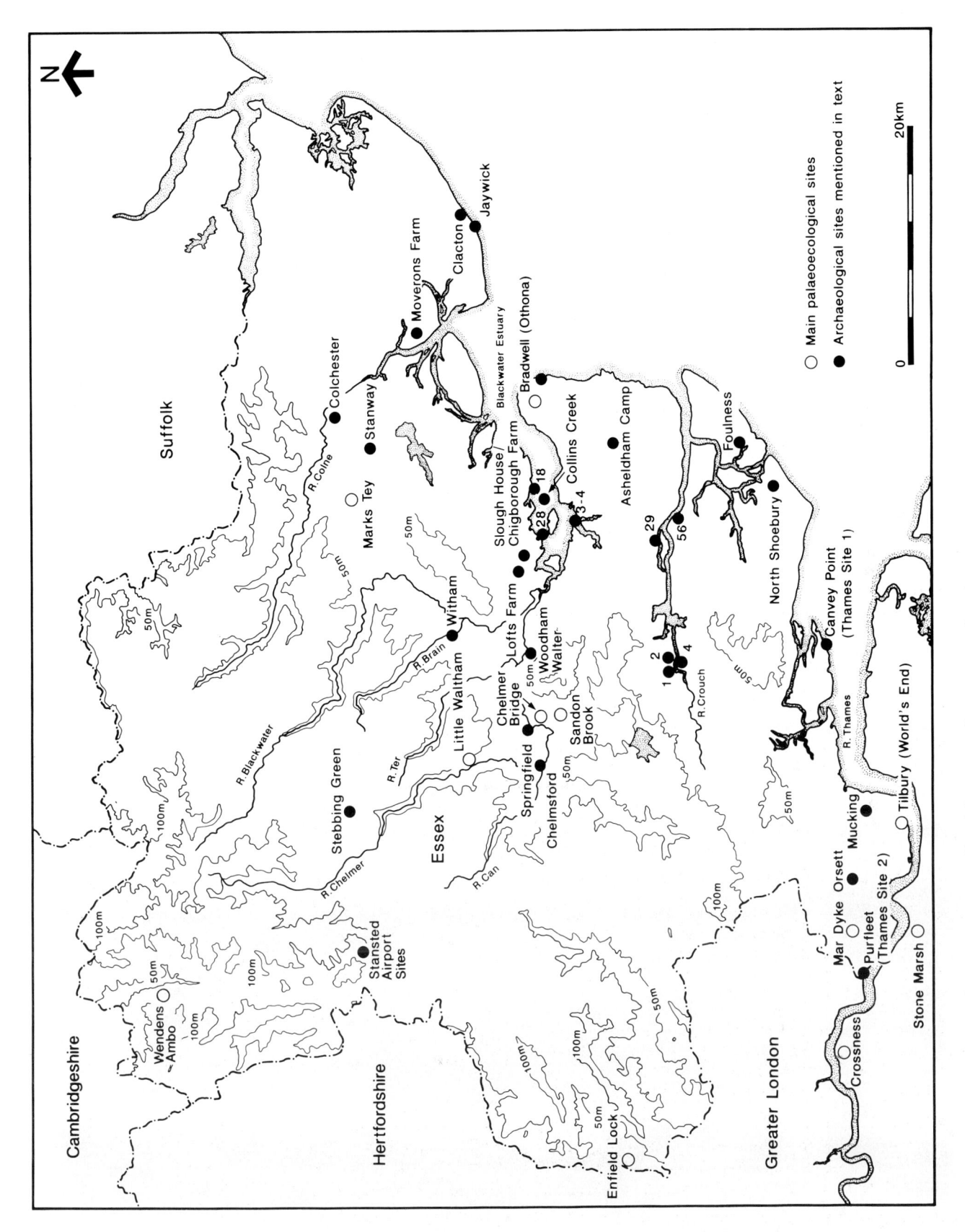

Fig. 1 Locations of main sites referred to in text

during the Early Mesolithic the proto-Thames flowed northwards from its present estuary, joining the proto-Crouch and Blackwater as one major estuary off Foulness, separated from the proto-Stour by an undulating interfluve. During the course of the Mesolithic this landscape was submerged. Basal peats on the old land surface are known from the Thames Estuary and Bradwell (see above).

Mesolithic sites at Hullbridge (Crouch Site 4: Plate 1) and Maylandsea (Blackwater Sites 3,4,33) lying in the modern intertidal zone were clearly quite unrelated to their contemporary coastline and are best regarded as inland base camps of long duration but intermittent occupation from which forays into the North Sea lowlands could be undertaken. Survey work at Hullbridge (Crouch Sites 4,5, 15 and 17) has shown that the Mesolithic site was focussed around a palaeochannel to the north of the present River Crouch. This would have been a freshwater channel, well inland (Wilkinson and Murphy 1995).

Priorities for future work
1. To provide more detailed information on the environmental impact of earlier Flandrian communities, it will clearly be necessary to undertake detailed analyses of micro- and macrofossils from sediments in close proximity to known archaeological sites. The coincidence of sites and sediments is, however, exceedingly rare in Essex. For this reason the demonstration that the Hullbridge sites relate to a palaeochannel of the Crouch is very significant. It is thought that, as a research project, coring along the predicted course of this palaeochannel to obtain samples for palaeoecological analysis is likely to be profitable.

2. There is no specific information on the economies of earlier Flandrian groups in Essex. Any site with the potential to yield bones or plant material directly associated with cultural deposits is of top priority. Sites sealed by penecontemporaneous sediments would be still more important since they might be surface-intact.

Neolithic - Early Bronze Age

Vegetation and Landscape
At the Mar Dyke, Zone MD:2, dated to just before 4650 ± 90 BP (HAR 4523) is characterised by a decline in elm pollen and the first appearance of pollen from cereals and *Plantago lanceolata* (ribwort plantain) with other herbs (Scaife 1988, 109). Devoy (1979) has reported a similar elm decline in the intercalated peats of the Thames Estuary sequence at Crossness (Thamesmead) and Stone Marsh, dated to c 5000BP. It is now thought that the elm decline was a consequence of human disturbance of woodland combined with disease (Peglar 1993); the concurrent (or preceding) rise in herb and cereal pollen marks the onset of clearance for farming. Clearances within the later Flandrian woods dominated by oak, lime and hazel may, however, have been of very limited extent: pollen analysis of palaeosols sealed by estuarine sediments in the Blackwater estuary only some 200m from known Neolithic sites indicates dense woodland cover. Only at one site (Blackwater Site 18, Rolls Farm) does a reduction in lime pollen percentages at the top of the palaeosol hint at any anthropogenic impact (Scaife 1995).

Mar Dyke Zone MD:3 registers a regeneration of secondary woodland with an expansion of elm, lime and ash, a phenomenon widely reported from sediments of later Neolithic date (Whittle 1978). Pollen of cereals and weeds is markedly reduced in this zone, though radiocarbon dates on charred cereals from Blackwater Site 28 (Table

Plate 1 River Crouch Site 4, South Woodham Ferrers, Essex. Riverbank section showing the basal palaeosol with Mesolithic flints, Lower Peat, Middle Clay, Upper Peat and Upper Clay. From Wilkinson and Murphy (1995)

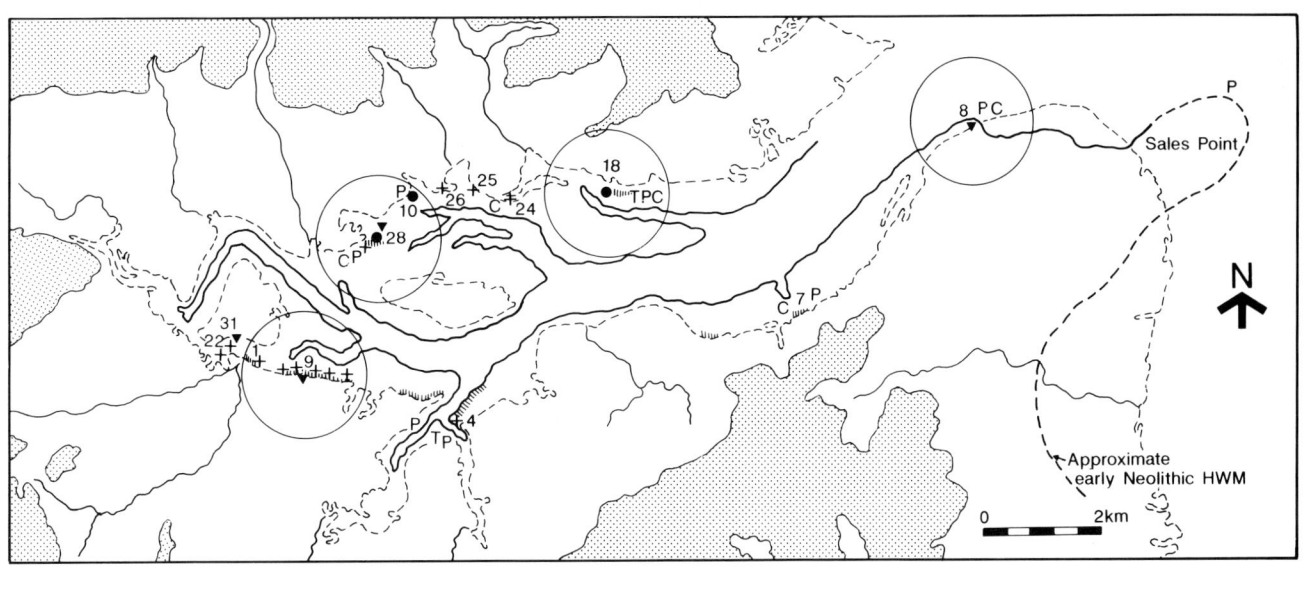

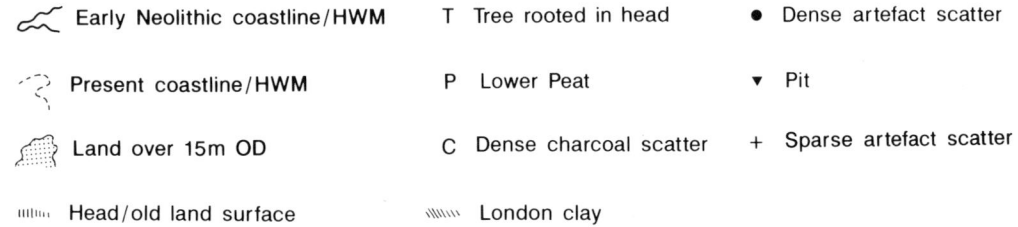

Fig. 2 The Blackwater Estuary in the early Neolithic. 1km diameter circles around main artefact scatters indicate probable relative importance of coastal and terrestrial resources in the catchments of these sites. From Wilkinson and Murphy (1995)

1: see below) certainly indicate continued cereal growing at this time. Similarly, extensive charcoal spreads mainly of later Neolithic date on a land surface under estuarine sediments elsewhere on the coast (Table 1: see below) indicate continued activity, possibly localised clearances.

Beyond the tidal limits of the main estuaries, where intercalated peats occur widely within estuarine sediments, river valley sediments of Neolithic date are at present unknown.

Coasts

The sequence of transgressive and regressive events defined by Devoy (1979; 1980) in the Thames Estuary is summarised in Table 1. Two of these are directly relevant to the Neolithic: the Tilbury III regression of c 5500-4000 BP, when there was extensive peat formation in the estuary; and the Thames III transgression, beginning c 4000 BP. During Tilbury III large areas of what is now the intertidal zone were available for settlement: abundant evidence for Neolithic activity has been detected during survey work (Wilkinson and Murphy 1986; 1995: Fig 2). The rise in relative sea level from c 4000 BP terminated this activity, sealing sites beneath estuarine sediments. The effects of this loss of land on coastal communities are difficult to assess, but clearly the consequent relocation of population could have created some economic stress.

Agrarian Economy and Food Collection

Information on the agrarian economies of prehistoric communities comes largely from charred remains of crops and animal bones retrieved from excavated sites. In Essex, most Neolithic contexts excavated have formed a component of multi-period crop mark sites on terrace gravels. In general fills are neutral to acid so that bone preservation is poor and sporadic. Densities of charred plant remains have usually proved to be exceedingly low. At Lofts Farm, for example, c 292 litres of soil from Neolithic features were flotated, yielding only two cereal grains, grass fruits, occasional hazel nutshell fragments and a scrap of sloe fruitstone (Murphy 1988). Similarly disappointing results have come from the excavations at Springfield, Slough House Farm and Chigborough Farm (Murphy 1990, 1991). Although Boyd (1987) reported some 80 grains of *Triticum aestivum* (bread wheat) from a pit at Woodham Walter, Neolithic features have generally produced only very diffuse scatters of charred cereals, nutshells and fruitstones. Furthermore, as these sites commonly remained foci of activity over long periods and are now truncated by ploughing there is a real likelihood of more recent charred material contaminating the deposits. Radiocarbon dates of 1570 ± 100 BP (OxA 3036) and 113 ± 1.2 BP (OxA 3035) on cereal grains from Neolithic pits at Slough House and Chigborough Farms show that such contamination has certainly occurred. Sites sealed by later deposits and thus protected from contaminants are clearly of considerable significance.

By far the largest assemblage of plant material currently available has come from the intertidal Blackwater Site 28 on a mudflat known as The Stumble, north of Osea Island (Murphy 1989; Wilkinson and Murphy, in prep). This site was submerged in Thames III and covered by estuarine sediments, only now being eroded away to expose it. About 300 soil samples were collected and the majority of these produced charred plant material. Plant remains were much more abundant at The Stumble than at the terrace sites, perhaps because there has been less physical weathering.

Radiocarbon dates on cereal grains and nutshells indicate activity over much of the Neolithic at this site. Within the general settlement spread discrete areas of earlier and later Neolithic activity have been distinguished, though it was not possible to define any significant differences between earlier and later Neolithic farming and foraging. Site 28D, with a late C14 date and late Neolithic pottery produced charred hazel nutshell and apple remains, but no cereals and appears to represent some specialised activity area where woodland foodstuffs were processed. A date from Site 28A on charred cereal grain, however, demonstrates continued cereal growing at this time.

The main crop was emmer wheat, with einkorn, bread wheat, naked barley and flax/linseed. Assemblage composition implies some crop processing in the vicinity. Remains of woodland plants - herbs, shrubs and trees - are well represented (Plate 2); in particular hazel nutshell and sloe fruitstones. There can be no doubt that the collection of wild foods in woodland remained an important part of the Neolithic economy here, as elsewhere in Britain (Moffett et al. 1989). As noted above, pollen analysis of buried soils in the Blackwater Estuary has indicated a largely wooded landscape with very little evidence for clearances (Scaife 1995). Charred roots, rhizomes and tubers, mostly unidentifiable at present, attest to other forms of foraging.

The Stumble seems to represent a settlement but other types of site are known from the coast (Wilkinson and Murphy 1995). On the foreshore at Purfleet (Thames Site 2), there is an exposure of Thames II estuarine sediments with drifted tree-trunks, the surface of which was sub-aerially weathered in Tilbury III. A thin soil formed on these sediments (MacPhail 1995) and mollusca from it indicate wooded conditions, within which stone and flint axes and other artefacts were deposited. There is no evidence for clearance, though a butchered femur of *Bos primigenius* hints at hunting. Elsewhere in the estuaries charcoal spreads on the palaeosol, mainly dated by C14 to the later Neolithic, seem to indicate continued woodland clearance. At The Stumble, twigs from a burnt flint mound gave a date immediately preceding Thames III, when the area must have been very wet. Later Neolithic sites in the Jaywick, Walton and Dovercourt Bay areas recorded by Warren et al. (1936) have now largely been lost by erosion, though a Beaker pit at Jaywick produced a few charred remains of emmer with pig and cattle-sized teeth fragments (Wilkinson and Murphy 1995).

Priorities for future work
1. Pollen and stratigraphic data are largely confined to coastal sequences in the estuaries of the main rivers. The identification and analysis of Neolithic valley sediments inland, exposed by quarrying or road construction, must take a very high priority.

2. Sampling Neolithic features at sites on terrace gravels has so far produced only sparse and often unreliable results, because of contamination. It would be unwise to assert that such sites will never produce useful results, but we cannot expect them to. Assessment of samples from such sites should continue, but the emphasis in research should be on other types of site. Those on calcareous subsoils should produce bone and land mollusc assemblages, at present extremely rare from excavated sites in the county. The importance of sealed, preferably surface-intact, sites has already been emphasised. Sites thought to extend under hill-wash deposits or valley sediments are potentially very informative.

Middle Bronze Age - Iron Age

Vegetation and Landscape
Valley sediments have been analysed for pollen and macrofossils in the Mar Dyke, Chelmer Valley at Little Waltham and the Chelmsford By-Pass and in the Stansted Brook.

In the Mar Dyke sequence, Zone MD:4 (3580 ± 70 BP: HAR 4524) is marked by a secondary elm decline with evidence for opening up of the remaining woodland canopy, with some birch scrub development. From this point on there is a continuous record of cereals and *Plantago lanceolata*. There follows a marked reduction in *Tilia* pollen, apparently indicating removal of lime woodland on the Thames terraces in the Iron Age (Scaife 1988).

At the Stansted Brook a thin biogenic deposit in clastic alluvial sediments was dated to 3810 ± 80 BP. Using this and another radiocarbon date from a biogenic band higher in the section, interpolated dates for the clastic sediments may be estimated. At about 3650 BP the site was enclosed by mixed woodland with lime and alder dominating. A subsequent wetter phase might relate to Bronze Age effects on hydrology. By about 3350 BP tree pollen and particularly lime declined, and deforestation associated with arable farming intensified from about 3000BP (Wiltshire 1991).

At Little Waltham, Peglar and Wilson (1978) report analysis of palaeochannel sediments dated to 3360 ± 80 BP, indicating a locally open landscape dominated by grasses with high *Plantago lanceolata*: amongst trees only alder pollen was abundant.

During construction of the Chelmer Bridge on the new A12 Chelmsford By-Pass palaeochannel sediments (detritus muds) dated to between 3710 ± 80 BP (HAR 6682) and 3200 ± 70 BP (HAR 6683) were seen, overlain by up to 185 cm of mineral alluvium. On macrofossil evidence (for pollen preservation was poor) the basal detritus muds formed in a channel fringed by dense alder fen woods with lime and other trees in the catchment; but towards the top seeds of weeds dominated the assemblages. The channel had largely silted up by 3200 BP (Murphy, Wilkinson and Wiltshire undated).

In short the evidence from these sites indicates new and extensive woodland clearance beginning in the Bronze Age around 3500 BP, perhaps a little later on the Boulder Clay Plateau at Stansted, intensifying further in the Iron Age with the removal of lime woodland. This activity resulted in increased alluviation and channel silting, as at the Chelmer Bridge.

Pollen and macrofossil analyses from archaeological deposits provide additional data on specific site environments. At Slough House and Chigborough Farms near Heybridge, studies of Bronze Age wells have indicated a landscape on the Blackwater terraces dominated by weedy grassland with isolated trees, including oak. There was localised scrub development on the abandonment of these features. Cereals and flax were grown or processed locally. Data from an Iron Age well also point to an open landscape and again there is evidence for cereal and flax growing (Wiltshire and Murphy 1993). Another Bronze Age well at Lofts Farm produced macrofossils indicating open weedy grassland (Murphy 1988). Charred macrofossils from the Bronze Age cremation cemetery at Moverons Farm, Brightlingsea included taxa indicative of rough grassland nearby (Murphy 1990). The buried soil under the Iron Age hillfort rampart at Asheldham Camp indicated pre-fort cultivation and downslope soil movement (MacPhail 1991). Pollen analysis of this soil defined a local landscape dominated by grassland with some cereal cultivation: there was little evidence for surviving woodland apart from some hazel scrub (Scaife 1991). All these sites were located in open landscapes largely cleared of woodland.

Nevertheless, wood from Bronze Age and Iron Age wooden structures at the intertidal sites Blackwater 18 and 28 (see below) illustrates the availability of roundwood, some probably from managed woodlands. Oak and hazel roundwood predominates in these structures, though field maple, the hawthorn group, ash and poplar were also used (Wilkinson and Murphy 1995).

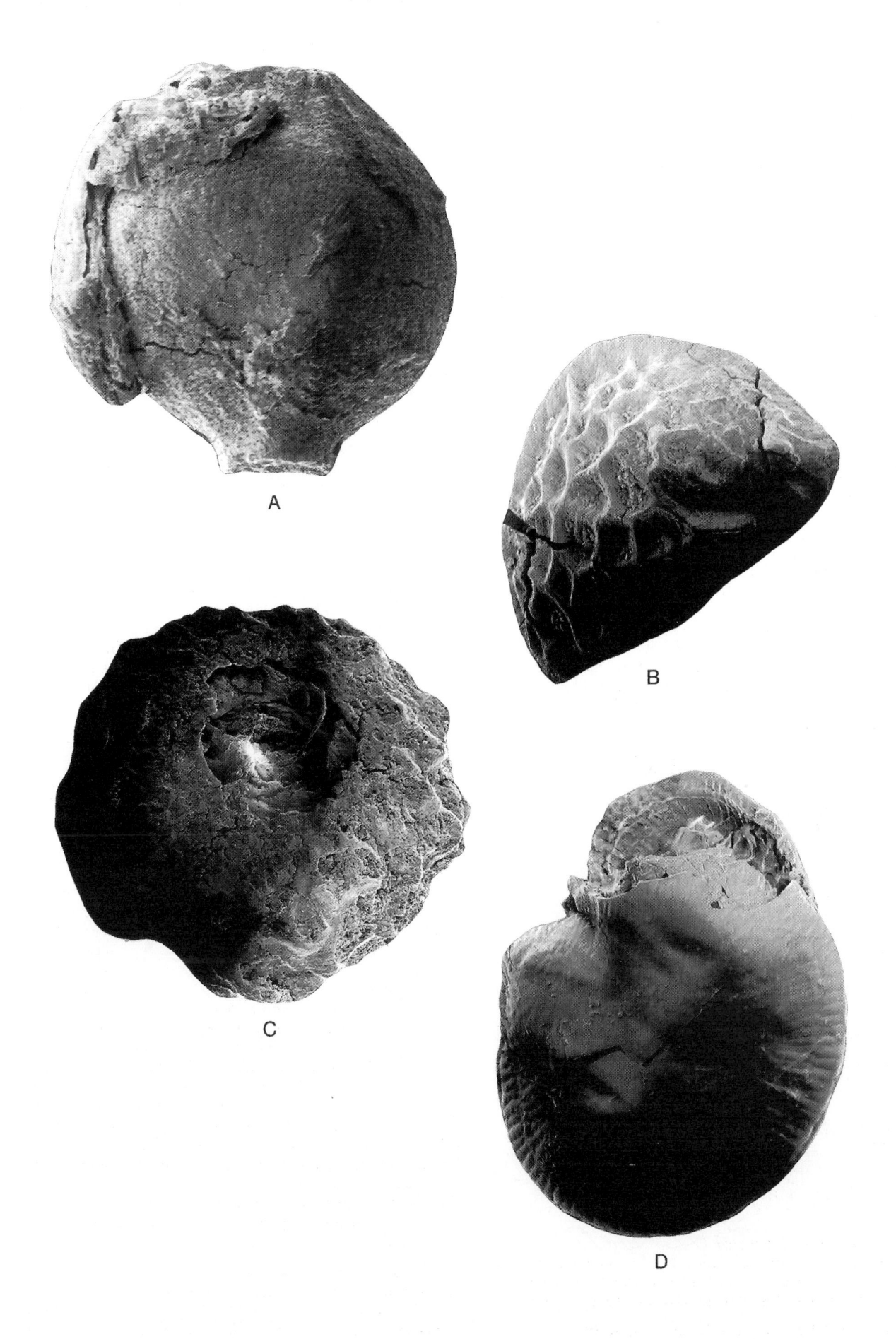

Plate 2 Charred remains of woodland plants from Neolithic features at The Stumble, Blackwater Site 28. A. *Tilia* sp (lime) immature fruit (length 1.1mm); B. *Rubus fruticosus* (bramble) fruitstone (length 2.0mm); C. *Quercus* sp (oak) immature cupule (width 4.1mm); D. *Moehringia trinervia* (three-veined sandwort) seed (length 0.8mm. From Wilkinson and Murphy (1995)

Coasts

Thames III, beginning about 4000 BP, resulted in extensive submergence of land occupied during the Neolithic (see above). The estuaries expanded towards their present margins and a long period of deposition of mainly fine-textured estuarine sediments with some intercalated peats began. Although settlements had been re-located onto the adjacent gravel terraces the present intertidal zone continued to be exploited (Wilkinson and Murphy 1995). Evidence for this comes primarily from wooden structures, apparently of varied functions, in the Crouch and Blackwater Estuaries. The association of human skulls with a wooden platform at Crouch Site 1 (Rettendon) suggests a ritual function, whilst other structures seem to have been more utilitarian - short lengths of trackway, hard-standings and probable landing-stages. A Bronze Age wooden paddle dated to 2900 ± 70 BP (BM 2339) from Crouch Site 56 (Canewdon) attests to river transportation. Channel fills at Crouch Site 29 (Latchingdon) with evidence for nearby Bronze Age activity included shells of winkle, whelk, mussel, oyster, cockle and eel bones - all potential food resources. At North Shoebury shells of mussel, oyster and cockle from Bronze Age and Iron Age features, together with a pleuronectid (flounder?) bone from an Early Iron Age pit, provide direct evidence for exploitation of coastal foodstuffs (Murphy 1995; Jones 1995).

The earliest known saltern from the area, at Crouch Site 2 (Woodham Ferrers) was dated to 3020 ± 90 BP (HAR 5733), but it was in the Late Iron Age that salt production expanded into a major industry. The locations of Late Iron Age and early Roman Red Hills provide a useful indication of coastline morphology around that period (Fig. 3).

Agrarian Economy

Information on the arable economy of the Bronze Age has come from features at Chigborough Farm, Slough House Farm and Lofts Farm, all near Heybridge, Springfield Lyons near Chelmsford and the Social Club Site at Stansted Airport. Assessment of samples flotated at the Late Bronze Age settlement at Windmill Field, Broomfield produced very little material (Fryer, unpublished).

Mention has already been made above of the pollen and macrofossil results from wells at Chigborough and Slough House Farms for Bronze Age cereal and flax cultivation, though there are grounds for suspecting a predominantly pastoral economy on the poorly-drained grasslands on the Blackwater terraces at this time (Wiltshire and Murphy 1993). In pre-Middle Iron Age features at these sites charred cereal remains were sparse (Murphy 1991). At Lofts Farm, however, the Bronze Age enclosure ditch produced charred cereal assemblages dominated by emmer, with a significant proportion of spelt as well as some barley, wild or cultivated oats and possibly horse-bean. (Murphy 1988). In Bronze Age pits at Springfield Lyons spelt chaff fragments were more abundant than those of emmer: other crops included bread wheat, barley and horse-bean (Murphy 1990). The charred cereal remains (again mainly spelt and emmer) from Late Bronze Age/Early Iron Age features at Stansted were sparse, suggesting that the occupants of this site on Boulder Clay soils were largely concerned with stock management rather than large-scale cereal processing (Murphy 1990). The results from these sites are thought to indicate variations in the relative importance of pastoral and arable farming, the former perhaps predominating on poorly drained or heavy soils. It is also now clear that spelt-growing was a Bronze Age innovation in this area.

During the Iron Age the relative status of spelt as a staple crop remains to be established. A large deposit of charred grain from an Early Iron Age storage pit at Rectory Road, Orsett seems to have been largely of spelt (Murphy 1988). The latest substantial charred cereal assemblage with a significant component of emmer came from a Middle Iron Age charred granary deposit at Asheldham Camp (Murphy

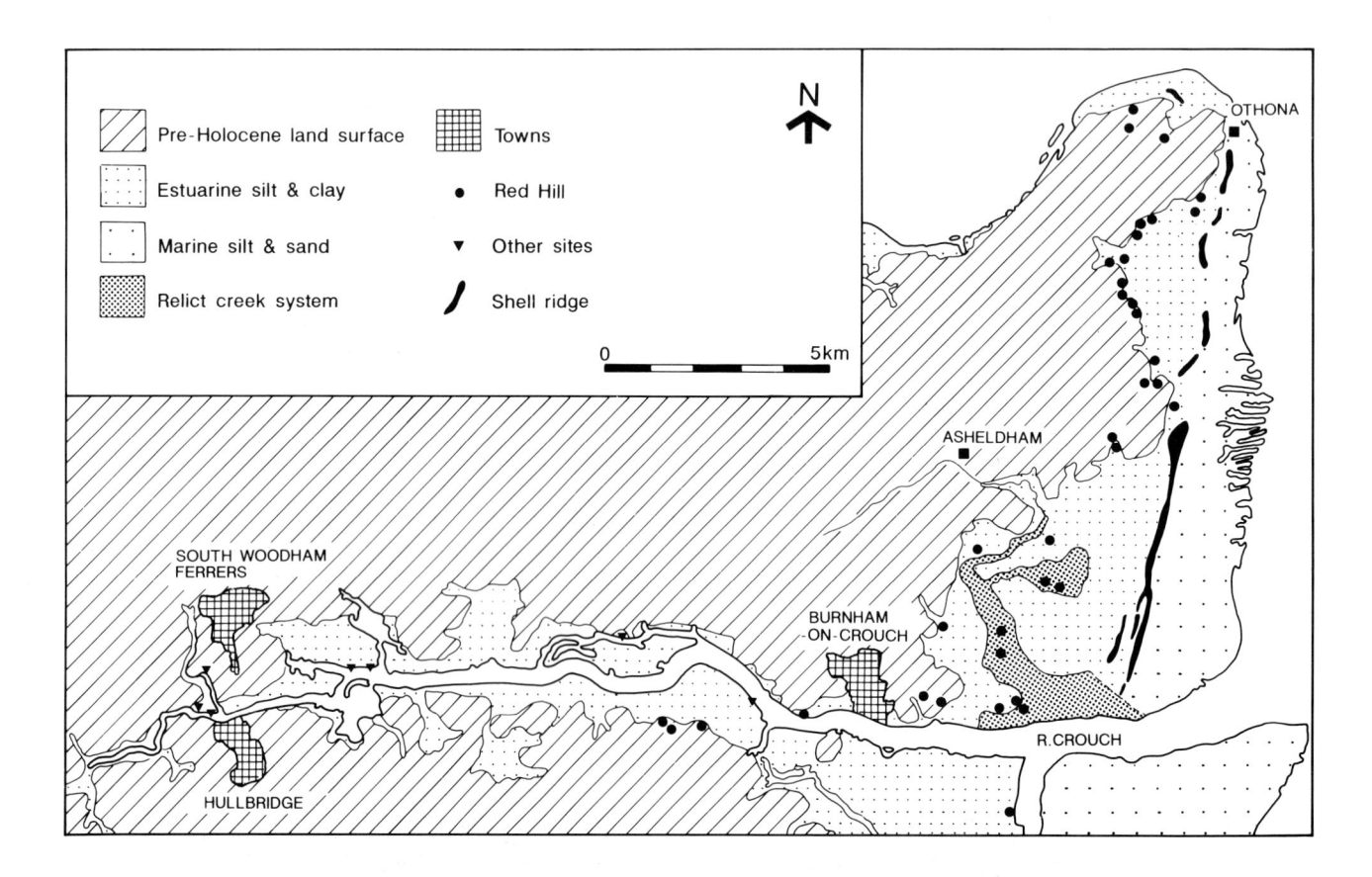

Fig. 3 The Dengie Peninsula in the 1st millennium AD. This map shows the location of Red Hills and other sites in relation to the main landscape elements. From Wilkinson and Murphy (1995)

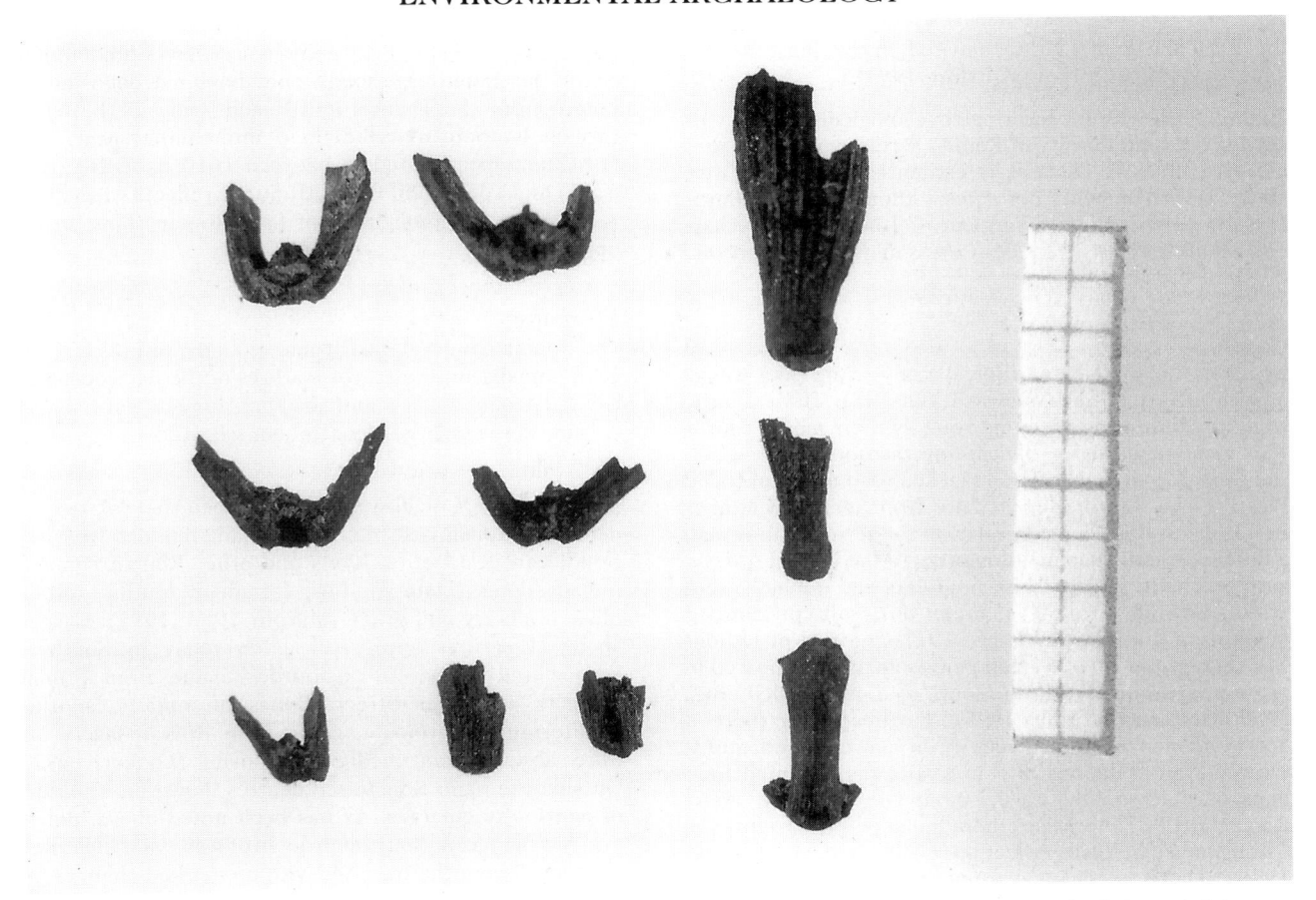

Plate 3 Charred cereal chaff from Iron Age contexts at Asheldham Camp. Top row. *Triticum spelta* (spelt) spikelet forks and glume base. Middle row. *Triticum dicoccum* (emmer) spikelet forks and glume base. Bottom row. *Triticum* sp terminal spikelet fork; *T. spelta* rachis internodes; *Hordeum* sp (barley) rachis internode

1991: Plate 3). Later Iron Age sites have either produced only sparse assemblages (eg Stansted Airport Catering Services Site, ACS: Murphy 1990) or few samples (eg North Shoebury; Ivy Chimneys, Witham: both Murphy, forthcoming; Stanway: Murphy 1992), but there are grounds for suspecting that spelt-growing increased in importance through the Iron Age.

The rarity of charred cereals at Stansted ACS may indicate a continued emphasis on a pastoral economy on Boulder Clay soils in the Iron Age, though elsewhere there is evidence for a Late Iron Age arable expansion. On the Blackwater terraces ditched field systems (in part, no doubt, for field drainage) are dated to the Late Iron Age/Early Roman period; densities of charred cereals were notably higher at Slough House and Chigborough Farms in features of this date than in earlier features (Murphy 1991).

Priorities for future work
Results available from Essex contrast with those from most other areas of the country in that, by chance, more information is available for the Later Bronze Age than the Iron Age. This applies to river valley sediments (there are at present no analyses of palaeochannel sediments dateable to the Iron Age) and to excavations of settlement sites. Continued inspection of valley sections exposed during road and bridge construction should eventually produce channel sediments and alluvium of demonstrable Iron Age date. There is also a clear need for extensive sampling at a total excavation of an Iron Age settlement in an area where soil conditions would favour an arable-based economy, ideally on a calcareous subsoil, where animal bones and shells should survive. Middle Bronze Age settlement sites, when located, must also take a high priority for investigation.

The Roman Period

Vegetation and Landscape
The Mar Dyke pollen diagram (Zone MD:4) indicates that the process of extensive woodland clearance on the Thames terraces, begun in the Bronze Age, continued into Roman times: in sediments estimated to be of Roman date tree pollen was as low as 10%, whilst cereal pollen was up to 5% (Scaife 1988, 109). The Upper Peat of the Crouch Estuary, which began to form in Late Roman times, has been analysed for pollen, though preservation was poor. High levels of grass pollen (76%) point to an open coastal landscape (Scaife 1995). In the Chelmer valley, at Moulsham Street, Chelmsford, pollen from a Roman ditch indicated a landscape of meadow or pasture with few trees (Scaife, unpublished). A palaeochannel of the Sandon Brook, a tributary of the Chelmer, dated to 1770 ± 70 BP (HAR 6580) at the base produced macrofossils indicating that the valley floor here, too, was open (Murphy, Wilkinson and Wiltshire unpublished). On the Boulder Clay plateau sediments of the Stansted Brook were exposed during construction of the Airport Rail Link (Wiltshire 1991). In mineral deposits of probable Roman date pollen preservation was too poor for analysis, though an organic band dated 1430 ± 60 BP (HAR 9238) was analysed indicating a cleared landscape with local reedswamp and mixed farming.

The pollen evidence for extensive clearance implies that some of the mineral alluvium underlying the modern river floodplains must be of Roman date, being derived from arable areas by erosion. In fact the lack of dating evidence makes it difficult to assess the magnitude of Roman alluviation compared to that of earlier and later periods. The only dated valley sediments of Roman date are those from the Sandon Brook (see above), whilst silty clays infilling the palaeochannel of the Stansted Brook must in part date from Roman times (Wiltshire 1991).

Taking these results from palaeoecological studies with the known high density of Roman settlements - in a sample area of N.W. Essex it is estimated that there were about 1.3 settlements per square kilometre (Williamson 1984) - a predominantly agricultural landscape, perhaps not wholly foreign to modern eyes, may be inferred over much of the county.

Coasts

By about 1750 BP Mean High Water Spring Tides was at +0.4m OD at Tilbury (Devoy 1980, 145). The estuaries would by then have taken up roughly their modern form. This was not, however, the case on the open coast, where the Roman coastline differed markedly from that of today. Plotting the distribution of Late Iron Age/Early Roman Red Hills on the Dengie in relation to the soil map reveals a Roman coastline some kilometres to the west of today's, with extensive salt-marshes, mud-flats and a major creek system which formed a focus for salt production (Wilkinson and Murphy 1986, 191). The fort of Othona was then at the tip of a small peninsula, now truncated by erosion, and bounded to the south by a now-infilled creek (Wilkinson and Murphy 1995). Further south there is good evidence for Roman activity on Canvey Island, and at Canvey Point (Thames Site 1) a site was occupied (perhaps only seasonally) at 0.7-0.8m OD, only just above Roman MHWST. Activities there included salt production, fishing and shellfish collection (Wilkinson and Murphy 1995). There is evidence from this site for intentional dumping of soil, refuse and quarried shell debris from nearby cheniers to raise the ground level. Recent work at Othona also indicates the importation of shell debris to raise ground levels or to improve drainage of clayey soils (Murphy, unpublished).

Deposition of clastic fine-textured sediments predominated in the estuaries, though thin biogenic deposits are known from the Thames and Roach. Only in the upper Crouch is there a well-defined intercalated peat. This *Phragmites* peat, dated to between 1610 ± 70 BP (HAR 5225) and 1380 ± 80 BP (HAR 5689) reflects widespread reedswamp development from Late Roman times in the upper estuary.

Economy

The Roman conquest clearly marked a major political and economic discontinuity, yet features of the palaeoecological and economic data indicate that some aspects of agriculture were essentially continuous with those of the Late Iron Age.

Excavations at Colchester have produced the clearest evidence for Romanised life. Exotic plant remains from the Boudiccan destruction levels and other Roman deposits include dates (Plate 4), figs, coriander, lentils, walnut, olive, mulberry and grape (Murphy 1984, 1992). Carpet-shells (*Venerupis* spp), still eaten today in Southern France and known as 'palourdes' came from Roman deposits at Culver Street. Bones of mullets, another Mediterranean favourite, came from Roman layers but were absent from medieval deposits (Locker 1992). Outside the main Romanised centres, however, a picture of continuity emerges. As has been noted above, pollen evidence suggests that the process of woodland clearance continued from the Iron Age with no marked changes. At Wendens Ambo Jones *et al.* (1982) found that assemblages of early Roman charred cereals (spelt and barley) resembled those of the Late Iron Age; only in the later Roman period was there evidence for a shift towards spelt-growing at the expense of barley.

Plate 4 Charred dates (*Phoenix dactylifera*) in Boudiccan destruction deposits at Lion Walk, Colchester. From Crummy (1984)

Charred cereal assemblages from rural Roman sites tend to be monotonously similar, irrespective of soil type. They usually include abundant spelt chaff, reflecting large-scale crop processing. Remains of other cereals - emmer, six-row hulled barley, bread wheat, oats, rye and pulses are also found. Assemblages of this type have come from sites on the coast (eg Canvey Point: Wilkinson and Murphy 1995), on gravel terraces (eg Slough House and Chigborough Farms: Murphy 1991) and on Boulder Clay soils (eg Duck End Farm, Stansted: Murphy 1990). At Stebbing Green assemblages from ovens dominated by spelt chaff but associated with sprouted grain were interpreted as debris from malting (Murphy 1989). A deposit of charred wheat malt with some barley from Culver Street, Colchester provides further evidence that some of the spelt crop was used for brewing (Murphy 1992).

Crop products charred within buildings during the Boudiccan sack of Colchester have come from several excavations. Typically they are very 'clean' with little chaff and few weed seeds. The field crops stored included spelt, emmer, bread wheat and flax/linseed (Murphy 1984, 1992). However, work at Culver Street has established that Colchester was not just a crop-consumer: there was agriculture within the walls. Besides structural evidence, micromorphological study of the re-worked debris from the Boudiccan fire indicates cultivation (MacPhail 1992), macrofossil assemblages interpreted as charred waste from byres or stables were recovered and marine invertebrates from the site were thought to indicate manuring with seaweed (Murphy 1992).

Priorities for future work
1. The volume of river valley alluvium of Roman date compared to that of other periods would give a measure of the intensity of arable farming. Continued inspection of valley sections exposed during construction work is clearly required.

2. The Boudiccan destruction layers at Colchester have produced a remarkable collection of closely dated samples representing stored crop products. Deposits of this type are extremely uncommon and every effort should be made to continue sampling at future excavations.

3. Deposits on the foreshore at Canvey Point are under active erosion. They have considerable potential for yielding data on Roman fisheries and the exploitation of the marginal coastal zone. Further sampling and analysis is required.

Saxon and Medieval Periods

Vegetation and landscape
A radiocarbon date of 1470 ± 80 BP (HAR 4526) places the top of the Mar Dyke sequence, Zone MD:5, in the early Saxon period. Pollen percentages of several tree taxa show slight increases at this level, particularly *Salix*, suggesting some extension of valley woodland in particular. However, cereal and *Plantago lanceolata* pollen also increase slightly at the top of the sequence (Scaife 1988). In the valley of the Stansted Brook a thin biogenic horizon dated to 1430 ± 60 BP (HAR 9238) again indicates an open landscape. The site was at first dominated by reedswamp and weedy grassland, and there was a subsequent increase in willow pollen and pollen of cereals. There was clearly early Saxon agriculture close to this site on the Boulder Clay plateau (Wiltshire 1991). In the Sandon Brook section (Murphy, Wilkinson and Wiltshire unpublished), sediments dated to 1770 ± 70 BP (HAR 6580) to 860 ± 70 BP (HAR 6570) produced macrofossil assemblages indicating persistence of locally open conditions and cereal cultivation over this period. On the gravel terraces of the Blackwater at Slough House Farm, pollen and macrofossil analyses of 7th century wells indicate very open landscapes - virtually treeless and dominated by weedy grassland (Wiltshire and Murphy 1993).

From the data available at present there seems to be no reason to think in terms of very large-scale woodland regeneration in post-Roman times, though no doubt on a local level some land was abandoned. Although dendrochronological work on Saxon well timbers from Slough House Farm does point to some regeneration beginning in the early 5th century AD (Hillam, forthcoming), the scale of this secondary woodland development could have been restricted.

Coasts
Devoy (1980, 145) estimates that by about 1750 BP MHWST was 2-3m below today's levels. Dated transgressive and regressive overlaps for the Saxon and Medieval periods are rare. In the Crouch estuary the top of the Upper Peat is dated 1380 ± 80 BP (HAR 6589), giving a calibrated date range (one standard deviation) of 604-681 AD (Wilkinson and Murphy 1995). On the Dengie Flats, Greensmith and Tucker (1971; 1971a; 1973) report a transgressive phase dated to about 1400BP. Both events, and the submergence of Roman occupation surfaces in the Thames estuary, must be broadly linked to Devoy's Thames V.

The main evidence for Saxon activity in the estuaries comes from a recently recognised group of extremely extensive fish trap complexes. One at Collins Creek in the Blackwater is currently being planned and assessed (ECC, undated). Calibrated radiocarbon dates so far obtained are 640-675 AD (UB 3485) and 882-957 AD (UB 3486). The Domesday Survey and later medieval documents show that there was a coastal salt industry and large-scale medieval land claim but both of these have so far proved rather archaeologically elusive. It is thought that low mounds on the modern salt-marsh probably relate to medieval salt production (Wilkinson and Murphy 1995). Only at Foulness has a medieval sea bank been excavated (Crump 1981). A timber framework within it gave dendrochronological and calibrated radiocarbon dates of the late 15th century.

13th-14th century layers at Canvey Point (Thames Site 1) have produced remains of shark, thornback ray, shad?, herring, conger eel, whiting, cod, haddock, mullet, horse mackerel and flatfish: these may relate to a fish-processing site (Jones 1995). Marine mollusc shells and mammal bones, mostly sheep/goat were also recovered (Luff 1995). At Culver Street, Colchester, medieval deposits included a higher density of fish-bones than Roman layers. The assemblages from this site are thought to reflect a medieval fishing industry specialised towards catching eel, herring and cod (Locker 1992).

Agrarian Economy
At present no early Saxon settlement in Essex has been extensively sampled for plant remains, though at Springfield Lyons cremation pit fills have produced charred plant material, predominantly remains of grassland plants with some charred crop remains: spelt, possibly emmer, bread-type wheat, barley, oats, rye and perhaps pea (Murphy 1990). Two other sites in Eastern England - West Stow, Suffolk (Murphy 1985) and Mucking, Essex (Van der Veen 1993) - have produced evidence for the continuation of spelt cultivation into early Saxon times. This may be some indication of continuity with Roman arable farming.

Late Saxon settlement features at Springfield produced much larger assemblages of charred crop and weed remains. Oats were the predominant cereal, with bread wheat, barley, rye and traces of spelt and emmer, the lat-

Peter Murphy

Table 1: Summary of key dated environmental and economic features of the post-glacial in Essex. For sources, see text.

Years BP (uncalibrated)	Vegetation Pollen Data	Vegetation Other Data	Coasts Transgression/regressions (Thames/Tilbury)	Coasts Other aspects	Agrarian Economy
0					
500				Foulness 15th century sea embankment. Canvey Point (Thames Site 1), 13th-14th century fishing site. Medieval salterns. Collins Creek. Blackwater Estuary. Saxon fish-traps	Round Wood Stansted. 13th century arable farming based on bread and rivet wheat with pulses important. Springfield Lyons. Late Saxon farming. Oats important, with other cereals, pulse and flax
1000	Slough House Farm 7th Century AD wells, Open grassland with some arable farming. 1430 BP. Stansted Brook. Open Landscape and mixed farming	1770-860 BP. Sandon Brook. Macrofossils indicate locally open conditions with cereal and flax cultivation nearby. Channel silting and alluviation		1610-1380 BP. Crouch Estuary Upper Peat with early Saxon wooden structure	Springfield Lyons. Early Saxon cremations produced cereals including spelt
1500	Moulsham St. Chelmsford. Valley floor pasture/meadow		Thames V About 1750 BP / Tilbury V	Canvey Point (Thames Site 1) Roman fishing, shellfish collection, salt production	Roman sites. Widespread evidence for arable farming based on spelt. Imported foodstuffs
2000	Asheldham Camp, Buried soil under rampart. Grassland nearby, few trees		Thames IV 2600 - ? BP	Red Hills	Asheldham Camp. Iron Age charred granary deposits give latest evidence for large-scale emmer cultivation
2500	Mar Dyke MD: 5 Lime decline: extensive clearance on Thames terraces. 2980 BP. Chigborough Farm. Bronze Age well: open grassland environment. 3350 BP, Stansted Brook, Decline in tree pollen, particularly lime. 3360 BP. Little Waltham, Grassland on Chelmer floodplain. 3580 BP. Mar Dyke MD: 4 Secondary elm decline; beginning of large-scale clearance	3490-3080 BP. Moverons Farm, Brightlingsea. Charred macrofossils from cremations indicate local grassland. 3710-3200 BP. Chelmer Bridge palaeochannel. Macrofossils indicate alder and lime woodland at base, open weedy vegetation at top	Tilbury IV / Thames III 3850-2800 BP	Blackwater and Crouch Estuaries. Bronze Age and Iron Age wooden structures, dated 3680, 3250, 2950, 2850, 2800, 2790, 2730, 2400, 2380, 2360, 2350, 2300, 2220, 2080, 1900 BP. 3020 BP. Crouch Estuary Site 2. Bronze Age saltern	2800-2680 BP. Lofts Farm. Cereal growing based on emmer, some spelt. 2830 BP. Springfield Lyons. Cereal crops include spelt and emmer. 2980 BP. Chigborough and Slough House Farms. Emmer and flax growing. 3490-3080 BP. Moverons Farm. Rare cereal remains in Bronze Age cremations
3000					
3500				3885 BP. The Stumble, Burnt flint mound. 3910 BP. Purfleet (Thames Site 2). Base of peat overlying palaeosol on Thames II sediments with Neolithic axes etc.	3830 BP. Jaywick. Beaker pit including sparse remains of emmer
4000	Mar Dyke MD: 3 Woodland regeneration.	Blackwater Estuary and open coast. Charcoal spreads, (mainly oak) on submerged Neolithic palaeosol dated 4690, 4180, 4020, 4000 and 3990 BP	Tilbury III		
4500	4650 BP. Mar Dyke: MD 2 Elm decline. 4930 BP. Stone Marsh, Kent. Elm decline				The Stumble. Charred hazel nutshell and emmer grains dated 4780, 4675, 4060 and 4020 BP
5000					
5500	5740 BP. Mar Dyle MD: 1 Oak, lime and hazel woodland with alder		Thames II 6575-5410 BP		
6000					
6500	6670 BP. Bradwell. Deciduous woodland, lime predominant		Tilbury II		
7000			Thames I 8200-6970 BP	Rapid submergence of southern North Sea basin. Sea level rise -25.5m to -8.9m OD between 8500 and 7000 BP	
7500	8500-7000 BP. Enfield Lock. Pine, hazel, elm woodland; oak and alder later immigrants				
8000	8170-7830 BP. Tibury World's End. Woodland of pine, elm and oak; early local dominance of alder		Tilbury I		
8500					
9000				9000 BP. Sea level 45m below today's. Major estuary offshore from Foulness (proto-Thames/Crouch/Blackwater)	
9500	9546 BP. Enfield Lock. Open vegetation dominated by sedges with some Late Glacial species				
10000					

ter two probably minor contaminants of other crops. Horse-beans, peas and flax were also grown. The abundance of oats might perhaps be related to the production of animal fodder, though since virtually no bone survived at the site there is no information on animal husbandry. There was no evidence for disposal of crop cleaning waste at the site: the assemblages are largely of semi-cleaned crop products. Although weed seeds are not common, the high frequency of *Anthemis cotula* (stinking mayweed) fruits is thought to indicate that, though the site is on loamy soil over gravel, areas of heavy clay soils were under cultivation (Murphy 1990).

Evidence for clay soil farming in the 13th century has come from the settlement at Round Wood, Stansted (Murphy 1991). Here wheats were the main crop, including both bread wheat and rivet-type wheat. Oats were relatively common, as were horse-beans, peas and vetches, though barley and rye were rare. Wheat processing was clearly an important activity, though possible differential preservation of grain and chaff during charring complicates definite interpretation of on-site activities. Compared to prehistoric and Roman sites at Stansted pulses are much more abundant, which hints at the importance of legume cultivation for maintenance of soil nitrogen levels at a time when manure was in short supply (Bolton 1980, 34).

Very few data are available from urban sites, though medieval latrine and refuse pits at Culver Street, Colchester produced some mineralised dietary residues of faecal origin origin with charred cereals (Murphy 1992). At the site of Grays Brewery, Chelmsford waterlogged 13th-century deposits have provided limited information on floodplain vegetation and domestic activities (Murphy forthcoming b).

Priorities for future work
1. The upper sediments in some valley sections have provided limited information on the early Saxon landscape. However, to detect archaeologically significant vegetational changes in the 5th and 6th centuries fine sampling for pollen with closely spaced radiocarbon samples will be required.

2. Further extensive sampling at large-scale excavations of rural settlement sites is needed. In particular at least one early Saxon settlement and one Medieval settlement on light soils, for comparison with Round Wood, should be investigated.

3. More work is needed on urban waterfront sites: in contrast to most other areas of the country little is known of such sites in Essex.

Early Modern
Very little work has so far been done on the environmental archaeology of early modern sites, largely because it is assumed that documentary evidence provides a fuller picture than that obtained from palaeoecological methods. This may, in general, be true, but occasions will arise where studies of micro- and macrofossils help to clarify particular aspects of sites. For example, macrofossils from 16th-century garden features at Hill Hall have provided a list of plants grown in the garden and some information on phases of dereliction and abandonment (summarised in Murphy and Scaife 1991). Other possible applications would include studies of sites involved in the use or processing of various biological materials.

Bibliography
Allen, R. H. and Sturdy, R. G. 1980. 'The Environmental Background', in Buckley, D. G. (ed.), *The Archaeology of Essex to AD 1500*, CBA Res. Rep. 34, 1-7

Ashton, N. M., Cook, J., Lewis, S. G. and Rose J. 1992. *High Lodge. Excavations by G. de G. Sieveking 1962-1968 and J. Cook 1988*, British. Museum Press: London

Bedwin, O. 1991. 'Asheldham Camp - An Early Iron Age Hillfort: Excavations. 1985', *Essex Archaeol. Hist.* 22, 13-37

Bolton, J. L. 1980. *The English Medieval Economy, 1150-1500*, Dent: London

Bridgland, D. R. 1994. *Quaternary of the Thames*, Chapman and Hall: London

Bridgland, D., Selby, I., Wymer, J., Preece, R., Boreham, S., Stuart, T., Peglar, S. and McNabb, J. 1992. 'An investigation of the Clacton channel deposits exposed during redevelopment of the the former Butlin's holiday camp, Clacton-on-Sea, Essex', Pre-publication draft

Buckley, D. G. (ed). 1980. *Archaeology in Essex to AD 1500*, CBA Res. Rep. 34

Boyd, P. 1987. 'Carbonised seeds', in Buckley, D. G. and Hedges, J. D. *Excavation of a Crop Mark Complex at Woodham Walter, Essex*, E. Anglian Archaeol. 33, 41

Chambers, F. M. and Mighall, T. 1990. 'Palaeoecological Investigations at Enfield Lock: Pollen, pH, Magnetic Susceptibility and Charcoal Analyses of Sediments', in Bedwin, O. (ed.) 'Archaeological Investigations: Former Royal Ordnance Factory, Enfield Lock 1990. Final Report'

Crummy, P. 1984. *Excavations at Lion Walk, Balkerne Lane and Middleborough, Colchester, Essex*, Colchester Archaeological Report 3

Crummy, P. 1992. *Excavations at Culver Street, the Gilberd School and other Sites in Colchester 1971-85*, Colchester Archaeological Report 6

Crump, R. W. 1981. 'Excavation of a Buried Wooden Structure at Foulness', *Essex Archaeol. Hist.* 13, 69-71

Devoy, R. J. N. 1979. 'Flandrian Sea Level Changes and Vegetational History of the Lower Thames estuary', *Phil. Trans. Roy. Soc. Lond.* B285 (1978-9), 355-407

Devoy, R. J. N. 1980. 'Post-glacial Environmental Change and Man in the Thames Estuary', in Thompson, F. H. (ed.) *Archaeology and Coastal Change*, Soc. Antiq. Lond Occasional Paper (NS) 1, 134-148

D'Olier, B. 1991. 'Sedimentary events during Flandrian sea-level rise in the south-west corner of the North Sea', in Nio, S. D., Shuttenhelm, R. T. and Van Weering, Tj. (eds), *Holocene Marine Sedimentation in the North Sea Basin*, 221-8. Blackwell: Oxford

Essex County Council. undated. 'Collins Creek, Blackwater Inter-Tidal Zone, Essex. Research Design for Survey, 1992-3', Archaeological Field Projects Service. Essex County Council: Chelmsford

Evans, A. 1995. 'Palynological investigations at Bradwell-on-Sea', in Wilkinson, T. J. and Murphy, P., *Archaeology of the Essex coast, vol. I: the Hullbridge survey*, E. Anglian Archaeol. 71, 51-6

Fryer, V. unpublished. 'Windmill Field, Broomfield, Essex. Assessment report on the Carbonised Plant Remains from Bronze Age Contexts'

Greensmith, J. T. and Tucker, E. V. 1971. 'Overconsolidation in Some Fine-Grained Sediments: Its Nature and Value in Interpreting the History of Certain British Quaternary Deposits', *Geol. en Mijnb.* 50 (6), 743-8

Greensmith, J. T. and Tucker, E. V. 1971a. 'The Effects of Late Pleistocene and Holocene Sea Level Changes in the Vicinity of the River Crouch, East Essex', *Proc. Geol. Assoc.* 82(3), 301-22

Greensmith, J. T. and Tucker, E. V. 1973. 'Holocene Transgressions and. Regressions on the Essex Coast, Outer Thames Estuary', *Geol. en. Mijnb.* 52(4), 193-202

Hillam, J. Forthcoming. 'Tree Ring analysis', in Wallis, S. and Waughman, M., *Archaeology and the landscape in the Lower Blackwater Valley*, E. Anglian Archaeol.

Jones, A. K. G. 1995. 'The Fish Remains', in Wilkinson, T. J. and Murphy, P., *Archaeology of the Essex coast, vol. I: the Hullbridge survey*, E. Anglian Archaeol. 71, 191-2

Jones, G., Halstead, P. and Morse, V. 1982. 'The Carbonised Seeds', in Hodder I., *The Archaeology of the M11. Excavations at Wendens Ambo*, Passmore Edwards Museum: London.

Lewis, J. S. C., Wiltshire, P. E. J. and MacPhail, R. I. 1992. 'A Late Devensian/early Flandrian site at Three Ways Wharf, Uxbridge: environmental implications', in Needham, S. and Macklin, G. (eds), *Alluvial Archaeology in Britain*, Oxbow Monograph 27, 235-247

Locker, A. 1992. 'The fish bones', in Crummy, P., *Excavations at Culver Street, the Gilberd School and other sites in Colchester 1971-85*, Colchester Archaeological Report 6, 278-80

Luff, R. M. 1995. 'Mammal, Bird and Amphibian Bones', in Wilkinson, T. J. and Murphy, P., *Archaeology of the Essex coast, vol. I: the Hullbridge survey*, E. Anglian Archaeol. 71, 192

MacPhail, R. I. 1991. 'Soil Report', in Bedwin, O., 'Asheldham Camp - an early Iron Age hill fort: excavations 1985', *Essex Archaeol. Hist.* 22, 35

MacPhail, R. I. 1992. 'Buried Soils', in Crummy, P., *Excavations at Culver Street, the Gilberd school and other sites in Colchester, 1971-85*, Colchester Archaeological Report 6, 273-5

MacPhail, R. I. 1995. 'Soil Micromorphology from section 2', in Wilkinson, T. J. and Murphy, P., *Archaeology of the Essex coast, vol. I: the Hullbridge survey*, E. Anglian Archaeol. 71, microfiche, appendix C

Moffett, L., Robinson, M. A. and Straker, V. 1989. 'Cereals, fruits and. nuts: charred plant remains from Neolithic sites in England and Wales and the Neolithic economy', in Milles, A. (ed.), *The Beginnings of Agriculture*, BAR International Series 496, 243-61

Murphy, P. 1984. 'Carbonised Fruits from Building 5; Charred Cereals from. Buildings 41, 45 and 38', in Crummy, P., *Excavations at Lion Walk, Balkerne Lane and Middleborough, Colchester, Essex*, Colchester. Archaeological Report 3, 40, 105, 108 and 110

Murphy, P. 1985. 'The Cereals and Crop Weeds', in West, S., *West Stow. The Anglo-Saxon Village. Vol. 1*, E. Anglian Archaeol. 24, 100-8

Murphy, P. 1988. 'Plant Macrofossils', in Brown, N., 'A Late Bronze Age Enclosure at Lofts Farm, Essex', *Proc. Prehist. Soc.* 54, 281-93

Murphy, P. 1988. 'Cereals and Crop Weeds', in Wilkinson, T. J., *Archaeology and Environment in South Essex*, E. Anglian Archaeology 42, 99-100

Murphy, P. 1989. 'Carbonised Plant Remains from the Stumble', an Intertidal Site in the Blackwater Estuary, Essex, England, *Circaea* 6 (1), 21-38

Murphy, P. 1989. 'Carbonised Plant Remains from Roman Contexts at Stebbing Green, Essex', Ancient Monuments Laboratory Report 112/89. English Heritage: London

Murphy, P. 1990. 'Springfield Lyons, Chelmsford, Essex. Carbonised Plant. Remains from Neolithic, Late Bronze Age, Iron Age, Roman, Early and Late Saxon Contexts', Ancient Monuments Laboratory Report 11/90. English Heritage: London

Murphy, P. 1990. 'Moverons Farm, Brightlingsea, Essex. Carbonised Plant Remains from a Bronze Age Cremation Cemetery', Ancient Monuments Laboratory Report 122/90. English Heritage: London

Murphy, P. 1990. 'Stansted Airport, Essex. Carbonised Plant Remains', Ancient Monuments Laboratory Report Series 129/90. English Heritage: London

Murphy, P. 1991. 'Cereals and Crop Weeds', in Bedwin, O., 'Asheldham Camp' - an early Iron Age hill fort: excavations 1985', *Essex Archaeol. Hist.* 22, 31-4

Murphy, P. 1991. 'Plant macrofossils from Multi-Period excavations at Slough House Farm and Chigborough Farm, near Heybridge, Essex', Ancient Monuments Laboratory Report Series 64/91. English Heritage: London

Murphy, P. 1992. 'Environmental Studies: Culver Street; Environmental Studies: Gilberd School; Charred Cereals and Flax from Building 152', in Crummy, P., *Excavations at Culver Street, the Gilberd School and other sites in Colchester*, Colchester Archaeological Report 6, 273-289 and 330-3

Murphy, P. 1992. 'Stanway, Essex. Plant Remains from Late Neolithic/Early Bronze Age and Middle Iron Age Pits and Late Iron Age Burials', Ancient Monuments Laboratory Report Series 29/92. English Heritage: London

Murphy, P. 1995. 'Mollusca, Botanical evidence', in Wymer, J. J. and Brown, N. R., *North Shoebury; settlement and economy in south-east Essex 1500BC-AD1500*, E. Anglian Archaeol. 75, 142-50

Murphy, P. Unpublished. 'Othona, Bradwell-on-Sea, Essex (73. 1991). Assessment of Macrofossils'

Murphy, P. forthcoming 'Grays Brewery, Chelmsford: Plant macrofossils'

Murphy, P. and Scaife, R, G. 1991. 'The Environmental Archaeology of Gardens', in Brown, A. E. (1991), *Garden Archaeology*, CBA Res. Rep. 78, 83-99

Murphy, P., Wilkinson, T. J. and Wiltshire, P. E. J. forthcoming. 'Valley Sediments of the Chelmer and Sandon Brook'

Peglar, S. M. 1993. The mid-Holocene *Ulmus* decline at Diss Mere, Norfolk, UK: a year-by-year pollen stratigraphy from annual laminations, *The Holocene* 3, 1-13

Peglar, S. M. and Wilson, D. G. 1978. 'The Abandoned River Channel', in Drury, P. J., *Excavations at Little Waltham 1970-71*, CBA Res. Rep. 26, 146-8

Rose, J., Allen, P. and Hey, R. W. 1976. 'Middle Pleistocene stratigraphy in Southern East Anglia', *Nature* 263, 492-4

Rose, J. and Allen, P. 1977. 'Middle Pleistocene stratigraphy in South-East Suffolk', *J. Geol. Soc. London* 133, 83-102

Scaife, R. 1988. 'Pollen Analysis of the Mar Dyke Sediments', in Wilkinson, T. J., *Archaeology and Environment in South Essex*, E. Anglian Archaeol. 42, 109-14

Scaife, R. 1991. 'Pollen analysis of the Iron Age Land Surface', in Bedwin, O., 'Asheldham Camp - an early Iron Age hill fort: excavations 1985', *Essex Archaeol. Hist.* 22, 35-6

Scaife, R. 1995. 'Pollen Analysis: Intertidal Sites (Blackwater. Sites 3, 18 and 28; Crouch Sites 9 and 8)', in Wilkinson, T. J. and Murphy, P., *Archaeology of the Essex coast, vol. I: the Hullbridge Survey*, E. Anglian Archaeol. 71, 43-50

Scaife, R. unpublished. 'Moulsham Street, Chelmsford (MTC 80): Pollen Analysis'

Singer, R., Wymer, J. J., Gladfelter, B. G. and Wolfe, R. 1973. 'Excavation of the Clactonian industry at the Golf Course, Clacton-on-Sea, Essex', *Proc. Prehist. Soc.* 39, 6-74

Turner, C. 1970. 'The Middle Pleistocene deposits at Marks Tey, Essex', *Phil. Trans. Roy. Soc. London* B257, 373-440.

Van der Veen, M. 1993. 'Grain Impressions in Early Saxon Pottery from Mucking, Essex', in Hamerow, H., *Excavations at Mucking Volume 2: the Anglo-Saxon settlement*, English Heritage Archaeological Report 21, 80-1

Whittle, A. W. R. 1978. 'Resources and Population in the British Neolithic', *Antiquity* 52, 34-52

Wilkinson, T. J. and Murphy, P. 1986 'Archaeological Survey of an Intertidal Zone: the Submerged Landscape of the Essex Coast, England', *Journal of Field Archaeology* 13(2), 177-94

Wilkinson, T. J. and Murphy, P. 1995. *The Archaeology of the Essex Coast, Vol. 1: the Hullbridge survey*, E. Anglian Archaeol. 71

Wilkinson, T. J. and Murphy, P. in prep. *The Archaeology of the Essex Coast Vol. 2*, E. Anglian Archaeol.

Williamson, T. 1984. 'The Roman Countryside: Settlement and Agriculture in N. W. Essex', *Britannia* 15, 225-30

Wiltshire, P. E. J. 1991. 'Palynological Analysis of British Rail Sections at Stansted Airport, Essex', Ancient Monuments Laboratory Report 8/91. English Heritage: London

Wiltshire, P. E. J. and Murphy. P. 1993. 'An Analysis of Microfossils and Macrofossils from Waterlogged Deposits at Slough House and Chigborough Farms, near Heybridge, Essex', Ancient Monuments Laboratory Report 66/93. English Heritage: London

Wymer, J. J. 1980. 'The Palaeolithic of Essex', in Buckley, D. G. (ed.). *The Archaeology of Essex to AD1500*, CBA Res. Rep. 34, 8-11

Wymer, J. J., Lewis, S. G. and Bridgland, D. R. 1991. 'Warren Hill, Mildenhall, Suffolk', in Lewis, S. G., Whiteman, C. A. and Bridgland, D. R., *Central East Anglia and the Fen Basin. Field Guide*, 50-8. Quaternary Research Association: London

Archaeological Research and the Essex Sites and Monuments Record

P.J. Gilman

"Any attempt to describe the British Archaeological Database must begin by recognising that there has not been a single successful attempt to compile a set of archaeological information that is complete and consistent" (Fraser 1993, 19).

"Research into the historic environment is a minority activity, yet it is also the most basic use because its results assist all other uses. It is also involved in questions of preservation because it can assess the relative importance of survivals" (Baker 1983, 65).

Introduction

The use of Sites and Monuments Records (SMRs) for research has received relatively little discussion in archaeological literature. During the conference at Writtle in 1993, it was noticeable that very few, if any, of the speakers made direct reference to the County Sites and Monuments Record during their contributions. This paper aims to establish that the Essex Sites and Monuments Record (ESMR) is an essential tool for archaeological research in the county. After outlining the history and development of the SMR, the paper describes its content and functions, before going on to outline a number of current initiatives which the Section is undertaking to enhance the SMR. The way in which the SMR is used as a tool for archaeological research is then described, and suggestions are provided for ways in which its largely untapped potential could be released. Finally, mention is made of the way in which the SMR may develop in the future to meet the demands which are increasingly being made upon it. This paper has been updated (in January 1996) to cover developments since the Writtle conference.

History and Development of Sites and Monuments Records

The Essex County Sites and Monuments Record (ESMR) forms part of a country-wide system of SMRs, most of which are maintained by County Councils. The history and development of this system of records has already been fully described in several published sources (e.g. Burrow 1984, Lang 1991, RCHME 1993a). A brief account will be sufficient here, therefore, to provide the context for the development of the ESMR.

The systematic creation of inventories of archaeological and historic monuments can be traced back to the creation of the Royal Commission on the Historical Monuments of England (RCHME) in 1908. The Royal Warrant instructed this Commission to *"make an inventory of the Ancient and Historical Monuments and Constructions connected with or illustrative of the contemporary culture, civilization and conditions of life of the people in England... from the earliest times to the year 1700, and to specify those which seem most worthy of preservation"*. To date, the RCHME has produced and published inventories for just over half the English counties, including Essex.

Later, the mapping of antiquities on Ordnance Survey (OS) maps lead to the development of a card index system, which was to become an essential source of information for the subsequent development of SMRs. This card system was maintained and revised because the OS maps were regularly revised. Visible antiquities were documented to a high standard as a justification for their depiction on maps. The cards were maintained by the OS's Archaeology Division, which was transferred to the RCHME in 1983. The record cards themselves formed the core of the National Archaeological Record, of which more later. At a local level, annotated maps and card indexes were often maintained by the OS's correspondents such as, in Essex, J.G.S. Brinson and M.R. Hull at Colchester.

In the 1960's, the increasing recognition of the threats posed to archaeological sites from development, resulted in the Walsh Report into the protection of field monuments (1969), whose recommendations included:

"A consolidated record of all known field monuments should be held by the County Planning Authorities so that they may be aware of all such monuments in their areas.

County Councils which have not already done so should consider whether adequate professional archaeological assistance is available to them and should examine whether the appointment of an archaeological officer on a full or part-time basis is called for in their areas."

Although these recommendations were not implemented directly, local SMRs eventually began to emerge in the 1970s, beginning with Oxfordshire (Benson 1974). The development of a national network was not uniform, but each English county now has a Sites and Monuments Record, under the direction of a qualified archaeological officer. Almost all of these records are maintained by County Councils, although their exact locations vary. Most are in Planning Departments, but others are in museums and Property Departments. There also exist other, more localised SMRs, e.g. for some historic towns, which are maintained by District Councils or Archaeological Trusts, such as Colchester. These are normally linked to the 'parent' county SMR.

A major impetus to the evolution of the network of SMRs came in the 1980s, with the development of archaeological rescue units, and project funding: *"In 1981-82, DOE attitudes towards the local service were revised with the realisation that a systematic and rational approach to preservation demanded a foundation of Sites and Monuments Records developed to a consistent and minimum level of completeness. DOE grants began to flow back to SMRs and field survey work"* (Baker 1983, 148).

DOE and, later, English Heritage, funding provided the basis for the recasting and computerisation of SMRs. Use of the form for recording Scheduled Ancient Monuments, the *AM107*, provided an initial data standard. English Heritage also provided software, in the form of the SUPERFILE package, which was adopted by just over half of the county SMRs.

Despite the public funding which went into the creation of SMRs, and the location of the majority of them in local government, there is little statutory basis for their maintenance. The 1988 Town and Country Planning Act General Development Order defined an archaeological site as one *"held within a Sites and Monuments Record maintained by a County Council"*. This definition was revised in the Town and Country Planning Act (General Permitted Development Order) 1995 to: *"Land which is ... or which is within a site registered in any record adopted by resolution by a county council and known as a County Sites and Monuments Record"*. The ESMR was adopted by resolution of Essex County Council's Environment Committee in October 1995. The importance of SMRs was given further recognition in 1990 when Planning Policy Guidance Note 16, dealing with the treatment of archaeological remains in the planning system, was issued by the Department of the Environment (DoE 1990). However, the lack of statutory support can, potentially, have negative effects on the staffing and funding of SMRs. In the current climate of uncertainty over local government, and especially following the recent review of Local Government Structure, there is understandable anxiety over the future of some SMRs.

Current and Future Developments with the ESMR

In 1989 the government decided that the lead role with regard to local SMRs should be assigned to the RCHME. This new responsibility was formally incorporated into a revised Royal Warrant in 1992. Since 1989 there has been an increase in cooperation between the Commission and SMRs, especially via the Association of County Archaeological Officers (ACAO). RHCME and ACAO have stated that SMRs and the NAR should be considered as jointly constituting the Extended National Archaeological Record. During 1991 and 1992 RCHME carried out a review of local and national archaeological records, subsequently published in 1993 (RCHME 1993a). This made a number of important recommendations which, if carried through, would result in the creation of a network of national, county, and local databases, which are curated at the appropriate level with the appropriate data for that level. The information within these databases would be compiled and maintained according to nationally agreed standards and would be exchanged between the partners in the network, according to data exchange agreements. A data standard for national and local SMRs has been compiled by a joint RCHME/ACAO working party (RCHME 1993b). To support its implementation, an integrated thesaurus of architectural and archaeological terminology has been published (RCHME and English Heritage 1995). Although the RCHME review provides much useful information about the resourcing, use and operation of SMRs, there is surprisingly little mention of the use of SMRs in research. Rather, the emphasis is on the use of SMRs for planning and management purposes.

One of the initiatives being mounted by the RCHME is the development of new software, based on the MONARCH system recently developed for the National Monuments Record. This will replace the now obsolete SUPERFILE database management system. The new software will be based on the ORACLE relational database management system, and is currently being tested in four 'pilot' SMRs, including Essex. Use of this system will enable SMRs to record archaeological information more comprehensively. It will also help to implement the nationally agreed data standards. This should bring about greater compatibility and consistency between national and local record systems.

The Essex Sites and Monuments Record

Essex County Council established an Archaeology Section in 1972 and one of the principal objectives was the creation of a Sites and Monuments Record (Hedges, 1975; 1977). Indeed, Essex was one of the very first SMRs to be set up, following the lead given by Oxfordshire. As initially created, the ESMR was based on the OS 1:25000 series maps, with sites and finds numbered sequentially on each sheet, e.g. TQ68-1. Each sheet had an associated file containing proforma record sheets for sites and artefacts, and supporting documentation such as offprints, drawings, maps etc. Sites were mapped using several conventions, the most numerous being outlined areas, which were usually drawn around the most convenient field and/or property boundaries. Findspots were indicated by dots, or by an area defined by a dashed line where the NGR was uncertain. Linear monuments, such as Roman roads, were shown by a dot- and dashed line. A simple index was provided for each file. To complement this system, crop marks were sketch-plotted onto OS 1:10560 overlay sheets.

It had been intended that the ESMR was to be computerised using the County Council mainframe, and the site and artefact sheets were designed with this in mind. Resources, however, could not be found for this, and the ESMR was maintained as a 'manual' system until 1983. Funds were then obtained from English Heritage for the recasting and computerisation of the SMR. This was at first carried out by a number of individuals but in 1984 a full-time post was created to ensure continuity and consistency of work.

In 1984 microcomputer database software was still in its infancy and the SMR entries were entered as 'non-document' word-processed files, using the Wordstar package. These files could be manipulated using a suite of programs developed by English Heritage and written in the BASIC computing language, which provided very simple facilities for sorting and searching of data. It is interesting to note that the way in which certain fields were handled had a great bearing on the future development of the computerised SMR and still does to this day. For example, to keep related information together, a number of fields were divided into subfields, separated by a "/", with groups of associated subfields separated by a semi-colon. A 13th-century moat would be entered as:

moat/earthwork/C13/-.

Likewise, a 2nd-century Roman silver coin would be entered as:

coin/find/C2/silver.

The relationships between these subfields were preserved when the Version 1 data was migrated across to the SUPERFILE system in 1986.

Contents of the Essex Sites and Monuments Record

The ESMR consists of the following:

1. *The computerised database* The records in this database include the location of sites and finds (their District, Parish, NGR). A summary description is provided, which may vary from a one line entry to several paragraphs of text. There then follows a set of grouped entries which list the site and artefact types represented within each record, their form (e.g. find, earthwork, crop mark, building etc.), their period and, where relevant, material (e.g. bronze for a socketed axe). Site and artefact types are entered using a wordlist agreed between the counties of Essex, Cambridgeshire, Norfolk, and Suffolk. This is of great value for helping to ensure consistency in regional SMR searches. Many of the other fields are also controlled by wordlists, to provide consistency of entry and retrieval.

Land classification and site status, ownership, and tenancy, geology and topography are entered, where known. There are fields for information about site assessment and site management. The site's archaeological history is recorded (i.e. the type of archaeological activity, such as survey or excavation, the name of the director of the work, and the date). Lists of visits to the site can also be entered, with the name, organisation, and date.

A very important part of each record is a bibliography of unpublished and published sources which will enable the enquirer to obtain further information should this be necessary. The SMR retains a set of files per 1:25,000 sheet from the old SMR, each of which contains much unpublished material such as letters, maps, drawings etc. Finally, the compilation date and compiler are recorded, as well as subsequent alterations.

ARCHAEOLOGICAL RESEARCH AND THE ESSEX S.M.R.

The SUPERFILE database software allows for great flexibility in searching. Simple and complex queries can be generated easily with the use of a computerised form. For example, it is possible to retrieve all Bronze Age palstaves from a particular District, or from a group of parishes, or from a block of land defined by grid references. Another search might be for all Roman sites excavated in Essex before a particular date, and for which there are no known published excavation reports. Complex searches can be built up using Boolean Logic, i.e. the use of operators OR, AND, NOT, in various combinations. The current machine in use allows for very fast retrieval, and hundreds of records can be accessed within minutes if not seconds. The retrieved records can be output in various formats, according to need, and the amount of data can also be varied, from a simple index print-out to the complete records on the database. To complement the database, a complete print-out is available to make access to information both easy and fast. The SMR staff have developed ways of producing good quality print-out, despite the inherent limitations of the SUPERFILE software.

2. *SMR Maps* All the sites and finds which can be mapped (i.e. those with 6-figure or more precise NGRs) are plotted onto maps covering the whole of Essex, at 1:10,000 scale (Fig. 1). Particularly complicated areas such as historic towns are also plotted at 1:2500 scale or even, in the case of Colchester, at 1:1250. Crop marks are sketch-plotted at 1:10560 scale and, for complex sites, rectified plots are made at 1:2500 (Fig. 2).

3. *Photographic archive* The SMR also includes a large photographic archive, containing aerial photographs, ground shots, and photos of artefacts. The bulk of this collection is made up of aerial photographs drawn from several sources, notably the RCHME's National Library of Aerial Photographs, the Cambridge University Collection (CUCAP), various local flyers such as the late Richard Farrands, and Ida McMaster, and the Section's own ongoing programme of aerial survey. The Section has a large slide collection which, as well as a forming a valuable part of the SMR, provides an indispensable visual aid for lectures and talks.

4. *Archives* Nowadays, original archives derived from fieldwork are almost always stored in the appropriate local museum with the finds. Where this occurs, a reference is made to this in the relevant SMR record. The SMR does, however, include much original material, often unpublished, such as letters, reports, sketches, drawings, maps etc. A great deal of this material is unique and irreplaceable.

5. *Library* The SMR also contains a library of archaeological publications, periodicals and off-prints, including substantial runs of national, county, and local journals.

Sources used to compile the SMR
In compiling the SMR, the Archaeology Section has drawn upon a wide variety of published and unpublished material. The former includes the Royal Commission on the Historical Monuments of England's Inventory of the Historic Monuments in Essex, published in four volumes between 1916 and 1923 (RCHME 1916, 1919, 1921, 1923). Essex is fortunate to have a complete Inventory although, because it was compiled between 1916 and 1923, it concentrates on historic buildings rather than archaeological sites. However, amongst the buildings there are thorough descriptions, often accompanied by photographs and plans, of the county's rich heritage of medieval churches.

For Roman sites, the third volume of the Victoria County History (VCH 1963), compiled by M.R. Hull was particularly useful, as was the same author's 'Roman Colchester', almost a mini-SMR in a book (Hull 1958). Another major source is the Ordance Survey record cards, of which the SMR has a virtually complete set. The SMR also has a copy of the card-index compiled by the moated sites research group, as well as gazetteers from other sources such as the CBA Mesolithic survey. During the creation of the SMR, and again in the recasting process, national, county, and local journals were systematically trawled for reports and notes on archaeological sites. One important source remains the annual round-up of archaeological work in the county which began in 1974, is published in *Essex Archaeology and History* (the transactions of the Essex Society for Archaeology and History) and which is collated and funded by the County Council.

As a result of PPG 16 there has been a great increase in the amount of archaeological work which is funded by developers. Such work is carried out by archaeological contractors working to a brief provided by the Archaeology Section's Archaeological Advisory Group. The brief will stipulate that a summary of the results must be provided to the SMR, normally within four weeks of the completion of fieldwork. For evaluations and other fieldwork, it is also stipulated that a copy of the final report should eventually be deposited with the ESMR.

The ESMR contains a rich variety of unpublished material from diverse authors, ranging from professional archaeologists to local observers. This material comprises letters, maps, sketches, reports, record cards, lists of sites, sketches on the backs of envelopes or record sheets etc. Other unpublished information includes dissertations written by students, using the ESMR as a source. Cartographic information is also included in the ESMR, such as a copy of the Chapman and Andre survey of the county in 1777, military maps from the last war, and old OS maps, notably a complete set of copies of the OS 1st edition 6" map of 1888. A remarkable item is two files entitled Wartime Contraventions, which appears to be a record of all the defence works which were recommended to be built in the county in World War II. It is believed that, in many counties, this information was destroyed - not so in Essex!

Many individuals have worked on the ESMR, over a period of over 20 years. It is impossible, therefore, to give an absolute guarantee as to the consistency and comprehensiveness of its compilation. The recasting exercise in the 1980's did, however, provide an opportunity to produce a more consistent and systematic Record. This was helped by the fact that the bulk of the recasting was done by one person (the author of this paper). The maintenance and enhancement of the ESMR is, moreover, done under the overall supervision of the ESMR Officer, thus helping to ensure that standards and consistency are maintained.

The Approach to the Recording of the ESMR
The ESMR embraces archaeological sites and finds of all periods from the Palaeolithic to sites from World War II such as pill-boxes. For the prehistoric to Roman periods, the ESMR aims to be as comprehensive as possible. From the medieval period onwards, a more selective approach has had to be employed. Historic buildings, for example, are only recorded where there is an obvious archaeological connection, such as a medieval church, or an early post-medieval building situated on a medieval moated site. Post-medieval artefacts are only recorded where they are of particular archaeological interest.

The way in which archaeological sites and finds are recorded on the ESMR has been subject to a number of constraints. For example, the SUPERFILE database only allows a certain amount of space for each individual record. A decision was therefore taken that sites should be subdivided according to logical and consistent criteria. These include major periods, land-parcel, and archaeolog-

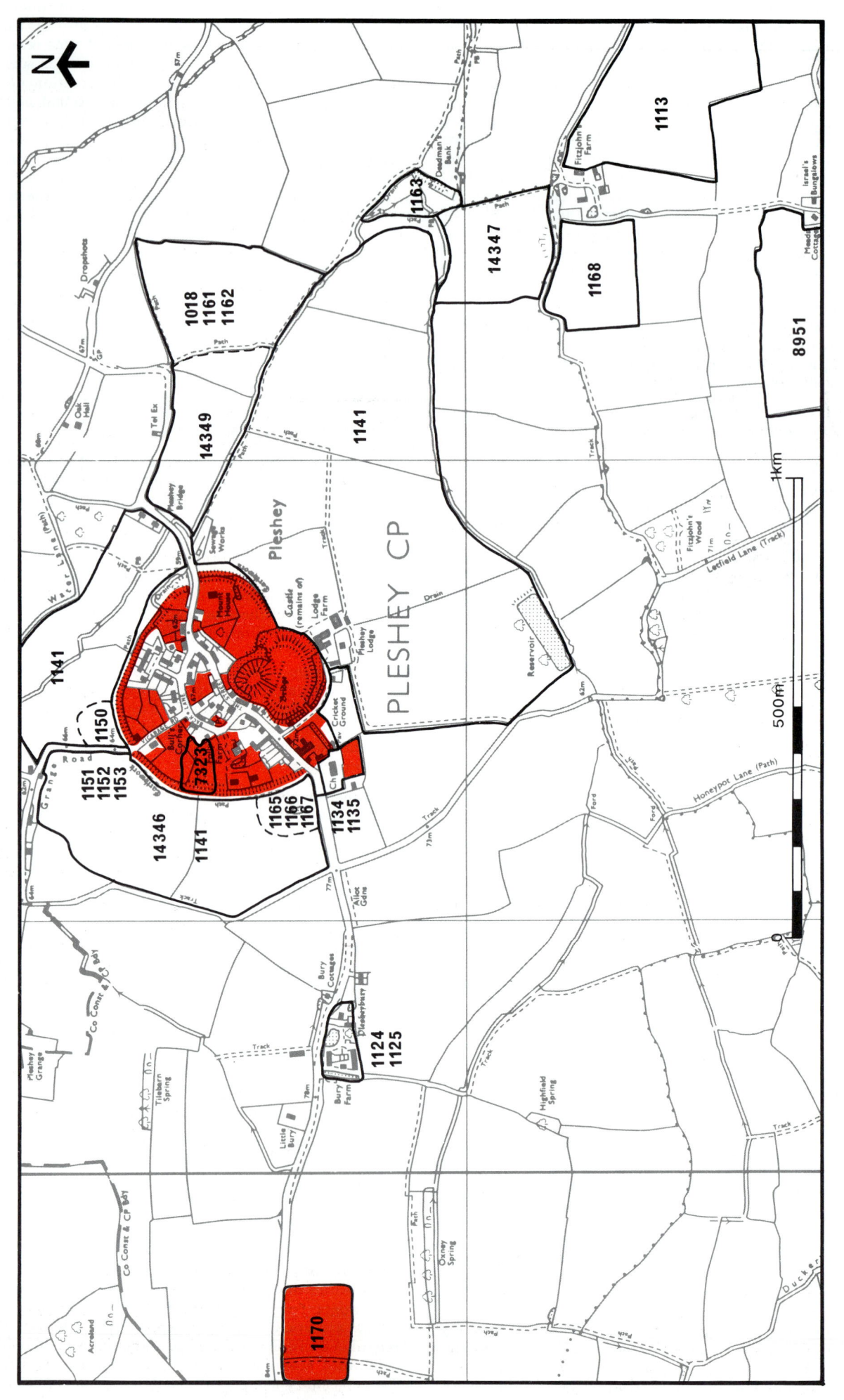

Fig. 1. Sample 1:10,000 SMR map

ical history. So, for example, Pleshey castle produced a number of records according to, first, land-parcel or component (e.g. inner bailey), period (e.g. Roman, medieval), and then archaeological history (e.g. excavations, watching brief, single finds). Where a site has been subdivided, cross-references are made to other relevant records.

Staffing levels of the Sites and Monuments Record
The SMR is located within the Archaeology Section's Archaeological Advisory Group, the Section's 'curatorial' wing. This group has a mixture of permanent and temporary staff, the numbers of the latter fluctuating according to the demands of project funding.

The Group consists of the following:

Permanent
Manager (Archaeological Advisory Group, the author of this paper)
SMR Officer
Development Control - two teams of two staff, each with one senior and one junior officer, for West and East Essex respectively
Project Officer (National Mapping Programme)

Temporary
Research Officer
Project Officer (Historic Towns Survey)
One SMR Assistant employed on the National Mapping Project and aerial survey
One SMR Assistant employed to maintain the SMR and to assist with the Historic Towns survey.

In addition, the Archaeology Section welcomes students on work experience placements, which normally involve some time working on the SMR.

This level of staffing helps to ensure not only that the SMR is maintained at an acceptable level, but also that a rapid response can be made to queries and that informed assistance is on hand for visitors to the SMR.

Access to the Sites and Monuments Record
The SMR has been compiled with public money and is available for public consultation. As office space is limited, persons wishing to visit the SMR are asked to make an appointment. In addition to personal callers, the SMR receives many telephone and written enquiries. In all cases, the Section is aware of the threat to archaeological sites which may be posed by unscrupulous individuals and enquirers are asked to state the nature of their research. The ACAO has published guidance to its members on the issues of access and charging (ACAO, 1993) and the Essx SMR follows this.

At present, a charge is normally made only to commercial users of the SMR (i.e. those who will profit from obtaining information from it). The charge is made to cover the staff time involved in providing information, rather than for the information itself. General research enquiries are normally dealt with free of charge, although with complex or lengthy enquiries, a charge may have to be levied to cover the staff time involved. Alternatively, researchers will be asked to visit the SMR in person to obtain the information personally.

Current use of the Sites and Monuments Record
As with other SMRs, the majority of enquiries are planning-related. These range from consultations from landowners, or prospective owners, anxious to know what is on their land, to developers weighing up several options for purchase, to the day to day querying of the database as part of the development control process. The SMR is of course consulted by the Archaeology Section's own staff, both from the 'curatorial' and the 'contractual' wings in the course of research on their own projects. External queries are very few in number, especially from academic institutions. Recent queries to the ESMR have included requests for information on long mortuary enclosures and barrows, for sites where Ipswich ware has been found, and for prehistoric sites in the Thames valley in Essex. The ESMR has also contributed information to national projects such as the Assessment of Assessments and the Monuments at Risk Survey.

Limitations of the ESMR
Because of the inherent limitations of the software and the way in which these have constrained the database, there can be problems in using the ESMR. For example, some database operations can be halted by large records causing problems with the computer's memory management. Other limitations are more fundamental. For most archaeological sites and finds, especially in rural areas, there is no difficulty in recording all the categories of information, at the most appropriate level. For others, notably urban sites, and large excavations, compromises have to be made. This leads to anomalous situations, such as the fact that a single find of a brooch or arrowhead may receive more attention than a similar find from a large excavation. This means that a researcher using the ESMR needs to be made aware of the fact that not all the artefact and site types will have been separately recorded for all the sites. Normally, this is not a great difficulty, if one assumes that researchers are aware of all the major excavations from the county. This problem does, however, emphasise the need for qualified, experienced staff to assist users of the Record.

Enhancement of the ESMR
The Archaeology Section is well aware that there are areas where the SMR could be profitably enhanced, and is constantly seeking funds for survey projects as is illustrated by the following case studies:

National Mapping Project Much of Essex is still devoted to arable cultivation and, as a result of this, and also of past agriculture, many of the county's archaeological sites only survive below ground, to be revealed as crop marks. Crop marks constitute the biggest single class of site recorded on the ESMR, with some 2,000 individual records. The bulk of these were entered in the early 1980's during a project funded by English Heritage. Crop marks are classified on the ESMR according to their form, using words from the East Anglian SMR wordlist.

The Archaeology Section had been aware for some time that its crop mark record was in need of an overhaul, for several reasons:

(i) the crop mark plot dated back a number of years, and was at 1:10560 scale, whereas the SMR constraint maps had been prepared at 1:10,000. The two therefore could not be overlaid and compared.

(ii) standards in plotting and classification had progressed since the bulk of the crop marks had been plotted

(iii) although the Section had received regular grants for aerial reconnaissance, funding had been less forthcoming for post-reconnaissance. As a result, the SMR was not as up-to-date as it ought to be, particularly since it had not been possible to do a regular trawl of other collections since 1987.

An answer to these difficulties has now been found in the shape of the RCHME's National Mapping Project (NMP) aims to ensure that *all* information derived from aerial photographs in England is plotted and classified consistently to a national standard. The Essex part of the NMP commenced in 1993 and will eventually result in the replacement of the current crop mark plots with a fresh set of 1:10,000 maps. As well as crop marks, the new maps will also include earthworks and other sites recorded by aerial photography. This information will help ensure that projects which analyse data on a regional and national basis have a consistent basis from which to work. A particular aim is to provide data for English Heritage's Monuments Protection Programme. However, this is not the only purpose and the NMP should be a valuable aid for research workers, whatever their area of study, be it a small area, a county, or greater. The NMP will take several years to complete but the work to date has already added many new sites and features to the ESMR. As well as crop marks they include many coastal sites such as salt working sites, oyster pits, and remains from the shipping and fishing industries.

Aerial Survey The Archaeology Section carries out a regular programme of aerial reconnaissance which, in recent years, has been directed to enhancing the ESMR for particular areas of the county where little flying has taken place hitherto, such as north-west Essex and the coast. The latter is proving particularly productive with whole categories of sites being added to the ESMR for the first time, such as wrecks and oyster pits (Strachan 1995). The choice of flight path is based on crop conditions, tide levels (for the coastal survey), knowledge of local geology and topography and also on existing information, or the lack of it, in the ESMR. This is a further illustration of the way in which the ESMR is used in survey and also in research.

World War II defences The importance of monuments from the Second World War has been increasingly recognised in recent years. Although there may be those within the archaeological profession who do not recognise these monuments as falling within the remit of mainstream archaeology, many feel that they are also to be valued and are worthy of study. This is particularly so when it is considered that defensive sites from the Second World War are disappearing, at an increasing rate, in many cases without record. Moreover, the people who built or were alive when these sites were constructed, are gradually dying out, taking with them their memories of 1939-45. In an attempt to assess the extent of WWII defences in Essex, five sample areas were examined in 1993 and, sub-

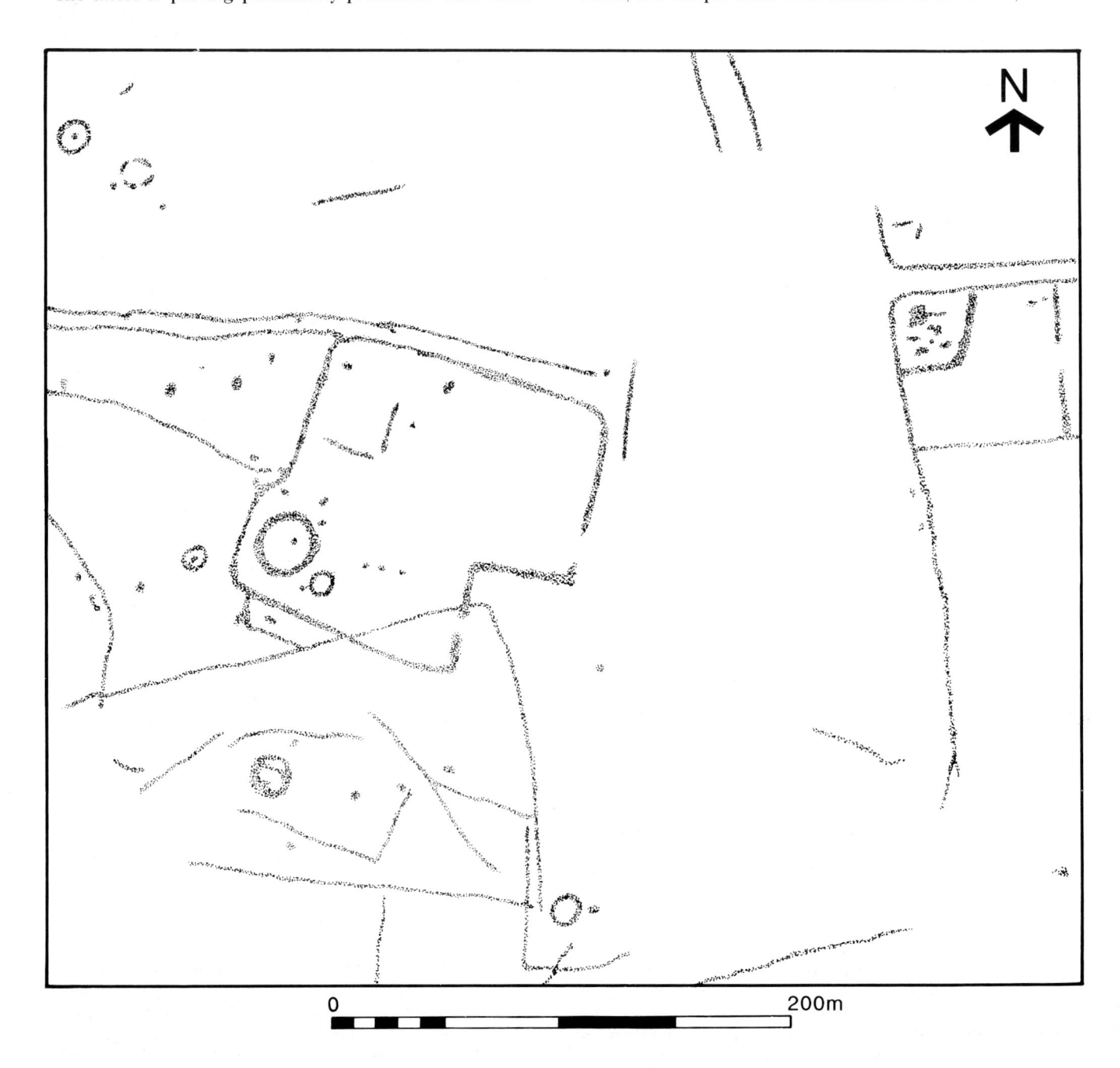

Fig. 2. Rectified crop mark plot

sequently, the survey was extended to the main lines of fortification.

The results to date indicate that, as a potential front-line county, Essex was very heavily defended indeed. As well as the coastal fortifications, three major lines of defences crossed the county (Gilman and Nash 1995). In addition, towns such as Chelmsford, and military installations such as the airfields and Royal Ordnance factories at Waltham Abbey, were protected by anti-aircraft and anti-tank installations and pill-boxes. Prior to the current survey, about 500 sites were known from Essex, many of which had been added to the ESMR. The results to date indicate that the overall total for the county is may be in the order of 3,000. The surviving sites include many rare and interesting examples, such as steel Alan-Williams turrets, anti-aircraft gun platforms, and minefield control towers (e.g. Fig. 3). The ESMR was used as a basis to select the pilot areas, and then to plan the surveys to visit known sites and to fill in the gaps by looking at likely locations. It is thus an excellent example of the way in which the ESMR can guide both survey and research.

Historic Towns This project, funded by English Heritage, aims to build on and replace a survey of the county's historic urban centres which was carried out in the early 1980's and which was adopted as Supplementary Planning Guidance (Eddy with Petchey 1983). The current survey will produce an analysis and assessment of archaeological and historic sites in each town. This will be based on the information in the ESMR which has been substantially enhanced and updated for the settlements to be considered during the survey. The project will use a Geographic Information System (GIS, see below) to record and analyse the wide range of spatial information (e.g. archaeological sites, Listed Buildings, Conservation Areas, planning permissions, cartographic and documentary information) which will be collected. The principal objectives of the project are to produce a framework for the management of urban archaeological sites and deposits and a set of research priorities to guide future archaeological work. The ESMR will play a pivotal role, initially by providing the main source of information to be used. However, the development of a GIS will enable the ESMR to become a dynamic tool which can be updated as urban archaeological work in the county progresses and which will, in turn, be used to revise the management and research frameworks.

Industrial Archaeology Following the appointment of an officer with a specialism in Industrial Archaeology to the Development Control team in 1994 efforts are being made to improve the ESMR's coverage of industrial monuments. A two-pronged approach is being adopted:

(i) thematic surveys of particular site types to provide a comparative basis for decisions about protection, preservation, research and recording;

(ii) detailed surveys of specific sites threatened by proposals for demolition and/or conversion.

At the time of writing, a major survey of the county's malt-houses had been completed and surveys were underway of lime kilns, breweries and milestones. Information from both types of survey is added to the ESMR which will enhance its role in guiding the definition of priorities for research.

Monuments Protection Programme

English Heritage's Monuments Protection Programme (MPP) aims to both increase the number of monuments protected as Scheduled Ancient Monuments, and to make the Schedule more representative of the country's archaeological heritage. County SMRs are the major source of information for the MPP which commenced in Essex with

Fig. 3. Minefield control tower, north of Crouch estuary

the scoring of particular monument classes. The scoring utilised the information held in the ESMR and the actual system used was based on the Secretary of State for National Heritage's non-statutory criteria for Scheduling (cf. Annex 4 of PPG 16). After the scoring exercise had been completed, and following consultation between the Archaeology Section and English Heritage, thresholds were drawn for particular monument classes. Sites scoring above this line would be visited by English Heritage's MPP fieldworker to assess whether they were worthy of scheduling. Certain sites below the line would also be visited, based on the exercise of local professional judgement. From August 1993 to April 1994, staff from the Archaeological Advisory Group were directly involved in site visits and the production of scheduling proposals, to assist in increasing the rate of progress with the MPP.

The MPP may not be 'research' in the classic sense of the word, but this exercise does illustrate the way in which the SMR is used in the protection of important monuments in the interests of future generations, interests which will include archaeological research.

Research and the Essex Sites and Monuments Record

It is a sad comment on the lack of awareness of SMRs in academic circles that the following comments, published in the proceedings of a conference on SMRs organised by the ACAO in 1984, are still valid today.

"Sites and Monuments Records are one of the success stories of the last twenty years in British archaeology. They have developed in a typically British way: somewhat haphazardly, with generally inadequate resources, but on the whole fairly efficiently. Archaeological perception of them varies. At one end of the scale is the 'public archaeologist', heavily into Heritage management and Information Technology. He or she regards the Sites and Monuments Record (SMR) as central to virtually all archaeological activity, from the essential bureaucratic drudgery of planning control up to the most abstract and rarefied of academic research projects. At the other end is the 'academic' archaeologist, whose view of the obsessive data-collecting

mentality of the local SMR curator may be less than enthusiastic, if indeed he or she is aware of the existence of SMRs at all.

These caricatures are drawn to highlight one particular theme of discussion at the conference. Academic input into the theory of archaeological record systems has been as minimal as the academic use that has been made of the information now available from them. Of the 120 or so participants at the conference, very few were from universities or other academic institutions. While acknowledging that SMRs are not the most entrancing of the issues facing British archaeology today, one cannot help but be concerned at the potential gulf between 'public' and 'academic' archaeology which this apparent lack of interest denotes" (Burrow 1984, 4).

This lack of awareness manifests itself in other ways, as is illustrated by the following extract from a letter which was sent to the ACAO by an undergraduate student in March 1993:

"I was wondering if you could help me at all. For part of the third year of my Archaeology degree course.... I have to write a dissertation. Mine is "The non-funerary features associated with earthen long barrows and allied monuments". I am aiming to make a few maps for my dissertation, showing the position of all the earthen long barrows, and another of Neolithic settlement, to establish any patterning (or lack) of the two. Is there any easy way to find out where these sites are? I was hoping there might be some kind of computer database, where the information could just be printed out".

Hopefully, this was an aberration, otherwise one is bound to question whether, and to what level, archaeology students are being taught about 'public' archaeology and SMRs.

Enquiries to the ESMR are, indeed, always welcome, but it does help if these are not too general and they should also be realistic. For example, shortly after the author commenced recasting the ESMR, he was asked if it was going to be possible to retrieve all 14th-century floor tiles of a particular size. In 1988, the following, rather ambitious request was received from a research student:

*"I am interested in the following stone tools.
1. Any stone implements from mining sites (including sites other than copper). For instance hammerstones, stone wedges and axes, which may be unmodified, grooved, notched and perforated.
2. Other sites, any stone implements which are grooved and notched".*

Clearly, it would be unreasonable to expect an SMR to cater for all such esoteric requests. An SMR is an aid to research, not a substitute.

One of the reasons for the lack of use of SMRs in general seems to lie in a general feeling that they are incomplete and inconsistent in both content and structure. This is important since archaeological distributions and research projects do not usually correlate with modern administrative boundaries. As a result, researchers will normally need to consult more than one county SMR.

It is indeed true that there is some basis for the concerns about completeness and consistency. Over the past decade, several surveys of SMRs and their contents have been carried out. For example, in 1987-88 English Heritage reviewed SMRs in connection with the Monuments Protection Programme (Chadburn 1989). This review did find that there was disparity in the way records were defined, the date range covered, and gaps in SMR coverage. These problems are due in part to the differential development of SMRs in various parts of the country, and also to the varying level of funding which they receive. Furthermore, in the early days of the development of the SMR network, there was a serious lack of guidance from national bodies as to how these Records should develop and how they should collect and store data. Nevertheless, the English Heritage review also found that there was substantial common ground in categories of evidence and data categories used. Furthermore, one of the most recent surveys of SMRs was able to claim that they:

"represent the most complete and consistent national source of data on British Archaeology available" (Lang 1992, 181).

If the lack of use of SMRs in academic research lies in a limited perception of their value and usefulness on the part of researchers, then this can only be overcome through greater communication between SMR-holding bodies and University Departments of Archaeology. The need for such communication is becoming more and more acute as the gap between 'academic' and 'public' archaeology continues to widen. One way in which this chasm could be bridged would be through greater participation of County Archaeologists and SMR Officers in University Teaching programmes, for example through regular seminars and, where appropriate, visits to SMR offices. Undergraduate and research students should be encouraged to make more use of SMRs in their undergraduate and postgraduate dissertations. The ESMR only appears to be regularly used for this purpose by students of one university (Reading). Moreover, to make the most efficient use of SMRs, both students and tutors should contact SMRs to identify potential topics for projects, and also potential pitfalls which might arise in particular areas. For their part, SMRs could offer work placements to students to allow them to gain direct experience of SMR work.

The ESMR and Research within the Archaeology Section

Development Control As has already been mentioned, the ESMR is most used in the planning process, as the primary source of information to inform recommendations to the local planning authorities. Through its use in the planning process, the ESMR is a major influence on archaeological research. This is because the recommendations which are based on the ESMR are the major factor, once planning decisions are implemented, in deciding what fieldwork is carried out, and which sites are preserved for future research.

In making their recommendations, whether for evaluation, excavation, watching brief, or for preservation of archaeological sites *in situ*, development control officers are guided by current research priorities. These priorities are also used in drawing up project briefs for archaeological fieldwork, as an aid to the setting of objectives. Following the 1993 conference, lists of the research priorities set out by the various speakers, were drawn up on a period by period basis, and are being used by the development control officers in their daily work. Moreover, at the time of writing the five county archaeological services (Cambridgeshire, Essex, Hertfordshire, Norfolk and Suffok) in East Anglia were preparing a series of period-based frameworks to guide research in the region as a whole.

Typological analysis Crop marks, as discussed above, constitute a major class of monument on the ESMR. However, they can be very difficult if not impossible to classify on the basis of their form alone. A first attempt at an assessment of excavated enclosures in Essex was made several years ago (Priddy and Buckley 1987). This found that circular enclosures were the easiest to classify, since the larger circular enclosures, or the smaller ring ditches, were most likely to be Bronze Age in date. However, rectilinear and rectangular enclosures were more difficult. For example, Late Bronze Age enclosures in Essex include both circular (e.g. Springfield Lyons) and square or subrectangular sites (e.g. Lofts Farm, Broomfield) (Fig. 4). The Archaeology Section aims to pursue the study of crop marks, through the sampling of particular enclosure types by trial-trenching, in order to refine crop mark classification. For example, an English Heritage-funded project commenced in 1995 to examine a number of circular 'hengiform' enclosures in the north-east of the county.

Landscape Research The ESMR provides an important aid to the Section's own field projects, as can be seen by its use in publications. For example, in a report on excavations at Coggeshall, the ESMR was used to provide a wider, landscape context for the excavated sites (Clarke 1988, 81-88). A more detailed example of this approach is provided in the report of rescue archaeology along the A13 in south Essex. In the concluding discussion in this report, site and artefact distributions drawn from the ESMR were carefully used as the basis for a discussion of settlement change through time (Wilkinson 1988, 115-121).

Future developments

Geographical Information Systems

One of the most exciting, potentially, recent developments in archaeological computing is the advent of Geographical Information Systems (GIS). Use of GIS could be particularly beneficial to the use of SMRs. Although SMRs such as the Essex record, provide an essential and vital source of information, they are very limited when it comes to answering spatial enquiries. The

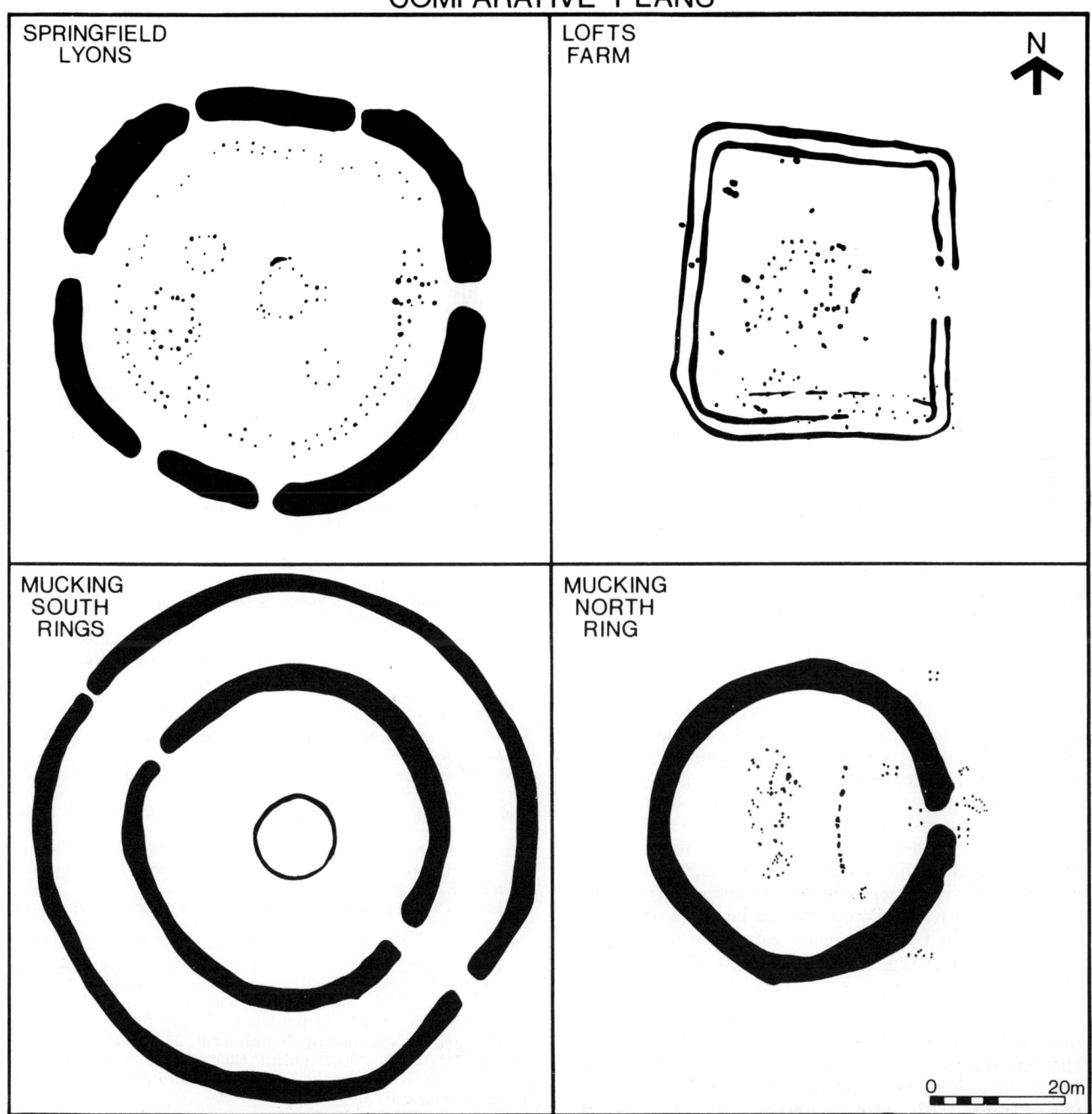

Fig. 4. A selection of Late Bronze Age enclosures in Essex

queries that can be handled are confined to the retrieval of information from particular administrative areas, or from within an area defined by NGR coordinates. This limitation is largely due to the way in which computing has developed, with GIS and other related systems such as CAD being a relative newcomer to the scene. Nonetheless, this is a very serious limitation given that the bulk of queries to the SMR, especially in dealing with the planning process, have a spatial element, i.e. the query is concerned with what sites lie within or near a particular location or land parcel. In fact the normal entry point for most queries is not the database, it is via the SMR constraint map. The searcher will then proceed to look up the sites of interest via the print-out or by interrogating the database directly. This can be a time-consuming process, particularly for very large developments such as major road-schemes or pipelines which cannot be neatly defined for a direct database search.

Use of a GIS would provide the means of carrying out this kind of spatial enquiry and of retrieving the database records simultaneously. Furthermore, GIS would provide the ability to link many other datasets which have a spatial component, such as historic buildings or historic landscape features. More usefully, GIS would provide a powerful tool for analysing site locations and distributions, and even has the potential for predictive modelling aimed at identifying possible site locations. The power that use of GIS could bring to an SMR has been demonstrated by pilot studies such as that carried out by Harris and Lock in Oxfordshire (1992). This study also points out the problems involved. It is too simplistic for archaeologists to assume that a GIS module can just be added to an existing database, even where that is a Relational Database system. Major restructuring of the database to allow for integration with GIS would be required. This is because SMR databases do not usually handle spatial data very well - normally only one NGR is given, often a centred reference, rather than an attempt to define the monument or site spatially.

When the need for such restructuring is added to the high cost involved in acquiring the hardware and software merely to run the GIS and, especially, in acquiring the basic map data one can see why, despite the interest, there have been relatively few large applications of GIS in archaeology to date. There are, however, some grounds for hope. GIS has much to offer within local government and many County Councils are establishing corporate GIS-based databases. This helps avoid duplication of effort, makes the best use of resources and can bring together data sets which were becoming fragmented as a result of the spread of microcomputers. In Essex, the Planning Department is the lead department for GIS within the County Council. The hardware and software are in place as is a pilot application. Digital, vectorised map cover at 1:1250 and 1:2500 scale has been acquired from the Ordnance Survey following conclusion of an agreement between the latter and the local authorities. Although the new Monarch system itself does not explicitly incorporate a GIS, it has been designed to allow information to be recorded which would be required by a GIS, i.e. the definition of shapes and lines by NGRs. The Historic Towns project (see above) will allow a start to be made on linking the ESMR to the GIS. Experience gained during this work will be used to extend the GIS to cover the rest of the database.

Integration with other records
The Archaeology Section is located within the Environmental Services Branch (ESB) of the Planning Department. ESB also contains separate Historic Buildings and Countryside sections, both of whom contain information which relates to, and complements that held within the ESMR, such as historic buildings, historic parks and landscape features. The use of GIS, the development of Open Systems and the rise of query languages such as SQL (Structured Query Language) as industry standards, provides the potential for the creation of a database which will embrace all aspects of the historic environment. Eventually, it may be possible to provide links to the documentary and cartographic information held in the Essex Record Office. The creation of an integrated database would facilitate greater coordination of specialist advice from officers in the three sections. It would also make it easier to carry out interdisciplinary studies, the need for which was stressed by many of the speakers at the conference in 1993.

Summary
There has been a great deal of progress with the ESMR since the original conference on the Archaeology of Essex held in 1977, most notably the establishment of a computerised database. However, it is clear that much remains to be done, especially in terms of raising awareness of the ESMR and its potential. The challenges for the next ten years will include the introduction of new software, the introduction of GIS, and moves towards greater integration of databases. These in turn will raise important issues, as it becomes necessary to make information more widely available, both 'in-house' within the host authority, and also externally to researchers and the general public. Questions of data security and of control of access to information will inevitably arise, and it may even become necessary to redefine the purpose of the Record itself. Is it primarily an in-house tool for use within the planning process, or should its wider role as an aid to research be given more prominence.

The history of the ESMR to date has already been both complex and eventful, and the next decade will be no different. If a third conference on Essex archaeology is held in ten years time, it is the hope of this particular author that the intervening years will have seen much more use of the ESMR, with consequent benefits for the database itself and for archaeological research in general.

Bibliography
Baker, D. 1983. *Living with the Past: the Historic Environment.*
Benson, D. 1974. 'A Sites and Monuments Record for the Oxford Region', *Oxoniensia*, 37 (1972), 226-237.
Buckley, D.G. *Archaeology in Essex to AD 1500.* Counc. Brit. Archaeol. Res. Rep. **34**.
Burrow, I (ed.). 1984. *County Archaeological Records: Progress and Potential* (ACAO).
Chadburn, A. 1989. 'Computerised County Sites and Monuments Records in England: an overview of their structure, development and progress' in Rahtz and Richards (eds) *Computers and Quantitative methods in Archaeology*, Brit. Arch. Reps Int. Ser., **548**, 389-398, Oxford.
Clarke, C. P. 1988. 'Roman Coggeshall: excavations 1984-85', *Essex Archaeol. Hist.*, 19, 47-90.
DoE 1990. *Planning Policy Guidance Note 16, 'Archaeology and Planning'*, HMSO.
Eddy, M. R. with Petchey, M. R., 1983. *Historic Towns in Essex*, Essex County Council.
Fraser, D. 1993. 'The British Archaeological Database' in Hunter, J. and Ralston, I.(eds.) *Archaeological Resource Management in the U.K.*, 19-29.
Gilman, P. J. and Nash, F. 1995. *Fortress Essex*, Essex County Council.
Harris, T. M. and Lock, G. R. 1992. 'Towards a Regional GIS Site Information Retrieval System: the Oxfordshire Sites and Monuments Record (SMR) prototype' in Larsen (ed.) 1992.
Hedges, J. 1975. 'Archaeology within a County Planning Department - Essex' in Rowley, R. T. and Breakell, M. (eds) *Planning and the Historic Environment*, 29-49, Oxford.
Hedges, J. 1977. 'Development Control and Archaeology' in Rowley, R. T. and Breakell, M. (eds) *Planning and the Historic Environment II*, 32-51, Oxford
Hull, M. R. 1958 *Roman Colchester*, Society of Antiquaries.
Lang, N.A.R. 1992. 'Sites and Monuments Records in Great Britain', in Larsen (ed.) 1992.

ARCHAEOLOGICAL RESEARCH AND THE ESSEX S.M.R.

Larsen, C. (ed.), 1992. *Sites and Monuments, National Archaeological Records*, the National Museum of Denmark.

Priddy, D. A. and Buckley, D. G., 1987. *An Assessment of Essex Enclosures*, East Anglian Archaeol. **33**, 48-80.

RCHME. 1916. *An Inventory of the Monuments in Essex, I*

RCHME. 1921. *An Inventory of the Monuments in Essex, II*

RCHME. 1922. *An Inventory of the Monuments in Essex, III*

RCHME. 1923. *An Inventory of the Monuments in Essex, IV*

RCHME. 1993a. *Recording England's Past: A Review of National and Local Sites and Monuments Records in England.* London.

RCHME. 1993b. *Recording England's Past: A Data Standard for the Extended National Archaeological Record.*

RCHME and English Heritage. 1995. *Thesaurus of Monument Types: A Standard for use in Archaeological and Architectural Records.*

Strachan, D. 1995. 'Aerial Photography and the Archaeology of the Essex Coast', *Essex J.* **30** (2), 39-46.

VCH, 1963. *A History of the County of Essex*, **III**

Walsh, D. 1969. *Report of the Committee of Enquiry into the Arrangements for the Protection of Field Monuments (1966-8)* Chairman Sir David Walsh. Command 3904 (HMSO 1969, reprinted 1972).

Wilkinson, T. J. 1988. *Archaeology and Environment in South Essex*, East Anglian Archaeol. **42**

The chronicle of an archaeological unit (1968-1988)

by N. P. Wickenden

Introduction

It is rare that one is able to chronicle the background to, birth, *floruit* and (purposeful) demise of an archaeological unit. However, that is precisely what this paper seeks to do. The archives of the Chelmsford Excavation Committee (later replaced by Chelmsford Archaeological Trust) are preserved in the archive store of Chelmsford Museums Service, and make fascinating reading. In addition, a complete signed set of minutes of the two bodies has been placed with the Essex Record Office.

The establishment of the early units is recorded in Barry Jones' *Past Imperfect. The Story of Rescue Archaeology* (1984). It was a pioneering era when archaeological strata were being bulldozed away in an ever-increasing haste, often with no records being made - the will was often there, but the funding and opportunity to get past the bureaucracy were generally sadly lacking. So it was in Chelmsford, and indeed the whole of the county, where no professional unit existed prior to 1968 except for Colchester.

The story is true of many ventures: difficult funding, local government bureaucracy, personality differences. On a national scale, the gradual establishment of archaeology as a professional, scientific discipline led to the corresponding erosion of the role of the amateur, until then the backbone of the archaeological response. That dichotomy has continued today; despite the huge interest in the subject by members of the public, keen to get involved on local digs, no proper method has been found in nearly twenty years to harness that interest, with the result that there is often public disillusionment and frustration, which may be partly responsible for the corresponding increase in metal detecting. Local societies still exist today, but few carry out active fieldwork. Chelmsford's last society, the Mid-Essex Archaeological Society, finally closed through lack of interest in the early 1990s.

Background

Essex archaeology (outside of Colchester) in the two decades after the Second World War was dominated by two men: Major Jack Brinson and Philip Rahtz. The latter, then a lecturer at Birmingham University, mounted two excavations of major medieval monuments at King John's Hunting Lodge, Writtle (1955-57) and at Pleshey Castle (1959-1963).

Major J.G.S. Brinson founded the Roman Essex Society in 1946, partly in order to examine the Roman masonry from a bath-house exposed in an ARP trench in Moulsham, Chelmsford. The Roman Essex Society flourished until 1952, excavating at sites such as Chelmsford, Great Chesterford, Little Laver and Rivenhall (Rodwell 1976). In 1952 the Society closed, merging its collections with those of the Chelmsford & Essex Museum, which resulted in the opening of the museum's 'Roman Room' on 30th August 1952, unveiled by the Mayor of Chelmsford, Alderman Hugh Wright.

Also in this period, from 1956 to 1959, small excavations in Chelmsford were carried out by the archaeological branch of the historical association of King Edward VI Grammar School (Drury 1988, 5).

In the 1960s, successive 'Museum Assistants' at the Chelmsford & Essex Museum, assistants to the Borough Librarian and Curator, Eric Reed, were encouraged to carry out small scale excavations in Chelmsford, in the absence of any professional body: Mr Woodward at the Prince of Orange, Hall Street in 1961, assisted by Mrs Elizabeth Sellers, nominally directed by Major Brinson; Gareth Davies in 1965 at the St Johns Service Station in Moulsham Street; and Ian Robertson, in 1965 at the Maltings Site in Mildmay Road, and in 1966 at Dovedales College in Moulsham Street. For these latter two sites, inmates from Chelmsford Prison at Springfield were used as labour, after the example set by the Ministry of Public Building and Works. It is worthy of note that several assistant curators have gone on to make considerable careers in the museum world.

In the later 1960s, development was growing at an exponential pace in Chelmsford. By 1967, it was clear that Phase 2 of the proposed Inner Relief Road was going to cut a huge swathe through Moulsham, across Moulsham Street, with the corresponding loss of several medieval timber-framed buildings, and unknown damage to the site of the Roman town of *Caesaromagus* and to the Dominican Friary. This latter monument was only known from surviving placenames, from the Walker maps, and from limited excavations in 1938 (Drury 1974, 51-3).

In response to this threat, buoyed up by increasing local (and national) interest in 'rescue' archaeology, Eric Reed held a public meeting at the Chelmsford and Essex Museum on 7 March 1968 and formed the Chelmsford Archaeological Group, an amateur arm of the museum with no constitution, officers or power, designed to carry out part-time excavations. Much of the credit for the origins of this group should actually be placed with a local school-teacher, David Saunders, who had approached the museum staff with the idea in the previous December. January and February had been spent sounding out people like Major Brinson, and Ian Robertson, by then the Curator of the Passmore Edwards Museum in Stratford. Reed was by profession a Librarian, although his duties encompassed those of Curator as well, and so most of the practical organisation of the group fell on his assistants, David Jones and Arthur Wright. Indeed David Jones, both as assistant to Reed, and later Curator himself, always ensured the museum's support of the unit throughout its life.

The meeting was chaired by Cllr R Jutton, the Chairman of the Borough Council's Public Library and Museum Committee. Announcements were made about planned excavations, a list was passed round for volunteers' signatures, and the public shown what to look for and how to record their findings. In the following month, on 8th April, Major Brinson, who had been unable to attend the inaugural meeting, gave a public lecture on the Roman remains at Chelmsford.

The Chelmsford Archaeological Group issued a series of four newsletters, produced by Eric Reed, starting in April 1968. In June 1968, the Group announced the establishment of a number of small scale excavations designed to test surviving stratigraphy. These were at 21-7 Moulsham Street (director Warwick Rodwell), the Midland Bank, New Writtle Street (Paul Drury), Cables Yard (David Jones, Assistant Curator of the Museum), 76 Mildmay Road (PJ Dalby), 42 Roman Road (Marion Wells) and the Friars School (David Saunders and Dan Biglin). It must be said that the impending major threat of the Inner Relief Road was carefully skirted around, although Warwick Rodwell tried to initiate large scale excavations in the 3 acre orchard at the rear of 21 Moulsham Street. The third newsletter in August was able to publish initial interim results. It also listed the work of Paul Drury, who had volunteered to record the timber-framed buildings before

CHRONICLE OF AN ARCHAEOLOGICAL UNIT (1968-1988)

their demolition. The last newsletter in November 1968 was very brief, announcing a slide show. The Group was never formally constituted, and was rather ill-defined. Before it had been in existence for more than six months, it had been overtaken by events.

The Chelmsford Archaeological Group had set up an advisory panel, shortly after its creation, comprising Major Brinson, Gareth Davies, Ian Robertson, and John and Elizabeth Sellers. This group, *inter alia*, soon advised the creation of an excavation committee under distinguished patronage with wide representation. Eric Reed was only too happy to hand over the responsibility for archaeology to a more expert and professional group. On 17th May 1968 he wrote to Major Brinson: 'Is the project now assuming sufficient proportions to justify the creation of an excavation committee as at Colchester and Winchester, partly with a view to raising funds?'

Thus the museum, which had taken on the responsibility for the foundation of the group, subsequently took its place on the sidelines, though it strove to smooth the path of applications to the Borough Council for funding, equipment and premises, and lent its name and status to give the group a stable background. It was also seen by all as the proper place for the deposition of the archives. Had the Museum Curator not been first and foremost the Borough Librarian (all this preceded the 1974 Local Government Reorganisation), events might have had a different outcome.

In June 1968, Major Brinson wrote to the Chelmsford Borough Council Town Clerk calling for a wider, professional approach to rescue archaeology, and suggesting the establishment of an excavation committee, independent of the Borough authorities. In July, with the Council's recognition forthcoming, and despite a short spell in hospital, Brinson formed a Steering Committee, comprising representatives from the Ministry of Public Building and Works, the Library and Museum Committee, and the Museum; and the following individual members: Miss M Arnett, Major Brinson, David Clarke (Colchester Museum), DG Davies, Miss Hilda Grieve, Warwick Rodwell, John and Elizabeth Sellers. Mr Ian Robertson had been proposed as Secretary to the Steering Committee.

The Chelmsford Excavation Committee was formed, and headed notepaper printed. The Lord Lieutenant of Essex, Colonel Sir John Ruggles-Brise, and the Mayor of Chelmsford had kindly agreed to be patrons, and their names duly appeared on the letter heading. Lord Petre was asked to be President. Major Brinson was elected as the first Chairman, a post he held until his death in November 1973. John Sellers was elected as the first Secretary. Straightway the officers entered into correspondence and negotiations with the Borough of Chelmsford regarding access to buildings and sites for recording purposes in advance of the relief road.

The *ad hoc* purpose of the Committee was: *to deal with the problems of archaeology in the Borough of Chelmsford, in particular the problem of recovering archaeological data which will be destroyed by major redevelopment plans.*

The operating principles were listed as:

1. The Committee will assess the archaeological situation within the Borough, plan necessary excavations and recording of buildings in phase with development, appeal for funds to carry out these excavations and surveys and control the expenditure of these funds for the intended purposes.

2. The Committee will control the excavations and recording and will be responsible for ensuring that these are adequately and competently carried out, properly recorded, and published in the Journal or Transactions of an appropriate learned Society.

3. The Committee will be self-governing and independent of the Local Authority, but will work in closest liaison with Local Authority departments, Borough Council Committee representatives, and with Officers of the Borough Council.

4. The responsibilities of the Committee will be carried out during the formative stage by an Executive Committee which will act in accordance with the Committee principles and purposes, and will represent that body.

5. The Executive Committee shall consist of members invited to serve by Major JGS Brinson (Chairman) or his proxy, as discussed by the Advisory Panel of the Chelmsford Archaeological Group, on 30 May 1968.

The objects of the Committee, as laid down in its constitution were: 'to promote in the County of Essex the study and advancement of education in archaeology and history and to make available to the public, through museums and other institutions and repositories for the collection, exhibition and study of archaeology and historical remains, such remains and objects as may be found during the Committee's excavations and research and to make available also reports of such excavations and research.'

The Committee consisted of member representatives from the Inspectorate of Ancient Monuments, the Society of Antiquaries of London, the Royal Archaeological Institute, the Institute of Archaeology, London, the Council for British Archaeology, the Society for Medieval Archaeology, the Universities of Essex, London and Cambridge, the Essex County Council Education Committee, the Chelmsford and District Chamber of Commerce, the Essex Record Office, the Essex Archaeological Society, the Chairman of the Chelmsford Library and Museum Committee, the Towm Clerk of the Council, the Borough Engineer and Planning Officer, the Borough Librarian and Curator, and other representatives as deemed necessary. The July 1968 document also names the Victoria County History, and the West Essex Archaeological Group. Other individual members of the Committee were the Lord Bishop of Chelmsford, Norman St John Stevas, MP, John Cherry, Dr MG Jarrett and Dr MS Tite.

By November 1968, the Executive Committee was named as Major Brinson (Chairman), John Sellers (Hon. Secretary), Miss Arnett, David Clarke and Mrs E Sellers (representing the Essex Archaeological Society), Gareth Davies, Miss Hilda Grieve, Warwick Rodwell, Ian Robertson and Miss Sarnia Butcher (representing the Inspectorate).

The first meeting of the Executive Committee was held at Major Brinson's house at Barnston on 17 December 1968. It was attended by Brinson, Sarnia Butcher, Miss B.R.K. Dunnett, Gareth Davies, Paul Drury, Warwick Rodwell, and John and Elizabeth Sellers. Already the Ministry of Public Building and Works had recognised the professional status of the 'unit' with a grant of £2,000, largely for director's fees for excavations. Ros Dunnett (now Niblett), then with the Colchester Excavation Committee, agreed to direct the first excavations under the auspices of the unit. These in fact took place in March to April 1969 on the 'Orchard' Site threatened by the line of the Relief Road 'Parkway', for which Rodwell had lobbied long and hard. Paul Drury reported on plans for building recording, and Hilda Grieve on documentary research.

Initially the embryo unit had no premises (and used the Museum as a post box for several years), nor equipment, which was borrowed from the Museum and Colchester. Eric Reed represented the Museum on the Executive

Committee but had no other involvement. The Chelmsford Archaeological Group, by now an amateur society operating on its own (ie not under the museum's wing) continued to excavate under Dan Biglin, until its eventual demise in March 1972. Biglin himself continued to excavate independently of the Excavation Committee, for the Mid Essex Archaeological Group, as well as sitting on the Executive. The MEAG had been formed out of Ian Robertson's evening classes in archaeology in the mid 1960s.

By May 1970, Paul Drury had become established as the Field Director of Roman sites, and Elizabeth Sellers for the Friary. Early Committee meetings were often acrimonious, as personality clashes occurred and members tried to establish ground rules.

In September 1971, Paul Drury was elected as Secretary, following Mr Sellers' distinguished period in office. Drury, more than anyone, was responsible for the success of the unit, which could have foundered on several occasions without his drive and hard work. Upon the death of Brinson in November 1973, Sellers became the Committee's Chairman, and remained in this post until the Trust closed in 1988. Gerald Dunning became the Committee's President, until his death in 1978, when Leo Biek took up the position. At the same time, Sir John Ruggles-Brise retired as Patron, and the position lapsed.

A number of distinguished archaeologists held the posts of Vice-President, including Sir Mortimer Wheeler, who wrote in December 1968 that he was 'delighted and honoured to help the new Chelmsford Excavation Committee and should like to be regarded as one of its Vice-Presidents'. In September 1972 he was due to make a visit to the town and lunch with the mayor. Wheeler had accepted Brinson's invitation in August 1972,

"*I have been reading your great budget with appropriate interest, and will gladly do anything that I can to stir up the local magnates.*

I don't think that writing is good enough in circumstances like these and would far rather see the whites of their eyes. For this purpose I could make myself free on Wednesday or Thursday, August 30th or 31st, or Friday, September 1st (when I see partridge shooting begins: we might include a few sitting potentates in our first drive, don't you think ?).

Yours most gratefully

Rik"

As a result of a misunderstanding and rather sensationalist reporting by local papers regarding an apparent 'snub' of Wheeler by the mayor, the meeting was cancelled and Wheeler never did come.

Policy building

Whilst continuing to respond as a 'rescue' unit, Paul Drury also strove to set policies and goals for the future. In the privately published *Excavations 1972-73. Interim Report*, Drury not only laid out the interim results of his excavations, including the first attempt at a proper town plan of *Caesaromagus*, but also set the groundrules for future work: the early development of the Roman town, the mansio, temple area, and Dominican Friary. He listed the forthcoming developments in 1973-74 and presented then threatened areas in a plan.

In September 1974, his follow-up document *Archaeology in Chelmsford. 1975-7 and beyond*, with a foreword by Professor Frere, summarised the increase in knowledge produced by the five years of the Committee's excavations, 1969-1974. The total expenditure during that time had been £35,000, met by the Department of the Environment, Chelmsford Borough and Rural District Councils, Essex County Council, the Pilgrim Trust and public donations. He again warned of impending development on a massive scale, by Trackrail Ltd in an area bounded by Hall Street, Moulsham Street, Parkway and Mildmay Road, and also in the heart of the medieval town. To meet this threat, the Committee required £40,000 in 1975/76 and at least £20,000 in the following year.

In 1982, the Chelmsford Archaeological Trust (as it had then become, see below) published a joint paper with the Essex County Council Archaeology Section (Drury and Eddy 1982). This again summarised the state of knowledge, and set the research agenda and priorities for the 1980s. This document was revised in 1986, and again in 1989 by the County Council and Borough's Museums Service.

Publication

One of the basic operating principles of the Committee was to publish in appropriate journals of learned societies. Drury's first interim report on the Temple and other excavations at Chelmsford was published in the 1972 Volume 4 of *Essex Archaeology and History* and remained the sole source of information for over a decade. An article also appeared in volume 41 (1973) of *Current Archaeology*. Early reports carried the statement that Chelmsford was a conquest-period foundation, a belief fostered by burnt Claudian samian in the Chancellor Collection, thought to have come from Chelmsford. Work by Drury and Rodwell later indicated that Chancellor had also collected in London, and the samian was far more likely to have come from the Boudican fire at London. Evidence for the pre-Boudican occupation of Chelmsford thus evaporated, although it still appears from time to time in print today. Another huge leap forward was the excavation of the *laconicum* and part of the mansio bath-house in 1975. Here, the old excavations of Chancellor in 1849 were unearthed by chance and realised for what they were. Chancellor, despite being a Surveyor, had failed to locate his excavations accurately enough, and they had 'floated' for over a century. Gradually the plan of the mansio evolved: the square courtyard plan, which appeared in Wacher's *Towns of Roman Britain* (1974, fig 43), soon gave way to the rectangular version we now know. Even the old square plan still pops up in print every now and then!

The Committee investigated different possibilities of publishing their monographs, originally conceived in the format of Frere's *Verulamium I* (Frere 1972), but later recast in the light of the 1975 Frere Report on *Principles of Publication*. Eventually the first of a series of Chelmsford Excavation Committee/Chelmsford Archaeological Trust reports appeared in the CBA Research Series, with the excavations at Little Waltham (Drury 1978). The Trust has now had a total of nine reports published in the CBA Research Series (out of a total of 80 at the time of writing). Another report appeared in East *Anglian Archaeology* (Wickenden 1988), but overall this series has not done justice to Essex archaeology.

Reports which were either not of sufficient importance or length to warrant a monograph appeared in the relevant journals, either national or regional. These have included *Antiquaries Journal, Archaeological Journal, Britannia, Essex Archaeology and History, Journal of the British Archaeological Association, Landscape History, Medieval Archaeology, Post Medieval Archaeology, and British Archaeological Reports*. A full list of publications by the staff appears as Appendix 1.

Publication has also included pottery reports for the Middle Iron Age, Roman and medieval and post-medieval periods which have become standard works of reference (Drury 1978, Going 1987, Cunningham and Drury 1985).

CHRONICLE OF AN ARCHAEOLOGICAL UNIT (1968-1988)

Buildings and accommodation
The Committee was initially given use of a terrapin building in the Civic Centre Car Park, by the Borough Council, and later a building at 36 Burgess Well Road. Storage space was provided in the museum's basement. In 1979, the museum converted a former cafe in Central Park for use as a joint museum and Committee store. From May 1975, the Borough Council also made available the former Cemetery Lodge in Writtle Road for offices and storage, on a peppercorn lease, and the Committee and Trust continued to use this building until the demise of the Trust in April 1988, when it was taken over as museum staff offices and the Headquarters of the Borough's Archaeological service and store.

A county-wide service
From 1973, proposals were being made to establish a county-wide rescue unit. The fact that Chelmsford was the only professional unit, apart from its sister at Colchester, in the county had meant that it was fulfilling a wider rescue role than simply Chelmsford. Paul Drury excavated in Little Waltham (1970-71), Braintree, Heybridge, Great Dunmow (1970-72), Danbury (1974) and Runsell Green (1977) on behalf of the Committee, as well as doing fieldwork in Colchester and Asheldham (1977) with Rodwell, and Radwinter (1979). Colleagues had also been carrying out excavations: Steven Bassett in Saffron Walden, Maldon and Harwich; Warwick and Kirsty Rodwell at Wickford (1965-1971) and Rivenhall; and Kirsty Rodwell at Kelvedon. Much of this programme was in conjunction with the Research and Fieldwork Committee of the Essex Archaeological Society.

An Essex County Council Archaeology Section had been created within the County Planning Department by John Hedges, the first County Archaeologist. When this body accepted responsibility for a wider fieldwork role from April 1976, the Excavation Committee changed its fundamental role to one of addressing its huge backlog of unpublished excavations. Despite this, it was in fact asked to co-ordinate the excavation of a further site in Orchard Street in 1977, directed by Robin Turner for the County (Site AR, Drury 1988). One of the flaws of the Unit system in the early 1970s was that as public money rolled in to excavate, little or no thought was given to the costs and timetable of a post-excavation programme. Indeed, English Heritage inherited this problem from the Department of Environment and only completed their automatic funding of a national pre-1973 backlog programme in March 1993.

The Committee continued to attract 100% Department of Environment funding for its backlog programme, and took on the post-excavation work for some of the other Essex backlog sites mentioned above. Job Creation Schemes were also of great help in basic finds cataloguing and first aid, firstly through the MSC from 1977, and then through STEP, from 1978 to 1979.

Nevertheless with no new rescue money coming in, Paul Drury became involved in the investigation of the standing structures of Audley End in January 1979, and later, in March 1981, Hill Hall, and even Norwich Castle keep (1983). Both the former two projects expanded to include excavation programmes, and they attracted much-needed funding for the Excavation Committee from the Guardianship Monument side (Properties in Care) of the Department of the Environment. Drury continued with the post-excavation programme, but developed his own interests in standing buildings, and in medieval tiles, co-hosting two annual Tile Seminars at Cambridge and at York in 1978 and 1979.

Computerisation
From the early 1980s the Committee invested in an Apple IIE computer and 8" disc drive, mainly to word-process its documents. However, it also commissioned specially-written software for the quantification of pottery (produced by EICON of Bar Hill, Cambridge). This involved the use of an Apple Graphics Tablet, then a rather new and quirky, temperamental piece of equipment, but which automatically read in rim diameters and surviving percentage (ie the EVES), using a touch-sensitive pen on a pre-programmed pad. The software was used to produce the statistics for the post-medieval pottery from Chelmsford (Cunningham and Drury 1985) and was subsequently also used by the Nene Valley Research Unit.

The later Trust was also involved with the computerised encoding of texts to simplify and enable in-house desk top publishing, in conjunction with the CBA, and even co-hosted a one-day conference on the subject in London in December 1985. The work involved complex coding of the text to establish the proper size and type and headings, tables etc, using the ASPIC system. Typeset bromides were then sent for checking by the interface company, Electronic Village, and corrected until a clean set was used for publication. It was a very lengthy procedure and the expected savings hardly materialised. The Reports on post-medieval Moulsham Street, the mansio Roman pottery, Rivenhall volume 1 and Kelvedon were produced in this way.

The Chelmsford Archaeological Trust
In common with a number of units, the officers of the Chelmsford Excavation Committee felt increasingly threatened by personal liability *inter alia*. In 1980, accordingly, it was proposed that the Chelmsford Archaeological Trust be formed as a limited company, and that the Excavation Committee be dissolved. New Articles and Memoranda of Association were prepared, and the first Council of Management met in November 1981. Mr Drury became Secretary of the Company, and John Sellers remained as Chairman. The last accounts of the Excavation Committee for the year 1981 revealed income of £58,675, of which nearly £57,000 came from the Department of the Environment.

The first members of the Trust were Miss M Arnett, Ken Bascombe, Leo Biek, Dan Biglin, Nancy Edwards, Jim Doran (for University of Essex), John Evans, Professor Frere, Cllr C Goodier, Vic Gray, Mark Hassall (representing the Institute of Archaeology), Cllr Mrs V Hutchings, David Jones (representing Chelmsford Museum), Cllr A Knight (representing Essex County Council), Jill Macaulay, Martin O'Connor (Treasurer), Warwick Rodwell, John Sellers (Chairman), Cllr Adrian Sharpe, and Hugh Thompson (representing Society of Antiquaries of London). Mike Eddy observed on behalf of the County Archaeology Section, and Philip Walker as the county's Inspector of Ancient Monuments, for the Department of Environment.

By 1984, the central core funding from the Department of the Environment (English Heritage from 1985) was split between 'backlog' funding - for those sites excavated before December 1972 - and 'current' - those since 1973.

Otherwise the work continued as before. The projects at Audley End and Hill Hall grew, with substantial excavation programmes built in, the former involving pioneering work examining the former plans of the formal gardens. In excavating the flower beds, the plan of the medieval Walden Abbey was also elucidated (Cunningham 1988b, fig 3).

By late 1986, it was becoming clear that the backlog grant from English Heritage was rapidly dwindling, and that the incoming grants from all sources together would not sustain a full Trust beyond March 1988. Indeed the work on Audley End and Hill Hall had largely sustained the Trust for several years. The Council of Management duly voted to 'cease activities' and to close the Chelmsford Archaeological Trust Ltd after the end of year accounts had been duly audited. The alternative would have been carry on with a much reduced staff with constant uncertainty about funding, or to effect a total change to the way archaeology was approached in the county.

Simultaneous with the Trust's winding down, the Chelmsford Museums Service within the Borough Council was expanding and appointing specialist keepers. (The Trust had previously been commissioned by the Borough Arts Committee to write a detailed brief for the redisplay of the Museum's Archaeology displays (something which eventually took place in Novemeber 1991)). Nick Wickenden accordingly left the Trust and joined the Museums Service as its first Keeper of Archaeology in October 1987. The Museums Service had agreed to take over the Cemetery Lodge when the Trust closed as its archaeological service for the Borough, and to buy the assets of the Trust, thus enabling the Trust to close its books in the black. Nick Wickenden continued to work at the Lodge, arranging for the smooth transfer of archives from the Trust to the Museums Service.

The final Council of Management meeting was held on 18 March 1988. Present were Cllr AS Knight (Acting Chairman, due to John Sellers' illness), Mrs Cunningham (Secretary), Miss M Arnett, Mrs N Edwards, John Evans, Mrs V Hutchings, David Jones, Adrian Sharp, Cllr F Sturt and Nick Wickenden. Observing were Dr Patricia Andrews (for Chelmsford Museums Service), David Buckley (for Essex County Council) and Paul Drury (by then working for English Heritage).

The final Annual General Meeting took place on 17 June 1988 at the Chelmsford & Essex Museum. Present were Cllr AS Knight (Acting Chairman), Mrs CM Cunningham (Secretary), S Berrett (Treasurer), Miss M Arnett, Paul Drury, Mrs N Edwards, John Evans, Vic Gray, Mrs V Hutchings, David Jones, Warwick Rodwell, Adrian Sharp, Cllr Mrs F Sturt and Nick Wickenden. Also attending were David Buckley, Raphael Isserlin, Miss Caroline Gait and Miss J Dixon.

The audited accounts showed income for the year 1987/88 of £93,271 (in fact the greatest income had been received the previous year - £110,868). Since the Trust was formed in 1980/81, a total of £660,032 had been received. In accordance with its charitable status, the Trust's financial balance, £735, was passed to a similar-minded institution, its sister unit, Colchester Archaeological Trust.

The publication programme of the Trust was still incomplete, however; the remaining staff of the Trust were made temporary officers of Essex County Council, thus ensuring no enforced redundancies, and post-excavation work continued throughout 1998/89, administered through the good offices of the Archaeology Section, and funded by English Heritage. The Director, Mrs Carol Cunningham, left Essex in the summer of 1988 to join her husband in the Hebrides. For a while, a number of members of staff joined her working on the last throes of post-excavation on the Isle of Lewis.

Substantial work was nevertheless left unfinished, and it was agreed that the archives and continuing post-excavation programme should be invested in the Chelmsford Museums Service. Thus the series of Trust reports, begun in 1978 with the Committee's report on Little Waltham, continues to grow still, and letters continue to be sent out to defaulting specialists!

Officers of the Chelmsford Excavation Committee and Chelmsford Archaeological Trust

President -1972 Lord Alport
1972-1978 Dr G Dunning
1978-1981 Mr Leo Biek

Chairman 1968-1973 Major JGS Brinson
1973-1982 Mr JE Sellers

Secretary 1968-1971 Mr JE Sellers
1971-1984 Mr PJ Drury
1984-1988 Mrs CM Cunningham

Employees

Directors
Mr PJ Drury 1970-1984
Mrs CM Cunningham 1984-1988

Field Officers
Mrs Kirsty Rodwell, periodic and 1977-1984
Mr Derek Gadd, Hill Hall

Faunal Remains Unit, Cambridge
Rosemary Luff
Miss Julie Douglass 1985-1986
Ms Jacqueline Mulville 1986-1988

Post-excavation assistants
Mrs CM Cunningham, latterly Assistant Director 1978-1984
Mr CJ Going 1979-1987
Mr NP Wickenden, latterly Assistant Director 1979-1987
Mr Michael Dawson 1985-1987
Mrs Anne Marriott 1985-1986
Mr Andrew Harris 1987-1988
Miss Kate Steane 1987-1988
Mr Raphael Isserlin 1987-1988
Mr Geoff Carter 1988

Roman pottery assistants
Mrs Barbara Ford 1983-1984
Miss Tracey Atkins 1985-1986

Illustrators
John Callaghan 1979-1983
Susan Holden 1979-1983
Caroline Rochester 1983-1984
Mark (Alf) Duncan 1984-1986
Graham Reed 1985-1986
Michael Sutherill (Hill Hall) 1985-1987
Richard Bellamy 1987
Leslie Collett 1988
Caroline Gait 1988

Appendix 1
Publications by Chelmsford Archaeological Trust (formerly Chelmsford Excavation Committee) and its staff

Bassett, S. R. 1982. *Saffron Walden: excavations and research 1972-80*, CBA Res Rep 45, Chelmsford Archaeological Trust Rep 2

Cunningham, C. M. 1984. 'Summary of the pottery produced in the kilns', in *Excavations at Lion Walk, Balkerne Lane, and Middleburgh, Colchester*, Essex. Colchester Archaeological Trust Rep 3, (P Crummy), 186-9

Cunningham, C. M. 1984. 'Colchester ware louvers', *ibid*, 211-4

Cunningham, C. M. 1984. 'Medieval pottery', in 'Excavations at St Mary's Church, Little Oakley, Essex, 1977' (M J Corbishley), *Four church excavations in Essex*, Essex County Council Occasional Paper 4, 24

Cunningham, C. M. 1984. 'Medieval pottery', in 'Excavations at St Mary's Church, West Bergholt, Essex, 1978' (B. R. Turner), *ibid*, 60-1

Cunningham, C. M. 1988a. 'Audley End House', in Egan G 'Post-medieval Britain in 1987', *Post Medieval Archaeol*, 22, 216-8

Cunningham, C. M. 1988b. 'Walden Abbey' , in Youngs, SM, Clark, J, Gaimster, DM and Barry, T 'Medieval Britain and ireland in 1987', *Med Archaeol*, 32, 241-3

Cunningham, C. M. and Drury, P. J. 1985. *Post-Medieval Sites and Their Pottery in the Moulsham Suburb of Chelmsford*, CBA Res Rep 54, Chelmsford Archaeological Trust Rep 5

CHRONICLE OF AN ARCHAEOLOGICAL UNIT (1968-1988)

Cunningham, C. M. and Farmer, P. G .and N. C. 1983. 'A Horse and Rider Aquamanile from Harwich, and the Significance of Scarborough Ware in Essex', *Essex Archaeol Hist* 15, 54-67

Drury, P. J. 1972. 'The Romano-British Settlement at Chelmsford: *Caesaromagus*', *Essex Archaeol Hist* 4, 3-29

Drury, P. J. 1973. 'Little Waltham', *Current Archaeology* 36, 10-13

Drury, P. J. 1973. 'Chelmsford', *Current Archaeology* 41, 166-176

Drury, P. J. 1973. 'Observations of Roadworks in Thurrock, 1969-70', *Essex Archaeol Hist* 5, 113-22

Drury, P. J. 1974. 'Chelmsford Dominican Priory: the excavations of the reredorter, 1973', *Essex Archaeol Hist* 6, 40-81

Drury, P. J. 1975. 'Roman Chelmsford - *Caesaromagus*', in *The Small Towns of Roman Britain* (eds W. J. Rodwell and R. T. Rowley), *British Archaeol Rep* 15, 159-73

Drury, P. J. 1975. 'Post-medieval Brick and Tile Kilns at Runsell Green, Danbury, Essex', *Post-Medieval Archaeology* 9, 203-22

Drury, P. J. (ed) (with S. R. Bassett, G. D. Pratt and others). 1976. 'Braintree: excavations and research, 1971-76', *Essex Archaeol Hist* 8, 1-143

Drury, P. J. 1976. 'Rettendon Ware Kiln-debris and other material from Sandon', *ibid* 8, 253-8

Drury, P. J. 1976. 'A Group of Mid-Thirteenth Century Pottery from Naylinghurst, Braintree', *ibid*, 267-73

Drury, P. J. 1976. 'Observations at Bardfield Saling Church', *ibid*, 275

Drury, P. J. 1976. 'A Medieval Water Pipe from Chelmsford', *ibid*, 278-9

Drury, P. J. 1977. 'Excavations at Rawreth, 1968', *Essex Archaeol Hist* 9, 20-47

Drury, P. J. 1977. 'The brick and tile', in *Pleshey Castle, Essex (12th-16th century): Excavations in the bailey 1959-63* (F W Williams, Brit Archaeol Rep 42, 82-124

Drury, P. J. 1978. 'Little Waltham and pre Belgic Iron Age settlement in Essex', in *Lowland Iron Age Communities in Europe* (eds B. W. Cunliffe & R. T. Rowley), *British Archaeol Rep* S48, 43-76

Drury, P. J. 1978. *Excavations at Little Waltham 1970-71*, CBA Res Rep, 26, Chelmsford Excavation Committee Rep 1

Drury, P. J. 1978. 'The MPRIA Prehistoric Pottery', in 'Excavations at a Neolithic Causewayed Enclosure, Orsett, Essex, 1975' (Hedges, J. and Buckley, D.). *Proceedings of the Prehistoric Society* 44, 288-9

Drury, P. J. 1978. 'A Saxon Loom-weight and medieval Tile Kiln at Blackmore', *Essex Archaeol Hist* 10, 234-6

Drury, P. J. 1978. 'Floor Tiles', in 'Exploratory Excavation within the Monastic precinct, Waltham Abbey, 1972', (A. E. S. Musty), *Essex Archaeol Hist* 10, 151-6

Drury, P. J. (ed) 1979. *Synopses of Papers presented to the Cambridge Tile Seminar, November 1978*

Drury, P. J. 1979. 'The floor tiles', in 'Excavations at St Michael's Church Latchingdon, 1976' (C. Couchman), *Essex Archaeol Hist* 11, 24

Drury, P. J. 1980. 'Non-classical Religious Buildings in Iron Age and Roman Britain: A Review', in *Temples Churches and Religion: Recent Research in Roman Britain* (ed W. J. Rodwell), *British Archaeol Rep* 77(i), 45-78

Drury, P. J. 1980. 'The Early and Middle Phases of the Iron Age in Essex', in *Archaeology in Essex to AD 1500* (ed D. Buckley), CBA Res Rep 34, 47-54

Drury, P. J. (ed) 1980. *Synopses of Papers presented to the York Tile Seminar, December 1979*

Drury, P. J. 1980. 'Floor Tile Fragments from Buxted, in Buxted Village Site' (C. F. Tebbutt), *Sussex Archaeol Coll*, 117, 261-2

Drury, P. J. 1980. '"No other palace in the kingdom will compare with it": the evolution of Audley End, 1605-1745', *Architect Hist* 23. 1-39

Drury, P. J. 1981. *Excavations in the east end of the South wing of Audley End House, 1979* (Level III report available from National Monuments Record)

Drury, P. J. 1981. 'The production of brick and tile in medieval England', in *Medieval Industry* (ed D. W. Crossley), CBA Res Rep 40, 126-42

Drury, P. J. 1981. 'Medieval Narrow Rig at Chelmsford and its possible implications', *Landscape History* 3, 51-8

Drury, P. J. 1982. 'An interpretation of the structures', in 'Great Oakley and other Iron Age sites in the Corby area' (D A Jackson), *Northants Archaeol* 17, 10-13

Drury, P. J. 1982. 'A mid-eighteenth century floor at Audley End', *Post-Medieval Archaeol*, 16, 125-40

Drury, P. J. 1982. 'Aspects of the origins and development of Colchester Castle', *Archaeol J.*, 139, 302-419

Drury, P. J. 1982. 'An introduction to the ceramic building materials of Norwich', in 'Norwich Survey 1982', microfiche

Drury, P. J. (ed) 1982. 'Form, Function, and the interpretation of the excavated plans of some large secular Romano-British Buildings' in *Structural reconstruction: Approaches to the interpretation of the excavated remains of buildings*, British Archaeol Rep, 110

Drury, P. J. 1983. 'Terracotta from Hill Hall, Theydon Mount, Essex', *Antiq J.* 63 (1983), 364-9

Drury, P. J. 1983. "A Fayre House, Buylt by Sir Thomas Smith": The Development of Hill Hall, Essex, 1557-81', *JBAA* 136, 98-123

Drury, P. J. 1984a. 'The Temple of Claudius at Colchester Reconsidered', *Britannia*, XV, 7-50

Drury, P. J. 1984b. 'De la couleur dans (l'edifice medieval: carreaux et carrelages gothiques: De l'Est Anglie aux Pays-Bas', *Revue de l'Art* 63 (1984), 74

Drury, P. J. 1984c. 'An unusual late medieval timber-framed building at Harwich', *Vernacular Architect* 15

Drury, P. J. 1984d. 'Joseph Rose Senior's site workshop at Audley End, Essex: Aspects of the development of decorative plasterwork technology in Britain during the Eighteenth Century', *Antiq J* 64, 62-83

Drury, P. J. 1984e. 'The Mirror', in *Antiq J* 64, 239-40

Drury, P. J. 1988. *The Mansio and Other Sites in the South-eastern sector of Caesaromagus*, Chelmsford Archaeological Trust Report 3.1, CBA Res Rep 66

Drury, P. J. & Gow, I. R. 1984. Audley End: *Official Handbook* (DoE)

Drury, P. J. and Norton, E. C. 1985. 'Twelfth Century Floor and Roof Tiles at Orford Castle', *Proc Suffolk Inst Archaeol* (1985)

Drury, P. J. and Petchey, M. R. 1975. 'Medieval potteries at Mile End and Great Horkesley, near Colchester', *Essex Archaeol Hist* 7, 33-60

Drury, P J and Pratt, G D 1975. 'A late 13th and early 14th century tile factory at Danbury, Essex', *Medieval Archaeol*, 19, 92-164

Drury, P. J. and Rodwell, W. J. 1973. 'Excavations at Gun Hill, West Tilbury', *Essex Archaeol Hist*, 5, 48-112

Drury, P. J. and Rodwell, W. J. 1978. 'Investigations at Asheldham, Essex: an interim report on the church and the historic landscape', *Antiq J*, 58, 133-51

Drury, P. J. and Rodwell, W. J. 1980. 'Settlement in the later Iron Age and Roman periods', in *Archaeology in Essex to AD 1500* (ed D. Buckley), CBA Res Rep 34, 59-75

Drury, P. J., Rodwell, W. J. and Wickenden, N. P. 1981 'Finds from the probable site of a Roman villa at Dawes Heath, Thundersley, Essex', *Essex Archaeol Hist* 13

Drury, P. J. and Wickenden, N. P. 1982. 'An early Saxon settlement within the Romano-British small town at Heybridge, Essex', *Medieval Archaeol*, 26, 1-40

Drury, P. J. and Wickenden, N. P. 1982. 'Four bronze figurines from the Trinovantian Civitas', *Britannia* 13, 239-42

Going, C. J. 1976. 'The Roman Villa at Chignall St James: A New Plan', *Essex Archaeol Soc Newsletter* 57, 12-13

Going, C. J. 1977. 'Romano-Saxon sherds from Corringham', *Panorama*

Going, C. J. 1977. 'An Iron Age Glass Bead from Lindsell, Essex', *Essex Archaeol Soc Newsletter* 60, 6-7

Going, C. J. 1978. 'Excavations at Stebbing, Essex: Interim Report *Essex Archaeol Soc Newsletter* 62, 17-18

Going, C. J. 1979. 'A Colchester potter who felt the cold?' *Essex Archaeol Soc Newsletter* 67, 16

Going, C. J. 1980. 'Interim Report on Stebbing 1979', *Essex Archaeol Soc Newsletter* 70, 7

Going, C. J. 1980. 'Review of Reece Beckwith, "Ancient Walls"' in *Aerial Archaeol*, 3

Going, C. J. 1981. 'Review of G D B Jones, "High Heritage: North Wales from the Air"', *Aerial Archaeol* 4

Going, C. J. 1981. 'Some Nene Valley Folded Beakers with Anthropomorphic Decoration', in Anderson and Anderson (Eds), *Roman Pottery Research in Britain and North-West Europe*, British Archaeol Rep S-123, 313-20

Going, C. J. 1987. *The Mansio and Other Sites in the South-eastern sector of Caesaromagus: The Roman Pottery*, Chelmsford Archaeological Trust Report 3.2, CBA Res Rep, 62

Going, C. J. 1988a. 'An archaeological gazetteer of Dunmow', in Wickenden 1988, 80-85

Going, C. J. 1988b. 'The countryside around Great Dunmow', in Wickenden 1988, 86-88

Going, C. J. 1992. 'The pottery', in Wickenden 1992, 92-115

Going, C. J. 1993a. 'The Roman pottery', in Rodwell and Rodwell 1993, 64-70

Going, C. J. and Buckley D. 1977. 'The Romano-British villa at Chignall St James', *Aerial Archaeology* 1, 27-9

Going, C. J. and Ford, B. A. 1988. 'Romano-British pottery' in Wickenden 1988, 61-76

Going, C. J. and Marsh, G. D. 1980b. 'A hut group from Tyddin Saddler, Anglesey, Gwynedd', *Archaeologica Cambrensis*, 101

Pearce, J. E., Vince, A. G., White, R., with Cunningham C. M. 1982 . 'A Dated Type Series of London Medieval Pottery Part One: Mill Green Ware', *Trans London Middx Archaeol Soc* 33, 266-298

Rodwell, K. A. 1988. *The prehistoric and Roman settlement at Kelvedon, Essex*, Chelmsford Archaeological Trust Rep 6, CBA Res Rep 63

Rodwell, W. J. 1972. 'Rivenhall', *Curr Archaeol*, 3, 184-5

Rodwell, W. J. 1972. 'The Roman fort at Great Chesterford, Essex', *Britannia*, 3, 290-3

Rodwell, W. J. 1973. 'The products of kilns II and III', in 'The Romano-British pottery kilns at Mucking' (M. U. Jones & W. J. Rodwell), *Essex Archaeol Hist*, 5, 13-47

Rodwell, W. J. 1975. 'Trinovantian towns and their setting', in The *'small towns' of Roman Britain* (eds W. J. Rodwell and R. T. Rowley), Brit Archaeol Rep, 15, 85-101

Rodwell, W. J. 1975. *Roman Essex* (privately printed)

Rodwell, W. J. 1976. 'Coinage, oppida and the rise of Belgic power in south-eastern Britain', in *Oppida in barbarian Europe* (eds B. W. Cunliffe & R. T. Rowley), Brit Archaeol Rep, 52, 181-367

Rodwell, W. J. 1976. 'The Roman Essex Society's projects c 1946-52', *Essex Archaeol Hist*, 8, 234-48

Rodwell, W. J. 1976. 'Early Anglo-Saxon pottery from Canvey Island', *ibid*, 8, 265-7

Rodwell, W. J. 1976. 'Trial trenching at Bradwell-juxta-Coggeshall', *ibid*, 8, 249-50

Rodwell, W. J. 1976. 'The archaeological investigation of Hadstock Church, Essex: an interim report', *Antiq J*, 56, 55-71

Rodwell, W. J. 1978. 'Relic landscapes in Essex', in *Early Land Allotment in the British Isles* (H. C. Bowen U. P. J. Fowler), *Brit Archaeol Rep* 48, 89-98

Rodwell, W. J. 1978. 'Rivenhall and the emergence of first-century villas in northern Essex', in *Studies of the Romano-British Villa* (ed M. Todd), 11-32

Rodwell, W. J. 1980. Temples, *churches and religion in Roman Britain*, British Archaeol Rep, 77

Rodwell, W. J. and Rodwell K. A. 1973. 'The Roman villa at Rivenhall, Essex: an interim report', *Britannia*, 4, 115-27

Rodwell, W. J. and Rodwell K. A. 1973. 'Excavations at Rivenhall church, Essex: an interim report', *Antiq J*, 53, 219-31

Rodwell, W. J. and Rodwell K. A. 1973. *4,000 Years of Rivenhall*, Essex Archaeol Soc

Rodwell, W. J. and Rodwell K. A. 1974 'Rivenhall', *Curr Archaeol* 4, 12-16

Rodwell, W. J. and Rodwell K. A. 1975. 'Kelvedon', *ibid*, 5, 25-30

Rodwell, W. J. and Rodwell K. A. 1976. 'The investigation of churches in use: a problem in rescue archaeology', in *The Archaeological Study of Churches*, (eds P. V .Addyman & R. K. Morris), CBA Res Rep 13, 45-54

Rodwell, W. J. and Rodwell K. A. 1977. *Historic churches: a wasting asset*, CBA Res Rep, 19

Rodwell, W. J. and Rodwell K. A. 1986. *Rivenhall: investigations on the villa, church and village, 1950-77*, Chelmsford Archaeological Trust Rep 4, CBA Res Rep 55

Rodwell, W. J. and Rodwell K. A. 1993. *Rivenhall: investigations of a villa, Church and village, 1950-1977*. Vol 2, CBA Res Rep 80, Chelmsford Arch. Trust Rep 4.2

Rodwell, W. J. and Rowley, R. T. (eds) 1975. *The small towns of Roman Britain*, British Archaeol Rep 15

Wickenden, N. P. 1984a. 'Review of "The Roman Small Finds from Excavations in Colchester 1971-9"' by N. Crummy, *Essex Archaeology and History*, 15, 180-1

Wickenden, N. P. 1984b. 'Small artefacts', in P. J. Drury, 'The Temple of Claudius Reconsidered', *Britannia*, 15, 44-6

Wickenden, N. P. 1987a. 'A copper alloy votive bar and a carved bone plaque from Chelmsford, Essex', *Britannia*, 17, 348-51

Wickenden, N. P. 1987b. 'The Prehistoric Settlement and Romano-British Small Town at Heybridge, Essex', *Essex Archaeol Hist*, 17, 7-68

Wickenden, N. P. 1987c. 'Appendix on Roman *cornu*', in M Dawson (ed), *Roman Military Equipment. The Accoutrements of War*, BAR, S336, 38-9

Wickenden, N. P. 1988a. 'Some military bronzes from the Trinovantian civitas', in J. C. Coulston (ed), *Military Equipment and the identity of Roman Soldiers*, BAR, S394, 234-56

Wickenden, N. P. 1988b. 'Excavations at Great Dunmow, Essex: a Romano-British Small Town in the Trinovantian Civitas', *East Anglian Archaeology*, 41

Wickenden, N. P. 1988c. 'The building materials and small finds', in P J Drury, *The Mansio and other sites in the south-eastern sector of Caesaromagus*, CBA Res Rep, 66

Wickenden, N. P. 1988d. 'An enamelled Roman plate brooch from Chelmsford', *Essex Archaeol Hist*, 19, 272

Wickenden, N. P. 1988e. Review of Buckley, DG & Hedges, J, *Excavation of a cropmark enclosure at Woodham Walter 1976*, in Essex Archaeol Hist, 19, 279-80

Wickenden, N. P. 1990. 'Caesaromagus', *Essex Journal*, 25.3, 58-63

Wickenden, N. P. 1991. *Caesaromagus. A History and description of Roman Chelmsford* (Chelmsford Museums Service)

Wickenden, N. P. 1992. *The Temple and other sites in the northeastern sector of Caesaromagus*, CBA Res Rep 75, Chelmsford Archaeological Trust Rep 9

Wickenden, N. P. 1993. 'Roman Vessel Glass', in Rodwell and Rodwell 1993, 54-6

Wickenden, N. P. & Going, C. J. 1986. 'Little Waltham, 2 Roman Road', *Essex Arch Hist* 16, 143-4

Wickenden, N. P. & Isserlin, R. M. Forthcoming. *Frontage sites in the northern sector of Caesaromagus*, CBA Res Rep.

Wickenden, N. P. & Rodwell W. J. Forthcoming. *The prehistoric and Roman settlement at Wickford, Essex*, East Anglian Archaeology

Archaeology in Essex since 1945: a review

Warwick Rodwell

Prologue

Antiquaries and archaeologists have been interested in the county of Essex for more than three centuries, and a roll-call would include some of the earliest and most influential writers on antiquities: Camden, Gough, Stukeley and Roach Smith, to name but a handful. Not surprisingly, Colchester was pivotal in their interests, but acknowledged ancient centres such as Chelmsford, Great Chesterford and Maldon also received a share of attention. So too did the various 'camps' and other earthworks, as well as the ever-attractive Roman villas. It was, however, the diligent observation and personal curiosity of a small number of local antiquaries in the later nineteenth century, and in the early years of the twentieth, that gave rise to some of the most important discoveries. Colchester naturally remained a honey-pot for scholars and collectors, but many lesser sites began to be noticed, and such localities as the foreshore at Clacton and Jaywick, and the riverine mud at Hullbridge, yielded artefacts of seminal importance to Stone Age studies. Warren's observations of material eroding from the Clacton foreshore were crucial to Piggott's work on Grooved Ware (originally called Rinyo-Clacton ware). Pollitt's work on the Bronze Age in south-east Essex (first published in 1935, then re-published in 1953 with an updated gazetteer) was the first to recognise the wealth of archaeology in that area.

Nevertheless, during the inter-war years, it was still Colchester that commanded the bulk of the archaeological attention in the county. Credit for most of the work carried out was due to the indefatigable Romanist, Mark Reginald (Rex) Hull (1897-1976). For 36 years he was Curator of the Colchester and Essex Museum (1927-63). In the early 1930s, the impending construction of the Colchester by-pass, through Sheepen, the site of pre-Roman *Camulodunum*, was seen as providing an unrivalled opportunity for research into a tantalisingly documented but ill-understood period at the threshold of British proto-history. The joint expeditions of the late Professor Christopher Hawkes and Rex Hull into Iron Age *Camulodunum*, and, separately, Hull's painstaking recording of evidence relating to the Roman town of Colchester, were exemplary. Publication was delayed until after the Second World War, when three volumes appeared that still stand as milestones in British archaeological publication (Hawkes and Hull 1947; Hull 1958; Hull 1963).

Post-war developments

Hull's work continued long after the war and, although his interests were centred on Colchester, he embraced the whole county insofar as he was able. Throughout his curatorship, Hull assiduously collected notes on discoveries relating to all aspects of Essex archaeology, marking and describing these on a set of 6-inch Ordnance Survey maps. He also piled notes, cuttings and photographs into a series of scrapbooks. Throughout the 1950s, Hull worked on the compilation of an archaeological gazetteer for Essex, the Roman part of which was published as the third volume of the Victoria County History (VCH 1963). Hull had intended that the prehistoric periods should also have been included, but they were axed by the editorial committee, even though the manuscript was to hand.

The other substantial contributor, besides Hull, to the VCH's *Roman Essex* volume was Major John G.S. (Jack) Brinson (1911-73). He was a self-taught antiquary, who came at the end of the era of the 'gentleman archaeologist', and who developed his latent interest in the subject during wartime service with the Royal Engineers in North Africa and Italy. He returned to Essex in 1945, and immediately set to work on the county's archaeology. The following year he founded the Roman Essex Society, an amateur body, the objects of which were implicit in its title. Excavations were begun at Little Laver in 1946, followed by Bradwell-on-Sea, 1947; Chelmsford, 1947-9; Great Chesterford, 1948-9; Rivenhall, 1948, 1950-52; and Little Waltham, 1948 (Rodwell 1976a).

Brinson cherished the novel idea of setting up a field rescue unit - an archaeological flying squad - to investigate sites threatened by post-war development. He began to put this into practice at Great Chesterford, where gravel quarrying was gouging away the northern part of the walled Roman town. Brinson conducted a series of excavations in 1948-49, on a semi-professional basis, on behalf of the Ministry of Works (a predecessor of English Heritage) but, for various reasons, the results were only published in summary form (in VCH 1963).

The Roman Essex Society had been formed largely because the Essex Archaeological Society (founded 1852) did not take an active role in fieldwork, and there was thus no vehicle for organized excavation in the county. Nor did the museums play a serious part in field archaeology, except at Colchester. Like so many bodies born of goodwill and enthusiasm, but without back-up resources, the Roman Essex Society foundered: technically, it was merged with the county Society in 1952.

Fragmentation and dissipation

There then followed a hiatus in Essex field archaeology, during which time a spate of independently organised excavations took place, and a steady trickle of locally-based societies emerged and began to undertake fieldwork. Local antiquarian and historical societies already existed in several places, such as Southend and Barking (founded in 1920 and 1934, respectively), but they were not generally active in the field in the later 1950s. A powerful thirst for excavation, encouraged by adult education classes in archaeology, led to the formation of new amateur groups. Prominent amongst these, as well as being long-lived, were the Waltham Abbey Historical Society (founded 1952), the Colchester Archaeological Group (founded 1956) and the West Essex Archaeological Group (founded 1958).

All three groups are still active, and publishing the results of their work. Colchester Archaeological Group has consistently issued an annual *Bulletin* containing a record of its work, whereas Waltham Abbey Historical Society has published its excavations in national and local journals, and the West Essex Archaeological Group has recorded its achievements variously in monographs and articles. Harlow Roman temple, a site made famous by Wheeler (1928), formed the focus of the early excavations by the last mentioned group, between 1962 and 1971 (France and Gobel 1985).

While Romano-British structures were once the favourite for local excavations, prehistoric sites also began to receive attention in the 1950s, albeit on a very small scale. For example, trenches were cut across the earthworks at Ambresbury Banks in 1956 and 1958 (Alexander *et al.* 1978), at Wallbury Camp (1959), and at the newly discovered 'henge' at Lawford (1962-3). The Lawford site was one of many revealed in the Tendring Hundred through aerial photography, a subject that was to make a dramatic impact on other areas of Essex archaeology in the 1960s.

Many of the local archaeological and historical societies in Essex were born out of university extra-mural classes organised by Dr John Alexander: some classes he led personally, while others were taught and inspired by Hull; a few benefited from the teachings of both. Such was the case with the Wickford Archaeological Society, founded on the membership of an evening class begun in 1963 (the origin of the present writer's involvement in Essex archaeology); a few years' later, Wickford's neighbour, the Billericay Archaeological Society, similarly emerged. Both carried out numerous concerted programmes of excavation on threatened sites. Numerous other local groups, with or without an interest in active fieldwork, sprang up during the 1960s, and many more have been founded subsequently.

Unfortunately, there was no overall leadership in the county, attempted co-ordination, or general recognition of standards of excavation and publication. Some of the societies were short lived. Enthusiasm for excavation often outstripped commitment to publication, to such an extent that it is now impossible to discover exactly when and where some excavations took place, let alone locate or reconsider what was found.

Alongside the organized work sponsored by local groups, there was a small number of individuals carrying out excavations privately. Two farmers who investigated extensive sites on their own land deserve particular mention. At Gestingthorpe, Harold Cooper excavated for a quarter of a century on the extensive villa complex that he discovered when deep ploughing in 1948; he subsequently amassed a remarkable collection of finds from the site (Draper 1985). The late Felix Erith farmed at Ardleigh, where in 1955 his plough discovered the classic Deverel-Rimbury Bronze Age cemetery (Erith and Longworth 1960). Both men were deeply committed to the study of their sites, and welcomed interest shown by visiting scholars.

Other private enterprises were less agreeable, and some were blatantly clandestine. Notorious was the late M.J.Campen, a treasure hunter who preceded the metal-detector age. In the 1950s, he sought out and dug into 'plum' sites, mostly Roman, all over the county: Lexden, Kelvedon, Great Tey, White Notley, Rivenhall and Stebbing, to list but a few. Hull attempted to keep track of his activities, and to note them. Some of Campen's finds entered museum collections, but none of his 'excavations' was properly recorded or published.

Professional forays: the first phase

Independent excavations of an altogether different nature also began to take place in Essex, funded by outside organisations and directed by persons for whom digging was a more or less full-time commitment. After the Second World War, the government, through the agency of the Ministry of Works (Inspectorate of Ancient Monuments), began to support rescue excavations on threatened sites around the country, either by sending in a paid freelance archaeologist with a team of labourers to carry out what was termed a 'direct excavation', or, less often, by grant-aiding an established local museum or excavation committee. Eventually, in the 1970s, the latter arrangement became the norm.

The ministry acted largely on information received from its network of County Correspondents, a role fulfilled in Essex by Brinson. He himself had carried out the county's first professionally funded excavation, at Great Chesterford, in 1948-49; and that was followed by another, outside the town wall, directed by Kenneth Annable and Dr Vera Evison in 1953-55 (Evison 1994). Another important excavation was conducted by (Professor) Philip Rahtz on the earthwork remains of King John's hunting lodge at Writtle (1955-57), a site that was due for destruction but which was subsequently reprieved and publicly displayed (Rahtz 1969).

As a by-product arising from the work at Writtle, Rahtz also excavated at Pleshey Castle (1959-63); but this was a research campaign sponsored by the enlightened landowner, the late J.J.Tufnell (Williams 1977). Both Writtle and Pleshey were additionally notable in that they were projects in medieval archaeology, a subject which had hitherto received scant attention. Offshoots from Pleshey included excavations at Maidens Tye (High Easter), and at a number of lesser medieval sites in central Essex, by Elizabeth and John Sellers (Sellers *et al.* 1988). At the same time, Southend Museum staff embarked on research excavations at Rayleigh Castle, 1959-61 and 1969-70 (Helliwell and MacLeod 1981).

Meanwhile, quarrying of the Thames terraces attracted attention to their archaeology, and several small-scale professional forays were undertaken in response to specific discoveries. Thus in 1955 Kenneth Barton led an excavation for the Ministry of Works on an Iron Age and Anglo-Saxon site at Linford Quarry, Mucking (Barton 1962). Not far away, at Chadwell St Mary, a sequence of Iron Age and Roman remains were excavated in 1959 (Manning 1962). A third site in the locality, at Orsett, was also investigated intermittently between 1956 and 1970. Attention had been attracted to this by the appearance of a double-ditched enclosure as a strong cropmark on an air photograph taken by the RAF in 1946. Prehistoric, Romano-British and Anglo-Saxon features were found (Rodwell 1974). A multi-period cropmark site, containing another major ditched enclosure, at West Tilbury was sampled as it too was engulfed by quarrying in 1969 (Drury and Rodwell 1973). The concept of multi-period occupation on a large scale, particularly on the river terraces, slowly began to be appreciated.

The most notable of all cropmark discoveries was undoubtedly at Mucking, the first photograph of which the late Dr J.K.S. St Joseph published in 1964, when destruction of the site was just beginning (St Joseph 1964). The following year, Margaret Jones and the late Tom Jones began a 'direct excavation' for the Ministry of Public Building and Works (as it was then termed), which continued almost non-stop until 1978 (Jones 1968; Clark 1993). It was the largest excavation ever to be seen in Britain, and its European status was rapidly acknowledged (Jones and Jones 1975).

Direct excavations in Essex, carried out by the Ministry, came to an end with Brian Davison's work at Chipping Hill, Witham in 1969 and 1971 (Rodwell 1993), and with excavations on the Guardianship site of Hadleigh Castle in 1971-72 (Drewett 1975). Thereafter, professional excavations were locally organized, and frequently grant aided. To assist this process, the Department of the Environment (successor to the Ministry of Public Building and Works) set up a countrywide series of Area Archaeological Advisory Committees in 1974-75, and Essex was grouped with Hertfordshire and Cambridgeshire. The committees were disbanded as part of the government's purge on quangos in 1979.

A reawakening and a new era

The archaeological community as a whole was slow to appreciate both the pace and the seriousness of post-war development in Essex. In the 1960s, towns, large and small, were being torn asunder, losing both their historic buildings and their buried archaeology. New housing developments and industrial estates began to spread into rural areas; road improvement schemes cut swathes through archaeologically uncharted territory; and quarries everywhere expanded their output to meet the demands of the construction industry. Anxiety was rife. Nevertheless, there was still a widespread feeling within the county that local people were sufficiently well equipped to cope with the threats to the archaeology of Essex. It was indeed a naive view, founded on the belief that a few small trenches would suffice to yield the archaeological sequence of a site.

Concern began to be expressed about the uncoordinated nature of archaeological and historical research in the county. But there was still no lead being given. The Essex Archaeological Society was substantially moribund at the time and, in consequence, a theoretically complementary - but essentially rival - organisation was set up in 1964, the Essex Archaeological and Historical Congress. Since 1966, it has published the *Essex Journal*, in succession to the demised *Essex Review*, which had ceased publication in 1957. Congress also set up sub-committees to look into aspects of the problems that were then looming. It published the county's first archaeological policy statement: *Archaeology in Essex: a policy for research* (1969). An archaeological symposium has been organized by Congress as an annual event since the later 1960s.

Meanwhile, Colchester and Chelmsford were both being blitzed. Through the efforts of Hull and Brinson, and with the prestigious support of the late Sir Mortimer Wheeler, the lapsed Colchester Excavation Committee (of the 1930s) was resuscitated in 1964. Rosalind Dunnett (now Mrs Niblett) was appointed as Director of Excavations, the first full-time, remunerated post to be created in field archaeology in Essex. For seven years she battled to stay one step ahead of the army of developers who appeared to be intent on razing everything of antiquity in the town, including stretches of its perimeter walls. In 1971, the archaeological mantle fell to Philip Crummy, and still the battle against archaeological annihilation goes on.

While in the 1960s there was widespread agreement that a large-scale, professional approach was both acceptable and necessary to deal with the threats to Colchester's archaeology, a different set of criteria obtained for the remainder of the county. This was somehow regarded as much less important, with only watching briefs and small-scale 'sampling' excavations being called for. These, it was widely held, could and should be conducted by local societies, without professional help or guidance. Some proceeded on that basis, while others sought grant aid and outside assistance. Thus at Wickford the local society conducted excavations on an extensive Iron Age and Roman site between 1967 and 1973, largely with funding from the Ministry of Public Building and Works.

In Chelmsford, the problem was more acute, and attempts to investigate its archaeology on an 'evenings and weekends' basis proved hopelessly inadequate. It was locally admitted in 1968 that the swathe which was about to be cut through the middle of the town by the construction of the inner relief road was to be written off archaeologically: it was simply too big a problem to tackle. A turning point in Essex archaeology had been reached. The impending loss was averted when a trial excavation was carried out by the writer, largely using a machine, on one of the relief road sites; this provided the essential stimulus for the creation of the Chelmsford Excavation Committee, and its future funding through local and national sources. Over the next decade, a major programme of excavations was implemented under Paul Drury's direction. The story of the Committee and its successor body, the Chelmsford Archaeological Trust, is told elsewhere in this volume (Wickenden, 192-8).

Chelmsford has become one of the best studied Roman 'small towns' in Britain, particularly for its *mansio* and temple complex. The results are now available as a series of monographs (Going 1987; Drury 1988; Wickenden 1992). Attention has been paid to its medieval successor too (Cunningham and Drury 1985). Besides work in the town, the Committee carried out a major excavation on the Iron Age village site at Little Waltham, 1970-71 (Drury 1978), and on a medieval tilery at Danbury, 1972-73 (Drury and Pratt 1975). Later it became involved in important projects in building archaeology at Hill Hall and Audley End (Drury 1980), and in garden archaeology at the latter house, 1984-87 (Priddy 1988, 266-8).

The late 1960s were dominated nationally by the formation of excavation committees designed to cope with major development threats, not only in urban centres but also along the routes affected by trunk road schemes. In Essex, it was the proposal to build the M11 motorway that gave rise to the formation of the M11 Archaeological Committee in 1971; its operations were divided into three geographical sections. Two of these lay within Essex, north and south, the third in Cambridgeshire. Fieldwork and excavations, mostly on a small scale, were carried out along the route of the motorway. The major known site to be affected was the Roman villa at Wendens Ambo (Hodder 1982). In 1992-93, preparations to widen the M11 gave rise to a new campaign of excavation, and led to the investigation, *inter alia*, of an Anglo-Saxon cemetery at Wicken Bonhunt.

While Colchester, Chelmsford and the M11 motorway were each large enough to require their own fieldworkers and management committees, there were many other places in need of archaeological attention, particularly the small towns. At this point, it was clear that a body with county-wide interests was needed to organize excavations and surveys, and to canvass for the necessary funds. Many saw this as a role that the Essex Archaeological Society should fulfil, and when Brinson assumed the presidency (for the second time) in 1971, the ideal became a reality.

After a long period of gentle decline, the Essex Archaeological Society was reinvigorated, first by becoming involved in running rescue archaeology projects, and secondly by restructuring its committees and publications. In 1972, its old style 'Transactions' were superseded by *Essex Archaeology and History*, and the first issue of *Essex Archaeological News* appeared in its current format. Under the auspices of the Society, excavations and building recording were organised at Great Dunmow, 1970-72 (Wickenden 1988), Kelvedon, 1970-73 (Rodwell 1988), Heybridge, 1971-72 (Drury and Wickenden 1982; Wickenden 1986); Rivenhall, 1971-73 (Rodwell and Rodwell 1985; 1993); Maldon, 1971-73, Braintree, 1971-76 (Drury 1976); Harwich, 1972; Saffron Walden, 1972-80 (Bassett 1982); and Hadstock, 1973-76 (Rodwell 1976b). Watching briefs and trial work were also undertaken on numerous other sites.

The 1970s saw much effort put into the preparation of 'implications' reports, that surveyed the problems facing archaeologists in many different fields. The first of these to be tackled in Essex, in 1973-75, under the auspices of the county Society, highlighted the archaeological problems relating to medieval churches (Rodwell 1977). The archaeological implications of development in Colchester District were also spelled out for planners and the interested lay public (Crummy 1975). At the same time, the publication of brief, well illustrated accounts of recent excavations became popular, bringing archaeology to the attention of a wider audience (e.g. Crummy 1974; 1979).

An archaeological service established

In the late 1960s, there was widespread pressure for local authorities to grasp the archaeological nettle, and to take it voluntarily into the planning process. Acceptance of this concept entailed the creation of an entirely new arm to the County Planning Department. First, an archaeological officer and support staff were required. Secondly, they needed a reliable database to draw upon, and to provide the archaeological input for constraint maps and constructive planning. Thirdly, there was a need to carry out archaeological appraisals, and to provide a positive field response to threatened sites.

Essex County Council duly created an Archaeology Section within the Planning Department, and appointed John Hedges as the first County Archaeological Officer in 1972. He was succeeded in 1983 by David Buckley. Hedges' initial task, the creation of a county-wide Sites and Monuments Record, was no mean undertaking, and its augmentation remains an ongoing task, as new sites and fresh information relating to known ones come to light.

The Archaeology Section continued with the preparation and publication of surveys of selected topics and areas. In the former category are the surveys of redundant churches (Couchman and Hedges 1976) and of historic towns (Eddy and Petchey 1983). In the latter category, the plotting and study of large areas of cropmarks has been a notable achievement, plus a preliminary classification of cropmark enclosures (Priddy and Buckley 1987).

In the mid-1970s the now-established Archaeology Section progressively took over the organization and running of major rescue excavations in the county, in succession to the Essex Archaeological Society and the Chelmsford Archaeological Trust, leaving those bodies to concentrate on the writing up and publication of a decade of intense field activity. In 1978 - fifteen years after the publication of the seminal *Roman Essex* volume (VCH 1963) - the Section organised the first-ever general conference on Essex archaeology, held at Clacton; this provided the opportunity for a synthesis and overview, period by period, of the knowledge gained through recent work, most of which was at that stage unpublished (Buckley 1980). Fifteen years later progress was again reviewed at a conference held at Writtle. The intervening period had seen not only sustained effort in the field, but also a considerable outpouring of publications.

The Archaeology Section identified several neglected areas where there was a pressing need to gain evidence from the field. The desirability of examining and dating at least some of the innumerable cropmark complexes that had recently been revealed through air photography in the river valleys of eastern and central Essex was a case in point; this led to excavation campaigns at Woodham Walter in 1976 (Buckley and Hedges 1987a), and Springfield Lyons in 1981-90 (Hedges and Buckley 1981; Buckley and Hedges 1987b). Smaller-scale excavations, designed to establish basic dating for certain cropmark features of suspected early prehistoric origin, were also undertaken at, for example, Orsett in 1975 (Hedges and Buckley 1978) and Rivenhall End in 1986 (Buckley *et al.* 1988).

Rescue excavations carried out by the Archaeology Section over the last two decades have been legion, and some have proved to be of seminal importance. Springfield Lyons, which falls into that category in respect of both the Bronze Age and the Anglo-Saxon periods, has already been mentioned. Equally important, for the Roman period, is the pagan and early Christian complex at Ivy Chimneys, Witham, examined between 1978 and 1983 (Turner 1982 and forthcoming). Advances in local knowledge of the Bronze Age have come from fortuitous discoveries at sites such as Broads Green, Great Waltham (Brown 1988a) and Lofts Farm, Great Totham (Brown 1988b). Several long known, but ill-explored sites have also yielded to study; these include Asheldham Camp (Bedwin 1991), Danbury Camp (Morris and Buckley 1978), and the enigmatic Maldon *burh* (Bedwin 1992).

Perhaps the major threat of the 1980s to Essex archaeology was the enlargement of Stansted airport, the knock-on effect of which will continue to the end of the century. Programmes of research, field walking and site sampling were organised by Essex County Council (Brooks 1987; 1989; 1993; Havis and Brooks 1991). Not surprisingly, these investigations added enormously to our understanding of the archaeology of north-west Essex. Moreover, some individual discoveries proved to be of wider significance, particularly the late prehistoric settlement found and excavated on the Airport Catering site.

Elsewhere in the county *ad hoc* expeditions have concentrated on particular sites and problems. Most notable have been John Wymer's investigations on the Palaeolithic type-site at Clacton, backed up by his gazetteer covering the whole of Essex and East Anglia (Wymer 1985). A wide-ranging study of the riverside deposits of the Blackwater and Crouch valleys has shed fresh light on the morphology and environment of early prehistoric Essex (Wilkinson and Murphy 1986). The construction of the Gray's by-pass in 1979-80 added another group of multi-period sites to Thurrock's archaeology (Wilkinson 1988).

Inevitably, work has continued on the Thames terraces, the major site, after Mucking, being at North Shoebury in 1981 (Wymer and Brown 1995), where excavation followed extensive rescue recording by D.G.MacLeod of Southend Museum. The colossal post-excavation programme that was required to complement the fieldwork carried out at Mucking is now well advanced, and the first two volumes of the definitive report have been published (Clark 1993; Hamerow 1993), as well as a report on the Bronze Age 'North Ring' (Bond 1988).

Numerous excavations have been carried out in south-west Essex by the staff of the Passmore Edwards Museum, and have included extensive work at two important sites: Uphall Camp (Greenwood 1989) and Barking Abbey (MacGowan 1987; Redknap 1991). Significant discoveries have also been made in the Lea Valley and its hinterland, as at Nazeingbury, where a Middle Saxon monastic site was fortuitously discovered (Huggins 1978).

Although opportunities for research excavations are rare, it sometimes happens that projects relating to the conservation of historic buildings or landscapes provide the stimulus, and the necessary support, for limited investigations intended to supply evidence that is needed for the implementation of the programme. The acquisition of the Cressing Temple Farm complex by Essex County Council in 1987, not only secured a site of national importance, but also provided an opportunity for the planned study of the medieval buildings, along with the associated buried archaeological deposits. This included a study of the historic garden (Andrews 1993).

While the Archaeology Section has become the principal agent for professional archaeology throughout the county, and in Chelmsford, the special problems faced at Colchester have continued to keep its own Excavation Committee (now Colchester Archaeological Trust) not only in being, but also extremely active both in the field and in publication. The fruits of the early years' work (1964-68) were collectively published in a volume of the Essex Archaeological Society's *Transactions* (Dunnett 1971). The next major excavation, at Sheepen Hill in 1970 - covering 13 acres of *Camulodunum* - provided the first opportunity since the early 1930s to examine a sizeable area of Iron Age and early Roman landscape within the dyke system (Niblett 1985).

More recently, attention has been turned to areas west and south-west of Colchester, to the dykes, to Gosbecks and Stanway, where discoveries of outstanding importance have been made.

ARCHAEOLOGY IN ESSEX SINCE 1945: A REVIEW

The development of areas within and immediately around the town walls reached manic levels in the 1970s and early 1980s, necessitating a series of large-scale urban excavations. First came Lion Walk (1971-74), then the relief road around the walls (1973-76), the redevelopment of Middleborough (1979), and finally Culver Street (Crummy 1984; 1992). Between these major set-piece excavations, many smaller sites were investigated. In addition to the publication of excavation reports - now itself an impressive series - Philip Crummy has taken the opportunity to offer several synthetic papers, bringing together the results of three decades of research in Colchester (e.g. Crummy 1981). The publication of *corpora* of artefacts recovered from the excavations at Colchester has been a further significant achievement (Crummy 1983; 1987; 1988). The temple of Claudius has also been reconsidered (Drury 1984).

Alongside the daily work of the professional archaeological units, responsible amateur groups have continued to make significant contributions to Essex archaeology through fieldwork and publication. Examples include a monograph covering a string of the smaller site investigations carried out by the West Essex Archaeological Group (Clark nd); a series of reports on Waltham Abbey (e.g. Huggins 1970; 1972; 1976 and 1988), culminating with a pair of papers on the archaeology of the abbey church (Huggins 1989; Huggins and Bascombe 1992); and a collective volume on the 'Red Hills' of Essex, prepared by the Colchester Archaeological Group at the end of a long campaign (Fawn *et al.* 1990). Detailed fieldwork, combined with careful observation, by the Maldon Archaeological Group has led to an improved understanding of the topography of that important yet relatively ill-known town (Brown 1986), and the millennium celebration of the battle of Maldon, fought in 991, inspired a group of scholars to study the history and archaeology of the event, and its contemporary context (Cooper 1993).

The huge increase in the volume and diversity of archaeological work being carried out in the county is readily apparent from the annual report of the Archaeology Section and the summaries of excavations published in *Essex Archaeology and History*, since 1976. These have become a regular and invaluable source of information on recent and current work; they include not only accounts of excavations, but also of field walking, air photography and building recording. The importance of these summaries and interim reports is emphasised by the inevitable time-delay between discovery and full-scale publication.

Regrettably, the average time taken for a full report to appear, following the completion of fieldwork associated with a substantial project, is seven to ten years. If, however, the project was of extended duration, the time lapse from inception to publication may be double that figure. Thus, many of the excavations conducted in the 1960s and 1970s did not appear in print before the mid 1980s, and not a few are still in the pipeline today. Reports on smaller excavations, published in journals, appear on average five years after completion. Of the 32 monographs cited in this paper, relating to post-war excavations, only four had been published by 1980 and 21 have appeared since 1985. On the national scale, Essex has a good publication record; archaeologists are simply tardy in the full reporting of their own work.

Epilogue; changing perspectives on Essex archaeology

This paper has outlined the development of field archaeology in Essex over a period of half a century. It has not attempted to assess the academic impact of fieldwork in respect of individual sites, or periods; that is the preserve of other contributors to this volume. It may, however, be appropriate to conclude this essay with a brief review of the changing perspectives on archaeology that we have witnessed over the past three decades, since the publication of Roman Essex (VCH 1963).

Three aspects of archaeological study have evolved to an extent that could never have been foreseen: a move away from the concept of 'sites', and of 'periods' based on cultural divisions; the birth of landscape archaeology; and the embracing of buildings and other structures by the discipline.

Sites and periods

In the 1950s and 1960s, archaeology was almost exclusively site oriented. The compendious VCH gazetteer of sites and finds of the Roman period bore witness to this, and distribution maps were essentially collections of dots suspended in space. The belief that most archaeological 'sites' had finite limits and were attributable to individual 'periods' was also endemic in both pre- and post-war scholarship, so much so that even in the early 1970s the Ministry of Public Building and Works was still supporting excavations expressly on a period basis. It recognised three divisions - prehistoric, Roman and medieval - and had one inspector to deal with each. Sites were excavated with a view to learning about particular periods or structures, and when seemingly extraneous material (earlier or later) came to light it was more often ignored than embraced. Medieval and post-medieval layers were commonly dug away unceremoniously, in order to reach the interesting deposits. Colchester fared particularly badly in this respect.

The period-dominated approach induced amazing levels of blindness in archaeological scholarship. Thus, when Wheeler caused excavations to take place at Chipping Hill, Witham, in the early 1930s, he did so primarily to recover artefacts of the late Saxon period. Having made the assumption that Chipping Hill was the site of Edward the Elder's *burh*, with little justification, it was taken for granted that the artefacts recovered would be almost exclusively tenth century. Iron Age pottery and coins were initially reported as 'Saxon', so too was late Roman glass; and an amphora fragment was explained as having been maliciously 'planted'. Eventually, when the sheer volume of Iron Age and Roman evidence overwhelmed Anglo-Saxon prejudice, the excavation was abandoned and was not published for another 60 years (Rodwell 1993). Moreover, when part of the site was re-excavated in 1988, a clear prehistoric sequence was established, accompanied by a dense scatter of flint flakes and implements. Amazingly, no flints had been retained, or even noted, by the excavators of the 1930s.

Likewise, excavations of the 1940s and 1950s on major Roman sites, such as Chelmsford, Kelvedon and Rivenhall, predictably yielded artefacts of that period, and virtually nothing else. Yet fresh excavations at these sites, during and since the 1960s, have changed the picture substantially. They and numerous other sites all yielded flint flakes and implements by the hundred, and in some cases by the thousand. Knowledge of prehistoric Essex began to expand rapidly in the early 1970s, largely by chance. Structures and finds dating from the Iron Age have been excavated beneath Roman levels at the three places just mentioned. Rivenhall additionally yielded early Anglo-Saxon features cut into the Roman levels.

Excavations since the 1960s have demonstrated how the single-period site was the exception rather than the rule in Essex. The only area of the county where multi-period occupation had hitherto been generally recognised was on the Thames terraces, where there had been a long history of the discovery of artefacts of all periods, from the Palaeolithic to the early Anglo-Saxon, in the gravel pits and brickearth quarries. Nevertheless, when early Saxon features were excavated in 1955 at Linford Quarry, Mucking, along with later prehistoric and Roman remains, they were greeted initially with disbelief. Even in the 1970s, there was reluctance to accept that Anglo-Saxon occupation could occur directly on Roman sites: a deeply entrenched myth had grown up that the physical remains of the two cultures were never found in close juxtaposition.

Equally disconcerting in the 1960s was the discovery of archaeological sites on heavy clay soils where, again according to received wisdom, they should not have occurred. Wickford, on the London Clay, was a classic case. While the exploitation of clay lands in the Roman period was coming to be appreciated, the discovery of Neolithic, Bronze Age and Iron Age remains at Wickford in the late 1960s was a startling revelation. Today there would be nothing remarkable about such a discovery, and Broads Green provides a recent example on Boulder Clay (Brown 1988a). Field survey in north-west Essex has revealed an unsuspected density of settlement on intractable land (Williamson 1986). Continuity of site use through many centuries, and often millennia, was clearly the norm, on both light and heavy soils.

Landscapes
At the same time as long sequences of occupation, spanning more than one cultural phase, were being established through excavation, other investigative techniques began to reveal spatial relationships between sites. The principal advances were made through the advent of aerial archaeology. A few classic sites, mainly Roman, had long been known from air photographs, such as the Gosbecks temple, the Orsett Cock enclosure and the supposed 'signal station' at Hadleigh, but throughout the 1970s and 1980s, fresh complexes were recorded annually by aerial photographers. While some of the discoveries were of finite features - enclosures, ring ditches, building foundations - many were of landscape complexes. Multi-phase settlements, cemeteries, enclosures, field systems, trackways, linear boundaries, and a host of indefinable features, often stretching over many acres, were revealed wherever soil and crop conditions permitted.

The realisation that these complexes not only existed but also interlocked meaningfully with the extant landscapes and settlements opened up new horizons. Landscape archaeology as a sub-discipline was only born in the 1970s. Since then, huge strides have been taken in understanding patterns of agrarian land use, and the evolution of settlement nuclei. The baseless but long-held supposition that the 'modern' Essex landscape is largely of recent creation, and that the winding lanes so characteristic of the countryside are medieval, has been demonstrated as fallacious. Localised studies have shown that field systems and road patterns in many parts of the country are prehistoric in origin; elsewhere, different systems seem to be of Roman or possibly Anglo-Saxon date (Rodwell 1978; Rippon 1991).

Not only is the framework of the landscape susceptible of elucidation through fresh archaeological approaches, but so too are some of its less tangible components, such as historic woodland. Much of Oliver Rackham's pioneering work in this field has been carried out in Essex (e.g. Rackham 1986).

Structures
The study of standing buildings has long been the preserve of architectural historians, whose skills are different from those of the archaeologist. Consequently, a rigid divide formerly existed between archaeologists on the one hand, who investigated the foundations and buried remains of lost structures that were no longer standing, and architectural historians on the other, who directed their attentions to upstanding monuments. Legislation and separate financial provision for archaeology, and for building recording, not only emphasised the division, but also enforced it. Such was the case in the late 1970s, and it was pioneering work in Essex that did much to precipitate a change of heart at national level.

The two key factors were, first, the general development of interest in medieval and post-medieval archaeology, and second, the increasing realisation on the part of archaeologists that historic buildings are often highly complex structures, and are susceptible of investigation in the same way as buried deposits. Architectural historians had, on the whole, concentrated on the form and decoration of buildings, and had failed to appreciate their hidden complexities. Moreover, little attention was paid to seemingly humble structures, such as 'ordinary' timber-framed houses and rubble-built churches. Essex abounds in both.

It was Cecil Hewett's applied study of the technology and construction of timber-framed buildings in the 1960s that began to reveal their archaeology and true chronology (Hewett 1969; 1974). The redating of the Cressing Temple barns was of seminal importance to the study of vernacular architecture; and the developments that were to follow could not have been foreseen (Andrews 1993). However, it was the advent of excavations inside and around churches that effectively forced the issue of collaboration between archaeology and architectural history. Rivenhall and Hadstock were pivotal in this process.

The systematic archaeological study of standing buildings, and of their sites, slowly gained general acceptance during the 1970s, and has now become commonplace. A spate of opportunities arose in relation to rural churches: Rivenhall, 1971-73 (Rodwell and Rodwell 1985; 1993); Hadstock, 1973-86 (Rodwell 1976b); Asheldham, 1975-76 (Drury and Rodwell 1978); Latchingdon, 1976 (Couchman 1979); Little Oakley, 1977 (Corbishley 1984); West Bergholt, 1978 (Turner 1984); West Thurrock, 1979 (Milton 1984); and Cressing, 1979 (Hope 1984); and in a suburban context, Woodford, 1970-71 (Litton and Clark 1977). More recently, opportunities for investigation have arisen in some of Colchester's churches too, and the archaeology of the Norman castle has also been subjected to scrutiny and detailed recording.

In conclusion, the history of archaeology in Essex may be viewed as an index of the development of the discipline in England as a whole. The local achievements have been wide ranging, and it has not been possible in this brief review to mention more than a modest number of examples; much of importance has inevitably been passed over without mention. Nevertheless, it is hoped that a reasonably balanced review of the organisational vicissitudes and the fields of endeavour, that have characterised the past half-century, has been conveyed. Knowledge is seldom easily gained in archaeology, and what has been achieved has been through a combination of professional expertise, collective amateur effort, and personal dedication, performed sometimes in the face of seemingly overwhelming difficulties. Long may all three continue: *Forti Nihil Difficile.**

*'Nothing is too difficult for the brave': Southend-on-Sea High School for Boys motto

Bibliography
Alexander, J. A.. Cotton, M. A. Robertson Mackay, R. and Warren, S. H. 1978. 'Ambresbury Banks, an Iron Age Camp in Epping Forest, Essex', *Essex Archaeol. Hist.* 10, 189-205
Andrews, D. D. (ed.) 1993. *Cressing Temple: a Templar and Hospitaller Manor in Essex* Chelmsford: Essex County Council
Barton, K. J. 1962. 'Settlements of the Iron Age and Pagan Saxon periods at Linford, Essex', *Trans. Essex Archaeol. Soc.* (ser. 3) 1, 57-104

ARCHAEOLOGY IN ESSEX SINCE 1945: A REVIEW

Bassett, S. R. 1982. *Saffron Walden: excavations and research 1972-80*, CBA Res. Rep. 45

Bedwin, O. 1991. 'Asheldham Camp - an early Iron Age hillfort: excavations 1985', *Essex Archaeol. Hist* 22, 13-37

Bedwin, O. 1992. 'Early Iron Age settlement at Maldon and the Maldon burh: excavations at Beacon Green 1987', *Essex Archaeol. Hist.* 23, 10-24

Bond, D. 1988. *Excavations at the North Ring, Mucking, Essex: a Late Bronze Age enclosure*, E. Anglian Archaeol. 43

Brooks, H. 1987. 'The Stansted project; a report on the first year's work', *Essex J.* 22, 43-6

Brooks, H. 1989. 'The Stansted project; a report on the second and third years' work', *Essex J.* 24, 6-10

Brooks, H. 1993. 'Fieldwalking and excavations at Stansted Airport', in J. Gardiner (ed.), *Flatlands and Wetlands; current themes in East Anglian Archaeology*, E. Anglian Archaeology, 50, 40-57

Brown, N. 1988a. 'A Late Bronze Age settlement on the boulder clay plateau; excavations at Broads Green, 1986', *Essex Archaeol. Hist.* 19, 7-14

Brown, N. 1988b. 'A Late Bronze Age enclosure at Lofts Farm, Essex', *Proc. Prehist. Soc.* 54, 249-302

Brown, P. N. 1986. *The Maldon burh jigsaw* Maldon: Maldon Archaeological Group

Buckley, D. G. (ed.) 1980. *Archaeology in Essex to AD 1500*, CBA Res. Rep. 34

Buckley, D. G. and Hedges, J. D. 1987a. *Excavation of a cropmark enclosure complex at Woodham Walter, Essex, 1976*, E. Anglian Archaeol. 33

Buckley, D. G. and Hedges, J. D. 1987b. *The Bronze Age and Saxon settlements at Springfield Lyons, Essex; an interim report*, Essex County Council Occ. Paper 5

Buckley, D. G., Major, H. and Milton, B. 1988. 'Excavation of a possible Neolithic long barrow or mortuary enclosure at Rivenhall, Essex', *Proc. Prehist. Soc.* 54, 77-92

Clark, A. 1993. *Excavations at Mucking, 1: the site atlas*, English Heritage Archaeol. Rep. 20

Clark, F. R. nd [c.1989]. *Exploration and discovery in south-west Essex*, West Essex Archaeol. Group

Cooper, J. (ed.). 1993. *The battle of Maldon: fiction and fact*

Corbishley, M.J. 1984 'Excavations at St Mary's Church, Little Oakley, Essex, 1977', in *Four church excavations in Essex*, Essex County Council Occ. Paper 4, 15-27

Couchman, C.R. 1979. 'Excavations at St Michael's Church, Latchingdon, 1976', *Essex Archaeol. Hist.* 11, 6-31

Couchman, C.R. and Hedges, J.D. 1976 *Redundant churches in Essex* Chelmsford: Essex County Council

Crummy, N. 1983 *The Roman small finds from excavations in Colchester, 1971-85*, Colchester Archaeol. Rep. 2

Crummy, N. (ed.) 1987 *The coins from excavations in Colchester, 1971-79*, Colchester Archaeol. Rep. 4

Crummy, N. 1988 *The post-Roman small finds from excavations in Colchester, 1971-85*, Colchester Archaeol. Rep. 5

Crummy, P. 1974 *Colchester: recent excavations and research*, Colchester Excavation Committee

Crummy, P. 1975 *Not only a matter of time*, Colchester Excavation Committee

Crummy, P. 1979 *In search of Colchester's past* (2nd edition, 1984), Colchester Archaeological Trust

Crummy, P. 1981 *Aspects of Anglo-Saxon and Norman Colchester*, CBA Res. Rep. 39

Crummy, P. 1984 *Excavations at Lion Walk, Balkerne Lane, and Middleborough, Colchester*, Colchester Archaeol. Rep. 3

Crummy, P. 1992 *Excavations at Culver Street, the Gilberd School, and other sites in Colchester, 1971-85*, Colchester Archaeol. Rep. 6

Cunningham, C.M. and Drury, P.J. 1985 *Post-medieval sites and their pottery, Moulsham Street, Chelmsford*, CBA Res. Rep. 54

Draper, J. 1985 *Excavations at Hill Farm, Gestingthorpe, Essex*, E. Anglian Archaeol. 25

Drewett, P.L. 1975 'Excavations at Hadleigh Castle, Essex, 1971-72', *J. Brit. Archaeol. Ass.* (ser. 3) 38, 90-154

Drury, P.J. 1976 'Braintree: excavations and research 1971-76', *Essex Archaeol. Hist.* 8, 1-143

Drury, P.J. 1978 *Excavations at Little Waltham, 1970-71*, CBA Res. Rep. 26

Drury, P.J. 1980 'No other Palace in the kingdom will compare with it: the evolution of Audley End, 1605-1745', *Archit. Hist.* 23, 1-39

Drury, P.J. 1984 'The temple of Claudius at Colchester reconsidered', *Britannia* 15, 7-50

Drury, P.J. 1988 *The mansio and other sites in the south-eastern sector of Caesaromagus*, CBA Res. Rep. 66

Drury, P.J. and Pratt, G.D. 1975 'A late 13th and early 14th century tile factory at Danbury, Essex', *Medieval Archaeol.* 19, 92-164

Drury, P.J. and Rodwell, W.J. 1973 'Excavations at Gun Hill, West Tilbury', *Essex Archaeol. Hist.* 5, 48-112

Drury, P.J. and Rodwell, W.J. 1978 'Investigations at Asheldham, Essex: an interim report on the church and the historic landscape', *Antiq. J.* 46, 133-51

Drury, P.J. and Wickenden, N.P. 1982 'An early Saxon settlement within the Romano-British small town at Heybridge, Essex', *Medieval Archaeol.* 26, 1-40

Dunnett, B.R.K. 1971 'Excavations in Colchester, 1964-68', *Trans. Essex Archaeol. Soc.* (ser. 3) 3, 1-130

Eddy, M.R. and Petchey, M.R. 1983 *Historic towns in Essex. An archaeological survey of Saxon and Medieval towns, with guidance for their future planning* Chelmsford: Essex County Council

Erith, F.H. and Longworth, I.H. 1960 'A Bronze Age urnfield on Vinces Farm, Ardleigh, Essex', *Proc. Prehist. Soc.* (ns) 26, 178-92

Evison, V.I. 1994 *The Anglo-Saxon cemetery at Great Chesterford*, CBA Res. Rep. 91

Fawn, A.J., Evans, K.A., McMaster, I. and Davies, G.M.R. 1990 *The Red Hills of Essex: salt-making in antiquity* Colchester: Colchester Archaeol. Group

France, N.E. and Gobel, B.M. 1985 *The Romano-British temple at Harlow*, Essex West Essex Archaeol. Group

Going, C.J. 1987 *The mansio and other sites in the south-eastern sector of Caesaromagus*, CBA Res. Rep. 62

Greenwood, P. 1989 'Uphall Camp, Ilford, Essex; an Iron Age fortification', *The London Archaeologist* 6, 94-101

Hamerow, H. 1993 *Excavations at Mucking, 2: the Anglo-Saxon settlement*, English Heritage Archaeol. Rep. 21

Havis, R. and Brooks, H. 1991 'The Stansted project; the fourth and fifth years' work', *Essex J.* 26, 40-3

Hawkes, C.F.C. and Hull, M.R. 1947 *Camulodunum*, Soc. Antiq. Lond. Res. Rep. 14

Hedges, J.D. and Buckley, D.G. 1978 'Excavations at a Neolithic causewayed enclosure, Orsett, Essex, 1975', *Proc. Prehist. Soc.* 44, 219-308

Hedges, J.D. and Buckley, D.G. 1981 *Springfield cursus and the cursus problem*, Essex County Council Occ. Paper 1

Helliwell, L. and MacLeod, D.G. 1981 *Rayleigh Castle*

Hewett, C.A. 1969 *The development of carpentry, 1200-1700: an Essex study* Newton Abbott: David and Charles

Hewett, C.A. 1974 *Church carpentry: a study based on Essex examples* Chichester: Phillimore

Hodder, I. 1982 *Wendens Ambo: the excavation of an Iron Age and Romano-British settlement*, Passmore Edwards Museum monograph 2

Hope, J.H. 1984 'Excavations at All Saints Church, Cressing, Essex, 1979', in *Four church excavations in Essex*, Essex County Council Occasional Paper 4, 28-42

Huggins, P.J. 1970 'Waltham Abbey: monastic site and prehistoric evidence, 1953-67', *Trans. Essex Archaeol. Soc.* (ser. 3) 2, 216-66

Huggins, P.J. 1972 'Monastic Grange and outer close excavations, Waltham Abbey, Essex, 1970-72', *Essex Archaeol. Hist.* 4, 30-127

Huggins, P.J. 1976 'The excavation of an eleventh-century Viking hall and fourteenth-century rooms at Waltham Abbey, Essex, 1969-71', *Medieval Archaeol.* 20, 75-133

Huggins, P.J. 1978 'Excavation of a Belgic and Romano-British farm with Middle Saxon cemetery and churches at Nazeingbury, Essex, 1975-76', *Essex Archaeol. Hist.* 10, 29-117

Huggins, P.J. 1988 'Excavations on the north side of Sun Street, Waltham Abbey, Essex, 1974-77', *Essex Archaeol. Hist.* 19, 117-53

Huggins, P.J. 1989 'Excavations of the Collegiate and Augustinian churches, Waltham Abbey, Essex, 1984-87', *Archaeol. J.* 146, 476-537

Huggins, P.J. and Bascombe, K.N. 1992 'Excavations at Waltham Abbey, Essex, 1985-1991: three pre-conquest churches and Norman evidence', *Archaeol. J.* 149, 282-343

Hull, M.R. 1958 *Roman Colchester*, Soc. Antiq. Lond. Res. Rep. 20

Hull, M.R. 1963 *The Roman potters' kilns of Colchester*, Soc. Antiq. Lond. Res. Rep. 21

Jones, M.U. 1968 'Crop-mark sites at Mucking, Essex', *Antiq. J.* 48, 210-49

Jones, M.U. and Jones, W.T. 1975 'The cropmark sites at Mucking, Essex, England', in R. Bruce-Mitford (ed.), *Recent archaeological excavations in Europe*, 133-87

Litton, J.W.S. and Clark, F.R. 1977 *St Mary's Church, Woodford, Essex* Passmore Edwards Museum monograph

MacGowan, K. 1987 'Saxon timber structures from the Barking Abbey excavations', *Essex J.* 22, 35-8

Manning, W.H. 1962 'Excavation of an Iron Age and Roman site at Chadwell St Mary, Essex', *Trans. Essex Archaeol. Soc.* (ser. 3) 1, 127-56

Milton, B. 1984 'Excavations at St Clements Church, West Thurrock, Essex 1979', in *Four church excavations in Essex*, Essex County Council Occ. Paper 4, 1-14

Morris, S. and Buckley, D.G. 1978 'Excavations at Danbury Camp, Essex, 1974 and 1977', *Essex Archaeol. Hist.* 10, 1-28

Niblett, R. 1985 *Sheepen: an early Roman industrial site at Camulodunum*, CBA Res. Rep. 57

Pollitt, W. 1953 *Southend before the Norman conquest*, Southend Museum handbook no.7

Priddy, D.A. (ed.) 1988 'Excavations in Essex, 1987', *Essex Archaeol. Hist.* 19, 260-71

Priddy, D.A. and Buckley, D.G. 1987 *An assessment of excavated enclosures in Essex*, E. Anglian Archaeol. 33

Rackham, O. 1986 *The woods of south-east Essex* Rochford District Council

Rahtz, P.A. 1969 *Excavations at King John's hunting lodge, Writtle, Essex, 1955-57*, Soc. Medieval Archaeol. Monograph 3

Redknap, M. 1991 'The Saxon pottery from Barking Abbey', *The London Archaeologist 6*, 353-60

Rippon, S. 1991 'Early planned landscapes in south-east Essex', *Essex Archaeol. Hist.* 22, 46-60

Rodwell, K.A. 1988 *The prehistoric and Roman settlement at Kelvedon, Essex*, CBA Res. Rep. 63

Rodwell, W.J. 1974 'The Orsett "Cock" cropmark site', *Essex Archaeol. Hist.* 6, 13-39

Rodwell, W.J. 1976a 'Some unrecorded archaeological discoveries in Essex 1946-75', *Essex Archaeol. Hist.* 8, 234-48

Rodwell, W.J. 1976b 'The archaeological investigation of Hadstock Church, Essex: an interim report', *Antiq. J.* 56, 55-71

Rodwell, W.J. (with Rodwell, K.A.) 1977 *Historic churches: a wasting asset*, CBA Res. Rep. 19

Rodwell, W.J. 1978 'Relict landscapes in Essex', in H.C.Bowen and P.J.Fowler (eds), *Early land allotment in the British Isles*, BAR 48, 89-98

Rodwell, W.J. 1993 *The origins and early development of Witham, Essex: a study in settlement and fortification, prehistoric to medieval*, Oxbow Monograph 26

Rodwell, W.J. and Rodwell, K. A. 1985 *Rivenhall: investigations of a villa, church and village, 1950-77*, 1, CBA Res. Rep. 55

Rodwell, W.J. and Rodwell, K.A. 1993 *Rivenhall: investigations of a villa, church and village, 1950-77*, 2, CBA Res. Rep. 80

St. Joseph, J.K.S. 1964 'Air reconnaissance: recent results', *Antiquity* 38, 217-8

Sellers, E.E., Ryan, P.M. and Walker, H. 1988 'Maiden's Tye: a moated site at High Easter', *Essex Archaeol. Hist.* 19, 176-95

Turner, B.R.G. 1982 *Ivy Chimneys, Witham: an interim report*, Essex County Council Occ. Paper 2

Turner, B.R.G. 1984 'Excavations at St Mary's Church, West Bergholt, Essex 1978', in *Four church excavations in Essex*, Essex County Council Occ. Paper 4, 43-63

Turner, B.R.G. forthcoming *Excavation of an Iron Age settlement and Roman religious complex at Ivy Chimneys, Witham, Essex, 1978-83*, E. Anglian Archaeol.

VCH 1963 *A history of Essex, 3: Roman Essex*, Victoria History of the Counties of England

Wheeler, R.E.M. 1928 'A Romano-Celtic temple near Harlow, Essex, and a note on the type', *Antiq. J.* 8, 300-26

Wickenden, N.P. 1986 'Prehistoric settlement and the Romano-British "small town" at Heybridge, Essex', *Essex Archaeol. Hist.* 17, 7-68

Wickenden, N.P. 1988 *Excavations at Great Dunmow, Essex*, E. Anglian Archaeol. 41

Wilkinson, T.J. 1988 *Archaeology and environment in South Essex: rescue archaeology along the Grays by-pass, 1979-80*, E. Anglian Archaeol. 42

Wilkinson, T.J. and Murphy, P. 1986 'Archaeological survey of an inter-tidal zone: the submerged landscape of the Essex coast, England', *J. Field Archaeol.* 13, 177-94

Williams, F. 1977 *Pleshey Castle, Essex; excavations in the bailey, 1959- 63*, BAR 42

Williamson, T. 1986 'The development of settlement in north-west Essex: the results of a recent field survey', *Essex Archaeol. Hist.* 17, 120-32

Wymer, J.J. 1985 *Palaeolithic sites in East Anglia*

Wymer, J.J. and Brown, N. 1995 *Excavations at North Shoebury: settlement and economy in south-east Essex 1500 B.C. to A.D. 1500*, E. Anglian Archaeol. 75

Essex Archaeology: Retrospect and Prospect

D.G. Buckley

Introduction

It is very pleasing to be asked to provide an epilogue to this volume having watched with interest the progress of the second Archaeology in Essex conference from inception, through to successful event, and now to publication of the papers. Naturally, throughout I have been reminded of the arrangements for the first (the 1978) conference, which I had the good fortune to be able to organise, and of the thinking which went into that event. At that time much had been written about different aspects of the archaeology of Essex, but the county lacked any archaeological overview comparable to those written for other parts of the country, for example that by Rainbird Clarke for East Anglia (1960) and by Curwen for Sussex (1954). However, the County Archaeology Section, although it had only been in existence for a few years, had already amassed considerable knowledge by collating existing information and from field survey and excavation. There was, therefore, a perceived need for a review of the current state of knowledge to guide future work. The brief given to speakers at the conference was that they should consider what had been achieved in Essex in respect of their area of expertise, as much as possible set this against the national picture, and to indicate priorities for future work in the county. The published papers (Buckley 1980) provided a basis for much of the work which was carried out over the next decade and considerable advances were made in our understanding of the historical development of the county. During the same period there was also a massive increase in the amount of archaeological work being undertaken throughout Britain such that by the early 1990s so much new information was available both locally and nationally, that a second Essex review was clearly required.

The growth in the amount of archaeological work taking place was linked to a period of exceptional change and expansion in the organisation of British archaeology and this process is reflected in the papers in this volume. 1995 marks for me twenty-one years of service with the Essex County Council Archaeology Section, initially as deputy and, since 1983, as Principal Archaeology Officer, and it is appropriate that I undertake an overview of how archaeology has come to be conducted under the auspices of the County Council. In doing so there is some overlap with the papers presented by Rodwell and Wickenden in this volume, but as much as possible I have sought to avoid repetition. Although a degree of introspection is timely given the changes which may shortly affect the organisation of conservation services in the county, not least those which could result from the current Local Government Review, this contribution endeavours to look optimistically to a continued development of the county wide archaeological service provided by Essex County Council.

Establishment of the Archaeology Section

Pressure for Action

Early concern for the heritage of Britain was particularly related to highly visible monuments such as standing stones, burial mounds, hillforts, Roman walls, castles and religious houses. This approach was reflected in the Royal Commission on Historical Monuments' (England) inventory of Essex, which was one of the first counties to be surveyed. The earliest Ancient Monuments Protection Acts, passed in 1882 and 1913, concentrated national protection on such visible sites. Throughout the early part of this century, although the scope and interest in archaeology grew, the subject largely remained the province of university staff, museum based academics and a relatively small number of dedicated amateurs and local Archaeological Society members. The 1960s saw a significant change which arose from a growing appreciation of the rate at which archaeological evidence was being destroyed, particularly by urban redevelopment and new road construction. Many more people became involved and across the country existing and newly established local archaeology societies endeavoured to organise rescue excavations and to record sites prior to their destruction. In 1971, the establishment of the RESCUE organisation as a major archaeological pressure group concentrated attention on the scale of archaeological destruction nationally.

In Essex this period saw initiatives by the Essex Archaeological Society and other local societies while various *ad hoc* excavation committees including the Mucking Excavation Committee, Chelmsford Excavation Committee (later Chelmsford Archaeological Trust), Colchester Excavation Committee (later Colchester Archaeological Trust) were set up and Rodwell and Wickenden provide details in this volume of events during this period and the organisations and individuals who initiated them. At the same time pressure was put upon the county council to try and obtain decisions preventing the destruction of sites or to seek the provision of funding for specific rescue excavations. However, like most local authorities, Essex County Council lacked the in-house archaeological information and advice required for the making of informed decisions. This situation and the need for improvement had been recognised by the Report of the Walsh Committee (1969) which recommended that County Planning Authorities maintain a record of field monuments and consider the appointment of archaeological officers to provide adequate assistance. From 1969 the Department of the Environment encouraged the establishment of County Archaeologist posts and the setting up of Sites and Monuments Records (SMRs).

County Council response

In 1972 Essex County Council was one of the first counties to respond with the appointment of John Hedges to the post of Archaeology Officer, based within the Planning Department as part of the Environmental Services Branch (ESB). The branch already had sections dealing with the Historic Built Environment and Landscape Conservation, and this association of disciplines enabled close co-operation. Further, it provided an opportunity to develop the use of existing provisions for scheduled areas, listed buildings, Conservation Areas, protected woodlands and various planning measures collectively to protect archaeological sites. A report produced by the archaeology officer for the Planning Committee, entitled *The Archaeological Heritage: A Policy for Essex* (Hedges 1973), set out a blueprint of the requirements considered necessary to ensure long term protection of the county's archaeological resource. It identified the need to have staff to cover a wide range of activity including excavation, planning control, education and the provision of archaeological advice for all those seeking it. The Local Government reorganisation of 1973 delayed implementation of the recommendations in the report. However, once the new two-tier structure had been established it was agreed that the County Council would continue to provide specialist advice for conservation matters, including archaeology, as a service available to the fourteen new District Councils. Following this decision additional posts within the Planning Department were advertised and in 1974 the Archaeological Officer was joined by three more archaeologists who comprised myself, Christine Couchman and Lily Savory. Our combined brief was to develop expertise in the areas of excavation, records, publications, aerial survey, information and archaeological advice. It is still instructive to refer to a *Manual of Procedures and Specialist Advice* produced at that time (ECC 1974) to see how quickly and broadly archaeology was integrated into the Planning process. These early years of the Section I remember as particularly enjoyable ones since we were an enthusiastic team eager to grasp the opportunity provided to develop archaeological expertise under the umbrella of the local authority, which was much more secure than the previous unsettled existence as short-term contract field archaeologists. It is from this beginning that the Section has grown to its present size and range of functions. In the following sections it is my intention to look more closely at the way different areas of the Section's work have developed and to point to avenues for future progress.

Development of the Section 1972-90

Policy For Archaeology

Appreciation of the scale of what has been achieved requires some knowledge of the legal situation which provides the basis for county archaeology policy. In 1972 it was generally considered that there was little legal support for a county maintaining a Sites and Monuments Record and running an archaeological service. It has only been through a sustained effort, by national bodies and locally based organisations, to apply and broaden the available provisions that workable arrangements have been put into place across the country.

The statutory basis for archaeology was, and still is, limited. It largely relates to the functions of the Department of National Heritage (formerly carried out by the Department of the Environment), and to English Heritage, their advisers. The Ancient Monuments and Archaeological Areas Act 1979 consolidated previous legislation relating to the definition and protection of scheduled monuments and added provision for rescue excavation in designated Areas of Archaeological Importance. In 1983 the National Heritage Act established the independent Historic Buildings and Monuments Commission (English Heritage). It transferred to it many of the responsibilities of the Secretary of State and while the DNH has ultimate responsibility for applying the relevant laws most archaeological work at national level is carried out by English Heritage. The Royal Commission on the Historical Monuments of England established in 1908 has a lead role for compiling the national record of England's ancient monuments and historic buildings.

The national legislation does not protect the large number of archaeological sites recorded locally within County SMRs. Protection and provisions for the investigation of the great majority of sites has come about through the recognition of archaeology as a material consideration in the planning process and as a consequence of the development of planning policy. The starting points for this process are the Structure and Local Plans which were introduced by the 1968 Town and Country Planning Act. This and earlier Acts were consolidated into the 1971 Town and Country Planning Act. The operation of this Act by the reorganised Local Government structure was controlled by the 1972 Local Government Act. Amendments to the legislation were made periodically during the 1970s and 1980s and in 1989 the legislation was clarified by consolidating it into The Town and Country Planning Act 1990. Although modifications have been made by the Planning and Compensation Act 1991, the 1990 Act stands as the principal instrument of town and country planning law in England. The first acknowledgement of the County Council's role in respect of archaeology in legislation appeared in the Town and Country Planning General Development Order 1988 which recognised sites registered in any record kept by a county council and known as a County Sites and Monuments Record. This was amended in 1995 to read *"adopted by resolution by a County Council and known as a Sites and Monuments Record"* and the County Council has duly adopted the SMR.

Since the inception of Development Plans as the main guide for decisions made by local authorities and other organisations, archaeologists have encouraged the inclusion of policies for the protection and management of archaeological sites. In Essex the first Development Plan (1957) contained only a very brief general statement aimed at the protection of areas of great landscape, scientific or historic value. In the mid 1970s this was broadened in the Approved Review Development Plan (1976) to include a policy for the protection of Ancient Monuments listed under the Ancient Monuments Acts 1913-53. However, when the Essex Structure Plan Approved Written Statement appeared (1982), it included for the first time information about archaeology and policies for the protection and/or recording of archaeological sites. These policies were positively revised in the Essex Structure Plan, Approved First Alteration Written Statement (1991), and further improved in the Second Alteration Written Statement (1995). These county-wide policies for archaeology are supported by more detailed information and policies contained in the County Minerals Plan and the numerous Local Plans, which have been produced in recent years by each of the 14 districts in the county. These provide the basis for specific decisions in respect of planning applications affecting archaeological sites. Additional provision is also made through archaeological input into various topic based reports, most produced by the County Planning Department in consultation with the District Planning Departments, which have included historic towns (Eddy and Petchey 1983), barns (ECC 1989), golf courses (ECC 1992), the coast (1994) and countryside (in prep.).

Sites And Monuments Record

In order to underpin development plan policies there has to be a sound information base and a primary task in 1972 was the creation of an Essex Sites and Monuments Record as the starting point for any archaeological enquiry (Hedges 1975; 1977). In its short history the Essex SMR has been through a number of stages of development (Gilman, this volume). The initial manual based record complemented by sites depicted on the OS 1:25,000 map series was culled from a wide range of existing published sources, including the Ordnance Survey Archaeological Record Cards, museum accession books and information provided by local societies and individuals. It was compiled rapidly and contained many errors and duplications but by 1979 was already established as a primary research source for those contributing to the first Essex conference. In 1983 work commenced on converting the SMR to a computer based record, with support from the DoE (later English Heritage). Sites were remapped to 1:10,000 O.S. scale, and a thorough check was carried out of all information held, thereby enhancing the value of the record. New sites continued to be added, not least from the Archaeology Section's own survey and excavations, and by the time of the second Essex conference the SMR contained more than 14,000 records.

ESSEX ARCHAEOLOGY: RETROSPECT AND PROSPECT

The development control process
The majority of planning applications are determined at District authority level apart from certain concerns, such as those relating to minerals extraction, which are determined by the County Council. These number many thousands each year, of which a percentage have significant implications for archaeological remains. Members of the Section therefore established a close working relationship with District Planning Officers and, as specialist advisers, seek to ensure that a screening process, involving a check against the SMR, successfully catches applications which might affect known archaeology. Appropriate arrangements can then be made to ensure an adequate level of survey, evaluation, excavation, recording and suitable publication of the results. It is now standard practice to have archaeological conditions attached to planning consents. In the 1970s, not only was this approach new, but its legality was also questioned and many local authorities were reluctant to apply archaeological conditions. However, a number of counties persisted and following success at public inquiries it became a nationally accepted practice. In Essex one such case in 1979 included an appeal over refusal of planning permission for new houses in Chipping Ongar located on the projected line of the medieval town enclosure ditch. This was dismissed by the Secretary of State and part of the site was later scheduled.

Of particular significance in 1982 was the inquiry into the application to locate the Third London Airport at Stansted. A detailed archaeological study was presented in a proof of evidence by John Hedges as part of the County Council case of objection to the airport expansion. It included an examination of both the immediate 'take area' proposed for the new airport and of a much wider impact zone which was based upon estimated travel times from the airport. This exercise drew upon information held in the four relevant County SMRs for Essex, Hertfordshire, Suffolk and Cambridgeshire. The substantial supporting evidence, which included the production of seven period distribution maps (Fig.1), was one of the first studies carried out on such a large scale and proved quite an undertaking prior to the existence of computerised records.

Assessments elsewhere in the county in advance of developments, contributed to the general acceptance of archaeology as a material consideration within the planning process. In more complex situations, Section 106 agreements under the 1990 Town and Country Planning Acts (previously known as Section 52 agreement under the earlier Act) started to be negotiated setting out the details of how archaeological work would be conducted in respect of a particular development project. In these ways during the 1980s a development control process by agreement was gradually established and this formed the basis for the rapid acceptance of improved arrangements following the publication of government guidelines set out in the Planning Policy Guidance Note 16: "Archaeology and Planning" (DoE 1990, see below).

Excavation
In the 1970s the increasing need for archaeological field work saw the establishment of permanent field units variously organised by counties, universities, museums or with independent charitable trust status. Essex County Council was one of several counties to establish and maintain an in-house service which extended to field projects. A major part of my job description when I was appointed in 1974 was a requirement to identify threatened sites, seek funding and build up the Section's field capacity to investigate them. A list of important sites under threat was compiled and it is with some satisfaction that I am able to look at this now with the knowledge that virtually all the sites identified were eventually investigated, with many significant results. The first excavation took place in an extension to the churchyard at Danbury which is located within an Iron Age enclosure (Morris and Buckley 1978). This work was grant aided by the County Council, for which the budget was £1,000. The system normally used at that time was adopted and a team of freelance archaeologists, local society members and interested individuals was recruited to carry out the excavation. Known as volunteers, they were employed on a subsistence payment basis. Other excavations soon followed and the Section began to build up a reputation for the range and quality of the work. Rodwell (this volume) gives details of the more significant sites so they are not repeated here, but Fig. 2 gives an indication of the field work which has been undertaken across the county since 1974. The projects range from small scale watching briefs to extensive landscape projects. The Section also established a good record for the publication of its work particularly in the Transactions of the Essex Society for Archaeology and History, but also when appropriate in the *East Anglian Archaeology* series (for which I am a member of the editorial committee) and national journals.

This expansion in the number and scale of field activities resulted in various other changes. A year-round programme of excavation and post-excavation required supervisory staff and specialist finds staff to be readily available and consequently a core team of permanent excavation staff came in to existence. This was linked to a wide network of specialist contacts whose services could be called upon as necessary. There was also a general improvement and expansion in the range of field techniques. As a result there was a substantial increase in the cost of excavations, field work and publication which could only be achieved through wide ranging support from not only the County Council, but also from English Heritage, the Royal Commission on Historical Monuments, District Councils, the Manpower Services Commission, academic societies, museums and increasingly, from the mid 1980s, developers. The level of financial support obtained over the years was significant and the sum of all grants obtained from outside sources between 1974-90, exceeded £2 million. I believe that the success in raising such a figure reflects the importance attached to the maintenance of a field team with knowledge and expertise related to the archaeology of a county.

As the level of fieldwork grew, the activities of many local societies, which had achieved so much (Rodwell in this volume), began to diminish. Also the established excavation committees disappeared, with the exception of Colchester Archaeological Trust which has continued to carry out extensive excavations in Roman and Medieval Colchester and its hinterland (Crummy, this volume). This led to a concern that there might be insufficient attention given to local views in the determination of priorities for the county. The County Council therefore established the Advisory Committee for Archaeological Excavation in Essex in 1975 as a forum for the discussion of rescue excavation projects. It was able to assess and agree projects and forward them for consideration to a Regional Advisory Committee covering Essex, Hertfordshire and Cambridgeshire. This had been established as part of a national network by the DoE to consider all proposed rescue projects in the region before passing them forward to a National Committee which made the final selection for government funding. These quangos were later removed as part of government savings but the Essex committee decided to continue meeting since its members considered that it had a valuable role. Membership includes representatives from the Essex Society for Archaeology and History, the Essex Archaeological and Historical Congress, the Museum

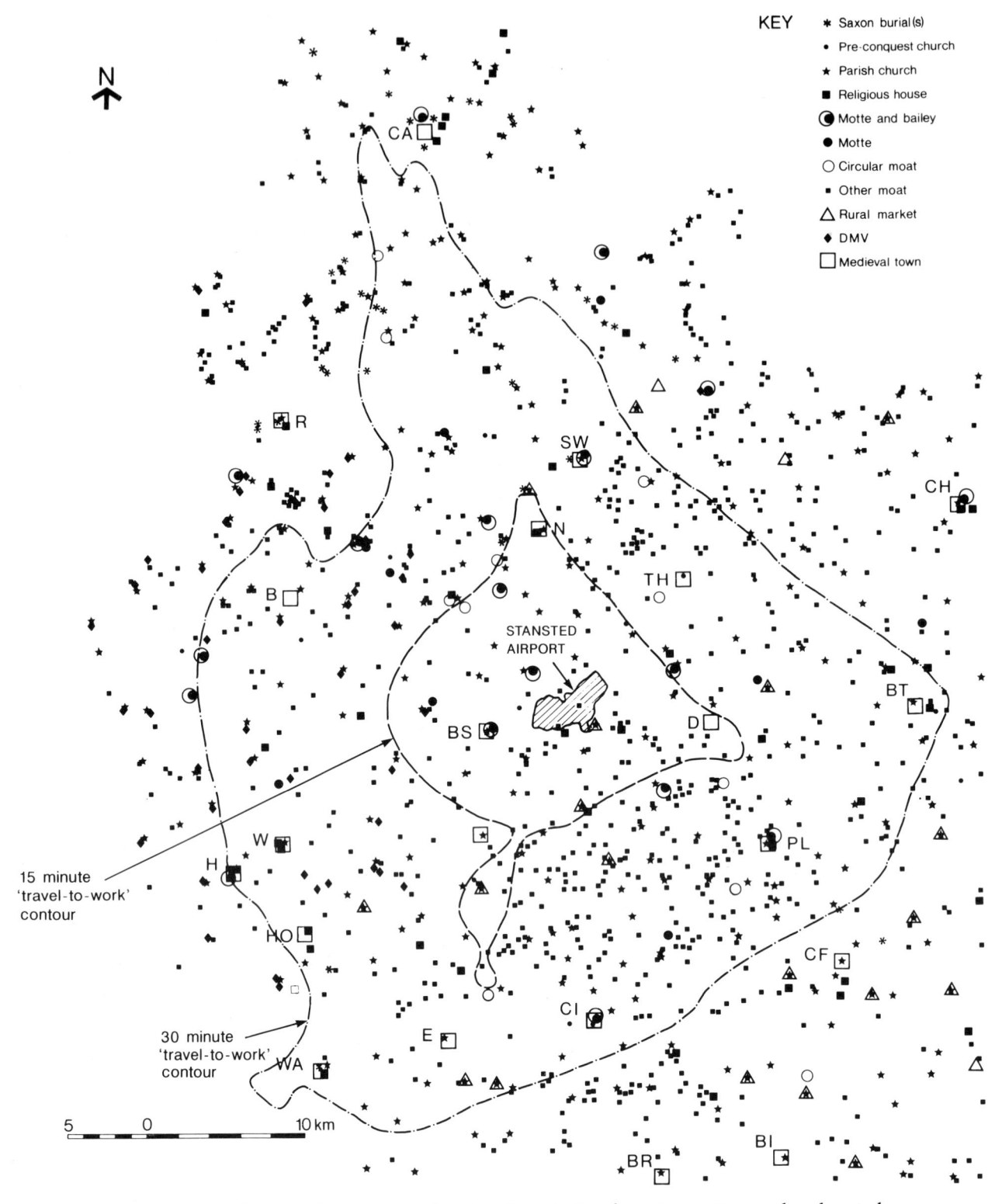

Fig. 1 Stansted Airport Inquiry plan of archaeological sites from 4 counties: medieval period

Curators Group, the Director of the Colchester Archaeological Trust and other groups and informed individuals. Members of the Archaeology Section have serviced the committee and attended to explain the level of development threats, proposed work programme, and results of work carried out while also taking note of the views and opinions presented. Throughout its existence the Committee has been chaired in turn by 3 elected county councillors (the late B Marriott, P Wawn and the late D Cotgrove), all of whom have given enthusiastic support for archaeology and helped to ensure feedback to the County Council Environment Committee about both concerns and achievements.

Advice, Education and Management

The SMR, planning and fieldwork roles of the Section were complemented by a broad-based approach aimed at increasing public awareness of the objectives in undertaking archaeological work. This was done in the belief that not only do people have a right to be kept informed, but also that education would help to ensure a

ESSEX ARCHAEOLOGY: RETROSPECT AND PROSPECT

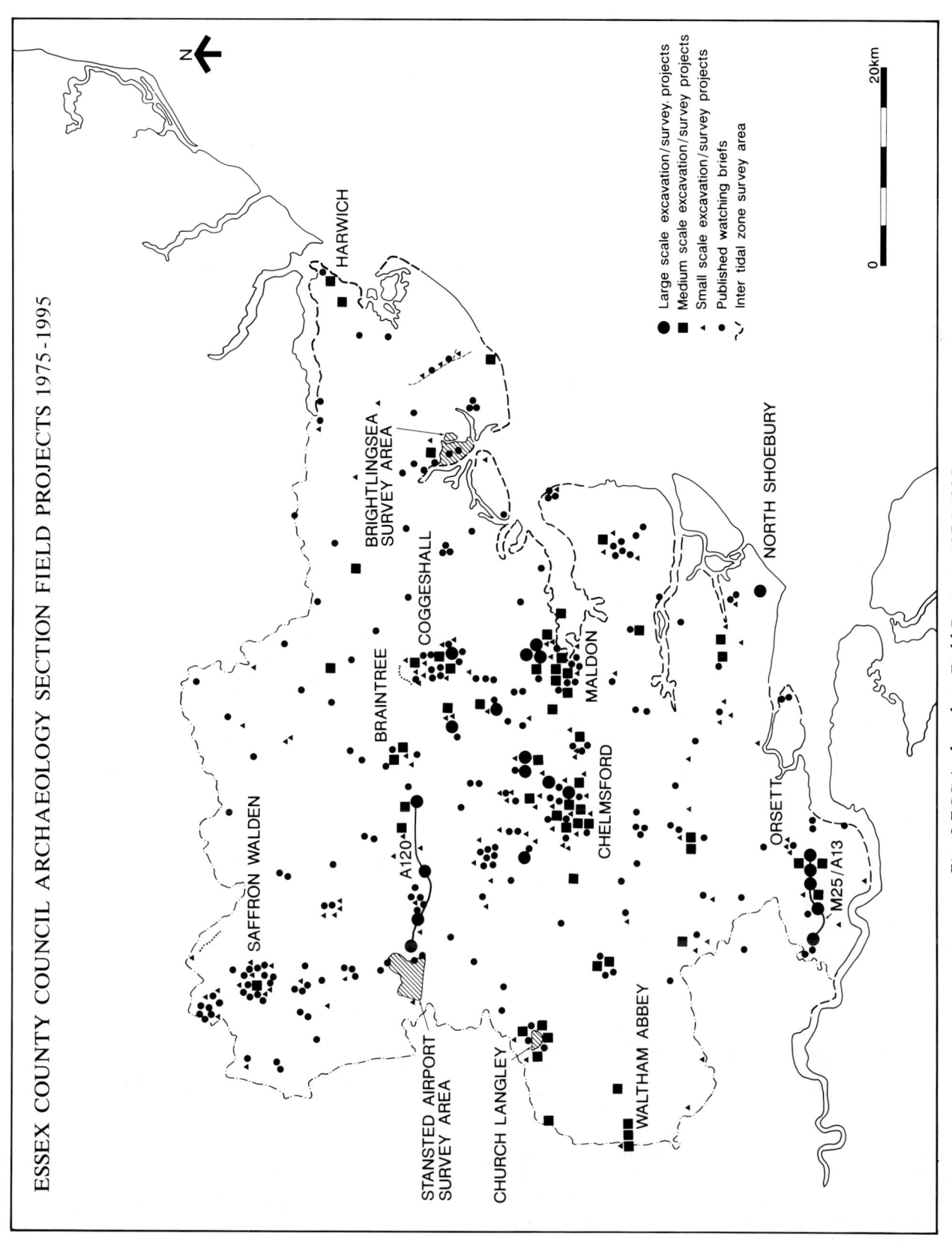

Fig. 2 ECC Archaeology Field Projects 1974-1990

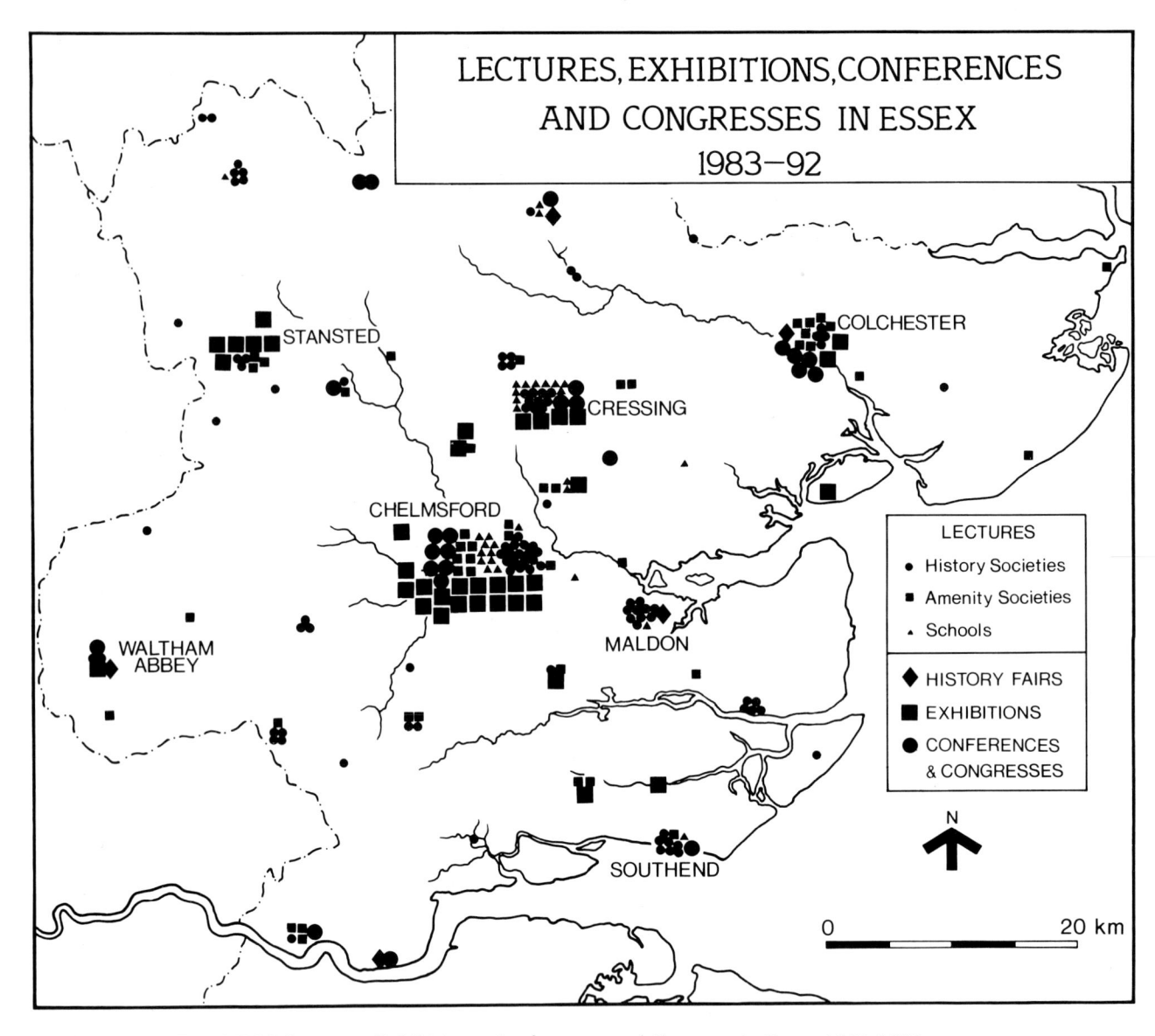

Fig. 3 ECC Lectures, Exhibitions, Conferences and Congress in Essex 1983-1992

sustainable future for the archaeology of Essex. It was felt that only through increased understanding would the need to safeguard our archaeological heritage be accepted, particularly where the ownership and desire to influence decisions in respect of the development and future management of land were concerned. Approaches adopted included the provision of information and advice through popular publications and the media. One initiative which has proved particularly successful has been the publication annually, from 1984, of a supplement in the *Essex Chronicle*. This has grown in size from 8 to 16 pages and in 1995 had a print run of 85,000. The Section has also been involved in a wide range of meetings, conferences and other events. Hundreds of lectures have been given to interested groups and numerous special exhibitions produced to support particular occasions. Of note has been the Section's involvement in the organisation of the Essex History Fairs since the first fair was held at Hedingham Castle in 1986. Measuring the success of these activities is difficult but the scale of presentation for the years 1983-92 indicated in Fig. 3 aims to demonstrate the level and county-wide nature of these efforts.

In addition to these activities, a contribution has been made towards measures for the better management of archaeological sites by providing assistance for their conservation and display. This was developed as a two-fold process involving grants to owners of sites and buildings while also being directed to historic buildings, woodlands and archaeological sites already in the Council's care. In addition, certain buildings and sites were specifically acquired by the council to ensure their protection. This policy had begun earlier with the acquisition of a representative range of wind mills and water mills. Its extension to archaeological sites started with the last open plot in Pleshey High Street providing a view of Pleshey Castle earthworks. This was purchased in the 1970s following the revokation of planning permission by the County Council and a display area was established. Management agreements were also agreed for that part of the Bartlow Hills group of Roman burial mounds located in Essex (now transferred to Cambridgeshire as a result of boundary changes) and the ruins of Alresford Church were taken into care following the disastrous fire in 1972. The most notable case came in 1987 when Cressing Temple came onto the market. As one of a group of County Officers involved in arguing the case for this remarkable site it was particularly satisfying to see the County Council raise the funds necessary to acquire, repair and maintain the monument and then set about making it accessible and presentable to the public. As a Scheduled Ancient Monument (Essex No. 211), it has been necessary to have an archaeologist on site throughout the conservation programme to record both the buildings and all ground disturbance. As a consequence much more is known about the history of the site and construction of the individual buildings (Andrews 1993).

ESSEX ARCHAEOLOGY: RETROSPECT AND PROSPECT

Reorganisation and progress 1990-1995

By the late 1980s there was a growing feeling that developers should be more responsible for the archaeological loss caused by their actions. At the national level the British Property Federation with the Standing Conference of Archaeological Unit Managers attempted, through the Developers Code of Practice (1986), to increase developer support and this was seen as taking the form of sponsorship for archaeology. The Archaeology Section put some effort into this approach (ECC 1984) and had some success. Although its most notable sponsorship, which was for the North Shoebury Project (Wymer and Brown 1995), was from the Mobil Oil Company who were not connected with the development. While this kind of funding tended to supplement that from central government, which was always inadequate, it became accepted that a developer should automatically be responsible for ensuring archaeological excavation, if required, on land earmarked for development. Major funding agreed with the British Airport Authority towards the cost of a four-year field programme in advance of the third London airport at Stansted was a particularly important early case in Essex (Brooks 1993; Havis and Brooks forthcoming). As a consequence of this principle that the polluter pays, the attachment of archaeological conditions to planning applications came to mean that a developer funded the archaeological work considered necessary. The issuing of PPG16 in 1990 formalised this procedure. However, this gave rise to the argument that developers have the right to choose the organisation undertaking the work, and so tendering for projects by archaeological field teams became an accepted part of the process.

In Essex, as in other counties, the development of a competitive market gave rise to an internal review of the work and composition of the Section. This took place in 1991 and led to a re-structuring to clearly separate what were seen as the curatorial and contractural roles. The new organisational structure (Fig. 4) reflects the separate areas of work carried out by the Section, comprising the Archaeological Advisory Group, the Field Archaeology Group and the Graphics Group, while also indicating a number of educational projects initiated since the new structure was established. Each of these areas of activity are considered below, but first, in order to appreciate the new arrangements it is necessary to have some understanding of the content of PPG 16.

Planning Policy Guidance Note 16: "Archaeology and Planning" (PPG 16)

PPG 16 has brought together much of what had been achieved through existing legislation, consolidated appeal decisions and the work of archaeological planners. It has resulted in a transformation in the way that archaeology is dealt with within the planning process nationally and consequently in the county of Essex.

The guidance states that it is intended for planning authorities in England, property owners, developers, archaeologists, amenity societies and the general public. It sets out the policy of the Secretary of State for the Environment on archaeological remains on land and how they should be preserved or recorded both in an urban setting and in the countryside. It gives advice on the handling of archaeological remains and discoveries under the development plan and control systems, including the weight to be given to them in planning decisions and the use of planning conditions.

In the document particular emphasis is placed upon the need to give priority to the preservation of archaeological remains *in situ*. Excavation, which is referred to as "preservation by record", can only ever be seen as the second-best option. The PPG advises that local authorities without the necessary in-house expertise should seek the advice of the County Archaeological Officer, or his equivalent, who maintains the Sites and Monuments Record which contains details of all recorded archaeological sites in the county. The note stresses that regardless of the circumstances, taking decisions is easier if the archaeological aspects of a development site can be considered early in the planning and development control process. In situations where archaeological remains may exist, but where there is insufficient information to make an informed decision on a planning application the DoE

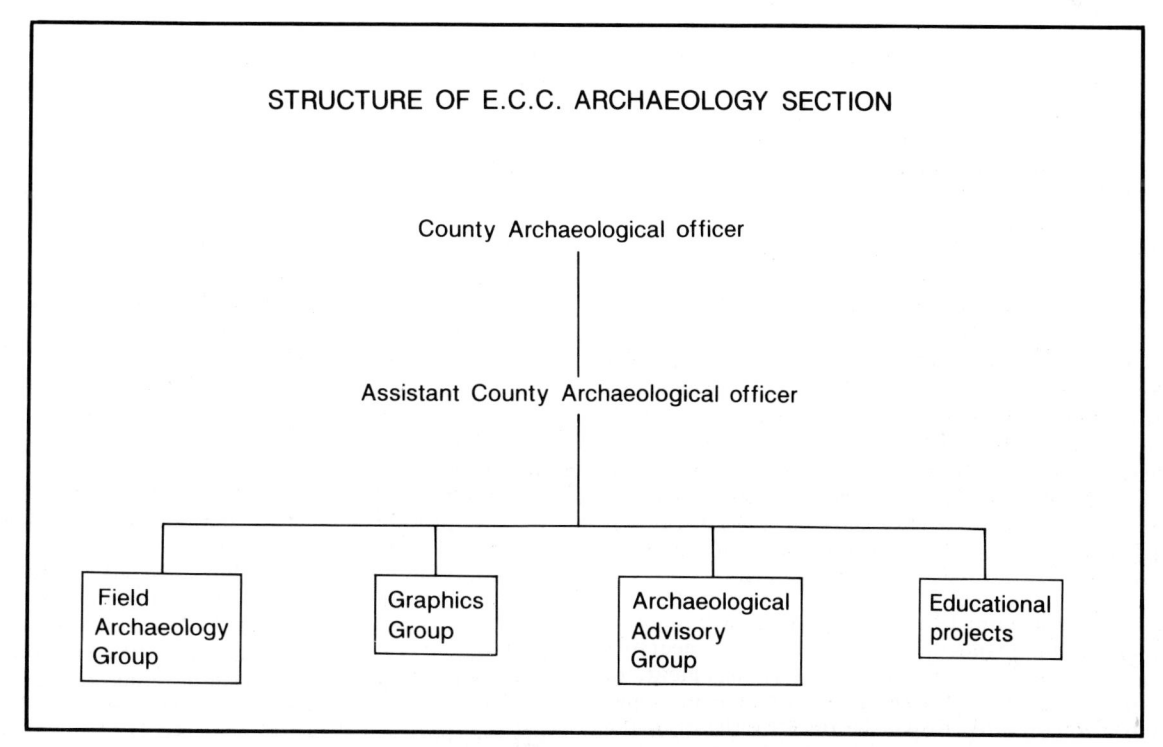

Fig. 4 Structure of the Archaeology Section following reorganisation in 1991.

advises that the local authority request developers to provide the necessary information in the form of an archaeological evaluation. The document also makes the point that the setting of a monument is a valid planning consideration and that developers should seek to protect this as well as the monument itself. Proposals which do not seek to protect the archaeological remains or their setting may be refused.

The PPG also addresses the question of who should pay when archaeological work is considered necessary. It states that it would be entirely reasonable for the planning authority to satisfy itself before granting planning permission, that the developer has made appropriate and satisfactory provision for the excavation and recording of the remains. In particular cases where the developer is a non-profit making community body which is unable to raise the funds to provide for excavation and subsequent recording without undue hardship, or in the case of an individual who similarly does not have the means to fund such work, an application for financial assistance may be made to English Heritage.

Whilst emphasising that Planning Authorities should seek to ensure that potential conflicts are resolved and agreements with developers concluded before planning permission is granted, the note considers that it is open to authorities to impose conditions designed to protect archaeological remains and ensure reasonable access for archaeologists to carry out their work. The application of positive planning and management is seen as the means to help bring about sensible solutions to the treatment of sites with archaeological remains and to reduce the areas of potential conflict between development and preservation.

PPG 16 clearly places the onus on the developer to state how sites will be affected by their development proposals and has resulted in a framework for dealing with these sites through a process of appraisal, assessment, evaluation and recording. Its success in securing mitigation strategies for archaeological sites, whether by preservation *in situ* or recording, has been confirmed by two reports into the impact of guidance commissioned by English Heritage (1992 and 1995). These show that throughout the country procedures are now in place to ensure that almost all applications for development submitted to local planning authorities are screened and appropriate archaeological advice provided.

Archaeological Advisory Group

The Archaeological Advisory Group (AAG) is responsible for the maintenance and enhancement of the SMR and the provision of information and advice relating to archaeological matters in connection with all types of development and monument management. It has been headed by Paul Gilman since its establishment, prior to which he had overseen the English Heritage funded project to computerise the SMR. The AAG has been active in ensuring input to Local Plans, implementation of PPG 16 by development control, extending provision of information and advice to all and in continuing to publicise widely the nature and extent of archaeological activity in the county. It has also been successful in seeking funding to carry out specific SMR enhancement projects.

The SMR is not a static data bank, but one which requires continuous maintenance and enhancement to meet the growing demands of conservation and management. In this context the Essex SMR is to be migrated to a new Oracle-based system developed by the RCHME from the national MONARCH system created for the NAR. When this is complete the next step will be development of multi-user facilities linked to the Geographical Information System (GIS) now being developed by the Planning Department. This will enable even better integration and analysis of data of various types, including that relating to the natural as well as the man-made environment. In the future, generation of new information is also likely to be focused as specific projects are set up to enhance particular topic areas. Current surveys of World War II defences, industrial sites and of the archaeology of the intertidal zone point the way in this process. Other enhancement work is a result of national initiatives which includes the organising of aerial reconnaissance and the systematic mapping of Essex sites as part of the National Mapping Programme, both grant aided by the RCHME. The AAG has assisted English Heritage with aspects of the Monuments Protection Programme for Essex and as part of this programme is currently undertaking a two-year survey of the historic towns of Essex, to replace *Historic Towns in Essex* (Eddy and Petchey 1983). It has also been able to contribute information for other important English Heritage sponsored national projects, such as the Assessment of Assessments (Darvill *et al.* 1994) and Monuments at Risk Survey (MARS) project (Darvill and Wainwright 1994) which will prove important in providing the figures on field activity and condition of sites which will be so important for the future management of the country's archaeology.

The development control process has become much more clearly defined under the new arrangements which saw four development control posts created within the AAG. Procedures are followed which have been generally recognised nationally, guidance having been provided by the Association of County Archaeological Officers (1993a) and the Institute of Field Archaeologists (in the form of a series of 'Standards and Guidance' documents for field and desk based investigations and recording). The development control officers monitor all planning applications submitted to the local planning authorities of 13 districts (Colchester has separate arrangements linked to the Colchester Archaeological Trust), as well as other new works and developments from a wide range of agencies like the Forestry Authority, the National Rivers Authority, the Countryside Commission and Utility bodies. In each case information relating to the archaeological implications and the best form of mitigation is given. Essex continues to have a high level of development and Table 1 indicates the consequent implications in terms of archaeological workload.

Where archaeological investigation is considered necessary a project brief is prepared for the developer by one of the development control officers setting out the archaeological requirements. This may relate to desk top assessment, fieldwalking, aerial and remote sensing survey, field evaluation and/or a full programme of excavation in advance of development as a condition of the planning permission (Figs 5 and 6). The stipulations in these briefs are in part standard, but in seeking to ensure that the archaeological work is relevant others are formulated in the light of current archaeological knowledge. In this respect the research frameworks set out in the 1978 conference proceedings and now in this volume provide important background. Specifications submitted in response are agreed and when the chosen contracting organisation has started fieldwork its progress is monitored to ensure that the work is carried out to a recognised standard. The final stage is submission of a report of the results which are then integrated into the SMR. The whole procedure aims to ensure the effective use of resources and retrieval of useful information.

The information and advice giving role of AAG has developed remarkably over recent years. In part this reflects the greater national concern for the heritage initiated at the popular level by the media and professionally by the various bodies responsible for the management and recording of historic sites, notably English Heritage. However, it also reflects the success of the long term policy adopted by the County Council to increase awareness of the diverse and rich archaeology of Essex. This has led to many more individual enquiries about sites and finds, but more importantly has seen growing contact developed with national and regional organisations wishing to include the management of archaeological sites in their thinking at local level. Examples include Forestry Authority planting schemes, Countryside Commission Stewardship and Set-Aside projects, MAFF Environmentally Sensitive Areas, National River Authority Coastal Management Plans and National Trust site management. Much closer links have also been developed with the Council's Recreational Land Management Section in respect of Country Parks. This has included field surveys and excavation, the results of which have been incorporated into park exhibitions and publications.

This growth of interest in archaeology is part of a wider concern for the environment and appreciation of the need to adopt a much more integrated approach to its protection and management. The question of sustainability is now a big issue and the outcome is certain to result in an even higher level of consultation.

Field Projects Service
The Field Archaeology Group (FAG) was set up to fulfil the role of archaeological contractor. Since its establishment it has been headed by Philip Clarke, previously a senior field officer responsible for several major excavations. He re-built the group following the loss of several field officers to the new curatorial group, has maintained the range and quality of fieldwork, introduced new techniques and adapted management procedures to meet the changing situation.

The FAG aims to follow best practice and recognised guidance for the organisation of field projects such as presented in the English Heritage publication *Management of Archaeological Projects* (1991a). However, the climate in which the group operates is much changed from that of the 1970-80s since it now has to compete for work with other contracting organisations. To date it has done this successfully and has maintained its position as principal contractor in the county. However, the situation can be complex when a single development might require up to four stages of attention comprising desk-top appraisal, fieldwalking or other non-intrusive investigation, evaluation by trial trenches, and full excavation. Each of these stages is accompanied by the need for a brief supplied by the curator with corresponding specification from the contractor, while a different contractor might be commissioned for different stages of the project. Although some projects are still commissioned by English Heritage and others by the County Council, developers now provide the main source of funding for the work.

The FAG carries out about 40-50 projects a year including evaluations, surveys, watching briefs and full scale excavations. Some of these are small jobs involving only a few staff for several days while others are sizeable requiring a substantial team operating in the field for several months followed by comparable post excavation programmes. It is not possible to detail all of these, but notable recent work has included survey of Saxon fish traps in the River Blackwater (Clarke 1993), excavation of Neolithic ring ditch burials at Brightlingsea (Lavender in prep) and Langford (Reidy in prep), late Bronze Age sites at Broomfield (Atkinson 1995b) and Boreham (Lavender in prep), topsoil stripping and selective excavation of Roman farm complexes at Down House Farm (Godbold in prep) and Great Holts, Boreham (Germany in prep). Most significant of all was investigation between 1993 and 1995 of part of a late Iron Age and Roman small town at Elms Farm, Heybridge (Atkinson 1995a and in prep). Once the potential of this site had been established using developer funding English Heritage agreed a grant of £1,039,000, the largest ever given for a single excavation in Britain. However, the national trend resulting from the successful application of PPG 16 is one of far fewer large excavations. The FAG is aware of this and is planning for a wider range of small scale projects. This has included the appointment of a geophysics specialist, the development of staff skills in both the survey of sites and the recording of standing buildings, the offering of training in archaeological site safety and the accepting of contracts from other units for the skills of specialist finds staff. It is through such diversification of its activities that FAG will continue to provide a locally based service for Essex.

Graphics Group
The maintenance of a separate graphics group helps to ensure that a full range of graphic material of a high standard is available to both the advisory and field groups. Over the years the group has been headed by several capable archaeological illustrators, Hazel Martingell, Alison McGhie and currently Roger Massey-Ryan. The high standard of illustrative work produced by the Archaeology Section is testimony to their efforts. In addition to publications covering research, survey and excavation projects an important and growing aspect of the group's work is related to promoting the archaeology of Essex to the public through exhibitions, popular booklets, and teaching material related to sites and themes of the county's archaeology.

Education Projects
It is now widely recognised that archaeological education programmes need to be expanded. English Heritage has had an education officer for some years and has supported various national and local inititiatives. Similarly the Council for British Archaeology has established a network of regional education officers, organised the annual National Archaeology Days to help introduce children to archaeology and is involved with other projects to introduce archaeology to a wider audience. The Essex committment to education has been mentioned above,

Calendar year	Total number of planning applications	Total number of appraisals made	Total number of detailed appraisals undertaken	Number of detailed appraisals revealing an archaeological dimension
1990	c. 20,500	c. 6,650	2,434	479
1991	c. 16,000	c. 6,300	2,077	455
1992	c. 15,500	c. 12,000	1,895	412
1993	c. 15,700	c. 13,500	2,028	349
1994	c. 16,000	c. 13,860	2,213	359

The great increase in planning application appraisals in 1992 reflects improved procedures following the issue of PPG 16; which included receipt of weekly lists of planning applications from all Districts

Table 1

Archaeological Projects in Essex 1988-1994

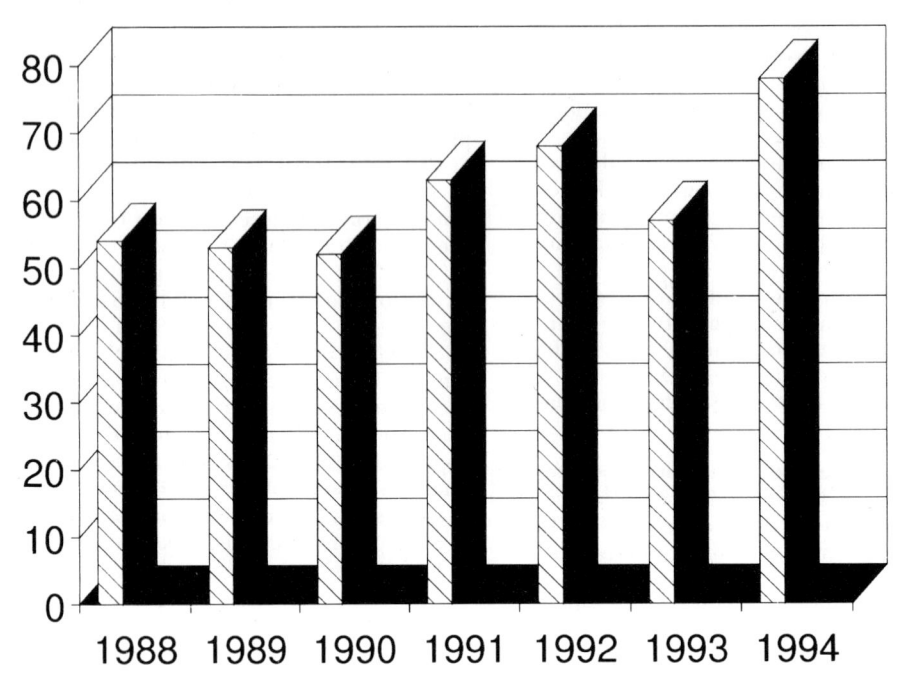

Fig. 5 Archaeological Projects in Essex 1988-1994

Types of Project: 1991-1994

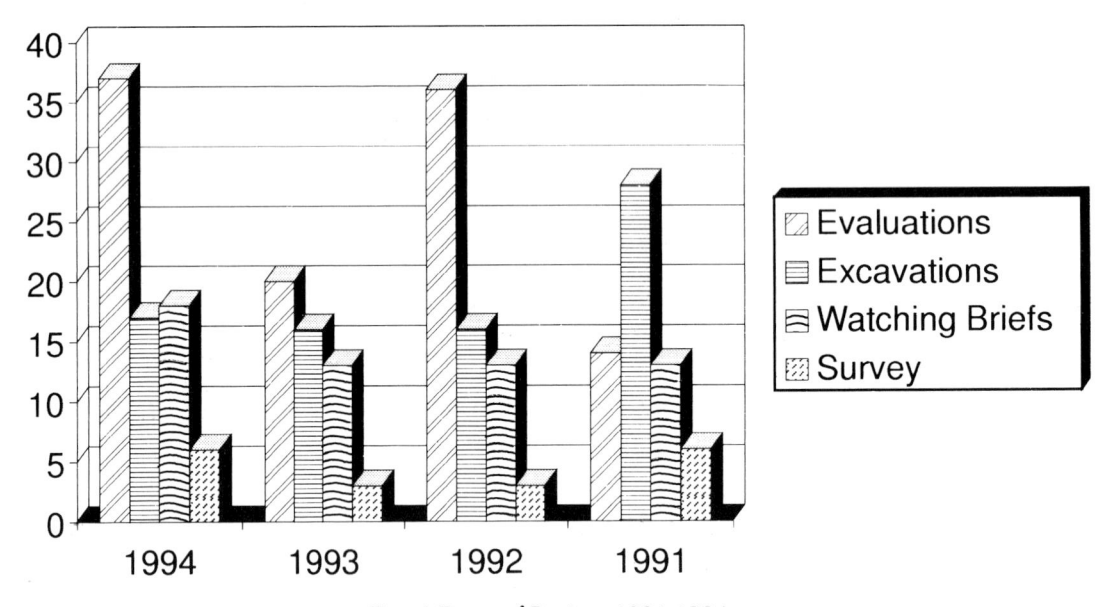

Fig. 6 Types of Project 1991-1994

but this has been boosted by a number of initiatives in recent years.

The Cressing Temple Charter states that opportunities for learning and research offered by a site of such importance will be used to enable present and future generations to be made aware of the county's history and their personal relationship to it. The organisation for the first time in 1994 of an Archaeology Field School and training excavation by the site archaeologist, Tim Robey, was a step in the development of this declaration. This addressed some of the specific research objectives identified at the site, enabling a fuller understanding of its history while offering individuals practical experience of archaeology. The opportunites for doing this have lessened with PPG 16, which reduced the possibilities for non-professional involvement in excavations.

The scale of the Elms Farm excavation in 1994 not only provided the opportunity for a significant level of local amateur participation, but enabled the involvement of two educational officers for the duration of the excavation. An exhibition on site and programme of weekend site-tours was set up, and a mini-excavation established to enable visiting school groups to gain hands-on experience of aspects of the process of archaeological investigation, recording and interpretation. Following the success of this initiative, it has proved possible to retain one of the educational officer posts to develop an archaeological outreach service. A programme of school visits has been directed primarily at junior schools. Teacher's packs have been prepared, exhibitions produced and lectures given to a wide range of groups. It is hoped to continue to develop educational activities, particularly those related to Cressing Temple, as part of an expanding programme of archaeological activities linked to the exhibition taking shape in the Wheat Barn and the proposed new visitor centre.

The Future

Recognition of the importance of the historic environment

The excessive destruction of the post-war decades has led to greater appreciation and effort to conserve the historic environment and in this local authorities play a pivotal role. Achieving this has required a great deal of dedication and no small measure of obligatory optimism. However, PPG 16 demonstrates success and government recognition of the importance of the archaeological heritage. Cross reference to archaeology has appeared in other PPGs and was recently reinforced by PPG 15 *Planning and the Historic Environment* (1994) which links below and above ground components of the archaeological record.

In September 1994 one event reflected the significant role now accorded to the country's heritage and of the concern for its proper management. English Heritage celebrated its tenth anniversary with a national conference which was attended by the Prime Minister and the Secretaries of State for both the Department of National Heritage and the Department of the Environment. The speakers gave repeated emphasis to the key role which local government has in achieving a heritage capable of sustaining social and economic well-being. It was recognised that local authorities, not only in their planning role, but also as direct managers of important components of the local environment, such as parks and museums, make a major contribution to the attraction of their area. In particular it was emphasised that the archaeological and historical heritage, its extensiveness, richness and local diversity, are important assets for both the local population and the external tourist market. Increased leisure time, a relatively affluent population, and the greater appeal of specialist holidays indicates considerable interest in the historic landscape. However, it was also acknowledged that the potential could only be realised if there is safeguarding, development and investment in our rich archaeological inheritance.

Local Government Review also focused the attention of all archaeological organisations on the implications of change for heritage services. As Chairman of the Association of County Archaeological Officers between 1992 and 1995 I was particularly involved in the association's consideration of the future of county archaeological services (1993b). The outcome of lobbying is demonstrated by the DNH's recent *Guidance to Local Authorities on Conservation of the Historic Environment* (August 1995). This acknowledges that England's archaeological and built heritage is a resource of unique cultural value and emphasises the Government's commitment to the heritage as reflected in the far reaching responsibilities and powers, both statutory and discretionary, that enable local authorities to deliver a conservation service at local level. The guidance is intended to assist new unitary authorities in meeting their responsibilities for the preservation and management of the historic environment and invites them to set out their proposals. In Essex, Southend is to have unitary status, and Thurrock may, and appropriate arrangements will need to be adopted to ensure a continued high level of archaeological service.

Research needs

Recognition of the importance of the historic environment and the need for its proper and sustained management requires both good databases and understanding of the need for new research. A view has been expressed by some members of the archaeological profession that archaeologists working within local authorities operate in a mechanistic fashion and that the outcome of their work does not directly benefit archaeological research (Biddle 1994; Barrett 1995). In Essex every effort has been made to ensure the integration of current research issues into our thinking. This applies not only to the input to plans and applications for development but also extends to the initiation and implementation of a range of projects specifically directed to answering questions and furthering understanding at county, regional and national level. It was in this context that both the 1978 and 1993 Archaeology in Essex conferences sought to provide a foundation for new work. Prior to 1970 the recorded archaeology of the county had a marked bias to the Roman period, especially that of Colchester and, to a lesser extent, Chelmsford. With a few exceptions earlier period sites were poorly represented in the record, similarly for the Saxon/early Medieval period there had been little study from an archaeological perspective. The contents of the two conference volumes illustrate how far the county has come in expanding our knowledge of all periods.

This pro-active approach has required a certain commitment on behalf of the County Council. First and foremost has been the maintenance of the Archaeology Section for over twenty years thereby ensuring a stable team with a range of archaeological expertise. Further, individual members of staff have been encouraged to develop and update their period and topic specialisations through training and membership of national and archaeological organisations. This has helped to ensure an awareness of ongoing research work and in particular the thinking of the major period societies on directions for future work. In recent years a specific research officer post has had a brief to identify and develop research projects and to seek funding for their implementation. Much has been achieved in the county but much remains which can be done. Since the scarce national resources for research are likely to be directed to a smaller number of major projects it will be for the archaeologists of Essex, whether full time professional or independent 'amateur', to work together on new projects and further understanding.

Attention to research needs has also been raised by English Heritage as part of a review of their policy in the light of the changed funding situation following the acceptance of PPG 16. *Exploring Our Past* (1991b) gives direction to those producing research designs for new projects for which grant aid is being sought. More recently English Heritage has also encouraged thinking about regional research frameworks. The county archaeologists of the Anglian region comprising Essex, Herts, Cambs, Norfolk and Suffolk, have met regularly for many years to discuss issues of common interest and ensure a consistent approach across the region. As early as 1981 this resulted in a combined survey of the barrows of East Anglia (Lawson et al 1981). Consequently the English Heritage lead has been taken up and recent meetings have actively pursued the drawing together of county information into period frameworks for the region. These will help to establish the agendas for future research.

In conclusion

I hope that this contribution to the conference proceedings has given an insight into the considerable progress which the organisation of archaeology in Essex has achieved with County Council support since 1972. It would not be possible for me to conclude without acknowledging the role of all those members of the Archaeology Section, past and present, who have contributed to this process. I have always considered myself fortunate to be the senior partner responsible for a team containing individuals with a very wide range of archaeological talent. These abilities have been collectively utilised and developed for the benefit of the archaeology of the county and it is therefore difficult to single out individuals. However, it is appropriate to recognise the inspiration and vision for the future which John Hedges provided. I also make special mention of the role played by Owen Bedwin who has contributed to the whole programme of work of the Section, but like all good deputies often fails to receive full recognition. The organisation and publication of the 1993 conference is clear testament to his ability. In turn the Essex conference proceedings demonstrate the positive approach to archaeology adopted in the county. This is an ongoing process necessitating the sustained investment which is proposed by Essex County Council for the archaeology of Essex into the 21st century.

Acknowledgements

In preparing this paper my memory has served me rather like that of Dylan Thomas in his "Memories of Christmas". I am therefore grateful to John Hunter, head of the Environmental Services Branch and member of the Planning Department since 1971 for reading and commenting on this paper. Also to John Davenport for his help with the planning content. Finally to Caroline Ingle for assisting in research and the numerous redrafts.

References

Andrews, D (ed). 1993. *Cressing Temple: A Templar and Hospitaller Manor in Essex*

Association of County Archaeological Officers. 1993a, *Model Briefs and Specifications for Archaeological Assessments and Field Evaluations*

Association of County Archaeological Officers. 1993b. *The future of County Archaeological Services in England*

Atkinson, M. 1995a. 'Elms Farm, Heybridge', *Current Archaeology* No. 144

Atkinson, M. 1995b. 'A Late Bronze Age enclosure at Broomfield, Chelmsford, *Essex Archaeol. Hist.* 26, 1-23

Barrett, J.C. 1995. *Some Challenges in Contemporary Archaeology*, Archaeology in Britain Conference 1995, Oxbow Lecture 2

Biddle, M. 1994. *What Future for British Archaeology* Archaeology in Britain Conference 1994, Oxbow Lecture 1

British Archaeologists and Developers Liaison Group. 1986. *Code of Practice* (British Property Federation and the Standing Conference of Archaeological Unit Managers)

Brooks, H. 1993. 'Fieldwalking and excavation at Stansted Airport', *E. Anglian Archaeology* No. 50, 40-57

Buckley, D.G. (ed). 1980. *Archaeology in Essex to AD1500*, CBA Res. Rep. 34.

Clarke, C.P. 1993. 'Collins Creek', in Gilman, P. J. (ed.), 'Archaeology in Essex 1992', *Essex Archaeol. Hist.* 24, 209

Clarke, R Rainbird. 1960. *East Anglia* (Ancient People and Places: Thames and Hudson).

Curwen, E.C. 1954. *The Archaeology of Sussex* (Methuen)

Darvill, T., Burrow, S. and Wildgust, D. 1994. *British Archaeological Bibliography supplement : The Assessment Gazetteer 1982-91. Resumes and bibliographic details for completed archaeological assessments, field evaluation reports, and environmental statements*

Darvill, T and Wainwright, G. 1994. 'The Monuments at Risk Survey: an introduction' *Antiquity* 68, 820-824

Department of the Environment. 1990. *Planning Policy Guidance Note 16: "Archaeology and Planning"* (HMSO)

Department of the Environment. 1994. *Planning Policy Guidance Note 15: "Planning and the Historic Environment"* (HMSO)

Eddy, M.R. and Petchey, M.R. 1983. *Historic Towns in Essex: An Archaeological Survey* (Essex County Council)

English Heritage. 1991a. *Management of Archaeological Projects (2nd ed.)*

English Heritage. 1991b. *Exploring Our Past: Strategies for the Archaeology of England*

English Heritage. 1992. *An Evaluation of the Impact of PPG 16 on Archaeology and Planning* (Prepared by Pagoda Associates Ltd)

English Heritage. 1995. *Review of the Implementation of PPG 16 Archaeology and Planning* (Prepared by Roger Tym & Partners and Pagoda Associates Ltd)

Essex County Council. 1974. *Manual of Procedures and Specialist Advice* (Planning Department Environmental Services Branch internal document).

Essex County Council. 1975. County of Essex Development Plan Written Statement

Essex County Council. 1976. Approved Review Development Plan Written Statement

Essex County Council. 1976. Essex Structure Plan: Approved Written Statement

Essex County Council. 1984. Your Company, Sponsorship and Archaeology.

Essex County Council. 1989. *Historic Barn Conversions: A Way Forward*

Essex County Council. 1991. Essex Structure Plan: Approved First Alteration Written Statement

Essex County Council. 1992. *The Essex Golf Report* (produced by the Essex Planning Officers Association) 2nd Ed.

Essex County Council. 1994. *Essex Coastal Strategy* (produced by Essex County Council and the Essex Coastal Districts)

Essex County Council. 1995. Essex Structure Plan: Adopted Second Alteration Written Statement.

Havis, R. and Brooks, H. forthcoming. *A Landscape Study: The Stansted Project 1985-1990* E. Anglian Archaeol.

Hedges, J.D. 1973. *The Archaeological Heritage: A Policy for Essex*, Essex County Council internal report.

Hedges, J.D. 1975. 'Archaeology Within a County Planning Department', in R. T. Rowley and M. Breakell (eds) *Planning and the Historic Environment*, 29-49

Hedges, J.D. 1977. 'Development Control and Archaeology', in R.T. Rowley and M. Breakell (eds). *Planning and the Historic Environment II*, 32-51

Lawson, J.A., Martin, A., Priddy, D., and Taylor, A. 1981. *The Barrows of East Anglia* E. Anglian Archaeol. No. 12

Morris, S. and Buckley D.G. 1978. 'Excavations at Danbury Camp, Essex, 1974 and 1977' *Essex Archaeol. Hist* 10, 1-28

Walsh, Sir David 1969. *Report of the Committee of Enquiry into the Arrangements for the Protection of Field Monuments (1966-8)*, (London HMSO)

Wymer, J. and Brown, N. 1995. *Excavations at North Shoebury: settlement and economy in south-east Essex 1500 BC-AD 1500*, E. Anglian Archaeol. 75

INDEX (by Peter Gunn)

Notes
1. Page references in *italic* indicate figures. Page references in bold indicate plates and tables.

2. References to footnotes are indicated by n following the page reference.

Abbess Roding, 162
Abingdon area, Upper Thames, 24
abuttals, 144, 144, 145, 146
Acheulian industry, 2, 3, 5, 6, 8
Addedomaros(us), 61, 76
Adminius, son of Cunobelinus, 62
adzes, 12, 22, 30n
aerial photography, 16, 202, 203
    Bronze Age sites, 40
    circular ditched enclosures, 30
    cropmarks, 200
    and ESMR, 183, 186
    and fish-weirs, 124
    Neolithic sites, 19
    Roman sites, 97, 98, 204
    Saxon features, 108, 115
    Tendring Hundred, 199
aerial reconnaissance, 15, 24, 95, 214
Aethelred II, King, 111, 125
Aethelstan, King, 125
agriculture
    Anglo-Saxon, 108, 110, 126, 177-9
    and animal power, 162
    and barrows, prehistoric, 114
    Bronze Age, 39, 43
        Early, 170, 171-2
        Late, 30, 32, 39
        Middle, 27, 174-5
    and enclosures, 149
    horticulture, 22
    Iron Age, 47, 51, 63-4, 174-5
    medieval, 105, 177-9
    Neolithic, 15-16, 22, 24, 170, 171-2
    open field, 141, 149
    post-medieval changes, 155
    Roman period, 100-1, 104, 105, 176-7
    and salt production, 29
    see also animal husbandry; cereals; crops; farmsteads; food; landscape
airfields, 187
Alban, Saint, 83
Aldermaston Wharf: Bronze Age finds, 39, 40
Alexander, Dr John, 200
Alfred, King, 122
All Cannings Cross, 35, 40
Almgren brooch, silver, 57
Alphamstone: cemetery, 19
Alresford: ring-ditch burials, 113
Alresford Church, 212
amber, 20
Amberley Lane, Barking, 122
Ambresbury Banks, Epping Forest, 47, 199
Ancient Monuments Protection Acts, 207
Angel Yard, Colchester, 73
Anglian Chalky Boulder Clay, 168
Anglian stage, 1, *1*, 2, 3, 5, 8, 168
Anglian Water, 98
Anglo-Saxon Chronicle, 117, 122
Anglo-Saxon period, 108, 202
    Colchester, 73
        Saxo-Norman mint, 74
    Early, 30, 87, 94, 108-15, *109*
    East Saxon Kingdom and Royal Estates, 105, 117-22, *119*, 125
    environmental archaeology, 177-9
    Great Chesterford cemetery, 77
    ironworking, 114-15
    landscape and rural settlement, 123-5
    Late, 111, 115
    London: East Saxon bishopric, 117
    Middle, 117, 120, 202
    Middle/Late, 30, 117-26, *118*
    Mucking cemetery, 101
    Norman impact on aristocracy, 129
    and Roman period, end of, 105
    and Roman population, 108-10, 115
    and Roman sites, 118, 121, 123, 203-4
    Saxo-Norman period: stone churches, 122
animal bone *see* bone, animal
animal husbandry, 51
    Anglo-Saxon, 115, 179
    Bronze Age, 27, 39, 174
    Domesday Book, 124, 125
    Iron Age, 47, 51, 63, 175
    medieval, 131, 179
    Neolithic, 15, 16, 22, 24
    and Red Hills, 101, 102
    Roman Chelmsford, 90, 93
    Roman period, late, 104, 105
    and stock exchange, 16
animal power, 98, 161-2
animal sacrifices, 42, 60, 80, 103
animal skins, 164-5
Annable, Kenneth, 200
antler, 10, 12-13
Antonine period, 80, 87, 103
    cremation burial, *102*
    fire at Colchester, 87
    Itinerary, 95, 97, 101
    Red Hills, 101
antoniniani (coins), 69
anvils, iron, 58
arch-bracing, 137, 138
Archaeological Advisory Group (AAG), 214-15
Ardale School
    Early Saxon cemetery, 110
    Iron Age
        Late: cemetery, 58
        pottery, 50, *53*, *56*, 57
        round house, 54
    North Stifford, 108
    pottery, *49*
Ardleigh, 97, 200
    barrow construction, 29
    cemetery, 26
    landscape change, 101
    structure, 33
    water mill, 100
arrowheads, 19, 24
    flint, 22
art, Iron Age, 52, 61
Ashdon, 77, 97, 103, 123
Asheldham
    church, 117, 122, 124, 126, 133, 204
    fieldwork, 195
    Viking axe, 122
Asheldham Camp, 32n, 202
    cereal cultivation, 63
    charred cereal remains, 174, 175
    Iron Age site, 47, 51, 172
Ashingdon, 123
Ashmolean library, Oxford, 95
Asklepios, depiction of, 80
assarting, 130, 131, 145
asses (coins), 77, 80
Association for Industrial Archaeology, 160
Audley End, 149, 152, 153, 195, 196, 201
    courtyard, 134
    estate papers, 145
    park, 95
Augustinian Order, 152
auroch, 8
Aveley, 7, 8
axes, 13, 15, 16, 30
    copper flat, 22
    flint, 22, *23*, 172
    metal flanged, 26
    miniature, 80&n
    Neolithic: Stickle Pike, 160
    Neolithic/earlier Bronze Age, 20, 22
    socketed, 30n
    Sompting and Breton (metal), 29
    stone, 15, 22, *23*
    "Viking Type", 122
    see also hand-axes

Bagshot/Claygate ridge, 12
Baker's Hole industry, 7
baking/cooking, 51, 132
Baldock, Hertfordshire, 63
Baldwins Farm, Barling, 29
Balkerne Gate, Colchester, 71
Balkerne Lane, Colchester, 69, 72
Balkerne Street, Colchester, 70
Ballintober sword, 26
Barbarous Radiates, 86
Barking, 199
    Anglo-Saxon period, 117, 121, 122
    church, 122
    creek: sword finds, 26
    estates, 123
    and trade, 125
Barking Abbey, 122, 144, 202
Barking Power Station, 165
Barling, 29, 30
Barling Hall, Barling Magna, 108
Barling Magna, 8, 108
Barlings, Lincolnshire, 152
barns, 51, 98, 139
    16th-century brick, 140
    aisled, 90, 100
    Coggeshall, 131
    Cressing, 131, 204
    machinery in, 162
    Roman, 100, 110
Barrington's Farm, Orsett, 108
Barrow Hills, Oxfordshire, 17
barrows, 16, 19, 24, 114
    Bronze Age, 24, 42, 57
    Chilterns, 19
    construction, 29
    Dedham, 19
    Mucking, 57
Bartlow Hills, 103, 212
Barton Court Farm, Oxfordshire, 100
Barton, Kenneth, 200
Basildon, Great Wasketts, 30&n
Bassett, Steven, 195
Bassingbourne Hall: manor, 124
bath-houses, 90, 91, 93, 97, 192
Battlesbridge, 97
Baythorne Hall, Baythorne End, 142
Beacon Green, Maldon: pottery, 33, 47, *48*
beads, 20, 52, 111
    shale, 20, 113
Beaker period, 19, 20, 22, 172
Beauchamps Farm, Wickford, 77
Beaumont Moates (Beaumont Otes), Chignall, 148, 148
beavers, 5, 11
Beckton: gas works, 165
Becontree Hundred, 121
Bedfordshire: stone quarries, 87
Beeleigh Mills, 162
Beeston Castle: Late Bronze Age, 41
Belchamp St Paul, 131, *132*
Belgae, 55
Belhus Park, Aveley, 7
belt fittings, 77, 80, *84*, 110, 111
Benedictine Order, 134, 145
Benfleet: Viking stronghold, 122
Berdon Priory, 162
Berkshire Downs, 39, 42
Biglin, Dan, 192, 194
Bigods Farm, Great Dunmow, 97
Billericay, 97
    Buckenham field, 93
    carpentry style, 137
    Iron Age, *53*, *56*, 76, 77
    Roman cremations, 87
Billericay Archaeological Society, 200
Birch, 97
Birchanger
    animal bone, 63
    Iron Age agriculture, 64
    Newcastle kilns, 163

INDEX

pottery, 50
skull burial, 51
Birchington, Kent: stamped bowl, 26
birds
  bone, 4, 83
  migratory, 11-12
Bishopstone, Sussex: Rookery Hill, 111
Black Death, 131, 161, 162
Black Park Terrace, 2
black powder *see* gunpowder
Blackpatch, East Sussex, 38
blacksmiths, 58, 59, 165
Blackwater estuary, 115, *171*
  Bronze Age settlement, 26, 174
  causewayed enclosures, 16-17
  fishing, 123
  Iron Age, 33, 174
  Langenhoe, 61
  pollen analysis, 170, 172
  see also Stumble, The
Blackwater, River, 5, 12, 101, 170, 171
  Anglo-Saxon/medieval environment, 108, 177, 215
  Bronze Age/Iron Age sites, 172, 175
  Mesolithic period, 170
  metalwork, 30, 115
  Neolithic/Beaker period, 20, **173**
  palaeolithic period, 2
  pottery, 20, 26
  Rapier, 26
  Saxon fish traps, 215
Blackwater valley, 19, 202
blades
  "long blade" technology, 10, 11, 13
  Mesolithic, 12-13
Blickling, Norfolk, 155
Bluelands Pit, Purfleet, 7
Boars Head site, Braintree, 76
Bobbitshole, Ipswich, 7
Bocking, 10, 61
Bohuns: at Saffron Walden, 133
bone
  artefacts, 12, 13, **35**, 77
  carved, 58
  comb, 33, 73, 83
  processing, 90
  Shirley's Bone Mill, Etruria, 158
  tools, 10, 32
  working, 93, 133
bone, animal, 5, 10, 13, 41, 51, 69, 121
  Anglo-Saxon/medieval remains, 177
  bird, 4, 83
  cat, 83
  cattle, 83
  Chelmsford finds, 83
  Colchester, 75
  dog, 51
  fish, 75, 174, 177
  goat, 177
  horse, 51, 83
  Iron Age agriculture, 63
  Neolithic remains, 172
  Neolithic/Bronze Age, 24
  pig, 51, 121
  prehistoric evidence, 171
  in Roman burials, 103
  sheep, 82, 177
  special animal bone deposit, 51
  survival of, 175
bone, human, 2, 13, 42
  Boxgrove, Sussex, 1
  Bronze Age skull finds, 29, 43
  cremation rites, 57
  cult of the severed head, 50-1
  from Bronze Age/Iron Age structures, 174
  Homo sapiens, 4
  and inhumation cemeteries, 58
  monastic cemetery, 133
Boreham, 97
  Late Bronze Age, 215
  New Hall, 155
  see also Bulls Lodge Quarry; Great Holts
Boreham Interchange: Late Bronze Age, 30, 31-2
Bos, 5, 172

Botany Pit, Purfleet, 7
bottle: kiln, 163
Boudica
  and Chelmsford, 194
  deposits of, 80
  revolt of, **77**, **88**, **91**, **93**, 103
  sack of Colchester, 71, 87, 176, *176*, 177
  sets fire to London, 194
Boulder Clay (till), 1, 22, 24, 32, 33, 36, 100, 101, 125, 172, 174, 175, 177, 204
Bovinger windmill, 165
bowl, omphalos, 57
Boxgrove, Sussex: pre-Anglian stage, 1
Boxted Wood, Stebbing, 98, 101
Boyn Hill, 2, 5
bracelets, 80, 83
Bracknell, Berkshire, 150
bracteate, gold, 113
Bradbury, D. W., 55
Bradfield church, Manningtree, 134
Bradwell: fish-weir, 124
Bradwell Nuclear Station, 165
Bradwell-on-Sea, 131, 168, 170, 199
Brain Valley Archaeological Society, 76
Braintree, 100, 163
  Belgic *oppidum*, 76
  Brands site, 91, 93
  building style, 138
  cemetery locations, 87
  excavation, 195, 201
  flint artefacts, 22
  London Road, 76, 77
  religious finds, 80
  Roman period, 93, 94, 103
  Tabor High School, 88
Brambleshot Grove cemetery, 76
Braughing, 97
Braughing-Puckeridge settlement, Hertfordshire, 60, 63
bread-making, 93
Breiddin: hillfort, 41
Brent Hall, 130
Brentwood, 137
  Brook Street hospital, 134
Breuil, Abbe, 5
brewing, 132, 177
brick: kilns, 163
brickearth, 7, 8, 27, 29
Bridge End, Saffron Walden, 141
bridle fittings, iron, 111
Brightlingsea
  cremation burials, 26
  Moverons Farm, 172
  Neolithic ring ditch, 19, 215
  Neolithic/Bronze Age, 24
  pottery, 22
Brinson, Major Jack, 192, 193, 194, 199, 200, 201
briquetage, 60, 61, 63
British Museum, 10, 12, 29, 61
British Quaternary sequence, 1, 5
Broads Green, Great Waltham, 29, 32, **34**, 202, 204
Broadstairs, Kent: stamp-decorated pot, 26
bronze
  bucket, 76
  casting moulds, 29, 31
  cockerel figurine, 83
  coinage, 47, 54, 59, 60, 61, 62, *62*, 62, 63
  decline in, 46
  dish, 58
  importing of, 55
  letters from inscription, 86
  Lofts Farm hoard, 52-4
  religious objects, 80
  ring, 51, 52, 54
  scabbard, 58
  tankard handle, 58
  vessels, 61
  working, 22, 42, 52, 122
  see also potin
Bronze Age, 199, 202, 204
  Ardleigh, 200
  burials, 43
  enclosures, 110, 188-9
  metalwork, 38, 39, 42, 43

pond barrow, 57
ringworks, 43
Springfield Lyons, 16, 110
woodland management, 101
Bronze Age, Early, 15, 22, 39
  artefacts, 24
  barrows, 24, 42
  burials, 22
  domestic sites, *19*, 20
  environmental archaeology, 170-2
  ring ditches, 19
  stonework, 20
Bronze Age, Late, 24, 26, 29-32, 51, 54, 58, 215
  crops, 32
  enclosures, 114, 189, *189*
  environmental archaeology, 175
  finds: North Shoebury, **35**
  future work, 33-6
  metalwork, 46
  pottery, 47
  settlements, 20, 26, 27, 33
  Springfield Lyons, 16
  woodland clearance, 15
Bronze Age, Middle, 26-9, 32, 39, 40-1, 44
  crops, 32
  enclosures, 40
  environmental archaeology, 172-5
  flint, 54
  future work, 33
  ring ditches/burials, 19
brooches
  Chelmsford, 80
  copper-alloy saucer, 111
  early Roman, 77
  gilt saucer, 113, *114*
  horse, 61
  Late Iron Age, 60
  pre-Flavian, 86
  pre-Roman, 74
  Saxon, 108, 111
  silver Almgren, 57
  small-long, 111
  as votive offerings, 82
Brook Hall, Mount Bures, 10
Brook Street hospital, Brentwood, 134
Brook Walden: medieval development, 130
Broomfield, 32, 174, 189, 215
Broomfield Borrow Pit, 115
Broomfield Road, Chelmsford, 87
Broxbourne, 10, 13
Brundon, Stour valley, 7
Buckenham field, Billericay, 93
buckets, 76, 111
Buckhurst Hill by-pass, 166
buckles, 80, 110, 111
Buckley, David, 202
Buildings Farm, Great Dunmow, 101
Bulls Lodge Quarry, Boreham, 98, *98*
Bulmer: medieval earthwork, 129
Bures: circular ditched enclosure, 30
Bures St Mary, Stour valley, 17
"Burgate", Rivenhall End, 121
Burgh Castle, 104
Burgh-by-Woodbridge, Suffolk, 62
burhs, Saxon, 118, 120, 121, 122, 202, 203
burials, 16, 19, 26, 58
  Anglo-Saxon, 101, 108, 110-13, *113*, 114, 118
    Heybridge, 120
    Late, 123
    Middle/Late: Colchester, 120
  animal, 41, 51, 80, 111, 123
  Beaker, 22
  Bronze Age, 19-20, 29, 33, 43, 44
  Colchester
    St Mary Magdalen churchyard, 134
    see also Butt Road
  cult of the severed head, 51
  flat graves, 19
  Great Braxted warrior, 58
  Iron Age, 33, 58
  megalithic tomb, 42
  Mucking, 100, 101
  Neolithic, 19-20, 215
  North Shoebury, 57
  Roman, 87, 93-4, 100, 102-3

INDEX

cemetery: Chignall St James, 98
Springfield cursus, 17
Stanway, 60
tribal, 55
"Viking", 123
see also funerary practices; grave goods and under enclosures
burins, 10
Bury, Hertfordshire: Little Wymondley, 142
Bury St Edmunds, 132, 142
butchery, 51, 90, 132, 172
Butlins Holiday Camp, Clacton-on-Sea, 5
Butt Road cemetery, Colchester, 69, 71, 72, 75, 84, 87

Caesar, C. Julius, 55, 59
Caesaromagus (Roman Chelmsford), 87, 88, *89*, 91-3, 192, 194
Caistor by Yarmouth, 104
Cam, River, 77, 95, 104, 129
Cambridge, 62, 95, 104
Cambridgeshire
  building style, 138
  Norman settlement, 129
  see also individual places
Campen, M. J., 200
Camulodunum, 90, 202
  as Anglo-Saxon royal vill, 120
  coins, 60, 62, *62*, 69
  industries, 93
  Iron Age, 69, 199
  Late Iron Age, 60, 61, 62, *62*, 63, 77, 87
  post-Boudica rebuilding, 91
  Roman, 69, 70-1, *71*, 77, 108
  defences, 88
  see also Colchester; Culver Street; Lion Walk; Sheepen; Stanway
Can, River, 77
Canewdon, 22, 174
Canonium, 88
  see also Kelvedon
Canterbury, 60, 110
Canute, King, 123
Canvey Island, 61, 103, 155, 162, 176
Canvey Point, 176, 177
Caratacus, 62
Carmelite friary: Maldon, 134
carpentry, 58, 132, *136*, 137-8
Carps Tongue sword, 30
Carter's Green, Matching, 130
Cassius Dio, 62
Castle Hedingham, 124, 129, 161
Castle Point Archaeological Group, 103
cat bone, 83
Catalan wine, 60
cattle
  bone, 83
  Chelmsford, 90, 93
  grazing of, 22
  Iron Age, 63
  Middle Bronze Age, 27
  remains, 172
  teeth, 20
  wild, 11, 15
Catuvellauni, 59, 61, 62, 63
causewayed enclosures, 16, *17*, 20, 22, 24, 30, 113
cave occupations, "Creswellian", 10
Celts
  coinage, 54, 60, 63, 86
  and cult of the severed head, 51
  Teutatis (war god), 58
  see also under temples
cereals, 20, 27, 51
  Anglo-Saxon period, 177
  barley, 20, 63, 64, 172, 174, 176, 177, 179
  bread wheat, 171, 172, 174, 177, 179
  Bronze Age, 170-1, 172, 174-5, **175**
  cultivation, 16, 39, 63-4, 105
  emmer, 20, 172, 174, 177
  grain processing, 27
  introduction of, 15, 16
  Iron Age, 172, 174-5, **175**
  medieval period, 131, 177
  milling, 162, 164

Neolithic, 22, 170-1, 172
oats, 27, 63, 174, 177, 179
pollen, 15, 170
Roman period, 175, 176, 177
rye, 63, 177, 179
spelt, 63, 174, 175, 176, 177
wheat, 22, 27, 63, 177, 179
see also corn driers; granaries
ceremonies, 24
ceremonial monuments: Neolithic, 16
  and cultivation, 20
  cursus monuments, 17
  henge monuments, 19
  and offerings, 42
Chadwell Heath: hand-axe finds, 5
Chadwell St Mary, 7, 200
Chadwell-Mucking area, pottery, 50
chalk, 8, 20, 27, 39, 163
  and Bronze Age settlement, 40
  figurine, 86
Chalk and Thanet Sand, 4, 7
Chalkney Wood, 95, 101
Chalton, Hampshire, 111-12
Chapman and André map, 129, *130*, *131*, *132*, 146, 147, 164, 183
charcoal
  Colchester, 75
  and industrial activity, 52
  making, 115
  Neolithic environment, 171
  radiocarbon dating, 13, 16, 17, 20, 29
Chardwell Farm, Clavering, 97
Charles I, King, 153
Cheddar/Creswell points, 10
Chells and Foxholes Farm, Hertfordshire, 101
Chelmer, River, 2, 26, 30, 77, 162, 175
Chelmer valley
  Bronze Age/Iron Age, 33, 36, 172
  causewayed enclosures, 16
  field system, 100
  metalwork, 42
  Neolithic/Bronze Age sites, 24
  ring ditches, 19
  Roman period, 175
  Springfield cursus, 17
Chelmsford, 84, 97, 202, 217
  A12 by-pass, 172
  and Boudica, 194
  bridges, 132
  Broomfield Road, 87
  Cramphorns site, *88*, 90
  defences, 80, 88, 93
    line: Golf Course, 150
    military landscape, *82*
    modern fortifications, 150, *151*
    post-Boudican fort, 77
    World War II, 187
  electrical equipment industry, 165
  excavations, 12, 50, 199, 201, 203
  Godfreys site, 77, 87, 88, 91, *92*, 93
  Grays Brewery, 179
  Grove Road, 91
  Hall Street, 87, 192, 194
  Hylands, 155
  Iron Age, Late, 76
  King Edward VI Grammar School, 192
  mansio, 76, 82, 83, 88, *90*, 91, *91*, 93, 94, 194, 201
  Mildmay Road, 192, 194
  Neolithic finds, 22
  New Writtle Street, 192
  octagonal temple, 80-2
  Parkway, 194
  post-medieval fieldwork, 150
  religious artefacts, 86
  Roman period
    building, 97
    Celtic religious influence, 83
    decline, 103
    defences, 88
    as Roman town, 77-80, *80*
  round houses, *81*, 94
  Springfield Road, 87
  surrounding landscape, 100, 101
  Walker's plan of, 148
  Writtle Road, 87

see also Caesaromagus; Moulsham Street; Springfield Lyons
Chelmsford Archaeological Group, 192-3, 194
Chelmsford Archaeological Trust, 76, 192, 194, 195-6, 201, 202, 207
Chelmsford and Essex Museum, 80&n, 192, 196
Chelmsford Excavation Committee, 76, 192, 193-4, 195, 196, 201, 207
chemical processes, 164-5
Cheshire/Droitwich region, 101
Chessington, MOD, 158
Chesterford Archaeological Group, 77
Chicago, University of, 5
Chichester: harbour area, 101
Chigborough, 20
Chigborough Farm, 114
  Bronze Age, 26, 172, 174
  Iron Age, 174, 175
  Mesolithic finds, 12
  prehistoric plant remains, 171
  Roman cereal remains, 177
Chignall St James, 98, 103, 124, 129, 148, **148**
Chigwell, 93
Child, Sir Josiah, 153, 155
Child, Sir Richard, 153
Chilterns, 15, 19, 24, 105
Chinese silk, 87
Chippenham, Cambridgeshire, 63
Chipping Hill Camp, Witham, 32n, 51, 63, 200, 203
  Bronze Age/Iron Age hillfort, 121
  Neolithic/Bronze Age, 24
  potin coinage, 54
  pottery, 22
Chipping Ongar, 10, 209
chisel, flint, 22
Chitts Hill cremation burials, 26
Chrishall, growth of, 130
Christianity
  adoption of, 86, 117
  artefacts, 80, *84*
  and burials, 71, 87
  Ivy Chimneys, Witham, 121, 202
  and Temple of Claudius, Colchester, 71, 72
  see also churches; monasteries
Church Farm, Fressingfield, Suffolk, 140, 142
churches
  Anglo-Saxon, 117, 122
  Colchester, 71, 72, 84, 204
  Early Saxon, 112
  medieval, 125, 126, 133, 134
  see also individual churches
Cirencester: Roman finds, 77
Cistercian Order, 133, 153
Clacton Channel deposits, 5
Clacton-on-Sea, 2, 97, 199
  carinated bowls, 22
  environmental archaeology, 168
  Golf Course excavation, 5, 6
  Neolithic period/Bronze Age, 20, 24
  Palaeolithic period, 202
  Roman burials, 102
Clactonian industry, 2, 3, 4, 5, 6, 7
Claudius, emperor, 50, 63, 72, 77
Clavering, 97, 125, 140
clay
  fired, 50, 57, 61, 115
  moulds, 30, 31, 41, 52
  pipes: Colchester, 74
  for pottery, 47
  slabs, perforated, 31, 32, 35, 43
Claygate/Bagshot ridge, 12
coal, 163
coal gas, 163, 165
coastline
  Anglo-Saxon/medieval environment, 177
  defences, 150
  Hoxnian Stage, 2
  Late Upper Palaeolithic/Mesolithic, 168-70
  marshes: salt production, 124
  Middle Bronze Age/Iron Age, 174

221

INDEX

Neolithic/Early Bronze Age, 15, 16, 171
post-medieval reclamation and change, 155
recession, 12
and Red Hills, 61
Roman period, 101-2, 176
World War II fortifications, 187
cobalt, 55
coffins
  fittings: Kelvedon, 103
  Late Iron Age burials, 58
  Roman burials, 87
  Saxon, 111
  stone, 87, 93, 103
Coggeshall, 103, 131, 132, 164, 189
Coggeshall Abbey, 161
coins
  Aethelstan, 125
  antoniniani, 69
  asses, 77, 80
  bronze, 54, 59, 60, 61, 62, *62*, 62, 63
  Celtic, 63, 86
  Colchester, 69, 74, 84
  Cunobelinus, 54, 58, 59, 60-3, 76, 86
  gold staters, 47, 59, 61, 62, 63
  Iron Age, 51, 59, 60, 61, 203
  introduction of, 54-5
  of Mercia, 117-18
  Merovingian, 120
  potin, 47, 51, 54-5, 76, 87
  Roman, 54, 63, 69, 83, 87, 101, 105
    late, 103, 104
    villa finds, 98
  Roman/post-Roman: Colchester, 74
  Saxon, 110, 117, 123, 124
  sceattas, 117, 118, 120, 121
  ship designs on, 60-1, *62*, 62
  silver, 62, 63
    Aethelred II, 111
    denarii, 77
  Southend: Gallo-Belgic hoard, 55
  staters, 47, 54, 61, 62, 63, 87
    Gallo-Belgic, 55, 59
  Tasciovanus, 59
  Theodosian, 83, 87
  Viking period, 123
  see also mints
Colchester, 1, 95, 97, 105, 132, 217
  Anglo-Saxon period, 117, 118, 125
  Balkerne Gate, 71
  Balkerne Lane, 69, 72
  Balkerne Street, 70
  Boudiccan sack of, 71, 87, 176, *176*, 177
  Butt Road, 69, 71, 72, 75, 84, 87
  by-pass, 199
  carpentry style, 137
  churches, 71, 84, 133, 204
  decline in Roman period, 103
  dykes, 57, 69, 202
  excavations, 195, 201, 202-3, 209
  expulsion of Vikings, 122
  Fordham: stone coffin, 103
  Gilberd School, 71, 77
  granary, 104
  hand-axes, 5
  Hyderabad Barracks, 61
  legionary fortress, 77
  medieval leper hospital, 134
  mint, 120, 125
  mirror find, 61
  Norman castle, 74, 129, 204
  Osborne Street site, 75
  post-Roman period, 73-4
  publications, 69-75
  River Colne at, 60
  Roman remains, 176
  St Botolph's Church, 133
  St Mary Magdalen churchyard, 134
  Speed's plan of, 147
  surrounding landscape, 100, 101
  Temple of Claudius, 71, 72, 80, 86-7, 203
  and trade, 125
  see also Camulodunum; Culver Street; Lexden Tumulus; Lion Walk; Sheepen; Stanway

Colchester Archaeological Group, 61, 95, 97, 101, 160, 199, 203
Colchester Archaeological Trust, 196, 202, 207, 210, 214
Colchester and Essex Museum, 10, 33, 95, 199
Colchester Excavation Committee, 201, 202, 207
Colchester Hall: manor, 124
College House, Braintree, 76
Collins Creek, 115, 124, 177
Colne estuary, 16-17, 103
Colne, River, 77, 162
  at Colchester, 120
  coin find, 60
  palaeolithic period, 2
  "Viking Type" axe heads, 122
Colne valley: Neolithic/Bronze Age sites, 24
Cologne, 162
Colville Hall, White Roding, 136
comb, bone, 33, 73, 83
Conservation areas, 187, 207
Constans, reign of, 104
Constantine
  Audience Hall of: Trier, 87
  period of, 105
Coombe Rock, 7
Cooper, Harold, 97, 200
Copford, 2, 134
copper: flat axes, 22
copper alloy
  bridle-bit, 61
  brooches, 111
  crucible for, 52
  figurines, 80
  objects, 77, 86, 93
  plaque, 83
coppicing, 101
Corbets Tey Gravel, 5, 7
core-adzes, Mesolithic, 12
cores, 2, 3, 10
  flint: Clactonian, 5, 6, 7
  Levalloisian, 7
  Upper Palaeolithic, 10
Corieltauvi: coins, 60
corn driers, 90, 97, 101
Cornwall: igneous stone axes, 22
Corringham: potin coins, 54, 55
Cotton Park Gardens, Romford, 93
court rolls, 145
crafts/industries, 39, 40, 160, 163-5
  Bronze Age, 39
  Chelmsford, 91-3
  cutlery, 132, 133, 163-4
  gunpowder, 155-8
  industrial revolution, 160, 161
  Iron Age, 52-4
  medieval, 131, 132, 133
  see also industrial archaeology; iron; metalwork; textiles
Cramphorns site, Chelmsford, *88*, 90
Cranborne Chase, 39
cremation burials
  Bronze Age, 19, 26, 29
  Chelmsford, 87
  Late Iron Age, 57-8, 76
  Mucking North Ring, 41
  North Shoebury, 29
  Roman, 83, 87
  Springfield Lyons, 110-11, 177
  Stansted, *102*
Cressing
  barn, 131
  church, 122, 204
  medieval holdings, 146
  religious house, 133
Cressing brook, 97
Cressing Temple, 152-3, 202, 204, 212, 217
  Charter, 216
Creswell/Cheddar points, 10
"Cresswellian" cave occupations, 10
Cromarty, Dorothy, 145
'Cromerian Complex' river system, 168
Crompton-Parkinsons, Chelmsford, 165
Crondon Park, Stock, 148

cropmarks, 24, 30, 200
  Anglo-Saxon settlement, 108
  Ardleigh, 26
  Asheldham Camp, 47
  burials, 103
  and circular enclosures, 33
  classification, 189
  enclosures, 202
  Gosbecks, 69
  and landscape change, 101
  M3 extension: Winchester, 40
  Neolithic, 113, 171
  Neolithic/earlier Bronze Age, 15
  of ring ditches, 19
  and Roman roads, 97
  Roman rural sites, 100
  and Sites and Monuments Record, 185-6, *186*, 188
crops, 27
  charred remains, 171, 177
  large-scale, 104, 105
  Late Bronze Age, 32, *32*
  processing, 31, 172
  see also cereals; plants
Crossness, Thamesmead, 170
Crouch estuary
  Anglo-Saxon/medieval environment, 177
  Bronze Age/Iron Age structures, 174
  Iron Age pottery, 57
  minefield control tower, *187*
  paddle find, 29
  Roman period, 175
Crouch, River, 102
  Mesolithic period, 170, **170**
  microliths, 12
  palaeolithic period, 2
Crouch valley, 202
crown posts, 138, 139, 141
Crowthorne Wood, Bracknell, Berkshire, 150
crucibles, 52
Crummy, Philip, 201, 203
Cudmore Grove, East Mersea, 5
Culver Street, Colchester, 69, 70-1, 72, 73, *73*, 93, 203
  cereal remains, 177
  flint/pottery scatters, 20
  medieval latrine/refuse pits, 179
  Neolithic/Bronze Age material, 24
  plant remains, 75
  pottery, 22
  Roman period, 74, 77, 176
  rural aspect of, 90
Cunningham, Mrs Carol, 196
Cunobelinus
  coinage, 54, 58, 59, 60-3, 76, 86
  trade with Rome, 60
Cups Hotel, Colchester, 73
currency bars, 59
cursus monuments, 17, *18*
  Springfield cursus, 17, 22, 24
customs duties, medieval, 133
cutlery industry, 132, 133, 163-4

Dagenham, 121
daggers, flint, 19, 22
Dalby, P. J., 192
Dallaunce, house at, 153
Danbury, 33, 97, 124, 195, 201, 202, 209
Danebury, Hampshire, 39, 42
  special animal bone deposit, 51
Danelaw, 122
Danes (Vikings), 117, 120, 122-3, 125
Darcy, Lord, 153
Darent valley: cemeteries, 113
Darenth valley: Saxon settlement, 110
Dartford Heath Gravel, 2
Dartmoor: Bronze Age settlement, 39
dating, 29
  Barking excavations, 122
  causewayed enclosures, 16
  of enclosures, 30
  Lofts Farm artefacts, 54
  Mesolithic period, 13
  see also radiocarbon dating

INDEX

Davies, Gareth, 192, 193
Davison, Brian, 200
Dawes Heath villa: religious find, 80
de Vere: earls of Oxford, 129
Dedham, 19, 138, 164
deer, 4, 5, 10, 11, 15, 16, 125
defences
    Camulodunum, 69, 71, 72
    Chelmsford, 80, 93
    coastline, 150
    Great Chesterford, 77, 104
    Roman towns, 76, 88
    World War II, 186-7, 214
denarii, silver, 77
dendrochronology, 13, 105, 115, 117, 177
Dengie peninsula, 61, 100, 117, *174*, 176, 177
Denmark: Neolithic period, 16
Denny, Sir Edward, 153
Denton, Norfolk: Lodge Farm, 140, 142
Denver Sluice, Norfolk, 165
Devensian stage, 3, 8
Dickleburgh, 100
disease
    Black Death, 131, 161, 162
    monastic, 133
    plague, 131, 150
    woodland, 153, 170
diverticulae (minor Roman roads), 97
documentary sources *see* Essex Record Office
dog bone, 51
Doggets Farm, Rochford, 162
Domesday survey
    Anglo-Saxon rural settlement, 123
    and churches, 122
    coastal activity, 177
    Havering, 121
    Horndon-on-the-Hill, 122
    mills, 162
    Newport, 121
    Norman settlement, 129, 130
    and royal vills, 118
    rural resources, 124
    sheep pasture, 63
    Stansted, 124
    urban/rural development, 125
    Viking names, 122
Dominican Friary, Chelmsford, 192, 194
Doreward's Hall, Bocking, 10
Dorset, 10, 39, 147
    see also individual places
Dortmund, 164
Dovedales College, Moulsham Street, Chelmsford, 192
Dover, 8, 29
Dovercourt, 5, 20, 150
Dovercourt Bay, 172
Down House Farm, Roman farm complexes, 215
dowries, 54
Drays Ditches, 42
drought (1975-6), 95
Drumcoltran: fortified hilltop, 42
Drury, Paul, 192, 194, 195, 201
Dubnovellaunos, 60, 61
Duck End *see under* Stansted Airport
Dun Ailine, Ireland, 41
Dunnett, Rosalind (Mrs Niblett), 201
Dunstable: Manshead Archaeological Society, 24
Durham House, Great Bardfield, 140
Durolitum, 93, 94, 97
Durotriges: coins, 60
Dutch 'adventurers', 155
Duvensee, North Germany, 13
dyestuffs, 161
dykes
    of Cambridgeshire, 105
    Colchester, 57, 69, 202

Earls Colne
    Hunt's of Earls Colne, 165, 167
    water pumps, 165
East Ham, 121
East India Company, 153

East Mersea
    16th-century fort, 150
    Cudmore Grove, 5
    tumulus, 103
East Saxon Kingdom (*East Seaxe*), and Royal Estates, 105, 117-22, *119*, 125
East Tilbury, 134, 150, 162
Edgar, Earl, 121
Edgars Farm, Stowmarket, Suffolk, 139
Edict of Milan, 87
Edith, Queen, 121
Edward the Confessor, 121
Edward the Elder, 118, 120, 121, 203
Edward III, King, 161, 164
Eifel region, 122, 162
electricity, 162, 163, 165
elephant, straight-tusked, 4, 5
Elizabeth I, Queen, 146, 153, 155
elk (moose), 11
Elm Road, Chelmsford, 87
Elmdon, 129, 130, 162
Elms Farm, Heybridge *see under* Heybridge
Elsenham, 95, 97, 103, 165
Elsenham Cross: Pledgdon: Mesolithic finds, 12
Ely, 121
enamel, 52
enclosure, landscape, 39, 146, 149
enclosures
    Bronze Age, 40, 110, 188-9
    Late, 27, 32, 189, *189*
    Middle, 39
    circular, 27, 30, *31*, 33
    funerary, 15, 16-17, *18*, 22, 57, 69, **70**
    rectangular, 121, 189
    see also causewayed enclosures; cropmarks
Enfield Lock: environmental archaeology, 168
engineering, 165
English Channel, 2, 8
English Electric, Chelmsford, 165
English Heritage, 38, 40, 93, 94, 181, 182, 185, 186, 187, 188, 189, 195, 199, 208, 209, 214, 215, 217
English Nature, 7
Environment, Department of, 181, 182, 195, 200, 208, 209, 217
environmental archaeology, 168-79, **178**
Epona worship, 83
Epping Forest, 12, 47, 199
Epping Forest District Museum, 158
Erbenhiem-type swords, 26
Erith, Felix, 200
Erkenwald, 121
Ermine Street, **77**
Essex Archaeological Society, 195, 199, 201, 202, 207
Essex archaeology
    conferences, *212*
    retrospect and prospect, 207-18
    review, 199-204
Essex Mills Group, 162, 166
Essex Police, 29
Essex Record Office, 143-9, 190, 192, 193
Essex Sites and Monuments Record (ESMR), 181-90, 208-9, 213, 214
estate maps, 147-8, 149, 162
Etruria, Staffordshire: Shirley's Bone Mill, 158
Evison, Dr Vera, 77, 200
Ewart Park metalwork, 29, 30, 31, 46
ewers, 77, 103

famines, medieval, 131
farmsteads, 99, 100, 104, 131, 215
Farningham, Kent: Iron Age, 50, 57
Farrand, late Commander R. A., 98
Farrands, R. H., 110
Faulkbourne Hall: medieval house, 129
fauna, 10, 11
    Anglian stage, 168
    Anglo-Saxon/medieval remains, **177**
    bone *see* bone, animal
    forest, 13

    Late Bronze Age, 33
    mammalian, 1, 2, 4, 5, 7
    marine
        cockles, 19, 64, 174
        eels, 174, 177
        molluscs, 2, 4, 5, 172, 177
        mussels, 27, 32, 64, 174
        oysters, 64, 174
        shellfish, 12, 15, 176
        shells, 19, 174
    North Shoebury, 27-9
    and radiocarbon dating, 10
    see also animal *and* individual animals
Feering: hand-axes, 5
Fengate, Cambs., 24, 39
Fenn Creek, 12, 29
Field Archaeology Group (FAG), 215
field books, 144-5, **145**
'field forts', 150
field systems, 24, 101
    Bronze Age, 39
    medieval, 144-5
    Roman, 100, 104, 125, 126
figurines, 80, 83&n, 86
finger rings, 80, 83
Fingringhoe, 29, 30, 61, **77**
fish bone, 75, 174, 177
Fisher's Green, Waltham Holy Cross, 13
fishing
    Blackwater estuary, 123
    fish-weirs, 124
    fresh/salt-water, 11, 12
    hunter-fisher-gatherers, 15, 16
    Roman period, 176
    Saxon period, 115
    traps, 131, 177, 215
Fitzwalter, Viscounts, 155
Flag Fen, 40, 41-2
flagons, 60, 87, 103
flakes
    flint, 2, 5, 6, 7, 8, 203
    Clactonian, 5, 6, 7
    High Lodge, Mildenhall, 1
    Levalloisian, 7
    Upper Palaeolithic, 10
Flandrian stage, 168, 170
Flavian period, 57, 87, 103
flax, 172, 174, 177, 179
flint, 43, 54, 93, 97, 203
    Bronze Age, 20, 24, 39-40
    as building material, 163
    burnt, 43, 57
    chisel, 22
    Clactonian industry, 5, 6, 7, 168
    fire-fractured, 20
    from Normandy, 166
    frost-shattered, 2
    and glaciation, 1
    Mesolithic, 170
    mining, 20, 22
    Neolithic, 15-16, 20, 24
    Orsett enclosure, 16
    scratched, 2
    Surrey/Sussex/East Hampshire, 12
    see also arrowheads; axes; cores; daggers; flakes; hand-axes; knives; sickles
food, 13, 39
    bread-making, 93
    consumption, 41
    cooking, 20, 132
    Bronze Age sites, 43
    cooking/baking, 51, 132
    Late Bronze Age remains, 41
    medieval remains, 179
    Mesolithic remains, 13
    and monastic diet, 133
    Neolithic sources of, 16
    as offering, 42
    processing industries, 165
    vessels, 20
    wild plant, 20, 22, 27, 172
    see also agriculture; crops
Fordham, Colchester: stone coffin, 103
forest *see* woodland
fortress: Camulodunum, 70-1, **77**

INDEX

forts
  early Roman, 76, 77, 80
  see also hillforts
fossils
  human, 10
  shells, 55
  see also macrofossil analysis; microfossil analysis
Foulness, 131, 155, 170, 177
Fountain site, Braintree, 76
Fox Hall: Bronze Age/Iron Age settlement, 33
Fressingfield, Suffolk: Church Farm, 140, 142
Frinton: Palaeolithic finds, 10
Frog Hall Farm, Fingringhoe: pottery, 29
Fryerning, 129
fulling mills, 162, 164
funerary practices, 26, 51
  Late Iron Age, 57-8
  native American, 42
  Roman, 103
  Saxon, 111, 113-14
  see also burials and under enclosures
funerary vessels, Belgic, 57
Fyfield Hall, 139

Galleywood Common, Chelmsford: defensive line, 150, *152*
gaming counters, 111
Gants Pit/Pounds Farm, Dovercourt: hand-axe site, 5
gas, 165
gatherers, 12
  hunter-gatherers, 15, 16, 168
  of wild plants, 20, 27
Gaul
  and burial practices, 103
  coinage, 54
  cremation rite, 57
  Gallic wars, 55, 58, 59, 60
  imports from, 60
  late Roman agriculture, 104, 105
  personal adornment, 61
  rural sanctuaries, 60
  warfare in, 54
Geographical Information Systems (GIS), 189-90, 214
Geological Society of London, 5
Gernon, Robert, 130
Gestingthorpe
  aisled buildings, 97
  excavation, 200
  farm buildings, 100
  figurine find, 80
  flat axes, 22
  Roman villa, 98
gift exchange, 20, 54
Gilberd School, Colchester, 71, 77
Glacial stage, 1-2, *1*, 8
  Early Post Glacial, 13
  interglacial, 2, 5, 7, 8, 168
  Late Glacial, 10, 13, 168
glass
  crucible, 52
  objects, 122
  palm cup, 103
  Roman, 69, 203
  vessels, 75, 87, 110, 111
  window, 93, 122
Globe Pit, Little Thurrock: hand-axe site, 7
goat, bone, 177
Gobions Farm, East Tilbury, 162
Godfreys site, Chelmsford, 77, 87, 88, 91, *92*, 93
Godmanchester, 104
Going, C. J., 58
Golands Bridge, Stebbing, 103
gold, 20, 52
  bracteate, 113
  coins, 47, 54, 59, 61, 62, 63
  hoarding of, 55
  ornaments, 42
  pendant, 113, *114*
  rings, 41
  thread, 122

Goldhanger see Chigborough Farm
goldsmiths, 163
Gosbecks, 69, 77, 202, 204
Gosfield, 100
Gosfield Hall, 162
Gower, Dr Foote, 95
graffiti, 58, 80
granaries, 51, 63, 90, 100, 104
grave goods, 22
  Anglo-Saxon, 108, 110, 111, 113
  Bronze Age, 39, 43
  and Christianity, 117
  Great Chesterford burial, 103
  Iron Age cremation burials, 58
  Roman, 87, 103
Grays
  by-pass, 101, 108, 202
  Clarence Road, 163
  flint artefacts, 22
  Palstaves, 26
Grays Brewery, Chelmsford, 179
Great Baddow, 22, 30
Great Bardfield
  Durham House, 140
  watermill, 166-7
Great Bardfield Hall, 129
Great Braxted: warrior burial, 58
Great Burstead church, 134
Great Canfield, 63, 83n
Great Chesterford, 24, 93, 97, 105
  Anglo-Saxon period, 121, 124
  excavation, 192, 199, 200
  iron work hoard, 104
  Late Iron Age, 76
  rich burial, 103
  Roman period
    defences, 104
    fort, 77
    road, 95
    as Roman town, 87
    Romano-Celtic temple, 83
  surrounding landscape, 101
  watermill, 100
Great Dunmow, 76, 95, 100
  Bigods Farm, 97
  Brewery, 165
  Buildings Farm, 101
  Domesday Book, 122
  excavation, 195, 201
  flint artefacts, 22
  Flitch Bacon factory, 165
  military equipment, 77
  Redbond Lodge, 103
  religious artefacts, 86
  Roman period
    cemetery, 87
    Roman town, 87, 88, 94
    villas, 98
  shrine, 83
Great Hallingbury: funerary inscription, 103
Great Holts, Boreham, 33, 100, 215
Great Leighs, 97
Great Lofts, Maldon, 101
Great Shelford, Cambs., 121
Great Tey, 97, 200
Great Totham see Lofts Farm; Slough House Farm
Great Wakering, 29, 33, 108
Great Waltham: Broads Green, 29, 32, 34, 202, 204
Great Wasketts, Basildon: Bronze Age hoard, 30&n
Great Wigborough: Red Hill 147, 63
Great Wymondley, Cambs., 100
Greenlands Pit, Purfleet, 7
Greensted Church, 117, 122
Grimes Graves, 41
Grove Road, Chelmsford, 91
Gun Hill, West Tilbury, 97
gunpowder production, 155-8, 164

Hadham, 93
Hadleigh, 33, 47, 77, 204
Hadleigh Castle, 200
Hadrian, period of, 82, 91, *102*, 103
Hadstock, 121, 122

church, 117, 133, 204
excavation, 201, 204
religious establishment, 122
villa, 98
see also Ashdon
Hall Farm, Mount Bures, 10
Hall Street, Chelmsford, 87, 192, 194
halls
  aisled, 110, *137*, 139
  base-cruck, 139, 140
  church-halls, 124, 126
  Harlowbury: great hall and chapel, 129
  Norse-type turf-walled, 121
  open-hall houses, 141
  post-built, 114
  raised aisled, *138*, 139-40
Hallsford: Lea Valley Co's pit, 10
Halstead, 95
hammers, iron, 58
Hampshire
  Deverel-Rimbury sites, 39
  see also individual places
hand-axes, 5-7, 8
  Acheulian Industry, 2, 3
  Boxgrove, Sussex, 1
  flint, 6
  interglacial period, 5
  palaeolithic, 2, 86
  Rochford, 2
Hanse merchants, 164
hare, 4
Harkshead, Suffolk, 8
Harlow
  cemetery locations, 87
  Early Saxon cemetery, 108
  Felmongers, 97
  flat axes, 22
  military metalwork, 77
  Minerva: carved head, 86, *86*
  Moor Hall, 32
  Old Harlow, 132
  religious finds, *84*
  as Roman town, 87
  Stafford House, 93
  temple, 51, 52, 59-60, 86, 199
    coinage, 54
    cremation, 57
    Early Saxon occupation, 110
    Iron Age coinage, 62
    late Roman find, 80
    and Tasciovanus, 61
Harlowbury, 129, 132
harness, 58
harness pendants, 77
Harwich, 97, 164
  dockyard crane, 161-2, *161*
  Dovercourt bypass: coastal gun battery, 150
  excavation, 195, 201
  medieval period, 133
Hatfield Broad Oak: medieval crafts, 132
Haughey's Fort, Northern Ireland, 42
Havering, 121, 123, 155
Hawkes, Professor Christopher, 199
Hayling Island temple, Hampshire, 60
hearths, 20, 51, 61, 93, 115
Hedges, John, 195, 202, 207, 209, 218
Hedingham Castle, 212
Helions Bumpstead: Horsham Hall, 131
Hemel Hempstead: Wood Lane End, 98
Hemigkofen-type swords, 26
henges, *18*, 19, 24, 30, 199
Hengistbury Head, Dorset, 10
Henham windmill, 162
Hertfordshire, 61, 62, 101, 114, 138
  see also individual places
Hewett, Cecil, 204
Heybridge, 97, 195, 201
  Elms Farm, 50, 54, 110, 215, 216-17
  Iron Age, 50, 60, 76, 77, 94
  Iron Age, Late/early Roman, 77
  Iron Age/Roman port, 76, 77, 94
  mansio, 91, 94
  Middle Bronze Age/Iron Age, 174
  as port, 76, 77, 80, 94
  pottery, 50, 55, 60

INDEX

as Roman town, 77, 87, 120
stone coffins, 87
sunken-featured buildings, 110
see also Maldon
High Beach, Epping Forest, 12
High Easter, 80, 200
High Lodge, Mildenhall, 1, 168
High Wood, Elmdon, 130
Hill Farm, Tolleshunt D'Arcy, 108
Hill Hall, 179, 195, 196, 201
Hill Wood clay pit, High Beach, 12
hillforts, 32n, 33, 41, 42, 47
    Asheldham Camp, 172
    Chipping Hill, 121
Historic Towns Project, 187, 190
Hoffmann and Belgian kilns, 163
Holbrooks, 60, 77, 86
Holderness: timber structures, 42
Holehaven: oil refinery, 164
Holland Gravels, 5
Holocene period: radiocarbon dating, 11
Homo erectus, 1
Homo sapiens, 1, 4
Horncastle, 104
Hornchurch, vill, 121
Horndon-on-the-Hill, 121-2, 125, 132
horns, cattle, 90-1
horses, 4, 5, 8, 10, 11
    bone, 51, 83
    burial, 111, 123
    harness, 58, 61
    Late Pleistocene, 10
    and power, 162
Horsey Island: The Wade, 10
Horsfrith Park Farm, 97
Horsham Hall, Helions Bumpstead, 131
"Horsham" points, 12
Horsley, John, 95
horticulture, 22
Horton Kirby cemetery, 113
Hoskins, W. G., 143
hospitals, monastic, 133, 134
Housham Hall, Matching, 130, 148
Howells Farm: Middle Bronze Age, 26
Hoxne, 105
Hoxnian stage, 2, 3, 4, 5, 7, 168
Hull, Mark, 199, 200, 201
Hullbridge, 199
    Fenn Creek, 12, 29
    Mesolithic period, 170
    survey, 15, 24, 102, 115
hundred centres, and royal vills, 118
hunting, 12, 43, 172
    hunter-gatherers, 15, 16, 168
Hunt's of Earls Colne, 165, 167
Hyderabad Barracks, Colchester, 61
Hygeia, depiction of, 80
Hylands, Chelmsford, 155
hypocausts, 108

ibex, 8
"Icanho": St. Botolph's monastery, 122
Iceni, 60, 62
Ickham, Kent: watermills, 100
Icknield Way, 77, 95, 97, 104, 105
Ickworth, Suffolk, 155
Ilford, 7, 8, 121
    see also Uphall Camp
industrial archaeology, 150, 160-7, 187
    manufacturing, 160, 163-5
    mining and quarrying, 160, 161, 163
    power supplies, 160, 161-3
    public utilities, 160, 165
    transport, 160, 165-6
    see also crafts
infirmary, monastic, 133
inflation: medieval period, 130
Ingatestone, 129, 130, 144, 148
Ingatestone Hall, 146
ingot, 30, 52
Ingrave, 130
Ingrave Common, *130*
Ingrave Hall, *130*
inhumations see burials
Inquisitions Post Mortem, 149
inscriptions, 77, 86, 103
internal combustion engines, 163

inventories, 146
Ipswich, 133
    Bobbitshole, 7
    growth of trade, 125
    pottery, 117, 121, 122
Ipswichian Stage, 3, 5, 7
Ireland, 40, 41, 43, 100
Ireland, Northern: Haughey's Fort, 42
iron
    bridle fittings, 111
    introduction of, 46
    ironwork hoards, 58-9, 59, 104
    ironworking, 54, 114-15
    keys, 111
    Little Waltham, 47
    miniature spearheads, 80
    objects, 93
    ore, 163
    production, 122
    shield, 58
    spear blade, 51
    and steel, 161, 164
    swords, 58
        miniature, 86
    tools, 60, 86
    see also blacksmiths; smiths
Iron Age, 27, 40, 46-64, 200, 201, 204
    agriculture, 63-4
    artefacts, 203
    burials, 19
    Camulodunum, 69, 199
    coins, 59, 61
    craft production, 52-4
    enclosures, 41
    environmental archaeology, 172-5
    field systems, 39
    Irish, 41
    landscape, 101, 202
Iron Age, Early, 26, 32&n, 33, 39, 46-7
    future work, 36
    pottery, 63
    settlement, 51
Iron Age, Late, 33, 46, 50, 55-63, 176
    art, 61
    coins, 61
    domestic architecture, 60
    funerary practices, 57-8
    landscape, 125
    metalworking, 52
    origins of Roman-British towns, 76
    pottery, 33, *53*, 57
    salt production, 61
    and town development, 93
    weapon burial: Kelvedon, 103
Iron Age, Middle, 33, 46, 47-55, 86
    domestic architecture, 50
    and introduction of coinage, 54-5
    pottery, 26n, 33, 57
    roundhouses, 32
    settlements, 51
Irons, Samuel, 163
ivory casket, 80
Ivy Chimneys, Witham, 84-6
    charred cereal remains, 175
    Iron Age religious activity, 59
    pagan and Christian complex, 121, 202
    temple complex, 84, *84*, 121

James I, King, 153
jars, 29, 51, 55, 57, 60, 63
Jaywick, 5, 172, 199
jet, 87, 94
jewellery, 63, 82, 83, 86, 87
John, King, 130
    Hunting Lodge (Writtle), 192, 200
Jones, David, 192
Jones, Margaret, 200
Jones, Tom, 200
Jupiter (god), 84, 86

Kelvedon, 12, 84
    circular temple, 83, 86
    Doucecroft site, 60
    excavation, 195, 201, 203
    graffito, 58
    hand-axes, 5

Iron Age, pottery, 61
Iron Age, Late, 77
    weapon burial, 103
    military fort, 76n
    pottery, 55, 61, 80
    rectangular houses, 60
    Roman period, 77, 87, 103, 200
    Saxon finds, 124
    shield binding, 77
    see also Canonium
Kennet valley, 38, 39
Kent
    Anglo-Saxon period, 117, 125
    carpentry style, 137
    coinage, 54, 62
    and Dubnovellaunos, 61
    Iron Age, 57, 62
    links with, 113
    monastic sites, 122
    and pottery, 50, 57
    Wealden houses, 140, 141
    West: sea-level changes, 15
    see also individual places
Kenyon, Robert, 77
Kesgrave sands, 1, 168
Kew: antler find, 13
keys, iron, 111
kilns
    bottle, 163
    brick, 163
    glass, 122
    limekilns, 163
    tile, 93
kilns, pottery
    Buckenham field, Billericay, 93
    Chelmsford, 93
    Colchester, 74
    Ivy Chimneys, Witham, 84
    Roman, 55
Kimmeridge
    shale bead, 113
    shale bowl, 51
King Edward VI Grammar School, Chelmsford, 192
King George's Reservoir, Sewardstone, 164
King Harry Lane, Hertfordshire, 58
Kings Lynn: King Street buildings, 142
King's Stables, Haughey's Fort, 42
Kingston on Thames, 43
knives, 10, 93, 111, 133
    flint, 17
    leather-working, 30
    Neolithic, 22
    shearing, 164
Knobs Crook, Dorset, 103

'laeti', 110
Lamarsh, 97
landscape, 204
    Anglo-Saxon, 123-5, 126, 177
    archaeology, 38, 43-4
    and Essex Sites and Monuments Record, 189
    Iron Age, 172, 202
    Late Upper Palaeolithic/Mesolithic environment, 168
    medieval, 143, 145-6, 177
    Middle Bronze Age environment, 172
    Neolithic/Early Bronze Age environment, 170-1
    post-medieval, 155
    Roman, 100-1, 104, 175-6, 202
Langenhoe, 54, 61, 101
Langford, 97, 162, 163, 215
Langley, parish of, 149
Langley tumulus, 97, 103
Lasts Garage, Chelmsford, 83
Latchingdon, 174, 204
latifundiae, 87, 104, 105
Latin, 143, 145
Lavenham, 138, 142
Lawford, 20, 164, 199
Layer-de-la-Haye, 20, 22, 52
Lea, River
    human skulls recovered, 29
    ironwork hoard, 58, 59
    sword finds, 26

225

INDEX

trade, 158
Waltham Abbey RGPF, 155
and watermills, 162
Lea valley, 202
  ancient boundaries, 100
  chemical industry, 164
  Enfield Lock, 168
  gravel pits, 163
  Mesolithic period, 13
  Neolithic/Bronze Age sites, 15, 24
  Saxon remains, 108
  Sewardstone, 164
  Viking stronghold, 122
Lea Valley Co's pit: Hallsford, 10
lead, 86, 87, 103
Leaden Roding, 100
leather
  industry, 132, 164-5
  leather-working knives, 30
  medieval tax on, 133
  remains: Colchester, 75
Leez Priory: religious house, 152
Leicester, Earl of, 153
Leigh-on-Sea: Viking burial, 123
leper hospital, Colchester, 134
Letchs Yard, Braintree, 93
Levalloisian technology, 3, 6, 7
Lexden: Roman site, 200
Lexden Tumulus, 57, 58, 60, 69
Leyton, 121
Leytonstone: hand-axe finds, 5
lignite bead, 113
Lilleshall Company, 162
limekilns, 163
linch pin, 58, 61
Lincolnshire: post-Dissolution monasteries, 152
Linford Quarry, Mucking, 200, 204
Linton, Cambs., 98
lion, 4, 5
Lion Pit Tramway Cutting, West Thurrock, 6, 7, 8
Lion Point, Jaywick Sands, 5
Lion Walk, Colchester, 69, 70-1, 72, 108-10, *176*, 203
Lisbon, 150
lithic finds *see* flint; stone
Little Bentley, Stour valley, 19
Little Braxted: Saxon cemetery, 121
Little Bromley, Stour valley, 19
Little Canfield, 162
Little Chesterford, 121
Little Clacton: microliths, 12
Little Domesday, 129
Little Dunmow: Lady Chapel, 153
Little Hallingbury, 29, 98
Little Holland, 124, 131
Little Holland Hall, 134
Little Ilford: timber church, 122
Little Laver: excavation, 192, 199
Little Leighs: medieval settlement, 129-30
Little Oakley, 97, 98, 110, 122, 204
Little Thurrock, 7, 163
Little Totham, 61
  Rook Hall, 26, 115
Little Walden: box burial, 103
Little Walsingham, Norfolk: Priory Gatehouse, 142
Little Waltham
  Belgic pottery, 55
  carinated bowls, 22
  excavations, 194, 195, 196, 199
  houses, 60
  Iron Age, 47, 50, 51, 57, 172, 201
  landscape, 100, 125
  Middle Bronze Age, 172
  pottery, 22, 46, 50, 55, 57
  rectangular shrines, 50
  roundhouse, 32
  Saxon finds, 124
Little Wool Hall, Lavenham, 142
Littlebury, 121
Llyn Fawr metalwork, 30, 46
Lodge Farm, Denton, Norfolk, 140, 142
Lofts Farm, Great Totham, 202
  Bronze Age, 29, 32, 172, 174
  building, **34**

Darmsden-Linton pottery, *48*
enclosure: land use, 39
flint/pottery, 20, *48*
Iron Age, 52-4, 174
Neolithic plant remains, 171
well, 33, 47, 172
see also Broomfield
London, 2, 5, 97, 105
  Antonine fire, 80
  Boudican fire, 194
  buildings, 136
  carpentry style, 137
  City Corporation, 153
  and East Saxon Kingdom, 117
  and Essex defensive line, 150
  food market in, 155
  Iron Age pottery, 57
  Museum of London, 13
  recaptured from Vikings, 122
  Roman, 104
  St Paul's Cathedral, 149
  south-west: burnt mounds, 43
  and steel imports, 164
  and trade, 120, 125, 131, 164
  Trafalgar Square, 7
London Clay, 7, 30, 32, 50, 125
long barrows, 16
Long Melford, 95
Longbridge Deverill Cow Down, 42
Longthorpe, 77
loomweights, 30, 33, 39, 114
  cylindrical, 26, 27, 29
  Iron Age, 63
Loughton by-pass, 166
Lower Gravel, 4, 5, 7
Lower Loam, 4
Lower Middle Gravel, 2
Luton, 24
Lynch Hill Terrace: Middle Thames, 5

M3 extension: Winchester, 40
M11 motorway, 7, 29, 33, 97, 201
maceheads, 22
Macleod, D. G., 27, 110, 202
macrofossil analysis, 5, 170, 172, 174, 175, 177, 179
Magnentius, 104
Maiden Bower: causewayed enclosure, 24
Maiden Castle, Dorset: coinage, 54
Maidens Tye, High Easter, 200
Maidstone, 50, 62
Maldon
  Anglo-Saxon period, 120, 121, 122, 125
  battle of, 203
  Beacon Green: pottery, 33, 47, *48*
  burh, 33, 202
  Carmelite friary, 134
  carpentry style, 137
  Early Iron Age settlement, 47
  excavation, 195, 199, 201
  Great Lofts, 101
  Langford waterworks, 162, 163
  Norman impact, 129
  salt production, 164
  Viking era, 123
  see also Heybridge; Woodham Walter
Maldon Archaeological Group, 29, 203
Maldon Hall Farm, 53, 57, 58
malting, 101, 177
Maltings Site, Mildmay Road, Chelmsford, 192
mammoth, 8, 10
Manchester: Metropolitan-Vickers, 160
Mandeville, Geoffrey de, 130, 134
Mandeville, William de, 133
Manningtree: Bradfield church, 134
manorial records, 129, 143-5
Manshead Archaeological Society of Dunstable, 24
mansiones
  Heybridge, 91, 94
  see also under Chelmsford
maps, 129, 146-9
  SMR, 183, *184*

see also Chapman and André map; Ordnance Survey; Walker maps
Mar Dyke, 7
  Iron Age pottery, 57
  pollen analysis, 15, 123, 168, 170, 172, 175, 177
Marconi, Chelmsford, 165
markets
  Late Saxon, 125
  medieval, 121, 132
  right of holding, 118
  Roman, 90
Marks Tey, 2, 5, 163, 168
Marlborough Downs, 38
Marlow, 2
Martello towers, 150
marten, 4
Matching: Housham Hall, 130, 148
Matching Green, 130
Matching Hall, 130
Matching Tye, 130
mattock, antler beam, 12-13
Mayland: River Blackwater, 12
Maylandsea: Mesolithic period, 170
Mayor's Parlour, South Street, Rochford, 142
medicine, and monastic houses, 133
medieval period, 76, 129-34
  agriculture, 105
  Asheldham Camp, 51
  Colchester, 73
  environmental archaeology, 177-9
  Great Dunmow, 88
  inflation, 130
  Irish sites, 41
  landscape, 101, 125, 143, 144
  Maldon, 120
  markets, 121, 132
  Mucking, 100
  Newport, 121
  rural settlement, 123, 126
  sources for archaeology, 143-9
  stone churches, 122
  town development, 90
  trade and communications, 40, 132
  vessel glass, 75
  Witham, 121
  see also Domesday survey; timber-framed buildings
Mediterranean, trade with, 50, 60
Medway, River, 1, 2, 5, 50
megalithic tomb, 42
Meonstoke, Hampshire, 98
Mercia, 117, 122, 125
Mercury (god), 83
Merovingian artefacts, 120
Mersea, 2, 103, 122, 123
  see also East Mersea
Mersea Island, 30, 124, 131
Merton College, Oxford, 140
Mesolithic period, 10, 168-70
  dating, 13
  and landscape change, 101
  lithic finds, 12
  sites, 11-13, *11*, 24
  White Colne, 8
Messing, parish of, 148
metal-detectors, 108, 123, 126, 200
metalwork, 165
  Anglo-Saxon, 110, 117
  Bronze Age, 26, 29-30, 32, 38, 39, 42, 43, 46
  Chelmer Valley, 42
  Ewart Park, 29, 30, 31, 46
  imported, 29
  Llyn Fawr, 30, 46
  medieval, 132
  military, 77, 80
  production/distribution, 41
  Scandinavian, 123
  see also bronze; coins; copper; iron
Metropolitan-Vickers, Manchester, 160
micro-wear studies, 5
microfossil analysis, 168, 170, 179
microliths, 10, 12, 13
micromorphological study, 177
midden sites

INDEX

Iron Age, 51, 57
islands, 40
Late Bronze Age, 41, 42
medieval refuse pits, 179
Neolithic deposits, 20
Saxon, 111
Middleborough, Colchester, 203
Middlesex, 26, 117
Midlands, 12, 59
Mildenhall, 105
  High Lodge, 1, 168
Mildmay Road, Chelmsford, 192, 194
military landscape, and Roman towns, 76-80
Millhead, Waltham Abbey, 158
mills, 122, 146
  animal-powered, 98, 162
  corn, 164
  see also fulling mills; tide mills; watermills; windmills
millstones, 111, 162
Minerva (god): Harlow, 86, *86*
mining and quarrying, 160, 161, 163
minsters, 122
mints
  Colchester, 60, 63, 73, 74, 120, 125
  Late Iron Age, 62
  Maldon, 125
  Newport, 121
  Saxon, 74, 118, 120, 121
mirrors, 61, *76*, **77**
Mistley, 95
Mobil Oil Company, 213
Moguntiacum, Rhine frontier, 77
Molehill Green site, 131
MONARCH software, 182
monasteries, 122, 129, 133, 134
  Dissolution, 133, 145, 152-3
  see also individual locations
monkey, 4
Montfichet, William de, 133
monuments
  Bronze Age, 15, 40
  ceremonial, 16
  funerary, 103
  Neolithic, 15, 16-20
  see also cursus monuments
Monuments at Risk Survey (MARS), 214
Monuments Protection Programme (MPP), 38, 187, 188
Moor Hall, Harlow, 32
Morgan and Ogilby: map, 147
morphology, 51
mortality, 131, 133
mortuary chamber, 57
mortuary (funerary) enclosures *see under* enclosures
mosaics, 69, 104
motorways, *see under* roads
Moulsham Street, Chelmsford, 80, 91, 94, 194
  bath-house, 192
  cemeteries, 87
  Cramphorns site, *88*, 90
  post-medieval, 195
  Roman period, 175
mounds, burnt, 43, 44
Mount Bures: Brook Hall, 10
Mount House, Braintree, 76
Mountnessing, 166
Moverons Farm, Brightlingsea, 172
Mucking, 202
  aisled structure, 100
  Anglo-Saxon period, 108, 110, 115, 117, 123
  Bronze Age, 20, 27, 29
  cemeteries, 19
    cremation burials, 57, 58
    Late Iron Age, 58
    ring ditches/burials, 26
    Roman, 103
    Saxon, 110, 111
  cereal cultivation, 177
  and Chadwell area: pottery, 50
  cropmark site, 200
  excavations, 33
  Iron Age, 51, 52, 57, 58

and Kentish links, 113
Linford Quarry, 200, 204
metalworking, 52, 54, 115
Roman period, *99*, 100, 101, 104, 105
round houses, 50
Mucking Excavation Committee, 207
Mucking Gravel, 8
Mucking North Ring, 29, 30, *31*, *34*, 41, 202
Mucking South Rings, 29, 30, 32, 41
Mucking Terrace, *7*
Museum of London, 13

Napoleonic wars, 150, 158
National Heritage, Department of, 208, 217
Navan, Ireland, 41
Navestock Hoard, 26
Nazeingbury, 63, **63**, 122, 202
Neanderthalers, 4, 8
Neckarburken, Baden Wurttemberg, 82n
Neolithic period, 15-24, 199, 204
  causewayed enclosure, 113
  cultivation, 12
  domestic sites, 20
  earlier, 16, *17*, 20, 24
  environment, 170-2, **173**, 174
  field systems, 39
  and human bones, 43
  later, *18*, 20, 22, 24
  long barrow, 114
  monuments, 16-20
  radiocarbon dating, 11
  ring ditch burials: Brightlingsea, 215
  Springfield enclosure, 30
  start of, 15-16
  Stickle Pike, Langdale Pikes, 160
  stonework, 20-2
Neptune, coins depicting, 63
Nevills (family), 153
New Hall, Boreham, 155
New Writtle Street, Chelmsford, 192
Newark-on-Trent, 150
Newcastle (brick) kilns, 163
Newham Hill: Ashdon, 97
Newman's End, Matching, 130
Newport, 121, 122, 125, 134
Newport Pagnell, 121
Niblett, Mrs R., 201
Norden, John: *Map and Description of Essex*, 146
Norfolk, 8, 12, 47, 123, 124
  see also individual places
Norfolk, earls of, 133
Norman Cross, Peterborough, 150
Norman period, 122
  conquest, 73, 117, 161
  impact on Anglo-Saxon society, 129
Norman-French, 143
Norsey Wood: defended settlement, 76
North Downs, Kent, 2
North Ockendon: farmstead, 131
North Sea: glaciation, 2
North Shoebury
  Anglo-Saxon cemetery, 110
  Bronze Age, 20, 27-9, 32, 33, *35*
  cemeteries, 57, 58, 110
  charred cereal remains, 175
  cremation burials, 57
  excavation, 124, 202
  flat axes, 22
  Iron Age, 33
  landscape, 126
  mussel shells, 174
  pottery
    carinated bowls, 22
    Iron Age pottery, 47
    stamp-decorated pot, 26
  Project, 213
  Roman landscape, 125
  sea food, 64
  skull burial, 51
  Viking stronghold, 122
North Stifford *see* Ardale School
Northamptonshire: water mills, 100
Northey Wood, Billericay, 97
Northfleet, Kent, 6, 113

Norton Fitzwarren, Somerset: fortified hilltop, 42
Norton Heath, 97
Norwich Castle keep, 195
Nun Coton, Lincolnshire, 152

oak
  barrels, 51
  coffins, 87
  well-lining, 115
  woodland, 15, 168
Oaklands Park, Elm Road, Chelmsford, 87
Ockendon, 7
Ogilby and Morgan: map, 147
oil refineries: Shellhaven/Holehaven, 164
oils, motor, 163
Old Harlow: medieval market, 132
Old Heath, Colchester, 120
Old Thorndon Hall, 143, 148
omphalos bowl, 57
Ongar, 97, 125
Orchard Street, Chelmsford, 195
Ordnance Survey, 95, 97, 129, 146, 147, 149, 150, 153, 181, 183, 190, 199, 208
Orsett, 20
  Barrington's Farm: Saxon features, 108
  Boyn Hill Gravels: hand-axes, 5
  earlier Neolithic pottery, 22
  enclosure, 16, 22
  excavation, 200, 202
  loomweights, 63
  metalwork finds, 26
  Rectory Road, 47, 63, 64, 174
  ring-ditch burials, 26, 113
  Saxon period, 108, *111*, 114
Orsett Cock, 19, 58-9, 77, 100, 204
Orsett Heath: flint scatters, 20
Orsett Heath Gravel, 2, 7
Orsett Lodge, **147**, 148
Osborne Street, Colchester, 75
Osea Island, 26, 171
osteoarthritis, 133
Othona, fort of, 176
ovens, 93, 101
ox, giant, 4
Oxford
  Ashmolean library, 95
  Merton College, 140
Oxford, earls of, 129

paddle, 29, 174
Pagans Hill, 82
Palaeolithic period, 1-8, *3*
  Clacton-on-Sea, 202
  environmental archaeology, 168
  flint mines, 20
  hand-axes, 86
  Late Upper, 8, 10, 168-70
  Lower, *1*
Palladian mansion: Wanstead House, 153
Palstaves, 26
palynological analysis, 15
parchment, 133
Parkway, Chelmsford, 194
parliamentary enclosures, 149
Pas de Calais, 2
Passingford Bridge, 97
patera, 77, 103
Paycocke's House, Coggeshall, 164
Peasants' Revolt, 161, 163
pebble and flake industries, 5
Pebmarsh: Roman farm buildings, 100
Peldon: Red Hill 117, 61
pendants, 77&n, *80*, 113, *114*
Pennines: Early Mesolithic sites, 12
Pentlow Hall: church-hall complex, 124
Petre family, 146
Petre, Sir John, 143
petrol, 163
petrological analysis, 50
Petters Sports Field: enclosure, 42
pewter, 83, 134
picks, 13
Piedmont, North Italy: jadeite axes, 22

INDEX

pigs
  bone, 51, 121
  burial of, 80
  grazing, 125
  Middle Bronze Age, 27
  remains, 172
  teeth, 20
  wild, 5, 11, 15
pill-boxes, 187
pilum head, 77
pin: Wicken Bonhunt, 123
place-names, 148
  Anglo-Saxon, 117, 123, 124, 126
  medieval, 130
  'Mill', 162
  Scandinavian, 123
plagues, 131, 150
Planning Policy Guidance (PPG 16), 213-14, 215, 216, 217
plants, 63
  Anglo-Saxon/medieval environment, 177
  apple remains, 171
  black henbane, 133
  Bronze Age, 15, 29, 33, 39, 170-1, 172, **173**
  carbonised remains, 20, 27, 31, 32, 171
  cherry stone, 20
  Colchester, 75
  coriander, 176
  dates, 176, *176*
  figs, 176
  flax, 172, 174, 177, 179
  fruitstones, 20, 171, 172
  grape, 176
  grasses, 20, 47, 172, 175, 177
  harvesting of, 15
  hazelnuts, 13, 20, 171, 172
  hemlock, 133
  herbs, 170, 172
  horse-beans, 174, 179
  Hoxnian interglacial, 168
  Iron Age, 172
  Late Glacial, 10
  Late Upper Palaeolithic/Mesolithic, 168
  lentils, 176
  macro fossils, 5
  monastic, 133
  mulberry, 176
  Neolithic, 15, 170-1, **173**
  nutshells, 171
  olive, 176
  peas, 177, 179
  pulses, 177, 179
  Roman period, 175-6
  salt-marsh, 115
  shrubs, 172
  sloe fruit, 171
  walnut, 176
  weeds, 170, 172, 177, 179
  wild, 20, 22, 27, 172
  see also cereals; crops; woodland
plate, metal, 123
platters, 60
Pledgdon, Elsenham Cross: Mesolithic finds, 12
Pleistocene stage, 2, 4, 10, 11, 13, 168
Pleshey, 103, 130
  Roman villa, 98
Pleshey Castle, 129, 185, 192, 200, 212
Plesheybury: Late Iron Age/early Roman, 77
Plumpton Plain: settlement, 40
points, 8, 10, 12, 13
poker, iron, 58
Poll Tax (1381), 163
pollen analysis
  Anglo-Saxon/medieval environment, 177, 179
  Asheldham Camp, 47
  Blackwater Estuary, 172
  Bronze Age, 24, 172, 174
  Clacton-on-Sea, 5, 168
  and landscape, 126
  Lea valley, 168
  Mar Dyke, 15, 123, 168, 170, 172, 175, 177
  Mesolithic period, 13

Middle Bronze Age/Iron Age environment, 172
Neolithic period, 24, 172
and palaeolithic period, 5
Roman period, 101, 175, 176
population
  of Colchester, 73
  growth
    Iron Age, 50
    post-conquest, 130
    post-medieval, 155
  late Roman period, 105
  later medieval decline, 131
  of Saxon Mucking, 110
  and sea-level rise, 104
Porters Hall villa, Stebbing, 98
potin coins, 47, 51, 54-5, 76, 87
Poterne, 42
pottery
  Anglo-Saxon, 108, 123, 126
    Early, 108, 110, 111, 117
    Late, 111, 124
      late 10th-11th-century, 122
    "Late Saxon Shelly Ware", 117
    Middle, 117, 120, 123
    Roman-Saxon, 105
    "Saxo-Norman" wares, 117
  Colchester, 74
  and cremation rite, 57
  industry, 163
  jars, 29, 51
  lamp chimney, 82
  manufacture and distribution, 41
  medieval, 132, 133
  Prehistoric
    Beaker, 16, 17, 19, 20, 22
    Bronze Age, 24
      Early, 20
      Late, *28*, 29, 30, 32&n, 40, 47
      Middle, 26, 27-9, *28*
    Iron Age, 60, 203
      Early, *28*, 32n, 33, 46, 47, *48*, 50, 52, 57, 63
      Late, 33, 46, *53*, 54, 55-7
      Middle, 26n, 33, 46, *49*, 50, 54, 55, 59
    Neolithic, 15, 16, 20, 22, 24
      late, 20, 171
  Roman, 50, 69, 76, 87, 88
    early, 55, 57
    late, 87, 101, 103
    Roman-Saxon, 105
  tool, 13
  trade *see under* trade
  TYPES
    amphoras(ae), 74, 77, 203
      Dressel 1, 50, 51, 55, 60, 69, 76
    Ardleigh Group, 26, 29, 33
    Belgic, *53*, 54, 57, 59, 60, 61, 76, 80
      wheel-thrown & grog-tempered, 46, 55
    bowls, 19
      carinated, 20, 22, *46*, 47
      Ebbsfleet, 22
      fine angular, 33
      form 13, 50
      Mortlake, 17, 22
      patterned, 50
      plain, 16, 17, 22
      rim footring, 50
      stamped (Kelvedon), 61
    coarse wares, 31
    Darmsden-Linton, 33, 46, *46*, 47, *48*, 50
    Deverel-Rimbury, 26, 29, 32, 39, 42, 43, 200
    fine wares, 26, 31, 39
    flint-tempered, 46, 47, 50, 55
    food vessels, 20
    German ware, 133
    Glastonbury ware bowl, 50
    glauconite-tempered, 50
    grass-tempered, 115, 117, 120, 121, 123
    grey ware, 80
    Grooved Ware, 16, 17, 19, 20, 22, 199
    haematite-coated ware, 47

    Hedingham ware, 133
    Ipswich Ware, 117, 120, 121, 123, 124
    London-type ware, 133
    Lower Thames Group, 26
    Mildenhall Ware, 22
    Mildenhall-style, 16, 19, 22
    Mucking-Crayford style, 50
    Mucking-Oldbury style, 50
    Oxfordshire oxidised wares, 104
    Oxfordshire red wares, 105
    Peterborough Ware, 17, 22
    post-Deverel-Rimbury, 29
    pre-Belgic, 62
    Rettendon-type wares, 93
    Rhenish, 124
    Rinyo-Clacton *see* Grooved Ware
    St Neots Ware, 117
    Saintonge ware, 133
    samian, 77, 80, 194
    sand-tempered, 46, 47, 50, 55, 117
    Scarborough ware, 133
    shell-tempered (STW), 47, 50, 51, 55-7, *56*
      'late', 104, 105
      St Neots-type, 117
    stamp decorated, 26
    Thetford Ware, 117, 120
    Thetford-type Ware, 117
    urnfield ceramics, 29
  see also kilns, pottery; urns
Pounds Farm/Gants Pit, Dovercourt: hand-axe site, 5
power supplies, 160, 161-3
Priory Gatehouse, Little Walsingham, Norfolk, 142
Prittlewell, 26, 113, *114*, 115
probate inventories, 146
Proto-Levalloisian technology, 3, 7
Public Buildings and Works, Ministry of, 192
Puckeridge *see* Braughing-Puckeridge
Purfleet, 7, 158, 163, 172

quarrying
  millstones, 162
  see also mining and quarrying
Quaternary stage, 1, 5, 7, 168
Queen post roofs, 139, 140
Quendon, 121
querns, 20, 27, 162
  lava, 93, 111, 122, 124
quernstones, 29

Radcliffe family, 155
radiocarbon dating
  Anglo-Saxon, 115
  and medieval environment, 177, 179
  Ardleigh, 26
  Bronze Age, 24, 29, 41, 174
    Early, 170
    Late, 38
    Middle, 32, 172
  fish-weirs, 124
  Flandrian stage, 168
  Iron Age environment, 172
  Late Glacial, 10
  Mesolithic, 11, 12, 13
  Neolithic, 11, 24, 170
    later, 20
  North Shoebury, 29
  Orsett enclosure, 16
  prehistoric plant remains, 171
  Roman environment, 175
  Springfield cursus, 17
  Waltham Abbey, 121
Radwinter, 95, 195
Rahtz, Professor Philip, 192, 200
railways, 163, 166
Rainham, Greater London, 19, 121, 132
Rams Hill, 40, 41, 42
Ransome, Hoffman and Pollard, 165
Rapiers, 26
Rathgall, Ireland, 41, 43
raven bones, 83
Rayleigh Castle, 129, 200
Rayne, 97, 98
Reading Business Park, 39, 40, 43

INDEX

Rectory Road, Orsett, 47, 63, 64, 174
Red Hills, 60, 101, 102, 105, 174, *174*, 203
  Iron Age agriculture, 63
  Late Iron Age/Roman period, 176
  Red Hill 89, 54
  Red Hill 147: Great Wigborough, 63
  salt extraction, 61, 64
Red Hills Exploration Committee, 61
Redbond Lodge, Great Dunmow, 103
Reed, Eric, 192, 193
refuse *see* midden sites
Reims, 104
reindeer, 10, 11
religion and ritual
  animal sacrifices, 42, 60, 80, 103
  and coinage, 54
  cult of the severed head, 50-1
  Iron Age
    Late: ritual and temples, 58-60
    Middle, 50-1
  medieval practices, 134
  Roman, 76, 80-7, *83*, 103
  special animal bone deposit, 51
  see also ceremonies; Christianity; churches; funerary practices; monasteries; shrines; temples; votive offerings
'rental' documents, 144, 145
Repton, Humphry, 153
reservoir, 98
Rettendon, 93, 174
Rhine, River, 4, 162
Rhineland, 57, 77, 122
rhinoceros, 4, 5
Rich, Lord, 152
rickets, 133
Rickling, 121
ring ditches, 17, 19-20, *19*, 24, 188, 204
  Anglo-Saxon, 113
  and cremation burials, 26&n
  Neolithic, 16
  North Shoebury, 29
ring gullies, Anglo-Saxon, 108
rings
  bronze, 51, 52, 54
  finger, 80, 83
  gold, 41
ringworks, Bronze Age, 40-1, 42, 43
Ripe, Sussex, 100
Riseley cemetery, 113
ritual *see* religion
Rivenhall
  church, 122, 124, 133, 204
  excavation, 192, 195, 199, 201, 203, 204
  Late Iron Age/early Roman, 77
  mirrors, 61
  proglacial lakes, 2
  Roman period, 77, 80, 200
    villa, 97, 100, 103, 108, 110
  Saxon period, 115
Rivenhall End, 15, 16, 20, 121, 202
Roach, River, 29, 176
roads, 160, 165-6
  by-passes
    A12 Chelmsford, 172
    Colchester, 199
    Dovercourt, 150
    Grays, 101, 108, 202
    Loughton, 166
    Rayne, 98
  medieval, 132
  motorways, 166
    M11, 7, 29, 33, 97, 201
    Winchester: M3 extension, 40
  Roman *see* Roman roads
Robertson, Ian, 192, 193
Rochford
  burial, 19
  Doggets Farm, 162
  hand-axes, 2
  landscape, 100, 101
  South Street, 142
Rochford Hundred, 15, 97
Rocque, John, 147, 153
Roding, River, 7, 51, 57, 122, 162
Roding Valley, 10, 97, 153

Rodings, the, 117, 123
Rodwell, Warwick, 192, 193, 194, 195, 207
Roman army
  First Cohort: Camulodunum, 71
  Legio XIV, 77
  Legio XX, 80
  and Saxon 'laeti', 110
  Thracian cavalry auxiliary, 77&n
Roman Catholic churches, 134
Roman Essex Society, 95, 97, 192, 199
Roman period, 201, 202
  and Anglo-Saxon settlement, 108-10, 115, 118, 121, 123, 203-4
  archaeological bias towards, 217
  burials *see* burials
  Caesar's invasion of Britain, 55
  Camulodunum, 69, 70-1, *71*, *72*, *73*, 74, 120
  coast, 101-2, 176
  collapse in Britain, 105
  domestic sites, 24
  early, 57
    cremations, 58
    house design, 60
    pottery, 55, 57
  Eastern Empire, 98
  environmental archaeology, 175-7
  fleet, 77
  glass remains, 75
  invasion and conquest, 51, 58, 59, 60, 61, 62, 73, 77, 176
  landscape/countryside, 95-105, 125, 202, 204
    agriculture, 100-1, 104, 105, 176-7
    farm complexes, 215
    field systems, 39, 126
    metal-detection at sites, 200
  Red Hills, 174
  salt extraction, 61
  temple: Ivy Chimneys, Witham, 59
  towns, 76-94, *78-9*
    death and burial, 87
    decline of, 103-4
    religion, 80-7, *83*
    see also Billericay; Braintree; Chelmsford; Colchester; Great Chesterford; Great Dunmow; Harlow; Wickford
  see also coins; pottery; Roman army; Roman roads; trade; villas
Roman roads, 95-7, 100
  diverticulae, 97
  Icknield Way, 77, 95, 97, 104, 105
  in medieval period, 132
  via Devana, 95, 100
Romchurch, vill, 121
Romford, Cotton Park Gardens, 93
roofs
  crown post, 138, 139, 141
  Queen post, 139, 140
  side-purlin, 138
  timber-framed buildings, 139-40
Rook Hall, Little Totham, 26, 115
Rookery Hill, Bishopstone, Sussex, 111
round barrows, 24
round houses, 34
  Chelmsford, 76, 80, *81*, 94
  Harlow, 59
  Iron Age, 47, 50, 51, 52, 54, 76
  Late
    Chelmsford, 80, *81*
    replaced by rectangular, 60
  Middle, 51, 86
  Late Bronze Age, 30, 31, 32
Round Wood *see under* Stansted Airport
Roxwell quarry, Chignall St James, 129
Royal Commission on the Historical Monuments of England (RCHME), 181, 182, 183, 207, 208, 209, 214
royal vills, 118-20, **120**, 121, 122
Royston, 97
Ruhr area, Germany, 164
Runneymede Bridge, 38, 40, 42
Runsell Green, 195
Russia: Ural Mountains, 5

sacrifices, animal, 42, 60, 80, 103

Saffron Walden, 95, 149
  Bridge End, 141
  excavation, 195, 201
  flint artefacts, 22
  gasworks, 165
  medieval period, 133, 145
  surrounding landscape, 100
  "Viking" burials, 123
Saffron Walden Abbey: brick barn, 140
Saffron Walden Museum, 61, 77n
St Albans
  Cathedral of, 83
  Vale of, 1
  see also Verulamium
St Botolph's Church, Colchester, 133
St Botolph's monastery: "Icanho", 122
St Clement's Church, West Thurrock, 134
St Johns Service Station, Moulsham Street, Chelmsford, 192
St Joseph, Dr J. K. S., 200
St Leonard's hospital, Newport, 134
St Mary Magdalen churchyard, Colchester, 134
St Mary's Church, Wanstead, 155
St Michael's Church, Woodham Walter, 155
St Neots, 121
St Osyth, 97, 153, 162
St Paul's Cathedral, London, 149
Salisbury Plain, 39, 40, 43
salt marshes, 63, 102, 105, 115, 176, 177
  erosion of woodland, 12
  and grazing, 124
salt production, 60, 101, 115, 164
  coastal, 124, 177
  Fenn Creek, 29
  Late Iron Age, 61
  Mucking North Ring, 30
  Red Hills, 64, 101
  Roman period, 176
  Woodham Ferrers, 174
sand extraction, 163
Sandon Brook, 175, 177
saunas, Bronze Age, 43
Saunders, David, 192
Sawbridgeworth: causewayed enclosure, 24
Saxton, Christopher, 146, 147
scabbards, 58
sceattas, 117, 118, 120, 121
Scheduled Ancient Monument, 38, 212
Scole, 100
scrapers, Upper Palaeolithic, 10
scurvy, 133
sea levels
  and glaciation, 2
  high: Boxgrove, Sussex, 1
  Neolithic/Bronze Age, 15
  rise
    Early Bronze Age, 171
    Flandrian stage, 168
    interglacial period, 4, 7, 8
    Mesolithic period, 12
    Neolithic period, 16, 171
    Roman period, 101-2, 104
sea-mammals, 12
sedges: Lea valley, 168
Sellers, Elizabeth, 192, 193, 194, 200
Sellers, John, 193, 195, 200
Sens, near Paris, 164
Sewardstone: Lea valley, 164
shafthole implements, 22
shale
  beads, 20, 113
  bowl, 51
  vessels, 76
Shaugh Moor settlement: Bronze Age, 39
sheep, 27, 93
  at temple site, 82
  bone, 82, 177
  Domesday Book, 124
  herding, 115
  Iron Age, 63
  lambs, 83
  late Roman period, 104
  pasture, 131
  sacrifice of, 60
  shearing, 164

INDEX

Sheepen, Colchester, 29, 60, 69, 95, 199, 202
Shellhaven: oil refinery, 164
Shepton Mallet, Somerset, 50
shields, 43, 54, 60, 111
  binding, 77
  hide-shaped, 52
  iron, 58
ships: images on coins, 60-1, *62*, 62
Shirley's Bone Mill, Etruria, Staffordshire, 158
Shoeburyness: Late Upper Palaeolithic finds, 10
shoes, hobnailed, 87
shrines, 34
  Great Dunmow, 83
  Holbrooks, 60
  isolated rectangular, 50
  Late Bronze Age, 32
  Little Waltham, 47
  Stansted Airport: Middle Iron Age, 51
sickles, flint, 22
silk, Chinese, 87
silver, 52
  Almgren brooch, 57
  coins, 62, 63, 77, 111
  hoarding of, 55
  mask, 83
  resources of, and war, 54
Sipsons Lane, Middlesex: stamp-decorated pot, 26
Site of Special Scientific Interest: Globe Pit, Little Thurrock, 7
slag, 54, 93, 115
Sledda: East Saxon King, 121
Slough House Farm
  Anglo-Saxon/medieval environment, 115, 177
  Bronze Age
    Middle, 174
    well, 172
  enclosure, 16
  flint/pottery, 20
  Iron Age, 174, 175
    Early, 33
  prehistoric plant remains, 171
  ring ditches/burials, 26
  Roman cereal remains, 177
  roundhouse, 32
Smeaton, John, 158
smiths, 51, 86, 93, 115, 132, 163, 165
SMR *see* Essex Sites and Monuments Record
Smyths (family), 153
Snettisham, Norfolk, 55
solar calendar, 19
Solingen, Dortmund, 164
Somerton, Suffolk, 63
Sompting and Breton axes, 29
South Benfleet: Mesolithic finds, 12
South Lodge Camp, 42, 43
South Ockendon, 5, 29
South Wales: timber structures, 42
South Woodford: Acheulian Industry, 6
South Woodham Ferrers, **170**
Southchurch, 22, 29, 52
  Thorpe Hall: cemetery, 19
  Thorpe Hall Brickfield, 26
Southchurch Hall, 10, 129
Southend Airport: crouched inhumation, 19
Southend Museum, 27, 110, 200, 202
Southend-on-Sea, 5, 199, 217
  coin hoard, 55
  confluence of rivers, 2
  metalwork finds, 26
  Mucking Gravel, 8
  Southchurch Hall, 10, 129
  see also Prittlewell
Spain: wine from, 60
spatula-like objects, **35**
spearheads, 80, 86, 114
spears, 58, 103, 111, 113
  iron, 51, 58, 59
  wooden: palaeolithic period, 5
Speed, John: map, 146-7
spindle whorls, 30, 32, 33, 39

Springfield: prehistoric plant remains, 171
Springfield cursus, 17, 22, 24
Springfield Lyons, 41, 42, 118
  Anglo-Saxon period
    cemetery, 108, 110-13, *113*, 115
    Early, burials, *112*
    Late, 124
    re-use of prehistoric site, 114
  artefacts, 30-1, 32
  Bronze Age, 20, 174
  cremation pit remains, 177
  earlier Neolithic pottery, 22
  enclosures, 22, 29, 30
    causewayed, 16, 24
    circular, 30, *31*, 189
  excavation, 202
  future work at, 33
  Iron Age, 174
  ironwork hoard, 58, 59
  moulds
    clay casting, 30, 31
    Ewart Park bronze-casting, 29
  occupation sequence, 33
  structure, **34**
Springfield Road, Chelmsford, 87
Sproughton, S.E. Suffolk: Palaeolithic finds, 10
Stafford House, Harlow, 93
Stainfield, Lincolnshire, 152
Stane Street, 88, 94, 97
Stansted Airport
  Airport Catering site (ACS), 51, *52*, 54-5, 175, 202
  Boulder Clay, 172, 174
  Bronze Age finds, 24
  cemetery, 58
  Duck End, 58, *102*, 103, 177
  excavation, 213
  housing, 141
  Inquiry, 209, *210*
  Iron Age, 33, 47, 60, **77**
  landscape change, 101
  Late Iron Age/early Roman, **77**
  medieval period, 129
  pottery, 33, 50, 60
  prehistoric collections, 15
  Rail Link construction, 175
  rectangular shrines, 50
  Round Wood, 108, 131, 179
  Saxon sites, 123, 124, *124*
  Social Club site, 47, *48*, 108, 174
Stansted Brook, 172, 175, 176, 177
Stansted village, 50, 55
Stanway, Colchester, 202
  charred cereal remains, 175
  funerary site, 57, 58, 69, **70**, 102
  Late Iron Age/early Roman, **77**
  rich burial, 60
  weapons grave, 103
Star Carr: organic artefacts, 12, 13
staters, 54, 55, 87
  gold, 47, 59, 61, 62, 63
status, and votive offerings, 22
steam power, 158, 162
Stebbing, 98, 101, 103, 200
Stebbing Green, 130, 177
steel, 161, 164
Steeple: wheel pump, 165
Stickle Pike, Langdale Pikes, 160
Stifford Clays: Iron Age finds, 51
Stock, 50, 97, **147**, 148
Stoke by Clare, 95
Stoke-by-Nayland: building style, 138
Stoke-on-Trent, 163
stone
  artefacts, 172
  axes, 15, 22, *23*
  coffins, 87, 93, 103
  lack of building, 137, 139
  mould, 43
  plaque: Witham, 85
  quarrying for building, 161
  replaces timber church: Waltham, 121
  Saxo-Norman churches, 122
  stonework: Neolithic period, 20-2
  tools, 10, 12
Stone Marsh, 170

Stone Point, Walton-on-the-Naze, 8, 12
Stort, River, 59, 77, 86, 95, 104
Stort valley, 15, 24, 86
Stour, River, 5, 95
  estuary, 8
  "long blade" technology, 10
  Mesolithic finds, 12-13
  Neolithic/Beaker pottery, 20
  palaeolithic period, 2
Stour valley, 164
  Brundon, 7
  Bures St Mary, 17
  causewayed enclosures, 16
  henge sites, 19
  Neolithic/Bronze Age sites, 24
Stowmarket, Suffolk, 139
Strabo, 63
Stratford, 22, 132, 164
Stratford Langthorne, 133, 134
Streetly Green, 121
Strethall, 124, 130, 131, *131*
structures, **34**, 204
  Anglo-Saxon, 110, 111-12, 121, 123
  Ardleigh, 33
  Blackpatch, East Sussex, 38
  Broads Green, 32, **34**
  Bronze Age, 40, 172, 174
    Late, 32
    Middle, 26
  Chelmsford, 91-3
  Colchester
    early timber, 70-1
    post-Roman, 73
    Roman period, 72, *73*
  Iron Age, 40, 51, 60, 172, 174
    Middle, 50
  Listed Buildings, 187
  Lofts Farm, **34**
  long-wall-jetty, 141
  longhouses, **34**
  Mucking North Ring, 30, **34**
  North Shoebury, 27
  post-and-slot building, Saxon, 112
  post-built, 50, 111, 115, 124
    Boreham Interchange, 32
    Great Holts, Boreham, 33
    hall, 110, 114
    houses: Bronze Age/Iron Age, 40
  rectangular, 32, 47, 51, 60, 64
  and ringworks, 41
  Springfield Lyons, **34**
  sunken-featured buildings, 108-10, 115, 120
  and textile industry: Dedham, 164
  timber, 29, 32, 40, 41, 80, 117
    1st-century, 76
    Anglo-Saxon, 115, 121, 122, 123
    Bronze Age/Iron Age, 172, 174
    Chelmsford, 91-3
    churches, 121, 122
    coastline structures, 61
    early Colchester structure, 70-1
    Flag Fen, 41-2
    rectangular, 60
    Roman buildings, 98
    temples, 84
    Wicken Bonhunt, 121
    see also timber-framed buildings
  see also barns; farmsteads; halls; mansions; monuments; round houses; shrines; temples; villas
Stumble, The, 61
  charred plant material, 171
  earlier Bronze Age sites, 20
  Neolithic, 15, 20, 22, 172, **173**
Sturmer: *tumulus*, 103
Stutton, Suffolk, 8
styli, 122
Sudbury, Suffolk, 7
Suffolk
  building style, 138
  microlith finds, 12
  pottery, 26
  Saxon period, 123, 124
  south-east: metalwork finds, 30
  timber-framed buildings, 139
  see also individual places

230

INDEX

Suidfred, King, 121
SUPERFILE software, 182, 183
Surrey, 47, 54, 117, 137
Sussex
    Bronze Age, 43
    East Sussex: sea-level changes, 15
    flint mining, 22
    hillfort, 42
    Wealden houses, 140
    see also individual places
Sussex, earls of, 155
Sutton: Temple Farm, 108
Swanscombe, 2-4, 5, 7
Sweden, 16, 164
swords, 42, 103, 113
    Ballintober, 26
    burials, 123
    Carps Tongue, 30
    chape of, 77
    Ewart Park, 30, 31
    flange-hilted, 26
    in ironwork hoards, 58, 59
    miniature iron, 86
    steel, 164
    Tumulous, 26
    "Viking Age", 122

Tabor High School, Braintree, 88
Takeley, 103, 124
tankard handle, bronze, 58
tannery, 132
tanning, 164
Tara, Ireland, 41
Tasciovanus, 59, 61, 62, 63
taxation, 131, 133, 149
    Poll Tax (1381), 163
Taylor, Isaac, 147
taylors, 132
Tayspells of Colchester (trade tokens), 164
teeth, 13, 20, 63
temenos, 84, 86
Templars, 164
Temple Farm, Sutton, 108
temples
    Gosbecks temple, 204
    Hayling Island, Hampshire, 60
    Ivy Chimneys, Witham, 59, 84-6, *84*, 121
    Kelvedon, 83, 86
    octagonal temple, Chelmsford, 80-2
    offerings, 54, 80
    Romano-Celtic, 80-2, 83, 84, 86, 93
    Temple of Claudius (Colchester), 71, 72, 80, 86-7, 203
    see also Harlow (temple)
Tendring, 95
Tendring Hundred, 15, 199
Tendring Plateau, 1
Tenterden area, 141
Teutatis: Celtic war god, 58
textiles, 122
    bag, 113
    building style, 138
    Chinese silk, 87
    evidence for, 39
    fulling mills, 162, 164
    industry, medieval, 131, 132, 133
    local industry, 164
    Roman/Saxon, 160
    spindle whorls, 30, 32, 33, 39
    spinning: Bronze Age, 39
    technical innovation, 161
    weaving, 33, 39
    wool industry, 164
Thames, River: estuary, 29, 33, 150
    clay slabs, 43
    coinage, 54, 61
    elm decline, 170
    Iron Age
        coins, 61
        pottery, 33, 50, 55, 57
    Late Upper Palaeolithic/Mesolithic, 168, 170
    metalwork finds, 30
    Neolithic/Early Bronze Age, 171
    Roman period, 177
    sea-level rise, 15

shell banks, 55
winged adzes, 30n
Thames, River, 122, 132
    basin: Neolithic flintwork, 15
    Bronze Age, 26, 29
    confluence with Rhine, 4
    diversion of, 7
    gravel terraces, 108
    ironwork deposition in, 59
    and island sites, 40
    Kew: antler find, 13
    Lower, 5, 29
    Lower Thames Group (pottery), 26
    Middle, 5
    Neolithic period, 15
    palaeolithic period, 1-2, 4, 5, 8
    Roman environment, 176
    sword finds, 26
    Tilbury: hand-axe finds, 8
    trade, 50, 113, 166
    Upper, 32, 51
    and water transport, 162
    wharves on, 163
Thames valley
    Bronze Age sites, 40
    island sites, 40
    Lower, 2, 4, 7-8, 111
    Middle, 2, 4, *4*, 39, 43
    palaeolithic period, 5
    ring ditches, 19
    Upper, 24, 43, 117
Thames-Medway: environmental archaeology, 168
Thamesmead: Crossness, 170
Thanet Bedrock, 4, 7
Thaxted, 95
    cutlery industry, 133, 163-4
    green, 130
    'Prouds', 140
    'The Borough', 140
    wine imports, 60
Theodosius, 83, 87, 104
Therfield Heath: Neolithic long barrow, 114
Thorndon Hall, 146
Thorndon Hall Excavation Group, 143
Thorpe Hall Brickfield, Southchurch, 26
Thorpe Hall, Southchurch: cemetery, 19
Thorrington, 162
Thracian cavalry auxiliary, 77&n
Three Mills Bromley-by-Bow, West Ham, 162
Thundersley, 12, 22
Thurrock, 2, 202, 217
    chalk quarrying, 163
    cropmark sites, 30
    hand-axe sites, 7
    and potin coinage, 54
    see also Little Thurrock; Mucking
Thurrock Chalk and Whiting Co., 166
Thwing, 41, 43
Tiberius, 77
tide mills, 162
Tilbury, 8, 130
Tilbury Fort, 150
tiles, 91, 93, 97, 98, 163
till see Boulder Clay
Tillingham, 80n
Tilty, 134, 153
Tilty Abbey, 161
timber see wood
timber-framed buildings, 130-1, 136-42, *141*, 204
    carpentry styles, *136*, 137-8, 142
    Chelmsford, 192
    'condensed plan', *140*, 141
    post-medieval pattern, 155
    Wealden houses, *139*, 140-1
    see also halls
Tiptofts, Wimbish, 136
Tiptree: jam factory, 165
Tiptree Churchyard, 10
Tithe Commutation Act (1836), 149
title deeds, 145, 146
Tofts Garage, Braintree, 88
Togodumnus, 62
Tollesbury, 22, 123, 162
Tolleshunt: Domesday Book, 123
Tolleshunt D'Arcy: Hill Farm, 108

tombs, 42, 103, 164
tongs, iron, 58
Toppesfield, 97, 103
Torres Vedras, Lines of, 150
Tovi (Canute's standard bearer), 123
Tower Hill, 42
Town and Country Planning Acts, 181, 208, 209
trade
    Barking as port, 122
    and causewayed enclosures, 16
    coinage, 54
    and Colchester, 120
    and East Saxons, 125
    in gold and silver, 63
    and industrial revolution, 161
    internal, 133
    and island sites, 40
    and London, 120, 125, 131
    medieval growth of, 132
    metalwork, 29, 55, 164
    in millstones, 162
    Normandy flints, 166
    pottery, 29, 32, 55, 122
        Iron Age, 50, 57
        medieval, 133
        Roman, 50, 57
        Saxon, 121
    and River Thames, 113
    with Roman world, 60-1, 62, 63
    tokens, 163, 164
    wine imports, 51, 55, 60
    with York: late Roman period, 87
Trafalgar Square, London, 7
Trajan, period of, 91
Trent Valley: timber structures, 42
Trier: Audience Hall of Constantine, 87
Trinovantes, 55, 59-60, 62, 77, 87, 91, 93
trumpet mouthpiece, 77
Tufnell, J. J., 200
Turner, Robert, 195
tuyere, pottery, 115
tweezers, 111

Uphall Camp, Ilford, 32, 50, 51, 57, 202
Upminster, Whitehill Wood, 32
Upper Gravel, 2
Upper Loam, 2, 5
Upper Middle Gravel, 2, 4
Ural Mountains, Russia, 5
urns
    biconical, 17, 39
    collared, 19, 20
    and cremation burials, 26
    globular, 26
    pedestal, 58
    Saxon cremation, 111

Vale of St Albans, 1
Valentinian, 104
Vange Hoard, 30&n
vellum, 133
Venus, figurines of, 80
Verulamium, 105
    Antonine fire in, 80
    burials, 103
    coin moulds, 62
    Folly Lane, 57
    religious finds, 82, 83&n
Victoria County History, 76, 95, 183, 193, 199
Vikings, 117, 120, 122-3, 125
villae regales see royal vills
villas, Roman, 97-8, 103, 104, 110, 199, 201
Virtue (god), 83
votive offerings, 22
    at Roman shrines, 83
    at temples, 82
    by Roman soldiers, 77
    Camulodunum, 69
    carinated bowl as, 20
    Celtic tradition, 86

The Wade, Horsey Island, 10
Walden, Manor of, 144
Walden Abbey, 134, 145, 195

INDEX

Walker maps, 129, 148, 192
Wallace, C. R., 50
Wallbury Camp, 199
Wallingford: Bronze Age site, 40
Waltham, manor of, 125
Waltham Abbey
  Anglo-Saxon period, 121
  excavation, 203
  medieval market-place, 132
  medieval religious house, 134
  minster church, 122
  as monastic foundation, 133
  post-Dissolution, 153
  pottery finds, 22
  religious art, 134
  Royal Gunpowder Factory, 155-8, *156-7*, 164
  Royal Ordnance factories, 187
  Town Mead: ironwork hoard, 58, 59
  Viking burials, 123
Waltham Abbey Historical Society, 199
Waltham Holy Cross, 13, 123
Waltham-in-the-Forest, 153
Walthamstow: Viking sword, 122
Walthamstow Electricity power station, 165, **165**
Walton-on-the-Naze
  Bronze Age, 24
  flint artefacts, 20, *22*
  "Horsham" point, 12
  Neolithic period, 20, 24, 172
  Palaeolithic finds, 10
  Stone Point, 8, 12
Wanstead: hand-axe finds, 5
Wanstead Golf Club, 153
Wanstead House and Park, 153-5, *154*
Ward, Dr Jennifer, 143, 155
Warenne, William de, 130
Warren Hill, 168
Warren, S. Hazzledine, 5, 10
warriors, 54, 58, 61, 123
wars
  English Civil War, 150
  Gallic wars, 55, 58, 59, 60
  Hundred Years War, 133
  Napoleonic, 150, 158
  Peninsular campaign, 150
  trophies of, 51
  World War II, 186-7, 214
water supply, 165
waterborne transport, 29
watermills, 100, 158, 162, 166-7, 212
waterways, 166
wattle and daub, Iron Age, 60
wattles, Iron Age, 50
Waylands Smithy: bronze ornaments, 42
Weald (Surrey, Sussex, East Hampshire), 12
Wealden houses, *139*, 140-1
"Wealdham" see Waltham
weapons, 40, 41, 42
  burials, 58, 103
  as grave-goods, 113
  Iron Age, 52, 59
  as offerings, 42
  see also arrowheads; shields; spears; swords
Weathercock Hill: bronze production, 42
Weaverhead Lane, Thaxted, 133
Webbe, Thomas and John, 164
weddings, 16
Wellcome collection, British Museum, 12
wells
  Bronze Age, 172, 174
  Lofts Farm, 32, 33, 47
  Mucking farmstead, 100
  Roman, 108, 110
  Rook Hall, 26
  Slough House Farm, 177
  timber-lined, 115
Wells, Marion, 192
Wendens Ambo
  agriculture, 101
  animal bone, 63
  cereals, 63, 176
  Domesday Book, 121

Iron Age, 50, 51, 55
  Roman charred cereals, 176
  Roman villa, 97, 201
  skull burial, 51
Wessex
  burials, 57
  chalk, 39, 40, 42
  contacts with, 47
  currency bars, 59
  Iron Age ritual, 51
  and Mercia, 117
  metalwork, 46
Wessex downland, 40
West Bergholt, 55
  church, 122, 204
West Cliff, Clacton, 5
West Essex Archaeological Group, 76, 199, 203
West Ham, 121, 162
West Harling, Norfolk, 30, 54
West Heslerton, Yorks., Neolithic field systems, 24
West Stow, Suffolk: cereal cultivation, 177
West Thurrock, 166
  churches, 122, 134, 204
  flint industry, 163
  Lion Pit Tramway Cutting, 6, 7, 8
West Tilbury, 97, 134, 200
Westhampnett cemetery, West Sussex, 58
Wheeler, Sir Mortimer, 194, 199, 201, 203
Wherwell, Hampshire: raised aisled hall, 139
White Colne, 8, 12
White Notley, 103, 122, 200
White Roding, 136, 162
Whitehill Wood, Upminster, 32
Wicken, estates, 123
Wicken Bonhunt, 20, 121, 123, 201
Wickenden, N. P., 47, 196, 207
Wickford, 87, 125, 195, 201, 204
  Beauchamps Farm, 77
Wickford Archaeological Society, 200
Wickham Bishops hoard, 30
Widdington, 121, 126
Widford, 129, 150
"Wigingamere" (Newport), 121
Wilburton metalwork, 29
William the Conqueror, 129
wills, 146
Wiltshire, 39, 100
  see also individual places
Wimbish: Tiptofts, 136
Winchester: M3 extension, 40
wind power, and Fens drainage, 162
Windmill Field, Broomfield, 174
Windmill Hill enclosure, Wiltshire, 16
windmills, 162, 165, 166, 212
windows, 93, 122, 138, 140
wine, 51, 55, 60, 77, 132
Witham, 163
  adoption of Christianity, 86
  Anglo-Saxon period, 117, 121, 122, 124, 125
  fulling mill, 164
  hand-axes, 5
  ironwork hoard, 58
  pottery, 22
  stone plaque, *85*
  temple, 83
  see also Chipping Hill; Ivy Chimneys
Wixhoe, 95
wolf, 4
Wolstonian Stage, 3, 5
wood, 130-1, 136-42
  Anglo-Saxon
    burials, 114
    and medieval environment, 177
    resource, 125
  artefacts, 12, 13
  barrels, 51, 63
  charcoals, 13
  and earthwork defences: Napoleonic period, 150
  as industrial fuel, 164
  mortuary chamber, 57
  oak, 15, 51, 115, 168
    coffins, 87

palisades
  Maldon, 47
  Orsett enclosure, 16
  remains: Colchester, 75
  spear: palaeolithic period, 5
  timber-lined wells, 115
  woodworking: Neolithic/earlier Bronze Age, 20
  see also carpentry; structures (timber); timber-framed buildings
Wood Lane End, Hemel Hempstead, 98
Woodford church, 204
Woodhall, Hertfordshire, 155
Woodham Ferrers: salt production, 174
Woodham Walter
  coin find, **77**
  deer-park, 155
  excavation, 202
  Mesolithic finds, 12
  Middle Iron Age enclosure, 52
  pottery, *53*, 55
  prehistoric plant remains, 171
  St Michael's Church, 155
woodland/forest, 100
  alder, 15, 168, 172
  Anglo-Saxon period, 108, 123, 125
  Anglo-Saxon/medieval environment, 177
  ash, 170, 172
  birch, 10, 168, 172
  Bronze Age, 15, 24, 170, 172, 175
  clearance, 15, 170
    Bronze Age, 172, 175
    Neolithic, 172
    Roman, 175, 176
    Saxon period, 123
  and coastline recession, 12
  deciduous
    Clacton, 5
    Neolithic/earlier Bronze Age, 15
  documentary sources, 144, 145, 147
  elder seed, 27
  elm, 168
    decline, 15, 168, 170, 172
    Dutch elm disease, 153
  fauna, 13
  hawthorn, 172
  hazel, 15, 168, 170, 172
  Holocene, 11
  Iron Age, 51, 172
  Late Upper Palaeolithic/Mesolithic, 168
  lime, 15, 168, 170, 172
  management of, 22
  Neolithic period, 15, 170, 172
  and Norman Conquest, 130
  oak, 15, 168, 170, 172
  pine, 10, 168
  poplar, 172
  post-Roman period, 123
  Roman management of, 101, 175, 176
  Wanstead Park, 153
  wild foodstuffs from, 172
  willow, 168, 177
  see also plants
wool industry, 164
Woolf Compound Beam engine, Beeleigh Mills, 162
Woolwich, 158
Woolwich Beds, 55
Works, Ministry of, 199, 200
Worlington, Suffolk, 104
Wormingford: Mesolithic find, 12-13
Wrabness Hall, 10
Wright, Arthur, 192
Writtle, 97
  King John's Hunting Lodge, 192, 200
  medieval castle, 129
  Peculiar of, 146
Writtle Road, Chelmsford, 87
Wuffing dynasty lineage, 118
Wyburn Height Estate, Thundersley, 12
Wymer, John, 202

Yarnton: burnt mounds, 43
Yorkshire: Late Bronze Age, 41